The Labor Force under Changing Income
and Employment

NATIONAL BUREAU OF ECONOMIC RESEARCH

NUMBER 65, GENERAL SERIES

The Labor Force under Changing Income and Employment

BY CLARENCE D. LONG

The Johns Hopkins University

A STUDY BY THE

NATIONAL BUREAU OF ECONOMIC RESEARCH, NEW YORK

PUBLISHED BY

PRINCETON UNIVERSITY PRESS, PRINCETON

1958

Long, Clarence Dickinson, 1908–   . The labor force
under changing income and employment. Princeton,
Princeton University Press, 1958.   464 p. 24 cm. (National
Bureau of Economic Research. General series, no. 65)
"A study by the National Bureau of Economic Research,
New York." 1. Labor supply. 2. Labor supply—U.S. I.
Title.   HD5706.L65   331.112   58–7119 ‡   Library   of
Congress

RELATION OF THE DIRECTORS

TO THE WORK AND PUBLICATIONS

OF THE NATIONAL BUREAU OF ECONOMIC RESEARCH

1. The object of the National Bureau of Economic Research is to ascertain and to present to the public important economic facts and their interpretation in a scientific and impartial manner. The Board of Directors is charged with the responsibility of ensuring that the work of the National Bureau is carried on in strict conformity with this object.

2. To this end the Board of Directors shall appoint one or more Directors of Research.

3. The Director or Directors of Research shall submit to the members of the Board, or to its Executive Committee, for their formal adoption, all specific proposals concerning researches to be instituted.

4. No report shall be published until the Director or Directors of Research shall have submitted to the Board a summary drawing attention to the character of the data and their utilization in the report, the nature and treatment of the problems involved, the main conclusions, and such other information as in their opinion would serve to determine the suitability of the report for publication in accordance with the principles of the National Bureau.

5. A copy of any manuscript proposed for publication shall also be submitted to each member of the Board. For each manuscript to be so submitted a special committee shall be appointed by the President, or at his designation by the Executive Director, consisting of three Directors selected as nearly as may be one from each general division of the Board. The names of the special manuscript committee shall be stated to each Director when the summary and report described in paragraph (4) are sent to him. It shall be the duty of each member of the committee to read the manuscript. If each member of the special committee signifies his approval within thirty days, the manuscript may be published. If each member of the special committee has not signified his approval within thirty days of the transmittal of the report and manuscript, the Director of Research shall then notify each member of the Board, requesting approval or disapproval of publication, and thirty additional days shall be granted for this purpose. The manuscript shall then not be published unless at least a majority of the entire Board and a two-thirds majority of those members of the Board who shall have voted on the proposal within the time fixed for the receipt of votes on the publication proposed shall have approved.

6. No manuscript may be published, though approved by each member of the special committee, until forty-five days have elapsed from the transmittal of the summary and report. The interval is allowed for the receipt of any memorandum of dissent or reservation, together with a brief statement of his reasons, that any member may wish to express; and such memorandum of dissent or reservation shall be published with the manuscript if he so desires. Publication does not, however, imply that each member of the Board has read the manuscript, or that either members of the Board in general, or of the special committee, have passed upon its validity in every detail.

7. A copy of this resolution shall, unless otherwise determined by the Board, be printed in each copy of every National Bureau book.

(*Resolution adopted October 25, 1926 and revised February 6, 1933 and February 24, 1941*)

TO THE MEMORY OF

MY FATHER

THE GREATEST TEACHER

I HAVE EVER KNOWN

PREFACE

IT IS always pleasant to recall debts that have enriched the borrower and, were it not that a long book ought to have a short preface, I should list my obligations in the full length they deserve. I am indebted to the Institute for Advanced Study for permitting me during the first half year of this book's preparation to complete a term of membership which I had begun before entering the service. I am grateful for the counsel of the late Walter W. Stewart, Leo Wolman, and the late Robert Warren, and for the inspiration which I received many years ago from that wonderful teacher and splendid man, the late Frank D. Graham. Finally, I owe Arthur F. Burns for nothing less than my appreciation of the meaning of scientific investigation, gained over many years of association with him at the National Bureau of Economic Research and the Council of Economic Advisers.

But no investigator can do his best without competent assistants to help him along or vigorous critics to keep him alert, and in neither respect have I been underprivileged. My assistants at one time or another in the past have been Donald Creecy, Susan Dischka, Esther Donahue, Harry Eisenpress, Rashi Fein, Louis Frisco, Stanley Kurta, Janette Rainwater, George Stepanovich, Fumie Yamamoto, and Margaret Chen. My critics have included Arthur F. Burns, the late Daniel Carson, Paul H. Douglas, Louis Ducoff, John Durand, Solomon Fabricant, Simon Kuznets, Wassily W. Leontief, Geoffrey H. Moore, Gladys Palmer, S. H. Ruttenberg, Leo Wolman, and W. S. Woytinsky. Emilie M. Hatfield edited the manuscript. H. Irving Forman drew the charts.

CLARENCE D. LONG

Baltimore, Maryland

CONTENTS

CONTENTS

CONTENTS

SUPPLEMENTARY APPENDIXES

(Mimeographed; on file at the National Bureau of Economic
Research, Inc., and in other economics libraries. Copies will be
furnished at cost on special request made to the National Bureau while the supply lasts.)

TABLES

xvii

CHARTS

The Labor Force under Changing Income
and Employment

CHAPTER 1

SUMMARY AND CONCLUSIONS

The Problem

WHY do people work? Some people work only to satisfy elemental needs, and lose much of their willingness to labor when their income is high enough to assure physical survival. Others toil for a wide variety of personal motives: one person to gratify an urge for consumption, display, or gambling; another to achieve wealth, rank, or social status; another to avoid criticism for being lazy; another out of habit, boredom, or loneliness; yet another out of altruism, or because he enjoys his work; and others for reasons such as earning social security benefits or forestalling the military draft by entering an essential occupation.

The external factors that may influence a person in his decision to work are even more manifold. They include the current level of remuneration; the incentive basis by which labor is paid (e.g. piece rates, over-time premium rates); the nonlabor income of labor; the hours and pace of a job; the jobs available in the neighborhood, occupation, or industry; the distribution of income among families and within families; the level and method of taxation; the amount of personal assets and their liquidity in time of need; the facilities for credit and the credit-worthiness of the individual; the availability of social security and assistance payments for the aged, the sick, or the unemployed, or for other persons of marginal employability; the restrictions or penalties affecting the earnings of social security recipients; the presence of children and other dependents, which may compel some to work and tie others to the home so they cannot work; the living standard of the community; the individual's demographic characteristics, such as age, sex, color, nativity, marital status, and residence; physical and mental health; and the extent of sports, entertainment and hobbies that compete for a person's time.

Such a lengthy list suggests that economic factors cannot completely explain labor supply behavior, and challenges the simple postulate of the classical economists: that people work less as wages increase, because higher wages enable them to satisfy their needs with less effort.

Nevertheless, we begin with an examination of this postulate, partly because this simple motivation, if enough people are swayed by it, may overshadow the other and more complex influences, and partly because two important studies made by Professor (now Senator) Paul Douglas indicate that such a claim was borne out by empirical investigation.

The Douglas studies refer *only* to the association between labor

3

force and earnings among large cities and at a given time (the first study covered 1920 and the second, 1930).[1] They did not investigate whether a similar association would appear over time—notably during peacetime growth, war mobilization or demobilization, or economic depression and recovery. They did not investigate the connection between labor force and employment (or unemployment) at a moment of time, the three-cornered relationship between these and income, nor the relationship between income and labor force among states, urban and rural areas of states, or nations. And, lacking the rich storehouse of materials provided by the 1940 and 1950 censuses—which frees us from the need to rely exclusively on the crude unit of a large city—they could not examine the labor force participation of wives according to the income levels of their husbands. Nor did they explore a great list of other factors which may influence labor force participation, either directly or through its connection with earnings: marriage, the size of the family; child-care responsibilities; the use of household appliances, factory-produced food, clothing, and commercial laundries and other services for the home; school attendance; educational attainment; social security; private retirement systems; the length of the workweek; income tax; and many others.

This volume has undertaken to fill these gaps in our empirical knowledge of labor force behavior and at the same time to seek some unified explanation for that behavior. The central questions are: (1) Has labor force participation been influenced by changes in income and in employment, and, if so, how and under what circumstances? (2) Are these two influences powerful enough to stand out over other possible influences, or do they reveal themselves only when the effects of the others are removed (held equal)? (3) Does any one among the other possible influences furnish a fairly complete explanation of labor force behavior, or must we seek an explanation in some combination of social, demographic, and economic forces?[2]

It is not easy to isolate the impact of these various factors. Many of them are so closely intercorrelated that they can act only jointly. Then, too, data are often lacking, or not easily related to labor force behavior. Fortunately, the statistical materials for this study have been unusually rich and comprehensive, as a result of the vast censuses of population and current sampling surveys—materials permitting separate examination of the labor force by age, sex, color, nativity, military status, child-

[1] Paul H. Douglas, *The Theory of Wages*, Macmillan, 1934, Chapter XI; Erika H. Schoenberg and Paul H. Douglas, "Studies in the Supply Curve of Labor," *Journal of Political Economy*, February 1937, pp. 45–79.

[2] The foregoing section on *The Problem* is a summary of Chapter 2. The concepts, materials, and methods are set forth in detail in the Appendixes and are summarized in Chapter 3.

care responsibilities of women, rural and urban residence, the density of population and the size of cities, income, school attendance, the amount of education completed, the employment status of the wife by the income or employment status of the husband, and hours of work. They also make it possible to study the labor force among different cities, areas, and nations at a moment of time, as well as within the same nation over the long and short run; the records of four foreign countries, as well as the United States, contribute abundantly. And they permit the testing of labor force participation not only as people become richer over time, but also as they grow poorer (as a result of wars or depressions). Such data open inquiry into the sequence of experience in a way that is impossible when only data on the moment-of-time behavior among localities are available, as in Douglas' case.

The Findings

The substantive results of the study are introduced in Chapters 4 and 5, which examine labor force participation among different areas and income groups at a moment of time. These "cross-sectional" analyses yielded the following results.

THE LABOR FORCE AND INCOME AT A MOMENT OF TIME AMONG CITIES, STATES, AND NATIONS (CHAPTER 4).

1. In general the labor force seems to vary more among cities, states, and nations, than would be expected from differences in the size or composition of population.

2. As was discovered by Paul Douglas, the variations in the proportion of a city's population in the labor force, i.e. its participation rate, appear to be inversely associated with variations in its average income per equivalent adult-male worker. The results amplify his findings, as follows: among 38 large cities in the United States, each 1 per cent higher real earnings (for equivalent adult males) was associated with a labor force that was typically about one-sixth of 1 per cent smaller for both sexes, one-half of 1 per cent for females 14 and older, one-fourteenth of 1 per cent for males 14 and older, and about one-third of 1 per cent for men 65 and older. Little or no association was manifest for males aged 18–64 or for females aged 16–24. There was a wide range in the amount of these inverse associations among teen-age boys and girls, but for the whole labor force of both sexes and of males and females 14 and older, the association remained rather constant.

3. The inverse associations were not found in all comparisons. Although Douglas' findings for the 38 cities in 1920 and 1930 were supported by our studies of the same cities in 1900 and 1940, they were not supported for *all classes* (whites and colored combined) or among

5

the same 38 cities in 1950. Nor were they upheld among the 48 states taken as wholes in 1940 or 1950, although different results might have been encountered had it been possible to adjust state-wide earnings for the diversity in the cost of living. (They were, however, upheld in 1940 among urban areas of the 48 states).

4. The inverse associations were not the spurious result of concentration of colored persons in certain low-income cities. They still obtained when the participation of whites was separated from that of the colored and correlated for the years 1920, 1930, and 1940 with male earnings of *all classes* (data on the earnings of whites and Negroes separately were not available by city before 1950). In 1950 the inverse association disappeared for white persons (as it did for *all classes*), but it was still pronounced between the participation and the earnings of Negroes.

5. Taking account of differences in unemployment among the cities did not change Douglas' results for 1930, nor those for the 1940 study. It might help to explain further the behavior of the labor force in 1950, but there was no dependable association for any group in any of these three years between labor force and unemployment, holding earnings constant.

6. Females did not tend to have higher participation in localities where the workweek was shorter.

7. The participation of women did not vary in any consistent way from one area to another with the participation of younger people or older men.

8. Neither single females, nor wives not living with their husbands responded noticeably in their participation to variations in female earnings.

9. Significant inverse associations were again found between real income per worker (or per capita) and labor force participation among 16 nations around 1930 and among 12 nations around 1950.[3] Difficulties of comparing income and labor force among nations make these findings less reliable than those among the 38 cities.

10. Some of the results of the study among nations were close to those among the 38 cities. In 1930, 1 per cent higher income was associated with 0.12 per cent lower participation for both sexes 15 and older, and with 0.40 per cent for females 15 and older (compared with 0.13 and 0.35 per cent respectively among the cities in the same year). A notable *difference* was that in 1950 the inverse association persisted internationally (in 12 nations) but had disappeared, except for Ne-

[3] The selection of nations was determined by availability of data; 9 of the nations were common to both dates.

groes, in the 38 cities. Another was the lack of any significant association for males 15 and older or for elderly males.

11. Among 11 nations around 1950, elderly males in the labor force showed some inverse correlation with the proportion drawing old age benefits. This association could signify either cause or effect; however, it was a modest one. It may be concluded that—whether or not the proportion drawing social security benefits is considered—there was still no significant association between participation of elderly men and the level of real income per labor force member.

12. A further moment-of-time examination was made of five nations (whose income and labor force behavior over time are extensively analyzed in later chapters). Associations among these—observable in 3 around 1900 and 1920, and in all 5 around 1930, 1940, and 1950— offer the advantage of having been based on more solid data than those of the 12- and 16-nation studies. For both sexes, males, and females, associations are inverse in all the censuses, and significant in the 5 nations in 1930, 1940, and 1950 in spite of the small number of observations. They are similar, numerically, in each of the latter three censuses and, on the whole, resemble those among the 16 nations around 1930 and among the 38 cities during 1900–1940.

THE LABOR FORCE OF FEMALES AND THE EARNINGS OF MALES IN DIFFERENT INCOME GROUPS AT A GIVEN TIME (CHAPTER 5).

1. As noted earlier, the 1940 and 1950 censuses made available data on labor force participation of wives according to wage and salary earnings of their husbands. These data apply to different income groups within a city and are separately classified by age of wife, color of wife, and possession of children. They reveal that mothers of young children have much lower participation rates than wives without young children, but that—with or without young children—the more prosperous the husband, the less likely that the wife is in the labor force. The weighted average for all income levels was about ⅓ of 1 per cent smaller labor force of wives for each 1 per cent higher income group of husbands. The same results are found in both 1940 and 1951.

2. The hypothesis that female participation varies oppositely with male earnings is strongly supported by data on wives classified by income groups of husbands *within* a city or nation. The evidence is more convincing than that based on a heterogeneous unit such as a city or state without this classification (and it is therefore unfortunate that data are available only for wives according to their husbands' incomes).

3. Although wives of more prosperous husbands are less apt to be in the labor force regardless of age, color, or responsibilities for the

care of children, colored wives are more prone to work than white wives, even when they are of the same age, have the same child-care responsibilities, and have husbands in the same income group.

4. There is no convincing evidence that the higher female participation rate in some areas results from greater employment opportunities —at least as measured by unemployment of males. Even within each city the participation of wives of a particular age, color, or child status was inversely related to the income of husbands, despite the fact that similar employment opportunities are presumably available to all women in any given city, regardless of husbands' income. This finding does not mean that job opportunities have no effect in determining whether or not women will enter the labor force.

5. Although the labor force tendency of *wives* does not depend on size of city, density of rural population, or educational attainment (below college level), the participation and employment of *all females* seems closely related to the extent of their education—more closely, indeed, than to their age. Among females whose maximum education is the completion of grammar school, the tendency to seek employment is less closely related to the amount of education than is the case for males, but among women who have completed one or more years of high school or college, the reverse is true.

THE FEMALE LABOR FORCE OVER TIME (CHAPTER 6).

1. Female labor force participation has increased in all of the five countries studied. In the United States the increase per decade has averaged 17 per 1,000 females aged 14 and older—about the median for the five countries—and has been reasonably parallel as between rural and urban areas.

2. The rate of increase has been much greater since around 1930 than before that time.

3. The increase has not appeared to be associated in any regular way with that in real disposable income of equivalent adult males, whether computed *per worker* or *per capita*.

4. The increase in participation has occurred among females in most of the age groups, in most of the nations, and over most of the decades, but has been greatest among women 20–64. Decreases have occurred among females 14–19, elderly women 65 and over, and, in recent decades, among American colored females of almost all age groups.

5. Among colored females in the United States participation was very high in earlier years. Between 1930 and 1950 it declined greatly, though still remaining higher than that of white females. This decrease may represent a tendency to converge toward the participation level of native white females, as rising incomes permit more and more colored

women to adopt living and working patterns of the American middle class. (Rising incomes have not reduced the participation of native white females, but they may have reduced that of colored women whose incomes have been rising much more sharply than those of white women, thus enabling them to realize a long-suppressed desire to follow the pattern of native white women.)

6. The rates of participation of foreign-born females in the United States have increased less than those of native white females. The labor force behavior of American-born descendants of the foreign-born has been closer to that of native offspring of native-born parents than to that of the foreign-born themselves.

7. In the two countries with data affording comparisons over time, females aged 14–24 have tended to increase their participation—even while more of them have tended to marry or attend school. There has been a great decline in the proportion of "inactive" females, i.e., those who do not attend school, do not work, and are not married.

8. Participation of females has varied widely according to age, marital status, and period studied; nevertheless, increases have characterized the behavior of young and old and married and single females, and have occurred in recent as well as in earlier years. Standardizing for marital status has accentuated the increases. The per-decade increases in female participation, standardized for age and marital status, were typically between 20 and 30 per 1,000 females and older, and differed surprisingly little among the nations.

9. Comparisons among nations show that there has been no close relationship between general gains in well-being and the increasing participation of females—both married and single—in the labor force.

10. The change in the proportion of females who are mothers of young children seems not to have significantly affected the participation rate of all females. This does not mean that female participation is not greatly influenced by the number of children to be cared for, but merely that the shift in the distribution of the burden of motherhood does not seem to have had an important effect.

FURTHER ANALYSIS OF THE INCREASES IN FEMALE LABOR FORCE PARTICIPATION OVER TIME (CHAPTER 7).

1. During 1890–1950, real disposable personal income per equivalent adult male employed nearly tripled, rising from about $1,000 to about $2,700 (in 1929 dollars). According to the moment-of-time association among 38 American cities discussed in Chapter 4, one would then expect female participation to decrease from 199 per 1,000 females 14 and older in 1890 to approximately 124 in 1950. Instead, it rose from 199 to 284—standardized for age and rural-urban residence. Thus the

9

excess of actual over expected labor force was 160 per 1,000 females 14 and older in 1950 and totaled about 9 million, or more than half the entire 1950 female labor force.

2. Illustrative estimates of the possible saving of female labor by the increased use of household appliances, commercial services, and manufactured food and clothing suggest the first two may not have been very significant but the third could have been more important.

3. In combination, developments in "technology for the home" could have released a substantial amount of female labor for gainful employment. However, there was only the crudest information as to their extent or the ultimate effect of the saving in labor, which could just as likely have gone into a higher standard of housekeeping or more leisure for the housewife as into the labor force.

4. A more accountable release of females to the labor force, traceable mainly to the lower birth rate since 1890, may stem from the great decline in the number of persons for whom the average wife, mother, or helping relative must keep house. Also important is the longer life span of women due to many fewer deaths from childbirth and disease. Computations for rural and urban areas, and white and colored populations in the United States, as well as in Great Britain and Canada (similar computations could not be made for New Zealand and Germany), indicate that such factors could have been the source of the entire rise in female participation in these nations, areas, and groups. Even so, it is still necessary to consider the employment opportunities and other inducements which might have determined whether and when employable women would, in fact, enter the labor force.

5. The data on labor force and earnings presented in the study do not support the hypothesis that the increase in female labor force has been due to the rising ratio of female to male earnings, at least in recent decades.

6. Agriculture lost, and trade gained, in relative importance as employers of female workers; but in general the industries with high proportions of female workers were about the same in both 1890 and 1950. Among occupational groups, virtually the entire rise in the ratio of female to male employment between 1910 and 1950 took place in clerical occupations. The other major groups—notably professional services, skilled, and unskilled occupations—maintained their ratio of females to males at a fairly constant level.

7. There was a strong moment-of-time tendency in the 1940 and 1950 censuses for women with education above high school to have higher participation the more years of education they had achieved. And there was a marked rise over time in the ratio of education completed by females aged 20 and older to that completed by older men (who re-

10

ceived their schooling in years of less educational opportunities and shorter school terms). The increase in the educational advantage of young and middle-aged females may help to explain why women showed an increase in participation while older men showed a loss. However, the decade-to-decade relationship between these developments has not been particularly close.

8. The increase in female participation over time was fairly closely related in the various countries and areas to the shorter standard workweek in industry. Many housewives, who would otherwise not have had time both to work and to take care of their homes and their children, may have been able to take gainful work.

MALES IN THE LABOR FORCE OVER TIME (CHAPTER 8).

1. Male participation has declined since 1890 in all five of the countries studied. Decreases among males aged 14 and older have clustered for the most part between 10 and 30 per 1,000 per decade, and almost without exception have accelerated in recent decades.

2. The declines have occurred simultaneously with increases in income per adult-male worker in all five countries; the relationship is such, considering the statistical difficulties, as to be consistent with at least the possibility that the two movements were associated with each other. Except in Germany, for which any income comparisons are probably unreliable, the declines have been about 5 to 11 per 1,000 males 14 and older for each $100 increase, or 0.1 to 0.2 for each 1 per cent increase in real personal disposable income per equivalent adult-male employed worker. The results for the English-speaking countries do not differ significantly whether the income data belong to the year in which the labor force was enumerated or to the average of that year and the two preceding years. *Per capita* incomes showed less similarity in the relation between male participation and income than *per worker* incomes.

3. Although considerable changes in the age composition of the male population have occurred in all five countries, the changes have had little net effect on the over-all male participation rate: the decline in the relative number of young males has been balanced by the rise in the relative number of elderly men.

4. In the United States the extensive migration to urban areas has also had little net effect on the average participation of males aged 14 and older, since the age groups whose participation differed markedly between rural and urban areas contributed only minor numbers to the labor force.

5. From 1890 to 1930, participation rates of Negro and foreign-born males were higher than those of native white males. But in 1940 and

1950 they declined sharply in all age groups—so sharply that in 1950 a thousand Negro or foreign-born males contributed fewer persons to the labor force than did a thousand native white males. Nevertheless, the predominance of native whites was such that the decline in male participation of all classes differed slightly from that of native whites.

6. Boys and young men under 25 reduced their participation in all five of the nations studied, in both earlier and recent periods. The decline for boys 14–19 was sizable in all the countries except Germany, but it varied widely. It was generally greater in the foreign countries than in the United States and was most marked in Britain. In the United States it was especially heavy for foreign-born and Negro boys, and for boys in urban areas. Most of it occurred before 1930, although it showed concentration for Negro boys in the United States in the period since 1930, and for British and German boys since World War II. The decline in participation of young men 20–24 has been largely confined to the United States, where, since 1930, it has been sharper than that for teen-age boys.

7. These declines have shown little relation to changes in income, but have reflected fairly closely the rise of school attendance in the countries for which data were available. It is uncertain whether the growth of school attendance was the cause or the consequence of the decline in labor force. Both of these changes may have resulted, variously, from compulsory school laws, increased awareness of the value of education, and higher incomes permitting parents to dispense with their children's earnings and to pay higher school taxes.

8. Males aged 25 to 64—the primary labor force age group—have also reduced their participation in recent decades, in almost all of the five countries. The reductions among men aged 25 to 44 were small and were probably caused by the post-World War II rise in school attendance among war veterans aged 25 to 34. The decline in participation of men aged 45 to 64 was larger, and undoubtedly reflects earlier retirement. There was a slight tendency of this kind before 1930, and it has since become much more pronounced. The causes of the declining participation of men aged 45 to 64 are probably best understood in the light of the labor force behavior of men aged 65 and older.

OLDER WORKERS IN THE LABOR FORCE (CHAPTER 9).

1. With some exceptions, men aged 65 and older have reduced their participation far more than have young men or teen-age boys. The reductions have been greater in recent than in earlier decades, greater in foreign countries than in the United States, and in the United States greater among Negroes than among native whites or foreign-born. In the United States the decline per decade has amounted to 50 per 1,000

12

elderly men, in New Zealand to well over 100. As a result the latest censuses show the participation of elderly men to be lower in the foreign countries than in the United States. Declines in the foreign countries were greater also in relation to income changes.

2. The reduced participation of older men has not been the result of their longer life span. It has not, in this country, been the result of their migration from rural to urban areas or their changing composition as to color and nativity—although such developments have probably been greater here than in the other nations considered in the study.

3. The extension of pensions and social security and assistance benefits may have influenced the withdrawal of elderly men from the labor force, especially over the past two decades, but they could not have been the major factor. Benefits, generally, have been modest; times when they were relatively meager have sometimes been accompanied by withdrawals, and times when they were more ample, by increases for the group 65 and over; and men under 65, though not ordinarily qualified as recipients, have also left the labor force.

4. If the retirement of elderly men has been influenced by rising real earnings—which might permit them to save or enable their children to support them—this influence does not stand out very clearly.

5. There is no evidence that older men have reduced their participation because they have been physically less able to work in recent years than older men were in earlier years.

6. Company rules and practices that compel retirement are widespread and are certainly responsible in many cases for the nonparticipation of older workers, but evidence is lacking that (aside from those rules and practices which are tied to pensions) they are a larger factor now than they were a generation ago. Certainly they have been in some effect since the turn of the century.

7. Statistics do not support hypotheses that the declining participation of older persons has been forced by the rapid advance of technology, by a decrease in self-employment, or by an increase in the size of firms (even though larger firms seem to hire smaller proportions of older men than do smaller firms).

8. There does seem to be some relationship between the declining participation of elderly men and the male unemployment rate. Elderly men have dropped out in periods of *very high* unemployment, with exodus apparently largest in those industries in which unemployment was greatest. They have returned in periods of *very low* unemployment. But the relationship holds only in the short run and for large changes in unemployment. In the long run and for mild changes in unemployment, the decline has not been closely related to the general unemployment level.

13

9. In both the 1940 and 1950 censuses, men participated in close relation to their education, measured in number of equivalent full-time years of school completed. In fact, for men without high school education, years of school completed seemed more important than age in determining how large the proportion of men of a given age would be in the labor force.

10. The reluctance of employers to retain or hire older men may therefore be due in some degree to the better training of the younger men and women in relation to the pay which they require or which humane employers feel obliged to give them.

11. This hypothesis receives some support from the great decline over the past four decades in the ratio of years of school completed by elderly men to those completed by young men and women—scarcely more than four-tenths in 1950 from nearly eight-tenths in 1910. This ratio was not closely related, in detailed movement, to the ratio of participation of elderly men to that of younger women. But it showed enough similarity of movement to leave the impression that inferior education and training is a factor, if only one factor, in the displacement of older men by younger and middle-aged women.

12. If elderly men are being squeezed out by their deficiency in education and training, they will continue to be at a disadvantage in competing for jobs with young men and women so long as the educational system continues to be highly dynamic; for the benefits of improved training accrue in the first instance to the young, and reach the elderly only after a lag of decades.

THE LABOR FORCE IN DEEP DEPRESSIONS (CHAPTER 10).

1. There are various theories about the response of participation to changes in employment. One is that large numbers of dependents are pressed into the labor force by widespread joblessness of family breadwinners during depressions. Another is that many persons of borderline employability or inclination to work are drawn into the labor force by the good wages and other job attractions that prevail during high employment. A third is that additions occur in response to both very low and very high employment, with withdrawals occurring during times of balanced prosperity.

2. The theory that net additions to the labor force accompany depressions, however plausible, seems to gain little support from the record. Statistics overwhelmingly indicate that more people have been driven out of the labor force by the unavailability of jobs (or by the unrewarding and exacting nature of the only ones available to secondary workers) than have been driven into it by joblessness of family breadwinners.

14

3. The only empirical evidence of net additions in depressions was provided by the special Enumerative Check Census, conducted in November 1937 by postal employees. The tendency revealed by that so-called census cannot be attributed to differences in concept; but it stands alone and is directly centradicted by the regular United States census conducted two and a half years later (when unemployment was almost as great as in November 1937). Such special surveys may tend to magnify what they set out to measure (though no such tendency appears in the special state surveys).

4. Under great unemployment the decline in participation was not confined to the nation as a whole in 1940 compared to 1930 and 1950, but extended also to rural areas, urban areas, large cities, and the forty-eight states. It appeared not only in the over-all labor force, but extended to most male age groups. Rises in participation were manifested by some young and old groups in certain areas and by some central-age female groups in others, but no age-sex group showed a consistent tendency toward higher participation in time of depression.

5. In 1940—a year of severe unemployment—white wives of unemployed husbands, standardized for age and child status, were much more apt to be in the labor force than wives of employed husbands, but only in the United States as a whole and in metropolitan areas; in the smaller urban places and in rural areas, the opposite was true. Colored wives were less apt to work if their husbands were unemployed, regardless of locale, and whether or not they had young children. Materials in the same detail have not yet become available for 1950. Sample summary data suggest that, as in 1940, there was a tendency for white wives to have had higher, and colored wives lower participation if their husbands were unemployed.

6. Conceivably, many persons who wanted jobs but did not seek them, believing no work was to be had, may not have been counted in the labor force. However, the last two censuses provided for the inclusion of such persons and, beginning with the 1940 census, one may perhaps assume that people who *strongly* desired jobs would have been counted in the labor force even though not actively seeking employment.

7. The depression behavior of labor force has been observed so far in comparisons with employment and unemployment but not with income. Real income per labor force member was depressed well below trend in every country (in 1940 for the United States and in the early thirties for the four foreign countries studied), and real income per employed worker was depressed in every country, with the possible exception of Germany.

8. With income per worker depressed, the participation of both sexes

15

and of females generally was lower per 100 rise in the number of unemployed males among the five countries. But the associations among the countries were too mixed to suggest a systematic tendency for the relationship between labor force and unemployment to have been affected by the depression of income.

THE LABOR FORCE UNDER SHORT-RUN CHANGES: WAR MOBILIZATION AND DEMOBILIZATION (CHAPTER 11).

1. In five years of World War II up to April 1945 the equivalent of 25 million full-time workers moved into civilian and military employment in the United States, raising the number of equivalent jobholders from 45 to 70 million—more than three for every two workers occupied in the spring of 1940.

2. These additions increased civilian employment by 13 million persons, (nearly 30 per cent) while the armed forces called up 12 million men. Over 5 million of the equivalent of 25 million workers came from increases in hours, mostly through overtime; nearly 8 million came from re-employment of persons who were in the labor force in 1940 but unemployed; and 11.5 million, who represented additions to the labor force itself, were largely persons who had been attending school, engaged in housework, or retired.

3. During the five-year period, the number of employed persons, including civilian and military workers, increased 42 per cent in the United States, which was slightly more than in Canada, three times as much as in Britain, and four times as much as in Germany. (This is so even if active armed forces and 7 million foreigners are counted in the German work forces; in fact if only German citizens are counted, the number of additional Germans mobilized for civilian and military employment barely rose at all). Civilian employment increased a sixth in the United States and possibly a fifth in Canada. Britain and Germany were less fortunate in this respect. Britain, with slower population growth and less prewar unemployment than the two North American nations, had suffered an actual diminution in its civilian employment of about 4 per cent by 1943 and 8 per cent by 1945; it was only possible to make up the 4 per cent decline in 1943 by asking the average worker to put in 9 per cent more hours in each workweek. German civilian employment fell and by mid-1943 it was over a fifth below 1939; if foreigners are counted, civilian employment was only a fifteenth below mid-1943. In the case of Germany, compensating extensions in hours were minor, for its workweek was lengthened only 4 per cent in the first two years and it lost most of that increase by 1944.

4. Excluding these, however, the labor force rose 8.5 million in the United States, 1.8 million in Britain, and 0.6 million in Canada. In the

16

United States, the rise was from 54.1 per cent of the population 14 and older before the war to 62.3 per cent at the war peak, or 8.2 per cent compared with 6.8 in Canada and 4.7 per cent in Great Britain. In some degree, the comparison with prewar is unduly favorable to the United States and Canada and unfavorable to Great Britain, for the labor force participation rates of the United States and Canada were depressed in 1940 or 1939 whereas that of Britain was expanded somewhat in view of the war mobilization already partly in effect in 1939. Based on *post-war* (1947) labor force participation, the wartime excess is 6.4 per cent in United States, 5.4 per cent in Britain, and 5.1 per cent in Canada.

5. On any basis of comparison Germany made the poorest record for wartime additions. Its labor force lost native Germans, even aside from war deaths; counting foreigners in its labor force, the expansion was still much less than that in the United States. The relative failure of Germany to get more of its citizens to seek work cannot be attributed to emigration, Allied bombing, "high" birth rates, small reserves of women in the peacetime labor force, or a more complete labor force mobilization at the start of the war.

6. The inflows to the labor force in the various countries were domi-nated by the military draft. Until the armed forces were enlarged, labor force expansion was negligible. With demobilization of nine-tenths of the peak armed strength, the United States labor force shrank eight-tenths of its excess over prewar size (disregarding the population growth). An average for the war of about 70 persons was added to the United States labor force for every 100 men taken into the armed forces. However, the addition was not uniform from year to year. It was rela-tively large—between 70 and 119—early in the war and relatively small —about 50—in the last two years of war. The five-year average, 72, was almost the same as Canada's during 1939–1945. Labor force increase measured against the military draft was very different in Great Britain, where it was 47 during 1939–1943 and a substantial negative amount during the two last years, and in Germany, where it was zero or nega-tive during 1939–1944.

7. In this country females accounted for slightly more than half the wartime addition to the labor force (including the part due to popula-tion growth); in Britain for eight-tenths. Excluding the part due to population rise, the United States added 35 females for every 100 fe-males at work before the war, Britain 21, and Canada 19 (compared with 1941); Germany relinquished 1. For every hundred males at work before the war the United States added 9, Canada 6, Britain 2, and Germany 0.3.

8. Besides the increases in employment and hours worked, there were large transfers from less essential to more essential jobs. The major

17

shifts to war production in all four countries named above probably occurred *within* industries. Nevertheless, mobility *between* industries was not lacking. In the United States all industry groups except agriculture gained workers early in the war. By 1943, industrial employment had exceeded 1939 levels by about half. By 1945, transportation had expanded almost three-fourths over 1939; services (including government) over a fourth; trade, distribution, and finance remained about steady.

9. Great Britain's industrial employment decreased after 1942, and in 1945 was lower than in 1939; however, the fluctuations were never wide. Agriculture, services, and transportation changed little during the six years, and commerce, trade, and finance lost heavily between 1939 and 1943. Britain built up its war industries and agriculture by severely curtailing domestic services, construction, trade, distribution, finance, and the manufacture of clothes, food, and beverages.

10. The Germans were less ingenious or less determined than the British in restricting nonessentials. Throughout the war, domestic service, employing chiefly native Germans, was almost undisturbed. Agriculture and industry parted with workers at first, but by the war's end had about retrieved what they had lost at the war's start. Employment fell in most service industries, also in commerce, trade, and finance. Transportation made negligible gains.

11. In none of the countries was direct compulsion the major factor in recruiting wartime labor. The United States never required civilians to work. Germany had universal conscription on paper but did not thoroughly enforce it until after the Allied landing, when it was too late to use the extra labor effectively. Half of Britain's additions were made before the National Service Act. Even after that, its policy was still persuasion. Coercion was not relied upon extensively until the last two years, during which, paradoxically, the labor force as a whole and essential employment both declined.

12. Wartime movements into the labor force may have been influenced by four factors: (1) reserves of labor among students, housewives, and the elderly; (2) the extent to which care of families prevented girls and women from taking gainful work; (3) government allowances to dependents of fighting men; (4) the strength of enemy blows. These factors help to explain the large proportion added in the United States, which had a larger reservoir of females outside its peacetime labor force than either Britain or Germany. Allotments to dependents of fighting men in the United States, though by no means niggardly, were smaller relatively than in Germany or Canada, but were not reduced if the recipient worked for pay, though they were in the other two countries.

18

13. Most additions to the labor force during the war came when the enemy was hitting hardest. In Britain six in ten of the additions were made before the U.S.S.R. entered the war; in this country two in three came during the two years before the Italian surrender in mid-1943; in Germany the few additional native workers entered after the Stalingrad disaster. Canada, an auxiliary belligerent, distributed its expansion fairly evenly throughout the five years of the war.

14. The homeward-bound armed forces of the three English-speaking victors trailed the exodus of civilians. Civilian workers, so many of them women, quit war industries first, shifting into less essential sectors perhaps, and then leaving the labor force to return home and await the returning warriors. The entire shrinkage of the labor force in the United States occurred between March 1945 and May 1946; it took longer in Canada and Britain but was about complete by early 1947.

15. Aside from the wartime increase in labor force attributable to population growth, the great bulk of additions proved to be temporary in three countries. (No satisfactory postwar comparisons can be made for dismembered Germany.) In America postwar participation did not decrease to the 1940 level, a fact that misled many into believing it was still expanded from the war. This mistake arose from the failure to perceive that the labor force at the turn of the 1940's had been somewhat depressed, probably by the widespread unemployment.

16. In the Korean conflict, the labor force showed signs of retracing its early World War II pattern by rising as the armed forces expanded. However, the ratio of its increase to recruitments was much less than half that in 1941–1943, possibly because in April 1940 the labor force had been, proportionately, depressed. With the approaching end of the conflict the labor force proportion returned to near peacetime proportions without any appreciable demobilization of armed forces.

THE LABOR FORCE UNDER SHORT-RUN CHANGES (CHAPTER 11, concluded).

1. In time of peace the total labor force in the United States has been a relatively stable proportion of the total population 14 and older in the short run. Since 1946 the maximum fluctuation in participation, seasonally adjusted, has been well under 3 per cent of the working-age population. The labor force data are based on interviews conducted each month with a representative sample of the nation's households, and a good part of the range of fluctuation—perhaps all of it—could have been the result of errors in sampling or in interviewing. The fluctuation in Canada has been slightly greater than in the United States, partly perhaps because the data during much of the postwar period in that country were quarterly estimates instead of quarterly averages.

2. An analysis by means of partial correlation (holding unemployment and armed forces constant) suggests that during the World War II period (1940–1946) there may have been a significant inverse association between real income and participation for all groups except persons 65 and older, and a significant positive association between money hourly earnings and participation, the same group excepted. But during the postwar period (1946–1952) the correlations showed little agreement in sign either from one group to another or from war to postwar years. On the basis of this evidence it is not possible to claim a dependable association between participation and income or earnings during the period from 1940 to 1952.

3. The armed forces have had a clear-cut association in size with the labor force in the United States, but only when the number of men in uniform has varied on a grand scale, as in World War II. There are theoretical reasons for believing that the armed force changes caused the labor force changes. The small-scale changes in the armed forces during the period between the end of World War II and the beginning of the Korean conflict had some association with the labor force in both the United States and Canada, but the association was not strong in the United States and it was weaker in Canada—doubtless partly because the small labor force changes were obscured by sampling and interview error.

4. The peacetime labor force behavior has not been *fundamentally* different in the short run from the long run, or in periods of "full" employment from periods of less than full employment.

5. What information we have on "gross changes" in the labor force (the sum of persons who enter and leave in any month) suggests that they have occurred at a regular rate and have not been responsive to variations in income and unemployment.

6. Neither the total labor force nor the major age-sex groups behaved in the relatively mild recessions of 1949–1950 or 1953–1954 in a manner to confirm any theory that unemployment drives a net number of workers into or out of the labor force. The partial correlations between labor force and unemployment in the postwar period (holding armed forces and income or earnings constant) suggest a larger participation when unemployment was larger, but they are generally insignificant or only mildly significant. There was no dependable reaction of participation to unemployment in these recessions.

THE STABLE LABOR FORCE UNDER RISING INCOMES AND HIGH EMPLOYMENT (CHAPTER 12).

1. The over-all labor force participation rate has been rather impressively stable from one high-employment census year to another. The stability has held for the United States since 1890 and possibly

SUMMARY AND CONCLUSIONS

since 1820; for Great Britain since 1911 and possibly since 1841; for Canada since 1911; for New Zealand during 1896–1951; and for Germany during 1895–1939. In none of the countries or rural and urban areas has the average variation been more than 1.7 per cent of the total working-age population. In the United States during 1890–1950 the maximum fluctuation between successive high-employment census dates was less than the normal seasonal variation in any given year.

2. The labor force has been a stable proportion of the working-age population—adjusted or unadjusted for undercounts and overcounts at certain censuses, and standardized or unstandardized for changes in the composition of the population. However, the over-all participation rate has been especially stable in the United States when standardized with respect to age, sex, rural and urban residence, color, and nativity, and in the other four countries with respect to age and sex (other standardizations not being possible).

3. In the United States the stability has also extended to rural areas, urban areas, and large cities taken in the aggregate, though not individually. In Canada, it seems much less marked; but requisite data are available only for 1941 (a World War II year) and 1951, and it has not been possible to standardize directly within rural and urban Canada for changes in age and sex composition.

4. Labor force participation has remained relatively stable in all the five countries during periods of increase in real annual disposable income per adult-male equivalent worker, or per capita. All the countries except Germany where income changes were small and uncertain manifested substantial income increases over the long run and for almost every decade.

5. The stability for the United States has been due to the behavior of the native white population. Both colored and foreign-born have reduced their participation by impressive amounts; in the case of Negroes nearly all of the reduction has occurred since 1930. The foreign-born, the native-born children of the foreign-born, and Negroes have all tended in recent decades to align their participation to the same level as that of native whites.

6. The over-all participation rate has remained stable in spite of marked changes for major age and sex groups. In all five countries participation has decreased to some extent for every male age group and increased for most female groups. The *net* change in the over-all labor force has generally been only a small percentage of the *gross* change.

7. The over-all stability of participation has also been marked when compared with changes in unemployment, or with seasonal changes in the labor force itself.

8. The stability of the labor force has been measured without regard

21

to the fact that some persons hold more than one job. Sample data in the United States over the last decade indicate that dual job-holding has been rather small and (until recently) constant despite great changes in the labor market. Recently dual job-holding seems to have increased somewhat, though what appears to be an increase may be the result of improvements in measurement techniques. Much of it is actually sequential (meaning that a person gives up one job on Tuesday and takes another on Thursday, thus holding two jobs in the same week), or nominal (holding two jobs but working at only one of them).

9. The stability of participation that we find in the United States in 38 large cities, taken in the aggregate, has been less impressive in those same cities taken individually.

10. Individual cities did not have very stable participation rates for whites. For Negroes the rates were extremely unstable, declining in every city for both sexes, for males, and for females.

11. The changes for whites and Negroes in the individual cities were not associated dependably with changes in size of city, with change in male earnings or in levels of male earnings, or with variations in job opportunity as reflected in unemployment rates.

12. White participation showed some tendency to rise in cities having small proportions of foreign-born.

13. White female participation rose in most cities simultaneously with a general decrease in the relative number of white children to be cared for, but the sizes of these changes were not significantly correlated. Among Negro females, however, the decline in labor force participation was significantly associated with the rise in the relative number of children (the latter occurring in nearly all cities as a result of a higher rate of survival of Negro children).

14. Participation rates of Negroes tended to decrease most in those cities where they had been highest to begin with, and were more nearly equal among cities in 1950 than in 1920. No such development could be discovered among the whites.

OVER-ALL STABILITY versus INTERNAL INSTABILITY IN A NATION'S LABOR FORCE PARTICIPATION (CHAPTER 13).

1. The fact that the over-all participation rate was stable in each of the five countries and in rural and urban areas of the United States, despite great internal changes, raises the question whether the stability has been due to some systematic tendency for the internal changes to offset each other.

2. There is, in fact, some statistical indication that in all the countries and areas participation rates of various female age groups have risen in a manner to offset the declines in male participation rates. The correlations between male and female participation have not been significant,

unless the data of war-torn Germany are excluded from the comparison, and in any case are not strong. Yet nearly all the coefficients are of the same inverse sign and, considering the element of randomness in the underlying data, seem to call for some explanation of how such a relationship could exist.

3. The hypothesis is advanced here that women may have both pushed and pulled young and elderly males from the labor force, to some extent seeking jobs that had been or were being sought by males, and to some extent being drawn into the labor force by the vacuum left by the exodus of males for other reasons.

4. The *source* of the influx of females could be their release from housework—as the result of the developing technology for the home, fewer children to be cared for, and the increased number of women surviving childbirth and disease. The *demand* could be explained by the expansion of clerical occupations which, with the great increase in educational attainment of the average female, opened new job opportunities to her. The *timing* could be reconciled with the shorter normal workweek in industry, which made it further possible for many females having household responsibilities to enter the labor force.

5. The hypothesis that the rising participation of females played a role in the declining participation of youths need not be discarded merely because that decline was reflected fairly closely in the rise of youths attending school. Some of those who entered school undoubtedly did so for cultural and legal reasons; as they left the labor force, a gap would have been created which women would have been called upon to fill. Others may have sought education because the good jobs were taken by the mature and better trained women. Many were able to remain in high school or college because working female relatives were contributing to family earnings.

6. The decline in the participation of older men—45 to 64, and 65 and older—has not been as easy to explain on independent grounds as that of the school-age males. No statistical evidence could be found, in either this or other studies, that the decline has been the immediate result of increases in real income, extension of pensions and social security, physical deterioration (compared with elderly men in earlier periods), or of changes in self-employment, the pace of industry, or the level of employment. Even if a tightening of company rules and practices against hiring and retaining older workers had been primarily responsible (there was no lack of such discrimination a half century ago), the reason for the tightening would need to be explained. Employers would surely have been less ready to part with this supply of labor had there not been available a new and better source—namely women.

7. It would seem plausible—in view of the close moment-of-time

23

relationship between education completed and participation, and of the great increase in the ratio of education completed by women to that completed by elderly men—that women displaced elderly men because of their better training for many clerical, personal service, and professional jobs in comparison to their relative wages. And financial assistance from a working daughter or wife—even her ability to support herself without help—doubtless aided many a sick or unemployed man to advance his retirement.

8. Over-all participation remained stable although the amount of leisure increased, the increase having taken the form of reductions in normal working hours for the average labor force member.

9. Reductions in the full-time workweek occurred in every one of the four nations for which standard hours data could be compiled, and they occurred between every census date, except in Hitler Germany between 1933 and 1939. The average reductions per decade were rather remarkably uniform among the four nations, but there were wide variations from one decade to the next. And there seemed to be no dependable association over the short run between reductions in hours and increases in income in the short run. Yet there was sufficient possibility that income increases played a long-run role (in the sense of inducing or enabling people to work less) to justify asking why reductions should have taken place in hours instead of in over-all participation.

10. There are grounds for believing that a reduction in hours offered a more convenient and more flexible device for distributing, among workers and over time, any increase in leisure that might be demanded as a result of rising incomes. The large rise in the number of households relative to the population has meant that a greater number of workers was needed merely to provide each household with a primary worker. The great majority of families had no more than one worker at the start and consequently could not have parted with a full-time labor force member—at least not permanently. Temporary or spasmodic periods away from work may jeopardize a person's job and in any case may result in an uneven distribution of leisure over the year.

11. If people have sought more leisure as a result of rising incomes, it is likely that all the members of a family wish to share in this leisure by means of a shorter workweek for all—instead of having some members continue to work an undiminished week and others withdraw altogether from the labor force; a reduction in hours therefore seems a more equitable device for distributing leisure among individuals and groups.

12. This latter expectation is apparently contradicted by the fact that the decline in the participation of males and the rise in the participation of females have shifted much of the burden of work from

24

men to women. But if account is taken of the decline in the housekeeping responsibilities of women as a result of technological and demographic developments, and of the extent to which men have taken over many chores formerly done by women in the home, servants, and maintenance services, it may be that the decrease in work and the increase in leisure have been fairly evenly distributed after all.

13. Workers who desired a longer workweek so as to allow other members of the family to withdraw altogether from the labor force are not likely to have influenced the average workweek appreciably. Technical conditions of production press toward uniform hours throughout a factory or store, regardless of the wishes of a minority.

14. Once normal working hours had been reduced, all sorts of obstacles would have prevented their being raised again: a tendency for shorter hours to be frozen into maximum hours, union agreements, factory shift schedules, commuting arrangements, and pace of work.

15. In the future, unions will probably play a leading role in initiating and furthering reductions in the full-time workweek, even if their role in the past has not been the dominant one. Unions are, of course, far more powerful now than during the years when most reductions in working hours occurred. And a curtailment in the workweek is likely to be more acceptable to unions than a reduction in the labor force, if only as a device for spreading work among as many workers as possible in a time of declining employment. It should not be surprising if reductions in the labor supply continue to take the form of fewer hours, and perhaps less effort per hour, rather than of reduced participation, nor if the over-all labor force continues to stay rather close to its present and past percentages of working-age population.

16. The decline in participation of the foreign-born and Negroes in the United States raises the question of why the native whites or the *all classes* did not also show declines. The explanation may be that these minority groups—as their more sharply rising incomes converged toward those of the native whites—tended to adopt the working habits of the latter. This view is supported by the fact that among the various cities participation rates of female Negroes tended to become not only more like those of native whites, but also more like those of other female Negroes in other cities. As the remaining barriers to equal participation in the economic life of the nation break down, the Negro may aspire in an increasing degree to live and work like other Americans of the same income group.

17. Participation rates have not been stable in individual cities over time even for whites, nor in cities where the instability could not be attributed to the presence of large numbers of foreign-born.

18. This lack of stability may occur because persons already com-

mitted to the labor force tend to migrate to cities of high pay and good job opportunities, but this explanation does not seem to have strong statistical support, and we are obliged to let the instability in individual cities stand as an unexplained exception to the stability we have found for over-all labor force participation over time.

Concluding Observations on the Main Question: Is the Labor Force Influenced by Changes in Income and Employment?

At the start of this investigation, we posed three central questions: (1) Has labor force participation been influenced by changes in income and employment? (2) Has the influence, if effective, been powerful enough to stand out over other possible forces? (3) Of these other possible forces, have there been any which account for that part of labor force behavior not explained by income or employment?

It is unfortunate that a detailed and protracted search into an unusually rich and varied lode of statistical material has left our answers incomplete. For all the economic, social, and demographic forces analyzed in this study, many others had to be neglected, among them some likely to be influential.[4]

Differences in family characteristics. Large and small families may have very different participation rates, as may families with high and low incomes per member—and differences remain after standardization for age, sex, color, or other demographic differences, or after taking into account the income of the head of the family. Unfortunately the census, while it has given a great deal of family information on both labor force and population, has never classified the data for computing participation rates of families; yet many of the decisions to enter or leave the labor force are family decisions.

Changing community attitudes. The family and the community have greatly altered their attitudes toward the question of whether wives and children should work. Is the change in attitudes the cause, or the effect, of the increased participation of females and the decreased participation of children? Possibly, both attitudes and participation changes gradually molded each other or both were shaped more or less simultaneously by still other social forces.

Differences in social class. A powerful motivating force in Western societies is the aspiration to advance oneself and one's children to a

---

[4] This study has omitted the analysis of the effects of income tax on labor force participation. However, the writer has presented such an analysis in a paper to a subcommittee of Congress: Clarence D. Long, "Impact of Federal Income Tax on Labor Force Participation," *Papers Submitted by Panelists Appearing before the Subcommittee on Tax Policy,* Joint Committee on the Economic Report, 84th Cong., 1st sess., Nov. 9, 1955, pp. 153–166.

higher social class. This aspiration may be realized by working harder, by a wife's gainful employment, by restricting the size of the family, and by sustaining children in school longer before they enter the labor force. Social aspiration may be more powerful than any of the tangible influences, but there are no statistics by which to measure its impact, and we can only derive insights through observation.[5]

Social life and the job. The growth of large cities and the increasing anonymity of urban life may have caused women and older people to depend more on their jobs for companionship or marriage opportunities. The impact of this development would be all the greater, of course, as the social conditions of work became more agreeable.

Changing conditions of work. The last half century has seen a distinct improvement in working conditions—cleaner surroundings, abundance of rest-room facilities, and safety measures, as well as the courtesy of supervisors, fairness of grievance procedures, seniority protection, and coffee breaks and adequate lunch periods, to name some—which may well have persuaded many women to enter or to remain in gainful employment.

Intensity of effort required of the employee. It seems impossible to say quantitatively that there has been a decline in the intensity of effort in an hour of work; at least one British observer has concluded that the pace of work is slower in Britain than it was in the nineteenth century,[6] but such judgments must rest largely on qualitative observations because of the tremendous difficulty of measuring personal effort. Participation would surely be affected to some extent by the ability or inability of women, older persons, children, and partially disabled persons to maintain the pace of work set by industry, and by the variations in physical and mental capability of individuals at different times and in different places. Almost nothing is known statistically about such variations and their relation to participation.

Changes in technology and machinery, improvement in lighting and air conditioning, greater subdivision of tasks, and so forth, should have influence on the degree of intensity of effort called for. The time required to travel to and from work might be included in intensity—or in the length of the working day.

Increases in supplementary or "fringe" benefits. Substantial increases

---

[5] The 1951 census of Britain offers a labor force classification by five social class groups, but does not accompany it with any similar classification of population that would enable us to compute labor force participation rates by social class. In any case "the grading is no more than a convenient rearrangement of occupational unit groups and must not be considered as if it were a separate classification of individuals." *Census of 1951,* Great Britain, Part I, p. XVIII.

[6] P. J. D. Wiles, "Notes on the Efficiency of Labour," Oxford, *Oxford Economic Papers,* June 1951, pp. 158–174.

in various benefits to employees have involved expenditures by employers that are not accounted for in straight-time wage rates. These include pensions and social security contributions by employers; paid sickness and hospitalization benefits; paid holidays; premium payments for holiday, overtime, and night shift work; unemployment compensation; and annual employment or wage guarantees. A recent pilot study of a very small number of manufacturing firms has been made on this question by the Bureau of Labor Statistics.[7] But we do not know how much these benefits have increased over time, to what extent they are available to the whole labor force, and what their effect may have been on labor force participation.

Changes in unionization. During most of the sixty-year period covered in the United States, union strength comprised less than a tenth of the labor force and consisted mainly of adult males who would have been in the labor force in any case. Unions could not, therefore, have had much effect on participation in this country in the earlier years. Their role may have been greater in the other nations, and, in the recent period, in this country; for between 1935 and 1947, unions grew to about a fourth of the United States labor force and have since stayed at approximately that level. They conceivably restrict job opportunities for women and children through qualifications and apprenticeship requirements and through rules on equal pay. Also they impose a "tax" on earnings in the form of union dues, although these are not high for most members. Influence of unions on labor force participation would be difficult to measure, and probably is confined to affecting which occupations and industries women and children enter. It is noteworthy that the accelerated influx of women into the labor force since 1930 could occur in the face of the greatest increase of unionization this country has experienced.

Changes in the distribution of income. In addition to increases in average real income in recent decades, there probably has been a considerable redistribution of income, before and after taxes. The structure of income distribution has many theoretical consequences for labor force—a notable one is its effect on rivalries in respect to living standards, and the need to work in order to keep up with (or ahead of) the Joneses. Materials for an investigation of these aspects exist, but it would be a considerable undertaking. Related to the income distribution among families is income distribution *within* families. Some wives may have entered the labor force because their husbands were unwilling, especially during inflation, to supplement fixed household allow-

[7] *Problems in Measurement of Expenditures on Selected Items of Supplementary Employee Remuneration, Manufacturing Establishments,* 1953, Bulletin 1186, Bureau of Labor Statistics, January 1956. The report was prepared by J. W. Bloch.

ances which may have lagged behind the prices of food and clothing, and even behind wages. It will be some time before there will be adequate statistics on family budgets for the study of such a factor.

Changing burdens of credit. Any change in the ease with which people can buy clothes, appliances, cars, and houses on the installment plan could influence participation. Heavy commitments of future income in order to buy durable consumer goods could easily oblige wives to enter or stay in the labor force. Here again, lacking information, we can only theorize from personal observation.

Changes in wealth and liquid assets. Whether an older worker, an unemployed worker, a partially injured worker, or an expectant mother can leave the labor force very likely depends to some extent upon past savings or any net wealth accumulated in other ways, and upon the liquidity of the assets. But there are no data through which to discover the nature or amount of the relationship to labor force participation.

Changes in leisure-time activities. The last half century has seen a great increase in the types and variety of non-gainful activities of the average person: the widening interest in sports; the popularization of movies, radio, and television; the use of automobiles for holiday and vacation trips; the development of summer camps for teen-agers; the extension of hobbies. All these have influenced participation, partly because they compete for a person's time, and thus may reduce participation; and partly because they may call for higher income, thereby increasing participation. Comment on the nature of this influence would be worth little in the absence of quantitative information.

Without systematic knowledge of the foregoing factors and many other elements of the problem, our answers to the central questions of this investigation are incomplete, hesitant, and speculative. Do changes in income influence labor force? Probably yes—provided other things do not change very much. Under comparatively static conditions, the higher the income the lower the participation, with rather great changes in income required to bring about moderate changes in the over-all participation rate.

There is, of course, the theoretical possibility that what we have seen, rather, is a reverse influence of labor force on income; i.e. a large labor supply might depress the level of wages. But such a reverse effect could scarcely amount to much. For one thing, the significance of a large or small labor supply depends much more on its size relative to the quantity of land, capital, management, and technique than on its size relative to population. For another, labor force size is only one dimension of labor supply—the others being hours, effort, and labor force quality—so that changes in labor force size are only one supply factor influencing wages. For still another, even if labor supply affects the level of wages, it would probably influence mainly the share of labor in the total income and would have only a small impact on the absolute level of earnings per worker; in view of the smallness of labor force changes relative to income changes, such a reverse effect would be a case of a small tail wagging a large dog. Finally, it is scarcely likely that, say, the high participation of a wife could be the cause of low earnings of the husband—unless one makes much of the occasional husband who relaxes his effeorts greatly because his spouse has taken over some of the breadwinner's responsibility.

There is the theoretical possibility that both labor force and income are jointly influenced by some third force. But what could it be? Age? Sex? Color? Nativity? Child-care responsibilities of women? All these have been taken fairly well into account by standardization. Employment opportunities? They may well affect participation, but they cannot explain away the inverse relationship between labor force and income; for that has been upheld *within* the same metropolitan areas, where the industrial and occupational structure is the same to poor and well-to-do alike. Education? A three-cornered relationship of education, income, and participation has been found for females; but since good education goes with both high income and high participation, it cannot explain away the inverse relationship between the last two. Thus, although we do not rule out the possibility that the inverse association between labor force and income at a moment of time has been the joint result of outside forces, we cannot easily imagine what those outside forces could be.

Is the labor force influenced by changes in employment? Probably yes, in the case of severe or great depressions, of the kind experienced during the 1930's—with, however, a very large increase in unemployment required to cause a small net decrease in the over-all labor force participation rate. Probably no, in the case of employment changes which are moderate and not associated with great changes in the size of the armed forces. Inasmuch as the violent unemployment fluctuation of the 1930's and early 1940's has been unique in our recorded history,[8] it would seem that, except under unusual circumstances, the labor force is not influenced by the *quantity* of employment opportunities, i.e. the per cent of those in the labor force who are able to find jobs. Whether labor force is influenced by the quality of employment opportunity is another matter. Many more women might be in the labor force if there were an abundance of physically light, clerical jobs, than if opportunities were confined to heavy, manual labor.

[8] Stanley Lebergott, "Annual Estimates of Unemployment in the United States, 1900–1954," in *The Measurement and Behavior of Unemployment,* Princeton University Press for the National Bureau of Economic Research, 1957.

If participation is explained only feebly or not at all by dynamic changes in income and employment, what does explain its behavior? What explains the rather generally declining participation of young and old people; the generally increasing participation of females (especially wives); and the generally stable participation of the whole working-age population, during both long- and short-run periods of peacetime and moderately high employment? What explanation will also fit the great increases in labor force during World War II and the decreases at the war's end—as well as the fact that, in the United States, the stability of over-all participation has been confined to native whites, with the participation of Negroes and foreign-born generally declining in recent decades?

No single factor or small number of factors could entirely explain such behavior in a complex and rapidly moving economy. In any case, it would be impossible to isolate the effects empirically, for some of the forces might well act jointly, and others send out waves of influence in all directions, waves which may eventually break upon the labor force after a considerable lag and as if deriving from other sources. Nevertheless, it may be possible to single out a few dynamic forces that are capable of explaining important elements of labor force behavior.

One of these may be the growing redundancy of working-age females as a result of the declining birth rate and the rising survival rate of women—which reduced the relative need for women in own home housework. The effect of these demographic developments was probably accentuated by the advancing technology for the home. Together, these reductions in the home housekeeping burden may account for the great secular increase in the availability of females for gainful work. And housekeeping responsibilities of women were further reduced temporarily during World War II by substantial amounts, as a result of the immense draft of men into the armed forces; this temporary reduction provides a possibly important contributing explanation for the large temporary influx of women into the labor force.

A second dynamic force was the dramatic increase in education of the average woman, both absolute and relative to that of older men. In conjunction with the growing need for clerical and service labor, this probably gave women a comparative advantage over the less well-trained and frequently overpaid older worker and the untrained child; and it may account for ability of the market to absorb the increased supply of women.

The increase of female workers may in turn have forced the exodus of the young and older males. Women—better trained and better suited for the jobs, and often willing to work for less—may well have out-competed males in the job market and made employers ready to pass rules against older workers (which to so many have appeared to be the real force in compelling earlier retirement). In addition, the earnings of the women could have helped finance longer schooling for the young males and earlier retirement for the older ones. This pressure exerted by women does not exclude independent reasons for the withdrawal of males—growing incomes and cultural and institutional changes undoubtedly played their parts, and the males who departed for these reasons left a vacuum which helped draw women into the labor force. But it is our hypothesis that the prime mover was the influx of female workers, and that their displacement of the male worker helps to explain the stability in over-all participation.

A third force would seem to have been the substantial reduction in the hours normally worked by the average labor force member, which occurred in greater or less degree in all the four nations with hours data. This reduction surely enabled many wives and mothers of school-age children to work and still have time to shop, cook, and do a minimum of house cleaning, rest a bit, provide husbands with some companionship, and partake of some occasional amusements. It would also help explain why the over-all participation of the whole working-age population has remained relatively stable, instead of declining as incomes doubled or tripled; for hours reductions were probably a more convenient, flexible, and equitable means of spreading leisure than were reductions in participation. A now powerful union movement will very likely find hours reductions the most acceptable way of effecting any future decreases in labor supply—whether those decreases represent rising demands for leisure, as incomes rise secularly, or a falling demand for labor, as employment declines in depressions. Union agreements—as well as maximum hour laws, factory shift arrangements, and growing suburbanization calling for longer commuting—would freeze at the lower levels any hours changes that have been made for other reasons. The demand for leisure has thus probably been definitely and irrevocably shunted onto the track toward fewer hours, so that any reductions in labor supply will continue to take the form mainly or wholly of fewer hours and less effort per hour, with the labor force staying close to its present and past percentages of working-age population.

These three main forces—the release of females from home housework and child care, the increase in the relative education of women, and the reduction in the normal workweek—may furnish a major part of the explanation of why participation rose for females, declined for young and older males, and remained stable for the whole working-age population, despite our expectation that rising income should have led all of them to decline. That interpretation is not inconsistent with our explanation of why foreign-born and Negroes tended to reduce

32

their over-all participation: for these minority groups were doubtless bringing their labor force tendencies into line with those of the dominant native whites. The breaking down of occupational barriers may have been partly due to rising incomes of the native whites, who could be expected to offer less resistance to the competition of minority groups for jobs when their own prosperity was relatively high—thus making increasingly feasible the adoption by minority groups of the living and working habits of the native whites.

The three dynamic factors emphasized do not explain all the labor force behavior our study has revealed; especially they do not explain the instability over time of the labor force participation of individual cities. And rarely do they furnish a "tight" explanation of any labor force development.

But this should not be surprising: many of the statistics used here were less than satisfactory in either concept or measurement, and data for the study of many factors were lacking altogether. Nor should it be surprising if income turned out to play a larger role in the dynamic behavior of labor force than our statistics could discover. Economic forces may exert their influence mainly through social or institutional channels, which wind in much the same way as do those of a great river to sea. While the general course is there, its direction or rapidity of movement at any one time or place depends on the terrain, in a manner hidden from a lone, pedestrian explorer, able to follow its meanderings for only a comparatively short part of the way.

CHAPTER 2

THE RELATIONSHIP OF LABOR SUPPLY TO ECONOMIC AND OTHER INFLUENCES

"Everyone but an idiot knows that the lower classes must be kept poor or they will never be industrious."

ARTHUR YOUNG

Some Theories of Labor Supply Behavior

EACH person may have a different reason or combination of reasons for working. Everyone may go through stages in his life when new influences appear and others fade away. These motivations could not depend merely on the personality of the individual. They are likely to spring from many external factors—differing among persons or during the life of a given person—which not only influence his motivation to work (given his personality) but also alter his personality.

The many reasons for working and the factors that nourish them are the product of social, cultural, or spiritual forces independent of—even at war with—economic motivations. Nevertheless, there are enough obvious roots in economic soil to warrant inquiring whether economic forces, such as employment opportunities or income, play an important role in determining the supply of labor.

A specific question that has always intrigued economists is: Does an increase in wages cause the labor supply to expand or to shrink? Many thinkers have concluded that once workers have satisfied their pressing needs for food, clothing, and shelter, they will be eager for surcease from honest toil. "This view [the view that low wages mean large labor supply]," said Maurice Dobb, "seems to have been exclusively held by earlier centuries to the neglect of other considerations." [1]

The belief that people will work less as they become more prosperous has not been the sole property of earlier centuries. For example, W. Stanley Jevons held that "English labourers enjoying little more than the necessaries of life, will work harder the less they produce; or . . . will work less hard as the produce increases. . . . The richer a man becomes, the less does he devote himself to business." [2] Frank Knight has suggested that one of the goods purchased with increased earnings is leisure.[3] Even J. A. Hobson, never one to cast his reflections in the classical mold, has conceded that, "Though workers . . . will hardly

---

[1] Maurice H. Dobb, *Wages* (*Cambridge Economic Handbook*), London, Cambridge University Press, 1948, p. 59.

[2] *Theory of Political Economy*, London, Macmillan, 4th ed., 1911, pp. 180–181.

[3] *Risk, Uncertainty, and Profit*, Houghton Mifflin, 1921, p. 117.

ever claim a shorter working day if they know it to involve an actual fall of wages, . . . they will sometimes risk the fall and more often they will forego a portion of a contemplated rise of wages, so as to get a shorter day." And the forward-looking Sir Sydney Chapman predicted, a decade after the turn of the century, that "the attempt would *almost* certainly be to buy more leisure with higher wages, all the more so since each hour of leisure is enriched by possession." He agreed with Schmoller that "the more complex the social organization, the more time its members must devote to family and recreation, education and general affairs." [4]

Most of the foregoing conclusions have been based more or less explicitly on the notion that people work less as they become more prosperous because the more goods a person commands as a result of his higher income, the less he is inclined to value any additional amounts and the less work he is inclined to do to acquire them. These conclusions have not, however, as Lionel Robbins [5] made clear, been founded on very precise analysis of how people do, in practice, value income in terms of effort. Increased affluence would, other things being equal, be accompanied by reduced labor supply *per dollar of income*, but could be perfectly compatible with either an increase or a decrease in the *total labor* supply. Since no two individuals would necessarily react in the same way, how can one know what the average person will do? Solely by measuring the differences in labor supply under varying wages.

The Relation of Labor Supply to Economic and Other Influences

The aggregate quantity of labor supplied to the market by the inhabitants of a nation or locality, as reflected by the labor force and, to some extent, by hours is the subject of this investigation. Determination of how much of the supply goes to individual firms is beyond the scope of the study, since migration and industrial and occupational mobility are even more complicated matters than the labor force. Also outside its range is group control of labor supply in the form of collective bargaining or other devices. It is impossible to measure the effects of such activity because of the subtle and complicated combinations of political and economic factors, the variety of union constitutions and practices, and the shortage of statistics. Indeed, to the extent that unions behave as monopolists and therefore try to maximize the income of their members, they must take the demand for labor into consideration in de-

[4] "Hours of Labour," *Economic Journal*, September 1909, pp. 357–358.
[5] "On the Elasticity of Demand for Income in Terms of Effort," *Economica*, June 1930, pp. 123–129.

termining the supply of labor; thus there can be no such thing as a supply independent of demand. Group control will no doubt be affected by some of the considerations that govern individuals acting independently; during a strike the union will not hold out as long, or for as favorable a settlement, if its members are anxious to get back to their regular earnings. But, in the main, the wages and other supplementary benefits it aims for will depend on what it believes to be the demand for labor.[6] We investigate the aggregate behavior of individuals in entering and leaving the labor force, or in working a long or short week, on the assumption that these decisions would not appreciably affect the wage of the individual or his family, and, as a corollary, that each individual acts quite apart from others insofar as any intention of manipulating wages is concerned.

It is not implied, however, that the individual makes up his mind to enter or to leave the labor force with complete independence. As we noticed earlier, he is influenced in a thousand ways: by the number of other adults in his family who are already in the labor force or ready to join it; by community attitudes that "woman's place is in the home" and the man should provide; by his neighbor's standard of living; and by an inclination to conform with fellow members in his union, lodge, and country club. He is bound by laws which keep his children out of the labor force and in school until a certain age, which set maximum hours or minimum wages and may, in cases of borderline employability, make it impossible for his wife (or perhaps his children, or himself) to get a job. And he is affected by rules laid down by employers in the interest of efficiency and humanity. They may prevent his wife from working half time and, since she must be home when the children are not in school, may thus prevent her from working at all; they may force him to retire at 60 or 65 although he is willing and able to continue working. Group influences on the individual are considered wherever possible, but this does not prohibit dealing with the relation between the labor force, on the one hand, and wages or income as an independent variable on the other.

With few exceptions, the labor force is expressed in this inquiry as a percentage of the population, and the forces that determine the size of the population are ignored. Nevertheless, the percentage of population in the labor force will vary with the characteristics of the population and these characteristics must carefully be taken into account. It will be higher if the inhabitants are predominantly men, if they are healthy, intelligent, well educated, adaptable, emotionally stable and

[6] F. H. Knight, "Supply," in *Encyclopedia of the Social Sciences*, Vol. XIV, p. 473; J. T. Dunlop, *Wage Determination under Trade Unions*, Macmillan, 1944, pp. 31–32.

therefore to a high degree employable, if they live in families of one
or two people, or if many of them are Negroes or city dwellers. It will
be lower if most women are married and have young children to care
for. In Western nations, it will be lower if most people live on isolated
farms or in small villages, where the only jobs are frequently too distant
for easy commuting.

Not to be overlooked as an influence on the percentage of population
in the labor force is the nature of industry. Business or labor organizations help to determine in what occupations or industries workers are
concentrated. More women may be in the labor force if the full-time
week is very short and flexible, or if there is an abundance of clerical,
service, and light bench jobs. Old or disabled men presumably have a
better chance of staying on if the pace of industry is not too fast. Young
people have more opportunities to get jobs after school or in summer
if there are no rigid union rules against child labor or apprentices.

Even climate may have something to do with willingness and ability
to work, though present-day geographers point out the weakness of
the evidence on this topic.

Finally, if wages or income influence the propensity to work they
need not do so in any simple way. Although the wage offered may be
the most obvious factor influencing a man's decision to work, he may
also take into consideration his nonlabor income, such as dividends,
interest, rent saved from living in his own home or other property income, and the incomes of other members of his family. In theory, his
decision can be affected by the amount and type of taxes to which he
is subject. More women might enter the labor force if, in computing
income tax, they could deduct the cost of maids, baby sitters, and
nursery schools. Some well-to-do persons might postpone their retirement if increased income taxes reduced their ability to save—or, conversely, if the income tax were made less steeply progressive, permitting them to keep a larger share of what they earn. We need to know
whether these theoretical effects of taxation on labor force participation have been realized in any noteworthy way in practice.

The reaction of labor supply to a given wage may, moreover, be
affected by the way income is distributed; for people not only work,
but spend, competitively. A family with a $5,000 annual income may
have very different labor force propensities depending on whether its
neighbors' incomes average $7,500 or $2,500. Also possibly significant
—and so far entirely overlooked—is the way income is distributed
among members of the same family. For example, wives, to a considerable extent, receive fixed incomes and may conceivably be pressed
into the labor force in increasing numbers during inflation by rising
costs of food, clothing, and cosmetics.

Also to be considered is the way in which incomes are received—whether the wage or salary is fixed per hour, week, or year; whether higher than proportional pay is received for overtime; whether the worker is on a commission or a piece rate; whether the income is regular or fluctuates so that a person must earn enough in good times to tide him over slack periods; and, finally, whether taxes are withheld each month, paid at the end of the year, or taken as excise levies on commodity purchases.

Closely related to income is wealth. Do a man's assets exceed his liabilities, can he draw on them readily, and how do they compare with his standard of living? Also related are claims on social security by an older man who ponders retirement; claims on unemployment insurance by a young wife who pretends to be seeking employment when her actual plan is to have a baby; claims on military allowances by a soldier's wife, who may discover in some countries that working does not yield enough extra to justify giving up the government subsidy; claims for educational allowances by a discharged veteran who is considering college or trade school. Akin to all these is credit: the ability to borrow from relatives, or to charge the expense of necessities during a brief period of unemployment or sickness, may make it unnecessary to withdraw children from school in order to help with the family support.[7]

To assess the impact of these various factors is not easy nor is it always possible. Data are often lacking, or are not easily related to labor force behavior—as in the case of credit, income distribution, community attitudes, health, intelligence, and emotional stability. Many of the forces are closely intercorrelated: high birth rates and heavy responsibilities for child care, which hinder women from entering the labor force, are often associated with low incomes, which may propel women into it. Participation among Negroes tends to be high; but is this due to their comparative poverty or to their cultural characteristics? Ideally, each factor should be examined separately, with the others held constant, as to its relation to the size of the labor force for different areas and groups, and over time. The factors should even be analyzed in various combinations, since, in economics as in chemistry, elements may act quite differently in combination than they do individually. But limitations of data make it necessary to settle for much less.

Nevertheless, the data drawn upon are unusually rich and varied.

[7] Hicks suggests that the behavior of the poor may differ from that of the rich. A reduction in income may oblige the former to draw, at least for short periods, upon their leisure, i.e. to do more work, whereas the latter could avoid this by drawing upon their savings. However, the worker could for very short periods use credit as the equivalent of savings.

Surely more money has been spent during the last half century in gathering statistics on population and the labor force than on any other major type of general-purpose statistics. These materials enable us to make a separate examination of labor force by age, sex, color, nativity, military status, child-care responsibility, rural or urban location, density of rural population or size of city, average income of adult city worker, income group, school attendance, education completed, employment status of wife by income or employment status of husband, and working hours. Particularly valuable are the cross classifications of the last two censuses, which enable us to answer hitherto puzzling questions, such as whether the participation of women is governed mainly by income or by opportunities of employment.

Studies over time are no longer confined to the decennial censuses, which formerly left us quite in the dark as to what was happening between census years. Since 1940 a survey has been conducted for one week in each month by interviews with a sample of the nation's households. The sample results are blown up into national estimates of the labor force, employment, and unemployment, with many of the same breakdowns as in the decennial census. In addition, the monthly surveys provide information on characteristics not available in the ten-year enumeration, such as labor force turnover, availability of employed and unemployed for full-time or part-time work, and reasons for not working.

These materials allow us to single out important relationships with fair precision. Where they are lacking in detail, other things may sometimes be made equal by "standardization." Such devices always beg some questions. The problems raised by standardization are summarized in Chapter 3, but they cannot be solved to complete satisfaction.

Indeed, a complete solution can never be obtained, even in theory, to the problem of "other things equal." For man's reactions are affected by his experience—even by the order of his experience: his decision to accept or turn down a certain job may (other things equal) depend upon whether he was once poor and is now well off, or was once well off and is now poor. If such sequences of experience are significant, as we believe they are, then the patterns of labor supply which we fit to cross-sectional data in this study are open to serious question. This is perhaps one of the reasons why the relation between the labor force and income over a period of time differs so markedly from the relation at a given moment of time.

Some Previous Empirical Findings

Observers alert for empirical evidence on the behavior of labor supply in response to changes in wages and incomes have not been lacking.

As early as the decade after the Napoleonic Wars, Sir Edward West, in his *Price of Corn and Wages of Labour*, advanced the evidence of "witnesses before Committees of both Houses that the labourer in a scarce year, when his wage will furnish him with a much less than the usual quantity of food, will, in order to attain his usual supply of necessaries, be willing to do much more work than usual, even at a reduced rate of wages." [8] Very recently, P. J. D. Wiles has marshaled quantitative evidence and the testimony of travelers to support his conclusion that the "will to work" of the British has declined as compared with earlier periods and with other nations, and has ascribed the decline in part to progress.[9] The first to measure labor supply systematically, however, was Paul Douglas in his great classic, *The Theory of Wages*. Douglas, taking each of 38 large American cities as a separate observation, paired two sets of data: earnings of factory hands in 1919, and proportions of population in the labor force in January 1920. Later, in an article with Erika Schoenberg, he did the same for 1929–1930.[10] His two investigations agreed closely in the following conclusions:

1. That there was at a moment of time a significant association among cities between the level of earnings and the rate of labor force participation.

2. That the labor force was smaller by approximately six workers per 1,000 population aged 14 and older (standardized for age and sex) wherever annual earnings of equivalent adult-male factory employees were higher by $100.

3. That the labor force tended, in relative terms, to be smaller by about ⅙ per cent (population remaining constant) wherever annual earnings were higher by 1 per cent.

4. That the tendency for a smaller labor force to be associated with higher adult-male earnings extended, with wide variations, to boys and girls, to females above school age, and to older men, but not to men 20–59.

These conclusions, though interesting and important, represent only the beginning of an empirical investigation into the behavior of the labor force under changing income and employment. This is no reflection on the work of Professor Douglas, who dealt remarkably well with this complex matter within one chapter of a monumental treatise. But many and far-reaching questions remain. It is merely hinting at them to

[8] London, John Hatchard, 1826, p. 75. (I am grateful to George J. Stigler for this citation.)
[9] "Notes on the Efficiency of Labour," *Oxford Economic Papers*, Oxford, June 1951, pp. 158–174.
[10] Paul H. Douglas, *The Theory of Wages*, Macmillan, 1934, Chapter XI; Erika H. Schoenberg and Paul H. Douglas, "Studies in the Supply Curve of Labor," *Journal of Political Economy*, February 1937, pp. 45–79.

ask if the tendency obtains in rural areas, throughout states and nations, among richer and poorer persons in the same place at the same time, and for expanding incomes over long and short periods of time. Such questions, and the many others posed in subsequent chapters, can be resolved only through extensive further research. Before pursuing them, let us examine what is meant by labor supply and labor force, what are the various influences to which they may respond, and how reliable are the statistics upon which knowledge of their behavior must rely.

CHAPTER 3

THE MATERIALS AND THE METHOD

The Meaning of Labor Force and the Materials

ALL the basic statistics on labor force in the United States used in this study were obtained by home interviews, either in complete enumerations of the population by the decennial census, or in sample surveys of representative cross-sections of the population by the census or some other official statistical agency. These statistics are gathered in accordance with a fairly rigorous definition of labor force.

In the United States the labor force is currently defined as the sum of all persons reported by the census to be employed or unemployed during a certain specified week. The "employed" category covers all persons 14 or older who have jobs or businesses for pay or profit, including employers and the self-employed, unpaid family workers in a store or on a farm who help produce a salable product or service, and employees of nonprofit enterprises and government agencies. The "unemployed" category includes persons 14 and older who have no job or business of the above-mentioned sort and are seeking such employment during the survey week.

This definition by the census is not wholly satisfactory from an economic point of view (or indeed from any well thought-out point of view). Among the employed it includes inactive persons: jobholders who are sick, on vacation, weather-bound, or on temporary layoff. The first three of these groups should not be classed as employed or in the economic labor force since they are not producing goods or services and are not currently available for productive effort. The fourth (temporary layoffs) is in the economic labor force because these people are available for productive effort, but they more properly belong under the unemployed heading since they are idle involuntarily and because of economic reasons.[1] Further, persons are included as employed without regard to the number of hours they work. Some put in as much as 90 hours per week, and others, less than 15. Many of the part-time workers want only part-time work and in a sense are only part-time members of the labor force; the others want full-time work and are therefore partly unemployed.

As to the unemployed category the definition not only fails to include the temporary layoffs and partly unemployed workers mentioned

---

[1] Beginning January 1957, the census reclassified from "employed to "unemployed" persons with jobs but not at work because of temporary layoff or because they were waiting to start new jobs. And persons in the latter category, who happened to be in school while waiting, were classified as outside the labor force.

above, but gives full-time weight to the unemployed who want only part-time work. It is based on no objective description of employability, so that its inclusiveness might vary depending on the quality of the interview, the job market, or the desperation of family need for income. The belief has often been advanced that there may at times be a considerable number of *fringe workers* who want and need work but, discouraged by the difficulty of finding jobs, cease to look and so are not enumerated as unemployed. Conversely, it has frequently been suggested that when family incomes decline many persons may leave school or housework and enter the labor force as *additional workers*.

No facts have been marshalled to suggest that these defects have significantly distorted the size of the labor force; rather, the contrary. Census surveys have indicated that in ordinary times no large number of fringe workers has been overlooked, and the present investigation suggests that the number wrongly left out might be balanced by the number wrongly counted in—persons claiming to be employable or to be seeking work in order to collect unemployment insurance, persons with unrealistic wage and job aspirations, some persons now classed as unemployed on the ground that they would have been seeking a job if well, and other persons on the brink of leaving the labor force.

Studies in this volume indicate that in severe depressions fringe workers discouraged out of the labor force have probably appreciably outnumbered additional workers. Also, in mild recessions since World War II the behavior of the labor force has not been such as to demonstrate the existence of either fringe workers or additional workers. Further studies for scattered months since World War II, when the census gathered special statistics on the preferences of workers for full- and part-time work, have made it possible to construct estimates of what might be called the "economic" labor force—the number of equivalent full-time persons actually at work, plus the number of equivalent full-time persons unemployed for economic reasons (including temporary layoffs). This economic labor force deviated from the reported labor force *seasonally* (because of weather, vacations, and sickness), but over the years the relationship between economic and reported labor force manifested no trend and no systematic response to the recession of 1949–1950 or the Korean conflict. Since such data are available only for scattered months, this volume must rely mostly on the labor force reported by the census; its conclusions apply only to those data and not to a more strictly defined economic labor force. But the results might not be strikingly different even if statistics on labor force were defined and collected according to a more rigorous economic definition.

The concept of the labor force so far discussed refers to recent years.

43

Some review of the history of the concept and measurement technique is therefore in order (detailed treatment being reserved to Appendixes E and F).

Labor force data have been collected in connection with most decennial censuses since 1820. Through 1860 the data were very inferior in concept, coverage, and accuracy, and in 1870 and 1880, though much improved, were still haphazardly collected and can be used only for rough comparison. Therefore, the figures before 1890 were utilized merely to show that the earlier behavior, so far as can be judged, was not inconsistent with the later results.

The 1890–1930 censuses counted the labor force with reasonable care, but required adjustments for this study, in certain years—to make age groupings uniform in 1890–1910, to compensate for very small undercounts or overcounts in 1890, 1910, and 1920, and to correct for minor differences in the months the censuses were taken (since 1930, always in April). These corrections largely canceled each other. They are not necessarily accurate, and the degree to which they affect the conclusions of the study has been evaluated at relevant points. The chief problem in comparing the "gainfully occupied," as they were called, lay in the fact that the respondent was not asked to specify the exact period of his employment, but was classified as gainfully occupied on the strength of a rather vague "usual worker" status. In April 1940 and July 1945, two innovations in measurement technique were introduced to remedy this vagueness. The first was intended to exclude a number of persons who were usual workers at other seasons of the year but not at the time of the enumeration. The second, made in the census sample survey, was intended to bring in some housewives and students who were defined as belonging to the labor force in the survey week but were being overlooked in practice because their status was different at the moment of enumeration. The census then attempted to adjust earlier data to make them comparable with the new results; but rather intensive analysis in the present study showed that the adjustments were without very solid statistical foundation. The census downward adjustment of the 1930 data to make them comparable with the new 1940 technique is rejected altogether (see Supplementary Appendix H); the census upward adjustment of its 1940–1945 monthly sample data to make them comparable with the technique applied after July 1945 is used because, although no great confidence is placed in the resulting absolute level, most of the month-to-month variations may have been left undisturbed.

In April 1940 the labor force enumerated by the census was slightly smaller than that estimated on the basis of the monthly sample survey (then conducted by the Works Progress Administration) for the same

44

month. In April 1950 both surveys were conducted by the census, but the labor force as enumerated by the regular census was about $3\frac{1}{2}$ million less than as estimated from the sample survey. Some persons have concluded that the sample was less accurate than the complete enumeration; but a number of tests by the census, including analysis of data from households visited by both surveys, indicate that the discrepancy was attributable to the inferior ability and training of temporary enumerators, compared with the permanent sample survey staff. All of our regular censuses may have thus undercounted, for the relative size of the 1950 labor force does not seem to differ much from that of the earlier censuses. The difference with the sample result is nevertheless disconcerting; and since adjustment is impossible, this study keeps the two sets of data completely separate, using the regular census for analysis of labor force behavior over the long run, and the sample survey for analysis over the short run.

Concerning the usefulness of the regular United States census data for long-run analysis, it may be said that, for all their defects, they have been surprisingly consistent over the decades in both concept and coverage. Statistically, this judgment is supported by many intercensal comparisons during 1890–1950; qualitatively, it is supported by the fact that much the same important groups have been included (or excluded) by all censuses since 1870.[2]

The data for the four foreign countries examined in the present study are probably not as rigorous conceptually, or as comparable over time, as those of the United States. Certainly these nations do far less work of testing and analyzing their concepts and survey methods. No satisfactory data are available in Britain before 1911 (except that data for 1841, 1881, and 1891 could be used for purposes of rough comparison), in Canada before 1911, in New Zealand before 1896, or in Germany before 1895. British data had to be estimated for 1939, as no decennial census was taken between 1931 and 1951. Canadian data have excluded many females in agriculture and school boys working part time, though the latter omissions were offset by the fact that the census was normally taken in June, when many boys were out of school and working on farms. New Zealand censuses are frequently vague on the question of coverage of young children, inexperienced workers, and the disabled. The German census figures suffer from drastic changes in territory as the result of World Wars I and II; and they very likely include in the labor force, as housewives, some who would be excluded from the count in the English-speaking nations. Several of the countries have

[2] The variation in formal coverage has involved minor groups, such as some inexperienced workers not covered before 1940, and some child workers 10–13 not covered in 1940 and 1950.

changed the month in which their censuses were enumerated, and only Canada (in 1951) followed the United States in adopting a more precise time reference in deciding whether a person was in the labor force at the time of the census. On the whole, however, in concept and coverage the censuses of these nations have not changed much over time and have been roughly comparable with United States data during comparable periods—though such a conclusion may not always be accepted by other investigators with different statistical problems.

The usefulness of the United States sample survey of the labor force for short-run analysis depends, of course, on the reliability of the survey methods. It was instituted by the WPA in early 1940 and has been administered by the census since August 1942. It has relied upon a sample of roughly 20,000 households, increased in May 1956 to 35,000, each of which is visited by enumerators for a number of months and is then replaced by a new household—in such a way that not all replacements occur in any one month.[3] The households are not scattered through all the 3,000 or so counties of the nation, but are selected at random from within a smaller number of areas chosen for administrative convenience and as being broadly representative from the standpoint of income levels, occupations, industries, and urban-rural distribution. An effort is made to ensure that the sample reflects any shifts in population. Nevertheless, these monthly estimates of labor force, employment, and unemployment differ from the results that would be obtained by a complete enumeration. The size of the sampling error depends on the size of the sample—the larger the sample the smaller the error. It also depends on the size of the estimate: the sampling error for unemployment will be a smaller number than that for the labor force, but, other things equal, it will be a larger percentage. Finally the sampling error will be greater at some times than at others, depending upon variability of behavior within the sample. Since this degree of internal variability could change every month—and is especially subject to change as the economy moves into recession—the census should, ideally, re-estimate each month its whole schedule of sampling error. However, the census published fresh computations only infrequently before early 1954. The indicated sampling error in the post-World War II period before 1954 was about ±650,000 for a labor force estimate of about 60,000,000— roughly 1 per cent of the labor force. (The percentage error for unemployment, a smaller estimate, would have been larger.) All the errors

[3] These are the households actually interviewed. There have always been several thousand additional households in the gross sample for which interviews could not be obtained because of absence of the householder, vacancy, and other reasons. Currently, about 7,000 households fall into this "visited-but-not-enumerated" category. From January 1954 to May 1956, the number was about 4,000. *Current Population Reports, Labor Force,* Series P-57, No. 168, p. 5.

were larger before 1948. This variability is called the "probable error." The probable error is twice the standard error. The chances are about two out of three that an estimate from the sample would differ from a complete census by less than the standard error. The chances are nineteen out of twenty that an estimate would differ from a complete census by less than the probable error.

Through 1953 there were 68 sampling areas falling within about 120 counties. Late that year the census experimented with a design consisting of the same number of interviewed households (roughly 21,000) scattered through more areas—over 230 in about 400 counties—to reduce sampling error and increase administrative convenience. The old 68-area sample was retained temporarily for purposes of comparison and the results of the two samples, purporting to give more or less independent estimates for the nation, were released for January 1954. The two results were expected to differ by not more than sampling variability. Actually, the January differences were substantially greater than probable sampling error, especially for unemployment. In February 1954 the difference was smaller, though both samples revealed a much greater increase in labor force and unemployment than had ever occurred at that time of year. The census then dropped the old design and continued with only the 230-area sample. Under this sample, the probable error was reduced to, typically, about 600,000 for a civilian labor force estimate of about 66 million.[4]

No change was made in the new design, for the census decided the discrepancy was due, not to defects in the samples, but rather to errors in interviewing. There probably have always been errors in censuses—whether conducted by sampling or by enumeration—arising from misunderstandings or violations of instructions; but during this trial period, errors could have been greatly increased as a result of administering two samples at once with a limited staff. Such difficulties were expected to disappear as the census concentrated its efforts on the new design. There is no way to test the soundness of this judgment; certainly the unhappy experience revealed that, whether because of sampling or of interviewing error, the monthly data may be subject to greater variability than had been anticipated. To reduce this month-to-month variability, though perhaps at the expense of introducing some more persistent bias, the census instituted, in early 1954, what amounts to a new smoothing technique, described as the "new composite estimating procedure." [5] Even so, the errors of month-to-month change have been

[4] *Current Population Reports, Labor Force,* Series P-57, No. 165, p. 7. This is twice the standard error reported in the March 1956 report, shortly before the sample was enlarged to 35,000 interviewed households.

[5] For description of this procedure, as well as a full review of the sampling and survey methods of the census, see *Report of the Special Advisory Committee*

47

sizable. For example, in April 1956 the error was roughly 360,000 for the civilian labor force and 200,000 for the unemployed.[6] Such errors are very large in relation to the normal change from one month to the next. However, errors are reduced somewhat in this study by bunching the monthly estimates into quarterly averages. The enlargement of the sample by the census in May 1956, to 35,000 enumerated households took in 330 areas and the sampling errors were further reduced— both in degree and in month-to-month change. In August 1956, for instance, the error was 500,000 or 0.7 per cent for the civilian labor force, which was estimated at about 69 million. And the probable error of the month-to-month change was about 360,000.[7]

The methods of constructing the monthly sample survey estimates still leave much to be desired—as is attested by the *Report of the Special Advisory Committee*—but they constitute a notable pioneering effort. They represent some of the best scientific technique yet applied to the problem, planned and administered by one of the ablest groups of experts in the world of statistics.

Only one foreign nation has constructed a sample survey estimate of labor force comparable in quality and period of time covered with that of the United States. This is Canada, where the survey was begun in the form of quarterly estimates in 1945 and has followed American methods closely. Since January 1953, Canada has made a survey one week each month. Canada's sample embraces almost the same number of households as that of the United States although her population is only a tenth of ours. For technical reasons, which need not be described here, sampling errors in Canada are roughly similar in relative size to errors in our estimates. For Great Britain, the short-run analysis of labor force experience during wartime had to rest on annual estimates made in this study from scattered British sources. The wartime analysis for Germany had to rest on estimates by the Strategic Bombing Survey from data which were undoubtedly subject to gaps and duplications.

The Method

Reference was made in the closing pages of Chapter 2 to Paul Douglas' finding of an inverse association between labor force and earnings among 38 large American cities at a given time. Douglas chose large cities as units of study because he had no breakdown by income and he felt that cultural and economic differences among states, counties, or small urban units were so great as to make it impossible to know

on *Employment Statistics*, Bureau of the Census, mimeographed, August 1954. The members of the committee, appointed by the Director of the Census, were Frederick F. Stephan (Chairman), Lester R. Frankel, and Lazare Teper.

[6] *Current Population Reports, Labor Force*, Series P-57, March 1956, p. 7.

[7] The actual change from July was a decline of 542,000.

whether a difference in labor force participation was truly associated with a difference in earnings.

For example, one small and prosperous town might have a lower labor force participation, not because of its prosperity but because of its remoteness from job opportunities offered in a large city; another town, equally small but unprosperous, might have a large labor force participation, not because people felt forced to work but because of their nearness to a large city where jobs were abundant. Large cities may come closer to providing homogeneity (or other things equal) than the other types of locality for which census data were available.

The *Census of Population* at that time provided no information on earnings of the labor force. Douglas, therefore, had to rely on the *Census of Manufactures* for 1919 and 1929 for an index of a city's earning level. He could not circumvent the difficulty that factory wages might not furnish a satisfactory index of average earnings of the labor force, since the majority of workers are usually in nonmanufacturing industries. An additional complication was that wages were not given separately by age and sex; they were computed by dividing the payroll by the number of workers. Average wages in a city might prove relatively low if its labor force is "loaded" with large numbers of women and children, who almost always earn less than men. Such a situation could create the illusion that many women and children are forced to work because of the low average of wages, when actually the low average wage could be the result, rather than the cause, of a large proportion of women and child workers. Douglas got around this obstacle by dividing the factory payroll by the number of men workers plus a number of women and child earners reduced to an adult-male-earner equivalent. He based the reduction on certain fragmentary information on what women and children earned in relation to men.

When faced with a similar lack of data on earnings of adult males, this investigation followed Douglas' device—for example, in studies of personal disposable income in five nations over time. Douglas also compared earnings both with and without adjustment for inter-area differences in cost of living. This practice is adopted here in inter-area studies; and short-period comparisons over time are made both with and without adjustment for intertemporal difference in the cost of living. But long-period comparisons in this study are made only with income adjusted for the cost of living on the ground that a decade, or a half century, would give workers ample time to see through the "money illusion" and think of their income only in real terms.

Since the cities differed among themselves in size, Douglas compared not the absolute size of the labor force, but the rate of labor force participation. He sought thereby to discover whether a city with a higher level of earnings, such as Pittsburgh or Detroit, tended to have a systematically different labor force participation rate than one with a lower level of earnings, such as Baltimore. Since persons of different ages and sex have different employment tendencies, Douglas compared first the labor force participation of a particular age-sex group in each city with the earnings of males in the same city; e.g., in Baltimore the labor force of women 25–44, per 1,000 population of women 25–44, was compared with the average wage or salary. A simple correlation coefficient, based on the least squares technique, was then computed for the 38 cities, to determine what the relation was and whether it was significant. Separate correlations with earnings of equivalent adult males were next computed for each of the age-sex groups. Finally, Douglas made a summary comparison between earnings and the labor force participation of the whole population of each city. Before doing this, he had to take account of the facts that each age-sex group has different work tendencies, and each city has a different age-sex composition. Thus a city with a larger proportion of children and a smaller proportion of men may have a lower average labor force participation rate.

In computing an over-all labor force participation rate for a city, these differences in composition are eliminated statistically by standardization. This process, which is the same as fixed-weighting in the construction of price indexes, consists of selecting population age-sex structure of a typical city (or even of the average of all the cities) and weighting the labor force participation rates of the various age-sex groups in each city by that standard composition instead of its own.[8]

[8] Let s_i = labor force of any age group

p_i = population of that age group

$l_i = s_i/p_i$, or the percentage of the population of that age group, which is in the labor force—the "labor force participation rate"

$r_i = p_i/P$, or the standard or fixed ratio of the number of persons, to the number 14 and older

L_m = percentage of the male population in the labor force

L_f = percentage of the female population in the labor force

L = percentage of the population of both sexes in the labor force

$\bar{L}$ = the same percentage standardized

Then
$$\bar{L}_m = \frac{\Sigma(l_m \cdot r_m)}{\Sigma r_m}, \; \bar{L}_f = \frac{\Sigma(l_f \cdot r_f)}{\Sigma r_f}$$

and
$$\bar{L} = \frac{\Sigma(l_i \cdot r_i)}{\Sigma r_i} = \Sigma(l_i \cdot r_i) \; (\text{since } \Sigma r_i = 1.0).$$

The method is outlined in three steps and illustrated through standardization of the 1940 Baltimore labor force by the composition of Chicago in 1930.

The percentage of each age-sex group in the work force, l_i, is listed below in column one. Each group's percentage is multiplied by its share in the standard population, r_i, in the second column. And the products, l_i times r_i, are added to

So weighted or standardized, the labor force participation rates of the various cities differ from each other only to the extent that labor force tendencies differ and not because population compositions differ. At least, this is the ideal result. Actually, standardization is subject to two biases. One may be called a *weight bias;* it arises out of the fact that no standard can be completely representative of all the situations to which it is applied and that different standards will in theory yield not only somewhat different average labor force participation rates but also different relationships among the labor force participation rates of any two cities or areas, or of two different dates. The other, called here *interdependence bias,* arises out of the circumstances that the labor force tendencies of a city or area, or at a certain date, may be interdependent with its population composition, and that substituting a standard population composition would yield a spurious or forced result.[9]

yield the sums for males, $\Sigma(l_m \cdot r_m)$, females, $\Sigma(l_f \cdot r_f)$, and for both sexes, $\Sigma(l_i \cdot r_i)$, in column three. They have been divided by their shares in the population 14 and older (Σr_i), and the following juxtaposes the standardized and the actual:

	Labor Force in Percentages of Population 14 and Older of the Same Sex		
	Actual (1)	Standard-ized (L)	Effect of Standardization (L–L)
Males 14 and older	80.5	82.0	1.5
Females 14 and older	32.9	34.8	1.9
Both sexes 14 and older	56.3	58.7	2.4

[9] Standardizing the labor force of a certain locality or date for population composition requires substituting the population composition of some other locality or date, which is called the standard. This process rests on the assumption that the percentage of the population of each subgroup in the labor force would be the same even if it were part of a very different population composition. The assumption need not be true. For example, the number of boys 14–19 has declined greatly during the past half century both in proportion to total population and in ratio to the number of adult males. The tendency of boys to participate in the labor force has also declined enormously. Standardization undertakes to eliminate the first effect—the decline in the relative number of boys in the population—but it is assumed that boys would have the same tendency to work regardless of what proportion of the population they represent.

Suppose, however, that the tendency of boys to work depends on the number of boys in any given family. In 1890, for example, a father with five sons 14–19 may have felt so hard pressed at having such a formidable responsibility that he sent all of them out to seek jobs, thereby encouraging a 100 per cent labor force participation for boys in his family. In 1940, a father of two boys may have felt so affluent because of his relatively light responsibilities for family support that he kept both boys in school, with a consequent participation of zero for boys in his family. Thus to the extent that his feeling of well-being stemmed from having fewer progeny (rather than more income), the decision for or against his children's gainful employment must have been conditioned by the population distribution; in such a case the process of standardization, which couples the 1890 population distribution with the 1940 tendency to be in the

51

The extent of the weight bias was approximated by experimenting with various standards. These experiments indicated that the weight bias was rather sure to be minor, because the portion of the population differently represented in different cities, areas, or nations—mainly children and old people—did not usually constitute a very large part of the over-all labor force. Since the extent of the interdependence bias could not be ascertained, the next best thing was to present the behavior of both standardized and unstandardized labor force participation rates. The differences in behavior proved small; hence the interdependence bias could not have been large.

Douglas' results for 1920 and 1930 were tested in this study by means of similar correlations among the same 38 cities for one prior, and two subsequent census dates—1900, 1940, and 1950.[10] That is, for those years the labor force participation rates of each of the cities were standardized by the composition of the population of Chicago in 1930. Much the same standardization technique was applied in analyzing labor force behavior among whole states, among the urban and rural areas of states, among different income groups in the same city, among nations, and from one census to the next for the same nation. In the case of the five nations used in the study of behavior over time, the labor force was standardized by the age-sex composition of the United States population in 1940. The United States labor force was also variously standardized over time for changes in the proportion of persons living in rural and urban areas or in the proportion of native whites, negroes, and foreign born. This was necessary since these groups have had very different labor force tendencies at various times and have changed their labor force participation at very different rates over time. Similar additional standardization could not be done for the other countries for lack of data, but the changes in the rural-urban and ethnic composition of their population seem to have been much less than in the United States.

---

labor force, offers a source of error. It is even possible that the composition of the population is in turn influenced by changes in tendency to be in the labor force. For example, wives have always been less prone to work than single women, but in recent years women have been marrying earlier in life and have been having fewer children than the women a half century before. At the same time there has been a rise in the proportion of females who are in the labor force. The process of standardizing for changes in marriage composition rests on the assumption that these two tendencies are independent of one another. But it may well be that a two-way dependency exists: (a) that fewer children mean easier house cares and greater freedom to take jobs, or (b) that the increasing tendency of wives to work, and thereby contribute to family support, in itself explains why couples wed at earlier ages but have fewer children.

[10] This study of the 38 cities omitted 1890 and 1910 because of the difficulty presented by the probability of varying degrees of overcount or undercount in these years in the different cities.

Even in the United States a full cross-standardization for all these changes in population composition was not possible because the rural and urban labor forces were not separately classified by color and nativity in the censuses. However, a device was developed in this study and termed "partial standardization." (See section on *Various Minority Groups* in Chapter 12.) It consisted of "piling" the differences between the labor force participation rate, standardized and unstandardized for rural-urban composition, upon the native white labor force participation rates. Still another device, called "destandardization," was developed to test the stability of participation in the United States and Britain during the nineteenth century, when lack of data on the rural and urban labor forces prevented direct standardization for rural-urban composition. The device (also set forth in Chapter 12) consisted of assuming that the participation rates of the rural and urban populations were the same during the nineteenth century as they have been in recent decades, and then using these assumed rates to compute hypothetical unstandardized labor force participation rates for the whole population at the various nineteenth century census dates. These were then compared with the actual unstandardized rates to see if they yielded similar results.

CHAPTER 4

THE LABOR FORCE AND EARNINGS OR INCOME IN DIFFERENT CITIES, STATES, NATIONS, AND INCOME GROUPS AT A GIVEN TIME

"The goal of war is peace, of business, leisure."
ARISTOTLE, *Politics*

Labor Force and Earnings among Large Cities

THE two investigations by Paul Douglas examined the moment-of-time relationship between labor force and earnings for 38 large United States cities in 1920 and 1930.

Following Douglas' practice of standardizing the labor force participation rates of each of the 38 cities by the composition of the population of Chicago in 1930,[1] this study tested his results by similar correlations among the same cities for a prior census date—1900—and for two subsequent census dates—1940 and 1950. Because of the difficulty presented by the probability of varying degrees of overcount or undercount in 1890 and 1910 in the different cities, these dates were omitted. The test revealed the following:

1. For all the census dates except 1950 there was a tendency for the total labor force participation of both sexes, standardized for age and sex, to be inversely associated with real earnings per equivalent adult-male worker (Table 1 and Chart 1). That is, in those cities where average earnings tended to be high, labor force participation tended to be low. The association was significant on the 95 per cent ($\pm 2\sigma$) level. In 1950 there was virtually no association between labor force and earnings. There were positive associations for some age-sex groups, but these were either insignificant or significant on the lower level. Adjusting real earnings to a 48-hour workweek basis—to eliminate differences in earnings due to longer or shorter workweeks—modified the results very little, and Chart 1 omits this comparison. Unstandardized, the labor force was not as closely associated with earnings as it was when standardized, but, even so, the association was significant on the 95 per cent level for 1900 and 1940 and on the 68 per cent level ($\pm \sigma$) for 1930. Thus the test generally corroborated Douglas' findings.

2. Much the same inverse relationship to earnings was found when the participation of males and females was examined separately, being

[1] See Chapter 3 in the section on *The Method*.

54

TABLE 1

Correlation between Labor Force and Earnings, 38 Large Cities, United States, Census Dates, 1900–1950

(Coefficients of correlation between variations in rate of participation in labor force—per 1,000 persons aged 14 and older of same age-sex group—and intercity differences in annual earnings per adult-male equivalent in previous year.) [a]

A. LABOR FORCE BY SEX—REAL AND MONEY EARNINGS

	Real Earnings			Real Earnings on 48-Hour Week Basis		
	Both Sexes	Males	Females	Both Sexes	Males	Females
(STANDARDIZED) [b]						
1900 (June) [c]	−0.53 **	−0.24 *	−0.51 **	−0.50 **	−0.22 *	−0.50 **
1920 (Jan.)	−0.70 **	−0.47 **	−0.65 **	−0.63 **	−0.48 **	−0.56 **
1930 (April)	−0.63 **	−0.42 **	−0.54 **	−0.59 **	−0.52 **	−0.46 **
1940 (April)	−0.59 **	−0.40 **	−0.50 **	−0.54 **	−0.31 *	−0.49 **
1950 (April)	+0.29 *	+0.22 *	+0.13	...	...	...

	Real Earnings			Money Earnings		
	Both Sexes	Males	Females	Both Sexes	Males	Females
(UNSTANDARDIZED)						
1900 (June) [c]	−0.45 **	−0.26 *	−0.49 **	−0.45 **	−0.26 *	−0.49 **
1920 (Jan.)	−0.10	−0.07	−0.59 **	−0.10	−0.07	−0.59 **
1930 (April)	−0.28 *	−0.31 *	−0.55 **	−0.31 *	−0.33 **	−0.56 **
1940 (April)	−0.45 **	−0.35 **	−0.57 **	−0.45 **	−0.36 **	−0.52 **
1950 (April)	−0.01	+0.09	−0.04	+0.07	+0.11	+0.04

continued on next page

TABLE 1, *continued*

B. LABOR FORCE BY SEX AND AGE GROUP—REAL EARNINGS

	14	15	16	17	18-19	20-24	25-44	45-64	65 and Older
					MALES				
1900 (June)c	...	...	...	...	...	...	-0.004	-0.37**	-0.42**
1920 (Jan.)	-0.64**	-0.61**	-0.36**	-0.27**	-0.26*	-0.26*	-0.07	-0.32**	-0.60**
1930 (April)	-0.61**	-0.69**	-0.60**	-0.41**	-0.18*	-0.17*	-0.05	-0.28*	-0.42**
1940 (April)	-0.30*	-0.56**	-0.70**	-0.70**	-0.60**	-0.37**	-0.04	+0.10	-0.43**
1950 (April)	+0.27*	+0.18*	-0.10	-0.23	-0.01	+0.11	+0.17*	+0.04	+0.18*
					FEMALES				
1900 (June)c	...	...	...	...	...	...	-0.46**	-0.46**	-0.44**
1920 (Jan.)	-0.49**	-0.36**	-0.07	+0.12	+0.16*	-0.11	-0.61**	-0.62**	-0.71**
1930 (April)	-0.58**	-0.48**	-0.30*	+0.001	+0.31*	+0.13	-0.53**	-0.56**	-0.56**
1940 (April)	-0.37**	-0.64**	-0.54**	-0.41**	+0.06	+0.8	-0.53**	-0.46**	-0.30*
1950 (April)	+0.37**	+0.28*	+0.07	+0.08	+0.25*	+0.15	-0.15	-0.05	+0.31

The 38 cities: Atlanta, Baltimore, Birmingham, Boston, Bridgeport, Buffalo, Chicago, Cincinnati, Cleveland, Columbus, Dallas, Denver, Detroit, Houston, Indianapolis, Kansas City, Los Angeles, Louisville, Memphis, Milwaukee, Minneapolis, Newark, New Haven, New Orleans, New York, Norfolk, Omaha, Philadelphia, Pittsburgh, Portland (Oregon), Providence, Richmond, Rochester, St. Louis, St. Paul, San Francisco, Scranton, Seattle.

Source: Appendix A. *Census of Manufactures, 1900*, Vol. VIII, Part 2, Table 2. *Census of Population: 1940*, Vol. III, *The Labor Force*, Part 1, Table 15; *1950*, Vol. II, *Characteristics of the Population*, Part 1, Table 185, Paul H. Douglas, *The Theory of Wages*, Macmillan, 1934, pp. 269–294, 514. Erika H. Schoenberg and Paul H. Douglas, "Studies in the Supply Curve of Labor," *Journal of Political Economy*, February 1937, pp. 45–79. *Bulletin 694*, pp. 98–99, and *Monthly Labor Review*, February 1951, p. 153, Bureau of Labor Statistics.

* Significant on the 68 per cent (±σ) level.
** Significant on the 95 per cent (±2σ) level.

a Appendix D explains the earnings data. For 1939 and 1949 earnings are given per male worker 14 and older, rather than per adult-male equivalent worker.

b Standardization of the labor force for age or age-sex composition is based on the population of Chicago in 1930. See Chapter 3 for explanation of the method and its limitations.

c Birmingham, Houston, Dallas, and Norfolk were not covered by the census in 1900. The study omitted 1890 and 1910 because of the difficulty presented by the varying degrees of overcount or undercount in the different cities in these years.

higher for females than for males, especially for the unstandardized comparison; but only in 1920 did the association for males (unstandardized) fail to be significant on at least the lower level. The associations were higher in 1920 and 1930—the years studied by Douglas— than in 1900 or 1940, but on the whole they appeared to remain surprisingly constant over all four decades.

3. In the various age-sex groups the correlation with real earnings of males was far from uniform. Through 1940, it appeared fairly high for boys, elderly men, and most women aged 25 and older; but it was not highly significant for males aged 18–24 and 45–64, and it was not significant at all for males 25–44. (For the last three groups, however, the tendency to work is not expected to be much affected by economic circumstances.) Only in 1940 was the correlation distinctly significant

CHART 1

Correlation between Labor Force and Earnings, 38 Large Cities, United States, Census Dates, 1900–1950

Labor Force per 1,000 population aged 14 and older of same sex, standardized for age and sex on basis of population of Chicago in 1930.

Annual wage or salary in previous year, in dollars of 1929 purchasing power in Chicago, per adult-male equivalent factory worker; adjusted for intercity differences in cost of living except in 1899.

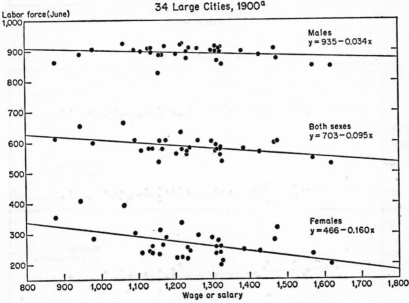

34 Large Cities, 1900[a]

Males
$y = 935 - 0.034x$

Both sexes
$y = 703 - 0.095x$

Females
$y = 466 - 0.160x$

Labor force (June)

Wage or salary

[a] Birmingham, Houston, Dallas, and Norfolk not covered by the 1900 census.

(chart continues on next page)

Correlation between Labor Force and Earnings, 38 Large Cities, United States, Census Dates, 1900–1950

Labor Force per 1,000 population aged 14 and older of same sex, standardized for age and sex on basis of population of Chicago in 1930.

Annual wage or salary in previous year, in dollars of 1929 purchasing power in Chicago, per adult-male equivalent factory worker; adjusted for intercity differences in cost of living except in 1899.

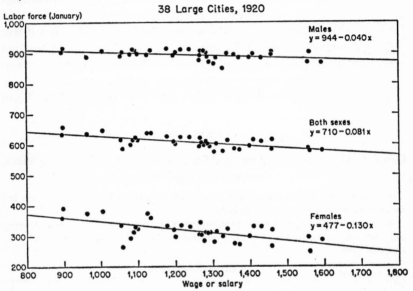

38 Large Cities, 1920

Males
$y = 944 - 0.040x$

Both sexes
$y = 710 - 0.081x$

Females
$y = 477 - 0.130x$

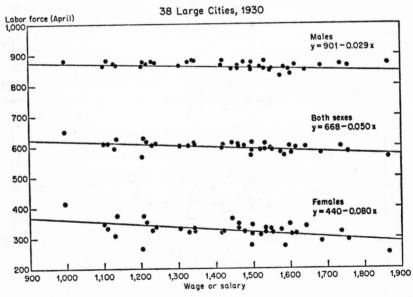

38 Large Cities, 1930

Males
$y = 901 - 0.029x$

Both sexes
$y = 668 - 0.050x$

Females
$y = 440 - 0.080x$

(concluded on next page)

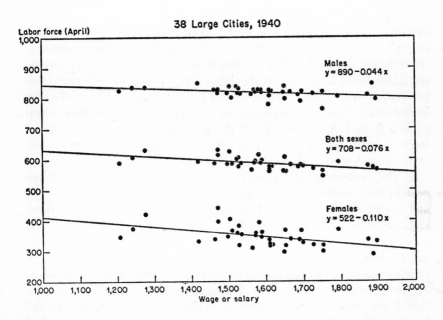

38 Large Cities, 1940

Labor force (April)

Males
y = 890 − 0.044 x

Both sexes
y = 708 − 0.076 x

Females
y = 522 − 0.110 x

Wage or salary

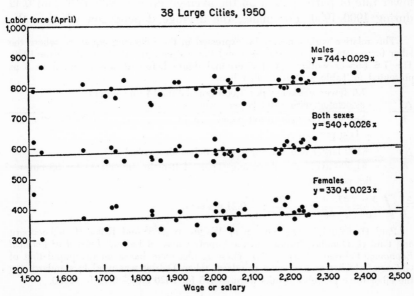

38 Large Cities, 1950

Labor force (April)

Males
y = 744 + 0.029 x

Both sexes
y = 540 + 0.026 x

Females
y = 330 + 0.023 x

Wage or salary

Source: Table 1 and Appendix Tables A-7A and D-1.

for males aged 18–24 and girls 16 and 17; in no year was it very significant for females 18–24.

4. During 1900–1940 the relationship was such that both sexes combined tended to have 8 fewer persons in the labor force, per 1,000 population aged 14 and older, for every additional $100 of earnings (Table 2).

Expressing the association between the labor force and earnings in numbers of people and in dollars makes comparison awkward. For example, a $100 gain in earnings has less significance when earnings are higher at the start, and an exodus from the labor force of 10 persons per 1,000 bulks larger when the labor force is around 500 per 1,000 population than when it is around 950 per 1,000. Accordingly, changes in the labor force and earnings are also presented in relative terms (Table 2, Part A, second line): the percentage by which the labor force of both sexes was lower in cities where real earnings per adult male equivalent were 1 per cent higher.[2]

5. The percentage differences accompanying a variation of 1 per cent in male earnings ranged from −0.13 in 1930 to −0.21 in 1940, and averaged −0.18 for the four decades—results very near to those of Douglas for 1920 and 1930.[3] Thus, during 1900–1940, wherever real earnings per adult male equivalent worker were up by 1 per cent, the labor force, standardized for age and sex, seemed to be down by roughly one-sixth of 1 per cent. The average for 1900–1950 was smaller: about one-eighth of 1 per cent. For females, the association was such that 1 per cent higher earnings of males were accompanied by 0.5 lower rate of participation on the average during 1900–1940 and 0.42 during 1900–1950. For males, the average depends on whether the

[2] This relative variation may be expressed in the following equation, where the labor force data are those for 1940 and the real earnings data are those for 1939. The 7.6 (fewer workers) is the original figure before it was rounded to 8 as presented in Table 2, Part A, first line.

$$\frac{\Delta l}{l} = \frac{\text{7.6 fewer workers (per 1,000 population 14 and older) associated with \$100 larger earnings}}{\text{585 workers (per 1,000 population 14 and older), average for 38 cities}}$$
$$= -1.30 \text{ per cent;}$$

$$\frac{\Delta e}{e} = \frac{\$100 \text{ larger real earnings (per adult-male equivalent)}}{\$1,590 \text{ average real earnings (per adult-male equivalent) for 38 cities}}$$
$$= 6.3 \text{ per cent.}$$

$$\frac{\Delta l}{l} \bigg/ \frac{\Delta e}{e} = \frac{\Delta l \cdot e}{l \cdot \Delta e} = \frac{-1.30}{6.3} = -0.21 \text{ per cent.}$$

[3] Paul H. Douglas, *The Theory of Wages*, p. 288, and Erika H. Schoenberg and Paul H. Douglas, "Studies in the Supply Curve of Labor," *Journal of Political Economy*, February 1937, p. 70. These results were based on the population of Chicago, which was used as a standard; when Detroit was used in standardizing the labor force Douglas' results were −0.15 for 1920 and −0.13 for 1930.

TABLE 2

Variations in Labor Force Associated with Differences in Earnings, 38 Large Cities, United States, Census Dates, 1900–1950

(Number of persons by which rate of participation in labor force—per 1,000 persons aged 14 and older of same sex and age group—was reduced for every additional $100 of annual real earnings per adult-male equivalent employed in previous year, and percentage by which rate of participation was reduced for every 1 per cent addition to real earnings.)

A. LABOR FORCE, BOTH SEXES

	1900 [a] June	1920 Jan.	1930 Apr.	1940 Apr.	1950 Apr.	1900–1940 Average	1900–1950 Average
Reduction per $100 additional real earnings (persons)	−10	−8	−5	−8	+3	−8	−6
Reduction per 1 per cent additional real earnings (per cent)	−0.20	−0.17	−0.13	−0.21	+0.09	−0.18	−0.12

B. LABOR FORCE, SEX AND AGE GROUPS

MALES

Reduction per $100 Additional Real Earnings (persons)

	14 & Older	14	15	16	17	18–19	20–24	25–44	45–64	65 & Older
1900 (June) [a]	−18	..	..	..	..	..	..	..	..	−20
1920 (January)	−4	−26	−35	−17	−11	−8	−4	n.s.	−3	−14
1930 (April)	−3	−9	−21	−29	−21	−5	−2	n.s.	−3	−7
1940 (April)	−4	−3	−14	−34	−42	−27	−7	n.s.	−1	−13
1950 (April)	+3	+6	+5	n.s.	−8	n.s.	n.s.	+2	n.s.	+3
1900–1940 Average [b]	−7	−13	−23	−27	−25	−13	−4	0	−2	−14
1900–1950 Average [b]	−5	−8	−16	−20	−21	−10	−3	+0.4	−1	−10

continued on next page

TABLE 2, continued

B. LABOR FORCE, SEX AND AGE GROUPS, continued

	14 & Older	14	15	16	17	18–19	20–24	25–44	45–64	65 & Older
FEMALES										
1900 (June) [a]	−16	...	...	...	...	...	...	−17	−20	−13
1920 (January)	−4	−15	−22	n.s.	n.s.	+8	n.s.	−16	−17	−12
1930 (April)	−8	−4	−13	−15	n.s.	+14	n.s.	−12	−12	−5
1940 (April)	−11	−1	−5	−20	−20	n.s.	n.s.	−16	−12	−5
1950 (April)	n.s.	+4	+4	n.s.	n.s.	+9	n.s.	n.s.	n.s.	+2
1900–1940 Average [b]	−10	−7	−13	−12	−7	+7	0	−15	−15	−9
1900–1950 Average [b]	−8	−4	−9	−9	−5	+8	0	−12	−12	−7
Reduction per 1 Per Cent Additional Real Earnings (per cent)										
MALES										
1900 (June) [a]	−0.65	...	...	...	...	...	...	n.s.	−0.04	−0.39
1920 (January)	−0.06	−2.39	−1.31	−0.36	−0.17	−0.12	−0.05	n.s.	−0.03	−0.29
1930 (April)	−0.05	−3.51	−2.96	−1.51	−0.63	−0.10	−0.03	n.s.	−0.02	−0.18
1940 (April)	−0.09	−2.38	−4.69	−3.51	−2.10	−0.66	−0.12	n.s.	n.s.	−0.54
1950 (April)	+0.07	+1.39	+0.84	n.s.	−0.40	n.s.	n.s.	+0.03	n.s.	+0.13
1900–1940 Average [b]	−0.21	−2.76	−2.99	−1.79	−0.97	−0.29	−0.07	0	−0.02	−0.35
1900–1950 Average [b]	−0.16	−1.72	−2.03	−1.35	−0.83	−0.22	−0.05	+0.01	−0.02	−0.27
FEMALES										
1900 (June) [a]	−0.74	...	...	...	...	...	...	−0.85	−1.55	−2.09
1920 (January)	−0.51	−2.56	−1.35	n.s.	n.s.	+0.16	n.s.	−0.65	−0.98	−1.73
1930 (April)	−0.35	−3.27	−2.66	−1.01	n.s.	+0.36	n.s.	−0.51	−0.73	−0.84
1940 (April)	−0.50	−2.57	−5.30	−2.71	−1.49	n.s.	n.s.	−0.65	−0.75	−1.05
1950 (April)	n.s.	+2.51	+1.58	n.s.	n.s.	+0.34	n.s.	n.s.	n.s.	+0.34
1900–1940 Average [b]	−0.53	−2.80	−3.10	−1.24	−0.50	+0.17	0	−0.67	−1.00	−1.43
1900–1950 Average [b]	−0.42	−1.47	−1.93	−0.93	−0.37	+0.22	0	−0.53	−0.80	−1.07

Source: See notes to Table 1.

n.s. = not significant.

[a] Birmingham, Houston, Dallas, and Norfolk were not covered by the census in 1900. The 38-city study omitted 1890 and 1910 because of the difficulty presented by the probability of varying degrees of overcount or undercount in these years in the different cities.

[b] In averages, n.s. is counted as zero.

extreme negative percentage in 1900 is included or excluded. On the whole it would seem best to exclude it, on the ground that the 1900 association was based on only 34 cities and did not benefit from an adjustment of earnings for intercity difference in living cost. If, in order to balance this exclusion, we also exclude the positive association for 1950—significant only on the lower level—the male labor force 14 and older tended to be smaller by 0.07 per cent when equivalent adult male earnings were higher by 1 per cent.

6. Among the individual age classes, each 1 per cent of higher real earnings per adult-male equivalent workers was accompanied during 1900–1940 by 0.17 to 5.3 per cent lower participation rates among boys and girls in their mid-teens, and by 0.18 to 2.09 per cent lower rates among the elderly.

The Possible Influence of Unemployment on the Relation between Labor Force Participation and Earnings

Douglas did not investigate the inverse relation between labor force participation and earnings as the possible result of intercity variations in the extent of unemployment. Under the additional worker theory, relatively high unemployment of men in a particular city could have forced many wives and young people into the labor market, bringing about a relatively high rate of labor force participation. High unemployment could also cause low labor earnings—so that the correlation between labor force and earnings would be a spurious one. But there is an alternative theoretical possibility. If the opposite of the additional worker theory were true—that is, if high unemployment discouraged many women, children, and older people, from seeking jobs —it is possible that labor force participation would be torn between being high as a result of low wages and low because of high unemployment.

These contingencies are investigated in Table 3 starting with 1930, because no satisfactory unemployment data were available for cities before that date. (In fact, these data were not gathered for the 1920 census and were not published in the 1910 census.) Table 3 begins with the same significant, inverse correlation between labor force of both sexes, of males, and of females and the real earnings of equivalent adult males that were given in Table 2. It next tests the correlation between labor force and unemployment. This it shows to have been generally inverse—like that between labor force and earnings; but also, to have been borderline or below in significance for all three groups at all three census dates. A third step is to test whether labor force has a significantly higher correlation with earnings and unemployment together, than with earnings alone. (Incidentally, the two "independent" variables, earnings and unemployment, are significantly correlated

TABLE 3

Simple, Multiple, and Partial Correlations: Labor Force Participation Rates by Sex, Real Earnings, and Unemployment of Males 14 and Older, 38 Large Cities, United States, Census Dates, 1930–1950

		1930			1940			1950		
		Both Sexes	Males	Females	Both Sexes	Males	Females	Both Sexes	Males	Females
Simple Correlations:										
Labor force and real earnings	$r12$	−0.64 **	−0.48 **	−0.53 **	−0.59 **	−0.40 **	−0.50 **	+0.29 *	+0.22 *	+0.13
Labor force and unemployed	$r13$	−0.33 **	+0.01	−0.38 **	−0.25 *	−0.02	−0.29 *	−0.26 *	−0.37 **	+0.02
Real earnings and unemployed	$r23$		+0.49 **			+0.07			+0.03	
Multiple Correlations:										
Labor force, real earnings and unemployed	$R1.23$	0.64 **	0.55 **	0.55 **	0.65 **	0.40 †	0.56 **	.39 †	0.44 †	0.14
Partial Correlations:										
Labor force and real earnings holding unemployed constant	$r12.3$	−0.58 **	−0.55 **	−0.43 **	−0.59 **	−0.40 **	−0.51 **	+0.31 *	+0.25 *	+0.13
Labor force and unemployed holding real earnings constant	$r13.2$	−0.02	+0.32 *	−0.16	−0.26 *	+0.01	−0.30 *	−0.28 *	−0.39 **	+0.02

Source: See notes to Table 1.

* Significant on the 68 per cent ($\pm\sigma$) level.
** Significant on the 95 per cent ($\pm2\sigma$) level.
† Significant on the 75 per cent level.

The variables are X_1, labor force per 1,000 persons 14 and older of same age-sex group, standardized for age-sex composition on the basis of the population of Chicago in 1930; X_2, real earnings per adult male equivalent in previous year adjusted for intercity differences; X_3, unemployed males 14 and older per 1,000 persons of same age-sex group.

only at the 1930 census and at that date the correlation is positive rather than inverse.) The results yield a multiple correlation $R_{1.23}$ only slightly higher than the simple correlation r_{12} for either 1930 or 1940, and appreciably higher in 1950 for both sexes and males but not for females.

Finally, the table examines whether the labor force is partially correlated with earnings, holding unemployment constant, and, if so, whether the correlation is stronger or weaker than that found when unemployment varied. The results show, on the whole, little difference. Holding unemployment constant weakened slightly the association between labor force and earnings in 1930, but left it almost the same in 1940 and 1950. There was no really significant association in any year between labor force and unemployment, holding earnings constant. Taking account of unemployment would not seem to have changed Douglas' results for 1930 or ours in 1940; but it might give some small additional explanation of labor force behavior in 1950.

The Possible Influence of Color and National Origin

Does the inverse relation between the labor force and income persist if the effects of color and of national origin are eliminated? In order to answer this question, Douglas constructed several partial correlations for 1920 and 1930, holding constant the share of Negroes, foreign-born, and native children of foreign-born in the population. His purpose was to learn whether the high labor force in cities where earnings were low was due to the presence of Negroes and foreign-born groups, whose high participation in the labor force may have been due to their color or national origin rather than to their poverty. His test did not modify his previous conclusion that the labor force of females was inversely related to income.[4]

This study proceeded with the same question in a very different way: in each city the *white* labor force was separately classified and expressed as a percentage of the white population. Data on the labor force by color were not available by age for 1900, but the procedure was carried out for each census from 1920 through 1950. Unfortunately, for 1920, 1930, and 1940 the labor force participation of whites could be correlated only with the earnings of all classes of males, rather than with the earnings of white males. Any distortion was kept to a minimum by confining the correlations to the 22 cities where the colored were a small proportion of the labor force—less than 10 per cent in 1940 (Table 4). The inverse association was upheld for both sexes 14 and older combined (standardized for age and sex),[5] for fe-

[4] Douglas, *op. cit.*, p. 293; Schoenberg and Douglas, *op. cit.*, pp. 72–73.
[5] The same general results were also obtained from correlations for 13 cities in which fewer than 5 per cent of the males in 1940 were *colored*.

males 14 and older standardized for age, for young females, and, to some extent, for elderly persons. The correlations for each of the years 1920, 1930, and 1940 also revealed a tendency for participation of the

TABLE 4

Correlation between Labor Force Participation of Whites and Real Median Earnings of Males of All Classes, 22 Large Cities with Relatively Few Colored to Distort the Median Earnings, United States, Census Dates, 1920–1940

(Coefficients of correlation between variations in rate of participation of white labor force—per 1,000 white persons aged 14 and older of same age-sex group—and intercity [a] differences in annual earnings of all classes in previous year per adult-male equivalent worker)

A. LABOR FORCE BY SEX [b]—REAL EARNINGS

	Both Sexes	Males	Females
1920 (January)	−0.37 *	−0.03	−0.39 *
1930 (April)	−0.45 **	−0.19	−0.38 *
1940 (April)	−0.47 **	−0.12	−0.46 **

B. LABOR FORCE BY AGE GROUP AND SEX—REAL EARNINGS

	14–19	20–24	25–44	45–64	65 & Older
			MALES		
1920 (January)	−0.13	−0.10	+0.09	−0.05	−0.43 **
1930 (April)	−0.39 *	+0.45 **	+0.19	−0.11	−0.54 **
1940 (April)	−0.16	−0.35 *	+0.08	+0.06	+0.08
			FEMALES		
1920 (January)	−0.51 **	−0.60 **	−0.23 *	−0.15	−0.02
1930 (April)	−0.42 **	−0.39 *	−0.16	−0.20	−0.33
1940 (April)	−0.52 **	−0.58 **	−0.26 *	+0.08	−0.30 *

Source: Appendix D. *Census of Population: 1920*, Vol. II, Chapter 3, Tables 15–17, and *Occupations*, Vol. IV, Chapter 4, Table 22; *1930*, Vol. III, Table 12, and *Occupations*, Vol. IV, Table 9; *1940*, Vol. III, *The Labor Force*, Parts 2–5, Table 5.

* Significant on the 68 per cent ($\pm\sigma$) level.
** Significant on the 95 per cent ($\pm2\sigma$) level.

[a] Less than 10% of the population in the following cities in 1940 was colored: Boston, Bridgeport, Buffalo, Chicago, Cleveland, Denver, Detroit, Los Angeles, Milwaukee, Minneapolis, Newark, New Haven, New York, Omaha, Pittsburgh, Portland, Providence, Rochester, St. Paul, San Francisco, Scranton, and Seattle.
[b] Labor force standardized for age or age-sex group composition on the basis of the population of Chicago in 1930.

white labor force to be lower in cities where earnings of all classes of males were higher.

Results for the labor force of whites were generally lower than those found in Table 1 and many of them were not individually significant. Nevertheless when most members of a large family of correlations have the same sign, the correlations must be accorded some respect, even if many of them are individually insignificant. Thus the results for white persons in Table 4 indicate that the inverse association between labor force participation and earnings found in the 38-city studies was not a spurious result of large concentrations of colored persons pulling down earnings and inflating labor force participation in some cities.

For 1950, the first census at which separate earnings became available for colored and white persons by cities, it was possible to correlate the labor force participation with male earnings for whites and for the colored independently (Table 5). It will be recalled that for all classes the inverse association between labor force and earnings disappeared

TABLE 5

Correlation between Labor Force and Real Median Male Earnings by Color, 38 Large Cities, United States, Census Date, 1950

(Coefficients of correlation between variations in rate of participation in labor force—per 1,000 persons aged 14 and older of same age-sex group—and intercity differences in annual earnings per adult-male equivalent employed in previous year)

A. LABOR FORCE BY SEX [a]—REAL EARNINGS

	Both Sexes	Males	Females
White Labor Force and White Earnings 1950 (April)	+0.32 **	+0.31 *	+0.07
Colored Labor Force and Colored Earnings [b] 1950 (April)	—0.53 **	—0.26 *	—0.51 **

B. LABOR FORCE BY SEX AND AGE GROUP—REAL EARNINGS

	14–19	20–24	25–44	45–64	65 & Older
MALES					
White Labor Force and White Earnings	+0.04	+0.35 **	+0.22 *	+0.41 **	+0.29 *
Colored Labor Force and Colored Earnings [b]	—0.70 **	—0.14	—0.12	—0.14	+0.28 *
FEMALES					
White Labor Force and White Earnings	—0.08	—0.15	+0.10	+0.12	+0.22 *
Colored Labor Force and Colored Earnings [b]	—0.42 **	—0.33 *	—0.48 **	—0.58 **	—0.43 **

Source: *Census of Population, 1950*, Vol. II, *Characteristics of the Population*, Part 1, Table 185, and Part 20, Tables 66 and 87. Appendix Table A-7A.

* Significant on the 68 per cent ($\pm\sigma$) level.
** Significant on the 95 per cent ($\pm2\sigma$) level.

[a] Labor force standardized for age or age-sex composition on the basis of the population of Chicago in 1930.
[b] Data were available for 23 cities only: Atlanta, Baltimore, Birmingham, Chicago, Cincinnati, Cleveland, Dallas, Detroit, Houston, Indianapolis, Kansas City, Los Angeles, Louisville, Memphis, Newark, New Orleans, New York, Norfolk, Philadelphia, Pittsburgh, Richmond, St. Louis, and San Francisco.

in 1950, and that the correlations, though individually insignificant, were positive. What do we find now? In the 23 cities with separate data, labor force participation and male earnings of the colored showed the same inverse correlation as that found for whites in 1920–1940 for both sexes combined, for males, and for females. They were inverse for all age-sex groups except males 65 and older. For males 14 and older they were significant only on the lower level and they were not significant at all in the 20–64 age groups. But the general pattern clearly suggests that the inverse tendencies between the labor force participation and earnings of the colored were still holding in 1950.

Not so, however, among whites in 1950, who showed generally positive correlations, not only for persons 14 and older, but for all the age-sex groups except females under 25. True, nearly all the correlations taken individually were either moderately significant or insignificant; but the fact that they were generally positive indicates the association between labor force participation and earnings to be no longer inverse for these groups of whites.

The previous section discussed additional tests made by this study to determine how unemployment affected the association between earnings and labor force participation of all classes. Such tests were made here for whites and colored separately in 1950 (Table 6). A significant inverse correlation on the higher level was found between the white male labor force and unemployed white males and, for the colored, between the labor force of the three groupings by sex and unemployed colored males—suggesting that adverse employment conditions may have had some effect in reducing the participation of these groups. For some groups, taking account of both earnings and unemployment measurably strengthened the correlation. Thus the multiple association of labor force, on the one hand, with earnings and unemployment, on the other, was significantly higher than that of labor force with earnings alone for white and colored males, and for whites of both sexes. But almost all the partial correlations were insignificant or borderline—not only those in which the labor force was associated with earnings, holding unemployment constant, but also those in which it was associated with unemployment, holding earnings constant. The labor force may have been associated with unemployment and earnings jointly, but it was associated only feebly, if at all, with either of these if the other was held constant.

The Effect of Child-Care Responsibilities on the Female Labor Force

We need to inquire here whether the lower labor force participation of wives in cities with higher male earnings may have been the con-

TABLE 6

Simple, Multiple, and Partial Correlations: Labor Force, Real Median Male Earnings, and Unemployed Males 14 and Older by Color, 38 Large Cities, United States, Census Date, 1950

	White			Colored [a]		
	Both Sexes	Males	Females	Both Sexes	Males	Females
Simple Correlations:						
Labor force [b] and real earnings r12	+0.32 **	+0.31 *	+0.07	−0.53 **	−0.26 *	−0.51 **
Labor force [b] and unemployed r13	−0.31 **	−0.47 **	+0.09	−0.55 **	−0.47 **	−0.44 **
Real earnings and unemployed r23		−0.26 *			+0.66 **	
Multiple Correlations:						
Labor force, [b] real earnings and unemployed R1.23	0.39 †	0.51 **	0.12	0.59 **	0.47 †	0.53 **
Partial Correlations:						
Labor force [b] and real earnings holding unemployed constant r12.3	+0.26 *	+0.22 *	+0.10	−0.25 *	+0.07	−0.32 *
Labor force [b] and unemployed holding real earnings constant r13.2	−0.24 *	−0.42 **	+0.11	−0.32 *	−0.40 *	−0.16

* Significant on the 68 per cent ($\pm\sigma$) level.
** Significant on the 95 per cent ($\pm 2\sigma$) level.
† Significant on the 75 per cent level.

[a] Data were available for 23 cities only: Atlanta, Baltimore, Birmingham, Chicago, Cincinnati, Cleveland, Dallas, Detroit, Houston, Indianapolis, Kansas City, Los Angeles, Louisville, Memphis, Newark, New Orleans, New York, Norfolk, Philadelphia, Pittsburgh, Richmond, St. Louis, and San Francisco.
[b] Standardized for age or age-sex composition on the basis of the population of Chicago in 1930.

cealed effect of differences in the proportion of child-care responsibilities. It was not possible to separate the labor force tendencies of females with and without young children, but it was possible to correlate among cities the labor force tendencies of white females and the ratio of number of children under 6 to number of wives 15 and older. To minimize the possible influence of earnings, only those cities were chosen where median real earnings of males of all classes were roughly similar—between $1,500 and $1,700 annually—and where less than 10 per cent of the male labor force was colored. There were 16 such cities.

The presence of young children is not expected to explain the inverse association. On the contrary, greater child-care responsibilities should prevent poorer wives from entering the labor force and thus offset the effect of poverty. In any case, no intercity correlation was found in 1940 between the labor force of white females and the proportion of children under 6. If the effect was there, it was too weak to manifest itself—even among cities where male earnings were rather similar and the proportion of colored was small.

The Effect of Prevailing Length of Workweek on the Female Labor Force

One might expect the labor force participation of women to be greater where a shorter workweek would allow them enough spare time for housekeeping. There is no evidence, however, that this is the case. A correlation was made among 38 cities in 1940 between the proportion of the population of either sex in the labor force and the median hours worked by males (assuming this median would roughly represent the required workweek for women). Male, instead of female hours were used to avoid a spurious correlation if large numbers of females were working part time. The correlation does not suggest that long hours tend to prevent females from working; if anything, there was a bare suggestion to the contrary. This may be the effect of the tendency for low incomes to result in both longer hours and higher participation. However, standardizing for income by examining the labor force tendencies of white wives, aged 25 to 29, without children, whose husbands were within a narrow wage or salary range ($1,000–1,499), disclosed no association between the labor force and hours (in this case the hours of females were used). Wives 25–29 who had children and whose husbands were in the same income range, showed a tendency to enter the labor force in higher proportions where the workweek was shorter, but it was faint and probably insignificant.

This lack of association between female labor force participation and working hours at a moment of time is in contrast to the apparently distinct association found over time (Chapter 6). But the range of variation in hours among the cities at a given time was very narrow, whereas over time it was very wide. The moment-of-time data were hours actually worked and may have included differences in part-time employment among localities; the data over time are standard or full-time and do not include such influences. In any case the associations over time hold only among peacetime periods of moderately high employment.

Interdependence among Age-Sex Groups

The entrance of women into gainful employment could conceivably displace many children and elderly people: either "pushing" them out through competition, or "pulling" them out when women's earnings enable young people to stay in school longer, or older people to retire earlier. This possibility was explored for 1930 by comparing the labor force participation of women aged 20–64 with that of youths 14–19 and persons 65 and older. To guard against the chance of income being the real influence, the comparison was confined to 27 cities where the yearly earnings of male factory workers were within a fairly narrow range—$900–1,550. The correlation was negligible. A further narrowing of the income range to $1,175–1,550 increased the correlation to bare significance, but it was necessary to exclude Pittsburgh in order to achieve even this. Thus women were not more apt to be in the labor force in areas where children and elderly people were less apt to be in gainful work—at least not at a given time. We shall see, however, that the relation over time is quite different.

Earnings of Females

So far this study has concentrated on male earnings; a word is called for on the response to variations in female earnings. A pairing of the wages or salaries of females employed for twelve months in 1939 with the participation rates of single women and of wives not supported by husbands reveals no significant association among cities of 100,000 to a million, among all urban areas, or among rural nonfarm areas. Higher female earnings either did not attract more women into the labor force, or were offset by some other factor, possibly the contrary influence of male earnings.

Labor Force and Earnings among the 48 States

The 1940 and 1950 censuses report the labor force and wages and salaries separately for rural and for urban areas of each state. In 1940, the urban areas of the 48 states showed about the same correlation between income and the labor force as did the 38 cities; but the rural

71

nonfarm areas and the states taken as units (standardized for age-sex and rural-urban composition) exhibited no association of any kind between income and the labor force in 1940 or in 1950. The association may not have existed among smaller cities, towns, and rural areas, or it may have been obliterated by other factors not present in large cities. In 1950, the urban areas of the 48 states revealed an inverse association only for females, and only half as pronounced as in 1940. The association for males was positive in 1950 but only moderately significant.

Association between Labor Force and Income: 12 to 16 Nations at a Given Time

Do lower-income nations tend to have higher labor force participation? This possibility was investigated among 16 nations using data for around 1930 and among 12 nations using data for around 1950. The nations are listed as follows, showing the years of labor force enumerations, with the first nine countries common to both lists.

Investigated for around 1930	Investigated for around 1950
Australia (1933)	Australia (1947)
Belgium (1930)	Belgium (1947)
Canada (1931)	Canada (1951)
Germany, excluding the Saar (1933)	Germany (Western) (1950)
Italy (1936)	Italy (1950)
Great Britain (1931)	United Kingdom (1951)
Netherlands (1930)	Netherlands (1947)
Sweden (1930)	Sweden (1950)
United States (1930)	United States (1950)
Czechoslovakia (1930)	Austria (1951)
Denmark (1930)	Finland (1950)
Estonia (1934)	Philippines (1948)
France (1930)	
Japan (1930)	
Norway (1930)	
Switzerland (1930)	

The nations were selected on the basis of available data. Labor force data for the 16 nations were accessible in a compilation of participation rates by broad age-sex groups published by the *International Labour Review* (Geneva, International Labour Office). The years referred to depended on when the census of each country was taken—the majority being 1930. In two nations the date was 1931, in two others, 1933, in one, 1934; and in Italy the census was taken as late as 1936. For all 16 nations, data on average annual national income per member of the labor force during 1925–1934, translated into United States dollars of 1925–1934 purchasing power, were available from Colin Clark's *Conditions of Economic Progress* (London, Macmillan, 1940).

The problems of comparing data of different countries are most perplexing. Censuses are not all taken at the same time or under the same economic conditions; they are planned and administered independently; and they do not always include the same types of worker. The United States excludes farm wives and daughters who do housework or churn butter solely for family consumption; Germany and the countries of Eastern Europe usually count them in. Moreover, something more than mere definition is involved in these differences, since farm women doubtless do far more field and commercial dairy work in these lands than in the United States. The foreign censuses have published little on definitions, less on instructions to enumerators, and still less on actual practices; in the extent and intensity of its pre-enumerative and post-enumerative studies the United States census is, so far as could be determined by this study, unique. Some of the uncertainties, however, involve minor segments of the population and they are not so troublesome as those encountered in other important economic magnitudes, including those of national income (Appendix F).

Income data, it should be noted, are not adjusted for income taxes, social security, or other deductions. They are not comparable therefore with the personal disposable income data which are used later for the studies of five nations over time. They are subject to formidable difficulties of comparisons in real buying power among nations with very different production and consumption patterns, and to problems presented by currency and exchange restrictions of various countries in translating their moneys into United States dollar equivalents.

Subject to such qualifications, there was for the 16 nations a significant inverse association between the over-all labor force participation rate of persons 15 and older, standardized for age and sex, and the real annual national income per labor force member, expressed in equivalent United States dollars of 1925–1934 buying power (Table 7 and Chart 2). The labor force was smaller by 11 persons (per 1,000 population 15 and older) for each $100 higher real income per worker, and by 0.12 per cent for each 1 per cent higher income. The labor force participation of females 15 and older and real income per worker were similarly associated, with 21 fewer females in the labor force per 1,000 females 15 and older for each $100 higher real income per worker, and

TABLE 7

Correlation between Labor Force and Income, 16 Countries around 1930 and 12 Countries around 1950

(Variations in rate of participation in labor force [a]—per 1,000 persons aged 15 and older of same age-sex group—correlated with income per labor force member in U.S. dollars) [b]

	Coefficients of Correlation Around:		Fewer Persons in Labor Force per $100 Additional Income Around:		Per Cent Smaller Labor Force per 1 Per Cent Additional Income Around:	
	1930	1950	1930	1950	1930	1950
Both sexes	−0.68 **	−0.54 *	−11	−3	−0.12	−0.07
Males	−0.20	−0.11	n.s.	n.s.	n.s.	n.s.
15–19	−0.52 **	−0.35 *	−16	−6	−0.14	−0.11
20–64	+0.38 *	−0.18	+1	n.s.	+0.001	n.s.
65 & older	−0.12	−0.19	n.s.	n.s.	n.s.	n.s.
Females	−0.65 **	−0.54 *	−21	−6	−0.40	−0.23
15–19	−0.50 **	−0.31	−22	n.s.	−0.27	n.s.
20–64	−0.62 **	−0.52 *	−22	−7	−0.42	−0.25
65 & older	−0.59 **	−0.53 *	−11	−4	−0.57	−0.54

Source (1930): *Income data:* Colin Clark, *The Conditions of Economic Progress*, London, Macmillan, 1940, pp. 34–40; *labor force data: Year Book of Labour Statistics, 1939,* Table 1, and *International Labour Review,* May 1940, pp. 546–549, Geneva, International Labour Office.

(1950): *Income data: National and Per Capita Income, Seventy Countries—1949,* Table 1, Statistical Papers Series E. No. 1, United Nations. *Labor Force data: Year Book of Labour Statistics, 1954,* Tables 1 and 2.

n.s. = not significant.

* Significant on the 68 per cent (±σ) level.
** Significant on the 95 per cent (±2σ) level.

[a] Standardized for age, or age and sex, on basis of population of United States in 1950.

[b] Income data for around 1930 are averages for 1925–1934; income data for around 1950 are for 1949.

The 16 countries: Germany, Australia, Belgium, Canada, Denmark, Estonia, United States, France, Great Britain, Italy, Japan, Norway, Netherlands, Sweden, Switzerland, and Czechoslovakia.

The 12 countries: Australia, Austria, Belgium, Canada, Finland, Germany, Italy, Netherlands, Philippines, Sweden, United Kingdom, and United States.

0.40 per cent fewer for each 1 per cent higher income. In the case of both sexes and females 15 and older, these percentage associations between income and labor force participation were similar to those among 38 United States cities. (Table 2.) There was no significant association in the case of males 15 and older or of males 65 and older and only a mildly significant association for men 20–64. However, all of the age-sex groups, except men 20–64, had associations with the same (negative) sign.

74

CHART 2

Correlation between Labor Force and Income per Labor Force Member: 16 Countries around 1930 and 12 Countries around 1950

Labor force 15 and older per 1,000 persons of same age group.
Income per labor force member in U.S. dollars.

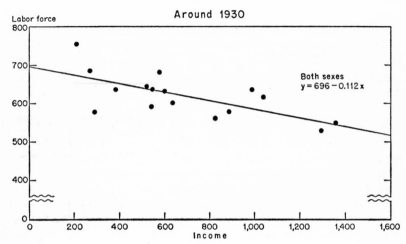

Around 1930

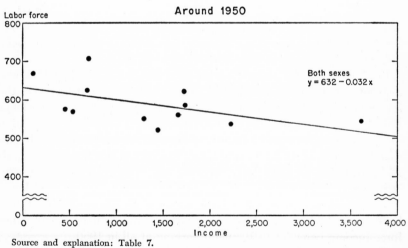

Around 1950

Source and explanation: Table 7.

No data were available for an analogous study of this many nations at any date before 1930, or for any date around 1940; the only other study that could be made among a substantial number of nations was for around 1950.

Selection of the 12 nations was determined primarily by the availability of income data of a certain quality. The United Nations Statistical Office computed the per capita income of 70 nations for 1949, translated into United States dollars. But data for only about twenty-four of the seventy were of "A" quality, based on official or semi-official estimates—and in only 12 of these had a labor force census been taken around 1950. In the 12 nations, three of the censuses were taken in 1951, five in 1950, one in 1948, and three in 1947.

Of all the age-sex groups analyzed, none had a significant association with income on the higher level; only both sexes combined, females, and teen-age males had even moderately significant associations. However the associations among the 12 nations were too similar in sign to be dismissed altogether. Almost identical inverse results were obtained when labor force participation was correlated with income *per capita*.

So far only a simple relationship with income has been considered. For some groups, labor force participation might also be influenced by other factors. Lacking data, it was not feasible to investigate most of these, but two of the most obvious were examined: child-care responsibilities and social security benefits.

The first was investigated by testing for a simple correlation between the labor force of women 20–64 and the ratio of females 15 and older to children 0–14—the higher the ratio, the lighter these responsibilities. The 1930 study gives no support to the rather popular notion that women in high per capita income countries would have relatively fewer children to care for; these two variables seem to have been independent.

But the study did show that female labor force participation was associated with lightness of child cares in the way expected, i.e. the fewer young children the average woman has, the higher the labor force participation becomes for women 20–64. The multiple correlation ($R_{1.23}$) with income and lightness of child cares was somewhat higher than the simple one with income alone. The partial correlations differed: the correlation of labor force with income, holding child cares constant, or with child cares, holding income constant, was slightly lower than the association of labor force with either singly. All in all, the burden of child cares adds only a little to the explanation of labor force-income behavior in 1930 and nothing at all in 1950.

The influence of relative availability of old age social security benefits was examined by correlating labor force participation of men 65 and older with the percentage of the population 65 and older of both sexes receiving old age benefits. This study could be made only for around 1950.[6] No account was taken of the amounts of such benefits in relation to the incomes elderly men could have earned, or of such

[6] Tables 6 and 7; *Year Book of Labour Statistics, 1954,* Geneva, International

conditions as restrictions on earnings while drawing benefits. Elderly persons receiving railroad retirement benefits and old age assistance (charity) were included in these figures in the United States, but no attempt was made to discover analogous supplementary benefits for the aged in the other countries. Excluded also were recipients of pensions under private plans. The study was confined to 11 countries, since old age benefit data for the Philippines were not available.

Despite the crudeness of data, there did seem to be some moderate correlation between labor force participation of older persons of a nation and the per cent of its older persons drawing old age benefits —either because the benefits enable men to retire or because men who retire are apt to try to qualify for them. A multiple correlation with income and per cent drawing old age benefits was substantially higher than the correlation with income alone, but it was significant only on the 75 per cent level. The partial correlation with income, holding the benefit factor constant, is not appreciably higher than the simple correlation with income alone. Whether or not social security benefits are taken into account, there is still no significant association between labor force participation of the elderly and the level of real income per labor force member among nations.

Association between Labor Force and Income among 3 to 5 Nations at a Given Time

A number of later chapters are devoted to a detailed examination of five nations *over time;* here they are examined at *a given time.* The study is at a disadvantage in correlating so few countries. But it has four advantages of selectivity. First, the labor force and income basic statistics are probably more sound (Appendixes D and E). Second, the same nations can be studied at various points in time. Third, the income data are adjusted to a personal-disposable basis, whereas those for the 12 and 16 nations did not allow for deductions from workers' pay (see Appendix D). Fourth, the income data are expressed as income per equivalent adult-male employed worker, while in the study of the 12 and 16 nations these data were expressed as income per member of the labor force. Using the employed-worker basis prevents distortion of correlations due to unemployed persons in the labor force. The adjustment to an equivalent adult-male basis is made because large numbers of women and children in the labor force could lower a nation's average income, not as the effect of poorly rewarded labor, but because women and children earn lower wages than men and often work only part of the year. A low average income could thus be the

Labour Office, Tables 2, 3, 4, and 32; *Statistical Abstract of the United States, 1954,* Bureau of the Census, p. 253.

statistical result, rather than the economic cause of high labor force participation among women and children. The adjustment tends to correct this spurious correlation, though it can be made only imperfectly from fragmentary data on earnings of women and child workers in relation to the earnings of males, principally in manufacturing (Appendix D).

Not all five countries could be studied in all the years covered by the United States census, but it was possible to make three-nation comparisons for around 1900 and 1920 and five-nation comparisons for around 1930, 1940, and 1950 (Chart 3). Graphically, at least, all seem to reveal the inverse association noted for the larger number of countries around 1930 and 1950, which association seems to be specially pronounced for both sexes and for females, and reasonably definite for males, except possibly around 1900. Since five nations were represented for each of the census dates around 1930, 1940, and 1950 it was possible to test the association by correlation (Table 8). These correlations had to be numerically high to be significant because of the small num-

TABLE 8

Correlation between Labor Force and Income, 5 Countries around
1930, 1940, and 1950

(Variations in rate of participation in labor force [a]—per 1,000 persons
14 and older of same age or age-sex group—correlated with personal disposable national income per adult-male equivalent
employed, in 1929 U.S. dollars.)

| | Coefficients of Correlation Around: | | | Fewer Persons in Labor Force per $100 Additional Income Around: | | | Per Cent Smaller Labor Force per 1 Per Cent Additional Income Around: | | |
	1930	1940	1950	1930	1940	1950	1930	1940	1950
Both sexes 14 & older	−0.81 *	−0.90 **	−0.86 *	−10	−11	−5	−0.23	−0.29	−0.17
Males 14 & older	−0.52 *	−0.81 *	−0.66 *	−3	−6	−3	−0.05	−0.11	−0.07
Females 14 & older	−0.79 *	−0.80 *	−0.84 *	−17	−16	−8	−0.79	−0.79	−0.50

Source and explanation of data: Appendixes A and D; notes to Chart 3.

* Significant on the 68 per cent ($\pm\sigma$) level.
** Significant on the 95 per cent ($\pm2\sigma$) level.

[a] Standardized for age or age-sex composition on the basis of the population of the United States in 1940.

The 5 countries: United States, Great Britain, Canada, New Zealand, Germany.

CHART 3

Correlation between Labor Force and Disposable Income, 3 to 5 Countries, Census Dates, 1900–1950

Labor force 14 and older by sex per 1,000 population of same sex and age group, standardized for age and sex on basis of United States population in 1940.

Personal disposable national income per adult-male equivalent employed, in 1929 U.S. dollars.

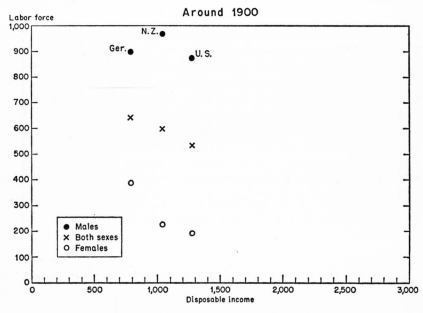

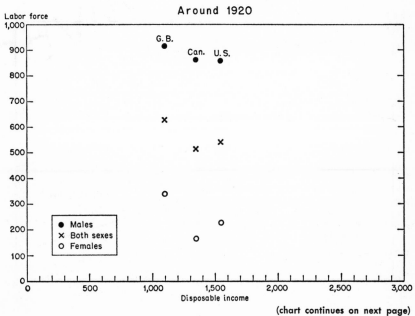

(chart continues on next page)

Correlation between Labor Force and Disposable Income, 3 to 5 Countries, Census Dates, 1900–1950

Labor force 14 and older by sex per 1,000 population of same sex and age group, standardized for age and sex on basis of United States population in 1940.

Personal disposable national income per adult-male equivalent employed in 1929 U.S. dollars.

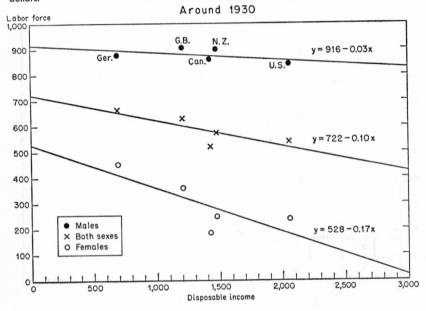

Around 1930

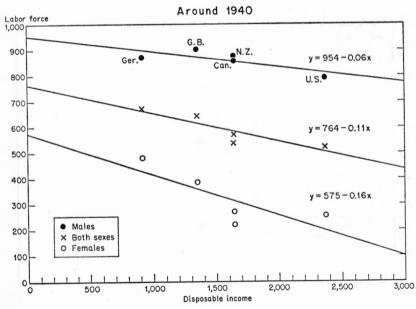

Around 1940

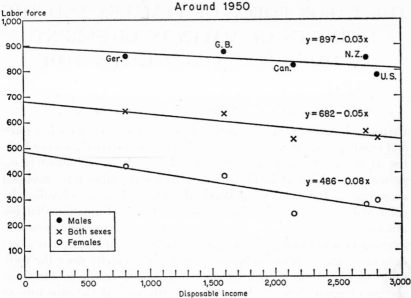

Around 1950

Labor force

Source and explanation: Appendixes A and D. Data on labor force and income refer to the nations and census years listed below (1910 being omitted for lack of comparable data). The income figure, when based on data of noncensus years, was adjusted to refer to the census year (Appendix D).

Around:	United States	Great Britain	Canada	New Zealand	Germany
1900	1900	...	...	1901	Av. 1895 & 1907
1920	1920	1921	1921	...	...
1930	1930	1931	1931	Av. 1926 & 1936	Av. 1925 & 1933
1940	1940	1939	1941	Av. 1936 & 1945	1939
1950	1950	1951	1951	1951	1950

ber of degrees of freedom; but all of them were at least moderately significant and one of them—both sexes around 1940—was significant on a 95 per cent level. All the associations were inverse. And for a particular sex group they were numerically very similar at each of the three censuses, especially in the case of females and both sexes.

It is difficult not to be impressed with the associations between labor force and income among these nations at a given time. No case is remarkable in itself, but like the associations among the cities, and to a considerable extent, states of the United States, the accumulating evidence of inverse association between labor force and income is not easily dismissed.

81

THE LABOR FORCE OF FEMALES AND THE EARNINGS OF MALES IN DIFFERENT INCOME GROUPS AT A GIVEN TIME

The Labor Force of Wives by Income Group of Husbands in the Same City or Type of Area

CITIES and states are unsatisfactory units for the study of labor force and earnings; they have been used only because better data were lacking. In the census statistics for 1940 and 1950, however, infinitely superior materials are at hand: namely, wives in the labor force grouped according to the incomes of husbands. These data are classified by color and age of wife and by age of children—information that enables us to eliminate many extraneous elements unfortunately present in inter-area comparisons. Some of the same elements, it is true, may affect even comparisons between income groups within a city since the well-to-do and the less prosperous do not normally reside in the same section of town. Nevertheless cultural patterns and the structure of industry are likely to be more homogeneous *within* a city than *among* cities; this suggests that there may be real advantages in studying the labor force by income groups.

Farm areas were excluded, largely because of defects in the wage and salary materials (Appendix D). All income groups for the rural nonfarm areas however, and for large, medium, and small cities yielded rather similar results (Table 9 and Chart 4). Wives were less apt to work if their husbands were well-to-do than if their husbands were poor—even when the wives were standardized for possession of young children and for age (to eliminate the possibility that the age factor kept wives out of the labor force). The effect of income was, moreover, pronounced. In 1940, the nonfarm labor force of married women ranged from 245 per 1,000 in the lowest income bracket to 64 in the highest, where incomes were $3,000 or more.[1] Furthermore, the higher the income level, the more women (percentagewise) dropped out with additional prosperity. At the lower range about 0.1 per cent fewer wives were in the labor force if income was 1 per cent higher; at the top of the range the figure was close to 0.9 per cent fewer. The weighted average for all levels was about —0.35 for the United States excluding farm areas and standardizing for age of wife and possession of young children. The unstandardized figure was only slightly different (—0.33).

[1] *Census of Population, 1940, Population, The Labor Force (Sample Statistics), Employment and Family Characteristics of Women*, p. 135.

TABLE 9

Variations in Labor Force of Wives Associated with Differences in Earnings of Husbands, United States, 1940

(Number of persons by which rate of participation of wives 18–64 in labor force—per 1,000 wives in same area, age, and income group—was reduced for every additional $100 of wage or salary earned by their husbands in the previous year, and percentage by which the rate was reduced for every 1 per cent addition to the husband's earnings. Husbands had no other income.)

	Income Level							Weighted Averages, All Income Levels [a]
	$100–300	$300–500	$500–800	$800–1,250	$1,250–1,750	$1,750–2,500	$2,500–3,250 and over	
A. ALL WIVES, STANDARDIZED FOR AGE AND POSSESSION OF YOUNG CHILDREN [b]								
Reduction per $100 Additional Income of Husband (persons)								
United States (except farm areas)	−19	−1	+0.3	−8	−8	−5	−3	−6
Metropolitan areas 100,000 and over	−14	−5	−4	−7	−9	−6	−4	−7
Cities 25,000–100,000	−35	−1	−8	−15	−9	−8	−3	−11
Cities 2,500–25,000	−26	−10	−2	−13	−10	−6	−2	−10
Rural nonfarm areas	−19	−3	+6	−7	−8	−3	−1	−5
Reduction per 1 Per Cent Additional Income of Husband (per cent)								
United States (except farm areas)	−0.08	−0.01	+0.01	−0.30	−0.61	−0.71	−0.87	−0.35
Metropolitan areas 100,000 and over	−0.05	−0.06	−0.10	−0.27	−0.60	−0.72	−0.93	−0.42
Cities 25,000–100,000	−0.10	−0.01	−0.14	−0.48	−0.58	−0.94	−0.79	−0.41
Cities 2,500–25,000	−0.08	−0.12	−0.05	−0.46	−0.76	−0.91	−0.85	−0.39
Rural nonfarm areas	−0.11	−0.06	+0.23	−0.37	−0.79	−0.60	−0.49	−0.19

TABLE 9, *continued*

	Income Level							Weighted Averages, All Income Levels [a]
	$100–300	$300–500	$500–800	$800–1,250	$1,250–1,750	$1,750–2,500	$2,500–3,250 and over	

B. WIVES WITHOUT CHILDREN UNDER 10 [c]

Reduction per $100 Additional Income of Husband (persons)

	$100–300	$300–500	$500–800	$800–1,250	$1,250–1,750	$1,750–2,500	$2,500–3,250 and over	Weighted Averages
United States (except farm areas)	−11	−3	−2	−6	−11	−7	−5	−6
Metropolitan areas 100,000 and over	−22	−7	−7	−7	−10	−7	−6	−8
Cities 25,000–100,000	−31	−4	−10	−16	−6	−7	−7	−11
Cities 2,500–25,000	−26	−15	−2	−4	−21	−8	−2	−10
Rural nonfarm areas	+7	−3	+5	−7	−9	−5	−2	−1

Reduction per 1 Per Cent Additional Income of Husband (per cent)

	$100–300	$300–500	$500–800	$800–1,250	$1,250–1,750	$1,750–2,500	$2,500–3,250 and over	Weighted Averages
United States (except farm areas)	−0.04	−0.03	−0.03	−0.18	−0.56	−0.66	−0.92	−0.32
Metropolitan areas 100,000 and over	−0.06	−0.06	−0.12	−0.21	−0.52	−0.66	−1.02	−0.39
Cities 25,000–100,000	−0.07	−0.03	−0.14	−0.41	−0.34	−0.59	−1.11	−0.35
Cities 2,500–25,000	−0.07	−0.14	−0.04	−0.12	−1.00	−0.91	−0.61	−0.35
Rural nonfarm areas	+0.04	−0.05	+0.14	−0.28	−0.72	−0.68	−0.64	−0.19

TABLE 9, *continued*

	Income Level							Weighted Averages, All Income Levels [a]
	$100–300	$300–500	$500–800	$800–1,250	$1,250–1,750	$1,750–2,500	$2,500–3,250 and over	
C. WIVES WITH CHILDREN UNDER 10 [c]								
Reduction per $100 Additional Income of Husband (persons)								
United States (except farm areas)	−12	−2	+3	−8	−6	−3	−1	−4
Metropolitan areas 100,000 and over	−13	−8	−1	−7	−7	−3	−1	−5
Cities 25,000–100,000	−41	+4	−5	−15	−6	−5	−4	−9
Cities 2,500–25,000	−25	−3	−3	−12	−7	−3	−2	−8
Rural nonfarm areas	−9	−3	+8	−8	−5	−1	−0.1	−2
Reduction per 1 Per Cent Additional Income of Husband (per cent)								
United States (except farm areas)	−0.08	−0.04	+0.12	−0.52	−0.91	−0.91	−0.66	−0.44
Metropolitan areas 100,000 and over	−0.08	−0.16	−0.04	−0.46	−0.92	−0.95	−0.59	−0.55
Cities 25,000–100,000	−0.15	+0.06	−0.12	−0.68	−0.71	−1.09	−2.38	−0.57
Cities 2,500–25,000	−0.12	−0.05	−0.09	−0.64	−0.92	−0.93	−1.62	−0.48
Rural nonfarm areas	−0.09	−0.11	+0.55	−0.60	−1.01	−0.35	−0.07	−0.15

Source: *Census of Population, 1940*, Vol. IV, *The Labor Force (Sample Statistics), Employment and Family Characteristics of Women*, Table 23, pp. 132–136.

[a] Weighted by number of wives 18–64 belonging to the various income levels.
[b] Standardized for age and child status on basis of total wives of the United States (except farm areas).
[c] Standardized for age of wives on basis of total wives of the United States (except farm areas).

CHART 4

Labor Force of Wives and Earnings of Husbands: Various Types of Nonfarm Areas, United States, April 1940

Labor force, per 1,000 of wives aged 18–64 and living with husband. Standardized for age on basis of total wives in same type of area.

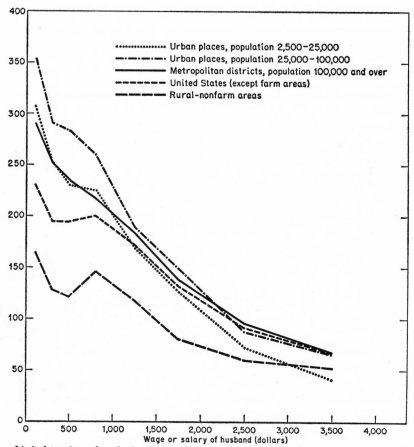

Limited to wives whose husband's income (in 1939) was entirely from wages or salary. The income groups are $1–199; 200–399; 400–599; 600–999; 1,000–1,499; 1,500–1,999; 2,000–2,999; and 3,000 and over. Readings are centered at midpoints of the ranges, except for the open-end class.

Source: *Employment and Family Characteristics of Women*, as cited in Table 9.

The association varied little among different-sized urban areas, but it was markedly lower for rural nonfarm areas.

The same data for 1940 allow separate analysis for wives with, and without children under 10. The participation of wives without young children had associations with husbands' income very similar to those of all wives (Table 9, Section B and Chart 6). This close similarity

CHART 5

Labor Force of Wives with and without Young Children, and Income of Husbands: United States, 1951 and 1956

Labor Force per 1,000 in Same Population Group

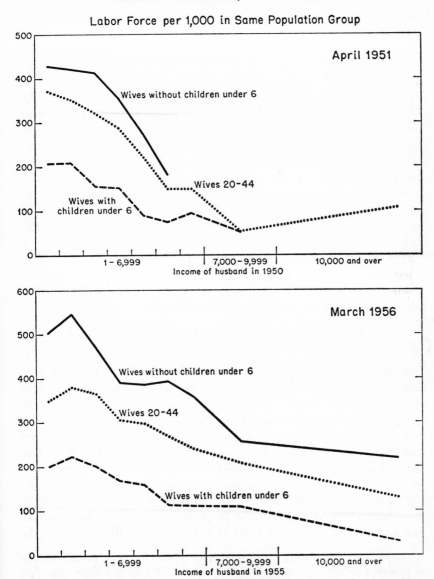

Source: For both years, "Marital and Family Status of Workers: 1956," *Current Population Reports, Labor Force*, Series P-50, No. 73, p. 14. Labor force not shown where sample base is less than 200,000. Income data are grouped at 500-dollar intervals up to $5,000, then $5,000–5,999, 6,000–6,999, 7,000–9,999, and 10,000 and over. Readings are centered at midpoints except for the open-end class.

was not surprising, since most wives in the labor force do not have young children and could be expected to dominate the average. Wives *with* young children (Table 9, Section C) showed somewhat different tendencies. Their labor force participation fell more sharply as the husbands' income rose (—0.44 instead of —0.32)—also not surprising, since this group would be more apt to leave jobs and care for their children, given the advantage of an increase in the husband's income.

At this writing the census has still not published similar tabulations for 1950. The only available data are a table from *Current Population Reports* which covers 1951 and 1956, and refers to wives aged 20–44 (Chart 5). Income groups differ, since the whole schedule of incomes had shifted upward. The table provides no data for younger or older wives or for standardizing for possession of young children. Nevertheless, the unstandardized association for 1951 was very similar to the unstandardized and standardized results for 1940 (Table 10). The associations for 1956 indicate a smaller reduction in labor force participation for wives associated with each higher income group of husband. The decline in the association was, in general, greater for the higher income groups.

These results must be regarded as far more reliable than correlations based on the crude unit of a city, and they would seem to establish a rather overwhelming presumption that, for wives at least, lower labor force participation accompanies higher income.

White and Colored Wives by Age of Wife and Possession of Young Children

The inverse association between wives in the labor force and husbands' earnings cannot be attributed to the presence of higher proportions of Negroes in the lower income groups. It is true that proportionately more Negro wives were in the labor force than white wives regardless of age, number of children, or income—perhaps because Negro women had less security, received lower average earnings, or carried a larger share of responsibility for the family. Yet, both Negro and white wives tended to enter the labor market in relatively fewer numbers, the higher their husbands' earnings. In the case of older women and of those with children under 10, the proportions were all on lower levels; but within each age [2] and child status group—as illustrated by the

[2] *Employment and Family Characteristics of Women,* as cited, p. 132. Mothers of preschool children were more likely to be in the labor force if there were older children to help care for the younger ones. Wives were least apt to work if all children were preschool, more apt if some children were of school age, most apt if no children were preschool. "Employment Characteristics of Household and Married Couples, April 1947," *Current Population Reports, Labor Force,* Series P-50, No. 5, May 7, 1948, p. 3, and Table 7, p. 10.

TABLE 10

Variations in Labor Force of Wives Aged 20–44 Associated with Differences in Income of Husbands in Previous Year, United States, 1951 and 1956

	Income Level (dollars)								Weighted Averages, All Income Levels [a]
	500–1,500	1,500–2,500	2,500–3,500	3,500–4,500	4,500–5,500	5,500–6,500	6,500–8,500	8,500–over 10,000 [b]	
April 1951									
Reduction Per $100 Additional Income of Husbands (persons) [b]									
All wives, 20–44 [c]	−2	−3	−4	−7	−7	0	−5	+1	−3.5
With children under 6 years	[d]	−5	[d]	−6	−2	+2	−2	...	−2.4
Without children under 6 years [e]	−1	−1	−6	−8	−9	...	...	...	−3.5
Reduction Per 1 Per Cent of Additional Income of Husbands (per cent) [b]									
All wives, 20–44 [c]	−0.03	−0.13	−0.28	−0.80	−1.48	0	−2.09	+1.31	−0.37
With children under 6 years	[d]	−0.31	−0.07	−1.44	−0.77	+1.58	−1.49	...	−0.33
Without children under 6 years [e]	[d]	−0.03	−0.35	−0.80	−1.51	...	...	...	−0.29
March 1956									
Reduction Per $100 Additional Income of Husbands (persons) [b]									
All wives, 20–44 [c]	+3	−2	−6	−1	−3	−3	−2	−1	−1.9
With children under 6 years	+2	−2	−3	−1	−5	[a]	[a]	−1	−1.5
Without children under 6 years [e]	+4	−8	−8	−1	+1	−3	−5	−1	−3.6
Reduction Per 1 Per Cent of Additional Income of Husbands (per cent) [b]									
All wives, 20–44 [c]	+0.45	−0.58	−0.42	−0.09	−0.45	−0.56	−0.45	−0.49	−0.20
With children under 6 years	+0.60	−0.18	−0.41	−0.16	−1.32	−0.05	−0.06	−0.94	−0.28
Without children under 6 years [e]	+0.44	−0.21	−0.43	−0.04	+0.10	−0.48	−0.93	−0.19	−0.21

Source: "Marital and Family Status of Workers: 1956," *Current Population Reports, The Labor Force*, Bureau of the Census. Series P-50, No. 73, p. 14; *Census of Population, 1950*, Vol. II, Part 1, *United States Summary*, p. 304.

[a] Weighted by the proportion of wives 14 and older belonging to different income levels as reported by the census of 1950.

[b] Number of persons by which rate of participation of wives 20–44 in labor force (per 1,000 wives of same age and income group) was reduced for every additional $100 of income of husbands in the previous year; and percentage by which the rate was reduced for every 1 per cent addition to the husband's income.

[c] Data could not be standardized for possession of young children. [d] Negligible.

[e] Wives with children under 18 but not under 6; wives with no children under 18 excluded.

CHART 6

Labor Force of Colored and White Wives with and without Young Children, and Earnings of Husbands: Metropolitan Districts Combined, United States, April 1940

Labor force per 1,000 in same population group.

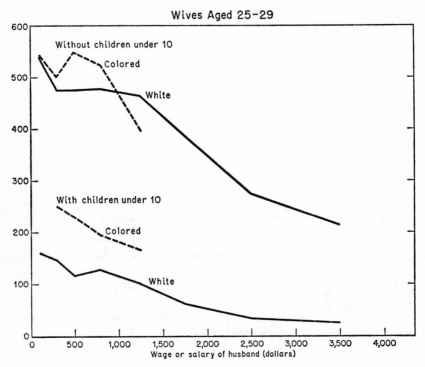

25–29 and 35–44 groups (Chart 6)—the inverse association persists regardless of color of wife, age of wife, or child-care responsibilities.

Employment Opportunities

Could the inverse correlation between female labor force and income be really due to the fortuitous effect of differences in job opportunities for women in different cities? A recent study by Nedra Belloc proposes that women, instead of being forced into employment by low earnings, are drawn into it by "abundant employment opportunities," which are measured by the ratio of females employed in manufacturing and domestic service to all females employed.[3] It would seem just as plausi-

[3] Nedra B. Belloc, "Labor Force Participation and Employment Opportunities for Women," *Journal of the American Statistical Association*, September 1950, pp. 400–410.

CHART 6, concluded

Wives Aged 35-44

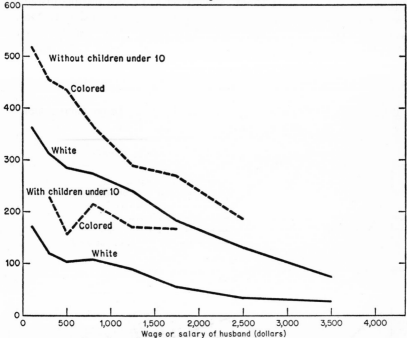

Wage or salary of husband (dollars)

Limited to wives whose husband's income (in 1939) was entirely from wages or salary. The income groups are $1–199; 200–399; 400–599; 600–999; 1,000–1,499; 1,500–1,999; 2,000–2,999; and 3,000 and over. Readings are centered at midpoints of the ranges, epcept for the open-end class. Metropolitan districts are urban areas with population of 100,000 or over.
Source: *Employment and Family Characteristics of Women,* as cited in Table 9.

ble to argue the reverse. In localities where women are obliged to work because men's incomes are meager, there tends to be a larger proportion of women available for factory jobs or for relatively low-paid domestic employment—attracting manufacturing industries that use female labor, and making it easier for middle- and upper-class women to hire domestic help. In any case, these two occupations have on the average, provided employment for scarcely one in four women; the main opportunities for female employment have always been furnished by stores, banks, insurance and real estate firms, beauty parlors, restaurants, schools, and government agencies.

Fortunately the problem has a solution. If it can be agreed that all women in any one city enjoy about the same job opportunities, the existence of an inverse association between labor force and income *within* the city would demonstrate effectively that the tendency exists and is not the spurious result of variations in opportunity among cities. This is what we find on examining separately each of eleven metropolitan districts of a million population or over (Chart 7). Classified by age, possession of children under 10, and color (for cities with large Negro populations), four or five times as many wives of low-income husbands were in the labor force as were wives of high-income husbands. Moreover, the higher the level of income, the more the participation of wives dropped for every additional $100 of earnings. This tendency

CHART 7

Labor Force of Wives and Earnings of Husbands: Large Metropolitan Districts, United States, April 1940

Labor Force, per 1,000, of Wives 18-64

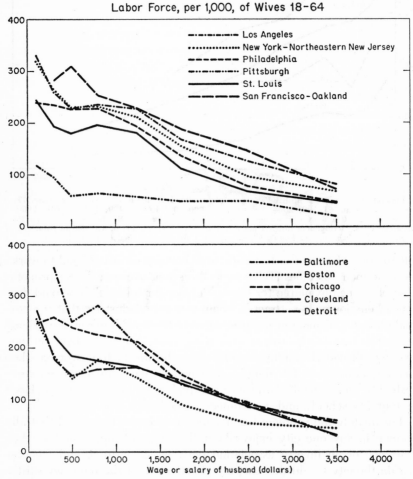

Limited to wives whose husband's income (in 1939) was entirely from wages or salary. The income groups are $1–199; 200–399; 400–599; 600–999; 1,000–1,499; 1,500–1,999; 2,000–2,999; and 3,000 and over. Readings are centered at midpoints of the ranges, epcept for the open-end class. Large metropolitan districts are those with population of 1,000,000 or over.
Source: *Employment and Family Characteristics of Women*, as cited in Table 9.

occurred for all groups except those in the $400–999 range.[4] The results do not demonstrate that job opportunities can be discarded as a factor, but they do suggest that the inverse relation cannot be attributed exclusively to them.

A different version of the influence of job opportunities could, of course, be urged—that female labor force participation may at any time tend to be high in those cities where unemployment is low and jobs are easy to get. This possibility was tested for 38 cities by correlating labor force participation rates of white females of various ages with unemployment rates of white men aged 25–44. (Male unemployment rates were used to avoid any tendency for both labor force and unemployment of females to be low merely because unemployed females had been discouraged from the labor market.) The relationship between female labor force and male unemployment appeared generally insignificant. The only exception was the correlation for young women 20–24, which exhibited a tendency that was positive and therefore, if anything, upsetting to the notion that white women would be in the labor force in greater proportion where jobs were easily found. As to colored females, the 23 cities with data for Negroes showed a significant tendency for their participation rates to be higher in cities where male unemployment rates were low and jobs presumably easier for colored women to get. The associations with male unemployment were inverse for all age groups of females and were significant on the 95 per cent level for all age groups except the 20–24 and 65 and older.

Rural Population Density and Size of City

No sign of any connection between the labor force and density of population was manifested for rural females; in all of the 48 states they were in the labor force without regard to the number of inhabitants per square mile. For example, Connecticut had relatively fewer females in jobs than Georgia, which was one-seventh as thickly populated. A slightly higher proportion of females was gainfully occupied in urban than in rural areas, and in big cities than in small towns; but no association with size of city was shown in the 38 cities, which ranged in population from 100,000 to 7 million, or in the 11 metropolitan districts of 1,000,000 or over, which also varied widely in size. The same findings resulted from a detailed study by color and age of wife, by child status of wife, and by income group of husband, e.g. white wives aged 25–29, with no children under 10, having husbands with a wage or salary of $1,000–1,499 [5] but no other income. Participation in the labor force in the four smallest metropolitan districts did not differ consistently from that in the four largest.

[4] *Employment and Family Characteristics of Women* as cited, pp. 152–163.
[5] *Ibid.* The computations separating white wives from all wives were the author's.

93

Education

Do not well educated persons have a better chance of getting jobs, and are they not therefore more apt to enter the labor force than the poorly educated or the illiterate? This expectation is not completely borne out in the case of wives. According to the 1940 census, married women living with their husbands were distinctly more apt to work if they were college graduates; but no similar association between education and employment was observable among women below the college level, even when they were also analyzed by age, and possession of young children. It is, of course, possible that well educated women had less need to earn money because their husbands were more prosperous on the average, and that the two counter-tendencies—the greater employability of the educated and their less urgent need to work—canceled each other out; but information was lacking for exploration of this possibility.

However, for all women, married and unmarried combined, the association between education and participation in the labor force was nothing short of powerful. Chart 8—which traces for 1940 and 1950 the rate of participation of women in the age groups 20–64 by color, by urban or rural-farm residence, and by years of school completed—brings out certain well defined tendencies.

One is that education seems to have been an even stronger factor than age in determining a woman's presence in the labor force. Among both whites and Negroes living in urban areas in 1940, the younger group, 20–24, had 200 more workers per 1,000 than did persons 55–64. Within each age group, on the other hand, women who had graduated from college were in the labor force at a rate typically about 250 or 300 more per 1,000 than those who had only a few years of grade school or no education at all. The patterns were different, however, in rural-farm areas. There age and education had little to do with the participation of persons who had not completed high school, but seemingly much to do with that of high school and college graduates. It may be that rural-farm women with less than a high school education had few chances to get jobs in nearby towns—at least jobs that paid enough to attract them—and that regardless of age or education they either worked on the farm as laborers and unpaid family workers or did no paid labor at all. But rural-farm women with a fairly good education could aspire to many types of jobs in stores and offices, and had greater opportunities the younger they were.

The second characteristic of the relationship with education is that for any given age, residence, or color the participation of females increases slowly with education up to high school, then rapidly up to

94

CHART 8

Labor Force of White and Colored Women and Years of Schooling: by Age Group, United States, for Urban and Rural Areas, 1940, and All Areas, 1950

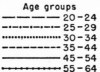

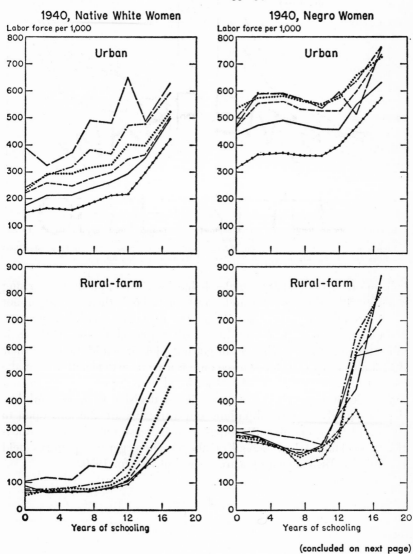

(concluded on next page)

CHART 8, concluded

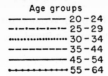

Age groups
————————— 20 - 24
—·—·—·—·— 25 - 29
·················· 30 - 34
————————— 35 - 44
——————————— 45 - 54
·——·——·——· 55 - 64

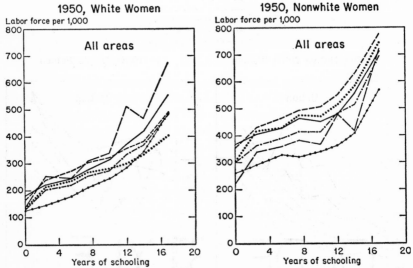

1950, White Women

Labor force per 1,000

All areas

1950, Nonwhite Women

Labor force per 1,000

All areas

Years of schooling

Years of schooling

Education data are for years of school completed—0, 1–4, 5–7, 8, 9–11, 12, 13–15, 16 and over—plotted at midpoint for the grouped years, except 16 and over.

Source: *Census of Population: 1940, Education, Educational Attainment by Economic Characteristics and Marital Status*, pp. 76–85; *1950, Education*, PE No. 5B, pp. 73–76.

college or beyond. That of males behaves in the opposite way, rising rapidly with education through grammar school, then slowly or not at all through high school or college. The explanation is fairly obvious. Most men must work if they are at all employable, and while their education affects their chances of getting a job, it would influence their decision to stay in the labor force only if it were so deficient as to make getting a job hopeless. On the other hand, females of any age do not automatically enter the labor force. Their decision to work doubtless depends partly on how abundant and attractive are the jobs open to them and these opportunities appear to increase rapidly with education, especially at high school or above. These general patterns held not only for 1940, a year of scarce jobs, but also for 1950.

CHAPTER 6

FEMALES IN THE LABOR FORCE
OVER TIME

The Upward Trend in the Female Labor Force

WE TURN to the five-nations data that enable us to examine changes over time. In all the countries during the last half century, the number of females in the labor force increased much faster than in the population.[1] And since about 1930 the increase has tended to be both greater and more uniform than it was in the earlier decades. An exception is Germany. World War II not only disrupted industry in that country but left people in the immediate postwar years with little incentive to work, since many had very large holdings of cash in relation to going wages—cash which, because of rationing, they could not use to buy the things they needed. In recent years a very large percentage of the population—as much as a fifth—has been receiving war and social security pensions which have been high in relation to earnings.[2]

In the United States female participation rose from slightly under 4 million in 1890 to over 16 million in 1950, a gain of about 17 per decade for every 1,000 females of working age (Table 11). This was approximately the median for the five countries; the increases varied from 11 per decade in Britain to 31 in Germany (up to 1939).

Compared with Changes in Income

Before comparing changes in labor force and income, a decision must be made as to what comprises income and who receives it and when.

If income has any influence on the labor force, it would surely be the sums actually paid out to persons as individuals: that is, national income less corporate profits withheld, and personal income taxes and social security contributions withheld or paid, plus government and business transfer payments to persons. In the recent decades the data, though they leave much to be desired, are readily available from the official income estimates of the four English-speaking countries. But no disposable personal income data have been available since World War II for Germany or in the earlier years for the other countries.

---

[1] Except for a decline in New Zealand in 1926, probably due to the fact that working children under 15, who had been included in the labor force by censuses through 1921, were left out beginning in 1926.

[2] "The pension system in West Germany is on so ruinous a scale that it has not been possible . . . to maintain it on a straight actuarial basis. Substantial subsidies have had to be voted by the federal and state governments." *New York Times*, Jan. 6, 1955, p. 6.

97

Consequently, it was necessary to make rough calculations (Appendix D).

Theoretically, labor would be influenced by non-labor income or by the lack of it, since a man may be under less pressure to work if, say, he receives rent, interest, dividends, a pension, or social security, than if his income is derived solely from current efforts. Therefore in

TABLE 11

Average Per-Decade Changes in Female Labor Force, 5 Countries, Various Periods, 1890–1951

	Change per 1,000 Female Population of Same Age (number)					
	14 & Older	14–19	20–24	25–44	45–64	65 & Older
	A. ENTIRE PERIOD					
United States:						
1890–1950	+17	−3	+20	+29	+27	−1
1890–1950 [a]	+20					
1890–1950 [b]	+14	−11	+8	+22	+23	−1
Rural areas,[a] 1890–1950	+15	−2	+20	+26	+16	−4
Urban areas,[a] 1890–1950	+14	−16	+1	+21	+28	0
Large cities,[a] 1900–1950	+22	...	...	...	...	...
Native white,[a] 1890–1950	+26	+7	+31	+33	+31	+2
Foreign-born white,[a] 1890–1950	+10	−45	−8	+29	+24	+1
Colored,[a] 1890–1950	−2	−33	−13	+15	+3	−24
Great Britain,[a, c] 1911–1951	+11	−6	+12	+16	+17	−16
Canada:						
1921–1951 [a]	+25	+23	+39	+29	+26	−4
1911–1951 [a]	+23	+10	+58	+24	+21	−1
New Zealand:						
1901–1951 [a, d]	+10	+31		+4	+7	−10
1896–1951 [a, d]	+12	+34		+7	+8	−17
Germany:						
1895–1939 [a]	+31	+42	+22	+43	+25	−13
1895–1950 [a]	+15	+12	+22	+25	+10	−18
	B. EARLY PERIOD					
United States:						
1890–1930	+14	−4	+29	+25	+15	−1
1890–1930 [a]	+16					
1890–1930 [b]	+10	−12	+15	+16	+13	−1
Rural areas,[a] 1890–1930	+10	−7	+22	+17	+10	0
Urban areas,[a] 1890–1930	+9	−17	+11	+16	+15	−1
Large cities,[a] 1900–1930	+17	...	...	...	...	...
Native white,[a] 1890–1930	+22	+5	+41	+29	+18	+2
Foreign-born white,[a] 1890–1930	+4	−34	+11	+11	+10	−1
Colored,[a] 1890–1930	+10	−19	−5	+24	+16	−7

TABLE 11, *continued*

	Change per 1,000 Female Population of Same Age (number)					
	14 & Older	*14–19*	*20–24*	*25–44*	*45–64*	*65 & Older*
	B. EARLY PERIOD, *continued*					
Great Britain,[a, c] 1911–1931	+7	+27	+28	+8	−10	−17
Canada:						
1921–1931 [a]	+20	−23	+73	+34	+6	−2
1911–1931 [a]	+18	−26	+93	+22	+7	+5
New Zealand:						
1901–1926 [a, d]	+4	+26		−2	−2	−8
1896–1926,[a, d]	+9	+32		+5	+1	−21
Germany,[a] 1895–1925	+35	+22	+32	+50	+35	−7
	C. RECENT PERIOD					
United States:						
1930–1950	+22	−2	0	+38	+50	−2
1930–1950 [a]	+28					
1930–1950 [b]	+24	−5	−7	+35	+45	−3
Rural areas,[a] 1930–1950	+25	+7	+14	+43	+29	−13
Urban areas,[a] 1930–1950	+22	−15	−21	+30	+55	+3
Large cities,[a] 1930–1950	+28	. . .	. . .	. . .	. . .	. . .
Native white,[a] 1930–1950	+34	+21	+11	+42	+56	+2
Foreign-born white,[a] 1930–1950	+24	−67	−47	+63	+53	+3
Colored,[a] 1930–1950	−24	−61	−30	−2	−23	−59
Great Britain,[a, c] 1931–1951	+15	−38	−3	+24	+44	−15
Canada,[a] 1931–1951	+28	+47	+23	+26	+36	−6
New Zealand,[a, d] 1926–1951	+16	+36		+9	+16	−12
Germany:						
1925–1939 [a]	+21	+86	0	+29	+1	−25
1925–1950 [a]	−9	0	+10	−6	−21	−32

Source: Appendix A.

[a] Labor force standardized for age composition on the basis of population of the United States in 1940.

[b] Labor force standardized for rural-urban composition and, in the case of age group 14 and older, for age composition on the basis of population of the United States in 1940.

[c] Age groups are available only for 14–17 and 18–24.

[d] Girls under 15 not included; 15–24 grouped together—no separate data available for girls 14–19 and women 20–24.

this comparison, disposable income includes property income and transfer payments. It would have been worth while to make a separate comparison with labor income alone, since this would be applicable to large segments of the population and labor force, who might there-

99

fore be insensitive to the behavior of property income (although the propensity to work might be influenced by an urge to "keep up with the Joneses," and the "Joneses" might have property income). Unfortunately the disposable income data of most countries before very recent years do not permit separate estimates of labor earnings; and even in recent years important segments of labor income are combined with property income and could be made to yield separate wage and salary estimates only by arbitrary assumptions. The long-run comparisons must therefore be based on total disposable income from all sources.[3]

It is not, of course, the aggregate amount of the income that is expected to influence labor force participation; rather, it is the amount in relation to the number of persons who share in it. Income per worker could in turn depend on whether income is computed per persons in the *labor force* (thus including the unemployed) or per persons *employed*. Both computations were made but since the difference is not important in the years of high employment, with which the study is primarily concerned, and since the most relevant comparison is with income per employed worker, the latter is used in the formal analysis. Still there remains a statistical problem. Income per employed worker could also vary because of changes in age and sex composition of the workers. Many women and young people work fewer hours than men and most of them earn less per hour—and separate data on the income of men, women and young people are lacking. A more rapid increase in the number of employed women would lower the averarge earnings or retard their increase, and could result in a spurious relationship between changes in average income per worker and labor force participation. This bias cannot be eliminated entirely, but it can be minimized by weighting the number of employed belonging to these groups by a crude measure of their average earnings. This was done in Appendix C, where the employed are adjusted to an equivalent adult-male basis. The income in this study therefore may be regarded as a rough approximation to income per equivalent adult-male employed worker. It may, of course, take time for people to react to a new level of income, causing current levels to influence future, rather than present, labor force participation. Moreover, the labor force has usually been enumerated in the spring, so that much of the census-year income is received after enumeration. Perhaps what we should use for comparison, then, is the income received prior to labor force participation.

[3] Short-run comparisons in a later chapter are based on both total disposable income and wage earnings; and inter-area comparisons have, of necessity, been based on labor earnings alone.

100

But should it be that for just the immediate preceding year or the average for several preceding years? Income may fluctuate for statistical reasons—because of difficulties of measuring income or of allocating its flow to a particular year. It may also fluctuate for cyclical reasons, and if the worker believes these fluctuations to be temporary and does not consider them in forming his decisions to enter or withdraw from the labor force, they may be less relevant to our purpose than the average of several years' income.

From some points of view it might have been best to use a five-year average but to do this would have involved fresh difficulties. In some instances, the materials were insufficient, e.g., German income data were available for one year only (1925) because of the inflation of the preceding years. In other instances, e.g. the United States in 1920, or Canada and Great Britain in 1921, the use of five years would have necessitated including income received in World War I, thus posing statistical and conceptual problems of measuring real income in wartime, and loading the average with income inflated or deflated by war and not applicable for peacetime. Therefore, averages for three years—the census year and the two preceding years—were used and were centered on the middle year.

Real income per equivalent adult-male employed worker doubled in the United States between 1890 and 1950; it increased substantially in Great Britain during 1911–1951, in Canada during 1921–1951, and in New Zealand during 1901–1951, and it rose even in Germany between 1895 and 1939, despite the disastrous military defeat in World War I. In Chapter 8, there is found to be very little difference in male labor force participation relative to income changes, whether the income changes were computed between census years or between three-year averages (each three-year average took in the census year and the two preceding years). Nor is any significant relative difference found here for females (Table 12). For the over-all period the differences were trifling except in Germany where, as it has been repeatedly pointed out, income comparisons are highly dubious in view of economic disruption, inflation, and the partitions that followed the two World Wars. For the early period the differences were negligible, except in Great Britain. For the recent period there was only a small difference for Germany.

Since income changes *per capita* are smaller, labor force variations in relation to these changes are larger. But there is the same lack of close relation in both the entire and recent periods as between labor force and real income.

101

TABLE 12

Average Per-Decade Changes in Female Labor Force per 1,000 Females 14 and Older, Associated with Average Per-Decade Increases in Income between Census Years and Three-Year Averages, 5 Countries, Various Periods, 1890–1951

	Change in Income (Dollars) between:[a]		Change in Labor Force[b] per $100 Increase in Income between:		Per Cent Change in Labor Force[b] per 1 Per Cent Increase in Income between:	
	Census Years (1)	3-Year Averages (2)	Census Years (3)	3-Year Averages (4)	Census Years (5)	3-Year Averages (6)
Entire Period						
United States 1890–1950	296	282	7	7	0.53	0.54
Great Britain 1911–1951	113	114	10	10	0.34	0.35
Canada 1921–1951	268	288	9	9	0.76	0.71
New Zealand 1901–1951	342	322	3	3	0.20	0.20
Germany 1895–1939	33	20	94	155	1.69	2.75
Germany 1895–1950	7	−7	214	−214	3.95	−3.87
Early Period						
United States 1890–1930	255	267	6	6	0.44	0.41
Great Britain 1911–1931	30	17	23	41	0.77	1.40
Canada 1921–1931	80	71	25	28	1.99	2.23
New Zealand 1901–1926	218	228	2	2	0.10	0.10
Germany 1895–1925	−43	−44	−81	−80	−1.48	−1.43
Recent Period						
United States 1930–1950	377	311	7	9	0.69	0.81
Great Britain 1931–1951	196	210	8	7	0.28	0.27
Canada 1931–1951	363	396	8	7	0.63	0.58
New Zealand 1926–1951	460	412	3	4	0.25	0.26
Germany 1925–1939	196	172	11	12	0.18	0.20
Germany 1925–1950	66	41	−14	−22	−0.25	−0.39

Source: Appendixes A and D.

[a] Real disposable income per adult-male equivalent employed, in 1929 dollars. Each three-year average took in the census year and the two preceding years.

[b] Labor force standardized for age composition on the basis of population of the United States in 1940.

Demographic Composition of Female Population

Now that we have observed the behavior of females in the labor force as a whole, let us concern ourselves with their behavior when classified by age, rural and urban residence, color, and place of birth.

AGE COMPOSITION.

The age composition of the female population has changed in about the same way as that of the male population. The increase in the number of women aged 45 and over has offset the decrease in those under 25, and the proportion of all females 25–45 has changed very little. In most age groups, in most nations, and in most decades female participation in the labor force has grown; women have entered the labor force most readily in the 20–64 age groups, though in the most recent census the number of those aged 20–24 dropped nearly everywhere except in Germany. Reductions for girls 14–19 occurred in the United States and Great Britain, and for women 65 and older in all the countries and areas, though these latter reductions were not substantial in Canada or among white persons in the United States.

One consequence of the changes was a marked shift in the composition of the female labor force from young women and girls to women aged 25–64. Standardization does not alter very greatly the participation rate of the female population as a whole, since the groups that changed the most never contributed large numbers and therefore had little weight in determining the over-all propensity.

RURAL AND URBAN RESIDENCE.

Many females in the United States have migrated to the cities, where their tendency to be in the labor force has been greater than in rural areas (Chart 9). The difference has narrowed somewhat—from twice as great in cities in 1890 to only half again as great in 1950, but otherwise the movements have been reasonably parallel.

Had labor force participation rates moved over the years in exact parallels, the higher level of urban participation might have resulted in a rise in the over-all rate as women moved into urban areas.[4] When female labor force participation, standardized for age and rural-urban residence, is compared with the proportion standardized for age only (Table 13), the increase is found to have been somewhat larger as a result of the migration. But the increase was great in any case, and it was just as notable in Britain where the rural-urban distribution of population had not altered materially since 1911.

[4] It is not certain, of course, that women who move from the country to the city will thereafter follow the labor force pattern of city women.

103

CHART 9

Females 14 and Older in Labor Force per 1,000 in Same Population Group: 5 Countries, Various Years, 1890–1951

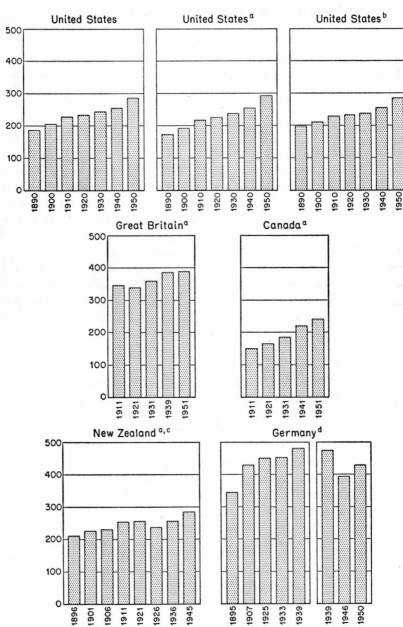

CHART 9, concluded

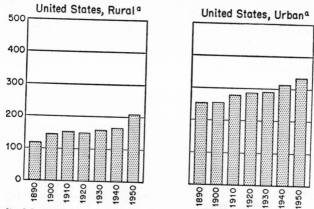

United States, Rural[a]

United States, Urban[a]

[a] Standardized for age on basis of population of United States in 1940.

[b] Standardized for age and rural-urban composition on basis of population of United States in 1940.

[c] Aged 15 and older.

[d] For 1895–1939, boundaries after World War I, without the Saar; 1939–1950, Federal Republic of Germany, without Berlin.

Source: Appendix A.

TABLE 13

Effect of Changes in Rural-Urban Residence on the Proportion of Females 10 and Older in the Labor Force, United States, Census Dates, 1890–1950

| | Female Labor Force per 1,000 Aged 10 and Older | | | | | | |
	1890	1900	1910	1920	1930	1940	1950
1. Changes in age eliminated [a]	162	180	201	209	219	233	267
2. Changes in age and rural-urban residence eliminated [b]	187	197	212	215	219	233	260
3. Effect of changes in rural-urban residence (line 1 − line 2)	−25	−17	−11	−6	0	0	+7

Source: Appendix A.

[a] Standardized for age on the basis of population of females 10 and older in the United States in 1940.

[b] Standardized for age and rural-urban residence on the basis of population of females 10 and older in the United States in 1940.

COLOR, ETHNIC COMPOSITION, AND PLACE OF BIRTH.

The population of each of the four foreign countries has been reasonably homogeneous; even in Canada, the relative numbers of British stock, French, and "Others"[5] have changed little in the last half century. Only in the United States has there been enough variation

[5] See Table 48.

CHART 10

Native White, Foreign-Born White, and Colored Females in the Labor Force per 1,000 in Same Population Group: by Age Group, United States, Census Dates, 1890–1950

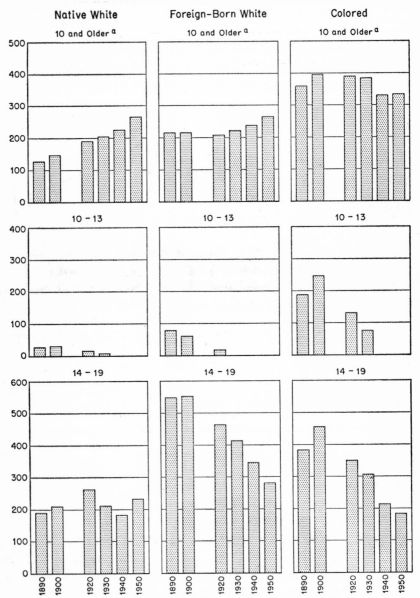

a Standardized for age on basis of United States female population in 1940.
Source: Appendix A.

CHART 10, concluded

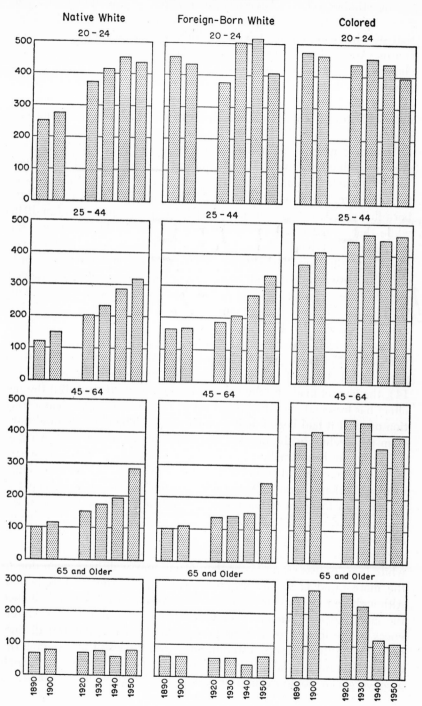

among ethnic groups to have had some effect on the labor force. The rate of participation of Negro females was several times higher than that of whites in 1890 and was still substantially higher in the latest census. And it has moved very differently—remaining relatively unchanged from 1890 to 1930, declining until 1940, and failing to rise significantly between 1940 and 1950 (Chart 10). But white females entered the labor force from 1890 to 1940 at much the same rate as did all classes of females (in which they are, of course, the major element).

Among teen-agers, both the foreign-born and Negroes showed the greatest reduction, and the participation rate for colored girls aged 14–19 was actually smaller in 1950 than that for native white girls of the same age. For females aged 20–24, the participation of the foreign-born fluctuated, and that of the colored declined, especially after 1940, while that of native white rose sharply. In the 25–44 age group, the participation of Negro women failed to rise after 1930, and for the 45–64 ages it declined between 1920 and 1940 and recovered only partially between 1940 and 1950. White women aged 25–64 moved into the labor market in large proportions. Native white and foreign-born women 65 and older manifested fluctuating but not declining tendencies, while Negro elderly women reduced their participation almost as much as Negro elderly men.

The effect of these great differences was to raise the rate of participation of all classes of females substantially but not enormously (Table 14), the impact made by the colored having been greatest. But the net effect has lessened over the years, and in 1946 was no more than a fraction of what it had been a half century earlier. The reasons could have been the decline in the number of foreign-born and the narrowing of differences in behavior between the various racial and national groups.

A word may be added on the behavior of the participation of Negro women. Perhaps it did not rise with that of native whites because it was so high to begin with; it was half again higher in 1890 than the level reached in 1950 by native white females after sixty years of rapid advance. It is also possible that the especially sharp decline in the participation of colored females since 1930, when the proportion for white females was rising faster than usual, may well have been due to the more rapid economic progress made by Negroes in this period. Although no real tendency has been discovered for income to influence the labor force of females over time, it is conceivable that as differences in the income of various groups grow smaller, cultural distinctions among these groups also diminish, with the effect of reducing the divergences in their labor force behavior. In the case of Negroes, such a convergence would mean a decline in participation. The decline has

TABLE 14

Effect of the Foreign-Born and Negroes on Rate of Female
Participation in the Labor Force, United States, Census
Dates, 1890–1950

	1890	*1900*	*1920*	*1930*	*1940*	*1950*
Rate of Participation [a]						
1. All classes	170	187	213	224	237	271
2. Natives (white and nonwhite)	160	182	214	225	237	272
3. Whites (native and foreign-born)	145	160	193	207	227	265
4. Native whites	127	147	190	204	225	265
Method No. 1						
5. Effect of foreign-born (line 1 minus line 2)	+10	+5	−1	−1	0	−1
6. Effect of colored (line 2 minus line 4)	+33	+35	+24	+21	+12	+7
7. Combined effect (line 1 minus line 4 or line 5 plus line 6)	+43	+40	+23	+20	+12	+6
Method No. 2						
8. Effect of foreign-born (line 3 minus line 4)	+18	+13	+3	+3	+2	0
9. Effect of colored (line 1 minus line 3)	+25	+27	+20	+17	+10	+6
10. Combined effect (line 8 plus line 9)	+43	+40	+23	+20	+12	+6

Source: Appendix A.

[a] Number of females 10 and older in the labor force (standardized for age composition on the basis of population of the United States in 1940) per 1,000 females of same age group, color, and place of birth.

Note: Data were not reported by the census in 1910.

probably been reinforced by the movement of southern Negroes from rural areas, where their tendency to be in the labor force was high, to urban areas, where it became comparatively low.

The fact that foreign-born women 20 and older live mostly in urban areas was clearly not responsible for their lower participation compared to that of native-born women of the same age; for foreign-born women were also found to participate less when compared with native-born women residing in the same city (Table 15). They may have been handicapped by language or training in getting jobs or perhaps they had more children to care for. Among immigrant teen-age girls the participation levels much above those of native-born girls reflected a greater economic pressure, which could reveal itself only where there was no responsibility for the care of children.

As the immigrants died off they were replaced by their native-born

109

TABLE 15
Labor Force by Sex and Age Group of Persons of
Varying National and Color Parentage per 1,000 of Same
Age and Parentage, Philadelphia, 1920

| | Native-Born Persons of: | | | |
Age	Native White Parents	Foreign and Mixed Parents	Foreign-Born Persons	Negroes
MALES				
10–19	340	327	488	393
20–24	923	937	945	946
25–44	966	972	975	973
45–64	937	948	945	973
65 and older	643	712	577	818
FEMALES				
10–19	273	285	414	268
20–24	513	559	382	568
25–44	299	317	183	529
45–64	219	226	158	530
65 and older	81	100	74	214

Source: *Census of Population, 1920*, Vol. II, p. 301, and Vol. IV, p. 463.

children. Would these children manifest the tendencies of their parents, the tendencies of descendants of native-born parents, or some mixture of the two tendencies? A fairly definite answer is provided by comparisons for the city of Philadelphia where, in 1920, persons born of foreign or mixed parents had rates of participation very similar to those of the same age who were born of native parents, and very unlike persons of the same age who were born abroad (Table 15). In this respect, the "melting pot" affected the first generation born on American soil.

School Attendance and Marriage

FEMALES UNDER 25.

The two countries for which statistical evidence is available on labor force participation, school attendance, and marital status both reveal similar developments for females aged 14–24. In the United States from 1890 to 1920 and in Canada from 1911 to 1951, these girls and young women increased their attendance in school, their participation in the labor force, and their tendency to marry as shown by a lower percentage of those who remained at home, presumably helping with the housework and looking toward marriage. The development in this country had gone almost as far as it could by 1920 (Canada did not reach the same stage until thirty years later), perhaps because in the

United States mass education had made an earlier start and because higher levels of well-being permitted younger marriages.[6] School attendance continued to grow in 1930 and 1940—in the latter year possibly because jobs were hard to get. And the proportion of young married women, which had been virtually constant for the previous half century, leaped ahead in 1950 as greater job opportunities, higher earnings, and veterans' benefits helped to finance matrimony at younger ages than ever before in this century. The absolute increase was largest among females aged 20–24, but the highest relative increase was among girls 14–19, of whom one in seven had husbands in 1950 compared to one in thirteen in 1890. The proportion of single girls of this age, who were not attending school and who were in the labor force, grew from a little over half in 1890 to over four-fifths in 1950.

In most of the five countries the ratio of wives—older as well as younger—to the female population has increased notably. The reason has doubtless been, partly, the lower incidence of death from childbirth. But in the English-speaking countries, early marriage was apparently encouraged by high employment and income and by relatively generous veterans' benefits following World War II—just as in Germany, as a result of the same conflict, it was probably discouraged by the loss of income and of marriageable men.

Single and married females aged 16 and older increased their participation in the four English-speaking countries (Chart 11). Widowed and divorced women, however, did so only in the United States; in Britain and New Zealand their participation decreased by amounts almost as large, in some cases, as the increase for single women and wives. In Germany wives showed sizable rises in participation up to 1939, while single, widowed, and divorced women—lumped together in the statistics—increased in the labor force, but only in very small amounts. The three latter groups and wives lowered their participation in Germany between 1939 and 1950—perhaps partly as an effect of the pensions which were referred to previously.

When the periods before and after 1930 (or approximately that date) are analyzed separately, both reveal increased participation of single and married women, but disclose no uniformity of behavior between the two periods. For wives, participation generally rose much more in the recent than in the earlier period, except in Germany, where the rise was much less. For single women there was a tendency in some countries for the reverse to be true.

Increases in participation were generally much smaller for females

[6] Females probably marry at younger ages in America than in most countries of the world. "Age of Marriage for Selected Countries," *Population Index*, April 1953, cover.

CHART 11

Single Females, Wives, and Widows and Divorcees 16 and Older in the Labor Force per 1,000 in Same Population Group: 5 Countries, Various Years, 1890–1951

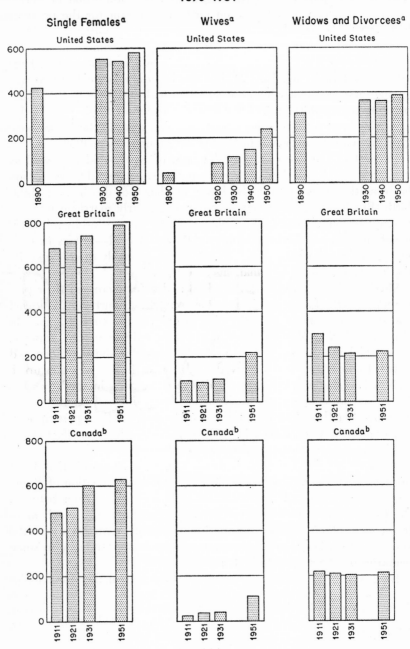

CHART 11, concluded

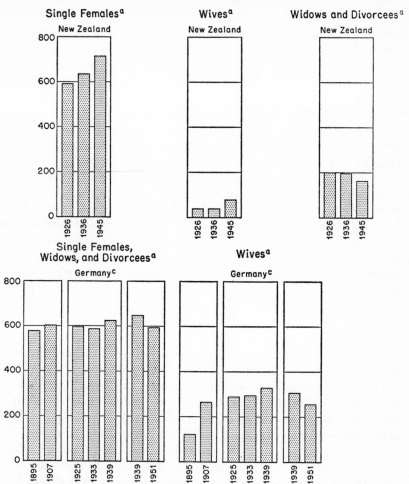

Single Females[a] Wives[a] Widows and Divorcees[a]

New Zealand

Single Females, Widows, and Divorcees[a] Wives[a]

Germany[c]

[a] Standardized for marital status and age on basis of female population of given country at latest census year before World War II.

[b] For 1921, standardized for marital status only.

[c] For 1895–1907, boundaries before World War I; 1925–1939, boundaries after World War I, without the Saar; 1939–1950, Federal Republic of Germany, without Berlin.

Source: Appendix A.

aged 45 and over—not so much in the United States as in Britain and Germany; in New Zealand, in fact, single women over 44 lowered their labor force activity, while younger women raised theirs enormously. The tendency for younger females to increase their participation more than older ones was generally characteristic of both early and recent periods—though in the United States older wives have increased their participation much more than younger wives in the recent period. In general it may be said that the rise of female participation, while it

113

varied widely according to age, marital status, and period studied, was nevertheless characteristic of both young and old, married and single, and of recent as well as of earlier years. When female participation is standardized for marital status and broad age groups, it reveals rates of increase per decade in the various countries that differ surprisingly little from those standardized for age only. Standardizing for marital status accentuated the increase, particularly in the United States, Great Britain, and New Zealand.

The rises in the rate of female participation, standardized for age and marital status, were typically between 24 and 33 per 1,000 per decade, and amounted to surprisingly small differences among the five nations. When they were related to changes in male income, however, the similarities disappeared, because of the wide difference in income behavior. Percentages varied from a rise of 0.47 in the labor force for each 1 per cent rise in male real income in New Zealand and Britain to 0.87 in Canada and upwards of 4.0 in Germany during 1895–1950. Standardizing for marital status seemed further to reduce any appearance of influence of income on the labor force participation of females.

Motherhood

Since young children tend to keep mothers out of the labor force, the propensity of women to participate will depend to some extent on how many of the nation's women have child-care responsibilities.

The interrelationships between marriage, motherhood, and labor force are complicated. A job for the young woman has undoubtedly helped to finance many early marriages that would otherwise have been postponed until the young man had finished school or achieved an adequate income in his job. On the other hand, wives may put off having children in order to keep the jobs that enabled them to marry at earlier ages. In general, the decline in the birth rate up to 1930 should have encouraged female labor force participation, and the rise in the birth rate and increase in the number of young mothers during the 1940's should have discouraged it.

Unfortunately only in the United States between 1940 and 1950 is it possible to determine with any degree of certainty what effect the changing proportion of women with young children has had on female participation. The effect in this decade may be seen from Table 16, line 11, to have been very weak—and opposite from what might have been expected. Despite the fact that more wives had young children in 1950, the mothers were a smaller proportion of all wives. If the proportion had been the same as in 1940, female participation would have risen less than it actually did, but by only 0.6 per cent of all fe-

114

TABLE 16

Women 16 and Older in the Labor Force, by Marital and Child Status, United States, 1890, 1940, and 1950

	1890	1940	1950	1890	1940	1950
NUMBER (IN MILLIONS)						
	Population			*Labor Force*		
1. Single	5.6	11.8	9.2	2.4	6.3	5.3
2. Widowed and divorced	2.3	8.1	9.5	0.7	2.9	3.6
3. Married	11.1 a	28.6 b	35.9	0.5 a	4.2 b	8.6
4. Without children under 10	5.1 a	18.0 b	24.1	0.3 a	3.4 b	7.6
5. With children under 10	6.0 a	10.6 b	11.8	0.2 a	0.8 b	1.4
6. Total, 16 and older	19.0	48.5	54.6	3.6	13.4	17.5
PER CENT IN LABOR FORCE						
	Unstandardized			*Standardized* c		
1. Single	43.1	54.2	58.1	40.4	52.7	57.8
2. Widowed and divorced	29.9	36.2	37.8	41.4	51.4	59.7
3. Married	4.6	14.7	23.8	4.5	14.7	24.0
4. Without children under 10	5.9	18.9	29.6	7.7	23.3	33.8
5. With children under 10	3.3	7.8	11.9	2.1	4.8	7.6
6. Total, 16 and older	19.0	27.9	32.0			
6. Total, 16 and older	19.0	27.9	32.0			
7. Standardized for age d				18.2	27.9	32.4
8. Standardized for age & marital status d				18.2	27.9	34.7
9. Standarized for age-marital-child status d				18.6	27.9	34.1
10. Effect of marital status (line 7 minus line 8)				0		−2.3
11. Effect of child status (line 8 minus line 9)				−0.4		+0.6
12. Combined effect (line 7 minus line 9)				−0.4		−1.7

Source: Appendix A. *Census of Population, 1940, Employment and Family Characteristics of Women*, pp. 9–10; *Current Population Reports, The Labor Force*, Bureau of the Census, Series P-50, No. 29, p. 8.

a The census of 1890 did not report the number of married women having children under 10, or the participation of married women in the labor force. These were estimated hypothetically from 1940 census data, on the assumption that the ratios in 1890 were the same as those in 1940 for southern rural-farm areas, where the proportion of married women in the labor force in 1940 was similar to that for the United States as a whole in 1890.

b The original data were for married women aged 18–64. The present figures were derived by assuming that no married women aged 16 or 17 or over 64 had children under 10.

c Lines 1 through 5, standardized for age on the basis of population of the United States in 1940.

d Standardized on the basis of female population of the United States in 1940. It was assumed that all mothers of young children were under 45. Child status of widows and divorcees was ignored.

males aged 16 and older. Indeed, the change in the proportion of mothers offsets to some extent the effect of the change in the proportion of wives, so that the combined influence of marriage and motherhood was less than that of marriage alone.

Although there were no actual data on the participation of mothers and non-mothers in the labor force in the United States before 1940, some indication was desired as to what the effect might have been within broad limits. Purely hypothetical figures for 1890 were constructed on the basis of the assumption that the proportions in 1890 were the same as those in the rural-farm South in 1940. (In 1940 the rural-farm South had much the same over-all female participation rate as did the United States as a whole in 1890.) On this assumption, the effect of changes in motherhood composition would have been small—less than 0.5 per cent of the female population aged 10 and older between 1890 and 1940. Unless the situation in 1890 was far more extreme than that assumed here, it may be concluded that the changing motherhood composition during 1890–1940 could not have had important effects. This does not mean that the number of children is not important in determining the proportion of females who work; the conclusion in the next chapter is that it may have been a major factor. It means simply that the mere distribution of females between mothers and non-mothers has in itself had little significance.

116

CHAPTER 7

FURTHER ANALYSIS OF THE INCREASES IN FEMALE LABOR FORCE PARTICIPATION OVER TIME

WHY did female labor force participation rise as income increased over time—instead of declining as might be expected on the basis of the behavior among different income groups and localities at a given time? This chapter inquires: (1) What has been the excess over the amount suggested by the moment-of-time relationship with real income? (2) What were the dynamic forces that might explain this excess?

Estimate of the Possible Excess of Actual Female Labor Force Participation over That "Expected" on the Basis of Rising Income

The excess in actual female labor force participation, over that suggested by the rise in real income, was estimated for the United States (Table 17). The first step (line 3) computed the increase in real income in each decade as a percentage of the income of the previous decade date.[1] The second step obtained the possible relationships between income and female labor force at a given time, i.e., other things remaining fairly equal. (See Chapter 4, where labor force was correlated with income among cities, states, and nations.) The most reliable comparison, because it offered the best chance of other things remaining equal, and because it allowed adjustment of earnings for inter-area differences in the cost of living, was the study of 38 large United States cities.[2] Its results varied from one decade to another, but as such statistics go the variations during 1900–1940 were moderate. The highest was —0.74 in 1900, the lowest —0.35 in 1930, and the remaining two were —0.51 in 1920 and —0.50 in 1940—equal to the average for the four decades. These are the percentages by which the female labor force participation was lower in cities where incomes were 1 per cent higher. In 1950 the inverse association disappeared.[3] We use these individual decade associations, despite the fact that the data were scarcely accurate enough to reflect real changes in the labor

---

[1] Actually, to reduce randomness, a three-year average was computed from incomes in each census year and the two preceding years.

[2] The study covered 1900 and 1920–1950. Because of the difficulty presented by the probability of varying degrees of overcount or undercount in the different cities in 1890 and 1910, these dates were omitted.

[3] It disappeared only for white females; for colored females, it was about what it had been for all females in the previous decades.

117

TABLE 17

Illustrative Estimate of the Difference between the Actual Rate of
Female Participation and the Rate Expected, Had the Female
Labor Force Been Inversely Related to Income over Time
as It Was at a Given Time in the 38 Large Cities,
United States, Census Dates, 1890–1950

	1890	1900	1910	1920	1930	1940	1950
1. Personal disposable income per adult-male equivalent employed (1929 dollars) [a]	1,011	1,203	1,418	1,486	2,079	2,293	2,701
2. Change in income, measured in 1929 dollars	–	+192	+215	+68	+593	+214	+408
3. Per cent of previous income	–	+19.0	+17.9	+4.8	+39.9	+10.3	+17.8
4. Per cent change in female labor force participation among 38 cities associated with 1 per cent higher incomes (Table 2)	–	−0.74	−0.53[b]	−0.51	−0.35	−0.50	0
5. Per cent decline in female labor force participation, if the percentage associations in line 4 are multiplied by the percentage income increases in line 3	–	−14.1	−9.5	−2.4	−14.0	−5.1	0
6. Expected rate of female labor force participation, on basis of actual rate in 1890 and the percentage reductions postulated in line 5 (per 1,000 females 14 and older)	199	171	155	152	131	124	124
7. Actual rate of female labor force (per 1,000 female population 14 and older) [c]	199	210	228	232	237	254	284
8. Difference to be explained (line 7 minus line 6)	–	39	73	80	106	130	160
9. Difference, in millions of females	–	1.0	2.3	2.9	4.7	6.6	9.1

Source: Appendixes A and D; Table 2.

[a] Three-year averages of income for each census year and the two preceding years.
[b] Average percentage for 1900, 1920, 1930, and 1940. See discussion in text.
[c] Standardized for age and rural-urban residence on the basis of population of the United States in 1940.

force-income relationship from decade to decade (even assuming that such changes actually occurred).[4]

[4] The association for 1900 had to be constructed from 34, instead of 38 cities, and without adjustment of earnings for inter-city cost-of-living differences; thus the −0.74 found in 1900 is probably not as accurate as the lower inverse associations for the later dates. For this reason the 1910 percentage, which had to be estimated in the absence of a 38-city study for that year, was assumed to be the average of the four decades 1900–1940 instead of the average of 1900 and 1920.

The third step multiplied these moment-of-time percentages by the percentage increases in real income per male worker between the various decade dates (line 3 × line 4), in order to discover what percentage declines in female labor force participation might have been expected (line 5).[5]

The fourth step used the percentages in line 5 to find the expected participation (line 6). This was done by a chain method: the actual rate in 1890 (199 per 1,000 female population 14 and older standardized for age and rural-urban residence) was reduced by 14.1 per cent, to get the 1900 rate of 171; this in turn was reduced by 9.5 per cent to figure the 1910 rate of 156; and so on until the 1940 rate of 124 was reached. The latter was allowed to remain constant to obtain the 1950 expected rate of 124 per 1,000 female population 14 and older.

The excess of actual over expected participation was arrived at in the fifth and final step (line 8). From 1900 to 1950, this excess increased from 39 to 160 per 1,000 female population 14 and older. Computed in absolute numbers it began at 1.0 million in 1900 and reached 9.1 [6] million—roughly half of the female labor force—in 1950. If these highly speculative calculations have any merit, the numbers of female labor force that have to be explained through so-called dynamic forces are enormous. Where shall we look to explain such magnitudes?

[5] In this connection there should be noted a number of differences in the income data between those used in the moment-of-time studies and those used over time: (1) The moment-of-time studies were based on wage or salary earnings, and during 1900–1930 rested on earnings of factory workers only; the incomes over time were real national disposable income divided by the number of employed workers of all kinds in all industries. (2) The moment-of-time earnings were not always those of an adult-male equivalent, since in 1939 and 1949 earnings of males 14 and older were used; the incomes over time were adjusted in all years to an adult-male equivalent basis. (3) The moment-of-time earnings data were unadjusted for income tax payments or withholdings; the income data over time were after income taxes (this tax difference could have been important only for the last decade). (4) The moment-of-time earnings were those of the calendar year preceding the census year in which the labor force was enumerated; the income data over time were averages of the census year and the two preceding years.
[6] Similar calculations might have been made for the four foreign countries, had there been moment-of-time studies by which to measure their internal labor force-income associations. Some consideration was given to basing the calculations for the foreign countries on the association found among the 38 United States cities, for these were not very different from the moment-of-time associations among the nations at various census dates (−0.40 for the 16 nations around 1930; −0.23 for the 12 nations around 1950; and, for the five nations, −0.79 around 1930, −0.79 around 1940, and −0.50 around 1950). But it was decided that the calculations would have been too tenuous even for illustrative purposes.

Possible Reduction of Housework as a Result of Technological Developments

HOUSEHOLD APPLIANCES.

Certainly the use of durable household appliances in the United States has greatly increased over the past half century (Table 18). Assuming that the stocks of appliances in homes at any census date are equal to output over the preceding ten years, the equipment per

TABLE 18

Illustrative Estimate of Female Labor Possibly Saved by Greater Use of Household Appliances, United States, 1890–1950

	1890	1900	1910	1920	1930	1940	1950
1. Stocks of household appliances a (millions of 1929 dollars)	763	1,200	2,394	3,245	5,483	7,654	11,299
2. Household labor possibly saved b (millions of hours)	254	400	798	1,082	1,828	2,551	3,766
3. Standard work year (hours)	3,300	3,100	2,870	2,670	2,600	2,150	2,050
4. Household labor possibly saved (thousands of person-years)	77	129	278	405	703	1,187	1,837
5. Excess over 1890 in line 4	–	52	201	328	626	1,110	1,760
6. Household labor possibly saved (females per 1,000 female population 14 and older)	–	2	7	9	14	22	31

Source: Appliances: 1890–1900, W. H. Shaw, *Value of Commodity Output since 1869*, National Bureau of Economic Research, 1947, p. 73; 1910–1950, R. W. Goldsmith, *A Study of Savings in the United States*, Princeton University Press, 1955, Vol. I, p. 681. Female population and labor force; Appendix Table A-2. Hours: the author's estimates of standard hours in major industry groups, weighted by employment in given year.

a Value of finished commodities produced for domestic consumption in the ten previous years; the 1890 figure is ten times the average of production in 1879 and 1889.

b It is assumed that each dollar's worth of appliances saves one-third hour of labor per year.

female increased between 1890 and 1950 about fivefold. Did these mechanical aids lighten housework materially, and did they release many housewives and daughters to the labor force? There can be no really satisfactory answer. If, for illustration, we make the modest supposition that each dollar's worth (in 1929 prices) released one-third hour of work per year,[7] the resulting saving of labor would have

[7] Based on the assumption that 3⅓ hours of labor were saved for each dollar's worth of appliances over a ten-year duration. The assumption is that the housewife valued her time at 30 cents per hour at 1929 prices. In the earlier decades housewives doubtless placed a lower value than this on their time and in the

120

equalled 2 out of 1,000 females 14 and older in the population in 1900, 7 in 1910, and so on, to 22 per 1,000 in 1940, and 31 per 1,000 in 1950. It is not certain, of course, that such labor-saving actually took place; perhaps many appliances were acquired not to save work, but to impress friends or improve the standard of housekeeping! In any case the figures suggested by the illustration are not large.

PURCHASE OF MANUFACTURED FOOD AND CLOTHING.

Housekeeping has been eased also by the transfer of much of the nation's production from the washboard, the cook stove, and the sewing circle at home to the commercial laundry, the restaurant, and the department store. The saving in household labor may be estimated from the increase in factory production and store distribution of food and clothing. An estimate—again illustrative—is made by dividing the potential earnings of housewives into the increase in value added through the manufacture of food and clothing (Table 19), yielding the number of equivalent full-time persons conceivably released from home production. The computation assumes that the value added in the factory roughly corresponds to the value of the labor saved by the housewife when she buys her supplies instead of processing the raw food and cloth herself.[8]

Table 19 suggests that the labor thus conserved substantially exceeded that saved by appliances. The possible saving was greatest in 1919, when high employment and income enabled housewives to buy many things ordinarily produced at home; the decline in 1939 may have represented a return to the family economy, as high unemployment and low purchasing power forced many wives to bake bread, can fruit, and make their own clothes.

SERVICES BOUGHT BY THE HOUSEWIFE.

There has been an increasing tendency for the housewife to buy services—mostly from commercial establishments—which she formerly performed herself. There are no statistics of value added for services

---

later decades, a higher value. The fact that the appliances have undoubtedly been improving in labor-saving faster than they have been increasing in cost has probably provided an offsetting bias.

[8] F. C. Mills objects in a letter that "the increase in value added reflects the play of many forces—fuller processing of food (packaging, etc.), quality changes, relative advances in cost of manufacture over part of the period covered," and he therefore questions the author's right to attribute the value of labor saved to the shift to the market. Mills' comment about the cause of the changes in value added is correct, but it does not destroy the present argument; for whatever the cause of the value added, it may be assumed that housewives would not have paid the prices required to create the value, had they not felt they were getting their money's worth.

TABLE 19

Illustrative Estimate of Female Labor Possibly Saved by Greater
Use of Manufactured Food and Clothing Formerly Produced
in the Home, United States, 1889–1949

	1889	1899	1909	1919	1929	1939	1949
1. Value added by manufacture to food and clothing (millions of 1929 dollars [a])	1,880	2,576	3,885	6,259	7,530	8,334	13,256
2. Same, per 1,000 females 14 and older [b] (thousands of 1929 dollars)	93.1	103.5	125.7	172.0	171.5	164.7	232.6
3. Excess over 1890 in line 2	–	10.4	32.6	78.9	78.4	71.6	139.5
4. Annual earnings per female worker [c] (1929 dollars)		690	765	835	1,170	1,375	1,881
5. Household labor of females possibly saved (line 3 ÷ line 4), in person-years per 1,000 female population 14 and older	–	15	43	95	67	52	74

Source: For value added, *Census of Manufactures: 1900*, Vol. VII, Part 1, p. cxlv ("value of product" minus "cost of materials used"); *1910*, Vol. VIII, *General Report*, p. 53; *1930*, Vol. III, p. 37. Also, *Statistical Abstract of the United States: 1946*, pp. 815, 817, 820; *1949*, p. 932; *1952*, p. 757. For population, Appendix Table A-2.

[a] In adjusting to 1929 prices for 1909 and earlier the cost-of-living index employed by Lebergott was used (*Journal of the American Statistical Association*, March 1948, p. 76). Since his data begin with 1890, his cost of living relative for that year was used to convert the value added for 1889. For 1919 and on, the base was the index of the Bureau of Labor Statistics for manual workers in large cities.

[b] Population data refer to 1890, 1900, 1910, 1920, 1930, 1940, and 1950.

[c] Female earnings were estimated roughly from the ratio to male earnings given in Appendix Table C-8. This ratio was multiplied by disposable income per adult-male equivalent employed given in Appendix Table D-4. Precisely speaking, these figures are not earnings of all females but rather disposable income of adult-female equivalent employed. The error is not significant for the rough illustrative purpose of this table.

as there are for commodities; the saving of household labor must be estimated from the number of workers engaged in cooking, waiting on table, chauffeuring, and generally performing for pay many tasks common to home life. The labor saved (per 1,000 females) is taken to equal the net growth in the number of persons so employed (Table 20). It is hard to tell whether this outside labor is as productive as that of the housewife in the home. One can only guess that a female does the same amount of work in gainful employment as she would do without pay for her own family; or whether efficiency in the performance of personal service has proceeded more rapidly inside or outside the household.[9] In any case the combined number of domestic servants

[9] Technological improvements in the store, restaurant, hotel, laundry, and barber shop have been appreciable, though many of the mechanical devices, e.g. electric mixers, toasters, refrigerators, and coffee makers, are also used in the home.

TABLE 20

Illustrative Estimate of Female Labor Possibly Saved by the
Rise in Domestic and Commercial Services Purchased by
Housewives, United States, 1890–1950

	1890	1900	1910	1920	1930	1940	1950
1. Persons in domestic service and service industries (millions) [a]	2.2	2.7	3.7	3.3	4.8	5.7	6.0
2. Same, per 1,000 female population 14 and older	104	108	119	91	109	113	105
3. Excess over 1890 in line 2 [b]	–	4	15	−13	5	9	1

Source: Persons in service: Daniel Carson, "Changes in the Industrial Composition of Manpower since the Civil War," *Studies in Income and Wealth, Volume Eleven*, National Bureau of Economic Research, 1949, p. 47; *Census of Population, 1950*, Vol. II, *Characteristics of the Population*, Part 1, p. 101. Population and labor force: Appendix Table A-2.

[a] Computed before rounding.
[b] This is taken as a rough measure of the amount of labor saved through purchases of services formerly performed by family members.

and personal service employees has changed very slightly in relation to the female population 14 and older. It rose in 1940 when office and factory jobs were scarce and unprofitable, and declined in 1920 when these jobs were plentiful and paid well.[10] But the fluctuations involved trifling numbers.

Less Housework because of Smaller Families

The burden of housework may depend less upon the size of the house or number of appliances than upon the size of the family. Some argue that the care of five small children is not much more confining than the care of one; but it is possible for five children to so range in age as to keep a woman tied down until her fifty-fifth year, and even to absorb the time of older sisters, maiden aunts, and grandmothers. Though easier by the dozen sounds intriguing, what mother really believes it? Certainly the 1940 census data indicate that the more young children she has, the less apt the wife is to be in the labor force. Among both white and colored wives, the rate of participation of those with three or more children was lower than that of wives with one child, and that of wives with one child was lower (to about the same degree) than that of wives with no children at all (Table 21).

A really satisfactory estimate of the "need" for females in their own homes would require decennial statistics on the number of families and

[10] "The class who usually seek employment in factories are such as would be usually employed as domestics in families." *Third Biennial Report, 1888–1889*, Maryland Bureau of Industrial Statistics and Information, p. 86.

TABLE 21

Wives in Labor Force from Families Having Male Head of House
and Specified Number of Children under 10, United States, 1940

	As Per Cent of Total Wives	As Per Cent by Number of Children			
		None	1	2	3 or More
All classes	11.9	15.0	9.0	6.4	4.9
White	10.8	13.8	8.1	5.5	3.4
Nonwhite	24.3	30.0	21.1	16.7	12.9

Source: *Census of Population, 1940, Families, Types of Families,* p. 214.

their distribution by size. It would also require information for some base date on the number of houseworkers (excluding paid domestic servants) in families of various sizes. Since the latter is not available, even for a single date, it is assumed that the need bears a simple proportion to the civilian population. Though a crude assumption, it may be tested against annual averages of monthly data (from *Current Population Reports*) on the number of females actually keeping house in each year during 1940–1954. The test supposes that the number needed in each year was the same proportion as in 1950—22 per cent. The estimated need, and the actual number during each of the fifteen years are compared in Table 22, which shows the discrepancies to be small, ranging from −03.4 to +03.2 per cent of the estimate. One of the largest appears for the post-World War II year, 1947, when about 1 million more females were in housework than were needed—perhaps because many women who had worked during the war desired to resume full-time family life. The discrepancies seem specially modest considering the margin of sampling and interview error and the huge changes in civilian population and in the need for females in housework resulting from World War II and the Korean conflict. For illustrative purposes it may be safe to use this method for calculating the same need from 1890 through 1940. This is done in Table 23 (line 3) where the number has been estimated as 21.3 per cent of the total civilian population, based on actual data at the decennial census of 1950.[11] Its rough reliability is attested by the fact that for 1940 the estimate was 28.0 million—only 0.4 million, or 1.4 per cent, different from the 28.4 million reported by the 1940 census.

To the number thus needed in home housework is added the number

[11] The difference between this 21.3 per cent, and the 22.0 per cent used in Table 22, arises from the fact that the 1950 census enumeration's labor force and not-in-labor-force results were rather different from those of the sample survey for the same month (Appendix F and Supplementary Appendix I).

TABLE 22

Need for Females in Housework Based on Population to be Cared for, Compared with Actual Number of Females (Not in Labor Force) Keeping House, United States, 1940–1954

(millions of persons)

	ANNUAL AVERAGES OF MONTHLY DATA							
	1940	1941	1942	1943	1944	1945	1946	1947
1. Total civilian population	131.7	131.6	130.9	127.5	126.7	127.6	138.4	142.6
2. Estimated need for persons in housework (line 1 × .220 ᵃ)	29.0	29.0	28.8	28.1	27.9	28.1	30.4	31.4
3. Actual number of females (not in labor force) who were keeping house	28.4 ᵇ	28.9	28.6	27.2	27.3	27.7	31.1	32.4
4. Excess of actual over need: millions (line 3 minus line 2)	−0.6	−0.1	−0.2	−0.9	−0.6	−0.4	+0.7	+1.0
Per cent excess was of need	−2.1	−0.3	−0.7	−3.2	−2.2	−1.4	+2.3	+3.2

	1948	1949	1950	1951	1952	1953	1954
1. Total civilian population	145.2	147.6	150.2	151.1	153.3	156.1	159.1
2. Estimated need for persons in housework (line 1 × .220 ᵃ)	31.9	32.5	33.0	33.2	33.7	34.3	35.0
3. Actual number of females (not in labor force) who were keeping house	32.8	33.0	33.0	33.0	33.3	34.2	33.8
4. Excess of actual over need: millions (line 3 minus line 2)	+0.9	+0.5	–	−0.2	−0.4	−0.1	−1.2
Per cent excess was of need	+2.8	+1.5	–	−0.6	−1.2	−0.3	−3.4

Source of data on which calculations were based: *Current Population Reports*, Bureau of the Census, 1940–1954.

ᵃ 1950 ratio of females in housework to total civilian population.
ᵇ April data.

in school (line 4) and the estimated number in institutions and unable to work (line 5).[12]

The sum of these three groups is the number of females "not available" for labor force at the various census dates (line 6). The number

[12] The benchmark for the latter was the actual number of females 14 and older in institutions and unable to work, as reported by the 1950 census: 2.4 million. It was assumed that, except for 1940, for which we have actual census data, the estimates at the earlier censuses would bear a constant ratio to the population of

TABLE 23

Illustrative Estimates of Female Labor Possibly Saved and Its Availability for Labor Force Participation due to Decline in Number of Females Needed in Own Home Housekeeping as Population to be Cared for Rose Less Rapidly than Number of Females 14 and Older, by Rural-Urban Residence and Color, United States, 1890–1950

(millions of persons, except where stated otherwise)

	1890	1900	1910	1920	1930	1940	1950
A. RURAL AND URBAN							
1. Civilian population	62.7	75.6	91.8	105.8	122.6	131.3	149.7
2. Females 14 and older	20.2	24.9	30.9	36.4	43.9	50.6	57.0
3. "Needed" in home housework (line 1 × .213 [a])	13.4	16.2	19.6	22.6	26.2	28.0	31.9
4. In school	1.6	1.9	2.7	3.0	4.3	4.4	4.5
5. In institutions and unable to work	0.9	1.0	1.3	1.5	1.8	2.7 [b]	2.4 [b]
6. Not available for labor force (sum of lines 3–5)	15.9	19.1	23.6	27.1	32.3	35.1	38.8
7. Available for labor force (line 2 minus line 6)	4.3	5.8	7.3	9.3	11.6	15.5	18.2
8. Available, per 1,000 females 14 and older	213	233	236	255	264	306	319
9. Actual labor force, per 1,000 females 14 and older [c]	199	210	228	232	237	254	284
10. Per cent actual was of available	93	90	97	91	90	83	89
B. RURAL							
1. Civilian rural population	40.7	45.6	49.2	51.5	53.7	57.1	54.4
2. Rural females 14 and older	12.1	14.0	15.2	16.2	17.4	19.8	18.6
3. "Needed" in home housework (line 1 × .213 [a])	8.7	9.7	10.5	11.0	11.5	12.2	11.6
4. In school	1.0	1.2	1.6	1.6	2.0	1.9	1.7
5. In institutions and unable to work	0.6	0.6	0.7	0.7	0.8	1.6 [b]	0.9 [b]
6. Not available for labor force (sum of lines 3–5)	10.3	11.5	12.8	13.3	14.3	15.7	14.2
7. Available for labor force (line 2 minus line 6)	1.8	2.5	2.4	2.9	3.1	4.1	4.4
8. Available, per 1,000 females 14 and older	149	179	158	179	178	207	237
9. Actual rural labor force, per 1,000 rural females 14 and older [d]	118	143	151	148	158	164	207
10. Per cent actual [d] was of available	79	80	96	83	89	79	87

[a] Ratio of actual number of females 14 and older not in the labor force and keeping house in April 1950 to the civilian population in April 1950. The number reported by the decennial census differs from the number reported by the *Current Population Reports*.

126

	1890	1900	1910	1920	1930	1940	1950
C. URBAN							
1. Civilian urban population	22.0	30.0	42.6	54.3	68.9	74.2	95.3
2. Urban females 14 and older	8.1	10.9	15.7	20.2	26.5	30.8	38.4
3. "Needed" in home housework (line 1 × .213 a)	4.7	6.5	9.1	11.6	14.7	15.8	20.3
4. In school	0.6	0.7	1.1	1.4	2.3	2.5	2.8
5. In institutions and unable to work	0.3	0.4	0.6	0.8	1.0	1.1 b	1.5 b
6. Not available for labor force (sum of lines 3–5)	5.6	7.6	10.8	13.8	18.0	19.4	24.6
7. Available for labor force (line 2 minus line 6)	2.5	3.3	4.9	6.4	8.5	11.4	13.8
8. Available, per 1,000 urban females 14 and older	309	303	312	317	321	370	359
9. Actual labor force, per 1,000 urban females 14 and older d	252	253	278	286	289	312	333
10. Per cent actual d was of available	82	83	89	90	90	84	93
D. WHITE							
1. Civilian white population e		54.8	66.4	94.9	110.1	117.8	134.0
2. White females 14 and older		17.9	22.0	32.7	39.5	45.7	51.3
3. "Needed" in home housework (line 1 × .22 a)		12.1	14.6	20.9	24.2	25.9	29.5
4. In school		1.5	1.7	2.7	3.9	4.1	4.0
5. In institutions and unable to work		0.7	0.9	1.3	1.5	2.3 b	2.0 b
6. Not available for labor force (sum of lines 3–5)		14.3	17.2	24.9	29.6	32.3	35.5
7. Available for labor force (lines 2 minus 6)		3.6	4.8	7.8	9.9	13.4	15.8
8. Available, per 1,000 white females 14 and older		201	218	239	251	293	308
9. Actual labor force, per 1,000 white females 14 and older d		156	173	210	225	244	289
10. Per cent actual d was of available		78	79	88	90	83	94
11. Actual labor force, per 1,000 white females 14 and older f		183	192	217	225	244	281
12. Per cent actual f was of available		91	88	91	90	83	91

b The 1940 and 1950 figures were those actually reported by the census.

c Standardized for age and rural-urban residence on the basis of population of the United States in 1940.

d Standardized for age on the basis of population of the United States in 1940.

e Includes a small number of armed forces during 1890–1930.

f Also "standardized" for rural-urban residence. This was actually a crude adjustment made by subtracting the female participation rate of all classes, standardized for age from that standardized for both age and rural-urban residence, and adding the difference to the rate of participation of white females standardized for age only. It thus assumes that the effect of rural-urban standardization of white females would be the same as that of females of all classes. The assumption is reasonably safe, since white persons constitute about 90 per cent of the total population.

g Ratio of persons in own home housework to population as reported by the *Census of Population, 1940*.

continued on next page

TABLE 23, *continued*

	1890	1900	1920	1930	1940	1950
E. NONWHITE (thousands of persons, except where stated otherwise)						
1. Civilian nonwhite population [e]	7,846	9,185	10,890	12,488	13,454	15,688
2. Nonwhite females 14 and older	2,299	2,867	3,667	4,361	4,944	5,688
3. "Needed" in home housework (line 1 $\times$ .1525 [g])	1,197	1,401	1,661	1,905	2,052	2,392
4. In school	141	165	321	388	425	528
5. In institutions and unable to work	141	175	224	267	378 [b]	348 [b]
6. Not available for labor force (sum of lines 3–5)	1,479	1,741	2,206	2,560	2,855	3,268
7. Available for labor force (line 2 minus line 6)	820	1,126	1,461	1,801	2,089	2,420
8. Available, per 1,000 nonwhite females 14 and older	357	393	399	413	423	425
9. Actual labor force, per 1,000 nonwhite females 14 and older [d]	374	409	414	412	360	364
10. Per cent actual [d] was of available	105	104	104	100	85	86

Source: Appendix Tables A-2 and A-3. *Abstract of the Census: 1900,* pp. 15, 27; *1920,* p. 405; *1930,* p. 262. *Census of Population: 1940, Characteristics of Persons Not in the Labor Force,* p. 17, and *Families, General Characteristics,* p. 24; *1950,* Vol. II, *Characteristics of the Population,* Part 1, pp. 94, 99, 206, and PB-1, p. 97.

"available" (line 7) divided by line 2, provides the "available participation," which may then be compared with the actual. The data used for comparison were standardized for age and rural-urban residence to help reconcile changes in participation due to larger proportions of females reaching adult age, or moving to urban areas where they were more pressed to work and where there were greater job opportunities.

As might be expected, in all years the actual was below the available female participation. But the percentage (actual of available) stayed remarkably constant. The lowest—83 per cent—occurred in 1940 when, as we shall see in Chapter 10, the female labor force was presumably depressed by the harsh difficulties faced in getting jobs. For the other six decade dates—all years of comparatively high employment—the percentage remained between 89 and 97, narrowing to between 89 and 91 for four of the six.

females 14 and older. There is some question whether the number unable to work and in institutions would bear such a constant relation to the female population. While there were relatively fewer older females at the earlier censuses thus indicating fewer unable to work, the level of medical care was lower and the hazards of industry and disease were much greater. These opposing trends, it is supposed, cancel out to yield a constant percentage of females 14 and older who were unable to work and in institutions.

Similar computations for rural and urban areas and for nonwhites and whites in the United States (Table 23—Section B–E), indicate that the relation between actual and available was on the whole less stable than that for the nation as a unit. While the rural and urban actual female labor force was below the available for all census dates, there was some fluctuation. This may have been due to defects in our estimates of rural and urban labor force before 1930. Of the color groups, the best explanation was offered in the case of the whites.[13] Among the nonwhites, the actual tends in the earlier years to slightly outnumber the available, probably because extreme poverty kept many colored females in the labor force despite the fact that they were needed in home housework, attended school, or had ailments that might have kept a white person out of gainful work. The actual remained fairly constant at 100 per cent or slightly more of the available during the first four decades, declining sharply to 85 per cent in 1940 and showing almost no change in 1950. The availability factor may thus have been the important one up to 1930; but after that date the decline in the labor force participation of colored females needs explaining. This question is deferred until Chapter 13.

Of the four foreign countries such illustrative computations have been made only for Canada and Great Britain from 1911–1951, since only these offer adequate statistics on female school attendance (Table 24). In the case of Britain the ratio of females needed in own home housekeeping was assumed to have been the same as in the United States.[14] The availability of women provides a good explanation for Great Britain—better than for the United States. In Britain the proportion of actual to available stayed between 83 and 90 per cent and was lowest in 1921 and 1931, when it may have been depressed by the fairly high unemployment.[15]

In Canada there was less agreement between actual and available. In part, this may have been because the actual participation cannot be

[13] The native and foreign-born whites had to be treated as a unit, rather than by nativity, as the native-born include persons in the families of the foreign-born. However, the explanation was not very satisfactory unless the actual labor force of whites was standardized for rural-urban residence. Since there were no data over this whole period cross-classified by color, age, and rural-urban residence, the device of "partial" standardization was used, the assumption being that the effect of standardizing whites for rural-urban composition would be the same as that for all classes. Since the population of whites is around 90 per cent of that of all classes, this assumption is not too risky. Thus standardized, the actual labor force (line 12 of Table 23, section D) is a very stable percentage of the available for all years except 1940; for the high-employment years 1890–1930 and 1950, it remains between 88 and 91 per cent.

[14] The level is not particularly important, since it does not affect the changes over the decades and it is with these changes that we are concerned.

[15] Actual labor force participation was standardized only for age and not for rural-urban residence; but rural-urban migration was minor in Britain during 1911–1951.

129

TABLE 24

Illustrative Estimates of Female Labor Possibly Saved and Its Availability for Labor Force Participation due to the Relative Decline in Number of Females Needed in Own Home House-keeping as Population to be Cared for Rose Less Rapidly than Number of Females 14 and Older, Great Britain and Canada, 1911–1951

	1911	1921	1931	1939	1951
A. GREAT BRITAIN (millions of persons, except where stated otherwise)					
1. Civilian population [a]	40.8	42.8	44.8	46.2	48.0
2. Females 14 and older	15.2	16.8	18.3	19.6	20.4
3. Needed in home housework (line 1 × 213 [b])	8.7	9.1	9.5	9.8	10.2
4. In school [c]	0.1	0.2	0.3	0.3	0.6
5. In institutions and unable to work	0.6	0.7	0.7	0.8	0.8
6. Not available for labor force (sum of lines 3–5)	9.4	10.0	10.5	10.9	11.6
7. Available for labor force (line 2 minus line 6)	5.8	6.8	7.8	8.7	8.8
8. Available, per 1,000 females 14 and older	382	405	426	444	431
9. Actual labor force, per 1,000 females 14 and older [d]	345	338	358	385	388
10. Per cent actual [d] was of available	90	83	84	87	90
B. CANADA (thousands of persons, except where stated otherwise)					
1. Civilian population [e]	7,192	8,775	10,363	11,180	13,939
2. Females 14 and older	2,274	2,845	3,477	4,130	4,948
3. Needed in home housework (line 1 × .226 [f])	1,625	1,983	2,342	2,527	3,151
4. In school	114	175	274	311	302
5. In institutions and unable to work [g]	61	76	93	110	132
6. Not available for labor force (sum of lines 3–5)	1,800	2,234	2,709	2,948	3,585
7. Available for labor force (line 2 minus line 6)	474	611	768	1,182	1,363
8. Available, per 1,000 females 14 and older	208	215	221	286	275
9. Actual labor force, per 1,000 females 14 and older [d]	149	164	184	219	240
10. Per cent actual [d] was of available	72	76	83	77	87
11. Actual labor force per 1,000 females 14 and older [h]	161	171	184	219	232
12. Per cent actual [h] was of available	77	80	83	77	84

Source: Appendixes A and B. *Census of Canada, 1951*, Ottawa, Dominion Bureau of Statistics, Vol. IV, *Labour Force*, Table 3.

[a] Total population during 1911–1931; total population minus armed forces in 1939 and 1951.

[b] Ratio of females needed in own home housework to population was assumed to be the same as in the United States.

[c] Estimated as one-half the total of both sexes 14 and older attending school plus the total of full-time female students in further education and universities.

130

standardized for rural-urban residence and thus manifests a rising percentage of the available over the period. Partial adjustment was made for this (line 11 of Table 24 B), by assuming that the effect of standardizing for rural-urban residence would be the same in Canada as in the United States. The resulting ratio on line 12 fluctuates somewhat; but its behavior is consistent with the possibility that the changing composition of population released females from own home housework to the labor force.

This method furnishes no proof that female labor force is thus determined by the relative abundance of working-age females.

One objection is that it seems to "predict" female labor force so closely as to leave no role for the other possible household labor-saving sources analyzed in this chapter. The various estimates of labor saving are summarized in Table 25 (lines 1–4). There the total labor saved (in excess of 1890) increased from 41 per 1,000 females in 1900, to 212 in 1950 (line 6). But not all of it was necessarily available, for it must also be assumed that the proportion *available* might have declined as income rose (Table 17, line 5) if some women had wished to have more leisure or to improve upon their housekeeping. Table 25, in line 7, gives an estimate of the saving in labor possibly available, which may be compared with the difference between the actual and expected labor force participation on line 8. The two estimates have very similar trends. However, in certain years—particularly 1920—there were substantial discrepancies.

There need be no surprise at these discrepancies; rather, it is surprising they were not greater. Only the crudest information was available on stocks of household appliances, purchases of food and clothing, and volume of services paid for by the housewife. And the grounds for translating their changes into household labor saved were most tenuous. It is just as likely that the standard of housekeeping or more leisure for the housewife, though adjusted for, would have absorbed the saving, as the adjustment was very imperfect. It treats all the females of the nation as if they belonged to one family. It ignores problems of aggregating the snatches of time and effort conserved by a great many women into full-time equivalents available for labor force participation. It uses the income-labor force associations in 38 cities at a moment-of-

---

[d] Standardized for age, but not for rural-urban residence.

[e] Total population 1911–1931; total population minus armed forces 1941 and 1951.

[f] Ratio derived by dividing population by number of females not in the labor force and keeping house as reported by the 1951 census.

[g] Figure for 1951 as reported by the 1951 census; earlier figures estimated to bear a proportion to the 1951 figure based on the population of females 45 and older.

[h] Also "standardized" for rural-urban residence. This was actually a crude adjustment for the effect of rural-urban migration, on the assumption that the effect was the same in Canada as in the United States.

TABLE 25

Further Illustrative Estimates to Show How Labor Saved in the
Home Might Explain the Excess of Actual, over "Expected"
Female Labor Force Participation, United States, 1890–1950

(per 1,000 females 14 and older)

	1890	1900	1910	1920	1930	1940	1950
Own home household labor possibly saved by:							
1. Increased stock of appliances (Table 18)	–	2	7	9	14	22	31
2. Purchase of goods and clothing (Table 19)	–	15	43	95	67	52	74
3. Services bought (Table 20)	–	4	15	–13	5	9	1
4. Total possibly saved by technology (sum of lines 1–3)	–	21	65	91	86	83	106
5. Labor possibly saved in the home as a result of fewer persons for the average female to care for (Table 23)	–	20	23	42	51	93	106
6. Total labor possibly saved in the home (sum of lines 4–5)	–	41	88	133	137	176	212
7. Estimated labor-saving possibly available for labor force participation [a]	–	41	82	124	112	147	182
8. Difference between actual and "expected" labor force, to be explained (Table 17, line 8)	–	39	73	80	106	130	160
9. Unexplained discrepancy (line 8 minus line 7)	–	2	9	44	6	17	22
10. Discrepancy as per cent of estimate on line 7	–	4.9	11.0	35.5	5.4	11.6	12.1

[a] Estimated by assuming that the availability for labor force participation would decline, as incomes rose, by the percentages given in Table 17, line 5.

time as if these were reliable indications of how much female participation might have varied over time, other things equal, when the city is not a completely homogeneous unit for labor force purposes and when many developments could have occurred over time besides those accounted for in Table 26. It overlooks the fact that income data over time could not be used for intercity comparisons as they were different from those used at a given time, and could not always be adjusted for cost-of-living differences among localities—and that the census materials themselves are not always reliable or comparable.

But even if the number of females made thus available could be estimated accurately, it must be concluded that they might not all enter the labor force or that they might enter only after long delay. We have also to consider the inducements and opportunities which might have determined whether and when these employable women would enter the labor force and find jobs.

Rising Ratio of Female to Male Earnings

A rise in the ratio of female to male earnings could mean that the gainful effort of females was being rewarded more favorably, that females had an increasing incentive to work outside the home and that males might encourage their wives, daughters, or mothers to seek employment, out of desire to prolong their own education or to hasten their own retirement. Or, depending upon the circumstances, the rise could mean that female labor was becoming more expensive relative to that of males—thus discouraging employers from expanding their hiring of females quite as rapidly as they would otherwise be inclined to do.

Separate data on the earnings of males and females are not abundant. One set consists of earnings in manufacturing in five countries, but it is not entirely satisfactory, since wages and salaries of factory workers do not necessarily reflect fees, commissions, and profits of employed and self-employed persons, nor wages and salaries of employees in other industries with very different occupational compositions. The material is also subject to variations because of changes in age composition. And it provides no means of assessing the dilution of earnings by labor turnover and part-time employment. We cannot therefore be certain that a rising ratio of female to male earnings really reflects better terms for females in jobs.

Such as they are, the data seem at first glance to support the hypothesis that the change in female relative to male participation was attributable to the change in the relationship between female and male earnings, for both ratios have moved upward. A closer look raises vigorous doubts. In the United States, the earnings ratio did not really begin to rise until after World War I, whereas the labor force ratio had been moving upward since 1890. In Canada no relative rise in female earnings occurred until after 1931, although female participation in the labor force, relative to that of males, had been advancing rapidly and steadily since 1911. In New Zealand the earnings ratio was virtually constant from before World War I until after World War II, but the labor force ratio rose after 1926. In Britain the two ratios moved almost oppositely throughout; and in Germany, they moved in contrary directions during 1925–1939. All in all, the ratio of female to male earnings in manufacturing does not help to explain the tendency of females to flow into the labor force more rapidly than males.

For 1940 and 1950, additional data are provided by the census which enable us to compute, separately for white and colored, the ratio of wage and salary earnings of females to those of males—not just for factory workers but for all employees. This ratio may be compared with the ratio of female to male participation at the same census dates.[16] The results show an actual decline in the relative earnings of both white and colored females, while the labor force of white females was making its greatest gain as compared to that of white males, and the labor force of colored females related to that of colored males was rising moderately.

A third set of data consists of annual earnings during 1944–1951. The ratio of female to male earnings and that of female to male labor force show no similarity of movement in either trend or fluctuation (Chart 12). Except for a sharp rise at the end of World War II, female earnings fell rather steadily, from nearly half of male earnings to scarcely over a third, while the ratio of female to male participation first declined to 1947 and then showed a fairly steady rise through 1951.

A fourth set of data gives ratios for major industries and occupational groups between 1940 and 1950.[17] Again there was no association between the female-to-male earnings ratio and the female-to-male *employed* ratio.[18] Manufacturing, which showed the only rise in the earnings ratio, had one of the lowest increases in its employed ratio. Finance, insurance and real estate, and retail trade, with the greatest decreases in female-to-male earnings ratio, had the largest increases in female-to-male employed ratio. But the other rankings were scattered. Much the same may be said for the occupational classifications.

Finally, it might be expected that females would be most attracted to those industries where the ratio of female-to-male earnings was already high and therefore need not be expected to rise. But no association could be discovered, at least from data of 1940 or 1950. The materials offer no evidence that the ratio of female-to-male earnings had anything to do with the ratio of female-to-male labor force.

[16] Earnings data are for the calendar year 1939. The source does not indicate whether the earnings pertain only to persons who worked the entire year; it must be presumed that they include income of persons whose participation in the labor force may have lasted only a few months. If so, the dilution might have been greater for female than for male earnings. However, the ratio for persons who worked twelve months in 1939 was practically the same as that for all persons, so that any relative dilution must have been insignificant. *Census of Population, 1940, The Labor Force (Sample Statistics), Wage or Salary Income in 1939,* pp. 39–41; Appendix A; "Income of Families and Persons in the United States: 1949," *Current Population Reports,* Bureau of the Census, Series P-60, No. 7, p. 36.

[17] "Income of Families and Persons in the United States: 1950," *Current Population Reports, Consumer Income,* Series P-60, No. 9, p. 39; *Census of Population, 1950,* Vol. II, *Characteristics of the Population,* Part 1, PB-1, pp. 102–104.

[18] A classification by industry for the labor force would have been much better for this purpose, but it was not available.

CHART 12

Ratio of Female to Male Labor Force Participation for Persons 14 and Older, and Ratio of Female to Male Median Wage or Salary Income: United States, 1944–1951

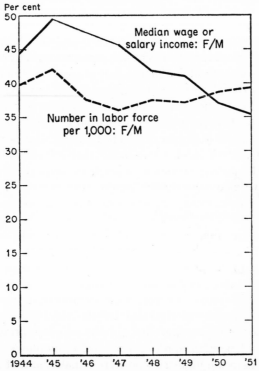

Source: Appendix B, and *Current Population Reports, Consumer Income,* Bureau of the Census, Series P-60, No. 7, p. 35.

Improving Employment Opportunities

The rise in the female labor force participation could scarcely have occurred without an expansion of opportunities for female employment. But where did these openings occur, and why? Was it because the usefulness of women was enhanced by their improved education and training, bcause girls and women were needed in bakeries, stores, and factories to produce and sell things which they were no longer producing in their own kitchens, or because women may have been better suited to do the paper work, the semiskilled labor, and the sales and service functions demanded by modern industry, than to do the heavy farm and factory work of earlier years? It is probably impossible to separate these causes one from another or to say which came first

135

or was more important. We shall, however, try to throw some light on them by considering each one separately.

EDUCATION.

Education is not necessarily related to skill or efficiency in a specific job, e.g., a man of little schooling may be a good pipe fitter and a girl with much Latin a mediocre stenographer. Nevertheless, the analysis in Chapter 5 brought out that education has probably been important—perhaps more important than age—in determining, at any given time, whether females would be in the labor force. Furthermore, in the United States there has been an impressive increase over the years in the amount of education completed by the average female aged 20 and older [19] (Chart 13), particularly in relation to that completed by the average older male (Chapter 9, Chart 19). But, the ratio of women's education to that of older men tended to rise less than the ratio of women's participation to that of older men. Also, the movements of these ratios were not very similar from decade to decade.

INDUSTRIES EMPLOYING FEMALES

The women who entered the labor force after 1890 did not, on the whole, select those industries that displaced their labor in the home, e.g. laundries, restaurants, hotels, beauty parlors, and factories processing food and making clothing.[20]

The industries that were the chief employers of females in 1890 tended to be the same in 1940 and 1950 (Table 26). Throughout the sixty years, domestic and personal service, manufacturing, and professional services led either in number of females employed or in percentage of workers in the industry who were females, and at some decades they led in both number and percentage. Conversely, transportation and communication, public service, and mining, which employed few females at the turn of the century, continued to employ few females in 1950. Only agriculture dropped drastically—from fourth place as a relative employer of females in 1890 to fifth place in 1930 and to seventh in 1940 and 1950. Trade and public services registered sharp rises.

Nor has there been any startling change in the ratio of females to males in broad occupational groups (Table 27). In most of these classifications—notably professional workers, proprietors, skilled and un-

---

[19] An even greater increase occurred among younger girls, but they are excluded from the comparison because their education is in many cases still going on and because time spent in further schooling would serve only to keep them out of the labor force.

[20] In these occupations, males and females combined were fewer, in relation to the female population aged 14 and older, in 1930 and 1940 than in 1890 and 1900.

136

CHART 13

Years of Schooling for Women 20 and Older, and Proportion in the Labor Force: by Age Group, United States, 1890–1950

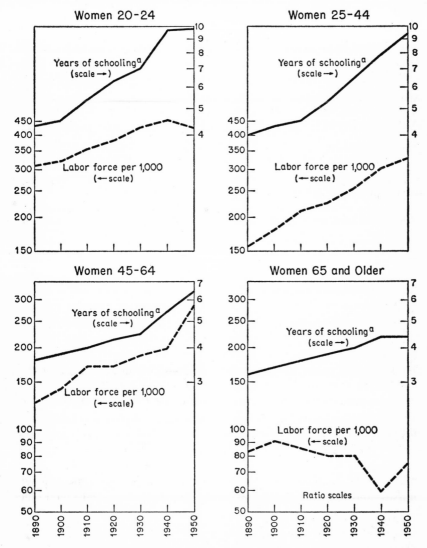

ᵃ Median equivalent full-time years of school completed, based on length of school year in 1940.

Source: Labor force, Appendix A. Years of school completed: *Census of Population, 1940,* Vol. IV, Part I, pp. 6–7, and *1920, Monographs V,* pp. 49–51, 113–114, Tables 30, 31; *Statistical Abstract of the United States,* Bureau of the Census, 1954, p. 125; *Census of Population, 1950, Education,* PE No. 5B, pp. 73–74.

TABLE 26

Industries Ranked According to Per Cent of Female Workers, United States, 1890, 1930, 1940, and 1950

	In Labor Force [a]				Employed [b]			
	1890		1930		1940		1950	
	Per Cent	Rank	Per Cent	Rank	Per Cent	Rank	Per Cent	Rank
Domestic and personal services	72.1	1	64.2	1	71.4	1	66.8	1
Professional services	35.7	2	46.9	2	56.7	2	58.1	2
Manufacturing, mechanical, and building	19.0	3	13.4	4	18.0 [c]	5	20.2 [c]	5
Agriculture, forestry, and fishing	7.9	4	8.5	5	5.8	7	8.5	7
Trade, finance, insurance, real estate	6.9	5	15.8	3	27.5	3	34.7	3
Transportation and communication	1.3	6	7.3	6	11.0 [d]	6	15.6 [d]	6
Public service (not elsewhere classified)	0.8	7	2.1	7	21.9 [e]	4	26.2 [e]	4
Extraction of minerals	0.1	8	0.1	8	1.2	8	2.5	8

Source: *Census of Population: 1940*, Alba M. Edwards, *Comparative Occupation Statistics for the United States, 1870 to 1940*, p. 187; *1950*, Vol. ii, *Characteristics of the Population*, Part 1, Table 124.

[a] Clerical occupations were omitted on the ground that they do not constitute an industry; it was not possible to assign them to the industries in which they belonged.

[b] Clerical workers included in the industries in which they were employed.

[c] Includes business and repair services.

[d] Includes other public utilities.

[e] Public administration.

skilled workers—the ratio of females to males remained fairly constant, and in the semiskilled group the ratio dropped. Virtually the entire rise in the female-to-male ratio was found in the clerical occupations—in 1950 there were nearly six times as many females as there had been thirty years before, and the proportion of females to males had risen from less than 30 per cent to over 50 per cent. Thus the labor released from housekeeping went to satisfy the demand for salesgirls, cashiers, office clerks, bookkeepers, typists, and telephone operators, teachers, nurses, and librarians.[21] The switch to sedentary and semiskilled office

[21] "Women in all businesses are supplanting men and in some branches have attained the place God intended them to have–a man measuring dry-goods will illustrate my point. Type-writing has greatly assisted the employment of females, and they have, especially in New England, displaced male book-keepers. I have especially inquired regarding their adaptability; they are, without exception considered more painstaking and trustworthy. Women cashiers and telegraph operators are also being substituted for men, they are quick and their sense of touch is such that the latter are selected for special work. I do not think that machinery has encouraged the substitution of women for men in the heavier departments;

TABLE 27

Major Occupational Groups Ranked According to Per Cent of Female Workers, United States, Census Dates, 1910–1950

	1910		1920		1930		1940		1950	
	Per Cent	Rank	Per Cent	Rank	Per Cent	Rank	Per Cent	Rank	Per Cent	Rank
Professional persons	44.0	1	48.2	1	49.2	1	45.4	1	39.4	2
Semiskilled workers	39.6	2	34.1	3	31.7	3	32.8	3	29.8	4
In manufacturing	44.7		38.3		36.8		} 32.8		} 29.8	
Other	29.6		26.1		24.9					
Clerks and kindred workers	28.4	3	38.6	2	38.7	2	41.0	2	51.9	1
Unskilled workers	24.8	4	20.3	4	22.1	4	23.5	4	30.9	3
Farm laborers	23.6		18.0		13.9		9.3		18.6	
Factory and bldg. const. laborers	3.3		5.4		3.7		} 2.3		} 3.7	
Other laborers	0.6		1.1		1.1					
Servants	76.6		69.9		69.3		64.3		62.9	
Proprietors, managers, and officials	4.6	5	4.6	5	5.2	5	5.8	5	8.5	5
Farmers (owners and tenants)	4.5		4.2		4.4		2.9		2.7	
Wholesale and retail dealers	5.5		5.7		6.3		8.8		} 13.5	
Other	4.6		5.6		7.0		10.3			
Skilled workers and foremen	2.2	6	1.8	6	1.3	6	1.7	6	3.0	6

Source: *Census of Population: 1940*, Alba M. Edwards, *Comparative Occupation Statistics for the United States, 1870 to 1940*, p. 187; *1950*, Vol. II, *Characteristics of the Population*, Part 1, Table 124.

and factory jobs was especially congenial to girls and women and would certainly facilitate the shift of females from housekeeping to gainful

---

until women are as strongly, physically developed, it would be impossible for them to compete. Sewing machines and light machinery is their work." *Third Biennial Report, 1888–1889*, Maryland Bureau of Industrial Statistics and Information, p. 78. "We are, on principle, opposed to their employment, but for certain operations we are compelled to employ them, as otherwise the work would be too expensive. This is especially the case where large numbers of small pieces have to be produced, the operations on which are simple but time-taking." *Ibid.*, p. 79. "We could not do our business without the employment of women and children. As you are aware, the hulling of peas, strawberries, and the packing of such vegetables belongs to women, they being so much neater and quicker, and more cleanly than men." *Ibid.*, p. 81. "Owing to the large hands which belongs to the sterner sex, they cannot become as neat and dexterous as female labor." *Ibid.*, p. 83. "I am of the opinion that some factories prefer female labor, because they can impose on them, at least, we have heard many reports to that effect." *Ibid.*, p. 84. (Statements made by dealers, engineers, packers, and an individual company.)

employment. But it may be doubted that this pull of opportunity was the sole, or the major factor drawing women into the labor force. In any case forces operating on the supply side were necessary to provide for the release of these additional females to the labor force.

Reductions in Working Hours

Very few working girls and women enjoy freedom from household cares, for some nurse babies or care for adolescent children, and many cook breakfast in the morning before they leave, and after they return prepare supper, wash underwear, iron clothes, and struggle with an occasional housecleaning; [22] and almost all go through bedside drudgery of curling hair and painting nails, since the female does not work for bread alone. Any attempt to account, therefore, for the large-scale transformation from housewife or mother's helper to secretary or grinding-machine operator, must consider whether the shorter workweek may have been a factor in allowing a female who has typed until five o'clock the necessary time in which to look for a cheap roast or a rich husband.

There need not be a simple connection between a reduction in working hours and an increase in the proportion of females in gainful activity. Some of the released time would be absorbed by improvements in housekeeping, child care, and personal toilet, some by commutation over longer distances. The influence of hours was examined in this study both for different areas at the same time (1940) and for the same area over time. The 1940 data disclosed no tendency for females to be in the labor force in large proportions in areas where the workweek was shorter, even when wives were standardized for age of wife, color of wife, presence of young children, or income of husband.

The comparisons over time made use of "standard" or "full-time" hours rather than hours actually worked. They were not, therefore, adjusted for time lost because of sickness, strikes, mechanical breakdowns, labor turnover, or layoffs, but represent the amount of time normally worked in all major branches of industry, including government and agriculture (though for farmers and other self-employed persons accurate data on hours are extremely difficult to obtain and even the concept of a workweek is obscure).

[22] "My sister and I . . . have no time to do our own cooking as we work eleven hours a day, so we must board out. We manage, however, to room ourselves which is more homelike, and we consider ourselves much better off than some of the girls who are obliged to board at the corporation boarding house." *Fifth Annual Report*, Maine Bureau of Industrial and Labor Statistics, 1891, p. 143. "After working hard all day many women stay up late at night to do cleaning and washing." *Ibid.* (Statements embodied in the report.)

140

In the four countries for which data were available, the full-time week fell about four hours per decade in the last half century, while the female labor force rose 10 to 30 for each 1,000 females aged 14 and older—about 3 to 10 additional female workers per 1,000 for every reduction of one hour.

What is the significance of these changes? Are there merely two long-run trends—downward in hours and upward in the labor force—but no real correlation? To answer this question we must study the census-to-census fluctuations. This was done for the United States as a unit and for its rural and urban areas, as well as for the three foreign countries (Chart 14), but we confine the comparison to censuses taken in time of high employment, since a severe depression may cut down the workweek and the labor force and thus interfere with the inverse relationship (Chapter 10). In the United States there was, apparently, a close association between the reduction in the average full-time workweek of all major industry groups and the increase in female labor force participation. It was almost perfect for the nation as a whole and was about as good as could be expected for rural and urban areas, since the urban labor force was compared with hours in manufacturing, and the rural labor force (which really represents also a wide variety of non-agricultural industries) with the workweek on farms. For example, there was little change in either hours or the labor force in the 1920's, but an enormous contraction in hours and a huge inflow of female labor force in the 1930's and 1940's. The rise in hours on farms between 1910 and 1920 was associated with the only instance of a drop in female participation.

The apparent affinity between hours and female labor force could not be tested fairly for certain of the census years—in Germany for 1907, in Canada for 1951, or in New Zealand for 1895–1951—owing to lack of satisfactory materials. Nor could it be tested in Great Britain and Canada for 1921 and 1931 or in Germany for 1939, 1946, and 1950, because these were years like 1940 in the United States when both hours and the labor force tended to be curtailed by unemployment. Thus the investigation in foreign countries covers only 1911–1939 and 1939–1951 in Great Britain, 1911–1941 in Canada, and 1895–1925 and 1925–1939 in Germany. The association between declining full-time hours and expanding labor force was close—though less so than in the United States—and it was still closer when the workweek in manufacturing was the measure of hours rather than the less well documented average for "all industries." These relationships do not warrant a final pronouncement that the reduction of the workweek in industry made it easier for women with household obligations to take outside jobs; but they require that this explanation be given serious consideration.

141

CHART 14

Increase in Female Participation in Labor Force Associated with Reduction in Full-Time Workweek: 4 Countries, Various Periods, 1890–1951

Percentage changes between census dates when employment was high: increase in number of females 14 and older in the labor force per 1,000 of same population group and decrease in full-time workweek (hours).

Labor force participation ratios standardized for age, and for other differences as noted, on basis of United States population in 1940.

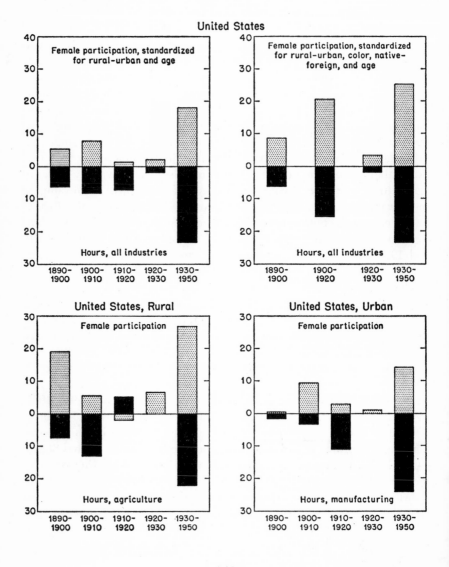

CHART 14, concluded

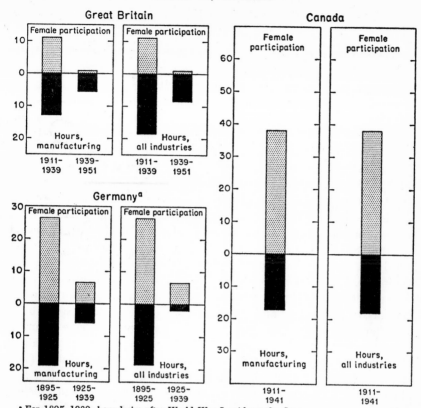

Great Britain
Canada
Germany[a]

[a] For 1895–1939, boundaries after World War I, without the Saar.

Data on females in labor force, Appendix A. Data on hours:

United States: Harold Barger and Sam H. Schurr, *The Mining Industries, 1899–1939*, National Bureau of Economic Research, 1944; Leo Wolman, *Hours of Work in American Industry*, NBER, Bulletin 71, 1938; *Survey of Current Business*, Department of Commerce; *Bulletin 604, Handbook of Labor Statistics*, and *Monthly Labor Review, Wages and Hours of Labor Series*, Bureau of Labor Statistics; *Census of Population, The Labor Force; Current Population Reports, The Labor Force*, and *Statistical Abstract of the United States*, Bureau of the Census; J. A. Hopkins, *Changing Technology and Employment in Agriculture*, Department of Agriculture, 1941; *Mixer and Server* (Hotel and Restaurant Employees International Alliance and Bartenders' International League of America); *Report on the Relations and Conditions of Capital and Labor Employed in Manufacturing and General Business, 1901*, United States Industrial Commission; *Statistics of Railways in the United States*, Interstate Commerce Commission; Carter G. Woodson, Editor, *Journal of Negro History; Journeyman Barber* (Journeyman Barbers' International Union of America), 1919–1920; W. J. Lauck and E. Sydenstricker, *Condition of Labor in American Industries*, Funk & Wagnalls, 1917; *Bulletin 126*, Women's Bureau, Department of Labor; reports and bulletins on labor statistics from different states.

Great Britain: International Labour Review, and *Year Book of Labour Statistics*, Geneva, International Labour Office; *Monthly Labor Review*, as cited; *Ministry of Labour Gazette, Monthly Digest of Statistics, Industrial Relations Handbook*, and *Abstract of Labour Statistics*, 20th edition, all London, H. M. Stationery Office; William Paine, *Shop Slavery and Emancipation*, London, P. S. King & Staples, Ltd., 1912; Royal Statistical Society, London.

Canada: Wages and Hours of Labour in Canada, Labour Gazette, Department of Labour, and *Labour Force*, Dominion Bureau of Statistics, both Ottawa; *International Labour Review*, and *Year Book of Labour Statistics*, as cited.

Germany: Colin Clark, *The Conditions of Economic Progress*, London, Macmillan, 1940; *Statistisches Handbuch von Deutschland, 1928–1944*, "München, Länderrat des Amerikanischen Besatzungsgebiets, 1945; *International Labour Review* and *Year Book of Labour Statistics*, as cited; *Statistical Annex to the Report of the Military Governor*, Wiesbaden, Office of Military Government for Germany; *Statistisches Jahrbuch*, Berlin, Statistisches Reichsamt; *Wirtschaft und Statistik*, Wiesbaden; Maxine Y. Sweezy, *The Structure of the Nazi Economy*, Harvard University Press, 1941; *Monthly Labor Review*, as cited; *Deutschland in Zahlen*, Köln, Wirtschaftswissenschaftliches Institut der Gewerkschaften.

CHAPTER 8

MALES IN THE LABOR FORCE OVER TIME

Behavior of the Male Labor Force

IN ALL five countries studied for approximately the last forty- to sixty-year periods, the male labor force, whether or not standardized for age composition, failed to rise as rapidly as the male population [1] and as a result showed a decrease per 1,000 male population in each country (Chart 15). Agreement among the five countries was reasonably close: most of the decreases were between 10 and 20 per decade for each 1,000 males of working age (Table 28), and almost without exception, accelerated in the recent period. Standardization of the labor force for age composition sharpens the decline a bit in the United States and modifies it in the other countries (changes in unstandardized data were not shown for the other countries) but on the whole makes scarcely any difference. The explanation is that the labor force participation rate does not differ much betwen elderly persons and teen-agers, or between men above middle age and youths in their early twenties, so that the age changes largely cancel out. Much greater variations have occurred in age composition. While men 25–44, the central age group, remained virtually unchanged throughout as a share of the male population (and of the male labor force), there were changes among the younger and older ages. The proportion of boys aged 10–13 fell from about an eleventh to a sixteenth of the total male population in the United States, in New Zealand, and in Germany, and that of young men 14–24 fell from a fifth to a sixth in all five countries. Also throughout the five countries the share of men aged 45–64 expanded enough to offset the shrinkage of that of youths aged 14–24; and the proportion of men 65 and older of the total male population doubled typically from 4 per cent in 1890 to 8 per cent in 1950. The composition of the labor force has reflected not only these changes in the population, itself, but also the impact of changes in the propensity of these various age groups to be in the labor force.

The effect of changing rural-urban residence can be measured only for the United States. Although in this country the movements of population from rural to urban areas have been on the largest scale, their

---

[1] In each of the five nations studied—the United States, Great Britain, Canada, New Zealand, and Germany—males have at various times over the past half century been more than half or less than half the population. But only in West Germany after World War II did the proportion of males and females become sufficiently out of balance to affect the labor force appreciably. In that country in 1946 there were scarcely more than two males for every three females aged 14 and older in the population.

144

CHART 15

Males 14 and Older in the Labor Force per 1,000 in Same Population Group: 5 Countries, Various Years, 1890–1951

Standardized for age, and for other differences as noted, on basis of United States population in 1940.

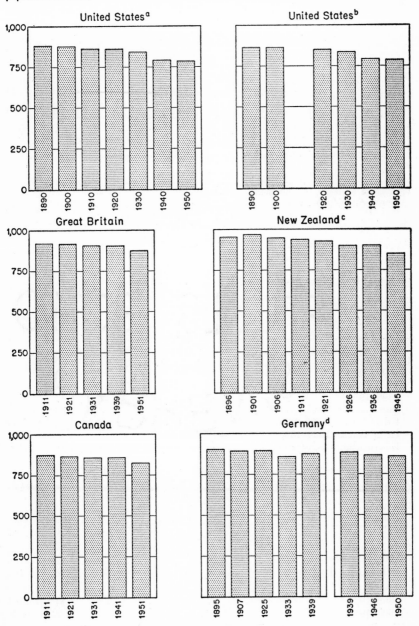

CHART 15, concluded

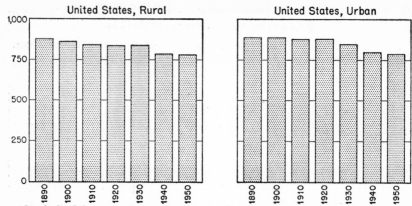

a Standardized for rural-urban composition as well as age.
b Standardized for rural-urban composition, color, and native-foreign composition, as well as age.
c Males 15 and older.
d For 1895–1939, boundaries after World War I, without the Saar; 1939–1950, Federal Republic of Germany, without Berlin.
Source: Appendix A.

TABLE 28

Average Per-Decade Changes in Male Labor Force, 5 Countries, Various Periods, 1890–1951

	Change per 1,000 Male Population of Same Age (number)					
	14 & Older	14–19	20–24	25–44	45–64	65 & Older
	A. ENTIRE PERIOD					
United States:						
1890–1950	−14	−29	−15	−8	−12	−54
1890–1950 a	−17					
1890–1950 b	−16	−29	−15	−7	−12	−49
Rural areas,a 1890–1950	−16	−18	−4	−9	−15	−54
Urban areas,a 1890–1950	−17	−41	−24	−7	−9	−44
Large cities,a 1900–1950	−19	...	...	...	...	...
Native white,a 1890–1950	−14	−21	−14	−6	−11	−70
Foreign-born white,a 1890–1950	−23	−64	−31	−7	−11	−51
Colored,a 1890–1950	−27	−43	−21	−15	−21	−73
Great Britain,a, c 1911–1951	−12	−66	−3	−0.3	+3	−62
Canada:						
1921–1951 a	−13	−39	−2	−1	−4	−66
1911–1951 a	−12	−41	−1	−2	−10	−34
New Zealand:						
1901–1951 a, d	−24	−25		−2	−22	−126
1896–1951 a, d	−19	−22		+0.4	−16	−106
Germany:						
1895–1939 a	−7	+5	+3	+2	−11	−66
1895–1950 a	+8	−17	−3	−2	−4	−58

	Change per 1,000 Male Population of Same Age (number)					
	14 & Older	14–19	20–24	25–44	45–64	65 & Older
	B. EARLY PERIOD					
United States:						
1890–1930	−8	−40	−5	−0.3	−3	−39
1890–1930 [a]	−11					
1890–1930 [b]	−10	−42	−7	+0.3	−2	−33
Rural areas,[a] 1890–1930	−9	−26	−1	−2	−3	−36
Urban areas,[a] 1890–1930	−11	−58	−11	+2	−0.3	−31
Large cities,[a] 1900–1930	−12	. . .	. . .	. . .	. . .	. . .
Native white,[a] 1890–1930	−9	−34	−4	+0.5	−2	−36
Foreign-born white,[a] 1890–1930	−17	−75	−7	−0.5	−4	−45
Colored,[a] 1890–1930	−10	−31	−2	−2	−5	−34
Great Britain,[a, c] 1911–1931	−8	−31	−3	−1	+1	−45
Canada:						
1921–1931 [a]	−4	−84	0	+9	+29	−26
1911–1931 [a]	−7	−66	+1	+3	+2	+19
New Zealand:						
1901–1926 [a, d]	−28	−25		−4	−22	−158
1896–1926 [a, d]	−18	−19		+0.3	−12	−115
Germany,[a] 1895–1925	−3	+5	−0.3	+1	−1	−38
	C. RECENT PERIOD					
United States:						
1930–1950	−26	−6	−36	−24	−31	−84
1930–1950 [a]	−30					
1930–1950 [b]	−29	−4	−32	−23	−32	−80
Rural areas,[a] 1930–1950	−29	−2	−10	−22	−40	−91
Urban areas,[a] 1930–1950	−29	−6	−50	−24	−27	−71
Large cities,[a] 1930–1950	−31					
Native white,[a] 1930–1950	−25	−7	−79	−18	−28	−88
Foreign-born white,[a] 1930–1950	−35	−42	−78	−19	−26	−63
Colored,[a] 1930–1950	−61	−68	−6	−42	−53	−151
Great Britain,[a, c] 1931–1951	−16	−102	−3	+1	+6	−80
Canada,[a] 1931–1951	−18	−17	−3	−7	−21	−87
New Zealand,[a, d] 1926–1951	−20	−25		+0.4	−22	−94
Germany:						
1925–1939 [a]	−16	+7	+9	+4	−31	−126
1925–1950 [a]	−14	−43	−6	−4	−7	−83

Source: Appendix A.

[a] Labor force standardized for age composition on the basis of population of the States in 1940.

[b] Labor force standardized for rural-urban composition and, in the case of age group 14 and older, for age composition on the basis of population of the United States in 1940.

[c] Age groups are available only for 14–17 and 18–24.

[d] Boys under 15 not included; 15–24 grouped together—no separate data available for age groups 14–19 and 20–24.

effects on the average proportion of the nation's population in the labor force have been negligible, not only for the whole period studied (1890–1950) but for any individual decade. The young and the old, the only groups whose tendencies to be in the labor force differed significantly between rural and urban areas, did not constitute enough workers to exert much influence on the total.

COLOR AND NATIONAL ORIGIN.

In 1890 Negro and foreign-born males both had a substantially stronger tendency to be in the labor force than did native white males. The tendency was found among all males aged 10 and older (standardized for age), and it was strongest in the case of boys and older Negro men (Chart 16). This higher tendency continued for the Negro males up to 1930. It still held in 1940 but their share of the total labor force was reduced more than that of native whites in all age groups, no doubt because of the greater incidence of unemployment among the colored (Chapter 10). And by 1950 the rate of participation of Negroes had fallen below that of native whites for all males combined and for men aged 25–64; for the young and elderly, it was about the same as the rate of the native whites. The fact that the decline among the colored was nearly double that among native whites over the half century is especially interesting, but the attempt to explain it is reserved until Chapters 11 and 12. In spite of disparities in level, differences in trend, and variations in the ratio of foreign-born to the total population, these minority groups have not had much effect on the participation of all classes in the labor force (Table 29). Their combined effect ranged from raising the labor force participation rate by 18 per 1,000 males 14 and older in 1890 to reducing it by a very slight 3 per 1,000 in 1950. The data on native whites, which provide the equivalent of standardizing for color and national origin, show that the decline in the proportion of native white males in the labor force was about seven-eighths as great as the decline for all classes of males.

Changes in Male Labor Force in Relation to Changes in Income

Changes in the male labor force and changes in real disposable income from all sources (per adult-male equivalent employed) between census years and between three-year averages over various periods ranging from 1890 to 1951, were compared for the five nations. Income data and the methods used were the same as those applied in studying the relation between changes in female labor force and changes in income over time, and are discussed in Chapter 6. For the four English-speaking nations over the entire period, income figures yielded by the three-year

148

CHART 16

Native White, Foreign-Born White, and Colored Males in the Labor Force per 1,000 in Same Population Group: by Age Group, United States, Census Dates, 1890–1950

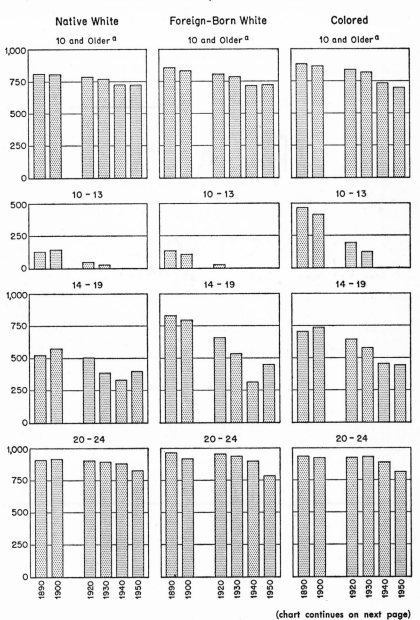

(chart continues on next page)

CHART 16, concluded

Native White, Foreign-Born White, and Colored Males in the Labor Force per 1,000 in Same Population Group: by Age Group, United States, Census Dates, 1890–1950

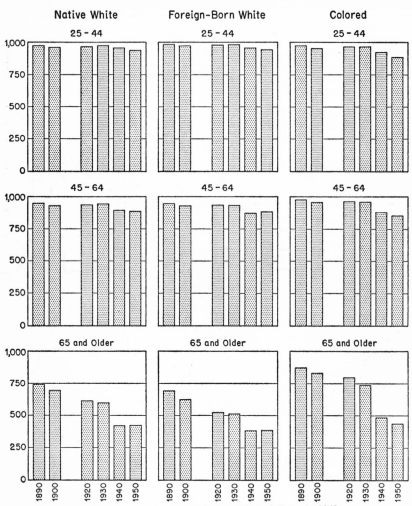

ᵃ Standardized for age on basis of male population of United States in 1940.
Source: Appendix A.

TABLE 29

Effect of the Foreign-Born and Negroes on Rate of Male Participation in Labor Force, United States, Census Dates, 1890–1950

	1890	1900	1920	1930	1940	1950
Rate of Participation [a]						
1. All classes	827	817	787	775	723	718
2. Natives (white & nonwhite)	820	814	783	774	724	718
3. Whites (native & foreign-born)	819	810	781	771	722	721
4. Native whites	809	805	775	768	723	721
Method No. 1						
5. Effect of foreign-born (line 1 minus line 2)	+7	+3	+4	+1	−1	0
6. Effect of colored (line 2 minus line 4)	+11	+9	+8	+6	+1	−3
7. Combined effect (line 1 minus line 4, or line 5 plus line 6)	+18	+12	+12	+7	0	−3
Method No. 2						
8. Effect of foreign-born (line 3 minus line 4)	+10	+5	+6	+3	−1	0
9. Effect of colored (line 1 minus line 3)	+8	+7	+6	+4	+1	−3
10. Combined effect (line 8 plus line 9)	+18	+12	+12	+7	0	−3
Discrepancy between Methods						
11. Effect of foreign-born (line 5 minus line 8)	−3	−2	−2	−2	0	0
12. Effect of colored (line 6 minus line 9)	+3	+2	+2	+2	0	0

Source: Appendix A.

[a] Number of males aged 10 and older in labor force (standardized for age composition on the basis of population of the United States in 1940) per 1,000 males of same age group, color, and place of birth.

averages were not significantly different from those of census years, whether expressed in terms of dollars or related to per-decade changes in the labor force (Table 30). In the early and recent periods, the differences were greater.[2] But, again, the differences were not significant for the four English-speaking nations with the exception that in Great Britain in the earlier period, the per-decade increase in income per worker was cut to nearly half and the decline in the male labor force per $100 rise in income nearly doubled, compared with the changes between census years.

[2] In the United States the reason was that the dividing date (1930) bordered on the depression of the 1930's so that the averaging in of some of the more prosperous years of 1928 and 1929 with the income figure for 1930 raised the increase of the earlier period and lowered the increase of the recent period.

TABLE 30

Average Per-Decade Changes in Male Labor Force per 1,000 Males 14 and Older, Associated with Average Per-Decade Increases in Income between Census Years and Three-Year Averages, 5 Countries, Various Periods, 1890–1951

		Change in Income [a] (Dollars) between:		Change in Labor Force [b] per $100 Increase in Income [a] between:		Per cent Change in Labor Force [b] per 1 Per Cent Increase in Income [a] between:	
		Census Years (1)	3-Year Averages [c] (2)	Census Years (3)	3-Year Averages [c] (4)	Census Years (5)	3-Year Averages [c] (6)
Entire Period							
United States	1890–1950	296	282	−6	−6	−0.12	−0.12
Great Britain	1911–1951	113	114	−11	−11	−0.15	−0.15
Canada	1921–1951	268	288	−5	−5	−0.09	−0.09
New Zealand	1901–1951	342	322	−7	−7	−0.13	−0.13
Germany	1895–1939	33	20	−21	−35	−0.19	−0.30
	1895–1950	7	−7	+114	−114	+1.03	−1.01
Early Period							
United States	1890–1930	255	267	−4	−4	−0.07	−0.07
Great Britain	1911–1931	30	17	−27	−47	−0.34	−0.61
Canada	1921–1931	80	71	−5	−6	−0.08	−0.09
New Zealand	1901–1926	218	228	−13	−12	−0.18	−0.17
Germany	1895–1925	−43	−44	7	7	0.06	0.06
Recent Period							
United States	1930–1950	377	311	−8	−10	−0.24	−0.28
Great Britain	1931–1951	196	210	−8	−8	−0.13	−0.12
Canada	1931–1951	363	396	−5	−5	−0.10	−0.09
New Zealand	1926–1951	460	412	−4	−5	−0.09	−0.10
Germany	1925–1939	196	172	−8	−9	−0.07	−0.08
	1925–1950	66	41	−21	−34	−0.20	−0.31

notes on following page

The same does not hold for Germany. For that nation the average income compared with the 1950 labor force actually rested on only two years, since there were no data for 1948. Nevertheless, the effect of including 1949 in the average was to convert a small per-decade rise in income into a small per-decade decline (1949 incomes were apparently much below those of 1950). The quantitative difference was not great, but the whole direction of movement was altered and the signs of the changes in labor force associated with the change in income were reversed. On the whole, it is probably best to disregard the German income changes as being unreliable: the territorial coverage has varied three times, explicit data on disposable income were not available for post-World War II years, and income comparisons over time are highly suspect for an economy as disrupted by war and military defeat as Germany's. It is not certain, therefore, what the quantitative change has been in German income per worker or whether the income change has been upward or downward.

The labor force-income analysis reveals that the proportion of males aged 14 and older in the labor force declined in all five countries during periods when annual real personal income (after income taxes) per employed adult male were rising. In the United States—as a nation, and in its urban and rural areas and large cities—the male labor force declined by 5 to 8 persons per 1,000 males aged 14 and older for each $100 increase in income. Much the same association was manifest in Great Britain, Canada, and New Zealand (income translated into United States dollars of constant purchasing power).

The association with income per worker seemed closer when expressed in percentages. For the entire period, a 1 per cent rise in real income was typically associated with a decline of 0.1 to 0.2 per cent in the labor force (the dubious comparison for Germany deviated significantly from this pattern). For the period since 1930, the United States as a whole and its urban areas showed a much greater decline in the male labor force relative to income per worker than they did in the earlier period. Canada revealed about the same changes in the two periods and Britain and New Zealand manifested recent changes that were substantially smaller than the earlier ones.

Notes to Table 30

Source: Appendixes A and D.

[a] Real disposable income from all sources per adult-male equivalent employed, in 1929 U.S. dollars.
[b] Labor force was standardized for age composition on the basis of population of the United States in 1940.
[c] Average of each census year and the two preceding years.

INCOME PER CAPITA.

Labor force participation may also be influenced by changes in income relative to consumer needs, which cannot be measured precisely, for people vary widely in their physical and social requirements for food, clothing, and shelter, depending on their age, sex, occupation, and income level. Although there is no satisfactory way of taking account of these differences, male labor force participation was compared with income per capita among the five nations and over the same periods of time studied for the comparisons with changes in income.

The results for the entire period show that in the United States about 16 males left the labor force (per 1,000 males 14 and older in the population) for each $100 rise in personal disposable income per capita—an exodus equivalent to a fall of 0.11 per cent in participation for each 1 per cent rise in income per capita. Except for Germany, which had a substantially larger relative decline, the results for the other countries were not very different from those of the United States.

For the recent period, the decrease in male participation showed the same comparatively uniform relation to increases in per capita income that was seen for the entire period; in fact, the degree of uniformity extended even to Germany for 1925–1939 (though not for 1925–1950). But for the early period all such uniformity was lacking. The declines in male labor force relative to increases in income per capita varied enormously from nation to nation, in a much wider range than that revealed by the comparisons with income per worker, with the principal variations again occurring for Great Britain and Germany.

Boys and Young Men

The proportion of young people under 25 who now participate in the labor force is much lower than it was fifty years ago. Boys have reduced their participation more than girls; children under 14, more than youths of high school age; and the latter, more than men of college age.

The reduction for boys aged 14–19 was sizable in all the countries studied except Germany and varied rather widely—from 18 to 66 per 1,000 per decade. The decline as a whole was generally greater in foreign countries than in the United States, and was most marked in Great Britain. In the United States it was especially noticeable for foreign-born and Negro boys and for boys in urban areas, and it has been sharp since 1930 for Negro boys. The decline for Britain was concentrated in the period after World War II, and that for Germany in the period since 1939. Otherwise, most of the shrinkage in the participation of teen-age boys seems to have occurred before 1930.

The decline for males aged 20–24 was generally smaller and mostly confined to the United States—where it has been heavy due to the recent rise in enrollment in institutions of higher learning. Also in the United States it has been much more acute in urban than in rural areas, and among the foreign-born and Negroes than among native whites.

The outflow of youths from the labor force was fairly well matched by the inflow into the classroom, at least in the United States, Canada, and Great Britain, where school attendance was reported or could be estimated by sex. It is not certain, however, that the rise of school attendance was the cause of the reduction in the labor force. Conceivably both developments may have been caused by some independent factor such as income, with school attendance rising as the young people no longer needed to work. In virtually all the countries and periods, participation of boys and young men in the labor force declined while income was rising.

However, among the countries in all periods the percentage changes in the labor force per 1 per cent rise in income have displayed very little uniformity. For boys aged 14–19 they ranged from +0.14 per cent in Germany (1895–1939) to as high as −0.86 per cent in United States urban areas or −2.33 per cent in Germany (1895–1950); for young men aged 20–24 they varied from −0.01 per cent in Canada to −0.36 per cent in Germany.

In the United States, the very marked change may have been owing, somewhat, to the movement of farm families to urban areas; in the cities the child labor laws were stricter and job opportunities for children were sparser—as revealed by the "voice of the farmers":

"The children of farmers are, as a rule, kept from school during the summer (spring) months to help along the work of the farm. . . . The children of town laborers get more schooling, because in these later years it is more difficult to find employment for them." [3]

The migration to the city was, of course, made possible as the advance in productivity reduced the labor requirements of agriculture. But it was also doubtless stimulated by the higher urban wages.[4] And the high and increasing urban wages must, in turn, have contributed to the extension of elementary, secondary, and advanced education by motivating parents to do without children's earnings and to vote for higher

[3] *Fourth Biennial Report,* Iowa Bureau of Labor Statistics, 1890–1891, pp. 58–96.
[4] There has undoubtedly been a large shift from rural-farm to rural-nonfarm areas which would reduce demand for child labor even in rural areas. A smaller absolute number of children under 16 were employed in agriculture in 1930 than in 1870. In 1900, the proportion was 1 in every 9 children aged 10–16; three decades later, it was only 1 in 30.

155

taxes to finance more schools, which at the turn of the century were often inadequate.[5] In fact, investigations by state bureaus of labor statistics give the impression that had there not been a considerable rise in incomes, the textbook might scarcely have triumphed over the plow or the workbench in the competition for the nation's children.

"As for children under 14 years of age we prefer not to employ them at all, as it is only now and then you will find one to keep their work up properly, but their parents often plead with us to take them with the plea that they must have them at work and other mills will work them. . . ."[6]

". . . if we drive the children out (as we often threaten to do), the mothers tell us they will have to go also. The children waste more than they do good, and we prefer not having them if we could get rid of them."[7]

Still more evidence on this score is the finding of the National Industrial Conference Board that in 1924 every second or third child who left the classroom to take a job did so in order to supplement the low income of his family.[8] It is not impossible also that many children left school and began work without being aware that their action was dictated by financial need, as their friends and relatives also commonly left school at an early age. High school attendance could not have become the norm for teen-agers without a considerable rise in incomes. Some tendency for higher real incomes to be associated in the short-run with reduced labor force participation of the young may be seen in Chapter 11. The labor force participation of persons aged 14–24 was partially correlated with real disposable personal income per equivalent adult-male employed worker, holding unemployment and armed forces constant. These associations—constructed from quarterly averages of monthly data and analyzed in two periods 1940–46 and 1946–52—were significant but they were also modest, and analogous associations with real hourly earnings were even more modest.

In any case economic developments can hardly have been the sole cause of the greater trend toward education. A field investigation thirty years ago by the United States Department of Labor found that one in three youngsters was then leaving school for lack of interest.[9] Although

[5] Testimony of David Blaustein, in *Report of the Industrial Commission on the Relations and Conditions of Capital and Labor Employed in Manufactures and General Business,* Government Printing Office, Washington, 1901, Vol. XIV, p. 128.

[6] *First Annual Report,* North Carolina Bureau of Labor Statistics, 1887, p. 148.

[7] *Third Biennial Report, 1888–1889,* Maryland Bureau of Industrial Statistics and Information, p. 81. See also *Twenty-first Annual Report,* 1912, p. 20.

[8] *Employment of Young Persons in the United States,* National Industrial Conference Board, 1925, p. 5.

[9] "Summary of the Report on Condition of Woman and Child Wage Earners

numerous instances were uncovered in which boys and girls took jobs to relieve desperate home conditions resulting from illness, alcoholism, death, or desertion, there was no absence of cases where children worked because of their dislike for school, desire for money, or their parents' indifference to education.

"At the home of a little girl of thirteen the surroundings point to a comfortable condition of life where the father earns $9 per week; the mother, $8; while the earnings of the child are $4 per week; the board paid by an aunt, and additional earnings from an older son, make the weekly income about $30. . . . There is no question but that the child at work could have received a better education without stint to the family." [10]

The significance of noneconomic factors is exemplified also in Great Britain, where income was relatively ample, and yet a high proportion of youngsters left school at an early age.[11] Although at any given time a smaller proportion of young people tends to seek employment if adult income is high (Chapter 4), over time the tendency does not seem to be immediately or strongly influenced by economic forces, though economic forces may well be an ultimate determinant.[12]

Men Aged 25–64

Of the 60 million members of the United States labor force in 1950, 57 per cent were men aged 25–64. The proportion was nearly the same

in the United States," Bulletin 175, Bureau of Labor Statistics, Women in Industry Series, No. 5, 1916, pp. 264–265. A study by the Maryland Bureau of Labor Statistics yielded similar results.

[10] *Twelfth Annual Report,* Maryland Bureau of Statistics and Information, a study by the Baltimore branch of the Consumers' League, 1903, pp. 117–119.

[11] The trend was modified somewhat in 1948 when the school-leaving age was raised by one year. The Education Act of August 3, 1944 (*The Public General Acts and the Church Assembly Measures of 1944,* London, The Council of Law Reporting, pp. 220–332, and *Keesing's Contemporary Archives,* Bristol, Vol. V, 7103/A) extended the age of compulsory school attendance from the end of the thirteenth to the end of the fourteenth year. Although the Act went into effect officially on April 1, 1947, its full effect was not realized until January 1949, when the number of pupils between 14 and 15 was 480,127, compared with 389,-900 in January 1948 and 150,101 in January 1947. The law contemplates a future rise in the school-leaving age to the end of the fifteenth year ("Education in 1949," *Ministry of Labour Gazette,* London, August 1950, p. 266).

[12] George Stigler has found that "if we classify states by per capita income and the racial composition of children—both of which are in a sense more fundamental and persistent than school age legislation—within the cells there is no evidence of a correlation between legislation and school enrollments. . . . Our brief study suggests . . . that the influence of legislation is a relatively weak factor, whose presumptive significance comes largely from the correlation of maximum age in the statute with incomes and racial composition," *Employment and Compensation in Education,* National Bureau of Economic Research, Occasional Paper 33, 1950, App. B.

in Canada and New Zealand, but in Great Britain and Germany it was lower because of the active female participation and the depletion of the male populations in the two World Wars. An overwhelming majority of men have tended to work, in all five countries over long periods. Nevertheless, men aged 25–44, who had maintained their rate of participation in the labor force at about 97 per cent from 1890 through 1930, reduced it to 95 per cent in 1940, and to 92.9 per cent in 1950. Men aged 45–64, who had maintained their proportion in the labor force at 94 per cent during the five decades through 1930, lowered it to 88.7 per cent in 1940 and to 87.7 per cent in 1950. This stability for five decades followed by a decline in the last two decades characterized the behavior of men in both rural and urban areas.[13]

The reduction in the labor force participation of men in the United States was greater than in the four foreign countries, and it was confined almost entirely to the recent period. Undoubtedly it occurred because more men aged 25–34 were attending college, graduate school, or vocational school. Roughly 700,000 fewer men of these ages were in the labor force in April 1950 than there would have been if the labor force had formed the same proportion of the population as in 1930. At the beginning of the school year, in October 1949, the school enrollment of men aged 25–34 was close to 500,000.[14] How much the enrollment in 1949–1950 exceeded that in 1929–1930 is a matter of guesswork [15]—though it is likely that the excess was large, since 93 per cent of those 25 and older who started school in the fall of 1949 were veterans. Reduced activity in the labor force was not, however, confined to men aged 25–34. It was also observable for men aged 35–44 in recent decades and for men aged 45–64—in both the early and the recent period. In fact, the reduction for men aged 45–64 was greater in some of the countries or areas than that for youths of 20–24.

[13] Before 1950 some labor force experts believed that the decline from 1930 to 1940 was due to the change in the technique of measurement in the 1940 census. It should be difficult to hold to this position now that the 1950 census, which used virtually the same technique as that of 1940, has revealed just as great a decline between 1940 and 1950.

[14] Some had doubtless dropped out between October 1949 and April 1950, and of those who stayed in, some were in the labor force part time.

[15] The census of 1930 did not report students aged 25 and older, possibly because they were not numerous enough to warrant separate classification.

158

CHAPTER 9

OLDER WORKERS IN THE LABOR FORCE

THE reduction in labor force participation among men aged 65 and older has been generally much greater than that among any other age group, as seen in Chapter 8 and Table 28.

In the United States the number of men of this age in the labor force decreased from around 700 per 1,000 males 65 and older in 1890 to 425 per 1,000 in 1950—a decline of about 50 per 1,000 per decade (Chart 17). The decline was smaller in Canada, but it was larger in Germany and Great Britain and it was enormous in New Zealand—well over 100 per decade. The result was that in the last census relatively fewer of the elderly men participated in the labor force in these countries than in the United States; the proportion was slightly lower in Canada in 1951, and it was much lower in New Zealand in 1951, in Germany in 1950, and in Great Britain in 1951.

The percentage decrease in the labor force of elderly men in the United States ranged from 0.57 to 0.84 (depending on area) for each 1 per cent rise in real annual disposable personal income per equivalent adult-male worker employed; in the foreign countries it was generally much larger. And except in Britain and New Zealand, the relative declines were greater in the recent period.

This chapter undertakes to explain why the labor force of elderly men has been shrinking in this and other countries since the turn of the century.

Demographic Changes within the Older Group

The widespread tendency for the 65 and older age group to grow in relation to the total population has been noted. Has there been an analogous tendency for the more elderly, say those of 70 or above, to increase in relation to the group 65 and older? In the United States, the ratio of those aged 70 or older to those aged 65 or older remained about the same throughout the period under study. In the other countries studied, the ratio rose on occasion, but in the more recent years it was equal to, or lower than that in at least some earlier years. Apparently not much had happened during the time covered to change the life expectancy of a person who had reached age 65 or more.[1]

Could one cause of the decline be the migration from rural to urban areas? Throughout 1890–1950, men aged 65 and older in the United States showed less participation in the labor force in urban than in

[1] *Man and His Years*, Federal Security Agency, 1951, p. 21.

CHART 17

Men 65 and Older in the Labor Force per 1,000 in Same Population Group: 5 Countries, Various Years, 1890–1951

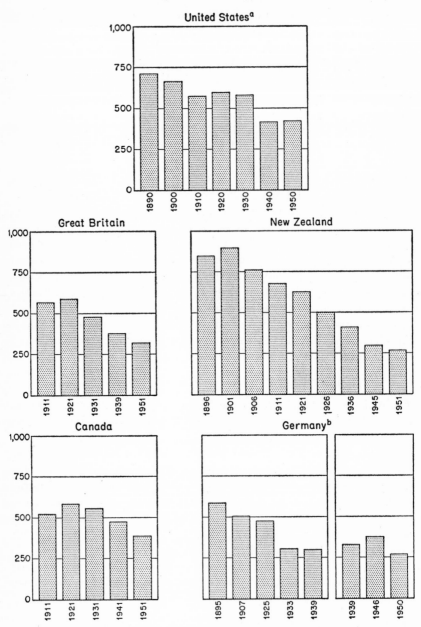

CHART 17, concluded

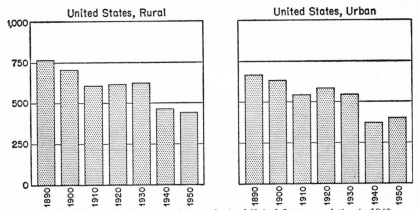

United States, Rural   United States, Urban

ª Standardized for rural-urban composition on basis of United States population in 1940.
ᵇ For 1895–1939, boundaries after World War I, without the Saar; 1939–1950, Federal Republic of Germany, without Berlin.
Source: Appendix A.

rural areas.[2] However, participation of elderly persons declined more in rural areas in both early and recent periods. And so sharp was the decline in both types of area that standardization for the effect of migration modified the decline in the total labor force of men aged 65 and older relatively little (Chapter 8, Table 28).

The effect of the changing composition of the population with respect to color and national origin may also be discounted. In the whole period, the rate of participation was higher for colored than for white men; but since Negroes have been a minority of the population, and a rather constant minority at that, their presence had only a light impact on the pattern of change of all classes. The foreign-born had a greater effect but in the opposite direction, so that the combined result was largely cancelled out, leaving only a negligible impact on the pattern of labor force change of the elderly (Table 31).

It is reasonable to conclude that the reason for the declining participation of elderly men does not lie in changes in the distribution of the population by age, residence, color, or national origin. Not without interest, however, is the fact that for elderly whites the decline halted between 1940 and 1950, but for the elderly colored it was intensified —yet employment opportunities for the latter were probably greater during the 1940's than ever before.

[2] This was probably true in comparison with farm areas rather than with rural-nonfarm areas, for in 1940 and 1950 men in each 10-year age group 35 and older participated in the labor force in generally smaller proportions in urban areas than in farm areas, but in higher proportions in urban than in rural-nonfarm areas.

161

TABLE 31

Effect of the Foreign-Born and Negroes on Rate of Participation of Elderly Males in the Labor Force, United States, Census Dates, 1890–1950

	1890	1900	1920	1930	1940	1950
Rate of Participation [a]						
1. All classes	739	683	601	583	415	420
2. Natives (white & nonwhite)	759	711	630	609	426	423
3. Whites (native & foreign-born)	725	668	585	573	410	418
4. Native whites	742	693	611	597	420	421
Method No. 1						
5. Effect of foreign-born (line 1 minus line 2)	−20	−28	−29	−26	−11	−3
6. Effect of colored (line 2 minus line 4)	+17	+18	+19	+12	+6	+2
7. Combined effect (line 1 minus line 4 or line 5 plus line 6)	−3	−10	−10	−14	−5	−1
Method No. 2						
8. Effect of foreign-born (line 3 minus line 4)	−17	−25	−26	−24	−10	−3
9. Effect of colored (line 1 minus line 3)	+14	+15	+16	+10	+5	+2
10. Combined effect (line 8 plus line 9)	−3	−10	−10	−14	−5	−1
Discrepancy between Methods						
11. Effect of foreign-born (line 5 minus line 8)	−3	−3	−3	−2	−1	0
12. Effect of colored (line 6 minus line 9)	+3	+3	+3	+2	+1	0

Source: Appendix A.

[a] Number of males aged 65 and older in labor force per 1,000 of same age group, color, and place of birth.

Old Age Security and Pensions

Recent years have brought improvements in private pensions, social security benefits, federal and state assistance, and various forms of direct or indirect charity. Do such subsidies offer a means or an incentive for elderly people to stop working? [3]

Here it is necessary to keep in mind two things. First, many elderly persons have dropped out of the labor force even when pensions were

[3] T. Lynn Smith has concluded that "since the social security program was instituted in the United States, there has been a strong tendency for persons less than 65 years of age to declare themselves old enough to qualify for old-age assistance." "The Recent Increase of Persons in the Social Security Ages," *American Sociological Review,* June 1945, pp. 414–418.

162

inadequate or nonexistent. They left in extremely large numbers in the United States during 1890–1910 and 1930–1934, when there were almost no government assistance and private pension plans,[4] and still more dropped out between 1930 and 1940, although old age assistance (charity payments) was inadequate during that decade and was not effectively supplemented by social security until after 1940. In New Zealand as many elderly males left the labor force between 1906 and 1926 as between 1926 and 1936, when benefits were definitely on the increase. Second, older workers actually re-entered the labor force or suspended their exodus temporarily during 1940–1950, despite the widespread extension of social security and private pension systems.[5]

Thus social security and pensions were far from being the main force (though they doubtless helped) in bringing about the withdrawal of elderly persons from the labor market. Indeed, there is evidence that elderly people desire to work as late in life as their health permits,[6] mainly because old age benefits rarely take the place of earned income even when they are comparatively generous. This is true not only of most company benefits but also of those paid by the Federal Old Age and Survivors Insurance System, which in 1941 remitted an average primary benefit of $23 per month; and few persons could live on this without help.[7] Between 1940 and 1945, the first five years during which benefits were paid, less than a third of all qualified men and women aged 65 and over who could have drawn old-age benefits by leaving employment, did so, and the rate of retirement from the labor force slowed down. For the next five years the rate speeded up again, but as late as June 1, 1950 two in five of the fully insured were still not drawing the allowances they were entitled to. "The psychological factor of hating to be put 'on the shelf' by poor health or the loss of a job makes many elderly workers resentful of enforced retirement."[8] "The

[4] In Massachusetts, Michigan, and Rhode Island participation of elderly persons in the labor force declined rapidly from 1930 to about 1935, despite large decreases in income.

[5] A return or suspension of withdrawal occurred only in the United States during the 1920's and 1940's, and in Nazi Germany after World War I.

[6] Only about 5 per cent of 2,380 men receiving old age benefits, visited in 1941–1942 by representatives of the Bureau of Old-Age and Survivors Insurance, said they retired and filed for insurance because they wished to do so, and while they were in good health. More than half the men reported that they were laid off by their employers, and about a third said they had left their jobs because of illness or failing health. Edna C. Wentworth, "Why Beneficiaries Retire," *Social Security Bulletin*, January 1945, p. 16.

[7] Some dwelt in joint households; some received family, public, or private assistance; many supplemented their income by working. Edna C. Wentworth, "Income of Old-Age and Survivors Insurance Beneficiaries, 1941 and 1949," *Social Security Bulletin*, May 1950, pp. 3–10.

[8] Edrita G. Fried, "Attitudes of the Older Population Groups Toward Activity and Inactivity," *Journal of Gerontology*, April 1949, pp. 141–151.

principal reason, however, is that without earnings they do not have resources enough to live at the level to which they are accustomed or even to meet the cost of their basic needs." [9]

Disposable Income

It might be expected that older men in borderline physical condition would tend to leave the labor force if they or their children were prosperous enough to provide for their support in retirement. Chapter 4 revealed that at a given time the labor force of men aged 65 and older was smaller in areas where incomes were higher. Is there an analogous relationship over time?

It is true that in the United States up to 1930 the inverse association over time was reasonably close to the association seen in Chapter 4. But when income per worker was rising very little or not at all, e.g. in Canada during 1921–1931 or in Germany during 1895–1925, more elderly men were leaving the labor force per decade than when income was rising rapidly, e.g. in the United States during 1940–1950. The outflow over time in different countries agreed more closely in absolute numbers than in relation to income changes which, then, either had no effect or were obscured by more powerful forces. Is one of these forces the fluctuations or trends, perhaps, in the ability to work?

The Older Man's Ability to Work

That certain capacities diminish with age, beginning almost at adulthood, is supported by considerable evidence. According to Miles of Stanford University, a man's manual mobility and reaction speeds reach an optimum in his twenties or thirties; [10] and his speed of learning reaches its peak shortly after his teens.[11] A. T. Welford, of the Cambridge University Psychological Laboratories, has concluded that as a man grows older he has increasing difficulty in comprehending verbal or visual data, particularly when they are new or unfamiliar, and as a result has to rely more and more on his past experience.[12]

Nevertheless it has been pointed out that this deterioration usually

[9] Margaret L. Stecker, "Beneficiaries Prefer to Work," Social Security Bulletin, January 1951, p. 16. This was also brought out by a sample survey of England and Wales in 1945 which revealed that 20 per cent of the men and women over 60 preferred to work; the rest could not afford to retire. Geoffrey Thomas, The Employment of Older Persons, Industrial Health Research Board, January 1947, p. 42.
[10] Walter R. Miles, "Measures of Certain Human Abilities Throughout the Life Span," Proceedings of the National Academy of Sciences, 1931, pp. 627–633.
[11] A. J. Carlson and E. J. Stieglitz, "Physiological Changes in Aging," Annals of the American Academy of Political and Social Sciences, January 1952, p. 22.
[12] A. T. Welford, Skill and Age: An Experimental Approach, Oxford, The Nuffield Foundation, 1951, p. 146.

occurs at a slow rate until fairly late in life.[13] And O. J. Kaplan reports that mental abilities are maintained without loss by some persons until late maturity, with losses occurring where they do largely because of disuse or lack of training; and that many of the test instruments and procedures are not relevant to the efficiency of elderly people in jobs.[14] "Although speed may decrease among older people," Welford concludes, "the deficiency is often more than offset by gains in quality and accuracy. Also it seems that even at the age at which most subjects show some fall in performing, there is a substantial number of individuals who maintain performance comparable with that of people in their twenties or thirties." [15]

It is not entirely certain, therefore, that elderly persons are actually less efficient workers, provided they are physically fit. But many older people name health as their reason for retiring, and it may be worth while to inquire as to whether, and how much, physical stamina has retrogressed in the past several decades. The life expectancy of the male in the United States has risen since 1900 by twenty years,[16] and for men of 65 it now stands at nearly fifteen years.[17] Are many of the less robust being preserved by medical science over longer life spans? Is the average man over 65 or over 45 a poorer specimen than one who was hardy enough to have achieved that age a generation or two ago?

Some light was focused on this question several years ago when Ernst Simonson asked "whether the increased life expectancy is associated with increased ability at work in the older age groups," and made a rather tenuous comparison between studies by Quetelet in 1836 of persons in different muscle groups in Belgium and studies by Rejs eighty-five years later of a group of 3,000 Dutch men and women. These comparisons could scarcely be said to offer rigorous proof, and Simonson pointed out other factors that might have helped to explain the result. Nevertheless he concluded that in 1921 maximum muscle strength was reached about a decade later in life than it was in 1836, and that "The decline of muscle strength at the age of 37 years in 1836 was about the same as that at the age of 50 years in 1921. In the same period, the life expectation for males in Holland increased from 34.9 years to 55.1 years. . . . The over-all trend is unquestionable, and

[13] Miles, *op. cit.*, p. 633.

[14] Psychological Aspects of Aging," *Annals,* January 1952, p. 36.

[15] Welford, *op. cit.*, p. 147.

[16] Harland Fox, "Utilization of Older Man Power," *Harvard Business Review,* November 1951, p. 43.

[17] Ray M. Peterson, F.S.A., *Description of a Modern Mortality Table, For Judging the Adequacy of the Funding Basis of Private Retirement Plans,* Equitable Life Assurance Society, 1953, paper presented at personnel meeting of American Management Association, February 16–18, 1953, Chart 3. The life expectancy of the 65-year-old female in 1953 was nearly eighteen years.

the comparison . . . seems to imply that the increased life duration is associated with a better maintenance of muscle strength, and possibly also of other functions important for the over-all working capacity." Life expectancy and peak strength were both prolonged, Simonson believed, by the improved standard of living.[18] Certainly the study lends no support to the hypothesis that older workers retired because they were not as strong as their forebears of equal age a generation or two ago.

Company Practices in Hiring and Retirement

Whether or not older employees are less efficient, many firms customarily retire their employees at a certain age. Over half the retirements in nonagricultural industries have been found by the Twentieth Century Fund to be compulsory,[19] and in 1950 about four in ten of several hundred companies told the Equitable Life Assurance Society, which insured their plans, that they required their employees, whether covered by the plans or not, to retire at a certain age, normally 65.[20]

No less common are rules against hiring new employees at ages above 45, 40, or even 35. A number of postwar surveys in New York State,[21] supported by two studies of the National Industrial Conference Board [22] and a nation-wide sampling of nearly 300 concerns by the National Association of Manufacturers in cooperation with the United States Chamber of Commerce, showed that between 25 and 40 per cent of all firms do not ordinarily employ personnel above these ages.[23] The rules are more strict in some cases than in others. Abrams

[18] Ernst Simonson, M.D., "Physical Fitness and Work Capacity of Older Men," *Geriatrics*, January–February 1947, pp. 110–112, 117. For a contrary view see W. J. Cohen in *Proceedings of the 3rd Annual Meeting*, Industrial Relations Research Association, December 1950, p. 329. Cohen sees reason to believe that the number of persons with disabilities is increasing, particularly in age groups approaching 65.

[19] Howard A. Rusk, M.D., in the *New York Times*, February 24, 1952, p. 67. Only 25 per cent were retired because of poor health.

[20] *Survey of Retirement Practices*, Equitable Life Assurance Society, June 1, 1950, p. 1. The replies came from a wide variety of occupations, including retailing, wholesaling, manufacturing, public utilities, finance, schools and hospitals, oil, steel, and insurance. The majority of companies treated both wage and salary earners alike (p. 2). See *289 Retirement Plans*, Bankers Trust Company of New York, 1948, p. 7.

[21] *Community Survey of Employment of the Elderly*, Rochester, N.Y., Industrial Management Council, January 1, 1948; Albert J. Abrams, "Industry Views Its Elderly Workers," in *Birthdays Don't Count*, New York State Joint Legislative Committee on Problems of the Aging, Leg. Doc. 61, 1948, pp. 152–153.

[22] "Maximum Age Hiring Practices Surveyed," *Factory Management and Maintenance*, January 1948, pp. 222–226, and "Personnel Practices in Factory and Office," *Studies in Personnel Policy No. 88*, National Industrial Conference Board, 1948.

[23] *Employment of the Physically Handicapped and Older Workers*, National Association of Manufacturers, 1949, p. 15.

has reported that they are applied rather rigidly in public utilities, in new industries (such as chemicals, plastics, and aviation), and in big firms in general, and more flexibly in small enterprises and service industries. They are probably enforced more generally when labor is plentiful and jobs are scarce, and they are apt to be found with private pension schemes.[24] In his Minneapolis studies of 168 firms with 57,000 employees, Fox also brought out that both salaried and hourly employees are utilized after age 65 much less in firms with pension schemes.[25] And such rules are likely to occur with company policies of hiring only at the bottom and promoting from within.[26] They are not on balance ameliorated by labor union rules governing seniority, apprenticeship, and transfers, or by the general unwillingness of unions to permit downgrading in pay and position as abilities decline.[27] And they may be aggravated by the medical examinations on which hirings are often based, which frequently search for disabilities that are no handicap in the job.[28]

Obstacles to retention of an existing employee beyond the age of 65, or to hiring a new one who is older than 35 or 45, appear unreasonable to the older man, who may believe that he is more productive than when he was a decade younger or that he is more efficient than younger people currently performing the same tasks.[29] Nevertheless these rules against older workers are often logical enough to the employer. A leading corporation executive—himself in his sixties—is reported as stating in early 1953 that "keeping older people with diminished capacity in the labor force appreciably reduces efficiency." [30] Some managements fear that the employee, where he has not yet deteriorated, will one day suddenly do so. Others believe, often without tangible evidence, that older persons have more serious accidents, do not get along well with younger persons, and are not receptive to new ideas.[31]

[24] A. J. Abrams, "Barriers to Employment of Older Workers," *Annals,* as cited, pp. 62–71. But even in times or places of labor shortage, it is not uncommon for defense plants and government agencies to advertise for workers under 45 or 35 (p. 65). Rules against hiring older workers are apt to be found with private pension plans, either because of the high cost of adequately pensioning off employees who have been with a company only a few years, or because firms are reluctant to hire short-term help who will be retired on a pittance (p. 67).

[25] Harland Fox, "Utilization of Older Man Power," *Harvard Business Review,* November 1951, p. 43. See also Sumner Slichter, "Economic Problems of Support of Retired Persons," in *Criteria for Retirement,* Geneva Mathiasen, editor, Putnam, 1953, p. 161.

[26] Lloyd G. Reynolds, *The Structure of Labor Markets,* Harper, 1951, p. 83.

[27] Abrams, *op. cit.,* p. 70.

[28] *Ibid.,* p. 68.

[29] See also "Older Workers Seek Jobs," *Survey in Four Employment Service Offices,* Bureau of Employment Security, August 1951.

[30] Abrams, *op. cit.,* p. 66.

[31] After surveying twenty-six large manufacturing companies employing chiefly

Still others may find it expedient to clear promotion channels in order to keep the more ambitious young people from leaving.[32] A consideration not easy to measure but important with regard to white-collar employees, is the effect of automatic raises, frequently made on the basis of years of service without close attention to efficiency. Gradually, older workers may reach wage levels above their productivity and consequently be replaced by younger and lower-paid men or women, wherever a good excuse presents itself.

Another consideration—often urged—is that an ever larger proportion of workers must now rely on jobs with firms for their livelihood, and that an ever smaller proportion earn a living on farms, in family enterprises, or in self-employment, where compulsory retirement rules have not been a factor.[33] Actually, there seems to be little factual evidence that the ratio of employees to self-employed has changed significantly in recent generations. In Great Britain, during three decades, only about one in every 100 gainfully occupied persons shifted from working on his own account to salaried employment, while nearly 30 in every 100 elderly men left the work force. In the United States, self-employed persons and employers dropped from just under 20 per cent of the labor force in 1910 to just under 19 per cent in 1940, again hardly more than one per 100, while the outflow of elderly persons was 17 per 100.[34] Although there was a noticeable decline in self-

skilled or semiskilled labor, Palmer and Brownell concluded that employers hesitated hiring older workers except where skill was needed, partly in the belief that they were less versatile. The tendency was to protect them on layoffs by applying seniority rules, even in nonunion plants, but to hire new workers under 35.

Their study could not find any general tendency for older workers to be less efficient or to be subject to more illness or accident. Many notions about the inferiority of the older worker prove on closer examination to be fanciful; see D. L. Palmer and J. A. Brownell, "Influence of Age on Employment Opportunities," *Monthly Labor Review*, April 1939, pp. 765–780.

This writer observed in a General Motors plant in 1947 that older women were preferred by many supervisors as being more industrious and reliable than the "bobby-soxers" and "jitterbugs." The plant employed many women in their fifties and even late sixties. One robust woman of 70 was doing a hard job polishing precision parts to close tolerances.

The industries in which the older worker finds it especially difficult to get a job are not those with a stable working force, but, rather, those in which seasonal or temporary work makes it easy to discriminate impersonally. Considerable discrimination against older workers occurs in insurance companies and in construction during a depression, and in chain stores, hotels, and restaurants, where the younger worker is more attractive to the customers.

[32] Fox, *op. cit.*, pp. 44, 51.
[33] Slichter, *op. cit.*, p. 159. See also, *Man and His Years*, Federal Security Agency, 1951, p. 26 (the section on population changes and their economic implications).
[34] Workers on own account, excluding employers: 1921, 12 and older; 1931, 14 and older; 1951, 15 and older. Source: Appendix A. Also, for the United States, *Census of Population: 1940, Comparative Occupation Statistics for the United*

employment of persons of all ages during 1920–1930, it was not accompanied by an appreciable exodus of elderly men from the labor force. Yet there was an actual recovery of self-employment during 1930–1940, when the outflow of elderly persons was greater than at any time since 1890. Any affinity between a decline in the proportion of the self-employed and a decline in the proportion of elderly men in the labor force has been very weak.

It has been argued that "with our rapid industrialization and the growth of large corporations . . . in the last fifty years . . . it became more difficult to make individual differences and compulsory retirement at an arbitrary age became the easiest way out. . . ." [35]

Some specially illuminating findings have recently become available as the result of a comprehensive sample survey of the experience and problems of older workers in major industry groups of seven labor market areas: Detroit, Los Angeles, Miami, Minneapolis and St. Paul, Philadelphia, Seattle, Worcester. This survey revealed that there was a rather definite tendency for the proportion of older workers—65 and older or 45 and older—to be smaller, the larger the number of employees in the establishment. There were cities in which this tendency was not observed in all industries; it did not occur without interruption or reversal; and it did not seem to hold at all for service establishments; but on the whole the tendency for the size of an establishment to work against the employment of older workers was fairly clear cut. [36]

But has the average size of firms been increasing enough to explain the decline in the participation of older workers? It is again illuminating to turn to some actual figures: this time on employees per firm in operation. [37] The usual difficulties of defining a firm are present, and

---

States, 1870 to 1940, pp. 63–72; Vol. III, The Labor Force, Part I, p. 7; 1950, United States Summary, PB1, p. 102. For Great Britain, Annual Abstract of Statistics, London, Central Statistical Office, No. 88, p. 15; No. 89, p. 14.

[35] Rusk, loc. cit.

[36] Older Worker Adjustment to Labor Market Practices, Dept. of Labor, BES No. R 151, September 1956, pp. 40 and passim. The survey was conducted by the United States Bureau of Employment Security with the cooperation of its state agencies and of four universities, and was based on a sample of employed workers in establishments having 8 or more workers covered by the state unemployment insurance law or by the Railroad Retirement Act. The writer is grateful to Mr. Sheldon Haber of The Johns Hopkins University for calling attention to this survey.

[37] The number of firms in operation by industry is from Dun and Bradstreet, Inc. (Statistical Abstract of the United States, Bureau of the Census, 1954, p. 502). The number of employees in private nonagricultural establishments is from the Bureau of Labor Statistics (ibid., p. 200), including all full- and part-time employees in pay periods ending nearest the fifteenth of the month. Proprietors, self-employed persons, domestic servants, and government employees were excluded.

the statistics doubtless reflect the improving efficiency of the fact-collecting agencies in locating tiny businesses that formerly escaped count. Such as they are, the data do not disclose any real increase in the average size of firms or any connection between changes in size of firm and the proportion of elderly men leaving the labor force. Between 1930 and 1940, while the participation of large numbers of older men was declining, the average size of firms dropped, though very slightly. This slight drop occurred because the number of private non-agricultural establishments grew a bit more rapidly than the number of employees of such firms. (There was, however, an appreciable rise in the number of employees per firm in manufacturing.) Then in the 1940's, while the average size of firm was rising (though slightly) the participation of elderly men in the labor force rose again. Serious doubt has also been thrown on the supposition that there has been increasing concentration of manufacturing in larger firms during the first four decades of the century.[38] If there has been a tendency for firms to standardize personnel policies so as to discriminate against men above middle age, it has not been the mechanical result of the increasing size or the concentration of business firms.

It would seem plausible that arbitrary discrimination is greater now than it was in the past, but this is by no means certain. A study in 1949 by the National Association of Manufacturers and the United States Chamber of Commerce found about the same proportion of firms with age barriers as a similar study by the N.A.M. in 1930.[39] These results for 1930 are not contradicted by those of another study of firms in New York state in the same year.[40] And over a half century ago the Commissioner of Labor Statistics of New York testified before the federal Industrial Commission, "We find in the free employment office conducted by the State that for a female who admits she is 45 years of age it is very difficult to get employment; and if a man admits an age much over 50 he also finds it very difficult. I saw . . . one case myself there . . . of an engineer whose hair was gray but who was physically a young, strong man, looked to be in the prime of life; in fact at a time to get the best work out of him, and he was refused employment on account of his gray hairs, and the Superintendent tells

[38] G. J. Stigler, *Five Lectures on Economic Problems*, London, Longmans, 1949, Lecture 5; G. Warren Nutter, *The Extent of Enterprise Monopoly in the United States, 1899–1929: A Quantitative Study of Some Aspects of Monopoly*, University of Chicago Press, 1951, pp. vi, 118–121. See review of these two works by Solomon Fabricant, "Is Monopoly Increasing?" *Journal of Economic History*, Winter 1953, pp. 89–94.

[39] Abrams, *op. cit.*, p. 62.

[40] Solomon Barkin, "The Older Worker in Industry," in *Report of the Joint Legislative Committee on Unemployment*, The State of New York, *Leg. Doc.* 66 (1933), pp. 190–204.

me that prevails pretty generally in the office." (*United States Industrial Commission Reports,* 1900, Vol. VII, p. 809.)

Could discrimination against older workers be shown to be on the increase, there would remain the question of why these rules and practices had been adopted.

The March of Technology

One explanation may be that the pace of modern industry is too swift for the physical and nervous energy of the older man. But it has not been proved conclusively that a person becomes less efficient, on balance, as he passes 45 or 65, especially since up-to-date machinery and methods may lighten the physical burden of the work and place a premium on judgment and experience.[41]

There are other aspects of technological progress that might, however, have serious consequences. As firms die, or processes become obsolete, or departments are reorganized, the older worker loses his place and with it his seniority or his moral claims on the employer. Protections erected by custom and humanity around him may not only fail to help, but may even work against him. Employers in new industries presumably will not wish to hire the older worker at a higher salary and on more liberal terms than would be necessary in hiring a younger man or woman, and they will hesitate to subject him to a lower grade than he has achieved. Long established firms may be so heavily committed to older persons already on their payrolls that they are not anxious to take on more such obligations.[42]

One might suppose that industries with the most rapid technological advance would have the fewest older employees. It is impossible to construct a really satisfactory index of technological progress in order to test this hypothesis. This study compares the annual percentage reduction in labor requirements per unit of output in a dozen manufacturing industries between 1899 and 1939, as computed by Solomon Fabricant, with the change between 1910 and 1940 in the ratio of men

[41] R. K. Burns, "Factors in Determining Retirement Age," *Proceedings of the Third Annual Meeting,* Industrial Relations Research Association, December 1950, p. 336; J. A. Hobson, *Work and Wealth,* Peter Smith, 1948. Hobson observes that the main trend of development of industrial machinery has been toward using tools and power to do work which men could not perform with the required regularity, exactitude, and speed, by reason of organic deficiencies (p. 72). While claiming there has never been an age or country where most labor was not toilsome, painful, monotonous, and uninteresting, he concedes it is probably less burdensome now than ever before (p. 76). P. J. D. Wiles in "Notes on the Efficiency of Labour" (*Oxford Economic Papers,* June 1951, pp. 158–180), has concluded, largely on the basis of qualitative material, that the pace of work is much less arduous in England now than it was a generation or two ago.

[42] Sumner Slichter stresses this factor, perhaps unduly in view of its lack of quantitative re-enforcement (*op. cit.,* p. 157).

aged 45 and older to all men in the chief occupations allied to these industries. There was some growth in the ratio of elderly workers to all workers, and some labor-saving in all industries, but these changes were in no way associated. Moreover, the outflow of elderly workers was smaller in the United States than in Britain and Germany, where there was less industrial progress.

But is there an association between growth in the size of an industry and decline in the proportion of elderly workers? Such a possibility is investigated for major industry groupings for the census dates 1910–1940 (Table 32). Do industries increasing most rapidly in number of

TABLE 32

Change in Ratio of Male Workers 45 and Older to All Male Workers, and Percentage Growth in Number Gainfully Occupied, Various Industries, United States, 1910–1940

	Percentage Change in Gainfully Occupied		Percentage Change in Ratio of Male Workers 45 and Older to All Male Workers	
	1910–1930	1910–1940	1910–1930	1910–1940
Public service	+129	+294	−7	−7
Trade	+108	+193	+10	+32
Professional services	+105	+133	+25	+23
Transportation	+68	+27	+38	+80
Manufacturing	+50	+46	+31	+38
Domestic and personal services	+28	+16	+23	+47
Mining	+20	+8	+53	+68
Construction	−8	−1	+25	+30
Agriculture	−15	−30	+30	+36
Entire labor force	+35	+46	+23	+34

Source: *Census of Population: 1930*, Vol. IV, *Occupations by States*, Tables 21, 22; *1940*, Vol. III, *The Labor Force*, Part I, pp. 197–198, and Alba M. Edwards, *Comparative Occupation Statistics for the United States, 1870 to 1940*, Table 14.

workers tend to manifest the slowest rise, or a decline, in the proportion of older men? Some such tendency is, of course, to be expected since rapid expansion would ordinarily occur by accession of new and young workers. Nevertheless, if a tendency was present, it was too feeble to indicate that rapid growth squeezes out older people, or that slow growth leaves an industry with a residue of aging workers. The proportion of older employees in manufacturing, in which employment rose by about half between 1910 and 1930, increased at about the same rate as that in agriculture, which reduced its work force, or in professional service, which doubled its work force.

Have older workers been replaced because industries employing them were supplanted by those employing younger people? Standardizing the ratio of elderly workers to workers of all ages in each industry

172

in 1940, according to the industrial composition of the labor force in 1910, raises the over-all ratio of older men less than 1 per cent. Inter-industry movements have affected the proportion of older workers negligibly, not because these movements were small—they occurred on a grand scale—but because the industries that grew in number of employees, notably trade and government, employed just as high proportions of older workers as those that diminished in work force, notably agriculture.

Unemployment

The three censuses of 1930–1950 revealed the following. The reduction in the proportion of older men in the labor force was closely connected with both the level, and the change of unemployment (Table 33). And the older the men, the closer was the connection. Among

TABLE 33

Outflow of Men from Labor Force, Level of Unemployment, and Change in Unemployment, 3 Age Groups, United States, 1930–1940, and 1930–1950

	1930–1940			1930–1950		
	55–64	45–54	35–44	55–64	45–54	35–44
Change in labor force per 1,000 of same age:						
Number per 1,000	−64	−44	−29	−73	−48	−34
Rank of age group	1	2	3	1	2	3
Average level of unemployment						
Per cent of labor force of same age	11.4	10.1	9.0	6.2	5.4	5.1
Rank of age group	1	2	3	1	2	3
Change in unemployment						
Per cent of labor force of same age	+8.1	+6.1	+5.2	−2.2	−3.2	−2.7
Rank of age group	1	2	3	1 [a]	3 [a]	2 [a]

Source: Appendixes A and C.

[a] Ranks for decreases in unemployment are inverted, in order to bring out the fact that the smallest decline in unemployment during 1930–1950 is the converse of the greatest increase and has the same effect of discouraging older men from staying in the labor force.

men of three age groups, 35–44, 45–54, and 55–64, unemployment was the least for those 35–44 in 1930, 1940, and 1950 and showed the smallest increase from 1930 to 1940 and from 1930 to 1950; and this age classification had the smallest decline in labor force participation over the 20-year period from 1930 to 1950. Men 45–54 showed a higher unemployment level for all three census dates, a sharper rise in the rate of unemployment between 1930 and 1940, and a steeper drop in labor force participation. And the third group—men 55–64—suffered the

173

most unemployment between 1930 and 1940, the greatest reduction in activity in the labor force in both of the two periods between 1930 and 1940, and 1930 and 1950. Men aged 65 or over withdrew from the labor force more slowly during times when unemployment was low, as in the 1920's and the 1940's, and faster when it was very severe. When unemployment of all persons rose from 6 per cent of the whole labor force in 1930 to 15 per cent in 1940, the ratio of elderly male workers to all male workers in the United States fell (although in view of the aging of the population it should have expanded).

There also seemed to be a clear association between reduction in the labor force of elderly males and unemployment of all males [43] among different industries (Table 34). Where unemployment of workers of all ages was extensive, as in construction, amusement, and mining, the proportion of elderly employees dropped sharply; where unemployment was on a minor scale, as in professional service, agriculture, finance, insurance, and real estate, there was only a small reduction, or even an increase, in the proportion of elderly workers.[44] All these findings are consistent with the possibility that elderly men left the labor force because they were discouraged by the lack of jobs.

Nevertheless, unemployment does not offer a complete explanation for the decline. "Full employment" conditions prevailed in Great Britain and Canada in 1951, in New Zealand in 1951, and in Germany in 1939. Employment in the United States in 1950, though not full, was not appreciably lower than in 1930. Yet participation of men aged 65 and older has in recent years been far below that in earlier years, even those of considerable unemployment, such as 1921 or 1931 in Britain and Canada, or 1936 in New Zealand. No doubt depressed conditions are responsible for a temporary exodus of the older worker. But for the powerful long-run forces responsible for their permanent withdrawal we must look elsewhere.

Education

Although at a given time the labor force participation of men in the primary working ages does not seem influenced by earnings, Chart 18 reveals that it has varied with the amount of education completed. This was true in both 1940 and 1950—years for which data by age,

[43] A. J. Jaffe and Charles D. Stewart found a tendency for major occupational groups with high unemployment rates to have high retirement rates for the year 1940 (*Manpower Resources and Utilization,* Wiley, 1951, pp. 231–232).

[44] Government, which had next to the least unemployment, was an apparent exception, in that it had the sharpest relative drop in the ratio of elderly to all employees. This drop occurred, not because of any net exodus of elderly persons, but because the expansion of government service during the 1930's naturally resulted in the hiring of more younger than older workers.

TABLE 34

Outflow of Men 65 and Older from Labor Force and Unemployment of All Males, by Industry, United States, 1930–1940

	Males Over 65 as Per Cent of All Males in Industry 1930 (1)	Males Over 65 as Per Cent of All Males in Industry 1940 (2)	Outflow (Col. 1 −Col. 2) (3)	Ratio of Outflow (Col. 3 ÷ Col. 1) (4)	Per Cent of Male Labor Force Unemployed 1930 (5)	Per Cent of Male Labor Force Unemployed 1940 (6)	Average Per Cent of Male Labor Force Unemployed, 1930–1940 (7)
Government	5.6	3.6	2.0	.36	2.4	3.0	2.7
"Not reported"	6.8	4.7	2.1	.31	25.6	51.4	38.5
Construction	5.3	4.4	0.9	.17	15.5	25.8	20.7
Amusement and recreation	3.2	2.7	0.5	.16	7.3	14.1	10.7
Manufacturing	3.3	2.8	0.5	.15	6.6	7.8	7.2
Mining	2.6	2.3	0.3	.12	7.8	12.6	10.2
Trade, wholesale and retail	4.1	3.7	0.4	.10	3.7	7.2	5.5
Transportation, communication, public utilities	3.0	2.8	0.2	.07	5.0	7.1	6.1
Professional and related services	7.3	7.1	0.2	.03	1.4	3.0	2.2
Agriculture, forestry and fishing	8.0	8.3	−0.3	−.04	1.3	4.4	2.9
Personal service	4.4	5.4	−1.0	−.23	5.3	8.5	6.9
Finance, insurance, real estate	5.6	6.9	−1.3	−.23	2.1	4.9	3.5

Coefficients of rank correlation $P_r = 1 - \left(\dfrac{6 \Sigma d^2}{n^3 - n} \right)$

					(5)	(6)	(7)
Including government					0.57	0.35	0.45
Excluding government					0.80	0.75	0.81

Confidence limits (Z test)

						(5)	(6)	(7)
Including government						insignificant		
Excluding government {	Upper					0.945	0.932	0.949
	Lower					0.376	0.282	0.406

Source: Censuses of the United States: 1930, Unemployment, Vol. I, Tables 9 and 10, and Population, Vol. IV, Occupations, by States, Table 21; 1940, Population, Vol. III, The Labor Force, Part I, Tables 78 and 80.

CHART 18

Labor Force of White and Colored Men and Years of Schooling:
by Age Group, United States, for Urban and Rural Areas,
1940, and All Areas, 1950

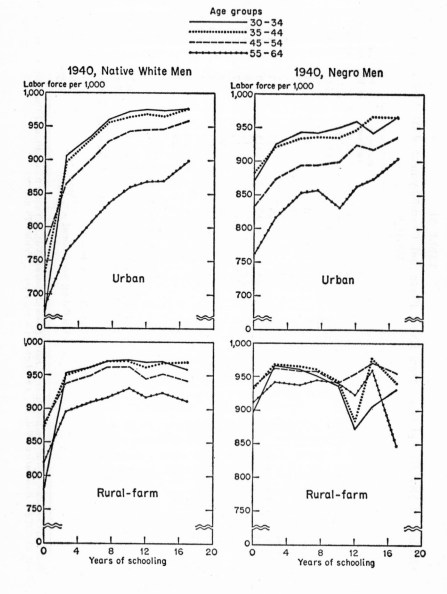

Age groups
———————— 30-34
•••••••••••••••• 35-44
——————— 45-54
•—•—•—•—• 55-64

CHART 18, concluded

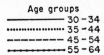

Age groups
——————— 30-34
•••••••••••••••••• 35-44
— — — — — — 45-54
•─•─•─•─•─• 55-64

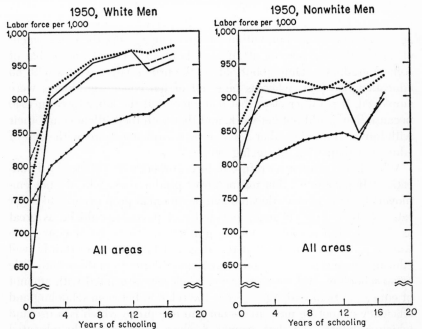

1950, White Men

Labor force per 1,000

1950, Nonwhite Men

Labor force per 1,000

All areas

All areas

Years of schooling

Years of schooling

Education data are for years of school completed—0, 1–4, 5–7, 8, 9–11, 12, 13–15, 16 and over—plotted at midpoint for the grouped years, except 16 and over.

Source: *Census of Population: 1940, Educational Attainment by Economic Characteristics and Marital Status,* pp. 76–85; *1950: Education,* PE No. 5D, pp. 73–76.

color, residence, and schooling have been made available.[45] The association with education was not so pronounced as that for women (Chapter 6), but it did show unmistakably that the fewer years of formal education a man had below a certain point, the less likely he was to be in the labor market. Among males in rural-farm areas the association was not strong; there it was significant only for those with no schooling at all. It was also weaker among Negroes; for those in rural-farm areas who had a high school education, the rate of participation in the labor force tended to be lower than for those with either more or less schooling.[46] The association was strongest among native whites in urban areas, where men with less than eighth grade attainment were in the labor force in much smaller proportions, the fewer

[45] The analysis begins with men aged 30 to 34, since many men under 30 are still in school, and therefore less likely to be in the labor force.
[46] There was a strong association for farm Negroes who were college graduates, but there must have been too few of these to indicate a genuine tendency.

177

years of school they had completed. For men 55–64 the reduction was extra sharp if they had not reached the college graduate level; indeed, their participation seemed to be more adversely affected by lack of education than by advancing age.

This same relationship was also reflected in actual employment. Within any given group of the same amount of education, the employment of men aged 55–64 was about 10 per cent under that of men aged 30–34 or 35–44; but, within any given age group, the employment of men with no schooling at all was about 40 per cent under that of college graduates. Only about half of the urban native whites with no education had jobs, whereas nine out of ten college graduates were employed. It is rather clear that many men left the labor force in 1940 because they could not get work, and that both their idleness and their withdrawal from the labor force were correlated more with lack of education than with advancing age.

Why should employers refuse to hire workers with substandard education? If poor education means lower productivity, why do not employers hire the poorly educated and pay them at proportionately lower rates, so that their efficiency per dollar of payroll would be as great as that of high school or college graduates? There is, of course, no way to prove empirically that this does not take place. Certainly well educated men command higher wages and salaries than those with little or no schooling, and earnings are more closely associated with amount of education than with age.[47] Since the relation between schooling and efficiency cannot be measured—nor can one prove which is cause and which is effect—the data cannot disclose whether poorly educated workers are underpaid or overpaid in relation to their output.

But in a land where elementary and high school education is almost free in urban areas, illiteracy or a negligible amount of schooling often reflects, at least for native whites, a lack of intelligence and of emotional stability.[48] And it is easy to understand why employers would be reluctant to hire very inefficient workers even at proportionate remuneration.

Moreover, any thoroughgoing attempt to pay the inefficient in strict proportion to their worth would violate minimum-wage laws and outrage the public. An employer will therefore normally find it more humane or less embarrassing to abstain from hiring substandard workers.[49] These people eventually become discouraged and cease to participate.

[47] *Census of Population, 1940, Educational Attainment by Economic Characteristics and Marital Status,* pp. 147 ff.

[48] Thus mental or physical defects, which happen to be correlated with lack of education, may bar many uneducated men from jobs, without employers being aware of, or immediately concerned with the lack-of-schooling factor.

[49] It must be emphasized that the concept of "substandard" used here is entirely

The effects would, of course, vary according to occupation and worker classifications. Agricultural workers could manage to stay in the labor force until a later age because the farm wage scale is flexible and many farm jobs involve little skill, liability, or supervision. So also might Negroes—even in urban areas—because they have been, for the most part, in unskilled occupations and, in the past, in low-wage jobs.

Over time, the amount of formal education possessed by elderly men has been rising more slowly than that of men and women below middle age: equivalent full-time years of education completed by men 65 and older has fallen from almost four-fifths of that completed by the young at the turn of the century, to about two-fifths in 1950. The elderly male has indeed fallen far behind in the ability to compete in the labor market if formal schooling is any index.

This was true when the comparison was made not only with women 20–24, but also with women 25–44. And in both cases the ratio of labor force participation of men 65 and older to that of younger women fell accordingly (Chart 19). In fact, there was some sympathy of detailed movement. The ratios of both education and labor force participation of elderly men to education and participation of women 20–24 fell a bit less rapidly during 1910–1930 than in the decades just preceding and following. Their brief opposite movement during 1940–1950 can be explained on the ground that the 1930's had an especially depressing effect on the labor force of older men, and need not rule out a long-run association. The two sets of ratios moved very similarly in the case of men 45–64 and women 20–24 during 1900–1940, if not in the decades just before and after. The detailed movements were not very close in the ratios of men 65 and older to women 25–44, and over the whole period the labor force ratio fell much more than the ratio of education. The education and labor force of men 65 and older and women 45–64 did not move together at all during the period up to 1930; from 1930 on the labor force ratio fell more than the education ratio. Finally, the outflow of elderly persons from the labor force has been just as heavy in countries where mass education has not forged ahead as it has in the United States. Nevertheless there is sufficient similarity of movement between relative educational attainment and relative labor force participation of older men and younger women to leave us with the feeling that inferior education is a factor, even if it is perhaps only one factor, in the labor force displacement of older men by young and middle-aged women.

---

relative to economic conditions. Many persons who would be substandard at times when profits were low and prospects dim would be valued employees in years of prosperity and labor shortage.

CHART 19

Ratios of Male to Female Labor Participation and Ratios of Male to Female Education: for Selected Age Groups, United States, 1890–1950

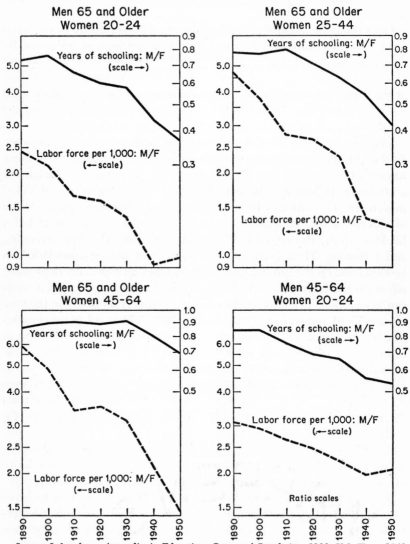

Source: Labor force, Appendix A. Education: *Census of Population, 1920,* Vol. II, p. 1043; *1940,* Vol. IV, Part I, pp. 6–7; *1950, Education,* PE No. 5B, pp. 73–74; *School Attendance in the United States,* Census Monograph V, pp. 49–51, 113–114, Tables 30–31. For method, see Appendix F, the section on Years of Schooling.

CHAPTER 10

THE LABOR FORCE IN SEVERE DEPRESSIONS

"The number of would-be wage earners and the number
of persons employed are in the main independent of one
another."

A. C. PIGOU, *The Theory of Unemployment*

The Additional Worker Theory

THE depression of the 1930's gave rise to the apparently new theory
that unemployment of the main breadwinner would make it necessary
for other members of the family normally engaged in housework, attending school, or retired, to follow the "help wanted" notices, and
would thereby result in additions to both the labor force and unemployment.[1] The "additional worker theory" turned out to have an
opposite version: persons unable to get jobs, or not wanting them in
normal times, are attracted into the labor force during times of ex-
ceptional prosperity by the higher wages and genial personnel interviews.[2] In the first version, an increase in supply comes from a *fall* in
demand; in the second, it comes from a *rise* in demand. The two ver-
sions seem to contradict each other, but some economists subscribe
to both. Woytinsky, for example, has suggested that both depression
and boom may bring about greater participation than "balanced prosperity." [3] Obviously, different people may react variously to depressions
but what is the net behavior? Can either of these theories find support
in actual experience?

[1] Several articles cover an early controversy on this subject between W. S.
Woytinsky and D. D. Humphrey; and some later studies by the author oppose the
theory. The Woytinsky view seems to have become the general opinion, but the
author believes that the statistics of the past and the events of the future will
demonstrate it to be wrong. See Humphrey, "Alleged 'Additional Workers' in the
Measurement of Unemployment," *Journal of Political Economy*, June 1940, pp.
412–419; Woytinsky, *Additional Workers and the Volume of Unemployment in
the Depression*, Social Science Research Council, Pamphlet Series 1, 1940, pp. 1,
17, 26, and "Additional Workers on the Labor Market in Depressions: A Reply to
Mr. Humphrey," *Journal of Political Economy*, October 1940, pp. 735–740; Clarence D. Long, "The Concept of Unemployment," *Quarterly Journal of Economics*,
November 1942, pp. 9–10, and *The Labor Force in Wartime America*, National
Bureau of Economic Research, Occasional Paper 14, 1944, pp. 24–26.

[2] J. H. G. Pierson, *Full Employment*, Yale University Press, 1941, pp. 18–19,
note 22: "For it is probable that if society were committed to providing job
opportunity for all those able and wanting to work, however numerous, certain
fresh supplies of labor not apparent at present would shortly be uncovered. . . ."

[3] W. S. Woytinsky and Associates, *Employment and Wages in the United States*,
Twentieth Century Fund, 1953, pp. 322–323, and a verbal discussion at the Decem-
ber 1952 joint meetings of the American Economic Association and the Industrial
Relations Research Association.

Surveys of the Labor Force during Depression

If a depression is "severe" when at least 10 per cent of the labor force is unemployed, six enumerations in the United States, and several in foreign countries, have measured the effect of severe depressions on labor force participation. The enumerations in the United States have included the *Enumerative Check Census* in late 1937, the decennial census in 1940, and state censuses by Massachusetts and Pennsylvania in 1934, Michigan in 1935, and Rhode Island in 1936. Those in foreign lands were made by Canada and Great Britain in 1931 (also in 1921), and by Germany in 1933. In all cases information on unemployment was obtained either from the censuses or from sources such as unemployment insurance.

The United States check census was taken as of late November 1937, almost at the bottom of the sharp recession that had started in the summer of that year. Designed partly as an audit of a voluntary postcard registration of employment taken earlier and partly as a sample enumeration that covered over a half million households on 50 of the more than 90,000 postal routes,[4] it resembled the 1940 census in concept, except that the enumerative check omitted unpaid family workers and jobholders temporarily absent the entire week of the survey because of sickness, strikes, or vacations.

The results seemingly upheld the theory that a depression causes the labor force to expand temporarily. The recession of late 1937 was very severe, for approximately 1 in 5 persons was out of work; and, in accordance with the theory, labor force participation appeared to be appreciably above that of 1930. In proportion to population aged 15–74, standardized for age-sex and rural-urban composition, the labor force rose to 58.0 per cent, a level that exceeded the 56.7 per cent in 1930, and the 55.3 per cent in 1940. The extra participants were mainly females. For every age group except 65–74 and for all females 15–74, female participation rose from 25.3 per cent in April 1930 to 29.8 per cent in November 1937, falling thereafter to 27.2 per cent in 1940. The conclusion was that the number of females employed or seeking jobs was nearly 3 million above "normal" (assuming 1930 to be normal). If, however, normal is computed by interpolating the participation between 1930 and 1940, and if labor force participation is standardized for age-sex and rural-urban composition, the excess in 1937 was about 1½ million females and ⅔ million males—somewhat more than 2 million altogether.

---

[4] It did not attempt to touch those places not having postal service. These included some but not all towns and villages of less than 2,500 population in 1930, undeveloped city suburbs, and remote rural areas—about 18 per cent of the nation's population.

182

It cannot be argued that the difference was due to the fact that the check census used an unusually comprehensive concept of labor force; in fact, the concept was rather restrictive. Nor can the difference be attributed to timing (November instead of April), for, judged by the seasonal pattern during 1946 to 1948, the labor force participation is usually about the same in these two months. The 1937 enumeration check has been criticized because it omitted certain rural places which did not enjoy postal service. But the urban estimates seem to reveal no fewer additional workers than the national ones. Conceivably the difference could be due to the fact that special enumerations of unemployment (quite aside from their reliance on a sample) may exaggerate unemployment, either by giving it disproportionate attention or by engendering an attitude in both interviewer and respondent that the survey is more successful if it reports a large number of unemployed.

But on the whole, it does not seem possible to explain the higher than normal participation by analysis and it is fortunate that we can look elsewhere for statistical light on this question.

THE FOUR STATE CENSUSES OF 1934–1936.

The Massachusetts census of January 1934, like the federal census of 1940, covered all persons 14 and older who were employed, and those who were able to work and seeking jobs, including first-job seekers and sick persons if the latter expected to resume the search for work after recovery. Excluded were housewives and students as such, inmates of institutions, invalids, and aged and retired persons not seeking jobs.

The Pennsylvania census [5] of February–April 1934, which covered 2 million households by interview, resembled the United States 1940 census except that it undertook to omit any persons who sought a job solely because the primary wage earner was involuntarily idle (though this is a highly subjective matter). The defect to be noted in this state's census was that the population was not counted and had to be interpolated. Consequently, there was no really firm foundation for computing labor force participation.

The Michigan Census of January 1935 used a concept similar to that of the 1940 United States census, and the Rhode Island enumeration of 1936 used the gainful worker concept of the 1930 United States census. The latter tabulated the inexperienced unemployed separately and included them as gainful workers. In other respects the Rhode Island census resembled those of the three other states.

---

[5] In addition to excluding farmers, this census omitted isolated residences. Unlike the 1930 and 1940 United States censuses, it excluded unpaid family workers, an omission of no moment, however, because it did not cover farms, where most of these workers are found.

None of the state enumerations was completely reliable. (The interviewers were largely inexperienced persons who were on relief.) They differed slightly in definition from each other and from the United States censuses in 1930, 1940, and 1950, with which they must be compared. And they were made for the most part in winter, when the labor force tends to be seasonally depressed,[6] while the federal censuses were taken in mid-spring, when labor force participation is usually higher.[7] The maximum seasonal difference between January and April, as reflected by the average pattern for 1946–1948 was about 8 workers per 1,000 population 14 and older—equal to the differences in participation between the regular national censuses in these four states in 1930 and 1940, and the 1934–1936 state surveys. However, the seasonal variation may have been smaller than in the nation as a whole, since agriculture doubtless had less influence in these industrial states.

In any case the four state comparisons do not corroborate the check census of 1937 (Table 35). The 1934–1936 labor force participation of both sexes combined was below the average of 1930 and 1940 by 3 to 10 persons per 1,000 population 14 and older, or by 5 to 28 persons per 100 unemployed adult males. If large-scale idleness had any effect, that effect was apparently to move more persons out of the labor force than into it.

But what has been the effect of depression on male and female participation considered separately? The measurement is complicated by the tendency of males to reduce their labor force participation from one high-employment period to the next and of females to increase theirs, so that the depression participation must be compared with the average at the preceding and subsequent censuses, when employment was higher. In three of the four states there was a smaller female participation during the depression than during 1930, 1940,[8] or 1950, the exception being Pennsylvania (which, paradoxically, tried to exclude additional workers from the concept). Yet the male participation in

[6] The year 1940 is also far from satisfactory as a recovery date; unemployment, though much lower than in 1934–1936, was still at record levels for any regular United States census.

[7] The practice of enumerating the United States population and labor force in April began in 1910. From 1840 to 1900 the census was taken as of June; in 1920, as of January; and in 1930, 1940, and 1950, as of April.

[8] By arbitrarily assuming that full-time housewives and students would not be seeking work, the Massachusetts survey may have excluded them from the possibility of being classed in the labor force. The explanation is rather obscure on this point. Before the new procedure was adopted by the census in July 1945, all labor force surveys may have omitted many housewives and students who were working part time or seeking gainful employment, because the enumerator may have assumed that his subject was a student or a housewife, and he may therefore have failed to press questions which might have revealed cases of job-hunting or part-time work.

184

TABLE 35

Number of Persons by Which the Labor Force of the Depression Years 1934–1936 Differed from That of the April 1930 and 1940 Average in Relation to Population and Unemployment, by Sex and Age Group, Four States

	Per 1,000 Population of Same Sex and Age				Per 100 Unemployed Men 25–64			
	Mass.,[a] 1934	Pa., 1934	Mich., 1935	R.I., 1936	Mass.,[a] 1934	Pa., 1934	Mich., 1935	R.I., 1936
Both sexes 15 and older	−8	−5	−3	−10	−8	−8	−5	−28
Males 15 and older [b]	+1	−28	+1	+2	+1	−42	+2	+6
15–24	−20	−13	−46	+5	−19	−20	−81	+14
25–44	+4	−58	+4	−22	+4	−88	+7	−61
45–64	+8	−18	+25	+16	+8	−27	+44	+44
65 and older	+19	+71	+40	+41	+18	+108	+70	+114
Females 15 and older [b]	−16	+16	−7	−20	−15	+24	−12	−56
15–24	−10	+58	−24	−17	−10	+88	−42	−47
25–44	−15	+2	−12	−9	−14	+3	−21	−25
45–64	−36	−8	+8	−25	−35	−12	+14	−69
65 and older	+17	+36	+34	−41	+16	+55	+60	−114

Source: Appendix F. Censuses of the United States: *1930, Unemployment*, Vol. I, pp. 455, 499, 837, 881, and *Population*, Vol. III, Part 1, pp. 1111, 1123, Vol. IV, pp. 797, 800, 802, 819, 1455; *1940, Population*, Vol. III, *The Labor Force*, Part 3, pp. 453, 588, Part 5, p. 14, Vol. IV, Part 3, pp. 191, 238–239, Part 4, p. 338. *1934 Report on the Census of Unemployment in Massachusetts*, Massachusetts Labor Bulletin No. 171, pp. 5–8. *Census of Employable Workers in Urban and Rural Non-Farm Areas, Pennsylvania, 1934*, State Emergency Relief Administration, Division of Research and Statistics, 1936, p. 1. *Michigan Census of Population and Unemployment*, First Series, No. 1, 1935, pp. 3, 4, 9. *Rhode Island Decennial Population Census of 1936: Story of the 680, 712*, Rhode Island Department of Labor, 1937, pp. 10, 23, 26.

[a] 14 and older.
[b] Standardized according to sex and age composition of the population of the United States in 1930.

Pennsylvania declined so much that the combined participation decreased. Participation of males 14 and older was slightly above the average in the other three states but by too slim a margin to be significant.

In view of the economic or industrial differences among these states, and of the fact that the censuses were conducted independently of each other, the general movements of participation among persons of the same sex and age are reasonably alike (Table 35). In three of the four states, the participation of young males under 25 was substantially below the average of 1930 and 1940, and the same may be said for females below 45, though not in the same three states. In two states men 25 to 44 were considerably below the 1930–40 average in their participation and in the other two slightly above it. For the most part, the participation of men 45 and older tended to be much above the average of 1930 and 1940, but only because the 1940 participation was very low—indicating that the main exodus of older workers may have occurred after the worst years of the deep depression.

Official censuses were taken in three foreign countries during the severe depression of the 1930's.[9] Great Britain and Canada suffered widespread joblessness in 1931 (and in 1921) when the participation rates of both countries were lower than in years when unemployment was low or moderate, namely 1911, 1939, and 1951 (Table 36). As in the United States, the trend of participation was downward for males and upward for females between periods of high employment. In depression the participation rates of males were above the trend but those of females were below—enough so to more than offset the tendency of males and to pull the combined participation rate down below the trend. In Germany it was the opposite. Female participation in the depression year 1933 was above the average of 1925 and 1939 and male participation was below trend, with the latter low enough to pull the combined participation of both sexes down below the trend. Support of the theory that there is a net number of additional workers is thus found wanting in all three foreign countries.

Among the various age and sex groups, there was no great uniformity of behavior (Table 36). Some "inflow" occurred among males, especially older men and some "outflow" among females (as in the four states). In every age-sex group, one of the three nations invariably moved in a direction away from the other two in its labor force tendencies.

Labor Force Behavior Revealed by the Regular United States Census of 1940, a Year of Partial Recovery in a Severe Depression

No regular censuses of the deepest depression dates in the United States have ever been taken, but the unemployment reported in the census at the time of the partial recovery of April 1940 was several times that in the high-employment census of 1930 or that in the 1950 census (Table 37).

The case for the additional worker theory in the United States as a whole in 1940 is even weaker than the ones already cited. Participation was well below the average of 1930 and 1950, for both sexes combined, for males and females separately and for every age-sex group except women 25–44. The deficit in participation of both sexes combined was 13 per 1,000 population 14 and older and 19 per 100 unem-

[9] New Zealand conducted one in 1936 revealing an idleness of 7 per cent, which was too low to be called severe in this study.

TABLE 36

Number of Persons by Which the Labor Force Average of the Depression Census Dates Differed from the Average of the Preceding and Subsequent Moderately High-Employment Census Dates, in Relation to Population and Unemployment, by Sex and Age Group, 3 Foreign Countries

	Per 1,000 Population of Same Sex and Age			Per 100 Unemployed Males 14 and Older		
	Great Britain, 1911–1921, 1931–1951 [a]	Canada, 1911–1921, 1931–1951 [a]	Germany, 1925–1933, 1933–1950 [b]	Great Britain, 1911–1921, 1931–1951 [a]	Canada, 1911–1921, 1931–1951 [a]	Germany, 1925–1933, 1933–1950 [b]
Both sexes 14 and older	−3	−4	−4	−3	−5	−3
Males 14 and older	+14	+13	−19	+14	+18	−13
14–24	+30	−19	+30	+30	−26	+20
25–44	−4	+5	+3	−4	+7	+2
45–64	−2	+9	−56	−2	+12	−37
65 and older	+90	+118	−70	+90	+162	−46
Females 14 and older	−19	−21	+13	−19	−29	+9
14–24	+17	−24	+10	+17	−33	+7
25–44	−28	−21	+30	−28	−29	+20
45–64	−51	−32	+1	−5	−44	+1
65 and older	+7	+11	−4	+7	+15	−3

Source: Appendixes A, C, and F.

[a] The depression labor force was the average of 1921 and 1931; the high-employment labor force was the average of 1911 and 1951.

[b] The depression labor force was for 1933; the high-employment labor force was the average of 1925 and 1950.

TABLE 37

Number of Persons by Which the Labor Force during the Severe
Unemployment of April 1940 Differed from the Average of the
Moderately High-Employment Census Dates April 1930 and
1950, in Relation to Population and Unemployment by Sex
and Age Group, United States and Its Urban and
Rural Areas

| | Per 1,000 Population of Same Sex and Age | | | Per 100 Unemployed Men 25–64 |
	United States [a]	Urban Areas [b]	Rural Areas [b]	United States [a]
Both sexes 14 and older	−13	−9	−23	−19
Males 14 and older	−22	−18	−26	−32
14–24	−30	−35	−35	−43
25–44	−2	+3	−10	−3
45–64	−22	−24	−19	−32
65 and older	−85	−101	−68	−123
Females 14 and older	−7	+1	−19	−10
14–24	−5	−4	−11	−7
25–44	+14	+28	−11	+20
45–64	−35	−34	−39	−51
65 and older	−18	−18	−105	−26

Source: Appendixes A, C, F, and Supplementary Appendix H. Censuses of the
United States: 1930, Unemployment, Vol. II, p. 250; *1940, Population,* Vol. IV,
Part I, pp. 90–93; *1950, Preliminary Reports,* PC-7, No. 2, pp. 21–23.

[a] Labor force was standardized according to the rural-urban composition of population of the United States in 1940; totals were standardized for age or age-sex.
[b] Labor force was standardized for age or age-sex, according to the composition of population of the United States in 1940.

ployed men 25–64. And the younger and older males and older females
showed very large deficits. Older men who lost their jobs apparently
failed to seek new ones, for the deficit in their participation in 1940
below the average of 1930 and 1950 was enormous in relation to the
excess in their unemployment above the average of 1930 and 1950.

Some students of labor force behavior have speculated that many
urban workers tend to lose heart during a depression and return to the
farms of parents or other relatives in order to find food and shelter
or stopgap work. It has been proposed that this "return" (actually,
most of it was a reduction in migration to cities) accounted for the lack
of additional urban workers [10] and constituted disguised rural unemployment. However, if there was such a "return" it did not result in
an increased participation in rural areas. The 1940 labor force par-

[10] Conference on Research in Income and Wealth, New York, November 1946,
Verbal comments of W. S. Woytinsky.

188

TABLE 38

Number of Persons by Which the Labor Force of the Colored and Whites during the Severe Unemployment of April 1940 Differed from the Average of the Moderately High-Employment Census Dates April 1930 and 1950, in Relation to Population and Unemployment, by Sex and Age Group, United States

| | Per 1,000 Population of Same Sex, Age, and Color | | Per 100 Unemployed Men 25–64 | |
	White	Colored	White	Colored
Both sexes 14 and older	−18	−9	−28	−10
Males 14 and older [a]	−28	+2	−43	+2
14–24	−35	−21	−54	−23
25–44	−9	+14	−14	+16
45–64	−26	−23	−40	−26
65 and older	−88	−82	−135	−91
Females 14 and older [a]	−9	−23	−14	−26
14–24	−10	−9	−15	−10
25–44	+10	−24	+15	−27
45–64	−36	−53	−55	−59
65 and older	−17	−53	−26	−59

Source: Appendixes A, C, F, and Supplementary Appendix H. Censuses of the United States: *1930, Unemployment*, Vol. II, pp. 250–251; *1940, Population*, Vol. III, *The Labor Force*, Part I, p. 90; *1950, Preliminary Reports*, PC-7, No. 2, p. 21.

[a] Standardized according to the age-sex composition of population of the United States in 1940.

ticipation was below the 1930 and 1950 average in both rural and urban areas, but it was relatively much more so in the former—perhaps because the depression had a greater impact on agriculture than on urban occupations, which benefited from the expansion of service industries. In the cities some inflow of females occurred, but it was overshadowed by the outflow of males. There was additional participation among men and women 25–44 in urban areas, but withdrawals were manifest in every rural group, without exception.

Among whites the 1940 participation was lower than the average of 1930 and 1950 in every age-sex category except women 25–44 (Table 38). For colored females it was depressed more than for white females. But the deficiency in the 1940 participation of the colored of both sexes combined, with respect to the 1930 and 1950 average, was only half that of whites although participation fell enormously between 1930 and 1940. The reason was that participation of Negroes decreased also from 1940 to 1950 thus lowering the average participation for 1930 and 1950, so that when compared with this lowered average, it yielded a smaller deficit (or in the case of males even an excess), compared to

189

the whites. With respect to unemployment, the deficiency in the 1940 participation of the colored was also much below that of the whites.

There is further evidence in the forty-eight states examined separately, that the deficiency in participation for 1940, compared to the average for 1930 and 1950, was not an accident of statistical aggregation. Every state manifested a deficit for males and for both sexes combined; and only seven scattered states showed additions—all small or negligible—for females. The deficit for both sexes ranged from 3 per 1,000 population 14 and older, or 9 per 100 unemployed in Delaware, to 49 per 1,000 population 14 and older, or 152 per 100 unemployed in Nevada (Table 39). There is no information by states on the rural and urban labor force in 1930, but in only eighteen states was urban participation higher in 1940 than in 1950 and in only thirteen was rural participation higher. The median deficit for the forty-eight states was 24 males per 1,000 male population and approximately 15 females per 1,000 female population, or 42 males and 88 females, respectively, per 100 unemployed. For both sexes combined the median deficit of 1940 participation below the average of 1930 and 1950 was 19 per 1,000 population and about 43 per 100 unemployed.

UNITED STATES CITIES, 1930, 1940, AND 1950.

The materials permit further study of the same 38 large cities used in intercity correlations in Chapter 4. Comparison was made within each city between the labor force groups 14–19, men 65 and older, and wives (all these groups being generally in a dependent status) and changes in the unemployment of men 25–44, the primary earning group.

The investigation indicated that among males, only for men 65 and older was there a significant correlation (and very slight, at that) between labor force participation and unemployment of males 25–44 for both 1930–1940 and 1940–1950. And only wives 35–44 in 1940–1950 had a correlation on the 95 per cent level (with unemployed men 25–44). Most of the labor force groups bore no significant correlation on any level with unemployment, although the fact that all the correlations were positive cannot be entirely ignored as a consideration supporting the additional worker theory.

It would also be interesting to compare changes in participation of these groups with changes in their own employment or unemployment. Unfortunately, such comparisons would present difficulties. An attempt to correlate with *unemployment* would be fruitless if the labor force fell in the same degree as employment, for unemployment could not change if people were abandoning the labor force as fast as they lost their jobs. And the correlation with *employment* is apt to be high simply because employment is so large a part of the labor force. Moreover, a high correlation would not necessarily mean that job conditions

TABLE 39

Number of Persons by Which the Labor Force 14 and Older during
the Severe Unemployment of April 1940 Differed from the Average
of the Moderately High-Employment Census Dates April 1930
and 1950, in Relation to Population and Unemployment,
by Sex, the 48 States, Their Urban and Rural Areas,
and 38 Large Cities

	Per 1,000 Population of Same Sex and Age				Per 100 Unemployed of Same Sex	
	States	Urban Areas [a]	Rural Areas [a]	Large Cities	States	Large Cities
Both sexes						
Number of places with additions	0	18	13	6	0	6
Number of places with deficits	48	30	35	32	48	32
Least deficit (or greatest addition)	−3	+26	+38	+14	−9	+43
Greatest deficit	−49	−58	−46	−46	−152	−219
Median deficit	−19	−9.5	−14	−15	−42.5	−35
Interquartile range	−15.5	−29.5	−28.5	−19	−33	−46
Males						
Number of places with additions	0			3	0	2
Number of places with deficits	48			35	48	36
Least deficit (or greatest addition)	−4			+13	−2	+289
Greatest deficit	−53			−51	−95	−208
Median deficit	−24			−23	−42	−47
Interquartile range	−12.5			−15	−30	−64
Females						
Number of places with additions	7			11	6	11
Number of places with deficits	41			27	42	27
Least deficit (or greatest addition)	+11			+30	+108	+181
Greatest deficit	−56			−32	−1867	−229
Median deficit	−14.5			−5.5	−88	−15
Interquartile range	−20			−23	−131.5	−81

Source: *Census of Unemployment, 1930*, Vol. I, Table XII–8, pp. 18–22. *Census of Population: 1930*, Vol. IV, pp. 66–67, 83; *1940*, Vol. III, *The Labor Force*, Parts 2–5; *1950*, Vol. II, *Characteristics of the Population*, Part I.

[a] Data on rural and urban areas were lacking for 1930. Deficits here were computed as the difference between 1940 and 1950. Since the trend is upward for females and downward for males, such deficits would be meaningless and are, accordingly, computed only for both sexes combined.

were influencing participation, i.e. youths and older men have evinced a long-run tendency to leave the labor force, and it is to be expected that this outward drift would have a depressing effect on their employment.

THE PROPORTION OF WIVES IN THE LABOR FORCE BY
EMPLOYMENT STATUS OF HUSBANDS.

This chapter has so far been confined to relationships over time. Comparisons are now made between wives with jobless husbands and wives with employed husbands in 1940. All wives of all classes, un-standardized, had virtually the same participation whether their husbands were employed or unemployed (Table 40). However, standardized for age, color, child status, and the size of the community in which they resided, wives of unemployed men had higher participation and showed varying tendencies with the age, color, child status, or residence of the wife. At 35 or over, the wife of an unemployed husband seemed somewhat more likely to be in the labor force than the wife of an employed husband, and less likely under that age. White wives of unemployed men were more likely to be in the labor force in greater proportion if they had no children; those with children manifested little reaction to their husband's unemployment. In communities of every size—both urban and rural—nonwhite wives, standardized for age, had a *lower* labor force tendency if their husbands were unemployed—whether or not they had young children. One explanation for this paradox may be that many colored fared better on relief in 1940 than if their breadwinners were employed, and it is supported by the fact that the disparity was somewhat larger in cities and rural nonfarm areas than in rural farm areas—where relief payments may not have been so ample.[11] Among *white* wives, the effect of residence varies. Wives who had unemployed husbands showed greater participation than wives of the employed if they lived in the metropolitan districts, a mixed tendency if they lived in a smaller city, and *less* participation if they lived in small urban places or rural areas (Table 40). The reason for this mixed behavior for white wives may well have been that, for them, the controlling factor was opportunity. Obviously in a large city the wife could seek work in many occupations other than the one in which her husband had been employed. In a rural nonfarm area, her search would often be confined to one or two firms, and the same forces causing her husband's disemployment could discourage her from even looking for a job.

Materials in the same detail in the 1950 census have not yet become available. But summary estimates of the *Current Population Reports* suggest that the patterns were not very different from those in 1940 (Table 41), although the similarity must be discounted by the fact that the data at hand for 1950 are unstandardized for age or, by color, for residence. As in 1940, white wives of the unemployed had a much higher participation than those of employed husbands; and in 1950 colored wives had a noticeably lower participation if their husbands were unemployed than if their husbands were employed.

[11] Married women with husbands not in the labor force, however, were themselves in the labor force to a much greater degree than the wives of either employed or unemployed men. This difference might have significance only if a substantial number of husbands were to drop out of the labor force.

TABLE 40

Number of Wives in the Labor Force per 1,000 Wives of the Same Husband-Employment Status, Child Status, and Residence, United States, April 1940

	Wives with and without Children under 10, Combined [a]				Wives with Children under 10 [c]		Wives without Children under 10 [c]	
	Unstandardized		Standardized [b]					
	Husband:		Husband:		Husband:		Husband:	
	Empl.	Unempl.	Empl.	Unempl.	Empl.	Unempl.	Empl.	Unempl.
WHITE AND NONWHITE COMBINED								
United States	137	136	150	204	73	74	203	208
Met. districts of 100,000 or more	162	173	177	195	72	86	241	271
Urban areas:								
25,000–100,000	192	192	203	199	106	122	265	276
2,500–25,000	180	168	193	181	105	108	247	254
Rural areas:								
Nonfarm	133	83	148	105	81	56	191	144
Farm	54	39	59	55	42	27	85	71
WHITE								
United States	125	118	139	200	62	63	190	292
Met. districts of 100,000 or more	150	158	164	190	66	79	230	263
Urban areas:								
25,000–100,000	171	157	183	184	95	105	241	236
2,500–25,000	161	134	172	162	91	85	227	213
Rural areas								
Nonfarm	123	71	138	94	73	44	182	126
Farm	38	32	50	47	24	21	67	65
NONWHITE								
United States	267	273	274	245	213	162	314	300
Met. districts of 100,000 or more	344	265	319	251	212	138	389	326
Urban areas:								
Nonfarm	455	383	427	370	312	266	504	440
Farm	429	396	419	393	346	328	468	436
Rural areas:								
Nonfarm	250	211	260	221	192	134	304	280
Farm	150	138	153	138	134	119	167	152

Source: *Census of Population, 1940, The Labor Force* (Sample Statistics), *Employment and Family Characteristics of Women*, pp. 164–175.

[a] Having husband present, i.e. reported as a member of the family though temporarily absent (on business trip, vacationing, or visiting) at time of enumeration.

[b] Standardized for age and child status; in the top section, also for color; in the case of the United States, also for residence.

[c] Standardized for age and, in the case of the United States, for residence.

TABLE 41

Number of Wives in the Labor Force per 1,000 Wives of the Same Husband-Employment Status and Residence, United States, March 1950

	Husband Employed	Husband Unemployed
WHITE AND NONWHITE COMBINED [a, b]		
United States	240	312
Urban areas	258	374
Rural areas		
Nonfarm	228	286
Farm	178	88
WHITE		
United States	228	333
Urban areas	. . .	. . .
Rural areas		
Nonfarm	. . .	. . .
Farm	. . .	. . .
NONWHITE		
United States	376	346
Urban areas	. . .	. . .
Rural areas		
Nonfarm	. . .	. . .
Farm	. . .	. . .

Source: *Current Population Reports, The Labor Force,* Bureau of the Census, P-50, No. 29, March 1950, pp. 8–9.

[a] Having husband present, i.e., reported as a member of the household though temporarily absent (on business trip, vacationing, or visiting) at time of enumeration.

[b] Standardized for residence in case of the United States. It was not possible to standardize for age.

The factor of relief could not well explain a second paradox: The participation of Negro wives with unemployed husbands was lower in 1950 (as in 1940) than that of Negro wives with employed husbands. By 1950 earnings had risen everywhere well above the public-assistance allowances. Nor does the answer lie in the fact that colored females reduced their participation between 1940 and 1950 while white females greatly expanded theirs, so that there is a long-run trend toward diverse behavior. It is possible that the difference might disappear if data were available to allow classification of colored women in 1950 by age residence, and child status.

On the whole, there is little or no support for the theory that unemployment drives net additions of workers into the labor force. Heneman made a further test of the theory, using case studies covering 1 per cent of the households in St. Paul, Minnesota, which were interviewed

194

by the University of Minnesota Employment Stabilization Research Institute each month from October 1941 through June 1942. The test could find no secondary unemployment. Heneman concluded that Woytinsky's methods, as far as that period of St. Paul experience was concerned, "were inappropriate and highly inaccurate." [12]

It would, of course, be too much to expect no instances of wives or children being driven into the labor force because the head of the household was unemployed. In households with severely curtailed means, some women might lay aside their aprons and some children their school books to seek jobs that would help meet the payments on the family house or car. But even during a depression there are still many more heads of households employed than unemployed, and many young girls or elderly men might discover that any pay they could earn would barely cover the extra expenses of working or that it would be too meager a reward for their efforts. Such persons might withdraw from the labor force; more so, if the young had access to free education or the elderly to old-age pensions.

There is, of course, considerable traffic into and out of the labor force at all times; statistics on gross movement gathered by the Current Population Surveys for 1948–1952 show that a 4 to 5 per cent withdrawal is replaced by a similar proportion each month—about 2½ per cent of which are males and 10 per cent females. This gross movement remained very much the same during the five years, notwithstanding the recession of 1949–1950. Thus a period of mild recession does not seem to give rise to either net or gross movement in the proportion of population in the labor force (Chapter 11).[13]

Some Questions concerning the Findings of This Investigation

During the years since these findings were reported in preliminary form [14] several scholars have cast doubt on the materials on which the findings rest, or on the conclusions they support.

[12] Herbert Heneman, "Measurement of Secondary Unemployment: An Evaluation of Woytinsky's Methods," *Industrial and Labor Relations Review*, July 1950, p. 567.

[13] For further analysis of gross movement, see the section on *Labor Force Turnover* in Chapter XI. Neither this stability, however, nor the net outflow in depressions revealed in this chapter, precludes the possibility of a rise in gross movement in a time of *severe* unemployment.

[14] "Size of the Labor Force under Changing Income and Employment," mimeographed paper presented to the Conference on Research in Income and Wealth, National Bureau of Economic Research, 1946; "The Labor Force and Economic Change," *Insights into Labor Issues*, edited by R. A. Lester and Joseph Shister, Macmillan, 1948, Chap. 13; "Labor Force, Income and Employment," mimeographed, National Bureau of Economic Research, 1950; "Impact of Effective Demand on the Labor Supply," *The American Economic Review*, May 1953, pp. 458–467; discussion by Theodore Leavitt and the author's reply, same journal, September 1954, pp. 637–647.

Durand and Ducoff have objected to the conceptual comparability of the four state censuses and of the 1940 census of the United States with the high employment enumeration of April 1930.[15] The sole objection to these state censuses is that the questions on labor force which they used differed somewhat from those used by the United States census. None of the critics, however, has made clear just how the questions could have led to an understatement of labor force sufficient in all four cases to convert the additions to, into subtractions from the labor force.

It will be rejoined that the study has been similarly remiss in dismissing the 1937 enumerative check census and its apparent additions after merely pointing out that such a special survey could easily be in error by the amount of the so-called additional workers. It should be kept in mind that, although no single state census need be regarded as more accurate than the enumerative check, there were four such censuses; they were conducted at different dates in the years of almost greatest depression; and notwithstanding their independence of each other, they showed similar results. Also, they did not differ much from the results of the foreign censuses. For separate surveys to yield the same general quantitative error in the same wrong direction would, indeed, be a coincidence. Moreover, this chapter, Chapter 3, Appendix F, and Supplementary Appendixes G and H show that actually the United States materials have been fairly comparable over the years, and that the three nations conducting censuses during severe unemployment—Great Britain and Canada in 1921 and 1931, and Germany in 1933—used the same concept and measurement technique as for the previous and succeeding high-employment years. It may be argued, of course, that the foreign countries do not furnish much information on technique and concept, so that there still remains the possibility of incomparabilities. But until indication has been provided that there are such incomparabilities, the data constitute serious evidence against the existence of net numbers of additional workers in severe or deep depression.

Finally, in the United States, the technique instituted in the 1940 census was continued with minor alterations into the 1950 census. Yet the 1940 participation was below the 1950 and 1930 levels by about the same amounts. True, an impressive discrepancy was discovered in

---

[15] Unpublished letters from John Durand and Louis Ducoff commenting on the author's "Size of the Labor Force under Changing Income and Employment." (See preceding footnote.)

196

April 1950 between the decennial census and the sample survey report (Appendix F), the latter seeming to show a recovery in participation between 1940 and 1950 greater than that shown by the former, and suggesting that a still greater labor force exodus occurred under the depression conditions than the census results show.

Durand has further objected that additional workers could have entered and left during the 1930's, before the 1940 census was enumerated, and that until a sufficient peacetime experience has been recorded by the *Current Population Reports*, the possibility remains that there are temporary additional workers during recession. However, records are now available covering ten years of such experience, including two mild recessions—one in late 1949 when joblessness rose to 7 per cent, and the other in 1954 when it rose to nearly 6 per cent. Yet the analysis of these records (Chapter 11) does not disclose a trace of corroboration for the hypothesis that there is a net number of additional workers in recessions.

ARE THERE ADDITIONAL WORKERS IN BOTH DEEP DEPRESSION AND HIGH PROSPERITY?

Woytinsky has suggested in a recent book and elsewhere that there may be additions in periods of both abnormally low, and abnormally high employment, with withdrawals in periods of balanced prosperity.[16] He argues that labor force additions appeared during the mid 1930's (at the time of the four state censuses), vanished by the time of the "balanced prosperity" of April 1940, and then reappeared during the subsequent war and postwar high employment. This thesis merits examination.

The 1940 census gave powerful evidence that the labor force was depressed rather than enlarged by the conditions then prevailing. Woytinsky has described these conditions as those of "balanced prosperity," thus presumably distinguishing them from the great depression conditions of 1934–1936 and 1937; and yet the April 1940 census enumerated 8 million persons who were either seeking jobs or on the public emergency work relief rolls. These 8 million persons were 15 per cent of the labor force,[17] or more than twice the highest percentage of unemployment that has ever been officially recorded by any other United States census. Was unemployment in 1934–1936 or 1937 so high above that of April 1940 as to raise a difference in degree to a differ-

[16] Discussion, at a session of the American Economic Association, of the author's paper, "Impact of Effective Demand on the Labor Supply," *American Economic Review*, May 1953, pp. 458–467; Woytinsky and Associates, *op. cit.* See also J. R. Hicks and A. G. Hart, *The Social Framework of the American Economy*, Oxford University Press, 1945, p. 79.

[17] Not counting several million other full-time equivalent unemployed, concealed among persons working part time or on layoff.

197

ence in kind? The National Industrial Conference Board estimates of unemployment for 1934–1936 were arrived at by interpolating between the 1930 and 1940 censuses—in order to estimate the working-age population and the labor force—and then subtracting estimates of employment which were secured by interpolating with various employment indexes for major industry groups.[18] These N.I.C.B. estimates, the four state censuses, and *The Enumerative Check Census* suggest that unemployment ranged from a fifth to half again higher in the great depression than in April 1940.[19] The argument that there were additional workers in 1937 but not in 1940 assumes that a decline of unemployment from 20 per cent to 15 per cent of labor force was powerful enough to drive out the additional workers by 1940. Is there a theory as to why there should be a critical rate between 20 and 15 per cent unemployment, at which additions to the labor force are converted suddenly into deficiencies? Surely without one we may presume that the greater the depression the greater labor force deficiency. In any case few instances of unemployment levels above those in April 1940 have been recorded either in the United States or in other countries. Unemployment was 12 per cent of the labor force in Great Britain in the censuses of 1921 and 1931, 15.7 per cent in Canada in the census of 1931, and 18 per cent in Germany in the census of 1933.[20] For depressions with up to 18 per cent unemployment it would seem possible to conclude that the statistics have shown no dependable evidence of additional workers.

HAS THE DIFFICULTY IN FINDING JOBS KEPT WORKERS OUT OF THE LABOR FORCE?

It is conceivable that there are additional workers who escape definition and measurement. A thoughtful reader has expressed these objections:

[18] See the discussion of these estimates by Russell A. Nixon and Paul A. Samuelson in "Estimates of Unemployment in the United States," *Review of Economic Statistics*, February 1940.

[19] Unemployment percentages for 1934–1936 in the United States are annual averages; they could not be found for actual seasons because of the lack of any index of seasonal variation of the labor force in these years. The ratio is computed, using the highest of the unemployment figures during 1934–1937. As observed earlier, the state censuses were taken in Massachusetts and Pennsylvania in early 1934, in Michigan in early 1935, and in Rhode Island in early 1936. *The Economic Almanac 1951–1952*, National Industrial Conference Board, p. 100; *Census of Partial Employment, Unemployment, and Occupations*, 1937, Vol. IV, *The Enumerative Check Census, passim*.

[20] Had the labor force participation varied widely in relation to population, it would have been better to express all unemployment as percentages of working-age population, but the comparative stability of the labor force rates made this step unnecessary.

"I wonder whether the census-taker's concept of labor force can be taken at face value? A man who has been out of work for two years, who had searched far and wide for a position, may feel so discouraged about prospects that he does not spend the fifty cents or dollar needed for moving around; he is not absolutely looking for a job in the census sense, but provided he is not demoralized, is it a sound view that he is no part of the labor force?"

The conception of labor force and unemployment is discussed in Appendix I. Certainly, the problem has complicated psychological aspects, and there is no doubt an almost infinite gradation of reactions of workers to unemployment or the threat of it. Nevertheless, we may mark off two main classifications of unemployed workers. The first is made up of those for families whose breadwinners have jobs. This is surely the largest, for even in the greatest depression the number of employed at least triples the number of unemployed. In this group, if job-seeking becomes hopeless or wages and working conditions unfavorable, some elderly men may, without sharp regret, retire, some young girls may take extended vacations or devote full time to the competition for the reduced number of financially eligible young males, and some youths may postpone leaving school. Such persons could not be regarded as unemployed—even psychologically. The others are persons who might be genuinely willing and able to work and therefore psychologically in the labor force, but not so classified statistically because they find job-hunting futile or too expensive. It is possible to conjure up hypothetical cases: the son who has had to interrupt his education and look for work because of his father's unemployment, but who finally gives up even looking; or the bookkeeper of 58 who cannot compete with young girls who are trained in the use of business machines and whose salary demands are lower.

However, even these people need not be overlooked, for the United States census rules since 1940 have required that enumerators be instructed to report as unemployed not only those persons who were actually seeking work but also those who would have been except for the fact that there was no work to be had, or no work to be had in their occupations.[21] And a similar provision has been included since 1940 in all the enumerations of labor force, beginning with the WPA monthly reports and continuing with the census monthly reports and 1950 decennial enumeration.[22] This provision would seem to go as far as house-

[21] *Census of Population, 1940,* Vol. III, Part 1, *United States Summary,* pp. 290–297, 512.

[22] *Monthly Report on Unemployment* of the Works Progress Administration, Schedule DRS 370C. *Current Population Reports* of the Bureau of the Census, Schedule SS-570cS14, Form P-1605bS21, August 1949; *Census of Population, 1950,* Vol. II, Part 1, pp. 460–461, 471–472. The 1950 census instructions to enumerators

to-house enumeration could in ensuring that such additional workers would not be overlooked.

WHAT HAPPENS DURING A DEPRESSION TO THE RELATION BETWEEN LABOR FORCE PARTICIPATION AND UNEMPLOYMENT, IF ACCOUNT IS TAKEN OF INCOME CHANGES OCCURRING AT THE SAME TIME?

This chapter has concluded that a rising tide of unemployment during a severe depression causes more people to leave than to enter the labor force, with the result that participation shows a net decline. But what happened to incomes during the depression studied? The investigation has not been able to detect any systematic impact of income in peacetime periods of high employment, but it may be that workers become accustomed to rising income and react only when it ceases to rise or when it declines. A comparison of the depression levels of income and labor force with the levels solely of the previous census date would have been obscured by the long-term upward trends in income and in female participation, and long-term downward trends in male participation. The depression levels of income and labor force are therefore compared with the trend levels—those that would have existed had the average rate of increase between the preceding and the subsequent high-employment census dates been maintained throughout the intervening period.

So measured, real income per worker was depressed in each of the four countries (see Table 42), whether expressed per labor force member or per employed worker.[23]

Under depressed income per worker, what was the behavior of labor force participation in relation to the unemployment of males? The participation of males showed a mixed relation to the change in their un-

stipulate (Par. 148): "you should also report a person looking for work if last week he was waiting to hear the results of attempts made within the last 60 days to find a job." They list as examples of "looking for work":

"(a) Registration at a public or private employment office.
(b) Being on call at a personnel office, at a union hiring hall, or from a nurse's register or other similar professional register.
(c) Meeting with or telephoning prospective employers.
(d) Placing or answering advertisements.
(e) Writing letters of application.
(f) Working without pay in order to get experience or training."

And paragraph 149 states: "Enter 'yes' for a person who would have been looking for work except for one of the following factors:

"(a) He was on indefinite layoff. That is, he was laid off from his job and was not instructed to return to work within 30 days of the date of layoff.
(b) He was temporarily ill or temporarily disabled.
(c) He believed no work was available in the community or in his line of work."

[23] The deviations were less when expressed per employed worker, but they were nevertheless observable for every country, except that one may be seen for Germany only if 1939 was used as the terminal high-employment date (instead of 1950).

TABLE 42

Depression Deviations in Labor Force Participation per 100 Unemployed Males, Associated with Percentage Depression Deviations in Real Disposable Personal Income per Worker, United States and 3 Foreign Countries

(Depression census dates, compared with the trend between the preceding and the subsequent peacetime, moderately high-employment census dates)

	United States 1940 compared with trend between 1930 and 1950	Great Britain 1921 and 1931 compared with trend between 1911 and 1951 (1921) (1931)		Canada 1931 compared with trend between 1921 and 1951	Germany 1933 compared with trend between: 1925 and 1939	1925 and 1950

Deviations in Labor Force Participation [a] per 100 Deviation in Male Unemployed [b]

Both sexes	−22	−5	−1	+2	−11	−6
Males	−30	+8	+8	+10	−14	−17
Females	−15	−18	−9	−6	−9	+6

Deviations in Income per Worker [c] in Equivalents of United States Dollars of 1929 Buying Power

Per employed worker	−2.5	−12.9	−12.1	−11.8	−7.4	+6.5
Per labor force member	−10.1	−20.7	−22.6	−21.8	−25.3	−9.8

Source: Appendixes A, C, and D.

[a] Standardized for sex and age composition on the basis of the composition of population of the United States in 1940.
[b] Males 14 and older.
[c] Adult-male equivalent employed.

employment, deviating below trend in the United States and Germany, and above trend in Great Britain and Canada. That of females declined in all four countries.[24] And that of both sexes combined declined in all countries except Canada.[25] But the amounts of labor force participation deviations bore no really systematic relation to the amounts of deviations in income. It is true that the United States, with the smallest depression in income, had the largest depression in participation relative to unemployment, and that Great Britain, with the largest income deviations, had below average deviations in participation relative to unemployment. But in Canada and Germany it was impossible to detect any systematic tendency for the relationship between labor force participation and unemployment to have been affected by the behavior of income during the depression period.

[24] Unless 1950 is used as the terminal date for Germany instead of 1939.
[25] The rise was very slight for Canada and must be discounted, because the lack of income data for 1911 made it necessary to use 1921 as the so-called previous high-employment date, despite the fact that it was actually a year of considerable unemployment.

CHAPTER 11

THE LABOR FORCE UNDER SHORT-RUN
CHANGES IN INCOME, EMPLOYMENT,
AND ARMED FORCES

"Labour is a commodity which cannot be increased and
diminished at pleasure."

DAVID RICARDO, *Principles of
Political Economy and Taxation*

THIS chapter and two occasional papers by the author [1] review the behavior of the labor force since 1939 in the United States, Great Britain,
Germany, and Canada. The more recent paper compares the labor
force at its wartime peak among these countries and uses annual data
to bring out how it was built up in the United States and Britain in
large relative amounts and in Canada in a small relative amount, and
its failure to rise at all in Germany; how it was demobilized in the
United States, Britain, and Canada at the war's end; and (briefly)
how it reacted in the United States and Canada to the conflict in Korea.
Its course in relation to mobilization in wartime and demobilization
is summarized in Chapter 1 of this volume. Here labor force is compared with fluctuations in earnings and income, unemployment, and
military strength during the years of war and transition. The comparison—further tested by multiple correlation analysis of quarterly data
—yields no evidence that the labor force has responded systematically
and dependably to short-run changes in income and in the demand for
labor, or to moderate peacetime changes in the armed forces.

As a proportion of the working-age population, labor force is derived
from census reports which have provided quarterly averages of monthly
estimates in the United States since 1940, quarterly estimates in Canada
since late 1945, and annual (June) estimates in Great Britain since
1939. Basic information for census estimates of employment, unemployment, and labor force in the United States during this period rests on
data obtained by enumerators in interviews with a random sample of
25,000 households located in 68 broadly representative areas throughout the country.[2] Every individual 14 years of age or over in each house-

---

[1] *The Labor Force in War and Transition: Four Countries,* Occasional Paper 36,
1952, and *The Labor Force in Wartime America,* Occasional Paper 14, 1944,
National Bureau of Economic Research.

[2] The gross number of households in the sample was 25,000 until May 1956.
Because of absences, vacancies, and other circumstances, the net number of
households actually interviewed was usually between 20,000 and 22,000. Beginning with May 1956, the size of the sample was increased to about 35,000

hold is classified as employed, unemployed, or not in the labor force, in accordance with the answers—given by some "responsible" member of the household—to a standard set of questions. The labor force figure is obtained by adding the estimates based on the number of persons reported to be employed and the number reported to be unemployed but seeking jobs.[3]

Using these data from each household, the Bureau of the Census computes the percentage of persons in each sex-color-age group who are employed, unemployed, or not in the labor force. National estimates are then derived by applying these percentages to independent estimates of the total civilian population by sex-color-age groups.[4]

Since estimates are based on a relatively small sample, there is a possibility of sampling error. The errors, and the steps taken to measure and minimize them, are presented in Supplementary Appendix I.

United States: Effect of Fluctuations in Armed Forces, Unemployment, Earnings, and Income on Labor Force Behavior in the Short Run

ARMED FORCES.

Until the armed forces began to expand, the labor force in this country remained stable in its relation to population (Chapter 12). Since most of the influx into the labor force occurred in the years when recruiting camps were jammed with inductees, it seems safe to infer that it was brought about by the military draft. The immense levies drew young men from schools into the armed forces and thus into the labor force; reduced the number of men at home for whom women had to keep house; deprived many households of their main breadwinners, making it necessary for wives, sisters, and mothers to work; and created a vacuum in the social life of women which millions of them filled by taking defense jobs.

Although the flow of new workers into the labor force during World War II kept close pace with the draft, the outflow began as early as the spring of 1945, several months before the end of the war and a full year before demobilization of the armed forces had neared completion.

interviewed households in 330 areas. (The number of sample areas had been increased to 230 in January 1954.)

[3] Persons 14 and older who are reported to be neither working nor looking for work are classified as not being in the labor force. Chapter 3 and Appendix E discuss further the census' definitions of employed, unemployed, and labor force. Chapter 3 also describes sampling methods more fully. Some examples of "looking for work," which were provided with questionnaires used by enumerators, appear in Chapter 10 under the heading, "Some Questions Concerning the Findings of This Investigation."

[4] Appendix E of the Economic Report of the President, Jan. 28, 1954.

The exodus of men 25–64 from the labor force had been completed in late 1945, that of women and young people in mid-1946, and that of the elderly in the fourth quarter of that year (Chart 20). Armed strength was still two million at the end of 1946, though servicemen were discharged rapidly, and did not reach the post-World War II

CHART 20

Labor Force Compared with Armed Forces and the Unemployed, United States, 1940–1956

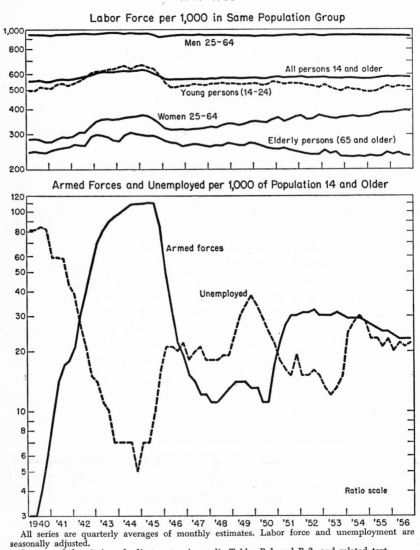

Labor Force per 1,000 in Same Population Group

Men 25-64

All persons 14 and older

Young persons (14-24)

Women 25-64

Elderly persons (65 and older)

Armed Forces and Unemployed per 1,000 of Population 14 and Older

Armed forces

Unemployed

Ratio scale

All series are quarterly averages of monthly estimates. Labor force and unemployment are seasonally adjusted.
Source and description of adjustments: Appendix Tables B-1 and B-2, and related text.

low of 1.2 million until the winter of 1948. It fluctuated moderately between 1948 and mid-1950, making no apparent impression on the behavior of the labor force (it declined slightly during the first half of 1950 when the labor force also showed a mild general decrease). It nearly reached peak expansion for the Korean operations—almost tripling—in the 12 months after the start of hostilities; during the same time, total labor force participation made most of its Korean expansion. The armed forces then remained rather constant for over three years, from mid-1951 through the third quarter of 1954, while the total labor force first fluctuated slightly and then lost its Korean additions, with its various subgroups moving diversely. In 1955, the services declined about one-fifth while the labor force increased slightly more than it had during the Korean conflict. A small amount of these labor force gains were lost in the last half of 1956, while armed forces remained constant.

THE UNEMPLOYED.

There was a strong association between unemployment and growth of the armed forces during World War II, and a significant but not so strong association during the postwar period. As the Army, Navy, and Air Force expanded in 1941, unemployment declined rapidly—about six months after Pearl Harbor it was less than 4 per cent [5] of the labor force and by mid-1943, less than 1 per cent. It was near this level for 24 months, while the armed services continued to expand to a peak of 12 million in early 1945. Then as millions of persons left both the armed services and civilian jobs during the last half of 1945, unemployment began to rise, reaching almost 4 per cent by early 1946—the end of the labor force contraction. Between early 1946 and late 1948 unemployment fell off a little while the labor force edged from 56.3 to 57.5 per cent of the working-age population. Participation of the age-sex groups was diverse—remaining virtually unchanged for men 25–64 after the second quarter of 1946, dipping slightly for elderly persons but showing no net rise or fall, expanding somewhat for young people, and continuing its steady, long-run increase for females. Between late 1948 and 1949 unemployment doubled, but this did not induce a significant change in the over-all participation rate, which, though dipping slightly in early 1949 was almost the same at the end of the year as it was at the end of 1948: approximately 57.5 per cent of the population 14 and older. Nor was the rise of unemployment accompanied by significant or systematic changes in the participation rates of the broad age groups. The rate for men 25–64 declined somewhat and that for women 25–64 rose even more (though slightly so) than the increase called for by the long-run upward trend in female participa-

[5] The percentage regarded as "normal" in this study.

tion. The rates for young and elderly persons remained approximately unchanged. Between late 1949 and the eve of the Korean action in the second quarter of 1950, unemployment declined substantially. At the same time the labor force as a whole and all major age groups manifested a decline in propensity in accordance with the additional worker hypothesis, but in opposition to the hypothesis that improved employment opportunities bring more persons into the labor force. This was the only instance in the period of systematic behavior of labor force in possible reaction to unemployment change. On the whole the period between early 1946 and the outbreak in Korea gave no real support either to the theory that higher unemployment results in additional workers or to the theory that it squeezes workers out of the labor force by depriving them of job opportunities.

Six months before the Korean action, unemployment began a decline which was to last, almost without interruption, for nearly four years— from the last quarter of 1949 to the second quarter of 1953. At the start of this decline before the Korean outbreak, the participation rates of men 25–64 remained substantially unchanged and those of persons 14–24 and 65 and older, of women 25–64, and of all persons 14 and older moved downward. As unemployment continued to fall from the Korean outbreak to the end of 1951, the total labor force reversed its movement, realizing almost all of its increase of the Korean episode; participation of young people showed a sharp, brief upturn, then began a long, general decline; that of women rose; and that of older people levelled off, then again slipped down. Unemployment still decreased gradually but steadily between the end of 1951 and the summer of 1953, as the participation of females moved generally upward and then declined, that of young and old people moved steeply downward (except for a temporary upturn in the first quarter of 1953), and that of all persons 14 and older first fluctuated, then decreased throughout 1953.

After the trough of this nearly four-year decline, unemployment, seasonally adjusted, rose moderately in the third and fourth quarters of 1953 and sharply in the first quarter of 1954, while the participation of the total labor force and that of young persons and women first declined and then rose, and the participation of elderly persons first rose and then declined. During most of 1954 unemployment rose somewhat further as the participation of young persons and of the total labor force decreased and that of women, men, and elderly persons remained about stable.

The decrease in total labor force participation during 1954 brought it down to about the same level as had prevailed during the two years before the Korean conflict (when, however, unemployment had been, first, appreciably lower, then appreciably higher, than in 1954).

In the first quarter of 1955 unemployment fell and was fairly constant during the rest of that year and throughout 1956; except for men and women, participation rose generally in 1955, failed to rise further during the first half of 1956, and then declined in the last half. The participation of men declined very gently during most of the two years and that of women was generally upward until the last quarter of 1956. Thus, the association of labor force with unemployment during these seven years followed no discernible pattern.

It may, of course, be argued that unemployment as a whole is not a dependable indicator of employment opportunity. Such an argument could proceed on two grounds.

Unemployment may fluctuate, not only from changes in employment, but also from changes in the labor force itself. This possibility can, however, be tested against the behavior of a group which does not enter and leave the labor force in any appreciable numbers, i.e. men 20–44. The test indicates that the unemployment of men 20–44 in this period followed the same course, essentially, as that of total unemployment. Except that it remained constant for the most part during mid-1951–1953 instead of gradually declining, and did not rise quite as much as total unemployment in 1953–1954, its movement was very similar.

But even this test may not be a good indicator of the effect of job opportunity. For example, an abundance of jobs might conceivably induce men 20–44 to alter their employment status if not their labor force status, by leaving one office or factory to seek work in another, thus increasing unemployment at a time when jobs were actually more plentiful. A better indicator might be the total hours worked, or overtime hours paid for at premium rates. An examination of these and other such factors would be most interesting, but they are beyond the scope of this study. The writer does not believe that labor force participation will respond any more sensitively or systematically to these other possible indicators than it has to unemployment, but a rigorous test must wait for some other investigation.

QUARTERLY INCOME.

Over the seventeen years from early 1940 through 1956, disposable personal income per adult-male equivalent employed rose 162 per cent —a 35 per cent rise after adjustment for the increase in the cost of living. As estimated by the census from sample surveys, the 1956 labor force was larger than that of 1940 by 3.3 per cent of population 14 and older, and as enumerated by the regular census in 1950, it was about the same as it had been in the censuses of 1890 through 1930 [6] —when the unemployment rate was also about the same (although

[6] Standardized for age-sex and rural-urban composition.

both money income and real income were much lower). The regular census also revealed that participation in 1950 was above 1940. It is possible that participation in 1950 or 1956 was higher than in 1940 because of the increase in armed forces and the decrease in unemployment in 1950 (Chapter 10). Changes in participation were associated neither with trends in income nor with deviations of income from the trends (which seemed to be a straight-line arithmetic movement throughout the entire seventeen years). In constant prices income seemed to move with labor force in only a few years—notably 1940–1942 and late 1943 through early 1945 (Chart 21).

CHART 21

Labor Force Compared with Disposable Income and Hourly Earnings, United States, 1940–1956

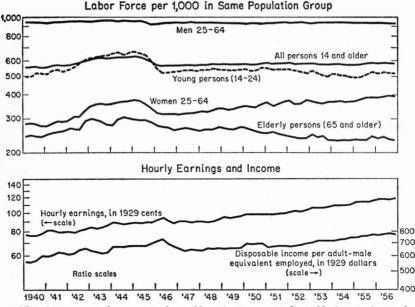

Labor Force per 1,000 in Same Population Group

All series are quarterly averages of monthly estimates, except disposable income (quarterly totals), and are seasonally adjusted.
Source and description of adjustments: Appendix Tables D-2, D-5, and B-2, and related text.

HOURLY EARNINGS.

Hourly earnings differ from quarterly income in that they exclude dividends, interest, and other non-wage receipts of wage earners, employers, and the self-employed. They cover earnings, approximately, for time worked and are unrelated statistically to employment or unemployment. And they are not adjusted here to an adult-male equivalent. Real hourly earnings rose about a fifth during 1940–1946, and remained rather constant during 1946–1948. They went up nearly 10 per cent by early 1950, changed very little during 1950–1951, and then climbed steadily during 1952–1956, so that by 1956 they were 30 per cent above 1946, and more than 50 per cent above 1940. So far as earnings were concerned, it was impossible to discern any influence on total labor force participation during this period, whether they were expressed in money or in real terms. Participation rates of the individ-ual groups were similarly lacking in systematic association. Participa-tion of females, of course, moved generally upward, as real hourly earn-ings rose over the seven-year period 1950–1956. The older and younger groups showed some positive agreement with real hourly earnings in certain detailed changes in participation rates during 1950–1956 but not in others, and they both moved in opposite directions from earn-ings during this period so far as trend was concerned.

Canada: Effect of Fluctuations in Armed Forces, Unemployment, Earnings, and Income on Labor Force Behavior in the Short Run

ARMED FORCES.

The crude annual data for 1939–1945 have suggested that in Canada the labor force during World War II increased by about the same amount in relation to armed forces as did the labor force in the United States. The Canadian estimates which have been available for every third month from late 1945 to the end of 1952, and thereafter for every month, showed that the labor force had lost its wartime addi-tions by the end of 1946, when demobilization of the armed forces was nearly complete (Chart 22). During the next four years (to mid-1950) the armed forces remained close to 4 or 5, and labor force participa-tion between 534 and 548 per 1,000 population 14 and older. In view of the fact that the sampling error of any figure was as much as 6, i.e. ±3 per 1,000 population 14 and older, these small variations scarcely uphold the existence of outside influences (Table 43). During the Korean conflict, Canadian armed services did not increase as much as the American armed services but, like the latter, they did remain al-most at Korean operation levels after the fighting had ended. Total labor force participation, instead of rising as in the United States, drifted downward and was about 1 per cent less during 1950–1952 than during 1946–1949. It declined further and by a similar amount in 1953 and 1954, then rose in the last half of 1955. Except that it held up slightly better in 1956 and manifested no increase in early 1954, total labor force participation in Canada during 1953–1956 be-

CHART 22

Labor Force Compared with Armed Forces and the Unemployed, Canada, 1945–1956

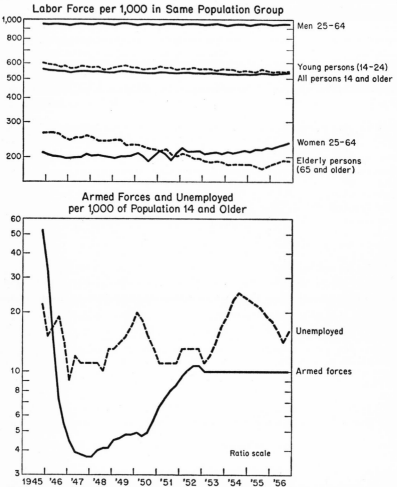

Quarterly estimates, seasonally adjusted (except armed forces). Source and description of adjustments: Appendix Tables B-6 and B-6A, and related text.

haved rather similarly to that in the United States during these years. But it showed less sign of association with armed forces.

UNEMPLOYMENT.

Unemployment in Canada remained lower [7] than in the United States throughout the decade ending in 1956 (Chart 22). There was some

[7] One of the striking features of United States-Canadian comparisons has been their agreement in movement of unemployment. Unemployment was lower in

210

TABLE 43

Variation in the Proportion of the Labor Force to Population and
the Corresponding Range of Error in the Labor Force Sample
Estimates, United States and Canada, 1946–1952

(per 1,000 population of same sex and age)

	Maximum Range of Labor Force Variation		Range Owing to Sampling Variability 2(2σ)
	Mid-1946– Mid-1950	Mid-1946– Mid-1952	
United States			
Labor force 14 and older	11	20	6
Males 14 and older	14	13	14
Females 14 and older	24	35	10
Young people 14–24	25	37	20
Men 25–64	13	14	20
Women 25–64	33	56	10
Elderly people 65 and older	11	31	20
Canada			
Labor force 14 and older	14	18	6
Males 14 and older	20	30	12
Females 14 and older	13	26	8
Young people 14–24	32	32	20
Men 25–64	21	21	20
Women 25–64	12	32	10
Elderly people 65 and older	37	60	20

Source of estimates of sampling variability: *Current Population Reports;* Series P-57, No. 118, p. 12; *The Labor Force,* November 1945–March 1952, *Reference Paper* No. 35, pp. 5–6. See also the author's comments in "Statistical Standards and the Census," in the *American Statistician,* February 1952, and Supplementary Appendix I.

fluctuation. Seasonally adjusted, it rose from about 2 per cent in 1948 to 3.8 per cent of the labor force in March 1950 and then declined to below 2.5 per cent. But it rose to near United States levels (about 4.5 per cent) only once—in the 1954 recession. There was a similar tendency for the labor force to rise in 1955 when unemployment decreased, as if in response to improved job opportunity, but there was no such association before and during the Korean operations.

The tendency of the total labor force participation to decline somewhat (instead of rising somewhat as in the United States) during the years following World War II is reflected in the behavior of the major age-sex groups. Men 25–64 showed a slight net rise, compared with a

average percentage in Canada, perhaps because of the great importance of agriculture. But the similarity of the detailed movements in the two countries during 1945–1950 was most impressive in view of the small samples on which the unemployment estimates rest.

slight net fall in the United States; but compared with this country the participation of young and elderly persons decreased much more, and that of women rose much less over the decade following 1946. The rise of unemployment in the 1949–1950 recession was not reflected in any significant rise or decline for any of these age-sex groups, and the post-Korean rise of unemployment in 1954 was met by a similar lack of systematic response. For most of this decade the participation of elderly men and young persons continued the downward trend without check or acceleration; that of women 25–64 continued its slow upward trend, also without change of pace. However, the slight increases in participation of all persons 14 and older, of young and old people, and the small acceleration in the increase of participation of women, which occurred in late 1955 and 1956, were associated with a moderate decline of unemployment.

QUARTERLY INCOME AND HOURLY EARNINGS.

Quarterly income and hourly earnings both soared in Canada during 1946–1956. Adjusted for the cost of living, hourly earnings rose about a third and income about a half. A trifling upswing of real income and earnings in early 1947 was accompanied by a very slight drop in labor force participation of all groups; a dip in real income and earnings during late 1947 and early 1948 was associated with a rise in the participation of women and elderly persons, and with a gentle decline in that of the young. On the whole, however, the labor force fluctuations were too restrained and unsystematic to suggest any response to changes in earnings or income of the kind that could be detected by graphical comparison.

Great Britain

Since Britain's annual estimates of the labor force are derived basically from registrations for social insurance rather than from surveys or censuses of population, they are not likely to reflect ordinary changes in labor force behavior, for a person is scarcely apt to withdraw his registration if he leaves the labor force briefly. They should, however, reflect the more long-lasting changes in his willingness or ability to be gainfully occupied.

British wartime additions to the labor force had entirely disappeared by mid-1946, about the same time as in the United States and about six months earlier than in Canada. Thereafter, participation declined from 60.6 per cent of the population 14 and older in 1946 to 58.8 per cent in mid-1949 (Chart 23), perhaps partly because of the small additional separations from the armed forces, but during 1951–1956 it climbed above the 1946 level and, in fact, to slightly above the level

CHART 23

Labor Force Compared with Armed Forces and the Unemployed,
Great Britain, 1939–1956

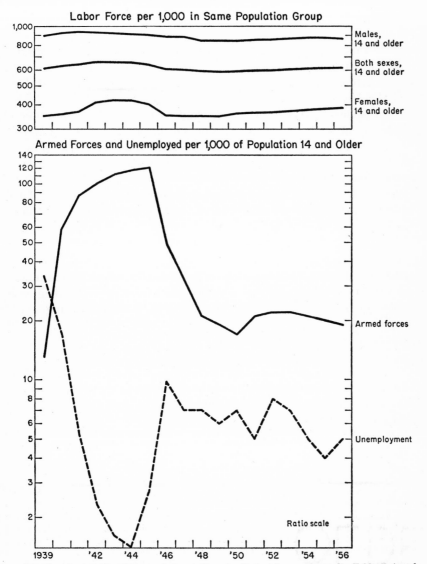

Annual estimates. For source and description of adjustments, see Appendix Table B-4 and related text, and Table B-5.

of 1939. Through the eleven postwar years, unemployment remained at very low levels—between 0.7 and 1.6 per cent of the labor force; and from 1948 forward the armed forces were at nearly constant strength. All in all, the British labor force participation was fairly stable—it was the same in 1951 as it had been in 1931, and almost the same as in 1921 and 1911.[8]

Recapitulation

In the United States, Great Britain, and Canada wartime additions had left the labor force by the end of 1946 and participation rates were close to those in previous periods of peacetime high employment. During the decade 1947–1956, the over-all participation in these three countries remained rather impressively stable, within a maximum range of 1.8 per cent in Great Britain, 2.3 per cent in the United States and 2.6 per cent in Canada—smaller than the normal range of variation in the United States or Canada between the winter and summer labor force of any given year.

In the United States and Canada males continued to leave the labor force as men above 45 retired earlier in life, and as boys and young men extended their years of schooling. Women above 25, chiefly wives, resumed their long-run labor force inflow in all three countries, though at a very moderate rate in Canada. These offsetting changes did not correspond in any consistent way to variations in armed forces, unemployment, or hourly earnings and disposable income, even when earnings and income were adjusted for changes in the cost of living.

The Joint and Several Effects of Armed Forces, Unemployment, and Income or Earnings

When a number of elements are present in any behavior, the effect of each may be so obscured by that of the others that it can be measured only after all of the elements have been examined in various combinations—by multiple and partial correlation.

Multiple correlations of United States data on labor force, armed services, unemployment, earnings, and income were tested for two

[8] Standardized for age and sex composition.

In a study of the British labor market for 1920–1938 Gerhard Tintner suggests that "it is not at all certain that there is any dependence of the supply of labor on wages and prices." His materials and his use of the term "industrial labor supply," indicate that he deals with shifts both into and out of the labor force and between industrial and nonindustrial occupations within the labor force. His measures therefore pertain to labor supply in relation to a group of important industries, and not to all labor (see Appendix B). However, the stability of the aggregate supply would be even greater than that of any segment of it. "An Econometric Investigation of the British Labor Market," *Econometrica*, July 1950, p. 268.

periods: the World War II period embracing the 26 quarters from 1940 through mid-1946, and the post-World War II period, covering the 24 quarters from mid-1946 to mid-1952 (Table 44). Labor force and unemployment were corrected for seasonal variations. (See text of Appendix B and Tables B-1 and B-2 for the seasonal indexes and a discussion of the method of adjustment and its reliability.) Labor

TABLE 44

Labor Force Correlated with Armed Forces, the Unemployed, Disposable Income, and Hourly Earnings, United States, 1940–1952

		Both Sexes 14 & Older	Males 14 & Older	Females 14 & Older	Persons 14–24	Persons 65 & Older
SIMPLE CORRELATIONS [a]						
World War II Period (1940–1946) [b]						
Labor force and:						
Armed forces	r_{12}	+0.956 **	+0.880 **	+0.968 **	+0.973 **	+0.924 **
Unemployed	r_{13}	−0.861 **	−0.783 **	−0.866 **	−0.883	−0.917 **
Income						
Real	r_{14}	+0.413 **	+0.297 *	+0.433 **	+0.485 **	+0.642 **
Money	r_{15}	+0.255 *	+0.273 *	+0.233 *	+0.250 *	+0.364 *
Hourly earnings						
Real	r_{16}	+0.399 **	+0.308	+0.407 **	+0.439 **	+0.466 **
Money	r_{17}	−0.405 **	−0.266 *	−0.443 **	+0.494 **	−0.599 **
Post-World War II Period (1946–1952) [b]						
Labor force and:						
Armed forces	r_{12}	+0.589 **	+0.328 *	+0.452 **	+0.363 *	−0.745 **
Unemployed	r_{13}	−0.129	−0.442 **	+0.053	−0.010	+0.587 **
Income						
Real	r_{14}	−0.256 *	−0.608 **	−0.054	−0.286 *	+0.151
Money	r_{15}	−0.361	+0.087	−0.360 *	−0.374 *	+0.173
Hourly earnings						
Real	r_{16}	+0.373 *	−0.240 *	+0.424 **	+0.323 *	−0.207
Money	r_{17}	+0.384 *	+0.773 **	+0.137	+0.304 *	−0.381 *
MULTIPLE CORRELATIONS [a]						
World War II Period (1940–1946) [b]						
Labor force, armed forces and:						
Unemployed	$R_{1.23}$	0.956 **	0.880 **	0.968 **	0.974 **	0.948 **
Real income	$R_{1.24}$	0.964 **	0.904 **	0.974 **	0.974 **	0.939 **
Money income	$R_{1.25}$	0.961 **	0.889 **	0.971 **	0.977 **	0.948 **
Real hourly earnings	$R_{1.26}$	0.961 **	0.893 **	0.972 **	0.975 **	0.924 **
Money hourly earnings	$R_{1.27}$	0.976 **	0.934 **	0.981 **	0.978 **	0.926 **

(table continues on next pages)

		Both Sexes 14 & Older	Males 14 & Older	Females 14 & Older	Persons 14–24	Persons 65 & Older

MULTIPLE CORRELATIONS [a] (cont.)

World War II Period (1940–1946) [b]

Labor force, armed forces, unemployed, and:

		Both Sexes	Males	Females	Persons 14–24	Persons 65 & Older
Real income	R1.234	0.973 **	0.919 **	0.979 **	0.978 **	0.950 **
Money income	R1.235	0.963 **	0.896 **	0.972 **	0.977 **	0.952 **
Real hourly earnings	R1.236	0.962 **	0.894 **	0.973 **	0.976 **	0.949 **
Money hourly earnings	R1.237	0.980 **	0.937 **	0.982 **	0.981 **	0.948 **

Post-World War II Period (1946–1952) [b]

Labor force, armed forces and:

Unemployed	R1.23	0.601 **	0.458 †	0.557 **	0.414 †	0.786 **
Real income	R1.24	0.639 **	0.687 **	0.454 †	0.459 †	0.760 **
Money income	R1.25	0.630 **	0.370 †	0.520 **	0.467 †	0.746 **
Real hourly earnings	R1.26	0.613 **	0.505 **	0.531 **	0.417 †	0.751 **
Money hourly earnings	R1.27	0.641 **	0.788 **	0.453 †	0.427 †	0.776 **

Labor force, armed forces, unemployed, and:

Real income	R1.234	0.689 **	0.712 **	0.572 †	0.534 †	0.790 **
Money income	R1.235	0.633 **	0.462 †	0.559 †	0.467 †	0.814 **
Real hourly earnings	R1.236	0.623 **	0.514 †	0.589 **	0.426 †	0.794 **
Money hourly earnings	R1.237	0.789 **	0.807 **	0.638 **	0.616 **	0.789 **

PARTIAL CORRELATIONS [a]

World War II Period (1940–1946) [b]

Labor force and armed forces holding constant unemployed and:

Real income	r12.34	0.838 **	0.628 **	0.881 **	0.876 **	0.621 **
Money income	r12.35	0.830 **	0.691 **	0.858 **	0.872 **	0.629 **
Real hourly earnings	r12.36	0.846 **	0.683 **	0.886 **	0.889 **	0.611 **
Money hourly earnings	r12.37	0.912 **	0.787 **	0.924 **	0.908 **	0.598 **

		Both Sexes 14 & Older	Males 14 & Older	Females 14 & Older	Persons 14–24	Persons 65 & Older

PARTIAL CORRELATIONS [a] (cont.)

World War II Period (1940–1946) [b]

Labor force and unemployed holding constant armed forces and:

		Both Sexes 14 & Older	Males 14 & Older	Females 14 & Older	Persons 14–24	Persons 65 & Older
Real income	r13.24	−0.477 **	−0.387 *	−0.446 **	−0.406 **	−0.408 **
Money income	r13.25	0.193	0.251 *	0.186	0.113	−0.275 *
Real hourly earnings	r13.26	−0.171	−0.076	−0.150	−0.253 *	−0.563 **
Money hourly earnings	r13.27	−0.362 *	−0.229 *	−0.292 *	−0.339 *	−0.539 **

Post-World War II Period (1946–1952) [b]

Labor force and armed forces holding constant unemployed and:

		Both Sexes 14 & Older	Males 14 & Older	Females 14 & Older	Persons 14–24	Persons 65 & Older
Real income	r12.34	0.659 **	0.248 *	0.567 **	0.468 **	−0.653 **
Money income	r12.35	0.464 **	0.067	0.444 **	0.219 *	−0.440 **
Real hourly earnings	r12.36	0.471 **	0.274 *	0.400 *	0.263 *	−0.461 **
Money hourly earnings	r12.37	0.738 **	0.345 *	0.610 **	0.517 **	−0.651 **

Labor force and unemployed holding constant armed forces and:

		Both Sexes 14 & Older	Males 14 & Older	Females 14 & Older	Persons 14–24	Persons 65 & Older
Real income	r13.24	0.336 *	−0.255 *	0.389 *	0.306 *	0.335 *
Money income	r13.25	0.073	−0.298 *	0.240 *	0	0.488 **
Real hourly earnings	r13.26	0.138	−0.108	0.224 *	0.096	0.397 *
Money hourly earnings	r13.27	0.600 **	0.286 *	0.503 **	0.492 **	0.226 *

World War II Period (1940–1946) [b]

Holding constant armed forces and unemployed Labor force and:

		Both Sexes 14 & Older	Males 14 & Older	Females 14 & Older	Persons 14–24	Persons 65 & Older
Real income	r14.23	−0.594 **	−0.562 **	−0.580 **	−0.406 **	0.176
Money income	r15.23	0.368 *	0.363 *	0.335 *	0.358 *	0.282 *
Real hourly earnings	r16.23	−0.351 *	−0.335 *	−0.389 *	−0.296 *	−0.101
Money hourly earnings	r17.23	0.721 **	0.681 **	0.665 **	0.497 **	−0.064

TABLE 44, *continued*

	Both Sexes 14 & Older	Males 14 & Older	Females 14 & Older	Persons 14-24	Persons 65 & Older
		PARTIAL CORRELATIONS [a] (cont.)			
		Post-World War II Period (1946-1952) [b]			
Holding constant armed forces and unemployed					
Labor force and:					
Real income r14.23	−0.384 *	−0.613 **	−0.154	−0.370 *	0.140
Money income r15.23	−0.160	−0.069	−0.059	−0.237 *	0.345 *
Real hourly earnings r16.23	0.076	−0.262 *	0.107	0.110	−0.191
Money hourly earnings r17.23	0.623 **	0.748 **	0.374 *	0.502 **	−0.117
		SIMPLE INTERCORRELATIONS [a] BETWEEN INDEPENDENT VARIABLES			
Unemployed and:					
Armed forces r32		−0.885 **		−0.503 **	
Real disposable income r34		−0.707 **		+0.207	
Money disposable income r35		−0.471 **		−0.447 **	
Real hourly earnings r36		−0.507 **		+0.339 *	
Money hourly earnings r37		+0.606 **		−0.652 **	
Armed forces and:					
Real disposable income r24		+0.539 **		−0.013	
Money disposable income r25		+0.165		−0.245 *	
Real hourly earnings r26		+0.504 **		+0.363 *	
Money hourly earnings r27		−0.590 **		+0.234 *	

Source and explanation: Income and hourly earnings, Appendix D. Labor force, armed forces, and unemployed, Appendix B. The variables are: labor force, X_1; armed forces, X_2; unemployed, X_3; real disposable income, X_4; money disposable income, X_5; real hourly earnings, X_6; money hourly earnings, X_7.

* Significant on the 68 per cent ($\pm\sigma$) level.
** Significant on the 95 per cent ($\pm 2\sigma$) level.
† Significant on the 75 per cent level.

[a] The labor force, armed forces, unemployed, and hourly earnings are quarterly averages of monthly estimates. Disposable income (per adult-male equivalent employed) was computed in three-month aggregates. Income and earnings were adjusted for linear arithmetic trend. All were adjusted where necessary for seasonal variation. Labor force, the armed forces, and the unemployed are expressed per 1,000 population aged 14 and older.
[b] The World War II period is from the first quarter of 1940 through the second quarter of 1946; the post-World War II period is from the third quarter of 1946 through the second quarter of 1952.

force, unemployment, and armed forces were expressed per 1,000 population 14 and older, to eliminate any trend introduced purely by rise in population. Disposable income was computed in three-month aggregates, and hourly earnings in three-month averages. Each was analyzed both with, and without adjustment for changes in the cost of living and for the straight-line arithmetic upward trend that seems to be observable in income and earnings.[9] There was no apparent over-all trend during 1940–1952 in the participation of either the total population or of males 14 and older. But there was an apparent straight-line *upward* trend in that of females 14 and older, and a straight-line *downward* trend in that of persons 14–24 and 65 and older. The correlations were constructed between the deviations from these trends. In all cases, the trends were derived from the entire 1940–1952 episode.

Table 44 seems to show that during the World War II period labor force participation was very strongly (and positively) correlated with armed forces—only for males 14 and older was this simple correlation below 0.900 (and very little below at that). And for three of the five labor force groups it was above 0.950. All of these correlations were significant well above the 95 per cent level. The correlation of labor force with unemployment was in all cases lower than it was with armed forces, but not much lower. This association was to be expected —as was the fact that it was uniformly negative—in view of another circumstance, to be noted in Table 44 under the heading of "Simple Intercorrelations between Independent Variables," that there was also a high and negative intercorrelation between armed forces and unemployment ($r_{32} = -0.885$). The three-cornered relationship raises a difficult question—to be asked whenever the so-called independent variables are not truly independent of one another. If labor force participation moved with armed forces, and if unemployment moved away from both, which of the three was the prime mover?

We are aided in answering this question by certain theoretical considerations. One is that the size of the armed forces was surely set almost entirely by the needs of the war and was therefore an independent variable, determined little or not at all by the levels of labor force participation and unemployment.[10] Another is that the other variables could not be regarded as independent of armed forces. Large scale mobilization could have the theoretical effects of (1) drawing young students into the armed forces and therefore into the labor force; (2) reducing the size of families, thus enabling adult females to move from unpaid housework into employment; and (3) reducing unemployment, by recruiting idle persons or by increasing the number of civilian jobs.

[9] The adjustment to upward trend was made to allow for the possibility that people become accustomed to a certain rate of rise in income and react only when the rise is specially slow or rapid.

[10] There was some chance that if labor force participation had been lower and unemployment higher, the government might have had to scale down armed force mobilization during World War II; but there is little evidence of such a contingency. It is more likely that the same armed strength could have been levied in any case, with lower labor force participation or higher unemployment resulting in less civilian production.

In support of these theoretical considerations, the multiple correlations of labor force with armed forces and unemployment ($R_{1.23}$) were the same or scarcely larger than the simple correlations with armed forces alone (r_{12}). But all of these multiple correlations were substantially larger than the simple correlations with unemployment alone (r_{13}).[11] And only for persons 65 and older was the multiple correlation of labor force and armed forces with *unemployment* larger than that with *income* or with *earnings*.[12] Although the simple associations of labor force with income or earnings were much weaker than those with unemployment, they were less dependent on the changes in armed forces, as shown by the simple intercorrelations in Table 44.

None of the simple correlations of labor force with income or earnings was very high, but more than half of them were significant on the 95 per cent level, and the remainder of them were significant on the 68 per cent level. Do these simple correlations demonstrate that income or earnings have influenced the short-run changes in labor force participation? Not necessarily, for both could have been influenced by a third factor—especially changes in armed forces.[13] Any such influence might be determined by two methods—multiple, and partial correlation.

Multiple correlation tests the effect on the size of the coefficient by adding a variable. Thus real income was added to the simple correlation between labor force participation and armed forces (with r_{12} becoming $R_{1.24}$) and to the multiple correlation of labor force with armed forces and the unemployed (with $R_{1.23}$ becoming $R_{1.234}$). Then money income, real hourly earnings, and money hourly earnings were substituted alternately for real income. None of the three-variable multiple correlations was substantially greater than the two-variable multiple correlations involving armed forces and unemployment, or than the simple correlation with armed forces. Yet they were very much greater than the simple correlations of labor force with income or earnings alone. This method suggests that income and earnings are not dominant in the explanation of labor force behavior during 1940–1946.

Partial correlation was used to see what the associations of labor force with income and earnings would have been if the other factors had not fluctuated. A first set indicates that the participation of various

[11] For persons 65 and older the difference was least substantial. This was also the only labor force group for which the simple correlation with unemployment was in excess of −0.900.

[12] In spite of the fact that the simple correlations of labor force with unemployment were much larger than the simple correlations with income or earnings.

[13] And the economic developments that occur with changes in the size of the armed forces.

age-sex groups was rather strongly associated with armed forces, holding unemployment and income, and unemployment and earnings constant. The correlations were all positive and significant on the 95 per cent level. A second set indicates that participation had a much weaker association with unemployment, holding armed forces and income or earnings constant. Some of the correlations in the second set were significant on the 95 per cent level, but most of them were significant on the 68 per cent level or not at all. And nearly all were inverse. A third set shows participation to be only moderately correlated with income or earnings, holding armed forces and unemployment constant. The partial correlations of labor force with real income except for persons 65 and older [14] were significant on the 95 per cent level and were inverse. Partial correlations of labor force with money hourly earnings were similarly significant, though positive, for all groups except persons 65 and older.

These uneven and moderate partial associations of the second and third sets may reflect some independent influence of unemployment, real income, and money hourly earnings on labor force participation, but the case is not a strong or a consistent one. All the above correlations —simple, multiple, and partial—make a clear case, however, for a close association between labor force and armed forces during the wartime period.

Nearly all of the correlations were much smaller during the postwar period. The simple correlations with armed forces were significant on the 68 per cent level for the participation of males 14 and older and young persons 14–24. For that of both sexes 14 and older, females 14 and older, and elderly persons, they were significant on the 95 per cent level, but only for the last group was the correlation at all high or negative. That it was negative, instead of positive as it had been during the war period, undermines its significance, since theoretical reasons are lacking for the participation of elderly persons to decline because armed forces rise, or to rise because armed forces decline. This perverse behavior in the postwar period extends also to the relation with unemployment—in this case the participation of the elderly seemed to rise and fall with unemployment [15]—though this behavior may have occurred as the result of incomplete elimination of trend. Of the other groups only for males 14 and older was the simple correlation of participation with unemployment significant in the postwar period.

The simple correlations of labor force with income or earnings were

[14] Thus possibly corroborating the moment-of-time results of this study.
[15] Thus seemingly supporting the additional worker theory.

for the most part substantially weaker than the simple correlations with armed forces.[16] Indeed, the signs of the postwar correlations—significant or insignificant—showed little agreement either from one group to another or within the same group, from wartime to the postwar period. Such evidence does not make it easy to claim a dependable association between labor force participation and income or earnings in either period.

When the various potential influences on postwar participation are added to form multiple correlations of various combinations ($R_{1.23}$ . . . . $R_{1.237}$) the results are all significant on the 95 or 75 per cent level. In the case of both sexes combined and for elderly persons, the multiple correlations were all significant on the 95 per cent level and were all much higher than the simple correlations with employment, income, or earnings. However, they were very little higher than the simple correlations with armed forces—suggesting that for these two groups other factors add little to the explanation, and that armed forces again wield the principal influence on participation. For males, and females taken separately, and young persons, the multiple correlations with armed forces, unemployment, and income or earnings were generally substantially higher than the simple correlations with armed forces alone, or than the simple correlation with any other single factor. For these groups no single factor would seem to offer an explanation of labor force behavior. It is possible that all the factors may combine to offer one—but none of the multiple correlations for these three groups was very high.

The conclusion that only armed forces adds much to the explanation of the postwar labor force behavior of both sexes and elderly persons is also upheld by the partial correlations. Holding unemployment and income or earnings theoretically constant, e.g. $r_{12.34}$ through $r_{12.37}$, labor force participation is correlated with armed forces on the 95 per cent level, though again we have the puzzling inverse association for elderly persons with a positive one for all other groups. Most of the partial correlations with unemployment, holding armed forces and income or earnings constant, e.g. $r_{13.24}$ through $r_{13.27}$, or with income or earnings, holding armed forces and unemployed constant, e.g. $r_{14.23}$ through $r_{17.23}$, are only moderately significant or are not significant at all.

The three groups—males, females, and young persons—showed partial correlations which again reveal no clear dominance of any fac-

[16] Of 20 simple correlations of labor force participation of the five groups with money and real income on the one hand, and with earnings on the other, seven were not significant at all and eleven were on the 68 per cent level, leaving only three significant on the 95 per cent level. Two of the three were for males 14 and older and had signs in reverse of those during the war.

tor. The great majority were significant on only the 68 per cent level, and those with unemployment and income or earnings frequently differed in sign from the war period. Of the few that were significant on the 95 per cent level, about half were with armed forces, holding unemployment and income or earnings constant, and nearly all were modest compared to those during the war. Perhaps the chief exception was the partial correlation with money hourly earnings, holding armed forces and unemployment constant.

How can we explain this general weakness of the postwar association of labor force participation with the various factors that seemed more influential during the war—specially that with the armed forces?

One reason may be that the powerful patriotic and other moral reinforcements that accompany all-out mobilization were missing during peacetime and during the limited military operation in Korea. Perhaps an equally important explanation is that the census estimates of labor force were subject to sampling errors which, though minor in proportion to the great movements in World War II, were large compared with the moderate changes of 1946–1952. A range of 6 persons per 1,000 aged 14 and older resulting from sampling error is appreciable if it is compared with fluctuations of 20, and the sampling variabilities are even more sizable, relatively, among individual groups (Table 43). The estimate of unemployment might vary from the sampling error within a range of 2 per 1,000 population. Still greater variations in the labor force and unemployment data could occur because of differences in the care exercised by census enumerators.

Incidentally, all correlations became much feebler when the labor force was given a lag of one year behind the independent variables.[17]

We might now consider briefly the rather interesting suggestion of Sumner Slichter that the effect of a wage increase on labor supply would depend on the level of earnings previously established.[18] For example, there is the possibility that more labor would be forthcoming at $7 a day if the prevailing wage had been $5 than if it had been $6, presumably because the lower the level from which a given increase starts, the greater is the relative change. This hypothesis was tested for the United States by correlating, separately for 1940–1946 and 1946–1952, the changes in the size of the labor force per 1,000 population 14 and older, with the *percentage* changes in real and money in-

[17] The labor force beginning with the third quarter of 1946, was correlated with armed forces, the unemployed, and real income in the same period of 1945. The multiple correlation dropped from 0.689 to 0.539, and the simple correlation with armed forces both declined and changed sign from +0.589 (Table 43) to −0.530. The associations with unemployed and real income became even more insignificant than before.

[18] *Modern Economic Society*, Holt, 1928, pp. 625–626.

come and earnings, which were computed by dividing the income or earnings of each quarter by those of the preceding quarter. The correlations thus obtained, however, had even less significance than those derived by associating the labor force with income or earnings expressed as percentages of the straight-line upward trend. The effect suggested by Slichter might conceivably be found in the behavior of the labor supply of a locality or of an individual firm, or in the behavior of unions in collective bargaining, but it has no apparent bearing on variations in labor force participation in the aggregate.

The foregoing discussion of factors influencing labor force has been limited to the United States. No correlations were computed for the British data, which covered only one month (June) each year.

For Canada we examine the participation of three groups 14 and older—both sexes combined and males and females separately (Table 45). The simple association with armed forces was found to be signifi-

TABLE 45

Labor Force Correlated with Armed Forces, the Unemployed, Disposable Income, and Hourly Earnings, Canada, Quarterly, February 1946 to August 1952

		1946–1952		
		Both Sexes 14 & Older	Males 14 & Older	Females 14 & Older
SIMPLE CORRELATIONS [a]				
Labor force and:				
Armed forces	r12	+0.365 [*]	+0.084	+0.396 [**]
Unemployed	r13	+0.169 [*]	+0.130	+0.092
Real income	r14	−0.199	−0.209 [*]	−0.097
Money income	r15	−0.061	+0.056	−0.199
Real hourly earnings	r16	+0.023	−0.155	+0.233 [*]
Money hourly earnings	r17	+0.170	+0.176	+0.045
MULTIPLE CORRELATIONS [a]				
Labor force, armed forces and:				
Unemployed	R1.23	0.379 [†]	0.143	0.396 [†]
Real income	R1.24	0.392 [†]	0.215	0.398 [†]
Money income	R1.25	0.365 [†]	0.111	0.418 [†]
Real hourly earnings	R1.26	0.366 [†]	0.185	0.440 [†]
Money hourly earnings	R1.27	0.396 [†]	0.191	0.397 [†]
Labor force, armed forces, unemployed and:				
Real income	R1.234	0.402	0.237	0.398
Money income	R1.235	0.385	0.218	0.423 [†]
Real hourly earnings	R1.236	0.379	0.223	0.440 [†]
Money hourly earnings	R1.237	0.439 [†]	0.291	0.398

	1946–1952		
	Both Sexes 14 & Older	Males 14 & Older	Females 14 & Older

PARTIAL CORRELATIONS [a]

Labor force and armed forces, holding constant unemployed and:

Real income	r12.34	+0.327 *	+0.033	+0.380 *
Money income	r12.35	+0.349 *	+0.074	+0.380 *
Real hourly earnings	r12.36	+0.344 *	+0.078	+0.377 *
Money hourly earnings	r12.37	+0.316 *	+0.020	+0.379 *

Labor force and unemployed, holding constant armed forces and:

Real income	r13.24	+0.096	+0.103	+0.013
Money income	r13.25	+0.131	+0.190	−0.078
Real hourly earnings	r13.26	+0.108	+0.126	+0.007
Money hourly earnings	r13.27	+0.207	+0.224 *	+0.031

Holding constant armed forces and unemployed

Labor force and:

Real income	r14.23	−0.146	−0.191	−0.036
Money income	r15.23	+0.077	+0.167	−0.162
Real hourly earnings	r16.23	−0.024	−0.173	+0.208
Money hourly earnings	r17.23	+0.240 *	+0.256 *	+0.037

SIMPLE INTERCORRELATIONS [a] BETWEEN INDEPENDENT VARIABLES

Unemployed and:

Armed forces	r32	+0.195
Real disposable income	r34	−0.108
Money disposable income	r35	−0.573 **
Real hourly earnings	r36	+0.066
Money hourly earnings	r37	−0.441 **

Armed forces and:

Real disposable income	r24	−0.159
Money disposable income	r25	−0.177
Real hourly earnings	r26	+0.109
Money hourly earnings	r27	+0.053

Source and explanation: Income and hourly earnings, Appendix D. Labor force, armed forces, and unemployed, Appendix B. The variables are: labor force, X_1; armed forces, X_2; unemployed, X_3; real disposable income, X_4; money disposable income, X_5; real hourly earnings, X_6; money hourly earnings, X_7.

* Significant on the 68 per cent ($\pm\sigma$) level.
** Significant on the 95 per cent ($\pm2\sigma$) level.
† Significant on the 75 per cent level.

[a] The labor force, armed forces, and unemployed are estimates for quarterly dates. Hourly earnings are quarterly averages of monthly data. Disposable income (per adult-male equivalent employed) is a quarterly total. All are adjusted where necessary for seasonal variations. Income and earnings are adjusted for linear arithmetic trend. Labor force, the armed forces, and the unemployed are expressed per 1,000 population aged 14 and older.

cant on the 95 per cent level for females, and on the 68 per cent level for both sexes; for males it was not significant. It was positive for all three groups. The correlation with real income was inverse for males on the 68 per cent level, and that with real hourly earnings was positive on the 68 per cent level for females. All other simple correlations were insignificant. Again, unemployment and income or earnings seemed to add little or nothing to the explanation of labor force behavior and the same can be said of the multiple and partial correlations. Only a few of the correlations revealed any significance, except where armed forces were involved, and even then they were on the lower levels. There were partial correlations with armed forces, holding unemployment and income or earnings constant, but these were significant only for both sexes and for females on the 68 per cent level. Thus the associations between participation and all the factors—even armed forces—were weaker in Canada than in the United States during the post-World War II years between 1946 and 1952. As in the United States, they were still weaker when the labor force was given a lag of one year to reveal the possible effect of changes in these variables.

Differences in Earnings and Attractiveness of Jobs among Industries

It is possible that average earnings would be raised statistically by the mere transfer of workers from low-paying agriculture and domestic service to high-paying manufacturing and trade, even if no wage rate had changed in any occupation or industry. A comparison of earnings weighted by the industrial distribution of employment prevailing at the time, with earnings weighted by the distribution at a fixed date, reveals that shifts in the composition of employment in industry had little effect on the amount or behavior of earnings in both the United States and Canada (Appendix Tables D-2 and D-3). Of course this does not mean that industrial composition has had no influence on the labor force. Any such influence depends also on the difference in attractiveness or irksomeness between the old and the new jobs. If both jobs were equally attractive to the worker or prospective worker, any transfer from lower to higher paid employments would presumably mean an increase in the effective reward per unit of effort, and would require no distinction from a rise in pay within each occupation. It would therefore require no standardization.

But if the new jobs at higher average pay merely compensated for the greater strain or longer travel involved, they would offer no better rewards, and it would be necessary to standardize the earnings for the changes in industrial composition.

Finally, if the industries whose employments were expanding were relatively more remunerative and more agreeable, standardization would eliminate the effect of a rise in average earnings but not the effect of betterment in average working conditions. Some persons might withdraw from the labor force because of the higher income resulting from the shift in employment composition; others might enter the labor force at the same time because the work was, on the average, more agreeable as a result of the shift. There is no way of dealing with this difficulty, and over the decades it could conceivably involve substantial numbers of workers. Within the years studied in this chapter, however, the changes in the peacetime industrial composition of employment would not suggest any significant net change in the attractiveness of jobs, in view of the minor changes in average earnings that have been found to result from these changes.

Labor Force Turnover

It would be possible for the net labor force participation to change very little and yet for the gross composition to change a great deal. In every household there occur endless reversals of plans, as girls leave gainful employment to marry, grandfathers enter retirement, husbands become disabled, high school graduates look for their first jobs, or divorced women seek a means of self-support (Chart 24). During 1948–1952 in the United States—the only period during which such data for the whole labor force have been available—the labor force lost and gained, on the average, around 4.5 per cent monthly and 10 per cent yearly. Annual turnover seems to be only double, instead of twelve times the monthly turnover, because many of the same persons enter and leave the labor force several times a year. It is not known how much of this turnover is real and how much is the result of errors in the answers of householders to the census enumerators' questions in different months or years.

Have these gross changes been influenced by the level of unemployment or incomes? The brief experience reveals that turnover has varied seasonally. It quickened in the spring as crops were planted and students left school and went to work or young women resigned their jobs to marry. It sped up in the summer as young people switched from one temporary employer to another and as crops were harvested in different months in different regions. It stayed fairly high in September because the students returned to school. And it finally dropped to a low in late fall and winter (perking up very little during the so-called Christmas rush). The range of the gross change was between 4 per cent in winter and 6 per cent in summer. The average was approximately 10 per cent a month for females and 2.5 per cent for males.

CHART 24

Gross Changes in Civilian Labor Force Compared with the Unemployed, Disposable Income, and Armed Forces: United States, 1948–1953

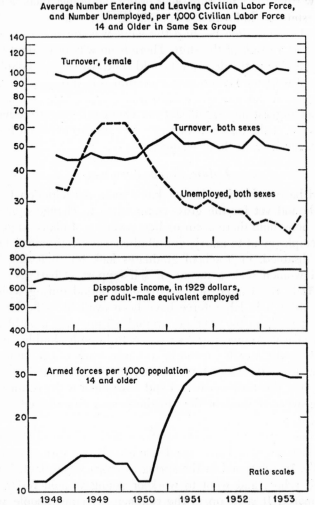

Average Number Entering and Leaving Civilian Labor Force,
and Number Unemployed, per 1,000 Civilian Labor Force
14 and Older in Same Sex Group

All series are quarterly averages of monthly estimates, except disposable income (quarterly totals). Source: Appendix Tables B-1 (labor force by employment, and armed forces) and D-5 (income); and *Current Population Reports*, Bureau of the Census, Series P-50, P-59.

Until mid-1950 when the mobilization of armed force brought on additional turnover, the proportion of population 14 and older who entered or left the labor force in any month was not influenced, apparently, by the levels of income and employment. The gross change continued substantially the same while unemployment fluctuated between 3 and

228

7.5 per cent.[19] During the last half of 1950 and early 1951, a small rise in civilian turnover seemed to be clearly associated with the increase of armed forces, as young men shifted out of jobs into the services and women and girls left school or housework to seek employment; but civilian turnover declined and then remained stable during the rest of 1951, while armed forces were rising and unemployment was still falling.

[19] This is also consistent with the conclusion of Mr. W. Lee Hansen of The Johns Hopkins University. Mr. Hansen has analyzed with some degree of intensity the data on gross additions to, and reductions from unemployment for 1948 through early 1956. He concludes that: "The absolute difference in gross movements during periods of high and low unemployment is due almost wholly to movement from the unemployed to a job or vice versa, rather than to differential movements into and out of the labor force. . . . An examination of gross movements in unemployment [in and out of the labor force] reveals no significant changes in the levels or their composition other than what might be expected because of seasonal variations." *Short-Run Behavior of the Labor Force: An Analysis of "Gross Change" Data*, mimeographed, Feb. 13, 1957, p. 19.

CHAPTER 12

THE STABLE LABOR FORCE UNDER RISING
INCOME AND HIGH EMPLOYMENT

"On the whole, it may be asserted that a slow and gradual
rise of wages is one of the general laws of democratic
communities."

DE TOCQUEVILLE (1833)

LABOR force participation in relation to population as a whole did not
change materially during peacetime periods of rising income and high
employment in the five countries studied. The most pronounced rise
was in Germany; the least, in Great Britain. And there was no association between the rather minor changes in participation and the substantial increases in real income that occurred in the English-speaking
countries.[1] Only in Germany were there no significant increases in
income per worker over the half century or so ending around 1950.

Total Labor Force in Five Countries in the
Last Half Century

For this study, major attention was focused on the periods since 1890
in the United States, 1911 in Great Britain and Canada, 1896 in New
Zealand, and 1895 in Germany. And for the United States and Great
Britain, the study went as far back as early 1800.

The 1950 census in the United States counted more than 112 million
persons aged 14 and older, of whom 60 million were in the labor force.
Although both the population and the labor force had increased enormously, the labor force bore almost the same relation to the population 14 and older in 1950 as in 1890 (Appendix Table A-2 and Chart
25). The maximum deviation from the average in any one of the decades was 34, and the average, 14 workers per 1,000 population. The
maximum includes variations due to changes in labor force concept,
in census practice, and in population composition. Even so, the variations were smaller than the normal seasonal changes in the early postwar period 1946–1948 (Chapter 13).[2]

[1] Increases in real income per worker ranged from 38 per cent in Britain during
1911–1951 to 166 per cent in the United States during 1890–1950. Increases in income per capita ranged from 59 per cent in Britain to 210 per cent in the United
States during these same periods (Appendix Table D-4).

[2] And they were no greater than the discrepancy in April 1950 between the labor
force as enumerated by the regular decennial census and that estimated from the
sample survey—both of which were collected or estimated by the same agency,
using the same concept and techniques of interviewing. (See the author's discussion on "Statistical Standards and the Census," *American Statistician*, February

230

CHART 25

Persons 14 and Older in the Labor Force per 1,000 in Same Population Group: 5 Countries, Various Years, 1890–1951

Standardized for age and sex, and for other differences as noted, on basis of United States population in 1940.

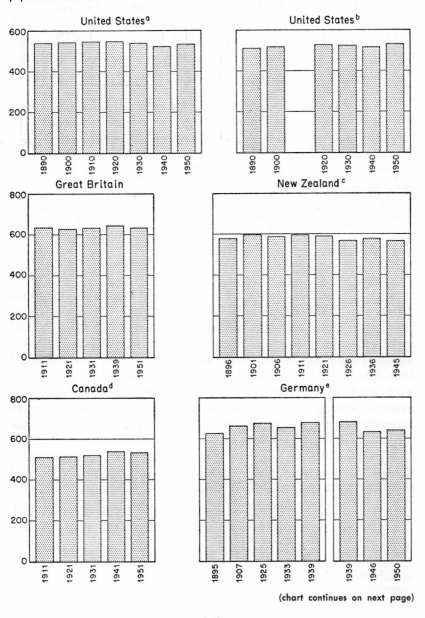

(chart continues on next page)

CHART 25, concluded

Persons 14 and Older in the Labor Force per 1,000 in Same Population Group

Standardized for age and sex

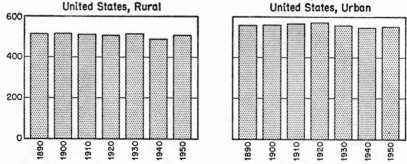

a Standardized for rural-urban composition as well as for age and sex.

b Standardized for rural-urban composition, color, and native-foreign composition, as well as for age and sex.

c Aged 15 and older.

d Partially standardized for rural-urban composition on the assumption that the effect of migration to urban areas would be the same in Canada as in the United States (in addition to standardization for age and sex).

e For 1895–1939, boundaries after World War I, without the Saar; 1939–1950, Federal Republic of Germany, without Berlin.

Source: Appendix A.

Much of the decade variation is eliminated by adjustment for miscounts and for differences in the season when the census was taken, thus reducing the maximum deviation in any one decade to 21, and putting the average at around 10 workers per 1,000 population of working age (Table 46). Still more of the decade variation was eliminated by standardizing for changes in population composition and residence. Such variations were very small compared with those which took place in income during these years. While variations in the labor force were generally less than 2 per cent of population, or 4 per cent of labor force over the whole period real annual disposable income per worker [3] nearly tripled, in terms of 1929 dollars (Chart 26 and Appendix D and Table D-4). Moreover, it went up in every decade whether computed between census years or between three-year averages.[4]

In the four foreign countries, the changes in participation were not,

1952.) The regular census enumerated the labor force as 534 per 1,000 population aged 14 and older; the estimate was 563—a difference of 29.

[3] Income per capita more than tripled (Appendix Table D-4).

[4] The three-year averages were for each census year and the two preceding years. Actually the changes in income did not differ significantly between the two computations. Real income also went up in every decade, per employed worker and per capita.

232

TABLE 46

Labor Force Aged 14 and Older per 1,000 of Same Age, 5 Countries, Various Periods, 1890–1951

	Average Number	Deviation from Average in Any One Census		Net Over-All Change
		Maximum	Average	
United States 1890–1950:				
Unadjusted for miscounts and season of census	546	34	14	−1
Adjusted but unstandardized	543	21	10	−6
Adjusted and standardized for age and sex [a]	534	12	5	+9
Adjusted and standardized also for rural-urban residence [b]	538	16	6	−7
Adjusted and standardized also for color and place of birth [c]	521	11	7	+20
Rural [a]	508	21	7	−6
Urban [a]	559	13	6	−6
Large cities (1900–1950) [a]	594	16	7	+4
Native white [a]	521	17	10	+34
Foreign-born white [a]	550	29	14	−38
Colored [a]	626	62	36	−85
Great Britain [a] 1911–51	633	11	4	−1
Canada 1911–51:				
Standardized for age and sex [a]	523	15	10	+21
Also partially standardized for rural-urban residence [e]	524	14	7	+11
New Zealand [a, d] 1896–1951	581	19	11	−18
Germany [a] 1895–1939	657	34	15	+53
Germany [a] 1895–1950	654	31	18	+15

Source: Appendix A. See also Supplementary Appendixes H (seasonal adjustment) and I (miscounts).

[a] Standardized for age and sex on the basis of population of the United States in 1940.

[b] Standardized for age, sex, and rural-urban composition on the basis of population of the United States in 1940.

[c] Standardized for age, sex, rural-urban composition, color, and place of birth on the basis of population of the United States in 1940.

[d] Aged 15 and older.

[e] Partially standardized for rural-urban residence on the assumption that the effect of migration would be the same in Canada as in the United States.

on the whole, greater than in the United States. In Germany the labor force rose by 53 workers for each 1,000 population during 1895–1939, and the maximum deviation at any one census from the average participation over the whole period was 34. In Great Britain labor force participation was almost the same in 1951 as in 1911, and the maximum deviation was 11. Maximum deviations in Canada and New Zealand were much the same as those in the United States (adjusted).

CHART 26

Labor Force Compared with Personal Disposable Income, 5 Countries, Various Years, 1890–1951

Labor force standardized for age and sex, and for other differences as noted, on basis of United States population in 1940. Income expressed in three-year averages.

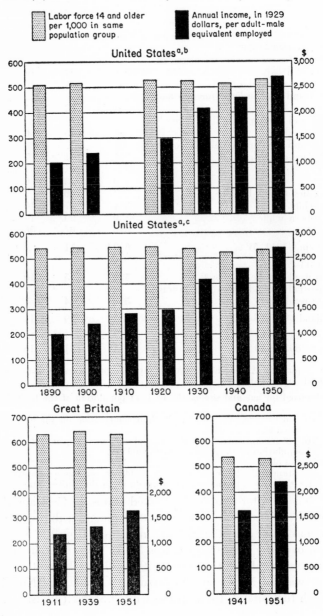

CHART 26, concluded

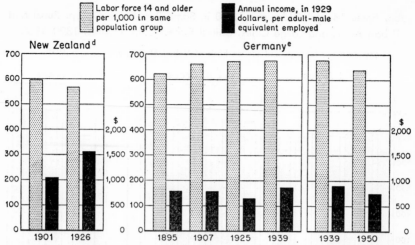

☐ Labor force 14 and older per 1,000 in same population group

■ Annual income, in 1929 dollars, per adult-male equivalent employed

New Zealand[d]

Germany[e]

[a] Income standardized for farm-nonfarm composition (on basis of U.S. population in 1940).
[b] Labor force standardized for rural-urban composition, color, and native-foreign composition, as well as for age and sex.
[c] Labor force standardized for rural-urban composition as well as for age and sex.
[d] Labor force 15 and older.
[e] For 1895–1939, boundaries after World War I, without the Saar; 1939–1950, Federal Republic of Germany, without Berlin.
Source: Appendix A (labor force) and Appendix Table D-4 (income).

The Labor Force in Rural and Urban Areas

In all of the five countries there has been an increase since the turn of the century in the proportion of the population living in urban, as compared to rural areas. Not much change has occurred in Canada and Britain since World War I, or in Western Germany since before World War II, but in the United States and New Zealand the increases have been marked and steady.

Unfortunately none of the four foreign countries provided data which throw clear light on whether the stability of total labor force participation was duplicated in rural and urban areas separately. (Some information was available for Canada—between 1941 and 1951.) However, data were available to allow a fair test of the stability of the aggregate labor force participation rate in each of these areas in the United States (Chart 27). True, rural and urban participation rates have sometimes moved in opposite directions.[5] But none of these small ebbs

[5] The urban rate was slightly higher in 1920 than in 1910 or in 1930 (572 per 1,000 of same age and type of area, compared with 567 and 557 respectively), while the rural rate was a trifle lower in 1920 (506) than in 1910 (511) or in 1930 (513). Real nonfarm income per worker rose from 1910 to 1920, but real farm income per worker fell substantially. There would seem to have been a real incentive for people to move to the city, especially when jobs were highly paid and abundant, as in early 1920 during the immediate postwar boom; and, since

235

CHART 27

Labor Force 14 and Older per 1,000 in Same Population Group: Rural and
Urban Areas and Large Cities, United States, Census Dates, 1890–1950

Standardized for age and sex on basis of United States population in 1940.

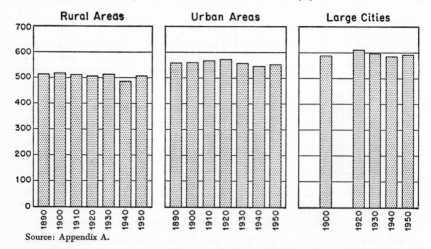

Source: Appendix A.

and flows has modified the conclusion that the labor force participation rate has been remarkably stable in the United States in rural areas,
in urban areas, and in large cities (taken as aggregates) as well as
in the nation as a whole—in the face of enormous increases in average
income.[6]

Stability was less marked in the rural and urban areas of Canada

---

a large proportion of the migrants were apt to be seeking work, the migration
may have produced the slight swell in urban labor force and the slight ebb in the
average rural rate. Statistics show that during recessions migration subsides, and
during depressions it becomes no more than a trickle. Conversely, during years
of high employment, such as 1922–1929, the loss of farm population became very
great indeed. (*Historical Statistics of the United States, 1789–1945*, Bureau of the
Census, pp. 18, 30.) When city jobs were less plentiful, as in 1930, there was
apparently a halt in the normal flow to cities or even in the return to farms; for
both the urban and the large-city rates decreased slightly, while the rural rate
increased appreciably—although real farm income was no larger in 1930 than in
1920, and real nonfarm income soared. But a really severe depression, such as still
persisted in 1940, seems to reduce participation somewhat in both city and
country; for when jobs are very scarce everywhere some persons with borderline
employability or desire to work may withdraw altogether (Chapter 10), a
tendency which does not seem to be observable during a moderate recession
such as 1948–1950, or 1953–1954 (Chapter 13).

[6] One cross-comparison may be of interest though it did not produce positive
results: individual cities were examined to determine whether the labor force
behaved differently when real weekly wages in manufacturing rose steeply than
it did when these wages rose gradually. No correlation could be discovered
either in absolute or in percentage changes.

between 1941 and 1951, when the rural labor force declined by 23 per 1,000 rural population and the urban labor force rose the same amount in relation to urban population (Table 47)—greater changes than any occurring in the United States between two successive census dates. The diversity of movement may simply have been the result of changes in the rural or urban age composition—lack of age detail by rural and urban areas having made it impossible to standardize for this factor.

TABLE 47

Rural and Urban Labor Force, Canada, 1941 and 1951

Labor Force ª	1941	1951	Change
Rural			
Both sexes	523	500	—23
Males	856	813	—43
Females	117	128	+11
Urban			
Both sexes	528	551	+23
Males	808	830	+22
Females	261	291	+30

Source: *Census of Canada*, Ottawa, Dominion Bureau of Statistics: *1941*, Vol. VII, Table 11; *1951*, Vol. II, Table 4, and Vol. IV, Table 18.

ª Per 1,000 rural or urban population 14 and older. Not standardized for age and sex because of lack of data.

But it may also have occurred because Canada's rural labor force in the war year of 1941 was somewhat augmented by substantial numbers of males of draft age who stayed on farms to evade military service, a hypothesis that derives some support from the fact that rural population and the labor force were both greater in 1941 than in 1951 and that the excess of 1941 over 1951 rural population was a trifle greater for males than for females. Certainly no such divergence in movement occurred for females. Female participation rates rose between 1941 and 1951 in both rural and urban areas, the rise having been greater in the latter than in the former areas. Even though participation may have been stable *within* these locales, in Canada as a whole it may have been affected by the migration to the cities. In English-speaking countries, white females are much more apt to work in urban areas—partly because they find light clerical and factory jobs congenial and partly because the higher standard of living calls for gainful employment. Thus any considerable migration might be expected to have *raised* the average participation of Canadian females. In Germany, conversely, where field labor is considered suitable for females, farm women are more apt to work than city women; and their migration to the city would have *lowered* female participation—depending on the number of women who moved, and the amount by which their participation in rural areas exceeded that in the cities.

A definite assessment of these movements and differences can be made only for Great Britain and the United States. In Britain, migration could not have been important, as a large and relatively unchanging proportion (three-fourths to four-fifths) of the population resided in urban areas throughout the period between 1911 and 1951. In the United States, the urban population grew from one-third of the national population in 1890 to two-thirds in 1950. But the effect of this huge relative shift on the labor force was no more than 4 persons per 1,000 of working age; and its effect on the stability of over-all participation was slight. The effects of migration would seem almost certainly to have been weaker in the other countries, where the shifts in population have been more limited. We shall pursue further the diversity of behavior over time among the various cities.

Various Minority Groups

Minority groups may tend to segregate and thereby perpetuate cultural and social differences that are in turn reflected in labor force behavior, with little relation to differences in income or employment opportunity. The economic differences might in the long run exert some influence on the cultural and social patterns, but it could vary from time to time and from nation to nation, largely for accidental reasons.

The problem was negligible in three of the five countries under study. Britain has had few nonwhites and no large number of aliens in its home islands during the last half century. There have been very few foreigners in Germany except during World War II, when many war prisoners and civilian workers were imported from occupied countries (these minorities were treated separately in Chapter 11 under the behavior of labor force in wartime). New Zealand has had a very homogeneous population (aside from Maoris, who are also not included in most of these figures). Canada, however, has had her French-language population and the United States has had considerable numbers of Negroes and immigrants. How have these social and ethnic groups affected the behavior of the labor force as a whole?

In Canada the number of "British Isles races," French, and "Other" have changed so little in relation to total population, and their differences in labor force participation have been so moderate (Table 48), that changes in racial composition could have exerted little influence on the total participation of the country. Moreover, the participation rates of the three main racial groups have remained quite stable during

1921, 1931, and 1951, the three peacetime censuses for which data were available by racial origin.

In the United States, slackening immigration reduced the foreign-born from a fifth of the entire population in 1890 to a ninth in 1940.[7] Such changes in the proportion of these groups to the population could alter the over-all labor force participation, even if the participation of each ethnic group had remained perfectly stable over time. But the rates of the ethnic groups have not been stable over time. The participation of native whites has been stable, but that of Negroes fell

TABLE 48

Labor Force by Ethnic Groups and Sex per 1,000 Population
10 and Older in Same Category, Canada,
1921, 1931, and 1951

	BOTH SEXES			MALES			FEMALES		
	1921	1931	1951	1921	1931	1951	1921	1931	1951
British Isles races	488	480	487	794	767	756	167	178	220
French	452	459	474	749	745	739	150	171	212
Other, including Indians	472	516	498	754	793	750	100	148	211
All Classes	476	481	485	775	767	750	153	170	216

Source: *Census of Canada*, Ottawa, Dominion Bureau of Statistics: *1931*, Vol. VII, Table 18; *1951*, Vol. II, Table 4, and Vol. IV, Table 20.

Data for 1911 were not available; 1941 was excluded not only because large numbers of males were in the armed forces but also because they constituted very different percentages for the British Isles races, the French, and "Other."

from 622 in 1890, to 516 in 1950 per 1,000 colored aged 10 and older. And the foreign-born labor force dropped from 536 in 1890, to 492 in 1950 per 1,000 foreign-born aged 10 and older.[8] In both instances these rates tended toward those of native whites (Chart 28). The tendency would indicate that as the propensity of Negroes and the foreign-born to work comes to resemble more closely that of native whites, and the native-born descendants of the foreign-born replace their forebears, much of the diversity in participation between major ethnic groups may disappear before very long.

Despite their characteristic behavior and their changing weight in

[7] Negroes remained close to a tenth of the population throughout the entire sixty years.

[8] The declining participation of the colored cannot be ascribed to their heavy rural-to-urban migration. On the contrary, had it been possible to standardize the colored for rural-urban residence, the decline would have been considerably greater, for the participation of colored females is much higher in urban areas than in either rural-farm or rural-nonfarm areas. *Census of Population, 1940, The Labor Force* (Sample Statistics), *Employment and Personal Characteristics*, pp. 31–32.

CHART 28

Labor Force of Native White, Foreign-Born White, and Colored Persons:
United States, Census Dates, 1890–1950

Persons in the labor force per 1,000 in same population group. Standardized for age and
sex (but not for rural-urban composition) on basis of United States population in 1940.

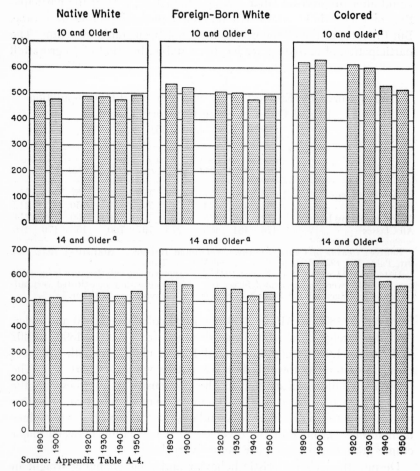

Source: Appendix Table A-4.

the population, the colored and foreign-born groups have not made an
impact on the total labor force (Table 49). Their participation rates
did not differ greatly from those of native whites, except in the case
of nonwhite women aged 25 and older, nonwhite boys aged 14–19,
and foreign-born girls aged 14–24. And such differences as occurred
were due in large part to dissimilarities in the age structure. For example, since mass immigration ceased some decades ago, foreign-born
persons in the United States have been much older, in the average,

240

TABLE 49

Effect of the Foreign-Born and Negroes on Labor Force,
United States, Census Dates, 1890–1950

	1890	1900	1920	1930	1940	1950
Labor Force [a]						
1. All classes	499	502	500	500	480	495
2. Natives (white & nonwhite)	490	498	499	500	481	495
3. Whites (natives & foreign-born)	483	486	487	489	475	493
4. Native whites	468	476	483	486	474	493
Method No. 1						
5. Effect of foreign-born (line 1 minus line 2)	+9	+4	+1	0	−1	0
6. Effect of colored (line 2 minus line 4)	+22	+22	+16	+14	+7	+2
7. Combined effect (line 1 minus line 4, or line 5 plus line 6)	+31	+26	+17	+14	+6	+2
Method No. 2						
8. Effect of foreign-born (line 3 minus line 4)	+15	+10	+4	+3	+1	0
9. Effect of colored (line 1 minus line 3)	+16	+16	+13	+11	+5	+2
10. Combined effect (line 8 plus line 9)	+31	+26	+17	+14	+6	+2
Discrepancy between Methods						
11. Effect of foreign-born (line 5 minus line 8)	−6	−6	−3	−3	−2	0
12. Effect of colored (line 6 minus line 9)	+6	+6	+3	+3	+2	0

Source: Appendix A.

[a] Labor force aged 10 and older per 1,000 population of same age and color, standardized for age on the basis of population of the United States in 1940.

than natives. After adjustment for age disparities, the total labor force participation of all classes differed from the native white participation only moderately in 1890 and very little in 1950.

Neither the rural nor the urban labor force has been classified by the census according to color and nativity. Hence, while we can standardize according to residence without regard to nativity or color, and can study the participation of native whites without regard to residence, we cannot cross-standardize the native white, nor the colored and foreign-born labor force for rural and urban residence. Our only recourse is to what we call a "partial standardization." This means standardizing the total labor force participation for rural and urban residence, measuring the difference between the standardized and unstandardized, and then adding this difference to the native white labor force (Table 50). This procedure is not as satisfactory as cross-standardization, but it would be seriously inaccurate only if the rural-urban composition were changing very differently in the native white population than in the colored and foreign-born populations. Happily, though the share of Negroes in the population was slightly higher in urban areas, and slightly lower in rural areas in 1950 than in 1890, by and large their rural-urban composition has changed about

TABLE 50

Two Alternative Methods of Partial Standardization of the Labor
Force for Rural-Urban Residence, Color, and Nativity,
United States, Census Dates, 1890–1950

	1890	*1900*	*1910*	*1920*	*1930*	*1940*	*1950*
Method No. 1: Add Effects of Rural-Urban Residence to Native White Labor Force							
Native whites in labor force per 1,000 population aged 10 and older of same sex, color, and nativity [a]:							
Males	809	805	...	775	768	723	721
Females	127	147	...	190	204	225	265
Both sexes	468	476	...	483	486	474	493
Effect of rural-urban residence, per 1,000 population aged 10 and older of same sex [b]:							
Males	−4	0	−1	0	−1	0	+1
Females	+25	+17	+11	+6	0	0	−7
Both sexes	+10	+8	+5	+4	−1	0	−3
Native whites in labor force, partially standardized for rural-urban residence, per 1,000 population aged 10 and older of same sex:							
Males	805	805	...	775	767	723	722
Females	152	164	...	196	204	225	258
Both sexes	478	484	...	487	485	474	490
Method No. 2: Subtract Effect of Color and Nativity from Labor Force of All Classes Standardized for Rural-Urban Residence							
Persons of all classes in labor force per 1,000 population aged 10 and older of same sex [b]:							
Males	819	814	793	790	771	722	716
Females	187	197	212	215	219	233	260
Both sexes	503	506	503	503	495	478	488
Effect of color and nativity, per 1,000 population aged 10 and older of same sex [c]:							
Males	+18	+12	...	+12	+7	0	−3
Females	+43	+40	...	+23	+20	+12	+6
Both sexes	+31	+26	...	+17	+14	+6	+2
Labor force partially standardized for rural-urban residence, color, and nativity per 1,000 population aged 10 and older of same sex:							
Males	801	802	...	778	764	722	719
Females	144	157	...	192	199	221	254
Both sexes	472	480	...	486	481	472	486

TABLE 50, *continued*

	1890	1900	1910	1920	1930	1940	1950
Discrepancy between Methods 1 and 2, per 1,000 population aged 10 and older of same sex:							
Males	+4	+3	...	−3	+3	+1	+3
Females	+8	+7	...	+4	+5	+4	+4
Both sexes	+6	+4	...	+1	+4	+2	+4

Source: Appendix A.

[a] Appendix Table A-4.

[b] Appendix Table A-2. Effects of rural-urban residence were obtained by subtracting labor force participation standardized for age and sex from labor force participation standardized for age-sex and rural-urban residence.

[c] Tables 29 and 49.

the same as that of native whites. The ratio of foreign-born to native white population fell somewhat more in rural than in urban areas, but did not change enormously. Thus the considerable changes in age-sex, rural-urban, and color-nativity composition of the population have not exerted enough weight to impair the stability of the total labor force participation, even in the United States. In the other countries where these changes have been generally on a smaller scale, it is likely that they would have had less effect. These results tend to confirm broadly the tentative conclusion of a paper written by the author which appeared in 1944 and which was perhaps the earliest comparative analysis of labor force behavior over time: "the propensity to be 'in the labor force' seems one of the most stable elements in the labor market, varying hardly at all except in long, slow trends, requiring years to consummate. It may be that the peacetime propensity is based not upon mere impulse, but upon deeply rooted habits, on the size and composition of families, on institutions of child care, education, and old age dependency, on the concentration of population, and on the structure and geography of industry. The labor force evidently does not expand or shrink under ordinary economic pressures." [9]

The Problem of Measuring Stability

There is, of course, no single criterion of stability or instability. A change meaningless in one situation can be significant in another. By the more obvious standards, few important magnitudes would seem to be as constant from one peacetime year to another as the total labor force participation. Nevertheless, before we are in a position to con-

[9] Clarence D. Long, *The Labor Force in Wartime America*, National Bureau of Economic Research, Occasional Paper 14, 1944, p. 37.

clude that the total labor force has been stable over the past half century, we must seek answers to a number of questions.

According to Durand, an authority on the labor force, this constancy is created partly by certain adjustments and partly by the dominance of males in the labor force.[10]

THE POSSIBILITY THAT THE APPARENT STABILITY IS DUE TO THE AUTHOR'S ADJUSTMENT IN THE CENSUS DATA.

My corrections for census undercount of labor force in 1890 and overcount in 1910 were somewhat larger than those made by Durand, but I made no correction for 1920 beyond a small one to shift the data from a January basis (the month of census enumeration in 1920) to an April basis (the month in which all United States censuses have been enumerated since 1930). Durand made substantial adjustments, which are discussed in Supplementary Appendix H, for both 1920 and 1930. Do the disparities between our adjustments explain how I obtained a comparatively high stability in the United States participation rate? On the contrary. If Durand had combined his male and female rates of participation instead of presenting them separately, he would have found that his total rate, while generally lower than mine as the result of his adjustments, would have been actually more stable (Table 51). My total participation rates have been stable in spite of the adjustments here, not because of them.

Indeed, for any of the nations or areas studied, except war-torn Germany after 1939, the maximum difference between one census and the next in either the standardized or the unstandardized labor force has been 3.4 per cent of the population of working age (Table 52)— smaller than the difference between the summer and the winter labor force in the United States in any normal year,[11] and only a fraction of the difference in unemployment between a good and a bad year. The average change in the labor force from one census to the next was half to two-thirds the maximum. Outside of Germany the average change was typically between 0.8 and 1.4 per cent of those of working age, or 1.4 to 2.4 per cent of the labor force itself.

WAS TOTAL LABOR FORCE PARTICIPATION STABLE BECAUSE OF THE STABILITY OF ADULT-MALE PARTICIPATION?

Actually the labor force participation of adult males has not been highly stable. In all of the five countries participation declined some-

[10] John D. Durand, in a letter to the author, 1950.

[11] The seasonal adjustments in Appendix Table B-1, footnote a, indicate a slightly smaller seasonal range than this, but they are based on quarterly averages which iron out some of the seasonal variation found in monthly data.

TABLE 51

Labor Force and Labor Force Changes as Computed by Durand and Long, United States, Census Dates, 1890–1950
(per 1,000 population of working age and same sex) [a]

	1890	1900	1920	1930	1940	1950	Average Change from Previous Decade	
							1890–1940	1890–1950
Males 10 and older:								
Durand:								
Labor force	755	781	764	744	729	–	–	–
Change from previous decade		+26	−17	−20	−15	–	20	–
Long:								
Labor force	792	795	783	762	722	729	–	–
Change from previous decade		+3	−12	−21	−40	+7	19	17
Females 10 and older:								
Durand:								
Labor force	166	184	206	215	236	–	–	–
Change from previous decade		+18	+22	+9	+21	–	18	–
Long:								
Labor force	170	188	212	220	233	265	–	–
Change from previous decade		+18	+24	+8	+13	+32	+16	+19
Both sexes 10 and older:								
Durand:								
Labor force	469	490	491	483	483	–	–	–
Change from previous decade		+21	+1	−8	0	–	7	–
Long:								
Labor force	490	499	504	495	478	494	–	–
Change from previous decade		+9	+5	−9	−17	+16	10	11

Source: Appendix A. J. D. Durand, *The Labor Force in the United States, 1890–1960*, Social Science Research Council, 1948, p. 208; *Census of Population, 1940*, A. M. Edwards, *Comparative Occupation Statistics for the United States, 1870 to 1940*, p. 93.

[a] Adjusted for miscounts but not standardized; see text of this chapter and Appendix A.

what for every male age group, without exception. In the United States between 1890 and 1950 the fall per 1,000 of corresponding age was 92 for men aged 20–24, 48 for men aged 25–44, and 73 for men aged 45–64. The reductions were roughly four-fifths of the increase for females in the 20–24 age group, one-fourth for ages 25–44, and one-half for ages 45–64. Indeed, when adjusted for miscounts, the total labor force participation—of persons aged 10 and older or 14 and older, standardized or unstandardized for age-sex, rural-urban composition, or color-nativity—did not change in any decade, or over all the decades between 1890 and 1950, by half so much as the change for the men 25–44.

Moreover, not all female groups showed an increase in participation. For example, in the United States in 1950 there were nearly a half million fewer girls aged 10–19 and women 65 and older in gainful occupations than there would have been had their rates of participa-

TABLE 52

Labor Force Stability: Census-to-Census Changes Measured in Percentages of Population of Working Age, 5 Countries, Various Periods, 1890–1951

	1890–1900	1900–1910	1910–1920	1920–1930	1930–1940	1940–1950	Change during Entire Period
							Over-Av. Max. All
United States:							
Unstandardized	+0.9	+0.8	−0.3	−0.9	−1.7	+1.6	1.0 1.7 +0.4
Standardized: [a]							
For age and sex	+0.5	0	+0.1	−0.3	−1.8	+1.3	0.7 1.8 −0.2
For age and sex and rural-urban residence	+0.3	−0.3	0	−0.8	−1.7	+1.0	0.7 1.7 −1.5
Native white, standardized for age and sex	+0.8	+1.7		+0.1	−1.2	+2.0	1.2 2.0 +2.4
Native white, standardized for age and sex and rural-urban residence [b]	+0.5	+1.2		−0.4	−1.1	+1.6	1.0 1.6 +1.8

	1911–1921	1921–1931	1931–1939	1931–1951	Change during Entire Period
					Over-Av. Max. All
Great Britain:					
Unstandardized	−1.8	−0.2	+0.4	−2.4	1.2 2.4 −4.0
Standardized for age and sex [a]	−0.5	+0.4	+1.3	−1.3	0.9 1.3 −0.1

	1911–1921	1921–1931	1931–1941	1941–1951	Change during Entire Period
					Over-Av. Max. All
Canada:					
Unstandardized	−1.3	+0.5	+1.0	−1.9	1.2 1.9 −1.7
Standardized:					
For age and sex [a]	+0.3	+0.8	+1.7	−0.7	0.9 1.7 +2.1
For age and sex and rural urban residence [c]	+0.1	+0.3	+1.8	−1.1	0.8 1.8 +1.1

TABLE 52, *continued*

	1896–1901	1901–1906	1906–1911	1911–1921	1921–1926	1926–1936	1936–1945	1945–1951	Change during Entire Period		
									Av.	Max.	Over-All
New Zealand:											
Unstandardized	+0.8	−0.8	+0.2	−2.6	−2.4	0	−3.4	−1.1	1.4	3.4	−9.3
Standardized for age and sex [a]	+1.8	−0.9	+0.7	−0.6	−2.0	+0.8	−1.2	−0.4	1.1	2.0	−1.8

	1895–1907	1907–1925	1925–1933	1933–1939	1939–1946	1946–1950	Change during Entire Period		
							Av.	Max.	Over-All
Germany:									
Unstandardized	+4.1	0	−2.7	+1.3	−8.7	+1.5	3.1	8.7	−3.5
Standardized for age and sex [a]	+3.8	+1.1	−1.8	+2.2	−5.0	+1.5	2.6	5.0	+1.5

Source: Appendixes A, C, and for German boundary changes, p. 429.

[a] Standardized on the basis of population of the United States in 1940.

[b] Partially standardized for rural-urban residence on the asumption that the effect of rural-urban migration would be the same for native-whites as for all classes.

[c] Partially standardized for rural-urban residence on the assumption that the effect of rural-urban migration would be the same in Canada as in the United States.

tion been the same as in 1890. If the population is standardized for age and sex, and the labor force involved in the increase of participation of women 20–64 is deducted from the labor force involved in the decrease of participation of males and of younger and older females, the net difference is only 223,000, or 1.6 per cent of the gross change between 1890 and 1950 of nearly 14 million workers (Table 53). In the four foreign nations the net change ranged from 3 per cent of gross change in Great Britain to a bit under 30 per cent in Canada.

We now examine the contention that males aged 25–64 have such a stable tendency to be in the labor force that any participation changes on the part of females or of younger and older males would be relatively unimportant. At this point, the position seems to be:

1. The total labor force participation rate is not stable.

2. How could it help being stable?

Actually, men aged 25–64 are less than one-third of the total population of working age, the other two-thirds consisting of teen-age boys and girls, women aged 25–64, and elderly people. For these so-called "marginal groups," the labor force averages 350 per 1,000; and a rise in the average participation of these groups in the United States to British levels, with no change in the rate for males, would raise the total United States participation from 534 to about the level reached in the peak

TABLE 53

Gross Changes in Labor Force of Males and Females Resulting
Solely from Variations in Their Rates of Participation,
Compared with Net Change, United States,
Census Dates, 1890–1950

It is assumed here that no change occurred in the sex and age composition of the
population.

| | Gross Changes (thousands of persons) | |
	Decreases	Increases
Males: [a]		
10–13	929	
14–19	1,403	
20–24	577	
25–44	1,042	
45–64	1,076	
65 & older	1,569	
Females: [a]		
10–13	274	
14–19	154	
20–24		760
25–44		3,834
45–64		2,243
65 & older	36	
	7,060	6,837
Sum of gross changes:		13,897
Net change:		−223
Net change as per cent of sum of gross changes:		−1.6

Source: Appendix A.

[a] Labor force standardized for sex and age on the basis of population of the
United States in 1940.

expansion of World War II.[12] The variations that could take place in
total labor force participation are therefore great,[13] and the reason no
large variations have occurred under peacetime high employment is
not that the labor force is in a "statistical straight-jacket," but that the
internal changes have offset each other.

HAS THE LABOR FORCE PARTICIPATION IN THE CENSUS MONTH BEEN
TYPICAL OF THE AVERAGE PARTICIPATION FOR THE YEAR?

There is a statistical possibility that the apparent stability was the
accidental effect of a shift over the years in the seasonal pattern of

[12] The proportion of males aged 25–64 in the population of Britain was about
the same as in the United States. So also was the tendency of this group to be in
the labor force.
[13] One has only to look to cities in the United States to see the widely varying

248

labor force behavior. Has the labor force as enumerated by the five countries [14] in spring, been unduly greater or less compared to the annual averages? Has there been a change in this relationship? Conceivably the 1890 labor force may have been a larger proportion of population in the spring than in the average for the year, and the 1950 labor force a smaller proportion in the spring. If so, a decline in the relationship between spring figures and the annual averages could have disguised, say, a rise in the average over time, thus making it appear falsely that the labor force was comparatively stable. Of course, other situations might also be proposed.

How were any such shifts in seasonal patterns to be tested? One way was to make use of the most detailed material available—monthly information in the United States since 1940, and quarterly and monthly information in Canada since World War II.[15] In both countries the peacetime differences between April or June participation and the annual average were small—nearly always less than 1 per cent of the population 14 and older—and they were, moreover, constant (based on data in Appendix B).

Before 1940 seasonal data were limited to the United States and provided only partial information on the behavior of the labor force. Data on employment in most branches of industry have been estimated by the National Bureau of Economic Research for 1920 and 1921, and by the Bureau of Labor Statistics for the period since 1929. These data show that the level in the spring quarter of the year has been very close to that for the annual average, and that no appreciable trend away from this relationship took place between 1920 and 1954.[16]

---

labor force tendencies in this country, even among northeastern cities (Appendix Table A-7A).

[14] The labor force has usually been enumerated in the early or late spring—the only exceptions having been January 1920 in the United States, September 1945 in New Zealand, and September 1950 in Germany. Also in Germany the 1946 census was taken in the fall, but was of little use because the German economy was, obviously, in a chaotic state. In the United States, adjustments were made for the differences in census seasons (Supplementary Appendix G), and for any differences between late spring (June) in 1890 and 1900, and early spring (April) in 1910, 1930, 1940, and 1950. There was no basis on which to make adjustments in New Zealand in 1945 nor in Germany in 1950, but these exceptions offered no serious problem.

[15] War years must be eliminated from the comparison, since changes during World War II and the Korean conflict would naturally produce abnormal differences.

[16] 1920–1921: Willford I. King, in "Changes in Employment in the Principal Industrial Fields, January 1, 1920 to March 31, 1922" (*Business Cycles and Unemployment,* National Bureau of Economic Research, 1923, pp. 82, 88), says, "Records were secured from employers who hire about one-tenth of all the employees in the United States. However, the proportion differs in different industries." 1929–1930: *Survey of Current Business,* Dept. of Commerce, March 1941, p. 17. 1953–1954: *Survey of Current Business,* March 1954, p. S-11;

Before 1920, seasonal information on unemployment was at hand only for trade unions, going back to 1897–98. These trade union data behave in the expected random fashion, but indicate no change in trend of the seasonal pattern of idleness.[17] However, the unemployment behavior of trade union members—largely in the printing, clothing, metals, and construction industries—would scarcely be significant for seasonal changes in labor force participation. Most of the members are males whose unemployment rates would change almost entirely because of variations in employment, whereas labor force participation varies largely because women and young people move in and out at different times of the year, such as during the Christmas and Easter seasons, and during the summer months.

Data on employment before 1920 were for manufacturing and could give no clue to the seasonal behavior in agriculture, services, trade, or of self-employment. They do, however, indicate what happened in one of the major segments of industry, and show that during 1900–1919, and for selected dates since, second-quarter employment remained close to the average for the year.[18]

It would of course have been more satisfactory to have had monthly data on participation during the census year, rather than that for only one month (or week) in the spring. Nevertheless the scanty material suggests that the average labor force participation over the year may have been very close to the spring figures, and that any differences may have stayed rather constant in direction and relative size. The conclusions as to the behavior of labor force participation over time, therefore, might not have been substantially different even if complete data had been available for the period studied.

Monthly Labor Review, Bureau of Labor Statistics, March 1955, p. 349; *Trends in Employment in Agriculture, 1909–1936,* Works Progress Administration National Research Project, p. 153; *Farm Labor,* Dept. of Agriculture, Jan. 12, 1955, p. 8.

[17] The fact that these data exclude employers, self-employed persons, unpaid family workers, domestic servants, and the unemployed allows the possibility that counter variations in seasonal participation could have occurred among these uncovered groups. *Report on the Relations and Conditions of Capital and Labor Employed in Manufactures and General Business,* United States Industrial Commission, 1900, Vol. VII, p. 30; Ernest S. Bradford, *Industrial Unemployment,* Bureau of Labor Statistics, Bull. 310, pp. 10, 47, 49.

[18] The dates chosen were years of relatively level employment. *Census of Manufactures: 1900,* pp. 20–55; *1919,* pp. 404–405; *1923,* pp. 1136–1137; *1947,* p. 81. E. S. Bradford, *Industrial Unemployment,* BLS, Bull. 310, p. 35; *Survey of Current Business,* March 1941, p. 17, and March 1954, p. S-11; *Monthly Labor Review,* March 1955, p. 349. The data for 1900–1929 cover wage earners only; those for 1947 and 1954, wage earners and salaried supervisory employees. The 1900 data on female employment cover females 16 and older. The data on female employment for 1954 were obtained directly from the Bureau of Labor Statistics and cover only employment in March, June, September, and December. The annual average is thus the mean of employment in these four months; the second quarter is taken as the average of employment in March and June.

DUAL JOBHOLDING.

The study is concerned primarily with how many people participate in the labor force and only incidentally with how hard or how long they work, or what kind of work they do. Still, variations in the proportion of persons who work concurrently at more than one job might be inter-related, as cause or effect, with changes in the number of persons in the labor force, and might serve as a partial substitute for such changes.

There is no information before 1940, but for five scattered dates since then the census has compiled sample survey information which suggests that dual jobholding is a relatively minor factor.[19] The first survey—though it was taken as of January 1943 during one of the busiest years of World War II—reported only 3.8 per cent of the employed civilian workers to have more than one job. The next two surveys—taken in early July of 1946 and 1950—indicated that the percentage was less than 3.5. The final survey—taken in early December 1950, when extra pre-Christmas job opportunities could be expected to increase dual job-holding in the light of economic mobilization for the Korean conflict —revealed a further drop to 3 per cent.[20] Not only was multiple em-ployment a relatively small factor during these years, but it was also relatively stable, considering the wide range of economic conditions covered by the surveys.[21] A fifth survey, published recently, indicates a somewhat larger percentage of dual jobholders (5.5 per cent) in July 1956. The census indicates that some of the difference may be attrib-utable to improved measurement techniques used in 1956, but suggests that there are reasons for believing that some actual increase has occurred.[22]

Even these data exaggerate the number of persons who were ac-

[19] Domestic service employees who usually work for several different employers during the week were considered to have only one job. Those who regularly work for only one employer, however, were counted as dual jobholders if they changed employers during the week. Persons operating two or more firms or business enter-prises (or combination of these) were considered as having only one job. To make results of the 1950 and 1946 surveys comparable with those of the 1943 survey, the census included persons who were self-employed. (From a mimeographed memorandum of December 1950, furnished by courtesy of Gertrude Bancroft of the Bureau of the Census.)

[20] The proportion of *jobs* held by dual jobholders could be expected to be somewhat greater than that of dual jobholders, since persons who hold more than one job may even hold more than two. No data were offered for 1943 on this proportion, but it was 5.6 per cent in July 1950, and 5.0 per cent in December 1950.

[21] This is also the conclusion of the Bureau of the Census in analyzing the data: "Except for seasonal differences, the extent of dual jobholding appears to have been remarkably constant, over the past several years. . . ." (Mimeographed memorandum cited in footnote 19.)

[22] "Multiple Jobholding: July 1956," *Current Population Reports, The Labor Force*, Bureau of the Census, Series P-50, No. 74, April 1957.

tually working "simultaneously" at more than one job. Some doubtless took a secondary job to supplement their vacation income, others to replace it if they had not been in primary jobs long enough to receive pay for vacation shut-downs.[23] Still others might have left one job and begun another later in the same week. Thus some of dual jobholding is actually sequential jobholding, or having two jobs but working at only one of them.

The true extent of genuine simultaneous work cannot be known until the census surveys precisely how many persons actually work at two jobs in the same day. But it is highly probable that *working* at more than one job has been less than even the modest percentages of *holding* more than one job reported by the census. As for earlier years, it must have been still less, for it is unlikely that people can work at two or more jobs in the same day unless the workday in primary employments is short. In earlier years, the workday was long.

Declining Participation of Negroes versus Stability among Whites

It has already been noted that the stability of the labor force participation of the total United States population and of the native white population does not extend to the foreign-born or to Negroes.

In 1930, the labor force participation of the colored in the United States was approximately the same as that of Germany's population. By 1950, it had fallen here almost to the level of the whites, i.e. from almost two-thirds to not much over half the population of working age. The decline was about the same whether or not standardized for age and sex—in fact, it occurred in nearly every age and sex group. It was specially pronounced for males and for young and old persons. And it occurred for females, while native white and some age groups of foreign-born females were increasing their participation.[24] How can we explain this instability?

COMPOSITION.

The reduction in labor force participation of Negroes has not been due to their large migration from rural to urban areas; on the contrary, the participation of the colored in urban areas has been appreciably above that of the colored in rural areas, both in the United States as a whole and in the South.[25] The migration may even have softened the decline.

---

[23] Vacationers working at secondary jobs may have been numerous at the time of the surveys in early July of 1946 and 1950.

[24] The only colored females who showed an increase in propensity to be in the labor force throughout 1890–1950 were those in the 25–44 age group.

[25] Standardized for age and sex. *Census of Population, 1940, The Labor Force,* loc. cit.

Nor has the decrease been due to changes among Negroes, Indians, Chinese, and others in the composition of the nonwhites, for Negroes have been so large a percentage of the whole nonwhite group as to dominate its labor force tendencies almost completely. Finally, it was not due to changes in age or sex composition, since the results were not modified appreciably by standardizing the colored labor force for age and sex.

One possible explanation may be that an increasing share of Negro females were kept out of the labor force by the rising responsibilities for the care of young children since 1930, for there has been a rise in the ratio of colored children under 14 to colored females of working age, no doubt as a result of the increase in the survival rate of the former. It is true that a decline in child-care responsibilities did not cause a rise in the participation of colored females before 1930, but the reason could have been that they had already reached their maximum potential in the labor force by that time.

THE SHORTER WORKWEEK.

In Chapter 7 (Chart 14), decreases in the length of the workweek seemed to be associated with increases in female participation—perhaps because they made it possible for many females to work in industry and still do their housework.

There are no analogous statistics by color. But to the extent that Negroes worked in the same firms or industries as white persons, they undoubtedly observed much the same standard hours. In recent decades Negroes have been moving rapidly out of relatively long-hour domestic service and agriculture into relatively short-hour manufacturing and service industries, a movement which could have produced an even greater decline in average hours for Negroes than for whites and permitted *more* rather than fewer Negro females to enter the labor force.

Large Cities Taken as a Whole and Individually

The stability of labor force participation rates over time observed for the four foreign countries, for the United States as a whole, for native whites in the United States, for the United States urban and rural areas, and for the 38 large United States cities in the aggregate, does not hold for all the cities examined, taken individually, in Canada or in the United States.

In Canada, participation was not highly stable either in individual cities or in all cities combined; in the cities combined, it rose per 1,000 population 15 and older from 581 in 1911 to 626 in 1951. In two-thirds of the 21 cities taken separately, the maximum change was greater than the maximum change when combined; in the other third, the maximum

TABLE 54

Stability of the Labor Force per 1,000 Population 14 and Older, by Color, 38 Large Cities, United States, 1920–1950

	OVER-ALL AND MAXIMUM [a] CHANGES IN LABOR FORCE [b]					
	Whites 1920–1950 [c]		Colored 1920–1950 [c]		All Classes 1900–1950 [c]	
	Over-All	Maximum	Over-All	Maximum	Over-All	Maximum
Atlanta	+34	34	−137	138	−30	33
Baltimore	+9	11	−154	154	−11	39
Birmingham	+46	46	−96	96	−40	40
Boston	−54	54	. . .	. . .	−35	72
Bridgeport	+20	29	. . .	. . .	+4	13
Buffalo	+30	30	. . .	. . .	+20	21
Chicago	+21	23	−89	89	+27	41
Cincinnati	−13	22	−122	122	−31	39
Cleveland	+35	35	−74	90	+38	38
Columbus	+13	24	. . .	. . .	+39	43
Dallas	+43	43	−76	76	+12	13
Denver	+39	44	. . .	. . .	+40	48
Detroit	+18	26	−95	95	+5	20
Houston	+18	18	−106	106	−35	35
Indianapolis	+42	44	−3	49	+55	55
Kansas City	+20	25	−96	102	+26	34
Los Angeles	+11	21	−39	39	+53	53
Louisville	−9	10	−166	166	−16	55
Memphis	+30	33	−88	88	−68	68
Milwaukee	+34	53	. . .	. . .	+45	53
Minneapolis	+34	42	. . .	. . .	+49	49
Newark	+18	18	−41	93	0	11
New Haven	−21	32	. . .	. . .	−6	45
New Orleans	0	6	−156	156	−23	65
New York	−15	15	−139	139	−3	29
Norfolk	+52	52	−95	95	−38	38
Omaha	−9	18	. . .	. . .	−7	19
Philadelphia	−10	22	−141	141	−23	32
Pittsburgh	−8	8	−117	117	−2	30
Portland, Ore.	+37	39	. . .	. . .	+37	39
Providence	−35	35	. . .	. . .	−40	55
Richmond	+41	41	−110	110	−8	31
Rochester	+4	16	. . .	. . .	+2	31
St. Louis	+7	7	−136	146	+16	44
St. Paul	+9	15	. . .	. . .	+20	24
San Francisco	+9	35	+15	21	+27	42
Scranton	−15	15	. . .	. . .	−17	28
Seattle	+20	28	. . .	. . .	+65	65
38 Cities						
Aggregate	+6	8	−109 [d]	109 [d]	+5	25
Median	+18	27	−96	102	−1	39

notes on following page

changes were 50 to 70 per 1,000 (based on Appendix Table A-13). Most of the changes occurred between 1941 and 1951 and seemed to stem largely from the male population. Male participation increased in 15 of the 21 cities, despite its general decline in recent decades in Canada as a whole. With male participation increasing, there was nothing to offset the rise for females.

In the United States, the stability observed in participation in all 38 large cities combined was largely due to fluctuations offsetting each other over time among the individual cities. In only 7 cities was the maximum change as small as that of the 38 combined, and about 29 had a maximum change of 30 to 72 per 1,000 population 14 and older.

Participation in individual cities was less than stable for whites alone as well as for all classes (Table 54), although the comparison had to be confined to 1920–1950, since data by color were not available for 1900. (The study of 38 large United States cities covered the census dates 1900 and 1920–1950.) Among white persons, participation was highly stable for all of the 38 cities combined (as was that of all classes), but all except three cities had maximum changes greater than the maximum change in the combined average, and 17 cities had maximum changes of 30 to 54 per 1,000. The changes for whites were small, however, compared with those for the colored. Colored persons are not numerous in many areas, and data were available for the full period 1920–1950 for only 23 cities. In all 23 except San Francisco, the colored labor force participation declined between 1920 and 1950; in all but a few it declined in every decade; in every city it fell between 1930 and 1940; and in only five was there a rise, which took place between 1940 and 1950. In 16 of the 23 cities the decline in colored participation occurred in the face of a rise in white participation. The decline averaged 109 per 1,000 colored population, but in seven cities it was more than 135—a fifth of the colored labor force in 1920. In the case of females, colored participation declined in all but four of the 23 cities (Indianapolis, Los Angeles, Newark, and San Francisco) while that of white females was rising in every one of the 38 cities. That of colored males declined without exception, and in 1950 was lower than white male participation in every one of the 23 cities. *It is noteworthy that*

Notes to Table 54

Source: Appendix A. *Census of Population: 1920*, Vol. II, Chapter III, Tables 15–17, and Vol. IV, *Occupations*, Chapter IV, Table 22; *1930*, Vol. III, Table 12, and Vol. IV, *Occupations*, Table 9; *1940*, Vol. III, *The Labor Force*, Parts 2–5, Table 5; *1950*, Vol. II, *Characteristics of the Population*, Part 1, Tables 86, 87.

[a] Difference between highest and lowest figures.

[b] Standardized for age and sex on the basis of the composition of population of Chicago in 1930.

[c] The study of 38 large cities covered 1900 and 1920–1950. Since data by color were not available for 1900, the comparison had to be confined to 1920–1950.

[d] Data were available for only 23 cities.

these declines in colored participation occurred despite the enormous increase in jobs available to Negroes.

This lack of stability in large cities demands explanation.

GROWTH OF CITIES.

Could the diverse behavior among the different cities have been related to changes in their size? That is, could the participation of whites have fallen in cities that were growing slowly, and risen in cities that were growing rapidly? The possibility that the latter offered more job opportunities to women, boys, and older men was tested by correlating, separately for whites and Negroes, the change between 1920 and 1950 in labor force participation [26] with the increase in population in each city. The test revealed some tendency for Negro participation to decline least in the cities with the most rapidly growing colored population. The correlation was not large ($r = 0.48$), though it was significant on the 95 per cent level; for whites it was much weaker and it was only moderately significant. There was no strong indication that changes in a city's labor force participation are tied to its population growth.

PROSPERITY OF CITIES.

Could the change in a city's labor force participation be associated with its relative prosperity? This question was examined in two ways: First, the changes in the white and colored participation between 1920 and 1950 were compared with the changes in real earnings of males of all classes.[27] Second, the changes in white and Negro participation in each city between 1920 and 1950 were compared with the *level* of earnings of white and Negro males in that city in 1949 respectively. But the changes in participation showed no association with *changes* in earnings for either whites or Negroes, and showed only a bare association with the *level* of earnings of whites ($r = 0.40$).

CHANGES IN JOB OPPORTUNITIES.

The labor force behavior in individual cities offers a chance to see whether participation rose in those cities in which unemployment declined most (or rose least), and fell in those cities in which unemployment rose most (or declined least). Accordingly, changes from 1930 to 1950 in labor force participation of whites were compared with changes in their unemployment rates [28]—with almost zero results. We have

[26] Standardized for age and sex.
[27] Adjusted to the purchasing power of the dollar in Chicago in 1930. All classes were used because separate earnings for whites and colored were not available in 1920.
[28] Comparisons between 1930 and 1940 and between 1940 and 1950 were made in Chapter 10 which dealt with the labor force in depressions.

already noted that the great decline in Negro participation between 1940 and 1950 occurred while job opportunities for colored people were surely becoming more abundant. Nevertheless, on the chance that the *size* of the changes may have been related—the changes in colored participation from 1930 to 1950 were correlated with the changes in the colored male unemployment rate among the 23 cities with separate data. Again, however, the correlation was too small to be significant.

INFLUENCE OF THE FOREIGN-BORN.

Did the total white participation rate rise in those cities where the foreign-born whites were few in number, and fall in those cities where they were relatively numerous and where their decreasing labor force propensity could exert more of a depressing effect? Some such tendency is borne out in a correlation between the change in white labor force participation between 1920 and 1950 and the ratio of foreign-born to whites in 1930. The correlation ($r = -0.43$) was significant on the 95 per cent level, though it was not large enough to justify placing great reliance on this factor as an explanation.

EFFECT OF CHANGES IN CHILD-CARE RESPONSIBILITIES OF WOMEN.

It has been suggested that more women could enter the labor force if there were fewer young children who required care at home, and that many women in their desire or need for jobs might postpone having children. It is true that white female participation rose in all cities, while the relative number of white children declined in all but four cities. But there was no significant correlation between the changes in the ratio of white children under 14 to white females 14 and older and the changes in white female participation. There was a significant similar correlation, however, for Negro females among the 23 cities for which data were available. In all the cities but 4 there were decreases in the participation of Negro women; and in all but 3 there were increases in the ratio of children to women—no doubt due to the decline in Negro infant mortality. And there was some tendency ($r = -0.48$) for colored female participation to decline most in cities where the increase in the relative number of colored children was greatest. The correlation did not assure that increases in child-care responsibilities were the dominant factor in causing the exodus of Negro women from the labor force, but it was significant on the 95 per cent level—high enough to require consideration.

257

THE TENDENCY OF NEGRO PARTICIPATION RATES AMONG CITIES
TO EQUALIZE.

In 1920 the colored labor force rates of 23 cities had an interquartile range of 80 [29] or 11½ per cent of the median rate; by 1950, this range had declined to 47, or less than 8 per cent. Between these dates the colored participation rate had declined most in those cities where it was highest at the start of the period ($r = -0.73$). This tendency to equalize, significant on the 95 per cent level, was observed entirely among the colored, and was not observable among the whites. It should not be surprising that as the working habits of the Negroes moved more closely to those of the whites, they would also move more closely to those of each other.

United States and Britain in the Nineteenth Century

UNITED STATES, 1820–1880.

Has the labor force been stable over the last sixty years because its potentiality for decline was exhausted in an earlier period? This conjecture is not supported by analyses available heretofore; the late Daniel Carson concluded that participation actually rose throughout the nineteenth century. However, examination of his materials [30] revealed no clear evidence that the total labor force participation changed at all, but suggested that a misleading impression was produced by the gradual improvement in census enumerations in the first three quarters of the nineteenth century, and by lack of standardization for age and rural-urban composition.

Whelpton [31] attempted to adjust for certain deficiencies in early enumerations but the data still indicated that labor force participation was rising. But there is serious doubt that Whelpton's adjustments were sufficient (Appendix F). And the rise may have been due also to a tendency for relatively more persons to be in the adult age groups, or to live in urban areas. Since 1890 data have allowed us to eliminate the effects of some demographic developments by standardizing the labor force for age, sex, and rural-urban compositions, but before 1890, the data did not permit such adjustment.

How are we to test this? Since information on rural and urban labor force were not available for the usual standardization, we resort to a device which we call "destandardization" (Table 55):

[29] Per 1,000 Negro population 14 and older.
[30] "Changes in the Industrial Composition of Manpower since the Civil War," *Studies in Income and Wealth, Volume Eleven,* National Bureau of Economic Research, 1949.
[31] P. K. Whelpton, "Occupational Groups in the United States, 1820–1920," *Journal of the American Statistical Association,* September 1926, pp. 335–343.

TABLE 55

Rural-Urban Destandardization Test of Stability of the Proportion
of Population 10 and Older in the Labor Force, United
States, Selected Years, 1820–1880

(labor force and population in thousands)

	1820	1840	1870	1880
Urban areas				
1. Population 10 and older	468	1,260	7,500	10,350
2. Assumed stable per cent in labor force (average of 1890–1940) [a]	52.2	52.2	52.2	52.2
3. Assumed labor force (line 1 × line 2)	244	658	3,915	5,403
Rural areas				
4. Population 10 and older	6,020	10,369	21,624	26,411
5. Assumed stable per cent in labor force (average of 1890–1940) [a]	46.4	46.4	46.4	46.4
6. Assumed labor force (line 4 × line 5)	2,793	4,811	10,034	12,255
United States				
7. Population 10 and older (line 1 + line 4)	6,488	11,629	29,124	36,761
8. Labor force (line 3 + line 6)	3,037	5,469	13,949	17,658
9. Per cent in labor force calculated by destandarization (line 8 ÷ line 7)	46.8	47.0	47.9	48.0
10. Actual per cent in labor force (Whelpton) [b]	44.4	46.6	44.4	47.3
11. Difference between Whelpton's [b] calculation of per cent in labor force and the calculation by destandardization (line 9 − line 10)	2.4	0.4	3.5	0.7

Source: Appendix A.

[a] This percentage is the average for 1890–1940 of the proportion of urban or rural population 10 and older in the labor force, standardized for age and sex on the basis of population of the United States in 1940.
[b] See footnote f, Appendix Table A-1.

Note: The data for 1830, 1850, and 1860 could not be used, for reasons set forth in Appendix F.

1. It is assumed that the participation rates in both urban and rural areas during 1820–1880 were the same as those standardized for age and sex during 1890–1940: urban, 52.2 per cent; rural, 46.4 per cent.

2. These assumed rates are multiplied by the actual urban and rural populations aged 10 and older during 1820–1880.

3. The resulting urban and rural labor forces are then added to obtain the combined labor force for the United States.

4. Finally, this sum is divided by the actual United States population 10 and older, in order to compute the destandardized rates for the United States as a whole. To the extent that the rise in participation was due to the more rapid growth of urban areas, with their higher participation levels, the rates thus "destandardized" for rural-urban composition should be reasonably close to those reported by the census and adjusted by Whelpton.

The expectation is approximately confirmed. Although the agreement was not precise (Table 55, line 11), the difference was only 0.4 per cent in 1840 and 0.7 per cent in 1880. Where the destandardized rate differed by a larger amount, i.e. 2.4 per cent in 1820 and 3.5 per cent in 1870, it could easily be more nearly correct than the Whelpton result, as the latter was subject both to errors in enumeration and to mistakes in adjusting for miscounts. On the accuracy of the adjustments for miscounts, Fabricant says:

". . . I am inclined to believe that Whelpton's estimates are no better than those obtained by assuming simply that for 1820–60 the ratios of gainful workers to total population 10 years and over lie between 44 and 50 per cent. If I *had* to narrow the range, I would put the limits at 46 and 48, and caution the reader against ascribing much validity to them." [32]

Our destandardized rate for 1820 is 46.7 per cent, which is within this narrower range.

For 1870, however, our understanding of the difference may be aided by the observation of Francis A. Walker, Superintendent of the Census at that time:

"The statistics of the census [of 1870] are not of uniform value. The census law of 1850 [under which it was conducted] was a purely tentative measure. Some of the inquiries which it proposed are such as the country is not even yet ripe for. In respect to others, no adequate machinery is provided; and the investigations from that census fail to accomplish worthy results. In respect to others, still, the compensation provided is so inadequate that, although the statistics are easily accessible, and the machinery for their collection is well adapted to the purpose, the motive force is wanting to secure the thorough performance of the duty. . . . Yet these statistics the authorities of the census are presumably bound to publish. . . ." [33]

[32] Solomon Fabricant, "The Changing Industrial Distribution of Gainful Workers: Comments on the Decennial Statistics, 1820–1940," *Studies in Income and Wealth*, Volume Eleven, NBER, 1949.
[33] *Census of 1870*, Vol. I, *Statistics of Population*, Part 1, p. xlvii.

A major reason for the defective enumeration of the census was that:

"the United States Marshals were left to appoint their assistants—the actual enumerators—without any check or control on the part of the Census Office . . . its right to make such a protest even being seriously a subject of question." [34]

In view of the shakiness of the data, the destandardization cannot prove that labor force participation, properly standardized, would have been stable during 1820–1880 or that it would have been close to the rates in later decades. It does indicate that the apparent rise in participation during 1820–1880 could be explained by the shift of population from rural areas, where participation was lower, to urban areas, where it was higher. The behavior is thus consistent with the hypothesis that the United States labor force participation has been fairly stable—aside from changes in age-sex or rural-urban composition—throughout the 130 years from 1820 to 1950.

ENGLAND AND WALES, 1841–1911.

The labor force of England and Wales in 1881 and 1891, adjusted for the minor omissions referred to in Appendix F, was almost exactly the same as in 1911 (Table 56, line 10).

In 1841, as originally reported, it was below these levels, but it did not include the unemployed in that depression year. If this omission were corrected by the addition of a hypothetical 10 per cent of the labor force, the participation rate of 1841 would be fairly close to the 1911 rate—particularly in view of the imprecision of the data.

But again it must be kept in mind that a larger share of the inhabitants lived in the lower-participation rural areas. What would be the result of applying the destandardization test? Assuming the participation rates in rural and urban areas were the same as in 1911, we find a destandardized rate for 1841 very similar to the "actual" (adjusted) rate for that year. It was less similar to the actual in 1881 and 1891. Even so, the destandardized and the actual labor force participation were apart by scarcely more than 0.5 per cent of the population aged 10 and older. The British, like the American experience, is consistent with the hypothesis that the labor force was a stable proportion of the population of working age in the nineteenth century, as it was in the twentieth.

[34] *Census of 1880, Compendium of the Tenth Census,* June 1, 1880, Part I, p. lx.

TABLE 56

Rural-Urban Destandardization Test of Stability of the Proportion
of Population 10 and Older in the Labor Force, England
and Wales, Selected Years, 1841–1911

(labor force and population in thousands)

	1841 [a]	1881	1891	1911
Urban areas				
1. Population 10 and older	5,803 [a]	13,143	15,925	22,269
2. Assumed stable per cent in labor force (same as in 1911) [b]	57.9	57.9	57.9	57.9
3. Assumed labor force (line 1 × line 2)	3,360	7,610	9,221	12,894
Rural areas				
4. Population 10 and older	6,287 [a]	6,163	6,129	6,250
5. Assumed stable per cent in labor force (same as in 1911) [b]	54.1	54.1	54.1	54.1
6. Assumed labor force (line 4 × line 5)	3,401	3,334	3,316	3,381
England and Wales				
7. Population 10 and older (line 1 + line 4)	12,090	19,306	22,054	28,519
8. Labor force (line 3 + line 6)	6,761	10,944	12,537	16,283
9. Per cent in labor force calculated by destandardization (line 8 ÷ line 7)	55.9	56.7	56.8	57.1
10. Actual per cent in labor force	50.5	57.3	57.3	57.1
Corrected for omission of unemployed in 1841:				
11. Assuming 10 per cent unemployed	56.1	–	–	–
12. Assuming 7 per cent unemployed	54.3	–	–	–
13. Assuming 13 per cent unemployed	58.0	–	–	–
14. Difference between "actual" per cent in labor force and the calculation by destandardization (line 9 minus line 10)	5.4	−0.6	−0.5	0
15. Same, assuming 10 per cent unemployed in 1841	−0.2	–	–	–
16. Same, assuming 7 per cent unemployed in 1841	1.6	–	–	–
17. Same, assuming 13 per cent unemployed in 1841	−2.1	–	–	–

Source: Appendix A.

[a] These figures were estimated by taking the rural population as 52 per cent of
the total population aged 10 and older.

[b] Actual per cent in labor force.

CHAPTER 13

OVER-ALL STABILITY VERSUS INTERNAL VARIATION IN A NATION'S LABOR FORCE PARTICIPATION

"A mighty maze, but not without a plan!"
POPE, *Essay on Man*

Statistical Relationship between the Exodus of Males and the Entrance of Females

PARTICIPATION rates of the over-all labor force in the five countries and in the rural and urban areas of the United States have changed rather little over the last half century. This comparative stability has been upheld in spite of occasional wide variations in unemployment and great increases in income per worker and per capita, and whether or not adjustment was made for changes in the composition of the population.

Why has over-all participation kept within such narrow limits, in view of the great changes in internal composition? Has the decrease in participation of one group been systematically interrelated with the increase in that of another?

Some interrelationship may be seen from Chart 29, where male participation is plotted from the base line for each country and area and female participation from the ceiling line. In all the places except Germany, the decline in male participation has been associated in a general way with the rise in female participation.

It would not have been prudent to attach great significance to these associations. Two strong trends in labor force participation over the decades—a declining one for males and a rising one for females— could produce this correlation. A real test was to correlate the deviations from these trends. Correlation was not practicable for the decade deviations, because of "random" variations due to interview error and to changes in the censuses in concept, measurement, and technique. But it was practicable for the broad "early" and "recent" periods. The early period ranges from 1911 through 1931 in Great Britain and Canada, from 1890 through 1930 in the United States, from 1896 through 1926 in New Zealand, and from 1895 through 1925 in Germany. The recent period takes in the census years from the end of the early periods through 1951 in Britain and Canada, 1950 in the United States, 1951 in New Zealand, and 1950 in Germany. In the United States the change in male participation during 1890–1930, minus

CHART 29

Association between Labor Force Participation Rates of Females and Males: 5 Countries, Various Years, 1890–1951

Number in labor force per 1,000 in same population group.
Standardized for age on basis of United States population in 1940, except as noted.

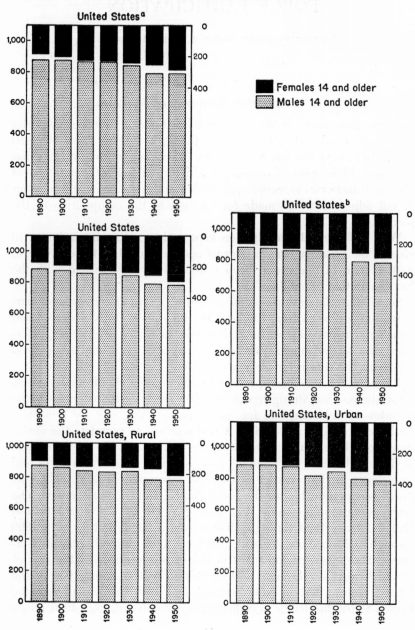

CHART 29, concluded

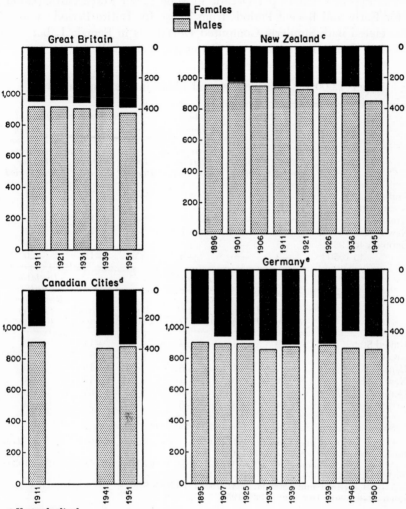

■ Females
□ Males

Great Britain

New Zealand [c]

Canadian Cities [d]

Germany [e]

[a] Unstandardized.
[b] Standardized for rural-urban composition as well as age.
[c] 15 and older.
[d] 15 and older. Age standardization on basis of population of Chicago in 1930.
[e] For 1895–1939, boundaries after World War I, without the Saar; 1939–1950, Federal Republic of Germany, without Berlin.
Source: Appendix A.

that throughout the entire period 1890–1950, was +6 (per 1,000 male population 14 and older). For females the analogous result happened to be —4 (per 1,000 female population 14 and older). Similar computations of male and female deviations were made for the recent period and for all of these periods in the other countries (Table 57).

TABLE 57

Deviations of Changes per Decade in Male Labor Force Participation for Early and Recent Periods from Those for Entire Period, Associated with Similarly Computed Deviations in Female Labor Force Participation, 5 Countries, Various Periods, 1890–1951

(per 1,000 of same sex 14 and older in the population)

	Males 14 and Older			Females 14 and Older		
	Early Period [a]	Entire Period	Deviation of Rate for Early from That for Entire Period	Early Period [a]	Entire Period	Deviation of Rate for Early from That for Entire Period
United States	−10	−16	+6	+10	+14	−4
Great Britain	−8	−12	+4	+7	+11	−4
Canada	−8	−12	+4	+12	+18	−6
New Zealand	−18	−19	+1	+9	+12	−3
Germany to 1939	−3	−7	+4	+35	+31	+4
to 1950 [b]	−3	−8	+5	+35	+15	+20
	Recent Period [c]	Entire Period	Deviation of Rate for Recent from That for Entire Period	Recent Period [c]	Entire Period	Deviation of Rate for Recent from That for Entire Period
United States	−29	−16	−13	+24	+14	+10
Great Britain	−16	−12	−4	+15	+11	+4
Canada	−17	−12	−5	+24	+18	+6
New Zealand	−20	−19	−1	+16	+12	+4
Germany to 1939	−16	−7	−9	+21	+31	−10
to 1950 [b]	−14	−8	−6	−9	+15	−24

Source: Chapter 8, Table 28; Chapter 6, Table 11; Appendix A.

[a] Great Britain and Canada, 1911–1931; United States, 1890–1930; New Zealand, 1896–1926; Germany, 1895–1925.

[b] 1895–1939: Boundaries after World War I, without the Saar. 1939–1950: Federal Republic of Germany, without Berlin.

[c] Great Britain and Canada, 1931–1951; United States, 1930–1950; New Zealand, 1926–1951; Germany, 1925–1950.

The correlation of the deviations from trend in participation between males and females was inverse, but it was not significant unless Germany was excluded.[1] Excluding Germany, the correlation was fairly high (−0.94) and was significant on the 95 per cent level: there were also mildly significant correlations in participation rates between women 25–64 and men 45–64 and 65 and older (Table 58). But sig-

[1] A case might be made for excluding Germany on the ground that this nation, dismembered territorially and upset economically by two great military defeats, did not offer the ideal conditions of peacetime high employment for labor force stability.

266

TABLE 58

Correlation between the Deviations of Changes per Decade in
Male Labor Force Participation for Early and Recent
Periods from Those for Entire Period, and the
Analogous Deviations in Female Labor Force
Participation, 5 Countries, Various Periods,
1890–1951

	COEFFICIENT OF CORRELATION	
	Five Countries [a]	*Four Countries (excluding Germany)*
Between males 14 and older and females 14 and older	−0.387 [*]	−0.942 [**]
Between females 25–44 and:		
Males 14–19	+0.007	+0.018
45–64	−0.045	−0.699 [*]
65 and older	−0.044	−0.691 [*]
Between females 45–64 and:		
Males 14–19	−0.152	−0.168
45–64	−0.089	−0.527 [*]
65 and older	−0.223	−0.719 [**]

The five countries: United States, Great Britain, Germany, Canada, and New Zealand.

Source: Data for computations, Appendix A; periods studied, Table 57.

[*] Significant on the 68 per cent (±σ) level.
[**] Significant on the 95 per cent (±2σ) level.
[a] Germany, 1895–1939.

nificant correlations of participation rates could not be found between females and boys 14–19.

All in all, these associations are not highly impressive. Nevertheless, with or without Germany, they were inverse in all but one correlation between female and male age groups (females 25–44 and males 14–19) and may perhaps merit some attempt at explanation of how such an interrelationship might exist.

Why Did Female Participation Rise While Male Participation Declined?

The great increases in female participation were not demonstrably associated with changes either in real disposable incomes of equivalent adult males or in the ratio of female to male earnings. Any judgments as to what did cause female participation to rise in the amounts and at the times it did must be highly tentative, in view of the inquiries of Chapter 7. These inquiries were speculative and provide at best an hypothesis, testable only when there are better statistical materials.

The hypothesis is that the increases in female participation over 60 years were due primarily to four factors:

1. The release of many women from the home as a result of the great decline in the ratio of the civilian population to the number of working-age females. The decline was due to a reduction in the birth rate and a rise in the female survival rate; and it occurred in a way that enabled millions of females, previously needed at home, to enter the labor force.

2. Labor saved in own home housework with the extended use of household appliances and the purchase of food and clothing formerly produced at home. The saving was probably too fragmentary and too scattered among females to have been responsible for many full-time female additions to the labor force. It was doubtless a marginal or contributing factor in many cases, though it most likely resulted in a higher standard of leisure and of family care. Still it was quantitatively important and, if it does not explain why females increased in the labor force, it may at least help to explain why their participation did not decline as income increased over time.

3. The expanding employment opportunities for females, arising with the extensive development of clerical occupations and service industries, and occurring *pari-passu* with the great increase in educational attainment of the average female, which qualified her for such employment.[2] This factor might not have moved women into the labor force if they could not have been spared at home, but it provided the demand.

4. The shorter workweek, making it easier for females to hold jobs and still carry out their household responsibilities which, though lightened, demanded a good deal of time and energy on the part of many women. (Reductions in the workweek were closely timed to the increase in female participation in the four countries for which data on hours were available.)

If declining household and child-care responsibilities, rising educational attainment, and shrinking hours of work had something to do with the increasing tendency of women to seek gainful jobs, we are led to the next link in the relationship between female participation and labor force behavior—that the large-scale entrance of females (chiefly aged 20–64) may in turn have been an active influence in the withdrawal of young and elderly persons.

It has been seen that men 45 and older reduced their participation by

---

[2] The increase in female education was both absolute and relative to the educational attainment of older men, whose schooling was limited by the lack of adequate schools at the times and in the places of their upbringing, by their disinclination to attend, or by their parents' financial requirements.

sizable amounts, and men 65 and older by far more—even more than young men and teen-age boys. This decline has not been closely related to the rise in real incomes (at least, since 1930), or to the extension of pensions and of social security (at least, before 1940), or to any discoverable deterioration in average physical ability to work (compared with men of the same age in earlier decades). It does not seem assignable to changes in self-employment opportunities, to rapidity of technological advance, or to the level of unemployment. There is a possibility that it has been due to a tightening in company rules and practices against hiring or keeping older workers; but it has not been definitely established that these rules have been more extensive than several decades ago when elderly men were in the labor force in much larger proportions. *In any case it seems doubtful that employers would have been so ready to part with this source of labor supply unless there had been new sources, namely women, available to take its place.*

Is it possible that the older men were to a large extent displaced by the entrance of better trained women, available at lower wages? There is some circumstantial support for such a thesis. At both the 1940 and 1950 censuses the participation of men was closely related at a moment-of-time to the amount of their education; for men with education *below* high school, years of schooling seemed far more important than age in determining participation (Chapter 9). A great decline occurred between 1910 and 1950 in the number of years of school completed by elderly men relative to the number completed by women 20–24 or 25–44. And a strong moment-of-time tendency was observable at the 1940 and 1950 censuses for women with education *above* high school to be in the labor force in larger proportions, the more years of schooling they had achieved.

Why would the influx of women into the labor force displace elderly men rather than depress the relative wages of women? Far from declining, the ratio of wages of women to those of men *rose*, but it might have risen even more—as a result of far better education and greatly expanded job opportunities for females in industry—had it not been held down by the very great rise in the ratio of females in the labor force.

How to explain the relation between the influx of women and the decline in participation of young people? As to young males the decline occurred in all five countries and in both recent and early periods, and was reflected fairly closely in greater school attendance in the countries for which data were available. Some of the rise in school attendance may have been cultural and institutional in origin and may have happened regardless of increases in income or in the female labor force. But many teen-agers may have stayed in school as a result of being squeezed out of the labor force by mature, better trained women. Employed sisters, mothers, and wives would also have helped to pay for the education of brothers, sons, and husbands.[3] Similarly, many elderly men have retired at earlier ages because of financial help from working daughters or wives and, in some cases, because their female dependents have become self-supporting.

An Attempt to Explain the Stability of the Over-All Labor Force in View of the Declining Hours of Work

But even if the declining participation of males was systematically interrelated with the rising participation of females, we should still have to explain why the two tendencies offset each other so completely as to leave the combined rate nearly stable. Have there been some economic or social forces at work to maintain the almost unchanging over-all rate despite rising income? We examine a number of possible explanations.

One explanation might be that man's aspiration tends to rise as fast as his income, so that instead of increasing his leisure, he strives for the things, e.g. better houses and cars, that a higher income can provide. Then, too, people live and spend competitively and their standard of living goes up with their income.

But in actual fact people have also increased their leisure: this leisure has taken the form of less working hours for the average labor force member.

In each of the four countries offering reasonably satisfactory data on the "standard," "normal," or "full-time" workweek, there have been marked reductions in the number of hours which the average labor force member has been called upon to work (Table 59). The workweek, weighted by the number of persons in the major industry groups (including agriculture, domestic service, and government), declined *per decade* by about 4.2 hours in the United States between 1890 and 1950, 3.3 hours in Great Britain between 1911 and 1951, 3.5 hours in Canada between 1921 and 1941, and 3.2 hours in Germany between 1895 and 1950 (3.1 hours between 1895 and 1939). The greater reduction in the United States was partly the result of the considerable transfer of workers out of long-hour industries, notably agriculture—shifts which did not seem to be responsible for significant differences in the length of the workweek in the other three nations. Standardization for

---

[3] Surveys made by various unions covering several thousand women members disclosed that up to a fourth of those who were married and separated or divorced gave the education of children as one of their chief reasons for working.

the shifts lowered the decrease per decade in the United States to 3.5 hours. Considering the roughness of the statistics, reductions in the workweek per decade have been much the same among the four countries measured in hours. In percentages (Table 59, line 3), they varied somewhat, ranging from 4.9 per cent per decade in Germany during 1895–1939 (or 5.3 per cent during 1895–1950) to 8.3 per cent in Great Britain (1911–1951).

Have reductions in hours been associated with increases in income? We seek the answers to this question in a number of additional computations in Table 59. First, we compute real income per hour (line 4). Second, we compute the percentage increases in income per hour for each decade date (line 5). Finally, we compute the percentage reduction in hours associated with a rise of 1 per cent in income per hour (line 6).

In all four countries, there were percentage decreases in hours associated with percentage increases in real disposable income per hour. For the entire periods they were: −0.27 in the United States, −0.34 in Canada, −0.62 in Great Britain, and −0.53 in Germany during 1895–1939 (or −0.91 during 1895–1950). The fact that the decreases relative to income increases were less similar among the four countries than the reductions in hours when not related to income would suggest that hours tended to fall at a certain rate per decade whether income was rising slowly or rapidly. And the lack of uniformity from one decade to another (line 6) further suggests that decreases in hours were not systematically associated with increases in income, at least in the short run. It would seem that shorter hours have at times been clearly precipitated by depressions and wars; for example in the 1930's they seem to have been instituted mainly to spread the smaller demand for labor among more workers. Of course the desire for a shorter workweek may well have been building up during the 1920's when income was rising but hours were stable. Or again, the greater demand for labor during World War I seems to have given workers, whether organized or unorganized, the bargaining and political power to win the leisure that income rises, before and during the war, had enabled them to afford. Nevertheless, higher incomes may have played a role in the long run—say, by creating the conducive social, political, and economic atmosphere. We therefore inquire why increased leisure, in the long run, took the form of a reduction in hours and not in over-all participation? Stated in another way, why did the participation of males fall just enough to be offset by the increase in the participation of females? In particular, why didn't the labor force participation of men 25–64 —the primary working ages—decline substantially instead of only

271

TABLE 59

Changes in Hours in Standard or Full-Time Workweek of the Labor Force Associated with Changes in Real Disposable Income per Hour, 4 Countries, Various Periods, 1890–1951

A. UNITED STATES, 1890–1950

	1890	1900	1910	1920	1930	1940	1950	Average Change per Decade 1890–1930	Average Change per Decade 1930–1950	Average Change per Decade 1890–1950
1. Hours in standard work week	66	62	57	53	52	43	41	–	–	–
2. Changes in hours, number	–	–4	–5	–4	–1	–9	–2	–3.5	–5.5	–4.2
3. Changes in hours, per cent	–	–6.1	–8.1	–7.0	–1.9	–17.3	–4.7	–5.8	–11.0	–7.5
4. Real disposable income per hour (1929 dollars) [a]	0.294	0.373	0.478	0.539	0.769	1.025	1.267			
5. Change in income, per cent	–	+26.9	+28.2	+12.8	+42.7	+33.3	+23.6	+27.7	+28.5	+27.9
6. Per cent change in hours per 1 per cent rise in income per hour (line 3 ÷ line 5)	–	–.22	–.29	–0.55	–0.04	–0.52	–0.20	–0.21	–0.39	–0.27

B. GREAT BRITAIN, 1911–1951

	1911 [b]	1921 [c]	1931	1939	1951 [a]	Average Change per Decade 1911–1931	Average Change per Decade 1931–1951	Average Change per Decade 1911–1951
1. Hours in standard work week	59	51.5	49.5	49	45	–	–	–
2. Changes in hours, number	–	–7.5	–2.0	–0.5	–4.0	–4.8	–2.3	–3.5
3. Changes in hours, per cent	–	–12.7	–3.9	–1.0	–8.2	–8.3	–4.6	–6.5
4. Real disposable income per hour (1929 U.S. dollars) [a]	.388	.424	.476	.523	.703			
5. Change in income, per cent	–	+9.3	+12.3	+9.9	+34.4	+10.8	+22.2	+16.5
6. Per cent change in hours per 1 per cent rise in income per hour (line 3 ÷ line 5)	–	–1.37	–0.32	–1.02	–0.24	–0.77	–0.21	–0.39

TABLE 59, *continued*

C. CANADA, 1921-1940

	1921	1931	1941	Average Change per Decade 1921–1931	1931–1941	1921–1941
1. Hours in the standard work week	63	60	56	–	–	–
2. Changes in hours, number	–	–3	–4	–3	–4	–3.5
3. Changes in hours, per cent	–	–4.8	–6.7	–4.8	–6.7	–5.8
4. Real disposable income per hour [a] (1929 U.S. dollars)	0.409	0.452	0.561	–	–	–
5. Change in income, per cent	–	+10.5	+24.1	+10.5	+24.1	+17.3
6. Per cent change in hours per 1 per cent rise in income per hour (line 3 ÷ line 5)	–	–0.46	–0.28	–0.46	–0.28	–0.34

D. GERMANY, 1895-1950

	1895 [e]	1907 [f]	1925	1933	1939	1950	Average Change per Decade 1895–[e] 1925	1925– 1939	1895– 1939	1895– 1950
1. Hours in the standard work week	64	58	53	48	52	48	–	–	–	–
2. Changes in hours, number	–	–6	–5	–5	+4	–4	–3.7	–0.7	–2.7	–2.9
3. Changes in hours, per cent	–	–9.4	–8.6	–9.4	+8.3	–7.7	–6.0	–0.8	–4.3	–4.9
4. Real disposable income per hour [a] (1929 U.S. dollars)	0.234	0.258	0.233	0.304	0.320	0.297	–	–	–	–
5. Change in income, per cent	–	+10.3	–9.7	+30.5	+5.3	–7.2	0	+26.7	+8.4	+5.3
6. Per cent change in hours per 1 per cent rise in income per hour (line 3 ÷ line 5)	–	–.91	+.89	–0.31	+1.57	+1.07	∞	–0.03	–0.51	–0.92

Source: Labor force, Appendix A; income, Appendix D; hours, notes to Chart 14.

[a] Per adult-male equivalent employed based on three-year averages in 1929 U.S. dollars.
[b] Hours data are for 1906.
[c] Hours data are for 1919.
[d] Hours data are for 1948.
[e] Hours data are for 1900.
[f] Hours data are for 1913-1914.

mildly?[4] Possibly shorter hours offered a line of less resistance than withdrawal from the labor force—especially among primary workers. Several considerations may suggest this.

In the first place, while the total labor force has remained almost constant in relation to the population, the average number of workers per household has fallen from about 1.75 in 1900 to 1.38 in 1950, as shown in the following table:

	1900	1930	1940	1950
Labor force 14 and older (millions)	28.1	48.7	52.8	60.1
Private households (millions)	16.0 a	29.9	35.1	43.5
Labor force per household (average)	1.75	1.63	1.51	1.38

Source: Labor Force: Appendix A. Households: *Census of 1900* (Special Reports), *Supplementary Analysis and Derivative Tables*, p. 379; *Census of Population, 1930*, Vol. VI, *Families*, pp. 7, 10; *Current Population Reports*, Bureau of the Census, Series P-20, No. 33, p. 15. The word "households" used in 1950 is synonymous with "families" at earlier dates.

a Source for 1900 data gave the distribution of all households, including quasi-family groups, by the number of persons per family. A percentage distribution of private families was computed after deducting all quasi-family groups from total families with seven or more members.

Note: Data were unavailable for 1910 and 1920.

This development has been the result of young and elderly men and women setting up separate and independent households. It is no doubt a reflection of the increasing well-being. But it also means that the way people have been choosing to live has made it more difficult for the labor force proportion to decline. There were no data on the distribution of families by number of workers in 1900; but in 1930, 1940, and 1950 almost seven in every ten families had only one worker or none at all.[5] Over two families in every ten had two working members; for these families a complete withdrawal of one worker, perhaps an elderly person or a youth, without replacement by another, perhaps a woman, might have meant an inconveniently large loss of income. And the fewest families—one out of every ten—have in recent decades included

[4] Actually, the decline was balanced by the rise in the relative number of men of that age in the population, which resulted in increases—ranging from slight to substantial—in the ratio of male workers 25–64 to the total labor force 14 and older of both sexes in four of the five countries. Only in Canada was there even a slight decline in the ratio.

[5] *Census of Population, 1930*, Vol. VI, *Families*, p. 8; *Current Population Reports*, Bureau of the Census, Series P-50, Nos. 5, 29. The 1940 data given in the P-50 reports are based on sample returns from the 1940 census. The 1950 estimates are based on data from monthly sample surveys.

An appreciable increase in 1940 and 1950 in the number of households with no workers was probably due mainly to the rise in the element of pensions, old age charity, social security, and perhaps personal savings—developments which have enabled many elderly men and women to set up or retain separate households after retirement.

three or more workers. These were the only households moderately able to adjust to the withdrawal of one member from the labor force.

It can be argued, of course, that a person need not withdraw permanently from the labor force in order to reduce participation and increase leisure. A woman might work only nine months instead of a full year, a schoolboy during the Christmas holidays but not in the summer; a family head might take an unpaid vacation or advance his retirement. Such reductions are often inconvenient or dangerous. Many breadwinners, and even secondary workers might jeopardize their jobs by taking unpaid vacations; and the failure to seek new employment immediately after losing a job might destroy the only chance of finding one or result in a prolonged period of unemployment. For most persons an easier and safer way to more leisure is through a shorter workweek. Also, the new leisure can be spread over the year instead of being concentrated in undue amounts in certain months.

More important, the psychological demand for leisure is surely a personal affair. If rising income made people desire more leisure, it is likely that all the members of any family wished to share in any additional leisure. A shorter workweek for all could better satisfy this wish than the withdrawal of one member of the household from the labor force.

Has the expectation been realized? Or is it not true that reductions in the participation of males and increases in the participation of females have redistributed a large part of the burden of work from males (especially youths and older workers) to females (especially women 25–64)? So far as participation is concerned, there certainly has been such a shift. But so far as the total burden of work—gainful and ungainful—is concerned, several other factors must also be considered.

There are no separate statistics on full-time hours for males and females. However, the great relative transfer of female workers since the turn of the century has been from long-hour occupations, such as domestic service and farm labor, into short-hour occupations, such as clerical work. The unskilled category, including laborers and servants, was the largest employer of females in 1910 but it was only the third largest in 1940 or 1950; the category of clerical and kindred work was the third largest employer of females in 1919 and in 1940 and 1950 it was the largest (Chapter 7). On the assumption that reductions in hours were the same for males and females in each of the countries— in the United States they must have been at least as much for females as for the whole labor force—male and female participation were multiplied by the length of the full-time workweek. For males, the weekly hours of labor force participation per 1,000 male population 14 and older showed a decline of 41 per cent in the United States during 1890–

1950, 27 per cent in Britain during 1911–1951, 17.5 per cent in Canada during 1911–1941, and 28.7 per cent in Germany during 1895–1950. For females, the decline in hours seemed typically to have more than offset the increase in participation, with the result that over the same periods hours of female participation fell 5 per cent in the United States, 14 per cent in Britain, and 7 per cent in Germany. Only in Canada was an increase manifested, but it had occurred up to 1941, a war year. If hours of participation fell during the next decade to the levels of the United States, they were about the same in 1951 as in 1911.

The above computations suggest that the total time females devoted to gainful work may have run counter to the great rise in their labor force participation. Nevertheless, there was probably a relative redistribution of gainful work from males to females, since the declines for females were in all cases much smaller than those for males. Is such a development consistent with the premise that if people desire more leisure as an effect of rising incomes it is likely that all members of a family wish to share in this leisure?

The answer requires that account be taken of a second factor: the burden of *nongainful* work in the home. Illustrative computations in Chapter 7 indicated that a great decline in the size of families and the advance in technology for the home could easily have resulted in more leisure for the average housewife (see Table 21).

These developments still do not amount to an easing in the woman's burden of work as great, relatively, as that apparently realized by a man from reductions in both hours and labor force participation. But females may be more likely to work close to home and therefore spend less time in commuting, as suburbanization pushes the population farther from their jobs.[6] And males very likely now bear a much greater part of the burden of home housework, shopping, and the many chores that go with "do-it-yourself" projects—painting, repairing, and so on. If these two developments could be measured in hours, it is possible that the reduction in total gainful and nongainful effort has not been very different between males and females.[7]

There still remains the question of why at least some workers or families might not have chosen to continue on a longer workweek and either not take the new leisure or take it in reduced participation. The answer is plain. Even had certain workers preferred an undiminished workweek (to allow one or more persons in their families to withdraw

[6] There are no statistics which reveal whether the time spent in traveling longer distances by auto has been greater or less than the time formerly spent traveling shorter distances by bus or trolley.

[7] Nothing has been said here about school attendance, for the number of males and females in school has been much the same to the extent that statistics can be relied upon.

altogether from the labor force), their wishes could scarcely have prevailed, unless they had been willing and able to hold a second job. For, if the great majority were able to win reduction in hours, the shorter workweek would have had to be standard for all workers in a factory or store.

So the shorter workweek may have offered a more convenient, flexible, and equitable "package" in which to obtain additional leisure evenly distributed among workers and over time as incomes rose gradually. Once working hours are reduced, all sorts of obstacles arise to prevent a revision upward. They tend to be frozen into laws on maximum hours and overtime pay; they become inherent in union agreements and factory shifts. Workers gradually buy or rent houses at distances that involve extensive commuting, and the pace of the work itself may increase so that a return to a longer workweek could be accommodated only by relaxing the intensity of effort. Even the employer himself may come to prefer the shorter week and to view a return to a longer week with little enthusiasm.

It would seem highly probable that the demand for leisure has been powerfully and irrevocably shunted toward fewer weekly hours of work and more rest periods and holidays for most persons, and not toward a downward trend in the proportion of population who work in a given week. In bringing about the past reductions in the workweek, the role of the unions, while considerable, has not been the dominant one. In the future, however, unions are likely to be much more important in initiating and pressing for shorter hours. For unions are far stronger now than during the years when most of the reductions occurred. Whether the demand for leisure arises from higher incomes or from the lack of demand for labor, a curtailment in the length of the workweek or additional rest periods, sick leaves, holidays, and vacations is likely to be more acceptable to unions than reductions in the size of the labor force, if only because the former means the possibility of getting higher than proportional wages for overtime at certain seasons of the year and in times of war emergency, or because declines in the labor force mean a loss of union membership and revenue from dues. It appears that any drop in labor supply will continue to take the form of fewer hours and perhaps less effort per hour, and that the over-all labor force will continue to stay rather close to its present and past percentages of working age population.

Some Troublesome Questions That Still Remain

Two difficulties remain.

One is that participation over time was stable only for native whites and that it declined sharply for Negroes and the foreign-born—in the case of Negroes, among females as well as among males. Perhaps the reason might lie in the greater improvement in the economic status of these groups relative to that of the native whites. There are no separate statistics on incomes of the foreign-born. However, since the huge immigration that occurred before World War I consisted mainly of the lowest economic class, and since a large proportion of the foreign-born obviously occupy very favorable economic and social positions at present, we may risk the assumption that their income has risen more sharply than that of the native whites. As for the Negro, there are no good income statistics before 1940, but it may be possible to make some judgment from mortality statistics. The fact that the death rate of nonwhites was relatively constant, at a level about half again as high as that of whites, between 1900 and 1930 makes it unlikely that the income of Negroes rose appreciably faster up to the latter year.[8] In the 1930's and 1940's, however, the death rates of nonwhites fell considerably more than those of whites; by 1940 the excess had fallen to a third, and by 1950 to a sixth. The relative decline during the 1930's was surely not due to a higher earned income—for wage rates were low and unemployment rates high for colored people throughout that depression decade—but, rather, to the great extension of welfare facilities to the Negro under the New Deal. During the 1940's censuses show an enormous rise in the relative earnings of nonwhites: the median wage or salary income of colored males 14 and older rose from 41 per cent of those of white males in 1939 to 61 per cent in 1950.[9] Negroes apparently benefited in two ways. Income rose more for the lesser educated workers and, since Negroes were more apt to be uneducated (and unskilled) the average Negro was more benefited than the average white by the great income redistribution of the 1940's. But the Negro also benefited as a Negro: age for age, the nonwhite males with education above the eighth grade (for whom there was undoubtedly a great denial of opportunity before World War II) manifested substantially greater increases of income than did the whites of the same educational attainment (Table 60).

But if the rise in income was greater for nonwhites and for the foreign-born than for native whites, and if Negroes and the foreign-born wished to work less as their income rose, why did their new leisure take the form of labor force reductions? The reasonable con-

[8] Death rates per 1,000 population by race and sex, for the death registration states: *Statistical Abstract of the United States, 1952,* Bureau of the Census, p. 67. Not to be overlooked, the death rates of both whites and nonwhites fell rapidly during these years—that of whites from 17 per 1,000 in 1900 to 9.5 per 1,000 in 1950, and that of nonwhites from 25 to 10.9 per 1,000.

[9] *Current Population Reports, Income of Families and Persons in the United States: 1950,* Series P-60, No. 9, p. 39.

TABLE 60

Median Income of Males by Age, Color, and Education Completed, United States, 1939 and 1949

	1939 [a]				1949			
	Native White	Index	Non-white	Index	White [a]	Index	Non-white	Index
30–34 Years of Age								
No school	$ 376	100	$ 319	100	$1,328	353	$1,167	366
1–4	445	100	365	100	1,647	370	1,175	322
5–7	667	100	486	100	2,190	328	1,560	321
8	967	100	613	100	2,631	272	1,818	297
9–11	1,227	100	667	100	3,026	247	2,059	309
12	1,443	100	714	100	3,380	234	2,227	312
13–15	1,625	100	759	100	3,680	226	2,456	324
16 or more	1,960	100	1,036	100	4,344	222	2,667	257
35–44 Years of Age								
No school	$ 390	100	$ 355	100	$1,444	370	$1,063	299
1–4	541	100	412	100	1,827	338	1,240	301
5–7	841	100	541	100	2,423	288	1,598	295
8	1,170	100	689	100	2,893	247	1,975	287
9–11	1,435	100	706	100	3,276	228	2,146	304
12	1,727	100	813	100	3,606	209	2,400	295
13–15	1,882	100	879	100	4,104	218	2,443	278
16 or more	2,432	100	1,118	100	5,381	221	3,142	281
45–54 Years of Age								
No school	$ 396	100	$ 293	100	$1,818	459	$ 962	328
1–4	583	100	370	100	2,022	347	1,205	326
5–7	859	100	540	100	2,525	294	1,636	303
8	1,195	100	667	100	2,973	249	2,038	306
9–11	1,481	100	667	100	3,294	222	2,167	325
12	1,810	100	865	100	3,798	210	2,286	264
13–15	1,885	100	909	100	4,315	229	2,417	266
16 or more	2,500	100	1,100	100	5,891	236	3,166	288
55–64 Years of Age								
No school	$ 282	100	$ 264	100	$1,881	667	$ 792	300
1–4	418	100	334	100	1,821	436	882	264
5–7	661	100	500	100	2,160	327	1,313	263
8	930	100	577	100	2,585	278	1,800	312
9–11	1,203	100	594	100	2,956	246	1,824	307
12	1,574	100	694	100	3,508	223	2,118	305
13–15	1,500	100	900	100	3,706	247	2,188	243
16 or more	2,143	100	999	100	5,429	253	2,688	269

Source: *Census of Population: 1940, Educational Attainment by Economic Characteristics and Marital Status*, Tables 29, 31; *1950, Education*, PE No. 5B, Table **12.**

[a] For 1939 the years of school completed are 5–6 and 7–8. Computed for 1949 by subtracting data for nonwhites from all classes.

279

jecture, expressed in Chapter 6, is that these groups were striving to follow the example of the native whites. A sameness in income for the various groups might well cause cultural attitudes to become the same also, dissolving differences in labor force tendencies. We saw in Chapter 12 that the labor force participation rates of Negro females tended not only to become more like those of the whites among the various cities, but also more like those of each other. The equalization need not, of course, have been due to the rapid rise in their income. The declines in Negro participation among the various cities were not related significantly to earnings of males of *all classes* in those cities (although separate earnings of colored males might have yielded such a relationship). It may instead have been due to a lowering, by 1950, of some of the social, occupational, industrial, and other barriers to the movement of colored persons. The social and economic mobility of the Negro might still flow in some degree from income changes, but one might expect that the flows would first be strained through the sieve of institutional changes and proceed at such different velocities in different communities as to lose their observable statistical connection with income changes.

Does this argument dispose of the previous one—that a reduction in full-time hours was an easier alternative than a reduction in participation? If Negroes and the foreign-born decreased their participation, why did the native whites not do likewise? Actually, the previous argument was not that a decline in participation was *impossible,* but that a shorter workweek was easier—at least for the native whites. For Negroes, a more rapid rise in income could not accomplish for them shorter hours than the whites were getting, since in most establishments the latter were dominant. The way for Negroes to acquire a more rapid increase in leisure than the whites as their income rose more rapidly, would have been to reduce their labor force participation which for decades had remained at uncomfortably high levels—presumably because of their low economic status. If these conjectures have merit, it might be supposed that as the remaining barriers to full participation in the economic life of the nation break down, the Negro will aspire in an increasing degree to the living and working patterns of any American in the same income group.

A second difficulty is to explain why the participation of whites has not been stable in a number of cities, even in some cities where the foreign-born whites were not significantly numerous. The greatest deviations from stability occurred during the 1940's. In two-thirds of the fifteen cities where white participation either rose, or showed a decline of more than 25 per 1,000 white population 14 and older over the period between 1920 and 1950, the change was either largely or entirely concentrated between 1940 and 1950. And these changes were found generally among both males and females. What is the explanation for this instability in the total labor force participation rate in many cities?

It is possible that those people who are committed to work prefer to live where pay and job opportunities are most satisfactory. Their movement would not result merely in some cities having an age and sex composition most likely to be in the labor force, for this factor has already been taken into account by standardization. Nor would it be reflected simply by a rapid rise in a city's population, for the study could discover no relation among cities between participation and population growth. Rather, those individuals who have higher labor force propensities than others of the same age and sex (but are not otherwise distinguishable according to objective characteristics) might move to localities where economic conditions are most favorable, leaving the people with relatively low propensities (for their age and sex) to work in areas of less favorable economic climate. This shift need not disturb the stability of participation of the nation as a whole.

In mild support of this thesis was a positive correlation among the cities between *changes* in the participation of whites from 1920 to 1950 and the *level* of real earnings of white males in 1949 [10] (Chapter 12). But the correlation was not high. No association was found between the level of the white labor force in 1950 and the level of earnings of white males in 1949 (Chapter 4). Nor was there any relation between changes in participation of whites and changes in their unemployment during 1930–1950 (Chapter 12), or between changes in their participation from 1920 to 1950 and changes in the proportion of the labor force in manufacturing. (The proportion of whites in manufacturing can perhaps be regarded as an index of abundance of good job opportunities in a city, since manufacturing tends to pay the highest of any major industry group.) Wanting a really satisfactory explanation, the lower degree of labor force stability among many cities as well as among Negroes and the foreign-born must stand as an exception to the rather high degree of stability in the over-all participation of the nation. Until some adequate reason can be discovered, we postpone any final conclusion that stability during peacetime periods of reasonably high employment is a universal or necessary feature of the total labor force participation.

[10] The lack of separate data on the earning of whites and nonwhites in 1919 prevented comparison of the *changes* in white earnings between 1919 and 1949.

APPENDIXES

APPENDIX A

The Labor Force and Population by Sex and Age Group, Decennial Enumerations

TABLE A-1

United States:
Labor Force by Sex and Age Group, 1820–1880

Age Group	MILLIONS [a]						Per Cent of Population of Same Sex and Age Group [a]					
	1820 [b]	1840 [c]	1850	1860	1870 [d]	1880 [e]	1820 [b]	1840 [c]	1850	1860	1870 [d]	1880 [e]
MALES												
10–15	...	...	...	...	0.6	0.8	...	...	...	...	19.3	24.4
16–59	...	...	...	...	9.8	13.0	...	...	...	...	91.0	93.4
60 & older	...	...	...	...	0.6	0.9	...	...	...	...	64.2	64.3
10 & older	...	...	...	...	11.0	14.7	...	...	...	...	74.9	78.7
FEMALES												
10–15	...	...	...	...	0.2	0.3	...	...	...	...	7.0	9.0
16–59	...	...	...	...	1.6	2.3	...	...	...	...	15.7	17.1
60 & older	...	...	...	...	0.1	0.1	...	...	...	...	5.4	5.2
10 & older	...	...	...	...	1.9	2.7	...	...	...	...	13.3	14.7
BOTH SEXES												
10 & older												
Census	2.5 [b]	4.8 [c]			12.9	17.4	38.3	41.3			44.4	47.3
Whelpton [f]	2.9	5.4	7.7	10.5	12.9	17.4	44.4	46.6	46.8	47.0	44.4	47.3
0 & older	2.9	5.4	7.7	10.5	12.9	17.4	25.8	28.1	33.2	33.5	32.5	34.7

[a] Totals and percentages were computed before data on population and labor force were rounded.

[b] Census of 1820, Book I, p. 2. Includes only agriculture, commerce, and manufacturing. Excludes professional, domestic, and personal services; forestry and fishing; and mining.

[c] Census of 1840, p. 475. Includes only agriculture, commerce, mining, manufacturing and trade, navigation of the ocean and inland waterways, and learned professions and engineering. Excludes domestic and personal services, and forestry and fishing.

[d] Officially corrected for the 1870 undercount of population and labor force in the southern states. Alba M. Edwards, *Comparative Occupation Statistics for the United States, 1870 to 1940, Census of Population, 1940,* pp. 91–92. Since no information was given for the 16–59 and 60 and older age groups the author assumes, as does Edwards, that the age-sex distribution of the adjustments to the labor force was the same as that of the labor force originally reported. No correction has been made for the fact that the labor force was probably underenumerated relative to the population.

[e] *Census of Population, 1880,* Vol. I, p. 714.

[f] P. K. Whelpton, "Occupational Groups in the United States, 1820–1920," *Journal of the American Statistical Association,* September 1926, p. 339; *Historical Statistics of the United States, 1789–1945,* Bureau of the Census, p. 63. Whelpton interpolated the totals for 1850 and 1860 linearly between the 1840 and 1880 labor force proportions of all persons aged 10 and over.

TABLE A-2

United States:

Population and Labor Force by Sex and Age Group, April, 1890–1950

Age Group[b]	POPULATION IN MILLIONS[a]							LABOR FORCE IN MILLIONS[a]						
	1890[c]	1900[c]	1910[c]	1920[c]	1930[c]	1940	1950[d]	1890[c]	1900[c]	1910[c]	1920[c]	1930[c]	1940	1950[d]
MALES														
0–9	7.8	9.1	10.3	11.7	12.2	10.8	15.1	...	...	...	...	...	...	...
10–13	2.9	3.3	3.6	4.3	4.9	4.7	4.6	0.5	0.5	0.3	0.2	0.1	e	e
14–19	4.0	4.6	5.5	5.7	7.0	7.4	6.6	2.3	2.8	3.1	3.0	2.9	2.5	2.5
20–24	3.1	3.6	4.6	4.5	5.3	5.7	5.6	2.8	3.3	4.2	4.1	4.8	5.0	4.7
25–44	8.9	11.1	14.1	16.2	18.3	19.6	22.3	8.7	10.7	13.7	15.8	17.8	18.7	20.8
45–64	4.3	5.5	7.2	9.2	11.2	13.4	15.2	4.1	5.1	6.7	8.6	10.5	11.9	13.4
65 & older	1.2	1.5	2.0	2.5	3.3	4.4	5.7	0.9	1.1	1.1	1.5	2.0	1.8	2.4
14–24	7.1	8.2	10.1	10.2	12.3	13.1	12.2	5.1	6.1	7.3	7.1	7.7	7.5	7.2
14 & older	21.5	26.3	33.4	38.1	45.1	50.5	55.4	18.8	23.0	28.8	33.0	38.0	39.9	43.8
10 & older	24.4	29.6	37.0	42.4	50.0	55.2	60.0	19.3	23.5	29.1	33.2	38.1	39.9	43.8
0 & older	32.2	38.7	47.3	54.1	62.2	66.0	75.1	19.3	23.5	29.1	33.2	38.1	39.9	43.8
FEMALES														
0–9	7.5	8.9	10.1	11.3	11.9	10.5	14.5	...	...	...	...	...	...	...
10–13	2.8	3.2	3.6	4.3	4.8	4.6	4.6	0.1	0.2	0.1	0.1	0.1	e	e
14–19	4.0	4.6	5.4	5.8	6.9	7.3	6.5	1.0	1.3	1.5	1.6	1.6	1.3	1.4
20–24	3.1	3.7	4.5	4.8	5.6	5.9	5.8	0.9	1.2	1.6	1.8	2.4	2.7	2.6
25–44	8.1	10.2	12.7	15.3	17.9	20.0	22.8	1.3	1.8	2.7	3.5	4.5	6.0	7.4
45–64	3.9	4.9	6.3	8.0	10.2	12.8	15.3	0.5	0.7	1.0	1.3	1.9	2.6	4.4
65 & older	1.1	1.5	2.0	2.5	3.3	4.6	6.6	0.1	0.1	0.2	0.2	0.3	0.3	0.5
14–24	7.1	8.3	9.9	10.6	12.5	13.2	12.3	1.9	2.5	3.1	3.4	4.0	4.0	4.0
14 & older	20.2	24.9	30.9	36.4	43.9	50.6	57.0	3.8	5.1	7.0	8.4	10.7	12.9	16.3
10 & older	23.0	28.1	34.5	40.7	48.7	55.2	61.6	3.9	5.3	7.1	8.5	10.8	12.9	16.3
0 & older	30.5	37.0	44.6	52.0	60.6	65.7	76.1	3.9	5.3	7.1	8.5	10.8	12.9	16.3
BOTH SEXES														
14 & older	41.7	51.2	64.3	74.5	89.0	101.1	112.4	22.6	28.1	35.8	41.4	48.7	52.8	60.1
10 & older	47.4	57.7	71.5	83.1	98.7	110.4	121.6	23.2	28.8	36.2	41.7	48.9	52.8	60.1
0 & older	62.7	75.7	91.9	106.1	122.8	131.7	151.2	23.2	28.8	36.2	41.7	48.9	52.8	60.1

TABLE A-2, *continued*

LABOR FORCE

Per Cent of Population of Same Sex and Age Group—Unstandardized [a]

Age [b] Group	1890 [c]	1900 [c]	1910 [c]	1920 [c]	1930 [c]	1940	1950
MALES							
10–13	17.8	17.7	9.2	6.0	3.3	e	e
14–19	57.1	61.1	56.2	52.6	41.1	34.4	39.9
20–24	92.0	91.7	91.1	90.9	89.9	88.0	82.8
25–44	97.6	96.3	96.6	97.1	97.5	95.0	92.8
45–64	95.2	93.3	93.6	93.8	94.1	88.7	87.9
65 & older	73.9	68.3	58.1	60.1	58.3	41.5	41.6
14–24	72.4	74.7	72.1	69.6	62.3	57.7	59.8
14 & older	87.4	87.3	86.3	86.5	84.1	79.0	79.0
10 & older	79.2	79.5	78.6	78.3	76.2	72.2	72.9
0 & older	60.0	60.9	61.5	61.4	61.3	60.5	58.2
14 & older f	88.3	87.4	85.9	85.8	84.1	79.0	78.2
10 & older f	82.3	81.4	79.4	79.0	77.2	72.2	71.5
FEMALES							
10–13	5.4	6.1	3.9	2.9	1.5	e	e
14–19	24.4	26.8	28.1	28.4	22.8	18.8	22.5
20–24	30.8	32.1	35.5	38.1	42.5	45.1	42.5
25–44	15.6	18.0	21.0	22.5	25.4	30.2	33.0
45–64	12.6	14.1	17.1	17.1	18.7	19.8	28.6
65 & older	8.3	9.1	8.6	8.0	8.0	5.9	7.6
14–24	27.2	29.2	31.4	32.8	31.5	30.5	32.0
14 & older	18.6	20.4	22.8	23.3	24.3	25.4	28.6
10 & older	17.0	18.8	20.8	21.2	22.0	23.3	26.5
0 & older	12.8	14.3	16.1	16.5	17.7	19.6	21.5
14 & older f	17.2	19.1	21.6	22.5	23.7	25.4	29.2
10 & older f	16.2	18.0	20.1	20.9	21.9	23.3	26.7

Per Cent of Population of Same Sex and Age Group—Standardized for Age-Sex, Rural-Urban, and Color-Nativity Composition [a]

Age [b] Group	1890 [c]	1900 [c]	1910 [c]	1920 [c]	1930 [c]	1940	1950
MALES							
10–13	16.3	16.9	8.1	5.5	3.3	e	e
14–19	57.8	61.5	56.6	53.0	41.0	34.4	40.2
20–24	92.5	92.1	91.2	91.0	89.9	88.0	83.5
25–44	97.3	96.5	96.7	97.2	97.4	95.0	92.9
45–64	94.7	93.4	93.7	93.8	94.0	88.7	87.7
65 & older	71.3	66.6	57.3	59.8	58.0	41.5	42.0
14–24	72.9	74.8	71.7	69.5	62.3	57.7	59.1
14 & older g	88.0	87.4	86.0	85.9	84.0	79.0	78.3
10 & older g	81.9	81.4	79.3	79.0	77.1	72.2	71.6
14 & older h	86.4	86.3	…	85.0	83.3	79.0	78.5
10 & older h	80.1	80.2	…	78.0	76.4	72.2	71.9
FEMALES							
10–13	5.0	5.7	3.6	2.6	1.5	e	e
14–19	27.7	30.2	29.9	29.6	22.8	18.8	21.9
20–24	36.2	36.9	37.9	39.2	42.3	45.1	40.9
25–44	18.8	19.8	22.3	23.2	25.3	30.2	32.2
45–64	13.8	14.7	17.7	17.5	18.8	19.8	27.8
65 & older	8.2	8.5	8.4	8.0	3.0	5.9	7.4
14–24	31.5	33.2	33.4	33.9	31.5	30.5	30.4
14 & older g	19.9	21.0	22.8	23.2	23.7	25.4	28.4
10 & older g	18.7	19.7	21.2	21.5	21.9	23.3	26.0
14 & older h	15.5	16.9	…	20.8	21.5	24.2	27.7
10 & older h	14.4	15.7	…	19.2	19.9	22.1	25.4

TABLE A-2, *continued*

LABOR FORCE

BOTH SEXES

	Per Cent of Population of Same Sex and Age Group—Unstandardized [a]								Per Cent of Population of Same Sex and Age Group—Standardized for Age-Sex, Rural-Urban, and Color-Nativity Composition [a]						
Age [b] Group	1890 [c]	1900 [c]	1910 [c]	1920 [c]	1930 [c]	1940	1950	Age [b] Group	1890 [c]	1900 [c]	1910 [c]	1920 [c]	1930 [c]	1940	1950
14 & older	54.0	54.8	55.7	55.6	54.6	52.2	53.4	14 & older [g]	54.0	54.2	54.4	54.5	53.8	52.2	53.3
10 & older	49.0	49.9	50.7	50.4	49.5	47.8	49.4	10 & older [g]	50.3	50.6	50.3	50.3	49.5	47.8	48.8
0 & older	37.0	38.1	39.4	39.4	39.8	40.1	39.7								
14 & older [f]	52.8	53.3	53.8	54.1	53.9	52.2	53.7	14 & older [h]	51.0	51.6	...	52.8	52.4	51.5	53.0
10 & older [f]	49.3	49.8	49.8	49.9	49.6	47.8	49.1	10 & older [h]	47.2	48.0	...	48.7	48.1	47.2	48.6

Source and concept: Chapter 3 and Appendixes E and F.

[a] Totals and percentages were computed before the data on population and labor force were rounded.

[b] Persons of unknown age were distributed among the age classifications in the same proportion as the rest of the population.

[c] Labor force and population during 1890–1920 were adjusted both for miscounts and for differences in month of enumeration. See Supplementary Appendixes G and H.

[d] Includes a half million persons, who were abroad or at sea and not counted by the census, comprising members of the armed forces, civilian citizens employed by the United States government, families of the foregoing, and crews of merchant vessels. *Census of Population, 1950, Characteristics of the Population*, Vol. II, Part 1, pp. 87, 247. (Based on 20 per cent sample.)

[e] The censuses of 1940 and 1950 did not count children under 14 in the labor force.

[f] Standardized for age-sex composition on the basis of the population of the United States in 1940.

[g] Standardized for age-sex and for rural-urban composition on the basis of the population of the United States in 1940.

[h] Standardized for age-sex, rural-urban, and color-nativity composition based on the population of the United States in 1940.

Explanation of standardization: Chapter 3, section on *The Method*.

United States:
Rural and Urban Population and Labor Force by Sex and Age Group, April, 1890–1950

POPULATION IN MILLIONS [a]

Age Group	RURAL							URBAN					
	1890	1900	1910	1920	1930	1940	1950	1900	1910	1920	1930	1940	1950
MALES													
0–9	5.6	6.0	6.3	6.5	6.2	5.7	6.3	3.1	4.0	5.2	6.0	5.1	8.8
10–13	2.0	2.2	2.2	2.4	2.5	2.4	2.1	1.1	1.4	1.9	2.4	2.3	2.5
14–19	2.7	3.0	3.2	3.1	3.5	3.7	3.0	1.6	2.3	2.6	3.5	3.7	3.6
20–24	1.9	2.2	2.3	2.1	2.3	2.5	2.0	1.4	2.3	2.4	3.0	3.2	3.6
25–44	5.4	5.9	6.7	6.9	6.9	7.8	7.5	5.2	7.4	9.3	11.4	11.8	14.8
45–64	2.8	3.4	3.9	4.4	4.9	5.5	5.2	2.1	3.3	4.8	6.3	7.9	10.0
65 & older	0.9	1.1	1.2	1.4	1.7	2.1	2.2	0.4	0.8	1.1	1.6	2.3	3.5
14–24	4.6	5.2	5.5	5.2	5.8	6.2	5.0	3.0	4.6	5.0	6.5	6.9	7.2
14 & older	13.7	15.6	17.3	17.9	19.3	21.6	19.9	10.7	16.1	20.2	25.8	28.9	35.5
10 & older	15.7	17.8	19.5	20.3	21.8	24.0	22.0	11.8	17.5	22.1	28.2	31.2	38.0
0 & older	21.3	23.8	25.8	26.8	28.0	29.7	28.3	14.9	21.5	27.3	34.2	36.3	46.8
FEMALES													
0–9	5.4	5.8	6.1	6.2	6.0	5.5	5.9	3.1	4.0	5.1	5.9	5.0	8.6
10–13	1.9	2.1	2.2	2.4	2.4	2.3	2.1	1.1	1.4	1.9	2.4	2.3	2.5
14–19	2.6	2.9	2.9	3.0	3.2	3.4	2.6	1.7	2.5	2.8	3.7	3.9	3.9
20–24	1.8	2.1	2.2	2.1	2.2	2.3	1.8	1.6	2.3	2.7	3.4	3.6	4.0
25–44	4.6	5.2	5.9	6.4	6.6	7.4	7.3	5.0	6.8	8.9	11.3	12.6	15.5
45–64	2.4	2.8	3.1	3.5	4.0	4.9	4.8	2.1	3.2	4.5	6.2	7.9	10.5
65 & older	0.7	1.0	1.1	1.2	1.4	1.8	2.1	0.5	0.9	1.3	1.9	2.8	4.5
14–24	4.4	5.0	5.1	5.1	5.4	5.7	4.4	3.3	4.8	5.5	7.1	7.5	7.9
14 & older	12.1	14.0	15.2	16.2	17.4	19.8	18.6	10.9	15.7	20.2	26.5	30.8	38.4
10 & older	14.0	16.1	17.4	18.6	19.8	22.1	20.7	12.0	17.1	22.1	28.9	33.1	40.9
0 & older	19.4	21.9	23.5	24.8	25.8	27.6	26.6	15.1	21.1	27.2	34.8	38.1	49.5
BOTH SEXES													
14 & older	25.8	29.6	32.5	34.1	36.7	41.4	38.5	21.6	31.8	40.4	52.3	59.7	73.9
10 & older	29.7	33.9	36.9	38.9	41.6	46.1	42.7	23.8	34.6	44.2	57.1	64.3	78.9
0 & older	40.7	45.7	49.3	51.6	53.8	57.3	54.9	30.0	42.6	54.5	69.0	74.4	96.3

TABLE A-3, continued

LABOR FORCE IN MILLIONS [a]

	RURAL							URBAN						
Age Group	1890	1900	1910	1920	1930	1940	1950	1890	1900	1910	1920	1930	1940	1950
MALES														
10–13	0.4	0.4	0.3	0.2	0.1	..	..	0.1	0.1	0.0	0.0	0.0	..	..
14–19	1.5	1.8	1.7	1.5	1.6	1.4	1.3	0.8	1.0	1.4	1.5	1.3	1.1	1.2
20–24	1.7	2.0	2.1	1.9	2.1	2.2	1.8	1.1	1.3	2.1	2.2	2.7	2.8	2.9
25–44	5.3	5.6	6.5	6.6	6.7	7.4	7.0	3.4	5.1	7.2	9.2	11.1	11.3	13.8
45–64	2.7	3.2	3.6	4.1	4.6	4.9	4.5	1.4	1.9	3.1	4.5	5.9	7.0	8.9
65 & older	0.7	0.8	0.7	0.9	1.1	1.0	1.0	0.2	0.3	0.4	0.6	0.9	0.8	1.4
14–24	3.2	3.8	3.8	3.4	3.7	3.6	3.1	1.9	2.3	3.5	3.7	4.0	3.9	4.1
14 & older	11.9	13.4	14.6	15.0	16.1	16.9	15.6	6.9	9.6	14.2	18.0	21.9	23.0	28.2
10 & older	12.3	13.8	14.9	15.2	16.2	16.9	15.6	7.0	9.7	14.2	18.0	21.9	23.0	28.2
0 & older	12.3	13.8	14.9	15.2	16.2	16.9	15.6	7.0	9.7	14.2	18.0	21.9	23.0	28.2
FEMALES														
10–13	0.1	0.1	0.1	0.1	0.1	..	..	0.0	0.1	0.0	0.0	0.0	..	..
14–19	0.5	0.6	0.5	0.5	0.5	0.4	0.4	0.5	0.7	1.0	1.1	1.1	0.9	1.0
20–24	0.3	0.4	0.5	0.5	0.6	0.7	0.6	0.6	0.8	1.1	1.3	1.8	2.0	2.0
25–44	0.4	0.6	0.8	0.9	1.0	1.4	1.7	0.9	1.2	1.9	2.6	3.5	4.6	5.7
45–64	0.2	0.4	0.4	0.4	0.6	0.7	1.0	0.3	0.3	0.6	0.9	1.3	1.9	3.4
65 & older	0.1	0.1	0.1	0.1	0.1	0.1	0.1	0.0	0.0	0.1	0.1	0.2	0.2	0.4
14–24	0.8	1.0	1.0	1.0	1.1	1.1	1.0	1.1	1.5	2.1	2.4	2.9	2.9	3.0
14 & older	1.5	2.1	2.3	2.4	2.8	3.3	3.8	2.3	3.0	4.7	6.0	7.9	9.6	12.5
10 & older	1.6	2.2	2.4	2.5	2.9	3.3	3.8	2.3	3.1	4.7	6.0	7.9	9.6	12.5
0 & older	1.6	2.2	2.4	2.5	2.9	3.3	3.8	2.3	3.1	4.7	6.0	7.9	9.6	12.5
BOTH SEXES														
14 & older	13.4	15.5	16.9	17.4	18.9	20.2	19.4	9.2	12.6	18.9	24.0	29.8	32.6	40.7
10 & older	13.9	16.0	17.3	17.7	19.1	20.2	19.4	9.3	12.8	18.9	24.0	29.8	32.6	40.7
0 & older	13.9	16.0	17.3	17.7	19.1	20.2	19.4	9.3	12.8	18.9	24.0	29.8	32.6	40.7

TABLE A-3, continued

LABOR FORCE AS PER CENT OF POPULATION OF SAME SEX AND AGE GROUP, UNSTANDARDIZED *

Age Group	RURAL							URBAN						
	1890	1900	1910	1920	1930	1940	1950	1890	1900	1910	1920	1930	1940	1950
MALES														
10–13	20.1	19.6	13.1	9.1	6.1	...	...	12.4	14.1	3.0	1.8	0.5	...	...
14–19	55.7	60.3	54.2	49.4	45.5	39.2	45.1	60.0	62.6	59.0	56.5	36.7	29.8	35.5
20–24	90.7	90.9	89.8	89.3	90.5	88.8	88.5	94.0	93.0	92.4	92.4	89.5	87.4	79.6
25–44	98.1	95.5	95.7	96.1	97.4	94.2	93.0	96.7	97.1	97.4	97.9	97.5	95.5	92.8
45–64	95.9	93.1	93.1	93.4	94.6	88.8	86.7	93.8	93.6	94.1	94.1	93.7	88.7	88.4
65 & older	76.5	70.4	60.9	61.6	62.2	46.4	44.1	66.6	63.1	54.0	58.1	54.2	37.0	40.0
14–24	70.2	73.5	69.3	65.5	63.4	59.5	62.6	76.4	76.8	75.5	73.9	61.3	56.1	57.8
14 & older	86.8	85.8	84.3	83.7	83.3	78.3	78.3	88.4	89.4	88.4	88.9	84.7	79.6	79.3
10 & older	78.3	77.7	76.1	74.7	74.5	70.5	70.7	80.9	82.3	81.4	81.6	77.6	73.6	74.2
0 & older	57.8	58.1	57.5	56.7	58.0	57.0	54.9	64.3	65.2	66.2	66.0	64.0	63.3	60.2
FEMALES														
10–13	6.1	7.0	5.3	4.8	2.9	...	...	3.9	4.4	1.8	0.4	0.2	...	...
14–19	17.9	19.0	18.1	17.2	15.2	13.5	16.5	36.2	39.8	40.0	40.3	29.4	23.3	26.5
20–24	18.0	20.2	22.0	24.0	26.9	29.0	29.6	47.9	47.7	48.1	49.0	52.3	55.5	48.2
25–44	8.7	12.1	13.3	13.5	15.4	18.6	24.0	24.8	24.3	27.6	28.9	31.2	37.0	37.1
45–64	10.5	13.0	14.5	13.1	14.3	13.3	20.1	15.8	15.7	19.7	20.2	21.6	23.7	32.5
65 & older	8.2	9.9	9.4	8.2	8.2	5.0	5.6	8.4	7.6	7.7	7.9	7.9	6.4	8.5
14–24	17.9	19.5	19.8	20.0	19.9	19.8	21.9	41.9	43.6	43.9	44.6	40.3	38.6	37.6
14 & older	12.3	14.7	15.5	15.1	16.0	16.4	20.4	28.0	27.8	29.8	29.9	29.7	31.2	32.6
10 & older	11.5	13.7	14.2	13.8	14.4	14.7	18.3	25.7	25.6	27.5	27.4	27.3	29.0	30.6
0 & older	8.3	10.1	10.5	10.3	11.0	11.8	14.3	20.7	20.4	22.3	22.2	22.7	25.2	25.3
BOTH SEXES														
14 & older	51.8	52.1	52.1	51.1	51.3	48.7	50.4	57.6	58.3	59.4	59.4	56.8	54.6	55.1
10 & older	46.7	47.3	46.9	45.7	45.9	43.8	45.3	52.7	53.7	54.7	54.5	52.1	50.7	51.6
0 & older	34.1	35.1	35.1	34.4	35.4	35.2	35.2	42.3	42.7	44.5	44.2	43.1	43.8	42.3

TABLE A-3, continued

PER CENT OF POPULATION OF SAME SEX AND AGE GROUP, STANDARDIZED FOR AGE AND SEX COMPOSITION [a, b]

LABOR FORCE

Age Group	RURAL							URBAN						
	1890	1900	1910	1920	1930	1940	1950	1890	1900	1910	1920	1930	1940	1950
MALES														
14–24	70.0	72.8	68.8	65.8	63.9	59.5	62.9	75.5	76.5	74.3	72.9	60.9	56.1	55.7
14 & older	87.4	86.0	84.0	83.4	83.7	78.3	78.0	88.5	88.5	87.5	87.7	84.3	79.6	78.5
10 & older	80.7	79.3	76.9	76.0	76.0	70.5	70.2	82.8	83.0	81.2	81.3	78.0	73.6	72.7
FEMALES														
14–24	17.9	19.5	19.7	19.9	19.9	19.8	21.8	41.8	43.6	43.9	44.4	40.3	38.6	36.8
14 & older	11.8	14.3	15.1	14.8	15.8	16.4	20.7	25.2	25.3	27.8	28.6	28.9	31.2	33.3
10 & older	11.2	13.5	14.1	13.7	14.4	14.7	18.6	23.7	23.8	25.9	26.6	26.9	29.0	30.9
BOTH SEXES														
14 & older	51.3	51.7	51.1	50.6	51.3	48.7	50.7	55.8	55.9	56.7	57.2	55.7	54.6	55.2
10 & older	47.4	47.8	46.8	46.2	46.5	43.8	45.5	52.4	52.6	52.8	53.2	51.7	50.7	51.2

Source and explanation: Notes to Table A-2 and Supplementary Appendixes G and H.

[a] Totals and percentages were computed before data on population and labor force were rounded.

[b] According to the sex and age composition of the population of the United States in 1940. For explanation of standardization, see Chapter 3.

TABLE A-4

United States:
Labor Force by Sex and Age Group, Color, and Nativity, April, 1890–1950

Age Group	NATIVE WHITE 1890	1900	1920	1930	1940	1950	FOREIGN-BORN WHITE 1890	1900	1920	1930	1940	1950	NONWHITE 1890	1900	1920	1930	1940	1950
							NUMBER IN MILLIONS [a]											
MALES																		
10–13	0.3	0.3	0.1	0.0	..	—	0.0	0.0	0.0	0.1	..	..	0.2	0.2	0.1	0.1	..	..
14–19	1.7	2.1	2.4	2.4	2.1	2.2	0.2	0.3	0.2	0.4	0.1	0.0	0.4	0.4	0.4	0.4	0.4	0.3
20–24	2.0	2.4	3.2	3.8	4.4	4.1	0.5	0.4	0.4	0.4	0.1	0.1	0.3	0.5	0.5	0.6	0.5	0.5
25–44	5.7	7.2	10.8	13.0	15.2	17.9	2.1	2.4	3.5	3.1	1.7	0.9	0.9	1.1	1.5	1.7	1.8	2.0
45–64	2.4	3.2	5.6	7.1	8.4	10.0	1.3	1.4	2.2	2.5	2.6	2.3	0.4	0.5	0.8	0.9	0.9	1.1
65 & older	0.6	0.7	1.0	1.3	1.2	1.7	0.2	0.3	0.4	0.5	0.4	0.5	0.1	0.1	0.1	0.2	0.2	0.2
14–24	3.7	4.5	5.6	6.2	6.5	6.3	0.7	0.7	0.6	0.5	0.1	0.1	0.7	0.9	0.9	1.0	0.9	0.8
14 & older	12.4	15.6	23.0	27.6	31.3	35.9	4.3	4.8	6.7	6.6	4.8	3.8	2.1	2.6	3.3	3.8	3.8	4.1
10 & older	12.7	15.9	23.1	27.6	31.3	35.9	4.3	4.8	6.7	6.6	4.8	3.8	2.3	2.8	3.4	3.9	3.8	4.1
0 & older	12.7	15.9	23.1	27.6	31.3	35.9	4.3	4.8	6.7	6.6	4.8	3.8	2.3	2.8	3.4	3.9	3.8	4.1
FEMALES																		
10–13	0.1	0.1	0.0	0.0	0.0		0.0	0.0	0.0	0.1	..	..	0.0	0.1	0.1	0.1	..	..
14–19	0.6	0.8	1.3	1.2	1.1	1.3	0.2	0.2	0.1	0.1	0.0	0.0	0.2	0.3	0.2	0.3	0.2	0.1
20–24	0.6	0.8	1.3	1.9	2.3	2.2	0.2	0.2	0.2	0.2	0.1	0.1	0.2	0.2	0.3	0.3	0.3	0.3
25–44	0.7	1.0	2.3	3.0	4.5	6.0	0.3	0.3	0.5	0.6	0.5	0.3	0.3	0.5	0.7	0.9	1.0	1.1
45–64	0.2	0.3	0.7	1.3	1.9	3.3	0.1	0.2	0.3	0.3	0.4	0.6	0.1	0.2	0.3	0.3	0.3	0.5
65 & older	0.1	0.1	0.2	0.3	0.3	0.4	0.0	0.0	0.0	0.0	0.0	0.1	0.0	0.0	0.0	0.0	0.0	0.0
14–24	1.2	1.6	2.6	3.1	3.4	3.5	0.4	0.4	0.3	0.3	0.1	0.1	0.3	0.5	0.5	0.6	0.5	0.4
14 & older	2.2	3.0	5.8	7.7	10.1	13.2	0.8	0.9	1.1	1.2	1.0	1.1	0.8	1.2	1.5	1.8	1.8	2.0
10 & older	2.3	3.1	5.8	7.7	10.1	13.2	0.8	0.9	1.1	1.2	1.0	1.1	0.8	1.3	1.6	1.9	1.8	2.0
0 & older	2.3	3.1	5.8	7.7	10.1	13.2	0.8	0.9	1.1	1.2	1.0	1.1	0.8	1.3	1.6	1.9	1.8	2.0
BOTH SEXES																		
14 & older	14.6	18.6	28.8	35.3	41.4	49.1	5.1	5.7	7.8	7.8	5.8	4.9	2.9	3.8	4.8	5.6	5.6	6.1
10 & older	15.0	19.0	28.9	35.3	41.4	49.1	5.1	5.7	7.8	7.8	5.8	4.9	3.1	4.1	5.0	5.8	5.6	6.1
0 & older	15.0	19.0	28.9	35.3	41.4	49.1	5.1	5.7	7.8	7.8	5.8	4.9	3.1	4.1	5.0	5.8	5.6	6.1

TABLE A-4, *continued*

PER CENT OF POPULATION OF SAME SEX AND AGE GROUP, UNSTANDARDIZED [a]

Age Group	NATIVE WHITE						FOREIGN-BORN WHITE						NONWHITE					
	1890	1900	1920	1930	1940	1950	1890	1900	1920	1930	1940	1950	1890	1900	1920	1930	1940	1950
MALES																		
10–13	12.7	14.1	4.3	2.2	...	...	13.3	10.2	2.4	...	...	...	46.8	41.3	19.3	12.2	...	...
14–19	52.3	57.4	50.2	38.6	33.1	39.9	83.1	79.7	65.9	53.2	31.1	44.8	70.3	73.7	64.1	57.8	45.5	44.3
20–24	90.7	91.6	90.1	89.3	87.9	82.6	96.6	91.9	95.4	93.8	89.9	78.2	93.7	92.3	92.6	93.1	88.9	81.2
25–44	97.3	96.0	96.9	97.5	95.2	93.9	98.4	97.3	98.0	98.2	95.8	94.4	97.6	95.4	96.8	96.8	92.3	88.4
45–64	94.9	93.0	93.5	94.2	89.3	88.6	94.7	93.0	93.5	93.3	87.2	88.2	97.9	95.9	96.4	96.0	87.9	85.4
65 & older	74.2	69.3	61.1	59.7	42.0	42.1	69.0	62.1	52.4	51.1	38.1	38.6	87.4	83.0	79.5	73.8	48.4	43.7
14–24	68.4	71.9	67.3	60.0	57.0	59.8	91.4	87.0	83.7	79.4	61.9	65.0	79.8	82.0	76.5	73.3	63.7	60.8
14 & older	84.9	85.7	84.8	82.5	78.7	79.9	93.8	91.3	90.9	89.3	80.2	75.3	90.3	89.9	89.5	88.2	79.9	76.8
10 & older	75.1	76.4	75.3	73.5	71.3	73.3	91.2	89.5	89.4	88.6	80.0	74.9	83.6	83.3	81.2	79.1	71.5	70.5
0 & older	54.3	55.6	56.4	57.1	58.8	57.7	88.1	87.8	88.2	87.4	79.0	74.0	58.6	61.1	62.4	62.4	56.7	53.2
FEMALES																		
10–13	2.7	3.0	1.5	0.7	...	...	7.8	6.0	1.6	...	...	...	18.8	24.6	13.0	7.5	...	...
14–19	19.0	21.0	26.2	21.1	18.2	23.2	54.8	55.2	46.3	41.3	34.4	28.0	38.2	45.5	34.9	30.5	21.3	18.3
20–24	25.1	27.5	37.3	41.4	45.1	43.5	45.6	43.3	37.6	50.1	51.4	40.7	47.3	46.2	43.7	45.5	43.8	39.5
25–44	12.0	14.9	20.2	23.4	28.5	31.7	16.2	16.6	18.6	20.7	27.1	33.3	37.0	40.9	44.4	46.5	44.8	46.2
45–64	10.0	11.5	15.1	17.3	19.3	28.5	10.0	10.9	13.8	14.1	15.2	24.6	37.4	40.9	44.7	43.8	35.8	39.2
65 & older	6.7	7.8	7.0	7.6	5.9	7.9	6.2	6.2	5.8	5.9	3.8	6.5	25.2	27.4	26.7	22.5	12.0	10.8
14–24	21.5	23.8	31.1	29.8	30.2	32.9	49.3	48.2	41.0	47.0	43.8	37.1	41.9	45.8	38.8	37.3	31.2	28.2
14 & older	15.0	17.1	21.8	23.0	25.0	28.7	19.9	19.5	18.7	18.9	18.0	22.0	38.5	42.2	41.7	41.8	36.8	37.0
10 & older	13.4	15.3	19.4	20.6	22.7	26.6	19.5	19.1	18.3	18.8	17.9	21.9	35.6	39.9	38.2	37.8	33.1	33.7
0 & older	9.7	11.1	14.6	16.1	18.9	21.2	18.7	18.7	18.1	18.5	17.8	21.6	24.9	28.9	29.4	29.8	26.6	26.1
BOTH SEXES																		
14 & older	50.4	51.9	53.5	52.8	51.7	53.8	60.2	58.3	58.4	56.7	50.8	48.9	64.7	66.2	65.8	64.9	57.8	56.3
10 & older	44.6	46.3	47.5	47.1	46.9	49.6	58.5	57.2	57.4	56.3	50.6	48.7	59.9	61.8	59.8	58.4	51.8	51.0
0 & older	32.3	33.7	35.6	36.7	38.8	39.3	56.4	56.0	56.6	55.4	50.5	48.1	41.9	45.1	46.1	46.0	41.4	39.4

TABLE A-4, continued

Age Group	NATIVE WHITE						FOREIGN-BORN WHITE						NONWHITE					
	1890	1900	1920	1930	1940	1950	1890	1900	1920	1930	1940	1950	1890	1900	1920	1930	1940	1950
	PER CENT OF POPULATION OF SAME SEX AND AGE GROUP, STANDARDIZED [a]																	
	MALES																	
14 & older [b]	89.3	86.7	85.3	83.8	79.1	78.8	92.5	89.9	87.8	85.7	78.4	78.8	92.3	90.9	89.9	88.5	80.1	76.4
14 & older [c]	89.0	86.7	85.4	83.7	79.1	78.9												
10 & older [b]	80.9	80.5	78.3	76.8	72.3	72.1	85.7	83.1	80.5	78.4	71.7	72.1	88.4	86.7	83.9	81.9	73.3	69.9
10 & older [c]	80.5	80.5	78.3	76.7	72.3	72.2												
	FEMALES																	
14 & older [b]	13.6	15.8	20.6	22.2	24.6	28.9	22.7	22.9	22.5	24.1	25.9	28.8	37.4	40.9	41.4	41.2	36.0	36.4
14 & older [c]	16.3	17.7	21.3	22.2	24.6	28.1												
10 & older [b]	12.7	14.7	19.0	20.4	22.5	26.5	21.5	21.5	20.7	22.1	23.7	26.4	35.9	39.6	39.0	38.4	33.0	33.3
10 & older [c]	15.2	16.4	19.6	20.4	22.5	25.8												
	BOTH SEXES																	
14 & older [b]	50.4	51.2	52.9	53.0	51.8	53.8	57.6	56.4	55.1	54.9	52.1	53.8	64.9	65.9	65.7	64.8	58.1	56.4
14 & older [c]	51.6	52.1	53.3	52.9	51.8	53.4												
10 & older [b]	46.8	47.6	48.7	48.6	47.4	49.3	53.6	52.3	50.6	50.3	47.7	49.2	62.2	63.2	61.5	60.2	53.2	51.6
10 & older [c]	47.8	48.4	49.1	48.5	47.4	49.0												

Source: Censuses of the United States: 1890, *Population*, Vol. I, Part 2, pp. 378–407; 1900, *Population*, Vol. II, Part II, pp. xxxvi–xxxix, and (Special Reports) *Occupations*, pp. 20–35; 1930, *Population*, Vol. II, p. 41; 1940, *Population*, Vol. IV, Part I, p. 90, and *Population, Education*, pp. 75–82; 1950, *Population, Employment and Personal Characteristics*, P-E, No. 1A, p. 62.

[a] Totals and percentages were computed before data on population and labor force were rounded.

[b] Standardized according to the age or age-sex composition of the population of all classes in the United States in 1940.

[c] Standardized according to the age or age-sex composition of the population of all classes in the United States in 1940. Partially standardized for rural-urban residence on the assumption that the effect of rural-urban migration would be the same for native whites as for all classes. This partial standardization was accomplished by taking the excess of the labor force participation rate of all classes, standardized for age or age-sex and rural-urban composition, over that standardized for age or age-sex alone, and adding the excess to the native white labor force participation rate, standardized for age or age-sex only.

Explanation of standardization: Chapter 3, section on *The Method*.

TABLE A-5

United States:

Armed Forces by Sex and Age Group, April, 1890–1950

Officers and Enlisted Personnel [a]

(Thousands)

Age Group [b]	1890	1900	1910	1920	1930	1940	1950
			MALES				
14–19	2	6	10	53	18	47	300
20–24	6	19	31	85	49	100	451
25–44	18	19	37	82	59	106	534
45–64	2	1	5	6	7	25	24
65 & older	–	–	–	–	–	–	–
14–24	8	25	41	138	67	147	751
14 & older	28	45	83	226	133	278	1309
			FEMALES				
14–19	–	–	–	–	–	–	2
20–24	–	–	–	–	–	–	5
25–44	–	–	–	–	–	–	13
45–64	–	–	–	–	–	–	1
65 & older	–	–	–	–	–	–	–
14–24	–	–	–	–	–	–	7
14 & older	–	–	–	–	–	–	21
			BOTH SEXES				
14 & older	28	45	83	226	133	278	1330
Stationed abroad	9	89	52	118	113	150	150
Total	37	134	135	344	246	428	1480

Source: H. *Exec. Documents*, 51st Cong., 1st sess., VIII, p. 52; 2d sess., II, p. 68; 56th Cong., 1st sess., XV, p. 67; 2d sess., II, p. 6. Annual reports of the Secretary of the Navy: *1920*, p. 220; *1930*, pp. 16–28; *1935*, p. 14; *1940*, p. 16. Annual reports of the Secretary of War: *1910*, I, p. 166; *1920*, I, p. 283; *1930*, p. 314; *1935*, p. 88; *1941*, p. 104. Census reports: *1890, Population*, Vol. I, Part 2, pp. 372–373; *1900* (Special Reports), *Occupations*, pp. 16–17; *1910, Population*, Vol. IV, pp. 428–429; *1920, Population*, Vol. IV, pp. 392–393; *1930, Population*, Vol. V, pp. 132–133; *1940, Population*, Vol. III, *The Labor Force*, Part 1, p. 99; *1950, Current Population Reports, Monthly Report on the Labor Force*, P-57, No. 94.

[a] Excluded were those stationed abroad and not considered as part of the population of continental United States during 1890–1940, and 150,000 in 1950. During 1890 and 1900 monthly averages of yearly census enumerations were used for April; for 1910–1940 estimates for April relied on monthly reports of the Army, and on interpolations of the June strength of the Navy and Marine Corps; and for 1950 Bureau of the Census estimates for April were used.

[b] Age distribution for 1890–1940 was based on returns at each population census covering the armed forces in continental United States; for 1950 it was based on information obtained from the Bureau of the Census (letter of July 10, 1950).

TABLE A-6

United States:

Females in the Labor Force by Marital Status and Age Group, April, 1890–1950

Age Group	Number in millions [a]							Per Cent of Female Population of Same Marital Status [a]						
	1890	1900	1910	1920	1930	1940	1950	1890	1900	1910	1920	1930	1940	1950
Single Women														
16–44	2.3 b	...	...	...	5.1	5.5	4.2	43.7	...	...	...	56.2	54.3	54.5
45 & older	0.1 b, c	...	...	...	0.6 b, c	0.7	0.9	34.5	...	...	...	47.5	45.7	49.8
16 & older	2.4 b	3.1 b	4.4 b	...	5.7 b	6.2	5.1	43.1	45.9	54.0	...	55.2	53.1	53.6
16 & older d								42.5	...	...	...	55.0	53.1	53.9
Married Women														
16–44	0.4	...	...	1.5	2.4	3.1	5.6	5.1	...	...	10.0	13.6	16.6	24.4
45 & older	0.1 c	...	...	0.4 c	0.7	0.8	2.1	3.5	...	...	6.6	7.8	8.6	16.6
16 & older	0.5	0.8	1.9	1.9	3.1	3.9	7.7	4.6	5.6	10.7	9.0	11.7	13.8	21.6
16 & older d								4.5	...	...	8.8	11.6	13.8	21.7
Widows or Divorcees														
16–44	0.3	...	...	...	0.9	1.4	1.6	52.0	...	...	...	67.5	61.8	61.5
45 & older	0.4 c	...	...	...	0.9 c	1.3	1.9	22.5	...	...	...	23.9	22.2	26.1
16 & older	0.7	0.9	1.1	...	1.8	2.7	3.5	29.9	32.5	34.1	...	34.4	33.7	35.5
16 & older d								31.0	...	...	...	36.4	33.7	36.4
All Women														
UNSTANDARDIZED														
16–44	3.0	4.0	6.2	6.6	8.4	10.0	11.4	21.7	23.6	29.3	27.9	29.7	32.4	34.3
45 & older	0.6	0.8	1.2	1.5	2.2	2.8	4.9	11.8	12.8	15.7	15.0	16.1	16.4	22.6
16 & older	3.6	4.8	7.4	8.1	10.6	12.8	16.3	19.0	20.6	25.5	24.0	25.3	26.7	29.7
STANDARDIZED d														
16–44	2.6	...	...	...	8.5	10.0	13.1	21.3	...	...	...	31.7	32.4	37.1
45 & older	0.9	...	...	...	2.5	2.8	4.5	12.6	...	...	...	16.7	16.4	22.7
16 & older	3.5	...	...	...	11.0	12.8	17.6	18.2	...	...	...	26.3	26.7	31.9

notes to table on following page

Notes to Table A-6

Source: Censuses of the United States: *1900* (Special Reports), *Statistics of Women at Work*, pp. 14-20; Joseph A. Hill, *Women in Gainful Occupations, 1870 to 1920, Census Monographs IX*, pp. 19, 23, 67-77, 230, 242-243; *1920, Population—Occupations*, Vol. IV, p. 692; *1930, Population*, Vol. II (Statistics by Subject), pp. 837-833, 843, 845-846, and Vol. V, *Occupations*, pp. 272-274; *1940, Population*, Vol. III, *The Labor Force*, Part 1, p. 22; *1950, Population, Employment and Personal Characteristics*, P-E No. 1A, p. 112.

a Totals and percentages were computed before data on population and labor force were rounded.
b Include "marital status unknown." Single women 16-44 in the population and labor force were derived by assuming that half of the girls 14-17 were 16 or 17, and that the number of girls 14 or 15 who were married, widowed, or divorced was negligible.
c Include "age unknown."
d Standardized according to marital status and age in 1940. For explanation of standardization, see Chapter 3.

TABLE A-7

United States:
Labor Force of Nonwhites per 1,000 Nonwhite Population of Same Age, Sex, and Type of Area, Urban and Rural Areas, 1940 and 1950

	14 and Older [a]		14-17		18-24		25-34		35-44		45-64		65 and Older	
	1940	1950	1940	1950	1940	1950	1940	1950	1940	1950	1940	1950	1940	1950
Urban areas:														
Males	775	744	217	205	823	746	931	866	926	908	859	851	363	380
Females	446	409	123	104	534	429	573	499	543	550	438	439	128	116
Both sexes	611	576	167	152	658	569	733	667	725	720	652	644	231	237
Rural nonfarm areas:														
Males	743	688	289	289	783	735	866	768	866	831	820	761	371	330
Females	342	303	131	113	386	285	398	351	425	400	361	349	111	100
Both sexes	542	495	209	201	575	518	635	561	650	612	604	558	245	211
Rural farm areas:														
Males	856	870	434	512	877	878	946	951	956	964	941	937	677	658
Females	230	226	163	149	280	250	245	253	242	260	247	241	128	92
Both sexes	543	548	301	338	586	564	600	583	594	606	622	606	434	409

Source: Censuses of the United States: *1940, Population, The Labor Force* (Sample Statistics), *Employment and Personal Characteristics*, pp. 31-32; *1950* (Special Reports), P-E No. 1A, pp. 62-67.
a Standardized for age or age and sex on the basis of population of the United States in 1940. For explanation of standardization, see Chapter 3.

TABLE A-7A

United States:
Labor Force as Per Cent of Population 14 and Older of Same Sex, 38 Large Cities, 1900–1950 [a]

STANDARDIZED FOR AGE AND SEX COMPOSITION [b]

	Males					Females				
	1900	1920	1930	1940	1950	1900	1920	1930	1940	1950
Atlanta	89.0	91.5	88.0	83.6	78.9	40.9	39.1	41.3	42.0	45.1
Baltimore	90.3	91.0	88.1	81.8	81.6	30.1	33.3	33.2	34.7	36.6
Birmingham	...	89.7	87.2	83.3	82.4 c	...	29.4	30.9	31.8	28.9 c
Boston	87.5	89.5	85.3	80.2	74.3	31.9	37.4	36.4	36.6	38.3
Bridgeport	91.0	90.0	88.0	82.9	81.6	28.5	31.0	32.4	39.3	39.0
Buffalo	89.0	88.5	85.8	82.1	82.2	22.1	27.2	27.5	29.9	33.5
Chicago	90.0	90.2	86.6	82.6	81.6	23.7	31.8	31.5	35.0	38.0
Cincinnati	91.5	89.3	86.0	81.0	79.5	28.8	31.9	31.0	32.4	34.8
Cleveland	89.9	89.5	86.2	82.6	82.9	21.8	26.5	29.5	31.9	36.6
Columbus	82.9	86.5	83.7	76.5	74.7	23.4	28.0	31.3	31.8	39.8
Dallas	...	89.2	87.1	83.0	83.6	...	33.4	35.2	39.5	41.7
Denver	85.1	87.7	84.9	79.9	79.9	23.3	30.4	33.0	31.7	36.9
Detroit	90.8	90.2	87.1	84.8	84.4	24.3	24.8	25.1	28.8	31.9
Houston	...	91.1	87.7	82.7	79.5	...	31.2	32.0	34.6	36.1
Indianapolis	89.9	90.2	86.6	82.2	84.2	23.8	29.7	32.0	32.7	40.9
Kansas City	89.9	88.9	87.4	83.9	81.5	24.7	30.9	34.3	36.7	38.6
Los Angeles	85.7	85.0	83.0	78.0	79.4	21.1	29.8	32.6	33.6	38.4
Louisville	90.5	90.8	87.7	83.0	82.2	28.5	35.9	32.6	33.8	33.6
Memphis	92.4	90.3	86.5	83.6	81.2	39.3	36.0	34.7	37.4	37.2
Milwaukee	90.9	90.6	86.1	81.5	84.8	23.8	30.2	29.0	31.9	39.2
Minneapolis	87.6	87.1	85.5	81.1	79.7	25.4	31.0	34.8	33.6	43.6
Newark	91.5	90.6	87.5	82.2	78.4	25.7	28.4	32.1	36.0	39.2
New Haven	86.8	89.9	86.4	81.8	74.4	27.7	32.4	33.2	38.2	39.3
New Orleans	89.5	90.8	88.0	82.7	77.3	25.9	32.9	33.3	34.6	33.7
New York	90.6	89.6	86.8	81.6	79.8	27.9	33.0	32.0	35.3	38.4
Norfolk	...	91.4	87.4	85.0	86.7 c	...	33.2	33.6	33.2	30.3 c
Omaha	89.9	88.5	85.1	82.5	81.4 c	25.9	29.8	31.5	32.2	33.4 c
Philadelphia	90.7	89.8	87.8	82.4	78.7	29.4	32.2	33.4	35.7	37.0
Pittsburgh	91.0	89.3	85.7	82.0	78.9	19.8	27.2	27.8	29.7	31.7
Portland, Ore.	90.8	87.0	86.3	81.2	82.3	23.9	29.4	33.4	33.5	40.3
Providence	92.0	90.6	87.5	83.9	76.6	33.6	38.1	37.3	40.4	41.2
Richmond	86.3	88.9	86.6	81.8	79.6 c	35.5	37.4	37.4	44.1	40.7 c
Rochester	88.7	89.1	84.9	80.6	79.6	31.2	34.3	33.9	36.8	41.1
St. Louis	90.9	91.1	88.0	83.9	79.6	24.4	32.9	32.2	35.9	39.3
St. Paul	88.6	88.5	85.4	82.1	81.2	26.3	31.2	32.0	33.9	38.0
San Francisco	88.5	88.4	85.1	79.2	75.7	24.2	32.8	34.6	36.6	42.8
Scranton	92.1	90.3	86.3	81.5	77.7 c	22.3	26.4	26.6	30.9	33.7 c
Seattle	84.9	86.8	85.3	79.7	78.9	20.0	28.5	32.0	32.9	39.4
All Areas	90.0	89.5	86.5	81.9	80.3	26.7	31.6	31.9	34.5	37.5

APPENDIX A

TABLE A-7A, *continued*

	1900	1920	Both Sexes 1930	1940	1950
Atlanta	65.3	65.6	65.0	63.1	62.3
Baltimore	60.6	62.5	61.0	58.6	59.5
Birmingham	. . .	60.0	59.4	57.9	56.0 c
Boston	60.1	63.8	61.2	58.7	56.6
Bridgeport	60.2	60.9	60.6	61.5	60.6
Buffalo	56.2	58.3	57.1	56.3	58.2
Chicago	57.4	61.5	59.5	59.1	60.1
Cincinnati	60.6	61.0	58.9	57.1	57.5
Cleveland	56.3	58.5	58.3	57.6	60.1
Columbus	53.6	57.7	57.9	54.5	57.5
Dallas	. . .	61.7	61.6	61.6	62.9
Denver	54.7	59.5	59.4	56.2	58.7
Detroit	58.0	58.0	56.5	57.2	58.5
Houston	. . .	61.6	60.2	59.0	58.1
Indianapolis	57.3	60.4	59.7	57.9	62.8
Kansas City	57.8	60.3	61.2	60.7	60.4
Los Angeles	53.9	57.8	58.2	56.1	59.2
Louisville	59.9	63.8	60.5	58.8	58.3
Memphis	66.3	63.5	61.0	60.8	59.5
Milwaukee	57.8	60.9	57.9	57.0	62.3
Minneapolis	57.0	59.5	60.5	57.7	61.9
Newark	59.1	60.0	60.2	59.5	59.1
New Haven	57.7	61.6	60.2	60.3	57.1
New Orleans	58.1	62.3	61.0	59.0	55.8
New York	59.7	61.7	59.8	58.8	59.4
Norfolk	. . .	62.7	60.9	59.5	58.9 c
Omaha	58.4	59.6	58.7	57.7	57.7 c
Philadelphia	60.5	61.4	61.0	59.4	58.2
Pittsburgh	55.9	58.7	57.2	56.2	55.7
Portland, Ore.	57.9	58.6	60.2	57.7	61.6
Providence	63.2	64.7	62.7	62.5	59.2
Richmond	61.2	63.5	62.4	63.2	60.4 c
Rochester	60.4	62.1	59.8	59.0	60.6
St. Louis	58.1	62.5	60.5	60.2	59.7
St. Paul	57.9	60.3	59.1	58.4	59.9
San Francisco	56.8	61.0	60.2	58.2	59.5
Scranton	57.7	58.8	56.9	56.6	56.0 c
Seattle	52.9	58.1	59.0	56.6	59.4
All areas	58.8	61.0	59.6	58.5	59.2

Source: *Census of 1900: Abstract*, pp. 109–111, and (Special Reports), *Occupations*, pp. 480–763. *Census of Population: 1920*, Vol. IV, pp. 452–454; *1930*, Vol. II, pp. 724–805, and Vol. IV, pp. 66–67, 96, 440; *1940*, Vol. II, Part 1, pp. 119–151, and Vol. III, *The Labor Force*, Part 1, pp. 65–68; *1950, Preliminary Reports*, series PC-5.

ᵃ The 38-city study omitted 1890 and 1910 because of the difficulty presented by the probability of varying degrees of overcount or undercount in the different cities in these years.
ᵇ The standard age and sex composition is that of Chicago in 1930. For explanation of standardization, see Chapter 3 in the section on *The Method*.
ᶜ Standard metropolitan area.

TABLE A-8

Great Britain:
Labor Force by Sex and Age Group, 1841, 1881, and 1891, Actual and Standardized

Age Group	Number in millions [a]			Per Cent of Population of Same Age Group and Sex [a]		
	1841	1881 [b]	1891	1841 [c]	1881 [b]	1891
			MALES			
10–19	0.8	1.7	2.0	42.7	55.0	56.9
20 & older	4.4	7.1	7.9	89.7	94.2	93.3
10 & older	5.2	8.8	9.9	76.4	82.9	82.6
10 & older [d]	5.6	9.4	10.7	79.4	85.6	85.3
0 & older	5.2	8.8	9.9	57.0	61.0	62.2
			FEMALES			
10–19	0.6	1.3	1.5	29.3	40.8	41.5
20 & older	1.2	2.6	3.0	23.6	31.1	31.3
10 & older	1.8	3.9	4.5	25.1	33.7	34.0
10 & older [d]	1.7	3.7	4.2	24.8	33.2	33.5
0 & older	1.8	3.9	4.5	18.9	25.3	26.1
			BOTH SEXES			
10 & older [c]	7.8 [c]	12.7	14.4	55.8	57.4	57.3
10 & older [d]	7.3	13.1	14.9	57.7	59.4	59.4
0 & older	7.8 [c]	12.7	14.4	41.9	42.6	43.6

Source, concepts, and discussion of statistical weaknesses: Chapter 3 and Appendix F.

[a] Totals and percentages were computed before data on population and labor force were rounded.

[b] Some persons 5–9 were reported as occupied; these were classified in the 10–19 group.

[c] Including an estimate of unemployed in 1841; unemployed workers were excluded from the original figures.

[d] Standardized for age and sex composition on the basis of the population of the United States in 1940. For explanation of standardization, see Chapter 3.

TABLE A-9

Great Britain:
Population and Labor Force by Sex and Age Group, 1911–1951

Age Group	POPULATION (millions) [a]					LABOR FORCE (millions) [a, b]				
	1911 Apr.	1921 June	1931 Apr.	1939 [c] June	1951 Apr.	1911 Apr.	1921 June	1931 Apr.	1939 [d] June	1951 Apr.
MALES										
14–17	1.5	1.6	1.5	1.6	1.3	1.3	1.3	1.1	1.3	0.6
18–24	2.5	2.4	2.7	2.6	2.1	2.4	2.3	2.6	2.5	2.2
25–44	5.8	5.7	6.2	7.1	7.1	5.7	5.6	6.1	7.1	7.0
45–64	3.1	4.0	4.6	4.8	5.4	2.9	3.7	4.3	4.6	5.2
65 & older	0.9	1.1	1.4	1.8	2.2	0.5	0.7	0.7	0.6	0.7
14–24	4.0	4.0	4.2	4.2	3.4	3.7	3.6	3.7	3.8	2.8
14 & older	13.8	14.8	16.4	17.9	18.1	12.8	13.6	14.8	16.1	15.7
0 & older	19.7	20.4	21.5	22.6	23.4	12.8	13.6	14.8	16.1	15.7
FEMALES										
14–17	1.5	1.6	1.5	1.6	1.3	0.9	1.0	1.0	1.1	0.5
18–24	2.7	2.7	2.8	2.5	2.3	1.7	1.8	2.0	1.9	1.8
25–44	6.3	6.7	7.0	7.5	7.4	1.9	1.9	2.2	2.5	2.6
45–64	3.5	4.3	5.1	5.6	6.3	0.8	0.9	1.0	1.1	1.8
65 & older	1.2	1.5	1.9	2.4	3.1	0.1	0.1	0.1	0.2	0.2
14–24	4.2	4.3	4.3	4.1	3.6	2.6	2.8	3.0	3.0	2.3
14 & older	15.2	16.8	18.3	19.6	20.4	5.4	5.7	6.3	6.8	6.9
0 & older	21.1	22.4	23.3	24.1	25.4	5.4	5.7	6.3	6.8	6.9
BOTH SEXES										
14 & older	29.0	31.6	34.7	37.5	38.5	18.2	19.3	21.1	22.9	22.6
0 & older	40.8	42.8	44.8	46.7	48.8	18.2	19.3	21.1	22.9	22.6

APPENDIX A

TABLE A-9, *continued*

		LABOR FORCE			
	PER CENT OF POPULATION OF SAME SEX AND AGE GROUP [a, b]				
Age Group	1911	1921	1931	1939 [c, d]	1951
		MALES			
14–17	82.6	77.9	76.5	80.9	56.2
18–24	96.9	96.9	96.4	97.0	95.8
25–44	98.5	97.9	98.3	98.5	98.4
45–64	94.1	94.8	94.3	95.0	95.4
65 & older	56.8	58.9	47.9	37.5	31.9
14–24	91.4	89.3	89.3	90.9	81.1
14 & older	92.7	91.8	90.5	89.7	86.3
14 & older [e]	91.9	91.6	90.4	90.3	87.3
0 & older	64.9	66.7	68.9	71.2	66.9
		FEMALES			
14–17	58.6	57.8	63.9	72.7	56.3
18–24	65.4	66.5	70.9	75.8	70.3
25–44	29.3	28.5	30.9	33.3	35.7
45–64	21.6	20.1	19.6	19.8	28.4
65 & older	11.5	10.0	8.2	8.5	5.3
14–24	62.9	63.3	68.4	74.6	65.4
14 & older	35.4	33.7	34.2	35.0	34.0
14 & older [e]	34.5	33.8	35.8	38.5	38.8
0 & older	25.5	25.4	26.8	28.4	27.2
		BOTH SEXES			
14 & older	62.7	60.9	60.7	61.1	58.7
14 & older [e]	63.2	62.7	63.1	64.4	63.1
0 & older	44.6	45.1	47.0	49.0	46.2

Source and discussion: Chapter 3 and Appendix F.

[a] Totals and percentages were computed before data on population and labor force were rounded.

[b] To adjust for the British practice after 1939 of counting a part-time worker as half a member of the labor force, persons occupied less than full time were treated as regular workers in this study for comparison with U.S. data.

[c] Population in 1939 was based on the National Registration in September. The estimate of 250,000 armed forces overseas and seamen at sea was added to the resident population. All reported ages were converted to uniform grouping by linear interpolation within the five-year age groups.

[d] For discussion of the 1939 labor force estimate see notes to Appendix Table B-4.

[e] Standardized for sex and age composition on the basis of the population of the United States in 1940. For explanation of standardization, see Chapter 3, section on *The Method*.

TABLE A-10

Great Britain:
Females in the Labor Force by Marital Status and Age Group, 1911–1951

Age Group	Number in millions [a]				Per Cent of Female Population of Same Marital Status and Age Group [a]			
	1911 April	1921 June	1931 April	1951 April	1911 April	1921 June	1931 April	1951 April
Single Women								
16–44	3.5 [b]	3.7 [c]	4.0	2.8	73.5	77.2	80.0	86.4
45 & older	0.3	0.4 [c]	0.5	0.7	46.5	47.7	48.1	46.2
16 & older [d]	3.8	4.1 [c]	4.5	3.5	70.1	72.5	74.0	73.7
					68.4	71.7	74.0	78.9
Married Women								
16–44	0.5	0.5	0.7	1.8	10.2	9.5	12.4	26.3
45 & older	0.2	0.3	0.3	0.8	8.6	7.4	7.0	15.5
16 & older [d]	0.7	0.8	1.0	2.6	9.6	8.7	10.1	21.5
					9.5	8.6	10.1	21.7
Widows or Divorcees								
16–44	0.1	0.2	0.1	0.2	61.5	45.5	47.3	66.1
45 & older	0.4	0.3	0.3	0.4	24.9	21.3	17.9	16.6
16 & older [d]	0.5	0.5	0.4	0.6	29.4	25.5	21.2	20.9
					30.0	24.0	21.2	22.2
All Women								
UNSTANDARDIZED								
16–44	4.1	4.4	4.8	4.8	42.3	42.5	44.8	46.3
45 & older	0.9	1.0	1.1	1.9	18.9	17.5	16.5	20.7
16 & older	5.0	5.4	5.9	6.7	34.7	33.5	33.5	34.1
STANDARDIZED [d]								
16–44	3.5	4.1	4.8	6.6	40.9	41.9	44.8	55.3
45 & older	1.1	1.1	1.1	1.6	19.0	17.6	16.5	20.8
16 & older	4.6	5.2	5.9	8.2	32.2	32.3	33.5	41.6

Source: *Censuses of England and Wales: 1911*, pp. 90–91, 165; *1921, Occupations*, p. 54; *1931, Occupations*, pp. 23, 39. *Censuses of Scotland: 1911*, Vol. II, pp. 227, 297, 378, 436 and LXXIV; *1921*, Vol. II, pp. 171–172; *1931*, Vol. III, pp. XVII, XXIII, XXV, XXVIII, 138. *Census of Great Britain: 1951*, Part I, p. 56.

[a] Totals and percentages were computed before data on population and labor force were rounded.

[b] Single women 15 and older in the labor force in 1911 were reported in quinquennial age subdivisions; the number aged 16–19 was regarded as five-sixths of the number aged 15–19.

[c] Single women were not classified separately in 1921; computations were made by subtracting the number of married and widowed women from the total female labor force.

[d] Standardized according to distribution by marital status and age in 1931. For explanation of standardization, see Chapter 3, section on *The Method*.

TABLE A-11

Canada:
Population and Labor Force by Sex and Age Group (Excluding Yukon and Northwest Territories), June, 1911–1951

Age Group	POPULATION (thousands)					LABOR FORCE (thousands)					LABOR FORCE (Per cent of population of same sex and age group)				
	1911	1921	1931	1941	1951	1911 [a]	1921 [a]	1931 [a]	1941	1951	1911	1921	1931	1941	1951
MALES															
14–19	424	493	629	676	647	274	295	323	378	311	64.6	59.8	51.4	55.9	48.1
20–24	385	351	465	517	538	355	324	429	491	494	92.2	92.3	92.3	95.0	91.8
25–44	1,146	1,324	1,486	1,662	2,015	1,113	1,280	1,451	1,625	1,941	97.1	96.7	97.6	97.8	96.3
45–64	537	708	939	1,140	1,285	507	651	890	1,064	1,164	94.4	91.9	94.8	93.4	90.6
65 & older	194	214	294	390	551	101	125	164	184	212	52.1	58.4	55.8	47.2	38.5
14–24	809	844	1,094	1,193	1,185	629	619	752	869	805	77.8	73.3	68.7	72.8	67.9
14 & older [b]	2,686	3,090	3,813	4,385	5,036	2,350	2,675	3,257	3,743	4,122	87.5	86.6	85.4	85.4	81.9
14 & older [c]	2,480	2,968	3,645	4,258	4,992	2,161	2,558	3,129	3,653	4,103	87.1	86.2	85.8	85.8	82.2
0 & older	3,812	4,522	5,367	5,891	7,089	2,350	2,675	3,257	3,743	4,122	61.6	59.2	60.7	63.5	58.1
FEMALES															
14–19	398	484	614	662	636	107	116	133	203	197	26.9	24.0	21.7	30.7	31.0
20–24	320	360	447	514	551	76	126	189	243	258	23.8	35.0	42.3	47.3	46.8
25–44	917	1,184	1,345	1,580	2,027	124	172	241	333	468	13.5	14.5	17.9	21.1	23.1
45–64	467	612	791	997	1,199	44	62	85	120	214	9.4	10.1	10.7	12.0	17.8
65 & older	172	205	280	377	535	9	13	17	21	27	5.2	6.3	6.1	5.6	5.0

TABLE A-11, *continued*

Age Group	POPULATION (thousands)					LABOR FORCE (thousands)					LABOR FORCE (Per cent of population of same sex and age group)				
	1911	1921	1931	1941	1951	1911ᵃ	1921ᵃ	1931ᵃ	1941	1951	1911	1921	1931	1941	1951
						FEMALES (cont.)									
14–24	718	844	1,061	1,176	1,187	183	242	322	446	455	25.5	28.7	30.3	37.9	38.3
14 & older	2,274	2,845	3,477	4,130	4,948	360	489	665	920	1,164	15.8	17.2	19.1	22.3	23.5
14 & older ᵇ	2,480	2,967	3,645	4,257	4,992	369	486	671	931	1,198	14.9	16.4	18.4	21.9	24.0
14 & older ᶜ											16.1	17.1	18.4	21.9	23.2
0 & older	3,380	4,253	4,996	5,599	6,920	360	489	665	920	1,164	10.7	11.5	13.3	16.4	16.8
						BOTH SEXES									
14 & older	4,960	5,935	7,290	8,515	9,984	2,710	3,164	3,922	4,663	5,286	54.6	53.3	53.8	54.8	52.9
14 & older ᵇ	4,960	5,935	7,290	8,515	9,984	2,530	3,044	3,800	4,584	5,301	51.0	51.3	52.1	53.8	53.1
14 & older ᶜ											51.6	51.7	52.0	53.8	52.7
0 & older	7,192	8,775	10,363	11,490	14,009	2,710	3,164	3,922	4,663	5,286	37.7	36.1	37.8	40.6	37.7

Source and concept: Chapter 3 and Appendix F.

ᵃ Minor adjustments were made during 1911–1931 to convert reported ages to uniform age groups. These adjustments did not disturb the labor force totals.

ᵇ Standardized for age and sex composition on the basis of the population of the United States in 1940.

ᶜ Standardized for age and sex composition on the basis of population of the United States in 1940, and partially standardized for rural-urban residence on the assumption that the effect of rural-urban migration would be the same in Canada as in the United States. This partial standardization was accomplished by taking the excess of the labor force participation rate of the United States, standardized for age or age-sex and rural-urban composition, over that standardized for age or age-sex alone and adding the excess to the labor force participation rate of Canada, standardized for age or age-sex only.

Explanation of standardization: Chapter 3, section on *The Method*.

APPENDIX A

TABLE A-12

Canada:
Females in the Labor Force by Marital Status and Age Group, 1921–
1951

Age Group	Number in thousands				Per Cent of Female Population of Same Marital Status and Age Group			
	1921	1931	1941	1951	1921	1931	1941	1951
Single Women								
16–44	...	486	677	619	...	52.1	63.0	64.4
45 & older	...	44	57	94	...	38.3	38.8	50.8
16 & older	388	530	734	713	48.1	50.6	60.1	62.2
16 & older a					48.1 b	50.4	60.1	62.7
Married Women								
16–44	...	49	71	270	...	4.0	5.0	13.5
45 & older	...	18	15	79	...	2.5	1.7	7.0
16 & older	35	67	86	349	2.1	3.5	3.8	11.2
16 & older a					2.1 b	3.4	3.8	7.0
Widows or Divorcees								
16–44	...	20	13	24	...	46.5	20.6	49.0
45 & older	...	40	69	68	...	16.1	20.2	16.0
16 & older	52	60	82	92	21.7	20.5	20.2	19.4
16 & older a					21.7 b	20.8	20.2	21.1
All Women								
UNSTANDARDIZED								
16–44	400	555	761	913	21.5	25.2	29.9	30.4
45 & older	75	102	141	241	9.2	9.5	10.3	13.9
16 & older	475	657	902	1,154	17.7	20.1	23.0	24.4
STANDARDIZED a								
16–44	...	538	761	1,101	...	25.3	29.9	35.9
45 & older	...	113	141	232	...	9.8	10.3	14.0
16 & older	495 b	651	902	1,333	18.5 b	19.9	23.0	28.2

Source: *Census of Canada* (Ottawa, Dominion Bureau of Statistics): *1931*, Vol.
VII, pp. 4–5, 36–38; *1941*, Vol. I, pp. 638–641, 802–803, Vol. III, pp. 14, 94–98, and
Vol. VII, pp. 12–13, 54–55; *1951*, Vol. IV, Table 11, and Vol. V, Table 17.

a Standardized according to distribution by marital status and age in 1941.
b Standardized according to distribution by marital status only in 1941.

Explanation of standardization: Chapter 3, section on *The Method*.

TABLE A-13

Canada:

Per Cent of Population 10 and Older in the Labor Force, 21 Cities, 1911, 1941, 1951

| | PER CENT OF SAME SEX GROUP | | | | | | | | |
| | Males | | | Females | | | Both Sexes | | |
	1911	1941	1951	1911	1941	1951	1911	1941	1951
Brantford	85.6	81.6	81.8	21.2	26.5	31.4	53.8	54.4	56.9
Calgary	80.6	77.6	80.0	15.0	21.0	29.9	48.3	49.6	55.3
Edmonton	84.1	77.3	79.8	20.9	23.8	29.0	52.9	50.9	54.7
Fort William	84.6	82.3	78.2	14.1	22.6	22.3	49.8	52.8	50.6
Halifax	81.3	78.8	79.5	22.6	28.7	31.6	52.4	54.1	55.9
Hamilton	84.7	80.8	81.8	23.9	25.8	32.0	54.7	53.7	57.3
Hull	85.8	76.8	80.6	17.7	22.0	26.5	52.2	49.8	53.9
Kingston	78.7	78.8	78.7	22.2	24.5	32.3	50.8	52.0	55.9
Kitchener	83.1	83.1	83.0	26.2	30.0	36.9	55.0	56.9	60.3
London	82.2	76.2	79.8	25.2	26.8	35.3	54.1	51.8	57.9
Montreal	82.2	78.1	79.1	21.2	27.4	30.7	52.1	53.1	55.2
Ottawa	83.4	77.6	78.4	22.5	33.2	35.1	53.3	55.7	57.1
Quebec	81.1	76.7	77.3	22.7	27.6	29.6	52.3	52.5	53.8
Regina	84.7	79.3	79.6	20.7	26.2	34.5	53.2	53.1	57.3
Saint John	82.1	79.4	77.6	20.8	25.6	28.8	51.9	52.8	53.5
Sherbrooke	84.4	79.1	79.0	23.6	32.1	30.5	54.4	55.9	55.1
Toronto	82.9	78.8	79.9	26.2	30.9	38.4	54.9	55.2	59.5
Vancouver	81.3	76.2	77.1	19.1	23.2	37.9	50.6	50.1	55.3
Victoria	80.8	78.6	77.0	14.9	24.1	34.5	48.3	51.7	56.0
Windsor	82.9	78.3	80.4	21.7	18.6	26.3	52.7	48.8	53.7
Winnipeg	84.5	77.4	79.5	22.0	26.2	35.6	53.7	52.1	57.9
Average									
10 and Older [a]	82.7	78.2	79.3	22.3	27.2	32.9	52.9	53.0	56.4
15 and Older [a]	90.9	86.8	87.9	24.4	30.2	36.5	58.1	58.9	62.6

Source: *Census of Canada*, Ottawa, Dominion Bureau of Statistics: *1911*, Vol. VI, pp. 280–469; *1941*, Vol. III, pp. 79–92, and Vol. VII, pp. 90–243; *1951*, Vol. I, Table 24, and Vol. IV, Table 7.

[a] Standardized for age or age-sex composition on the basis of the age and sex composition of the population of Chicago in 1930. For explanation of standardization, see Chapter 3.

TABLE A-14

New Zealand:

Population and Labor Force by Sex and Age Group, 1896–1951

Age Group	1896 (April 12)	1901 (March 31)	1906 (April 29)	1911 (April 2)	1921 (April 17)	1926 (April 20)	1936 (March 24)	1945 [a] (Sept. 25)	1951 [a] (April 17)
				Population [b] (*thousands*)					
Males									
15–24	75	84	94	94	102	122	135	131	129
25–44	97	111	144	176	188	196	215	245	264
45–64	58	61	66	74	106	128	163	168	177
65 & older	13	19	25	28	32	36	49	71	83
15 & older	243	275	329	372	428	482	562	615	653
0 & older	371	406	471	532	623	686	756	826	917
Females									
15–24	75	84	88	90	102	116	131	129	122
25–44	83	100	125	151	187	199	213	242	260
45–64	39	44	51	60	92	115	156	174	181
65 & older	8	12	16	20	27	32	49	75	92
15 & older	205	240	280	321	408	462	549	620	655
0 & older	332	367	418	477	596	658	735	822	909
Both Sexes									
15 & older	448	515	609	693	836	944	1,111	1,235	1,308
0 & older	703	773	889	1,009	1,219	1,344	1,491	1,648	1,826
				Labor Force (*thousands*)					
Males									
15–24	70	79	88	88	93	107	123	106	104
25–44	95	110	142	172	185	192	212	239	259
45–64	56	60	64	71	100	119	151	147	155
65 & older	11	17	19	19	20	18	20	21	22
15 & older	232	266	313	350	398	436	506	513	540
0 & older	232	266	313	350	398	436	506	513	540
Females									
15–24	29	35	36	42	53	56	70	79	70
25–44	15	20	25	33	40	39	46	58	57
45–64	5	6	7	10	13	15	21	23	31
65 & older	1	1	2	2	2	2	2	2	3
15 & older	50	62	70	87	108	112	139	162	161
0 & older	50	62	70	87	108	112	139	162	161
Both Sexes									
15 & older	282	328	383	437	506	548	645	675	701
0 & older	282	328	383	437	506	548	645	675	701

TABLE A-14, *continued*

Age Group	1896	1901	1906	1911	1921	1926	1936	1945 ᵃ	1951 ᵃ
				LABOR FORCE					
		(per cent of population of same sex and age group)							
Males									
15–24	93.3	94.0	93.6	93.6	91.2	87.7	91.1	80.9	80.6
25–44	97.9	99.1	98.6	97.7	98.4	98.0	98.6	97.6	98.1
45–64	96.6	98.4	97.0	95.9	94.3	93.0	92.6	87.5	87.6
65 & older	84.6	89.5	76.0	67.9	62.5	50.0	40.8	29.6	86.5
15 & older	95.5	96.7	95.1	94.1	93.0	90.9	90.0	83.4	82.7
15 & older ᶜ	95.1	96.9	94.8	93.7	92.3	90.3	89.9	84.9	84.8
0 & older	62.5	65.5	66.5	65.8	63.9	63.6	66.9	62.1	58.9
Females									
15–24	38.7	41.7	40.9	46.7	52.0	48.3	53.4	61.2	57.4
25–44	18.1	20.0	20.0	21.9	21.4	19.6	21.6	24.0	21.9
45–64	12.8	13.6	13.7	16.7	14.1	13.0	13.5	13.2	17.1
65 & older	12.5	8.3	12.5	10.0	7.4	6.3	4.1	2.7	3.3
15 & older	24.4	25.8	25.0	27.1	26.5	24.2	25.3	26.1	24.6
15 & older ᶜ	21.0	22.6	23.0	25.4	25.6	23.7	25.6	28.4	27.6
0 & older	15.1	16.9	16.7	18.2	18.1	17.0	18.9	19.7	17.7
Both Sexes									
15 & older	62.9	63.7	62.9	63.1	60.5	58.3	58.1	54.7	53.6
15 & older ᶜ	58.0	59.8	58.9	59.6	59.0	57.0	57.8	56.6	56.2
0 & older	40.1	42.4	43.1	43.3	41.5	40.8	43.3	41.0	38.4

Source and concepts: Chapter 3 and Appendix F.

ᵃ Population and labor force include 44,000 in the armed forces overseas for 1945 and 2,000 for 1951.

ᵇ Including only non-Maoris resident in New Zealand proper.

ᶜ Standardized for age or age-sex composition on the basis of the population of the United States in 1940. For explanation of standardization, see Chapter 3.

TABLE A-15

New Zealand:
Females in the Labor Force by Marital Status and Age Group, 1926–1951

	Number in thousands				Per Cent of Female Population of Same Marital Status and Age Group			
Age Group	1926	1936	1945	1951 ª	1926	1936	1945	1951 ª
Single Women								
16–44	82	103	108	97	63.1	69.6	79.4	82.2
45 & older	7	10	12	13	41.2	37.0	37.5	37.1
16 & older	89	113	120	110	60.5	64.6	71.4	71.9
16 & older ᵇ					59.2	63.5	71.4	73.3
Married Women								
16–44	5	7	22	29	3.1	4.0	10.4	11.1
45 & older	4	5	6	13	4.3	3.9	3.9	7.7
16 & older	9	12	28	42	3.5	4.0	7.7	9.7
16 & older ᵇ					2.7	3.7	7.7	9.7
Widows or Divorcees								
16–44	4	4	5	7	40.0	50.0	55.6	53.8
45 & older	6	8	7	8	15.8	16.0	10.8	10.7
16 & older	10	12	12	15	20.8	20.7	16.2	17.0
16 & older ᵇ					20.0	19.7	16.2	17.1
			UNSTANDARDIZED					
All Women								
16–44	91	114	135	133	30.1	34.5	37.9	33.8
45 & older	17	23	25	34	11.6	11.2	10.0	12.2
16 & older	108	137	160	167	24.1	25.6	26.4	24.9
			STANDARDIZED ᵇ					
All Women								
16–44	72	95	135	155	27.3	30.2	37.9	39.2
45 & older	23	24	25	35	12.4	10.9	10.0	12.6
16 & older	95	119	160	190	21.2	22.2	26.4	28.3

Source: *Population Census* (Wellington, Census and Statistics Office): *1926*, Vol. IX, p. 96; *1936*, Vol. X, pp. 59, 76; *1945*, Vol. IX, pp. 61, 78; *1951*, Vol. II, p. 49, Vol. IV, p. 79.

ª Including Maoris.
ᵇ Standardized according to distribution by marital status and age in 1945.

For explanation of standardization, see Chapter 3, section on *The Method*.

TABLE A-16

Germany:
Population and Labor Force by Sex and Age Group, 1895–1950

	POPULATION (millions) [a]								LABOR FORCE (millions) [a]							
	Post-World War I Boundaries without the Saar					Federal Republic of Germany without Berlin			Post-World War I Boundaries without the Saar					Federal Republic of Germany without Berlin		
Age Group	1895 (June)	1907 (June)	1925 (June)	1933 (June)	1939 (May)	1939 [b] (May)	1946 [c] (Oct.)	1950 [d] (Sept.)	1895 (June)	1907 (June)	1925 (June)	1933 (June)	1939 (May)	1939 [b] (May)	1946 [c] (Oct.)	1950 [d] (Sept.)
MALES																
14–19	2.8	3.2	3.9	2.6	3.3	2.0	2.0	2.2	2.3	2.7	3.3	2.1	2.9	1.8	1.5	1.6
20–24	2.1	2.4	3.1	3.1	2.0	1.2	1.2	1.7	2.0	2.3	2.9	2.9	1.9	1.1	1.0	1.7
25–44	5.9	7.5	8.3	9.9	11.3	6.5	5.0	5.9	5.7	7.3	8.1	9.7	11.0	6.4	4.8	5.6
45–64	3.3	3.9	5.8	6.4	6.6	3.8	4.5	5.2	3.0	3.5	5.3	5.5	5.8	3.3	4.1	4.7
65 & older	1.0	1.2	1.6	2.1	2.5	1.4	1.8	2.0	0.6	0.6	0.8	0.6	0.7	0.5	0.7	0.5
14–24	4.9	5.6	7.0	5.7	5.3	3.2	3.2	3.9	4.3	5.0	6.2	5.0	4.8	2.9	2.5	3.3
14 & older	15.1	18.2	22.7	24.1	25.7	14.9	14.5	17.0	13.6	16.4	20.4	20.8	22.3	13.1	12.1	14.1
0 & older	22.5	27.2	30.2	31.7	33.3	19.3	19.6	22.4	13.6	16.4	20.4	20.8	22.3	13.1	12.1	14.1
FEMALES																
14–19	2.8	3.2	3.9	2.5	3.5	2.0	2.1	2.1	1.7	2.2	2.6	1.7	2.7	1.6	1.6	1.4
20–24	2.2	2.4	3.1	3.1	1.9	1.2	1.9	1.8	1.3	1.5	2.1	2.1	1.3	0.8	1.0	1.3
25–44	6.0	7.5	9.7	11.0	11.6	6.7	7.4	7.6	1.6	2.8	4.1	4.9	5.4	2.9	2.7	3.1
45–64	3.7	4.4	6.2	7.0	7.8	4.3	5.6	6.3	1.0	1.6	2.2	2.4	2.8	1.6	1.7	2.0
65 & older	1.2	1.4	2.0	2.5	2.9	1.5	2.1	2.4	0.2	0.3	0.4	0.3	0.4	0.3	0.3	0.2
14–24	5.0	5.6	7.0	5.6	5.4	3.2	4.0	3.9	3.0	3.7	4.7	3.8	4.0	2.4	2.6	2.7
14 & older	15.9	18.9	24.9	26.1	27.7	15.7	19.1	20.2	5.8	8.4	11.4	11.4	12.6	7.2	7.3	8.0
0 & older	23.4	27.8	32.2	33.5	35.0	20.0	24.1	25.3	5.8	8.4	11.4	11.4	12.6	7.2	7.3	8.0
BOTH SEXES																
14 & older	31.0	37.1	47.6	50.2	53.4	30.6	33.6	37.2	19.4	24.8	31.8	32.2	34.9	20.3	19.4	22.1
0 & older	45.9	55.0	62.4	65.2	68.3	39.3	43.7	47.7	19.4	24.8	31.8	32.2	34.9	20.3	19.4	22.1

TABLE A-16, *continued*

LABOR FORCE
AS PER CENT OF POPULATION OF SAME SEX AND AGE GROUP [a]

Age Group	Post-World War I Boundaries without the Saar					Federal Republic of Germany without Berlin		
	1895	1907	1925	1933	1939	1939	1946	1950
MALES								
14–19	83.6	86.1	85.0	82.6	86.0	91.1	73.7	74.2
20–24	95.1	95.7	95.0	94.5	96.2	95.7	89.7	93.4
25–44	97.2	97.4	97.4	97.2	98.0	97.6	95.9	96.3
45–64	91.8	89.4	91.4	84.9	87.0	86.9	91.0	89.6
65 & older	58.8	50.2	47.4	30.1	29.7	32.7	37.2	26.7
14–24	88.6	90.2	89.4	89.1	89.8	92.8	79.5	82.8
14 & older	90.7	90.5	89.9	86.3	86.9	87.9	83.7	83.0
14 & older [f]	90.2	89.3	89.4	85.7	87.2	87.9	85.5	84.9
0 & older	60.6	60.4	67.6	65.5	67.1	67.7	61.8	63.2
FEMALES								
14–19	60.6	67.8	67.2	68.3	79.2	81.3	75.7	67.3
20–24	58.3	62.0	67.8	69.7	67.8	68.6	53.7	70.4
25–44	26.9	37.6	41.9	44.2	45.8	44.2	37.0	40.5
45–64	25.6	35.5	36.3	33.7	36.4	36.9	29.1	31.0
65 & older	19.7	21.6	17.6	13.3	14.1	17.3	13.3	9.7
14–24	59.6	65.3	67.4	69.1	75.2	76.6	65.1	68.7
14 & older	36.2	44.1	45.7	43.7	45.5	46.1	38.0	39.3
14 & older [f]	34.5	42.8	45.0	45.2	48.0	48.1	40.4	42.7
0 & older	24.7	30.0	35.3	34.1	36.0	36.2	30.1	31.4
BOTH SEXES								
14 & older	62.7	66.8	66.8	64.1	65.4	66.4	57.7	59.2
14 & older [f]	62.3	66.1	67.2	65.4	67.6	68.0	63.0	63.8
0 & older	42.3	45.0	50.9	49.3	51.2	51.7	44.3	46.3

Source and concepts: Chapter 3 and Appendix F. *Wirtschaft und Statistik*, Wiesbaden, Statistisches Bundesamt, 1952, pp. 256*, 352. *Deutschland in Zahlen*, Köln, Wirtschaftswissenschaftliches Institut der Gewerkschaften, 1950, pp. 12, 31. *Population of the Federal Republic of Germany and West Berlin*, United States Bureau of the Census, Series P-90, No. 1, pp. 55, 66, 73.

[a] Totals and percentages were computed before data on population and labor force were rounded.

[b] Resident population, including 655,000 in military and labor services.

[c] Data for 1946 exclude occupation forces, prisoners of war, civilian internees, and those in displaced persons camps, but include those in county refugee camps. The population aged 14 was treated as one-fifth of that aged 10–14.

[d] Excluding occupation forces; including all inmates of camps except those of the International Refugee Organization.

[e] Labor force was given for youths under 18 and 18–24, and was redistributed into 14–19 and 20–24 age groups. The proportion 20–24 in the labor force was assumed to be the average of the two classifications originally reported, 18–24 and 25–34. This estimated proportion was then multiplied by the population 20–24 to obtain the labor force for youths 20–24, which was then subtracted from that under 24 to obtain labor force 14–19. The labor force of persons 45–49 was estimated by averaging the labor force proportions for those 35–49 and 50–64. It was then subtracted from the reported labor force of persons 25–49. Both procedures of estimating were repeated separately for each sex.

[f] Standardized for age and age-sex composition on the basis of the population of the United States in 1940. For explanation of standardization, see Chapter 3.

TABLE A-17

Germany:
Females in the Labor Force by Marital Status and Age Group, 1895–1950

Age Group	Number (millions) [a]							Per Cent of Female Population of Same Marital Status and Age Group [a]						
	Pre-World War I Territory		Post-World War I Territory [c]			Federal Republic of Germany [d]		Pre-World War I Territory		Post-World War I Territory [c]			Federal Republic of Germany [d]	
	1895	1907	1925	1933	1939	1939	1950 [b]	1895	1907	1925	1933	1939	1939	1950 [b]
Married Women														
16–39	0.6	1.4	1.7	2.0	2.5	1.3 [e]	1.2	11.9	24.2	27.5	28.9	33.2	30.3 [e]	26.6
40 & older	0.5	1.4	1.9	2.2	2.7	1.5 [e]	1.6	12.2	28.2	29.8	29.4	32.3	30.8 [e]	23.9
16 & older	1.1	2.8	3.6	4.2	5.2	2.8 [e]	2.8	12.0	26.0	28.7	29.2	32.7	30.6 [e]	25.0
16 & older [f]								12.1	26.3	28.7	29.2	32.7	30.6	25.2
Single, Widowed, or Divorced Women														
16–39	3.6	4.4	5.6	5.4	4.9	2.9	3.5	69.2	75.2	78.0	80.4	86.1	87.5	82.8
40 & older	1.3	1.4	1.5	1.5	1.8	1.0	1.3	44.8	42.7	39.0	33.9	35.3	40.5	32.2
16 & older	4.9	5.8	7.1	6.9	6.7	3.9	4.8	60.7	63.7	64.7	62.1	62.5	67.6	57.7
16 & older [f]								57.9	60.1	59.9	58.8	62.5	65.7	59.3
All Women														
UNSTANDARDIZED														
16–39	4.2	5.8	7.3	7.4	7.4	4.2	4.7	42.7	50.0	54.7	54.7	56.0	55.0	54.3
40 & older	1.8	2.8	3.4	3.7	4.5	2.5	2.9	25.2	33.8	33.1	31.1	33.4	34.0	27.1
16 & older	6.0	8.6	10.7	11.1	11.9	6.7	7.6	35.4	43.3	45.3	43.6	44.7	44.8	39.1
STANDARDIZED [f]														
16–39	3.1	4.6	5.8	6.5	7.4	4.1	4.9	36.6	46.2	49.3	51.1	56.0	54.9	50.8
40 & older	2.0	3.4	3.9	4.0	4.5	2.6	2.6	24.3	33.6	33.2	31.1	33.4	34.4	27.0
16 & older	5.1	8.0	9.7	10.5	11.9	6.7	7.5	30.4	39.9	41.2	41.1	44.7	44.7	38.9

Source: *Statistik des Deutschen Reichs*, Neue Folge, Band 103, p. 126, and Band 203, Part II, p. 5, Berlin, Statistisches Reichsamt. *Wirtschaft und Statistik*, 1941, pp. 47–50, 1952, pp. 353–354, and *Statistisches Jahrbuch, 1952*, p. 26, Wiesbaden, Statistisches Bundesamt. *Population of the Federal Republic of Germany and West Berlin*, United States Bureau of the Census, Series P-90, No. 1, p. 69.

[a] Totals and percentages were computed before data on population and labor force were rounded.
[b] Without Berlin.   [c] Without Saar.   [d] Without Berlin.
[e] Excludes all camp inmates.
[f] Same age distribution assumed as for Germany post-World War I territory.

APPENDIX A

TABLE A-18

Germany:
Labor Force in Cities Having Population of 100,000 or More, 1895–
1933

| Age Group | PER CENT OF POPULATION OF THE SAME SEX AND AGE GROUP | | |
	1895 [a] (28 cities)	1925 [a] (45 cities)	1933 [a] (52 cities)
MALES			
14–19	80.1	80.0	...
20–24	94.0	92.3	...
25–44	97.5	97.2	...
45–64	90.0	92.1	...
65 & older	48.2	42.7	...
14 & older	90.9	89.9	85.1 [b]
14 & older [c]	90.7	90.6	...
FEMALES			
14–19	56.6	62.9	...
20–24	61.9	68.0	...
25–44	28.6	35.3	...
45–64	23.9	21.3	...
65 & older	13.6	8.6	...
14 & older	36.6	37.6	35.4 [b]
14 & older [c]	35.0	38.9	...
BOTH SEXES			
14 & older	62.7	61.9	58.5 [b]
14 & older [c]	63.3	65.2	...

Source: *Statistik des Deutschen Reichs: Textband 1895*, Neue Folge III, pp. 11,
20; *Band 408 (1925)*, p. 12; *Band 458 (1933)*, p. 99, Berlin, Statistisches Reichsamt. *Wirtschaft und Statistik, 1926*, Sonderheft 3, p. 24; *1934*, Sonderbeilage 24,
p. 23, Wiesbaden, Statistisches Bundesamt.

[a] Territory as at each census: *1895*, Pre-World War I; *1925* and *1933*, Post-
World War I without the Saar.
[b] The labor force actually includes some workers under 14.
[c] Standardized for sex and age-sex on the basis of the population of Chicago in
1930. For explanation of standardization, see Chapter 3, section on *The Method*.

Labor Force, Employment, Unemployment, and Armed Forces, Annual and Quarterly Estimates

TABLE B-1

United States:

Labor Force by Employment and Military Status, 1940–1956

ANNUAL AND QUARTERLY AVERAGES, ADJUSTED WHERE NECESSARY FOR SEASONAL VARIATIONS [a]

(millions) [b]

	Labor Force (Civilian & Military) Both Sexes	Males	Females	Armed Forces Males	Civilian Labor Force Both Sexes	Unemployed Both Sexes Old Defini- tion [c]	New Defini- tion [c]	Civilian Employed Old Defini- tion [c]	New Defini- tion [c]
1940	56.0	41.9	14.1	0.4	55.6	8.3		47.3	
I	55.7	41.5	14.2	0.3	55.4	8.2		47.2	
II	55.9	41.7	14.2	0.3	55.6	8.2		47.4	
III	56.4	42.2	14.2	0.4	56.0	8.5		47.5	
IV	55.9	42.2	13.7	0.6	55.3	8.4		46.9	
1941	57.4	42.8	14.6	1.5	55.9	5.6		50.3	
I	56.1	42.2	13.9	0.9	55.2	6.0		49.2	
II	57.4	42.9	14.5	1.4	56.0	6.0		50.0	
III	58.1	43.2	14.9	1.7	56.4	6.0		50.4	
IV	57.8	42.7	15.1	1.9	55.9	4.4		51.5	
1942	60.1	44.1	16.0	3.8	56.3	2.6		53.7	
I	58.4	43.4	15.0	2.3	56.2	4.0		52.2	
II	59.6	43.8	15.8	3.2	56.4	2.8		53.6	
III	60.3	44.2	16.1	4.2	56.1	2.2		53.9	
IV	62.2	45.0	17.2	5.6	56.6	1.6		55.0	
1943	64.4	45.7	18.7	8.8	55.6	1.0		54.6	
I	63.6	45.3	18.3	7.3	56.3	1.4		54.9	
II	64.4	45.5	18.9	8.5	55.9	1.1		54.8	
III	64.7	45.7	19.0	9.3	55.4	1.1		54.3	
IV	64.9	46.1	18.8	9.9	55.0	0.7		54.3	
1944	65.9	46.4	19.5	11.0	54.6	0.7		53.9	
I	65.5	46.4	19.1	10.3	55.0	0.7		54.3	
II	66.0	46.6	19.4	10.9	54.9	0.7		54.2	
III	65.8	46.2	19.6	11.4	54.2	0.7		53.5	
IV	66.4	46.6	19.8	11.6	54.5	0.5		54.0	
1945	65.2	45.9	19.3	11.1	53.8	1.0		52.8	
I	67.0	46.9	20.1	11.6	55.1	0.7		54.4	
II	66.3	46.4	19.9	11.8	54.2	0.7		53.5	
III	64.7	45.7	19.0	11.7	52.8	1.1		51.7	
IV	62.6	44.5	18.1	9.0	53.4	1.7		51.7	
1946	60.8	44.0	16.8	3.2	57.6	2.3		55.3	
I	60.8	43.8	17.0	5.2	55.6	2.2		53.4	
II	60.5	44.0	16.5	3.4	57.1	2.3		54.8	
III	60.9	44.1	16.8	2.4	58.5	2.2		56.3	
IV	61.0	44.2	16.8	2.0	59.0	2.4		56.6	

ANNUAL AND QUARTERLY AVERAGES, ADJUSTED WHERE NECESSARY FOR
SEASONAL VARIATIONS [a]
(millions) [b]

	Labor Force (Civilian & Military)			Armed Forces Males	Civilian Labor Force Both Sexes	Unemployed Both Sexes		Civilian Employed	
	Both Sexes	Males	Females			Old Defini- tion [c]	New Defini- tion [c]	Old Defini- tion [c]	New Defini- tion [c]
1947	61.6	44.7	16.9	1.4	60.2	2.1	2.3	58.1	57.9
I	61.2	44.4	16.8	1.6	59.6	2.0	2.2	57.6	57.4
II	61.6	44.8	16.8	1.4	60.1	2.2	2.4	57.9	57.7
III	61.8	44.8	17.0	1.3	60.5	2.3	2.5	58.2	58.0
IV	61.8	44.7	17.1	1.3	60.5	2.0	2.2	58.5	58.3
1948	62.8	45.2	17.6	1.3	61.5	2.1	2.3	59.4	59.2
I	62.3	44.9	17.4	1.2	61.1	2.0	2.3	59.1	58.8
II	62.3	44.9	17.4	1.2	61.1	2.0	2.3	59.1	58.8
III	63.2	45.5	17.7	1.3	61.9	2.1	2.3	59.8	59.6
IV	63.3	45.5	17.8	1.4	61.9	2.1	2.3	59.8	59.6
1949	63.6	45.5	18.1	1.5	62.1	3.4	3.7	58.7	58.4
I	63.4	45.5	17.9	1.5	61.9	2.6	2.9	59.3	59.0
II	63.2	45.5	17.7	1.5	61.7	3.3	3.6	58.4	58.1
III	63.5	45.5	18.0	1.4	62.0	3.8	4.1	58.2	57.9
IV	64.2	45.6	18.6	1.4	62.8	4.1	4.4	58.7	58.4
1950	64.5	45.9	18.6	1.5	63.0	3.0	3.2	60.0	59.8
I	64.4	45.7	18.7	1.4	63.0	3.8	4.0	59.2	59.0
II	64.0	45.7	18.3	1.3	62.7	3.2	3.4	59.5	59.3
III	64.3	46.0	18.3	1.3	63.0	2.8	3.0	60.2	60.0
IV	65.4	46.1	19.3	1.9	63.5	2.5	2.7	61.0	60.8
1951	66.0	46.7	19.3	3.1	62.9	1.9	2.1	61.0	60.8
I	65.9	46.3	19.6	2.5 [d]	63.4	2.1	2.3	61.3	61.1
II	65.4	46.6	18.8	3.1 [d]	62.3	1.8	2.0	60.5	60.3
III	66.0	47.0	19.0	3.4	62.6	1.7	2.0	60.9	60.6
IV	66.7	47.0	19.7	3.4	63.3	2.1	2.3	61.2	61.0
1952	66.5	47.0	19.5	3.5	63.0	1.7	1.9	61.3	61.1
I	66.7	46.9	19.8	3.5	63.2	1.7	2.0	61.5	61.2
II	66.1	47.0	19.1	3.6	62.5	1.7	1.9	60.8	60.6
III	66.4	47.2	19.2	3.7	62.7	1.8	2.1	60.9	60.6
IV	66.7	46.8	19.9	3.4	63.3	1.7	1.9	61.6	61.4
1953	67.4	47.7	19.7	3.5	63.8	1.6	1.8	62.2	62.0
I	67.7	47.8	19.9	3.5	64.1	1.5	1.7	62.7	62.5
II	67.2	47.5	19.7	3.5	63.6	1.4	1.7	62.3	62.0
III	67.3	47.7	19.6	3.5	63.7	1.5	1.7	62.2	62.0
IV	67.1	47.6	19.5	3.5	63.5	1.8	2.1	61.8	61.5
1954 [e]	67.8	47.9	19.9	3.4	64.4	3.2	3.5	61.1	60.8
I	67.7	47.7	20.0	3.4	64.3	2.9	3.2	61.4	61.1
II	67.9	47.9	20.0	3.4	64.5	3.3	3.7	61.2	60.8
III	67.9	48.0	19.9	3.4	64.5	3.5	3.8	61.0	60.7
IV	67.7	47.7	20.0	3.4	64.4	3.3	3.6	61.0	60.7
1955 [e]	68.9	48.1	20.8	3.1	65.9	2.7	2.9	63.1	62.9
I	67.7	47.6	20.1	3.2	64.5	2.7	2.9	61.8	61.6
II	68.5	48.0	20.5	3.1	65.4	2.7	2.9	62.7	62.5
III	69.4	48.3	21.1	2.9	66.4	2.5	2.6	63.9	63.8
IV	70.2	48.6	21.5	3.0	67.1	2.7	3.0	64.4	64.1
1956 [e, f]	70.3	48.6	21.7	2.9	67.5	2.6	2.8	65.0	64.8
I	69.8	48.5	21.3	2.9	66.8	2.4	2.7	64.5	64.2
II	70.6	48.7	21.9	2.9	67.7	2.6	2.9	65.2	64.9
III	70.7	48.8	21.9	2.8	67.8	2.5	2.8	65.4	65.1
IV	70.4	48.5	21.9	2.8	67.5	2.7	3.0	64.9	64.6

TABLE B-1, *continued*

	ANNUAL AND QUARTERLY AVERAGES, UNADJUSTED (millions) [b]								
	Labor Force (Civilian & Military)			Armed Forces Males	Civilian Labor Force Both Sexes	Unemployed Both Sexes		Civilian Employed	
	Both Sexes	Males	Females			Old Definition [c]	New Definition [c]	Old Definition [c]	New Definition [c]
1940	56.0	41.9	14.1	0.4	55.6	8.3		47.3	
I	54.5	40.9	13.6	0.3	54.2	9.3		44.9	
II	56.2	41.8	14.4	0.3	55.9	8.2		47.7	
III	57.7	43.0	14.7	0.4	57.3	8.3		49.0	
IV	55.7	41.9	13.8	0.6	55.1	7.1		48.0	
1941	57.4	42.8	14.6	1.5	55.9	5.6		50.3	
I	54.6	41.5	13.1	0.9	53.7	6.9		46.8	
II	57.8	43.0	14.8	1.4	56.4	6.1		50.3	
III	59.5	44.0	15.5	1.7	57.8	5.4		52.4	
IV	57.5	42.5	15.0	1.9	55.6	3.8		51.8	
1942	60.1	44.1	16.0	3.8	56.3	2.6		53.7	
I	57.1	42.7	14.4	2.3	54.8	4.0		50.8	
II	60.0	44.0	16.0	3.2	56.8	2.8		54.0	
III	61.7	45.1	16.6	4.2	57.5	2.2		55.3	
IV	61.8	44.6	17.2	5.6	56.2	1.5		54.7	
1943	64.4	45.7	18.7	8.8	55.6	1.0		54.6	
I	61.7	44.4	17.3	7.3	54.4	1.3		53.1	
II	65.4	46.3	19.1	8.5	56.9	1.1		55.8	
III	66.4	46.6	19.8	9.3	57.1	1.1		56.0	
IV	64.4	45.7	18.7	9.9	54.5	0.7		53.8	
1944	65.9	46.4	19.5	11.0	54.6	0.7		53.9	
I	63.7	45.6	18.1	10.3	53.2	0.7		52.5	
II	66.5	46.8	19.7	10.9	55.4	0.7		54.7	
III	67.4	47.2	20.2	11.4	55.8	0.7		55.1	
IV	66.0	46.3	19.7	11.6	54.1	0.5		53.6	
1945	65.2	45.9	19.3	11.1	53.8	1.0		52.8	
I	65.3	46.1	19.2	11.6	53.3	0.6		52.7	
II	66.8	46.6	20.2	11.8	54.7	0.7		54.0	
III	66.2	46.6	19.6	11.7	54.3	1.1		53.2	
IV	62.4	44.2	18.2	9.0	53.2	1.8		51.4	
1946	60.8	44.0	16.8	3.2	57.6	2.3		55.3	
I	59.5	43.2	16.3	5.2	54.3	2.6		51.7	
II	60.9	44.0	16.9	3.4	57.5	2.4		55.1	
III	62.1	44.8	17.3	2.4	59.7	2.1		57.6	
IV	60.8	43.9	16.9	2.0	58.8	2.0		56.8	
1947	61.6	44.7	16.9	1.4	60.2	2.1	2.3	58.1	57.9
I	59.8	43.8	16.0	1.6	58.2	2.4	2.6	55.8	55.6
II	62.1	44.9	17.2	1.4	60.7	2.3	2.6	58.4	58.1
III	63.1	45.7	17.4	1.3	61.8	2.2	2.6	59.6	59.2
IV	61.5	44.4	17.1	1.3	60.2	1.6	1.8	58.6	58.4

318

TABLE B-1, *continued*

ANNUAL AND QUARTERLY AVERAGES, UNADJUSTED
(millions) [b]

	Labor Force (Civilian & Military)			Armed Forces Males	Civilian Labor Force Both Sexes	Unemployed Both Sexes		Civilian Employed	
	Both Sexes	Males	Females			Old Defini- tion [c]	New Defini- tion [c]	Old Defini- tion [c]	New Defini- tion [c]
1948	62.8	45.2	17.6	1.3	61.5	2.1	2.3	59.4	59.2
I	60.8	44.2	16.6	1.2	59.6	2.4	2.7	57.2	56.9
II	62.8	45.1	17.7	1.2	61.6	2.0	2.3	59.6	59.3
III	64.4	46.2	18.2	1.3	63.1	2.0	2.3	61.1	60.8
IV	63.0	45.1	17.9	1.4	61.6	1.8	2.0	59.8	59.6
1949	63.6	45.5	18.1	1.5	62.1	3.4	3.7	58.7	58.4
I	61.9	44.8	17.1	1.5	60.4	3.0	3.3	57.4	57.1
II	63.6	45.6	18.0	1.5	62.1	3.4	3.7	58.7	58.4
III	64.9	46.4	18.5	1.4	63.5	3.7	4.0	59.8	59.5
IV	64.0	45.4	18.6	1.4	62.6	3.5	3.7	59.1	58.9
1950	64.5	45.9	18.6	1.5	63.0	3.0	3.2	60.0	59.8
I	62.9	45.1	17.8	1.4	61.5	4.4	4.6	57.1	56.9
II	64.6	45.9	18.7	1.3	63.3	3.2	3.5	60.0	59.7
III	65.5	46.6	18.9	1.3	64.2	2.6	2.8	61.6	61.4
IV	65.2	45.9	19.3	1.9	63.3	2.1	2.3	61.2	61.0
1951	66.0	46.7	19.3	3.1	62.9	1.9	2.1	61.0	60.8
I	64.3	45.7	18.6	2.5 [d]	61.8	2.3	2.5	59.5	59.3
II	65.9	46.8	19.1	3.1 [d]	62.8	1.8	2.0	61.0	60.8
III	67.3	47.7	19.6	3.4	63.9	1.7	2.0	62.2	61.9
IV	66.5	46.7	19.8	3.4	63.1	1.7	1.9	61.4	61.2
1952	66.5	47.0	19.5	3.5	63.0	1.7	1.9	61.3	61.1
I	65.2	46.3	18.9	3.5	61.7	2.0	2.2	59.7	59.5
II	66.6	47.1	19.5	3.6	63.0	1.7	2.0	61.3	61.0
III	67.6	47.8	19.8	3.7	63.9	1.7	2.0	62.2	61.9
IV	66.7	46.6	20.1	3.4	63.2	1.4	1.6	61.8	61.6
1953	67.4	47.7	19.7	3.5	63.8	1.6	1.8	62.2	62.0
I	66.6	47.2	19.4	3.5	63.0	1.8	2.0	61.2	61.0
II	67.4	47.8	19.6	3.5	63.9	1.5	1.8	62.4	62.1
III	68.3	48.4	19.9	3.5	64.7	1.4	1.7	63.3	63.0
IV	67.2	47.4	19.8	3.5	63.7	1.8	2.0	61.9	61.7
1954 [e]	67.8	47.9	19.9	3.4	64.4	3.2	3.5	61.1	60.8
I	66.6	47.3	19.3	3.4	63.2	3.5	3.8	59.7	59.4
II	68.0	48.1	19.9	3.4	64.6	3.4	3.8	61.2	60.8
III	68.8	48.7	20.1	3.4	65.4	3.2	3.5	62.2	61.9
IV	67.7	47.4	20.3	3.4	64.3	2.8	3.0	61.5	61.3
1955 [e]	68.9	48.1	20.8	3.1	65.9	2.7	2.9	63.1	62.9
I	66.7	47.1	19.6	3.2	63.5	3.3	3.5	60.2	60.0
II	68.6	48.1	20.5	3.1	65.5	2.7	3.0	62.8	62.5
III	70.3	48.9	21.4	2.9	67.4	2.3	2.5	65.1	64.9
IV	70.0	48.2	21.8	3.0	67.0	2.3	2.5	64.7	64.5
1956,[e, f]	70.3	48.6	21.7	2.9	67.5	2.6	2.8	65.0	64.8
I	68.6	47.8	20.8	2.9	65.7	2.9	3.1	62.8	62.6
II	70.8	49.0	21.8	2.9	67.9	2.7	3.0	65.2	64.9
III	71.7	49.4	22.3	2.8	68.9	2.3	2.6	66.6	66.3
IV	70.4	48.2	22.2	2.8	67.6	2.3	2.5	65.3	65.1

TABLE B-1, *continued*

ANNUAL AND QUARTERLY AVERAGES, ADJUSTED WHERE NECESSARY FOR SEASONAL VARIATIONS [a]

(*per cent of population 14 and older of same sex*) [b]

	Labor Force (Civilian & Military)			Armed Forces Males	Civilian Labor Force Both Sexes	Unemployed Both Sexes (per cent of labor force)	
	Both Sexes	Males	Females			Old Definition [c]	New Definition [c]
1940	55.2	82.8	27.8	0.8	54.8	14.9	
I	55.2	82.4	28.1	0.6	54.9	14.7	
II	55.2	82.4	28.1	0.6	54.9	14.7	
III	55.6	83.2	28.0	0.8	55.2	15.1	
IV	54.9	83.0	26.9	1.2	54.3	15.0	
1941	55.9	83.5	28.5	2.9	54.5	9.8	
I	55.0	82.8	27.2	1.8	54.1	10.7	
II	56.1	83.9	28.3	2.7	54.7	10.5	
III	56.6	84.3	29.0	3.3	54.9	10.3	
IV	56.1	83.1	29.3	3.7	54.3	7.6	
1942	58.0	85.3	30.8	7.3	54.4	4.4	
I	56.6	84.3	29.0	4.3	54.5	6.8	
II	57.6	84.8	30.4	6.2	54.5	4.7	
III	58.1	85.4	30.9	8.1	54.1	3.6	
IV	59.8	86.8	33.0	10.8	54.4	2.6	
1943	61.5	87.5	35.7	16.8	53.2	1.7	
I	61.0	87.1	35.0	14.0	54.0	2.2	
II	61.6	87.3	36.0	16.3	53.5	1.7	
III	61.7	87.5	36.1	17.8	52.8	1.7	
IV	61.7	88.0	35.6	18.9	52.3	1.1	
1944	62.4	88.3	36.7	21.0	51.9	1.0	
I	62.2	88.4	36.1	19.6	52.4	1.1	
II	62.5	88.6	36.6	20.7	52.2	1.1	
III	62.2	87.8	36.9	21.7	51.4	1.1	
IV	62.6	88.4	37.1	22.0	51.7	0.7	
1945	61.1	86.7	35.9	20.8	50.8	1.7	
I	63.1	88.9	37.6	22.0	52.2	1.1	
II	62.3	87.8	37.1	22.3	51.2	1.1	
III	60.6	86.3	35.4	22.1	49.6	1.7	
IV	58.5	83.9	33.6	17.0	50.1	2.7	
1946	56.5	82.6	30.9	6.1	53.5	3.7	
I	56.7	82.4	31.5	9.8	51.9	3.6	
II	56.3	82.6	30.5	6.4	53.1	3.8	
III	56.5	82.7	30.9	4.5	54.3	3.6	
IV	56.5	82.7	30.8	3.7	54.6	3.9	
1947	56.7	83.2	30.8	2.7	55.4	3.5	3.7
I	56.5	82.9	30.7	3.0	55.0	3.3	3.6
II	56.8	83.5	30.6	2.8	55.4	3.6	3.9
III	56.8	83.4	30.9	2.4	55.6	3.7	4.0
IV	56.7	83.0	31.0	2.4	55.5	3.2	3.6
1948	57.3	83.6	31.7	2.4	56.1	3.3	3.7
I	57.1	83.3	31.5	2.2	56.0	3.2	3.7
II	56.9	83.1	31.4	2.2	55.8	3.2	3.7
III	57.6	84.0	31.8	2.4	56.4	3.3	3.6
IV	57.5	83.8	31.9	2.6	56.2	3.3	3.6

APPENDIX B

TABLE B-1, *continued*

ANNUAL AND QUARTERLY AVERAGES, ADJUSTED WHERE NECESSARY FOR
SEASONAL VARIATIONS [a]

(*per cent of population 14 and older of same sex*) [b]

	Labor Force (*Civilian & Military*) Both Sexes	Males	Females	Armed Forces Males	Civilian Labor Force Both Sexes	Unemployed. Both Sexes (*per cent of labor force*) Old Defini- tion [c]	New Defini- tion [e]
1949	57.4	83.2	32.1	2.7	56.0	5.5	5.8
I	57.5	83.6	32.0	2.8	56.1	4.1	4.6
II	57.1	83.3	31.6	2.7	55.7	5.2	5.7
III	57.2	83.0	32.0	2.7	55.8	6.0	6.5
IV	57.6	83.0	32.9	2.6	56.3	6.5	6.9
1950	57.4	82.8	32.7	2.6	56.1	4.8	5.0
I	57.6	82.9	33.0	2.5	56.3	5.9	6.2
II	57.0	82.6	32.1	2.3	55.9	5.0	5.3
III	57.1	82.9	32.1	2.3	56.0	4.4	4.7
IV	58.0	82.9	33.7	3.4	56.3	3.8	4.1
1951	58.1	83.5	33.4	5.6	55.4	2.9	3.2
I	58.2	83.1	34.1	4.5 [d]	56.0	3.2	3.5
II	57.6	83.4	32.6	5.5 [d]	54.9	2.8	3.1
III	58.0	83.9	32.9	6.1	55.0	2.6	3.0
IV	58.5	83.7	34.0	6.1	55.5	3.1	3.4
1952	58.0	83.4	33.4	6.3	54.9	2.6	2.9
I	58.4	83.5	34.1	6.2	55.3	2.6	3.0
II	57.7	83.5	32.8	6.4	54.6	2.5	2.9
III	57.9	83.7	32.9	6.6	54.6	2.6	3.2
IV	58.0	83.0	33.9	6.0	55.1	2.5	2.8
1953	57.8	82.9	33.3	6.1	54.7	2.4	2.7
I	58.3	83.4	33.8	6.1	55.3	2.3	2.5
II	57.7	82.7	33.4	6.1	54.7	2.1	2.5
III	57.6	82.8	33.1	6.3	54.5	2.2	2.5
IV	57.3	82.5	32.9	6.1	54.3	3.1	3.6
1954 [e]	57.5	82.4	33.4	5.7	54.7	4.8	5.2
I	57.7	82.5	33.5	5.8	54.8	4.3	4.7
II	57.7	82.6	33.5	5.8	54.8	4.8	5.4
III	57.5	82.6	33.2	5.7	54.6	5.2	5.6
IV	57.2	81.9	33.3	5.6	54.4	4.9	5.3
1955 [e]	57.9	82.2	34.4	5.2	55.3	3.9	4.2
I	57.1	81.6	33.4	5.4	54.4	4.0	4.3
II	57.6	82.1	34.0	5.2	55.0	3.9	4.2
III	58.2	82.4	34.9	5.0	55.7	3.7	3.8
IV	58.7	82.8	35.4	5.0	56.2	3.9	4.3
1956 [e, f]	58.5	82.4	35.6	4.8	56.1	3.7	4.0
I	58.3	82.7	35.0	4.9	55.9	3.5	3.9
II	58.7	82.5	35.8	4.9	56.4	3.7	4.1
III	58.6	82.6	35.8	4.8	56.3	3.6	4.0
IV	58.2	82.0	35.6	4.8	55.9	3.8	4.3

Source: *Current Population Reports, The Labor Force,* Bureau of the Census; *The Battle for Production,* Fourth Quarterly Report to the President by the Director of Defense Mobilization, January 1, 1952.

[a] To adjust quarterly data, seasonal indexes were computed by averaging the ratios of original percentage figures to four-term moving averages, a method pre-

321

APPENDIX B

Notes to Table B-1, *continued*

sented by Arthur F. Burns and Wesley C. Mitchell in *Measuring Business Cycles* (National Bureau of Economic Research, 1946, pp. 46–50). The computation yielded the following indexes. (No adjustment was required for the armed forces.) For further discussion, see text at the end of this appendix.

| | Labor Force Civilian and Military | | | Civilian Labor Force | Unemployed | Civilian Employed |
	Both Sexes	Males	Females	Both Sexes	Both Sexes	Both Sexes
1940–1952						
I	97.5	98.4	95.2	97.3	116.6	96.6
II	100.8	100.4	101.7	100.8	102.6	100.7
III	102.2	101.9	103.1	102.4	96.7	102.7
IV	99.5	99.3	100.0	99.5	85.1	100.0
1953–1956						
I	98.4	98.8	97.5	98.2	119.0	97.6
II	100.2	100.4	99.7	100.1	102.5	100.1
III	101.4	101.4	101.3	101.6	90.2	101.8
IV	100.0	99.4	101.5	100.1	88.3	100.5

ᵇ Totals and percentages were computed before data were rounded.

ᶜ Beginning January 1957, the census reclassified from "employed" to "unemployed" persons with jobs but not at work because of temporary layoff or because they were waiting to start new jobs. And persons in the latter category, who happened to be in school while waiting, were classified as outside the labor force. The data for 1947–1956 have been revised in this study to conform as closely as possible with the new definition. No adjustment could be made for the persons with new jobs but still attending school. However, these were probably negligible in number. The seasonal adjustment index for the combined group of those who were on temporary layoff and those waiting to start new jobs is: I, 95.0; II, 115.0; III, 110.0; IV, 80.0 The index was based on the period 1947–1956.

ᵈ Estimated.

ᵉ From January 1954 through April 1956, data were based on a 230-area census sample. (Through 1953, there were 68 sample areas.)

ᶠ Beginning May 1956, data have been based on an enlarged sample of 35,000 interviewed households spread over 330 areas, comprising 638 counties and independent cities.

TABLE B-2

United States:
Labor Force by Sex and Age Group, 1940–1956

ANNUAL AND QUARTERLY AVERAGES, ADJUSTED WHERE NECESSARY FOR
SEASONAL VARIATIONS [a]
(millions) [b]

	Males 25–64	Females 25–64	Young Persons 14–24	Elderly Persons 65 and Older
1940	31.3	9.2	13.3	2.2
I	31.2	9.2	13.1	2.2
II	31.3	9.3	13.1	2.2
III	31.4	9.2	13.6	2.2
IV	31.3	8.9	13.5	2.2
1941	31.6	9.5	13.9	2.4
I	31.3	9.1	13.4	2.3
II	31.6	9.4	14.1	2.3
III	31.7	9.7	14.3	2.4
IV	31.8	9.7	13.9	2.4
1942	32.2	10.4	14.9	2.6
I	31.9	9.8	14.2	2.5
II	32.1	10.3	14.7	2.5
III	32.3	10.4	15.1	2.5
IV	32.4	11.2	15.8	2.8
1943	33.0	12.2	16.4	2.8
I	32.6	12.0	16.1	2.9
II	33.0	12.3	16.2	2.9
III	33.1	12.3	16.5	2.8
IV	33.3	12.2	16.7	2.7
1944	33.3	12.6	17.1	2.9
I	33.3	12.4	17.1	2.7
II	33.2	12.6	17.3	2.9
III	33.3	12.8	16.7	3.0
IV	33.3	12.9	17.2	3.0
1945	33.0	12.8	16.4	3.0
I	33.4	13.2	17.4	3.0
II	33.4	13.1	16.9	2.9
III	32.9	12.7	16.1	3.0
IV	32.3	12.1	15.3	2.9
1946	33.1	11.4	13.5	2.8
I	32.6	11.4	14.0	2.8
II	33.1	11.3	13.3	2.8
III	33.4	11.4	13.3	2.8
IV	33.4	11.5	13.4	2.7

TABLE B-2, *continued*

ANNUAL AND QUARTERLY AVERAGES, ADJUSTED WHERE NECESSARY FOR
SEASONAL VARIATIONS [a]
(millions) [b]

	Males 25–64	Females 25–64	Young Persons 14–24	Elderly Persons 65 and Older
1947	33.7	11.7	13.4	2.8
I	33.5	11.5	13.4	2.8
II	33.6	11.6	13.6	2.8
III	33.8	11.7	13.5	2.8
IV	33.8	11.9	13.3	2.8
1948	34.1	12.3	13.5	2.9
I	33.9	12.1	13.5	2.8
II	34.0	12.0	13.4	2.9
III	34.3	12.4	13.6	2.9
IV	34.3	12.6	13.4	3.0
1949	34.5	12.8	13.3	3.0
I	34.3	12.7	13.4	3.0
II	34.4	12.5	13.3	3.0
III	34.5	12.7	13.3	3.0
IV	34.6	13.2	13.3	3.1
1950	34.9	13.4	13.2	3.0
I	34.6	13.4	13.3	3.1
II	34.8	13.2	13.0	3.0
III	35.0	13.2	13.1	3.0
IV	35.1	13.8	13.5	3.0
1951	35.8	14.1	13.1	3.0
I	35.3	14.2	13.4	3.0
II	35.7	13.6	13.0	3.1
III	36.0	13.9	13.1	3.0
IV	36.2	14.5	13.0	3.0
1952	36.5	14.4	12.6	3.0
I	36.2	14.6	12.9	3.0
II	36.5	14.0	12.6	3.0
III	36.7	14.2	12.5	3.0
IV	36.6	14.8	12.2	3.1
1953	37.4	14.6	12.1	3.2
I	37.1	14.7	12.6	3.3
II	37.4	14.4	12.2	3.2
III	37.6	14.4	12.0	3.3
IV	37.6	14.7	11.7	3.1

TABLE B-2, *continued*

ANNUAL AND QUARTERLY AVERAGES, ADJUSTED WHERE NECESSARY FOR
SEASONAL VARIATIONS [a]
(millions) [b]

	Males 25–64	Females 25–64	Young Persons 14–24	Elderly Persons 65 and Older
1954 [c]	37.8	14.9	11.9	3.2
I	37.6	14.8	12.1	3.2
II	37.8	15.0	11.9	3.2
III	37.8	14.9	12.0	3.2
IV	37.8	15.0	11.7	3.2
1955 [c]	37.9	15.7	12.1	3.3
I	37.7	15.1	11.7	3.2
II	37.9	15.5	11.8	3.3
III	37.9	16.0	12.2	3.3
IV	38.0	16.0	12.7	3.5
1956 [c, d]	37.9	16.3	12.7	3.4
I	37.9	16.0	12.4	3.4
II	37.9	16.3	12.8	3.5
III	37.9	16.5	12.8	3.4
IV	37.8	16.4	12.7	3.4

TABLE B-2, *continued*

ANNUAL AND QUARTERLY AVERAGES, ADJUSTED WHERE NECESSARY FOR
SEASONAL VARIATIONS [a]
(*per cent of population of same sex and age group*) [b]

	Males 25–64	Females 25–64	Young Persons 14–24	Elderly Persons 65 and Older
1940	94.4	27.9	50.6	24.4
I	94.5	28.2	49.7	24.4
II	94.5	28.3	49.7	24.6
III	94.5	28.1	51.6	24.3
IV	94.2	27.1	51.2	24.2
1941	94.4	28.4	52.8	25.4
I	93.7	27.3	50.9	24.8
II	94.4	28.3	53.4	25.3
III	94.8	29.0	54.3	25.5
IV	94.8	28.8	52.7	25.9
1942	95.2	30.8	56.9	27.1
I	95.1	29.2	53.9	26.6
II	95.4	30.5	55.8	26.3
III	95.4	30.5	57.5	26.3
IV	95.2	32.9	60.2	29.1
1943	96.0	35.5	62.5	29.0
I	95.2	34.9	61.6	29.8
II	96.0	35.7	61.8	29.4
III	96.2	35.8	63.1	29.0
IV	96.5	35.4	63.5	27.7
1944	96.1	36.2	65.0	29.5
I	96.3	35.6	65.0	27.7
II	95.9	36.1	65.8	29.8
III	96.1	36.5	63.5	30.6
IV	95.9	36.7	65.5	30.0
1945	94.4	36.0	63.2	29.3
I	95.8	37.3	66.7	29.7
II	95.7	37.0	64.7	29.3
III	94.0	35.6	62.0	29.4
IV	91.9	34.0	59.2	28.7
1946	93.5	31.7	52.5	27.0
I	92.4	31.9	54.3	27.7
II	93.6	31.5	51.7	27.2
III	94.1	31.6	51.6	27.0
IV	94.0	31.8	52.2	26.1

TABLE B-2, *continued*

ANNUAL AND QUARTERLY AVERAGES, ADJUSTED WHERE NECESSARY FOR
SEASONAL VARIATIONS [a]
(per cent of population of same sex and age group) [b]

	Males 25–64	Females 25–64	Young Persons 14–24	Elderly Persons 65 and Older
1947	93.9	31.8	52.8	26.5
I	93.8	31.5	52.2	26.5
II	93.9	31.8	53.4	26.8
III	94.1	31.9	53.0	26.6
IV	93.9	32.1	52.7	26.2
1948	94.0	33.0	53.7	26.5
I	93.8	32.6	53.6	26.0
II	94.0	32.3	53.6	26.4
III	94.2	33.2	54.1	26.4
IV	94.0	33.7	53.6	27.1
1949	93.6	33.7	53.7	26.7
I	93.7	33.7	53.8	26.7
II	93.5	33.0	53.5	26.4
III	93.6	33.5	53.6	26.4
IV	93.4	34.5	53.9	27.1
1950	93.1	34.7	53.9	26.1
I	92.9	34.8	54.0	26.9
II	93.2	34.3	52.9	26.2
III	93.2	34.2	53.3	25.7
IV	93.1	35.6	55.3	25.4
1951	93.9	35.9	54.1	25.2
I	93.1	36.3	54.7	25.4
II	93.9	34.8	53.5	25.7
III	94.1	35.5	54.1	25.0
IV	94.3	36.9	54.0	24.6
1952	94.0	36.4	52.7	24.0
I	93.9	37.1	53.9	24.4
II	94.2	35.4	53.0	23.9
III	94.2	35.8	52.5	23.7
IV	93.5	37.4	51.7	23.9
1953	94.3	36.4	51.2	24.3
I	93.7	36.8	53.5	25.1
II	94.4	36.1	51.3	24.1
III	94.6	36.0	50.5	24.6
IV	94.6	36.5	49.6	23.2

TABLE B-2, *continued*

ANNUAL AND QUARTERLY AVERAGES, ADJUSTED WHERE NECESSARY FOR
SEASONAL VARIATIONS [a]
(per cent of population of same sex and age group) [b]

	Males 25–64	Females 25–64	Young Persons 14–24	Elderly Persons 65 and Older
1954 [c]	94.6	36.9	50.3	23.2
I	94.5	36.8	51.1	23.2
II	94.8	37.1	50.4	23.2
III	94.7	36.6	50.4	23.4
IV	94.4	36.9	49.3	23.2
1955 [c]	94.2	38.2	50.6	23.6
I	94.1	37.0	49.1	23.6
II	94.4	37.9	49.6	23.3
III	94.3	38.9	51.2	23.5
IV	94.3	38.9	52.9	24.5
1956 [c, d]	94.0	39.4	52.1	23.9
I	94.0	38.9	51.6	23.9
II	94.1	39.3	52.9	24.4
III	94.1	39.8	52.3	23.6
IV	93.9	39.6	51.6	23.5

Source: Table B-1.

[a] For information on the method of computing these seasonal adjustments of quarterly data, see note *a* to Table B-1 and text at end of this appendix. The computations yielded the following indexes for sex and age groups. (No adjustment was required for males 25–64, as their participation did not seem to fluctuate in any seasonal pattern.)

	Females 25–64	Young Persons 14–24	Elderly Persons 65 and Older
1940–1952			
I	96.5	93.1	97.0
II	102.2	101.1	100.1
III	101.0	108.5	101.6
IV	100.3	97.3	101.3
1953–1956			
I	98.2	93.0	98.2
II	100.0	101.0	100.6
III	99.2	108.6	100.6
IV	101.6	97.4	100.6

[b] Before rounding.

[c] From January 1954 through April 1956, data were based on a new 230-area census sample.

[d] Beginning with May 1956, the data have been based on an enlarged sample of 35,000 interviewed households, spread over 330 areas, comprising 638 counties and independent cities. The change to an enlarged sample does not seem to have affected significantly the estimates of labor force, employment, and unemployment during the two months when the results of both samples were published.

TABLE B-3

Great Britain:
Population and Labor Force by Sex and Age Group, 1939–1948

(June)	POPULATION (millions) [a]					LABOR FORCE (number in millions) [a]					LABOR FORCE (per cent of population of same sex and age group) [a]				
Age Group	1939 [b]	1943 [c]	1945 [c]	1947 [d]	1948 [e]	1939	1943	1945 [f]	1947	1948 [e,g]	1939 [b]	1943 [c]	1945 [c,f]	1947 [d]	1948 [e,g]
MALES															
14–17	1.6	1.4	1.4	1.3		1.3	1.2	1.1	1.1		80.9	84.7	82.7	80.6	
18–24	2.6	2.6	2.5	2.4		2.5	2.6	2.5	2.3		97.0	98.3	98.3	96.5	
25–44	7.1	7.3	7.3	7.3		7.1	7.2	7.2	7.2		98.5	98.5	98.5	98.5	
45–64	4.8	4.9	5.0	5.2		4.6	4.7	4.8	4.9		95.0	95.7	95.5	94.7	
65 & older	1.8	2.0	2.1	2.1		0.6	1.0	0.9	0.7		37.5	51.6	43.2	32.3	
14–24	4.2	4.0	3.9	3.7		3.8	3.8	3.6	3.4		90.9	93.7	92.9	90.9	
14 & older	17.9	18.2	18.3	18.3	18.5	16.1	16.7	16.5	16.2	15.7	89.7	91.6	90.2	88.2	84.9
FEMALES															
14–17	1.6	1.4	1.3	1.3		1.1	1.1	1.0	1.0		72.7	79.8	78.3	75.9	
18–24	2.5	2.6	2.6	2.4		1.9	2.1	2.1	1.8		75.8	81.2	79.8	74.3	
25–44	7.5	7.5	7.5	7.4		2.5	3.4	3.2	2.6		33.3	45.3	43.5	35.1	
45–64	5.6	5.9	6.0	6.1		1.1	1.7	1.6	1.5		19.8	28.0	26.5	25.5	
65 & older	2.4	2.6	2.8	2.9		0.2	0.2	0.2	0.1		8.5	6.9	5.7	4.2	
14–24	4.1	4.0	3.9	3.7		3.0	3.2	3.1	2.8		74.6	80.7	79.3	74.9	
14 & older	19.6	20.0	20.2	20.1	20.2	6.8	8.5	8.1	7.0	7.1	35.0	42.3	40.2	35.0	35.1
BOTH SEXES															
14 & older	37.5	38.2	38.5	38.4	38.7	22.9	25.2	24.6	23.2	22.8	61.1	65.8	63.9	60.4	58.9

TABLE B-3, *continued*

(June)	Civilian Labor Force: Number (in millions)[a] 1939[b]	1943	1945[f]	1947	1948[e,g]	Per Cent of Civilian and Military Population of Same Sex and Age Group[a] 1939[b]	1943[c]	1945[c,f]	1947[f]	1948[e,g]
					MALES					
Age Group										
14–24	3.5	2.1	2.0	2.6		84.7	51.8	51.3	69.8	
25–44	6.8	4.7	4.2	6.8		95.7	64.1	58.6	92.9	
45–64	4.6	4.6	4.7	4.8		94.6	93.5	92.8	94.0	
65 & older	0.7	1.0	0.9	0.7		37.5	51.6	43.1	32.3	
14 & older	15.6	12.4	11.8	14.9	14.9	87.0	68.0	64.8	81.4	80.5
					FEMALES					
14–24	3.0	2.9	2.8	2.7		74.6	71.9	71.7	73.5	
25–44	2.5	3.3	3.1	2.6		33.3	43.9	41.7	34.9	
45–64	1.1	1.6	1.6	1.6		19.8	28.0	26.4	25.5	
65 & older	0.2	0.2	0.2	0.1		8.5	6.9	5.7	4.2	
14 & older	6.8	8.0	7.7	7.0	7.1	35.0	40.0	38.0	34.7	35.1
					BOTH SEXES					
14 & older	22.4	20.4	19.5	21.9	22.0	59.8	53.3	50.7	57.0	56.8

Source and discussion: Appendix Table B-4, Chapter 3, and Appendix F.

[a] Totals and percentages were computed before data on population and labor force were rounded. The British practice after 1939 was to count a part-time worker as half a member of the labor force. Workers occupied less than full time were treated here as regular workers for comparison with U.S. figures.

[b] The population in 1939 was based on the National Registration in September. The estimate of 250,000 armed forces abroad and seamen at sea was added to the resident population. The ages of the population, as reported by the registration, were converted to the uniform grouping by linear interpolation within the five-year age groups.

[c] The 1943 and 1945 age classifications of the English and Welsh populations were derived by linear interpolation of 1939 and 1947 data within five-year age groups. The civilian population of Scotland in 1943 as reported by the 1943 issues of the *Monthly Digest of Statistics* (London, Central Statistical Office), was subdivided by age, on the basis of data for 1945 derived from the report of the Registrar General on civilian population, and added to armed forces and seamen, distributed as in England and Wales in 1945. The Registrar General excluded seamen at sea from civilian population in 1943–1947. We leave out only H. M. Armed Forces and Women's Services.

[d] Revised population totals of England and Wales in June 1947 (*Monthly Digest of Statistics*, June 1948, p. 1) were subdivided by age on the basis of the distribution in December. The data on Scotland for June 1947 were used as published.

[e] Revised 1948 totals, which are used here, were not available in time to permit computation of breakdown by age groups.

[f] Included in the mid-1945 British labor force were 150,000 or more workers from Northern Ireland, Eire, Norway, France, and the Low Countries (*Ministry of Labour and National Service Report, 1939–1946*, London, pp. 54–57). On the other hand, 300,000 armed forces were killed, missing, and captured, all of whom would have been in the labor force, and 60,000 civilians were killed (*World Almanac*, 1948, p. 552, official figure), a loss of perhaps 35,000 gainfully occupied. War losses were thus compensated to some extent by the gain of foreigners. Not included, but working, were 224,000 German and Italian prisoners of war (*Ministry of Labour and National Service Report, 1939–1946*, p. 57; *1947*, p. 77). Their inclusion would swell both the wartime labor force and the additions to normal high employment.

[g] The 1948 total labor force is from the new series on manpower, revised (*Monthly Digest of Statistics*, November 1956, p. 4). Armed forces for 1948 were classified in the same way as in 1947.

TABLE B-4

Great Britain:

Additions to "Working Population" to Compute Labor Force, by Sex, 1943–1948

(thousands)

	1943	1945	1947	1948 [a, b]
MALES				
Working population 14–64 [c]	15,028	14,881	14,628	
Undercount 14–64 [d]	626	676	803	
Domestics 14–64 [e]	26	36	47	
65 and older [f]	1,020	891	689	
Labor force	16,700	16,484	16,167	15,657
FEMALES				
Working population 14–59 [c]	7,628	7,218	6,104	
Undercount 14–59 [d]	255	266	293	
Domestics [e]	232	323	417	
60 and older, excluding domestics [f]	346	293	214	
Labor force	8,461	8,100	7,028	7,123

[a] The labor force figures for 1948 are from the new series on manpower. *Monthly Digest of Statistics*, London, Central Statistical Office, March 1949, p. 9.

[b] Revised 1948 totals, which are used here, were not available in time to permit computation of the various breakdowns.

[c] The working population figures include armed forces and part-time workers. No part-time workers were reported in 1939; there were 750,000 in 1943, 900,000 in 1945, 730,000 in 1947, and 800,000 in 1948. *Ibid.*, p. 3; *Ministry of Labour and National Service Report, 1939–1946*, London, Sept. 1947, pp. 65, 125. The British practice during 1939–1948 had been to count each part-time worker as half a member of the labor force, but this study gives full count during this period to all workers for comparison with U.S. data. Further discussion follows notes to this table.

[d] The undercounts, in percentages of nonworking population of insurable age in June 1948, were: males, 51; females, 3. These percentages were multiplied in each of the earlier years by the total population of insurable age, minus working population.

[e] The number of insured private domestics in June 1948 as reported in the *Ministry of Labour Gazette*, London, February 1949, p. 43, was assumed to represent the total number in service. The number in 1943 was taken to be half that in 1948. The numbers in intervening years were interpolations.

The few male domestics 65 and older were counted with occupied men of those ages. Female domestics were estimated as a whole, with those 60 and older taken to be 8 per cent of all domestics, as in 1948.

[f] It is calculated that in 1939 there were 296,000 women 60 and older in the labor force, excluding domestics. According to the *Ministry of Labour and National Service Report, 1939–1946*, p. 54, females 60 and older in the industrial population increased 50,000 from mid-1939 to mid-1953. The number in 1948 was given in the *Ministry of Labour Gazette*, February 1949, pp. 40, 43. The number in 1945 was derived by linear interpolation of data in 1943 and 1948; that in 1947 was taken to be the same proportion of female population of those ages as in 1948.

The number of occupied men 65 and older was assumed to be 350,000 greater in 1943 than in 1939 (*Ministry of Labour and National Service Report, 1939–1946*, p. 54). The number in 1948 was given in *Ministry of Labour Gazette*, February, 1949, p. 40, and that for 1945 was estimated by linear interpolation of data in 1943 and 1948. The percentage of the total male population 65 and older in the labor force was taken to be the same in 1947 as in 1948.

APPENDIX B

METHODS AND MATERIALS USED TO MAKE THE BRITISH WORKING POPULA-
TION DATA OF 1939–1948 COMPARABLE TO LABOR FORCE DATA.

The estimated numbers of males and of females 14 and older are believed to be reliable. But the age groupings are rough and though adequate for standardization are usable only with caution for other purposes.[1]

For 1939 the proportions of males and females 14–15 and 65 and older
in the labor force rest upon estimates by H. Frankel in "The Industrial
Distribution of the Population of Great Britain in July, 1939," *Journal
of the Royal Statistical Society* (London, Parts III–IV, 1945, pp. 392–
430). The number of boys and girls 16–17 and the age subdivision of
women 16–64 rely upon the 1931 proportions of persons of these ages
in the labor force. Males in other age groups were calculated by assuming the following percentages: age 18–24, 97; 25–44, 98.5; and 45–
64, 95.

The June 1939 distribution of population by age derives from the
September National Registration, which differed somewhat from
Frankel's calculations and is regarded here as being more accurate.
The registered populations in various age groups were multiplied by
the labor force proportions in order to obtain the labor force by age,
which was slightly greater for males than was Frankel's—though the
corrected population for males 14 and older was less—for it included 250,000 armed forces abroad and seamen at sea. However, since
the estimate of females 14 and older in the population was smaller, the
author's estimate of the labor force of both sexes combined was slightly
less than Frankel's. The 1943–1947 distributions rely on school attendance and unemployment insurance registration, and on the presumption that the participation of various age groups does not vary much
from one year to the next. Except for a small residual, boys 14–17 were
treated as being either in school or in the labor force.[2] Since school attendance data were unavailable for 1943, the labor force of that year
was estimated on the supposition that the number insured made up 86

[1] The age distribution of the labor force, as derived from unemployment compensation data, is probably biased by the greater chance that younger workers will
be insured. *Ministry of Labour Gazette*, February 1948, p. 48.

[2] Data on school attendance for 1946 and 1948 were available from the *Annual
Abstract of Statistics, 1935–1946*, London, H. M. Stationery Office, Central Statisti-
cal Office, No. 84, 1948, pp. 74–100, and *The Times Educational Supplement*,
London, December 25, 1948, p. 726, and were used to interpolate that for 1947.
School boys 14–17 in 1945 were estimated as a residual of changes in insurance
coverage.

The number of young people 14–17 in school during 1945–1948 was estimated
to be (in thousands): *1945*, boys 231, girls 202; *1946*, boys 247, girls 216; *1947*,
boys 257, girls 233; *1948* (15–17) boys 146, girls 134.

per cent of the labor force from this age group—slightly higher than in 1945. In 1948 no 14-year-old workers were counted. Males 18–24 not in school nor in the labor force were taken to be 1.5 per cent in 1939 and in 1947, and 0.75 per cent in 1943 and 1945. With the exception of these, the number 18–24 in the labor force consisted of individuals not attending institutions of learning.[3] The proportion of men 25–44 in the labor force was presumed to be 98.5 per cent throughout the period, 1939–1947. The 45–64 range was arrived at by subtracting the estimates for the above age subdivision from the total male labor force aged 18–64.

Insured girls 14–17 were assumed to be 86 per cent of girls of these ages in the labor force in 1943 and 85 per cent in 1945, thus well above the percentage in 1939 (when a larger share of female workers were uninsured domestics). The proportion neither in school nor in the labor force was taken to be 6 per cent of the total population of these ages in 1947. Women 60 and older in the labor force were estimated partly on the assumption that in each year as in 1948, 8 per cent of domestics were of these ages. Women 65 and older were then taken to be half the number 60 and older in the labor force, roughly the same ratio as in 1931. Women 18–64 were subdivided into uniform age brackets, in proportion to the ages of those registered for insurance in 1945 and 1947 according to the *Ministry of Labour and National Service Report, 1947* [London], p. 82. Part-time workers were divided evenly between women 25–44 and 45–64. Separate estimates were made for 1945 and 1947. The proportions in 1945 were used to distribute the labor force 18–64 for 1943.

[3] Men in college were assumed to be 18–24. Attendance data for 1939–1947 were given in the *Annual Abstract of Statistics, 1937–1947*, No. 85, p. 89, and for 1949 in *The Times Educational Supplement*, February 5, 1949, p. 89. The figures were (males only, in thousands): *1939*, 38; *1943*, 24; *1945*, 24; *1947*, 50.

TABLE B-5

Great Britain:
Labor Force by Employment and Military Status, Annual Estimates,
1939–1956

| (June) | Civilian & Military | | | Armed Forces Males | Civilian | | |
	Both Sexes	Males	Females		Both Sexes	Unemployed Both Sexes	Employed Both Sexes
				Number (millions of persons 14 and older)			
1939	22.9	16.1	6.8	0.5	22.4	1.4	21.0
1940	23.7	16.6	7.1	2.2	21.4	0.7	20.7
1941	24.1	16.8	7.3	3.3	20.7	0.2	20.5
1942	25.0	16.8	8.2	3.8	20.9	0.1	20.8
1943	25.2	16.7	8.5	4.3	20.4	0.1	20.3
1944	25.0	16.6	8.4	4.5	20.0	0.1	19.9
1945	24.6	16.5	8.1	4.7	19.5	0.1	19.4
1946	23.3	16.2	7.1	1.9	21.2	0.4	20.8
1947	23.2	16.2	7.0	1.2	21.9	0.3	21.6
1948	22.8	15.7	7.1	0.87	22.0	0.27	21.7
1949	22.8	15.7	7.1	0.74	22.1	0.25	21.8
1950	23.0	15.7	7.3	0.67	22.3	0.27	22.0
1951	23.2	15.8	7.4	0.80	22.4	0.18	22.2
1952	23.3	15.9	7.4	0.85	22.4	0.30	22.1
1953	23.4	15.9	7.5	0.84	22.4	0.27	22.2
1954	23.7	16.0	7.7	0.82	22.9	0.22	22.6
1955	23.9	16.1	7.8	0.78	23.1	0.17	22.9
1956	24.0	16.1	7.9	0.75	23.2	0.19	23.0
		Per Cent of Population 14 and Older of Same Sex					Per Cent of Labor Force
1939	61.1	89.7	35.0	2.7	59.8		5.5
1940	62.7	92.4	35.7	12.3	56.7		2.7
1941	63.9	93.4	37.0	18.2	54.9		0.8
1942	65.8	92.9	41.3	21.0	55.1		0.3
1943	65.8	91.6	42.3	23.6	53.3		0.2
1944	65.1	90.4	42.0	24.6	52.1		0.2
1945	63.9	90.2	40.2	25.5	50.7		0.4
1946	60.6	88.5	35.1	10.3	55.3		1.6
1947	60.4	88.2	35.0	6.8	57.0		1.1
1948	58.9	84.9	35.1	4.4	56.9		1.2
1949	58.8	84.4	35.0	4.0	56.9		1.1
1950	59.0	84.0	36.1	3.6	57.2		1.2
1951	59.9	85.9	36.3	4.4	57.7		0.8
1952	59.9	85.5	36.6	4.6	57.7		1.3
1953	60.5	86.7	37.1	4.6	57.9		1.2
1954	61.1	87.4	37.7	4.5	59.0		0.9
1955	61.3	87.2	38.0	4.2	59.2		0.7
1956	61.6	86.8	38.5	4.1	59.5		0.8

Source: *Monthly Digest of Statistics*, London, Central Statistical Office: March 1949, pp. 3, 9; July 1953, p. 3; January 1955, p. 3; November 1956, p. 5. *Statistical Digest of the War: History of the Second World War*, London, United Kingdom Civil Series, ed. by U. K. Hancock, 1951, pp. 1, 2, 8. *Ministry of Labour and National Service Report, 1939–1946*, London, September 1947 pp. 65, 125. *Ministry of Labour Gazette*, London, February 1949, pp. 40, 43.

334

TABLE B-6

Canada:

Labor Force by Employment and Military Status, Annual and Quarterly Estimates and Annual and Quarterly Averages, 1939–1956

Number (millions of persons 14 and older)

		Civilian and Military			Armed Forces Males	Both Sexes	Civilian Unemployed Both Sexes	Employed Both Sexes
		Both Sexes	Males	Females				
ANNUAL ESTIMATES (Actual Decennial Census for June 1941) [a]								
1939	Aug.	4.44	...	...	0.01	4.43	0.70	3.73
1941	June 1	4.66	3.74	0.92	0.31	4.35	0.37	3.98
1942	June 1	5.00	...	...	0.49	4.51	0.23	4.28
1943	June 1	5.10	...	...	0.67	4.43	0.10	4.33
1944	June 1	5.30	...	...	0.77	4.53	0.08	4.45
1945	June 1	5.33	4.16	1.17	0.70	4.63	0.11	4.52
ANNUAL AVERAGES AND QUARTERLY ESTIMATES [b]								
1945	Nov. 17	4.97	3.87	1.10	0.47	4.50	0.19	4.31
1946		4.96	3.88	1.08	0.13	4.83	0.14	4.69
	Feb. 23	4.97	3.87	1.10	0.28	4.69	0.13	4.56
	June 1	4.98	3.89	1.09	0.12	4.86	0.15	4.71
	Aug. 31	4.96	3.88	1.08	0.07	4.89	0.17	4.72
	Nov. 9	4.94	3.87	1.07	0.05	4.89	0.13	4.76
1947		4.98	3.91	1.07	0.03	4.95	0.10	4.85
	Mar. 1	4.89	3.84	1.05	0.04	4.85	0.09	4.76
	May 31	4.98	3.92	1.06	0.03	4.95	0.11	4.84
	Aug. 16	5.02	3.95	1.07	0.03	4.99	0.10	4.89
	Nov. 8	5.03	3.95	1.08	0.03	5.00	0.10	4.90
1948		5.02	3.95	1.07	0.04	4.98	0.10	4.88
	Feb. 21	5.00	3.92	1.08	0.03	4.97	0.10	4.87
	June 5	5.05	3.98	1.07	0.04	5.01	0.10	4.91
	Sept. 4	5.01	3.95	1.06	0.04	4.97	0.09	4.88
	Nov. 20	5.03	3.97	1.06	0.04	4.99	0.12	4.87
1949		5.13	4.04	1.09	0.05	5.08	0.14	4.94
	Mar. 5	5.04	3.98	1.06	0.04	5.00	0.12	4.88
	June 4	5.12	4.03	1.09	0.04	5.08	0.13	4.95
	Aug. 20	5.13	4.05	1.08	0.05	5.08	0.14	4.94
	Oct. 29	5.23	4.12	1.11	0.05	5.18	0.16	5.02
1950		5.13	4.04	1.09	0.05	5.08	0.17	4.91
	Mar. 4	5.22	4.08	1.14	0.05	5.17	0.20	4.97
	June 3 [c]	4.91	3.87	1.04	0.04	4.87	0.18	4.69
	Aug. 19	5.18	4.13	1.05	0.05	5.13	0.15	4.98
	Nov. 4	5.22	4.10	1.12	0.06	5.16	0.14	5.02
1951		5.29	4.14	1.15	0.08	5.21	0.11	5.10
	Mar. 3	5.29	4.09	1.20	0.07	5.22	0.11	5.11
	June 2	5.29	4.13	1.16	0.07	5.22	0.11	5.11
	Aug. 18	5.27	4.18	1.09	0.08	5.19	0.11	5.08
	Nov. 3	5.30	4.15	1.15	0.08	5.22	0.11	5.11

TABLE B-6, *continued*

		Civilian and Military			Armed	Civilian		
		Both Sexes	Males	Females	Forces Males	Both Sexes	Unem- ployed Both Sexes	Employed Both Sexes
ANNUAL AVERAGES AND QUARTERLY ESTIMATES [b]								
1952		5.42	4.24	1.18	0.10	5.32	0.13	5.19
	Mar. 1	5.41	4.19	1.22	0.09	5.32	0.13	5.19
	May 31	5.42	4.24	1.18	0.10	5.32	0.14	5.18
	Aug. 16	5.40	4.28	1.12	0.10	5.30	0.13	5.17
	Nov. 22	5.43	4.23	1.20	0.10	5.33	0.13	5.20
ANNUAL AVERAGES AND QUARTERLY AVERAGES OF MONTHLY ESTIMATES [b]								
1953		5.49	4.30	1.19	0.10	5.39	0.14	5.25
	I	5.44	4.28	1.16	0.10	5.34	0.12	5.22
	II	5.50	4.31	1.19	0.10	5.40	0.12	5.28
	III	5.52	4.32	1.20	0.10	5.42	0.15	5.27
	IV	5.51	4.32	1.19	0.10	5.41	0.18	5.23
1954		5.53	4.31	1.22	0.10	5.43	0.24	5.19
	I	5.45	4.24	1.21	0.10	5.35	0.20	5.15
	II	5.52	4.32	1.20	0.10	5.42	0.24	5.18
	III	5.55	4.33	1.22	0.10	5.45	0.27	5.18
	IV	5.60	4.37	1.23	0.10	5.50	0.25	5.25
1955		5.70	4.44	1.26	0.10	5.60	0.23	5.37
	I	5.59	4.37	1.22	0.10	5.49	0.24	5.25
	II	5.69	4.43	1.26	0.10	5.59	0.24	5.35
	III	5.77	4.50	1.27	0.10	5.67	0.23	5.44
	IV	5.77	4.48	1.29	0.10	5.67	0.20	5.47
1956		5.81	4.48	1.33	0.10	5.71	0.18	5.53
	I	5.71	4.40	1.31	0.10	5.61	0.19	5.42
	II	5.79	4.47	1.32	0.10	5.69	0.18	5.51
	III	5.85	4.52	1.33	0.10	5.75	0.16	5.59
	IV	5.90	4.53	1.37	0.10	5.80	0.17	5.63

TABLE B-6, *continued*

Per Cent of Population 14 and Older of Same Sex

| | | Civilian and Military | | | Armed Forces | Civilian | Civilian |
		Both Sexes	Males	Females	Males	Both Sexes	Unemployed Both Sexes (per cent of labor force)
ANNUAL ESTIMATES (Actual Decennial Census for June 1941) [a]							
1939	Aug.	52.9	...	...	...	52.9	15.9
1941	June 1	54.8	85.4	22.3	7.2	51.1	5.6
1942	June 1	57.8	...	...	...	52.0	4.0
1943	June 1	58.2	...	...	...	50.2	2.0
1944	June 1	59.7	...	...	...	50.7	1.9
1945	June 1	59.4	90.9	26.5	15.3	51.6	2.0
ANNUAL AVERAGES AND QUARTERLY ESTIMATES [b]							
1945	Nov. 17	56.2	85.6	25.3	10.3	50.8	3.9
1946		55.1	84.8	24.5	2.8	53.7	2.9
	Feb. 23	55.5	84.8	25.0	6.1	52.3	2.7
	June 1	55.3	85.1	24.6	2.7	54.0	3.0
	Aug. 31	55.0	84.7	24.3	1.4	54.2	3.2
	Nov. 9	54.7	84.5	24.1	1.1	54.2	2.5
1947		54.5	84.3	23.8	0.8	54.2	2.0
	Mar. 1	53.8	83.2	23.5	0.8	53.4	1.8
	May 31	54.6	84.5	23.7	0.8	54.3	2.2
	Aug. 16	54.9	84.9	23.9	0.7	54.6	2.0
	Nov. 8	54.8	84.6	24.1	0.7	54.6	2.0
1948		54.2	84.4	23.3	0.8	53.8	2.1
	Feb. 21	54.3	84.2	23.7	0.7	53.9	2.0
	June 5	54.7	85.1	23.5	0.8	54.2	2.0
	Sept. 4	54.0	84.2	23.1	0.8	53.5	1.8
	Nov. 20	53.9	84.2	22.9	0.8	53.5	2.4
1949		54.3	84.4	23.3	0.9	53.8	2.7
	Mar. 5	53.9	83.9	23.0	0.9	53.5	2.5
	June 4	54.6	84.7	23.6	0.9	54.1	2.5
	Aug. 20	54.5	84.8	23.3	0.9	53.9	2.7
	Oct. 29	54.0	84.0	23.3	0.9	53.5	3.1
1950		53.4	83.3	22.9	1.0	52.8	3.2
	Mar. 4	53.8	83.1	23.7	1.0	53.2	3.9
	June 3 [c]	53.5	83.4	22.8	0.9	53.0	3.5
	Aug. 19	53.1	83.7	21.8	1.0	52.5	2.8
	Nov. 3	53.3	82.8	23.1	1.1	52.6	2.6
1951		53.5	83.3	23.3	1.5	52.7	2.0
	Mar. 3	53.8	82.9	24.4	1.3	53.1	2.0
	June 2	53.6	83.3	23.5	1.5	52.9	1.9
	Aug. 18	53.2	84.0	22.0	1.6	52.4	1.9
	Nov. 3	53.2	83.0	23.1	1.7	52.2	2.0
1952		53.4	82.9	23.4	2.0	52.4	2.4
	Mar. 1	53.6	82.3	24.4	1.9	52.7	2.5
	May 31	53.5	83.2	23.4	2.0	52.5	2.5
	Aug. 16	53.1	83.6	22.2	2.1	52.1	2.3
	Nov. 22	53.2	82.4	23.7	2.0	52.1	2.4

APPENDIX B

TABLE B-6, *continued*

| | Civilian and Military | | | Armed Forces | Civilian | |
	Both Sexes	Males	Females	Males	Both Sexes	Unemployed Both Sexes (per cent of labor force)
ANNUAL AVERAGES AND QUARTERLY AVERAGES OF MONTHLY ESTIMATES [b]						
1953	53.1	82.5	23.1	2.1	52.1	2.6
I	53.0	82.4	22.8	2.1	52.0	2.2
II	53.4	82.6	23.2	2.1	52.4	2.3
III	53.1	82.4	23.3	2.1	52.1	2.6
IV	53.0	82.2	23.1	2.1	52.0	3.3
1954	52.6	81.6	23.4	2.0	51.6	4.4
I	52.5	80.9	23.6	2.1	51.5	3.7
II	52.6	81.8	23.2	2.0	51.6	4.4
III	52.6	81.6	23.3	2.0	51.6	4.8
IV	52.8	81.9	23.4	2.0	51.8	4.5
1955	53.0	82.0	23.6	2.0	52.0	4.0
I	52.3	81.8	23.1	2.0	51.3	4.4
II	52.9	81.6	23.6	2.0	51.9	4.2
III	53.4	82.4	23.7	2.0	52.4	3.9
IV	53.2	81.8	24.0	2.0	52.2	3.5
1956	53.2	81.7	24.5	2.0	52.2	3.0
I	52.6	80.7	24.2	2.0	51.6	3.4
II	53.1	81.7	24.4	2.0	52.1	3.1
III	53.4	82.2	24.4	1.9	52.4	2.7
IV	53.6	82.0	25.0	1.9	52.6	2.9

Source and concepts: Chapter 3 and Appendix F.

[a] Canadian labor force and armed forces for June 1941 are from the decennial census, and for June 1942–1945 from *Estimates of the Canadian Labour Force and its Composition 1941–7*, a mimeographed table prepared by the Research and Statistics Branch, Department of Labour, Ottawa. These estimates are merely rough projections from the census of 1941, and are not strictly comparable in definition with the quarterly survey instituted in November 1945. They omit both students and women gainfully occupied on farms or in farm homes. The August 1939 employment and armed forces are from *Estimated Manpower Distribution*, also prepared by the Department of Labour. Unemployment for that date could only be approximated, by giving it the same ratio to 1941 as trade union idleness. *Canada Year Book, 1945*, pp. 767–768, *1947*, p. 620, and *Census of Canada, 1941*, Vol. VII, *Occupations*, p. 12, Ottawa, Dominion Bureau of Statistics.

[b] Quarterly data were adjusted where necessary for seasonal variations by computations which yielded the following indexes. For information on the method of

computation, see note a to Appendix Table B-1 and text at the end of this appendix. (No adjustment was required for the armed forces.)

	Labor Force Civilian and Military Both Sexes	Males	Females	Civilian Labor Force Both Sexes	Unemployed Both Sexes	Civilian Employed Both Sexes
1945–1952						
I	97.5	98.7	93.2	97.5	158.5	95.8
II	100.3	99.9	101.9	100.3	81.6	100.8
III	102.6	101.6	106.3	102.7	70.5	103.5
IV	99.6	99.8	98.6	99.5	89.4	99.9
1953–1956						
I	98.8	98.8	98.1	98.8	155.5	96.7
II	99.7	99.9	99.8	99.7	98.6	99.8
III	101.9	102.2	101.7	101.9	61.9	103.5
IV	99.6	99.1	100.5	99.6	84.0	100.0

c Excluding Manitoba which was not enumerated because of flood conditions.

TABLE B-6A

Canada:

Labor Force by Sex and Age Group, Annual and Quarterly Averages, 1945–1956

PER CENT OF POPULATION OF THE SAME SEX AND AGE, ADJUSTED WHERE NECESSARY FOR SEASONAL VARIATION [a]

		Males 25–64	Females 25–64	Young People 14–24	Elderly People 65 and Older
1945	Nov. 17	95.0	21.1	60.4	26.5
1946		94.5	20.1	58.5	26.1
	Feb. 23	94.2	20.5	59.3	26.6
	June 1	94.8	20.2	58.8	26.6
	Aug. 31	94.8	20.1	57.6	26.2
	Nov. 9	94.3	19.7	58.4	24.8
1947		94.4	20.0	57.2	25.0
	Mar. 1	93.2	19.7	56.6	24.3
	May 21	94.9	19.8	56.9	25.2
	Aug. 16	95.0	19.9	58.2	25.0
	Nov. 8	94.6	20.6	57.2	25.5
1948		94.9	20.1	56.4	24.4
	Feb. 21	94.1	20.2	57.1	25.0
	June 5	95.3	20.3	57.4	24.2
	Sept. 4	95.3	20.1	55.2	24.1
	Nov. 20	94.7	19.9	55.9	24.1
1949		94.8	20.0	57.4	23.7
	Mar. 5	94.0	19.7	57.0	24.3
	June 4	95.3	20.0	57.6	24.5
	Aug. 20	95.3	20.0	58.0	22.9
	Oct. 29	94.7	20.2	56.8	23.1
1950		94.1	20.0	56.0	22.4
	Mar. 4	93.3	20.9	56.8	23.1
	June 3 b	94.7	20.1	55.3	22.5
	Aug. 19	94.5	18.9	56.0	22.0
	Nov. 3	94.0	20.1	56.0	21.8

TABLE B-6A, *continued*

PER CENT OF POPULATION OF THE SAME SEX AND AGE, ADJUSTED WHERE
NECESSARY FOR SEASONAL VARIATION [a]

		Males 25–64	Females 25–64	Young People 14–24	Elderly People 65 and Older
1951		94.4	20.5	56.6	21.0
	Mar. 3	93.6	21.4	57.7	21.2
	June 2	94.6	20.6	56.3	21.9
	Aug. 18	94.9	19.1	56.9	20.5
	Nov. 3	94.6	20.8	55.4	20.2
1952		94.4	21.0	56.0	20.1
	Mar. 1	93.7	22.1	56.0	20.9
	May 31	94.9	21.1	55.8	20.3
	Aug. 16	94.8	19.5	56.7	19.6
	Nov. 22	94.2	21.3	55.4	19.6
1953		94.3	20.7	55.6	18.9
	I	93.8	20.5	55.7	19.0
	II	94.6	20.8	55.9	18.7
	III	94.9	21.0	54.9	19.0
	IV	93.9	20.6	55.9	18.7
1954		93.9	21.2	54.8	18.3
	I	92.6	21.2	55.3	18.2
	II	94.1	21.8	55.2	18.3
	III	94.7	21.1	53.9	18.3
	IV	94.1	21.5	54.9	18.3
1955		94.2	21.7	54.5	17.8
	I	93.0	21.2	54.2	18.3
	II	94.3	21.8	53.9	17.8
	III	95.0	21.6	55.7	17.4
	IV	94.5	22.2	54.3	17.8
1956		94.3	22.8	54.0	18.8
	I	93.4	22.1	53.9	18.4
	II	94.3	22.6	54.1	18.7
	III	94.9	23.0	53.7	19.1
	IV	94.5	23.5	54.4	19.0

Source and concepts: Chapter 3 and Appendix F.

[a] For information on the method of computing these seasonal adjustments of
quarterly data, see note *a* to Table B-1 and text at end of this appendix. The
computations yielded the following indexes for sex and age groups. (No adjustment
was required for males 25–64, as their participation did not seem to fluctuate in
any seasonal pattern.)

	Females 25–64	Young Persons 14–24	Elderly Persons 65 and Older
1945–1952			
I	93.1	94.8	94.4
II	103.4	99.6	100.5
III	104.9	107.1	102.9
IV	98.6	98.5	102.2
1953–1956			
I	98.9	95.4	95.7
II	101.0	98.4	100.8
III	99.1	109.1	103.2
IV	101.0	97.1	100.3

[b] Excluding Manitoba which was not enumerated because of flood conditions.

APPENDIX B

TABLE B-7

Germany, Including the Saar, Austria, and the Sudetenland:
Population and Labor Force by Sex, 1939-1944

(May)	1939	1940	1941	1942	1943	1944
POPULATION 14 AND OLDER (millions) [a]						
Germans, including armed forces before losses						
Males	30.1	30.4	30.6	30.8	31.0	31.2
Females	32.2	32.4	32.6	32.8	33.0	33.1
Both sexes	62.3	62.8	63.2	63.6	64.0	64.3
Armed forces (assumed to be entirely males)						
Before losses	1.4	5.7	7.4	9.4	11.2	12.4
Losses	0	0.1	0.2	0.8	1.7	3.3
Active	1.4	5.6	7.2	8.6	9.5	9.1
LABOR FORCE (millions) [a]						
Germans, including armed forces before losses						
Males	25.9	26.1	26.4	26.3	26.7	26.6
Females	14.6	14.4	14.2	14.4	14.8	14.8
Both sexes	40.5	40.5	40.6	40.7	41.5	41.4
Foreigners [b] and prisoners in labor force						
Males	0.2	1.0	2.6	3.5	4.8	5.4
Females	0.1	0.2	0.4	0.7	1.5	1.7
Both sexes	0.3	1.2	3.0	4.2	6.3	7.1
PER CENT OF POPULATION IN LABOR FORCE [a]						
German labor force as per cent of German population of same sex, including armed forces before losses						
Males	85.9	86.0	86.2	85.4	86.1	85.1
Females	45.3	44.4	43.5	44.1	44.9	44.7
Both sexes	64.9	64.5	64.2	64.1	64.9	64.3
German and foreign [b] labor force as per cent of German and foreign [b] population of same sex, including active armed forces						
Males	86.0	86.4	87.3	86.6	87.4	86.0
Females	45.4	44.7	44.1	45.2	47.3	47.4
Both sexes	65.1	65.1	65.7	65.9	67.2	66.3

Source: Data and discussion on labor force, Chapter 3 and Appendix F. The population in 1939 by sex was derived from the census of that year. *Statistical Year-Book of the League of Nations, 1941-1942*, Geneva, 1943, Table 3, p. 26. For 1940-1944 the population represented the interpolation of data for 1940 and 1945, estimated by Frank Notestein in *Future Population of Europe and the Soviet Union*, Geneva, League of Nations, 1944, pp. 256-257 and 264-265. The Notestein data, which excluded the Saar and the Sudetenland, were not used directly but served as indexes for extrapolating the population reported by the 1939 census.

[a] Totals and percentages were computed before data on population and labor force were rounded.
[b] Belgians, Dutch, Poles, and others in Germany on contract, compulsory, or semi-compulsory labor services.

341

APPENDIX B

Seasonal Adjustments of Quarterly Data

The seasonal adjustments of the quarterly data for the United States in Appendix Tables B-1 and B-2 and for Canada in Tables B-6 and B-6A were based on the method of averaging ratios of original figures to four-term moving averages, "centered" on the third month.[4] Adjustment was made of the percentages, rather than of the absolute data, and the seasonally-adjusted data in millions were then computed from the seasonally-adjusted data in percentages. No seasonal adjustment was made, of course, for the armed forces in either country. And none was made for the labor force of men 25–64 (since it did not seem to fluctuate in any seasonal pattern), or for the unemployed in the United States during the World War II years, 1942–1945, when the decline of unemployment to extremely low levels seemed to have largely ironed out seasonal variations. For the United States during 1940–1952, the base period of the seasonal indexes covers the second quarter of 1940 to the second quarter of 1950; for Canada during 1945–1952 the base period covers November 1945 to June 1950. For both countries during 1953–1956, the base period of the seasonal indexes covers all of these four years.

Since these computations were made, two United States government agencies have constructed seasonal indexes based on somewhat different methods and different periods. The Bureau of the Census used an "Improved Ratio to Moving Average" method, based on data for 1947–1949. The Bureau of Labor Statistics used the link-relative method based on data for 1946–1953. These indexes were constructed for monthly data, but are here clustered into quarterly averages for comparison with the seasonal index of the study used for 1940–1952. Following are the three sets of indexes, compared for the seasonal adjustment of unemployment.

	This Study Ratio-to-Moving-Average Method, Based on Data for 1940 to 1950 [a]	Bureau of the Census "Improved Ratio to Moving Average" Method, Based on Data for 1947–1949 [b]	Bureau of Labor Statistics Link-Relative Method, Based on Data for 1946–1953 [c]
I	116.6	116.4	116.1
II	101.6	99.2	100.7
III	96.7	95.6	95.6
IV	85.1	88.8	87.7

[a] Base data cover the second quarter of 1940 to the second quarter of 1950.
[b] *Current Population Reports, Annual Report of the Labor Force 1954*, Bureau of the Census, Series P-50, No. 59, p. 13. Among the refinements was a provision for moving seasonal adjustment factors so as to reflect changing seasonal patterns with only a moderate time lag. The Bureau of the Census is now making an intensive review of its seasonal adjustments of unemployment and the labor force.
[c] "Revised Indexes of Seasonal Variations in Labor Force, Employment, and Unemployment," Bureau of Labor Statistics, Unpublished Memorandum, July 13, 1954, Table 1.

[4] Arthur F. Burns and Wesley C. Mitchell, *Measuring Business Cycles*, National Bureau of Economic Research, 1946, pp. 46–50.

342

APPENDIX B

As may be seen in the above comparison, the indexes differ very little. So far as unemployment is concerned, the methods and the periods used do not seem to have been critical despite the fact that the seasonal pattern of unemployment is far from being a regular one from year to year.

In the case of the labor force, the independent seasonal adjustment of the component age-sex groups and the total labor force 14 and older would have created some disparities, since the former would not have added up precisely to agree with the latter. Therefore the total seasonally adjusted labor force was computed in this study by combining the seasonally adjusted participation of the broad age-sex groups (omitting seasonal adjustment for men 25–64 and 65 and older since their participation did not seem to vary seasonally). The seasonally-adjusted data for females 14 and older were also computed independently and subtracted from the seasonally-adjusted total labor force to obtain the seasonally-adjusted data for males 14 and older.

The Bureau of the Census and the Bureau of Labor Statistics have constructed seasonal indexes for the civilian labor force only, the latter including the total 14 and older, males and females 14–24 separately, and males and females 25 and older separately. Since a labor force group 25 and older is not presented here, the comparison is confined to the total labor force and to males and females 14–24.

	This Study	Bureau of the Census [a]	Bureau of Labor Statistics [b]
		Total Civilian Labor Force 14 and Older	
I	97.3	97.5	97.9
II	100.8	100.8	100.4
III	102.4	102.4	101.9
IV	99.5	99.3	99.8
		Males 14–24	
I	93.5	. . .	92.8
II	101.6	. . .	101.7
III	108.6	. . .	110.3
IV	96.3	. . .	95.1
		Females 14–24	
I	92.1	. . .	92.7
II	100.4	. . .	100.4
III	108.2	. . .	107.2
IV	99.3	. . .	99.7

[a] *Measuring Seasonal Variation in Labor Force Components*, Bureau of the Census, Memorandum, March 1, 1951, Table 1. The census did not provide seasonal adjustments for males and females 14–24.
[b] Bureau of Labor Statistics, *op. cit.*, Table 4.

The greatest disparity was found for males 14–24, but the index of this study includes the armed forces. Even these disparities are not large, and the similarities for females 14–24 and for the total civilian labor force are very close.

Although the seasonal adjustments based on data for 1940–1950 seemed satisfactory for the period prior to the Korean conflict, they were less satisfactory for the period after that, since repetitive movements appeared in the quarterly data on females and total labor force during 1951, 1952, and thereafter. No revisions were made here in the adjustments for 1951 and 1952, because so many correlations based on these data would have had to be recomputed. New seasonal adjustments were made, however, for 1953–1956 on the basis of the data for those years. The seasonal patterns underlying these adjustments for 1953–1956 (footnotes *a* to Tables B-1 and B-2), indicate substantially smaller seasonal fluctuations, in the labor force, especially for females and both sexes, but greater seasonal fluctuations in unemployment, than those for the period 1940–1950. The same revisions for 1953–1956 were made for Canada, with substantially similar differences in pattern (footnote *b* to Table B-6 and footnote *a* to Table B-6A).

APPENDIX C

Labor Force, the Unemployed, and the Employed in Adult-Male Equivalents

TABLE C-1

United States:
Labor Force, the Unemployed, and the Employed in Persons 10 and Older and in Adult-Male Equivalents, 1890–1950

(millions)

	1890	1900	1910	1920	1930	1940	1950
				PERSONS			
April							
Labor force	23.2	28.8	36.2	41.7	48.9	52.8	60.1
Unemployed	...	...	1.3 [a]	... [b]	3.2 [c]	8.0 [d]	2.9 [e]
Employed	...	...	34.9 [f]	...	45.7 [f]	44.8	57.2
Monthly average							
Labor force [g]	23.6	29.3	36.8	42.4	49.7	54.1 [h]	61.1 [h]
Unemployed	1.2 [i]	2.2 [i]	1.3	1.6 [j]	5.7 [k]	7.7 [h]	2.6 [h]
Employed	22.4	27.1	35.5	40.8	44.0	46.4	58.5
	MONTHLY	AVERAGE	ADULT-MALE	EQUIVALENTS	[l]		
Labor force	19.6	24.3	30.9	35.9	42.9	46.9	53.9
Unemployed	1.1	2.0	1.2	1.5	5.3	6.9	2.2
Employed	18.5	22.3	29.7	34.4	37.6	40.0	51.7

Source and concepts: Appendix Table A-2, Chapter 3, and Appendixes E and F.

[a] The census of 1910 had asked a question on unemployment but had never published the returns. At the author's request in 1948 a special tabulation was made. Since it covered only wage and salary workers 16 and older, the small degree of idleness among own-account workers and children 10–15 was estimated. Estimates were based on the relation of the unemployment rates of these groups to those of employees 16 and older, as reported by the 1930 census.

[b] No question on unemployment was included in the 1920 census.

[c] Class A and B unemployed. *Census of Unemployment, 1930*, Vol. I, p. 13. For discussion of the problems of classifying the idle in 1930, see Supplementary Appendix H.

[d] The 8 million in April 1940 consisted of 5.1 million seeking jobs and 2.9 million on the rolls of federal emergency relief agencies, excluding the National Youth Administration. The census enumerated 2.5 million emergency workers but accepted the larger number registered. *Census of Population, 1940*, Vol. III, *The Labor Force*, Part 1, p. 3.

[e] *Census of Population, 1950*, "Employment and Income in the United States by Region," *Preliminary Reports*, 1951, PC-7, No. 2, p. 21.

[f] Labor force minus the number of unemployed.

[g] The average in each decade year 1890–1930 was approximated by enlarging the labor force figure for April by 1.7 per cent, the mean excess of the monthly average, over the April labor force in 1947, 1948, and 1949. *Current Population Reports, Monthly Report on the Labor Force*, Series P-57, Bureau of the Census. These years were selected because they embraced a period when the seasonal pattern of employment would not be disturbed by cyclical or war-induced variations.

[h] The labor force count of April 1940 by the decennial census was increased by 2.4 per cent of its absolute amount, and the unemployment figure was reduced by

3.6 per cent. These changes relied on the ratios of annual averages to April estimates. *Current Population Reports, Labor Force, Employment, and Unemployment in the United States, 1940 to 1946*, Series P-50, No. 2, p. 11. The labor force and unemployment decennial figures of April 1950 were multiplied by 1.016 and 0.886 respectively, ratios derived from *Current Population Reports, The Labor Force*, Series P-50, No. 31, p. 15.

[1] In 1890 and 1900 the census reported unemployment for 1–3 months, 4–6 months, or 7–12 months during the years June 1, 1889 to May 30, 1890, and June 1, 1899 to May 30, 1900. The census turned the results into yearly means by taking the duration in each group as the mid-point. The method was not wholly satisfactory. Census reports: *1890, Report on Population of the United States*, Vol. I, Part 2, p. cxxxvii, and *Compendium of the Eleventh Census*, Part 3, p. 387; *1900* (Special Reports), *Occupations at the Twelfth Census*, pp. ccxxv–ccxxxiv. To shift the means for the two years ended May 30, 1890 and 1900 to those for the calendar years, it was decided, after study of employment and output data, that since unemployment was probably not greatly different in the last halves of 1890 and 1900 from that in the last halves of 1889 or 1899, the percentages in 1889–1890 and 1899–1900 could be used for 1890 and 1900. See: Clarence D. Long's monthly index of building permits in United States cities during 1889–1890 and 1899–1900, in *Building Cycles and the Theory of Investment;* Princeton University Press, 1940, chart following p. 98; The American Telephone and Telegraph Company's index of "general business" in Wesley C. Mitchell, *Business Cycles, The Problem and Its Setting*, National Bureau of Economic Research, 1927, p. 296; Committee on Unemployment and Business Cycles of the President's Conference on Unemployment, and a Special Staff of the NBER, *Business Cycles and Unemployment*, McGraw-Hill, 1923, Chart 10, p. 62; W. H. Shaw, *Value of Commodity Output since 1869*, NBER, 1947, pp. 34–35, 39, 51–52, 62.

[j] Since the 1920 census did not include a question on unemployment, the average here relies on Leo Wolman's estimate (1.4 million) for nonagricultural employees, supplemented to cover the small degree of unemployment among own-account workers and farmers, based on the 1930 ratios of unemployment rates of these groups to those of nonagricultural employees. Committee on Recent Economic Changes of the President's Conference on Unemployment, and . . . the NBER, *Recent Economic Changes in the United States*, 1921, p. 478. The 0.6 million figure, published by the National Industrial Conference Board in the *Economic Almanac* (1950, p. 163), is almost certainly too low. Clarence D. Long, *The Labor Force in Wartime America*, NBER, Occasional Paper 14, 1944, pp. 39–46.

[k] A special census survey was made for January 1, 1931, covering 21 selected urban areas with a combined population of over 20 million. The means of the unemployment percentages of these same areas as of April 1, 1930 and January 1, 1931, were used to extend the April rate to the whole country for the year. *Census of Unemployment, 1930*, Vol. II, pp. 365–366.

[l] For explanation of the weights used in converting the labor force of women and teen-agers to adult-male equivalents, see text of this appendix. The same weights were used for the employed and the unemployed.

TABLE C-2

United States:
Labor Force, the Unemployed, and the Employed in Adult-Male
Equivalents, 1940–1956

(millions)

ANNUAL AND QUARTERLY AVERAGES,[a] ADJUSTED FOR SEASONAL VARIATIONS [b]						
	Labor Force	Unemployed [b]	Employed		Labor Force	Unemployed	Employed
1940	47.7	7.1	40.6	1945	54.1	0.9	53.2
I	47.4	7.0	40.4	I	55.5	0.6	54.9
II	47.6	7.0	40.6	II	54.9	0.6	54.3
III	48.0	7.2	40.8	III	53.8	0.9	52.9
IV	47.7	7.2	40.5	IV	52.1	1.4	50.7
1941	48.8	4.8	44.0	1946	51.9	2.0	49.9
I	47.8	5.1	42.7	I	51.8	1.9	49.9
II	48.9	5.1	43.8	II	51.7	2.0	49.7
III	49.3	5.1	44.2	III	52.0	1.9	50.1
IV	49.0	3.7	45.3	IV	52.1	2.0	50.1
1942	50.6	2.2	48.4	1947	52.9	1.8	51.1
I	49.4	3.4	46.0	I	52.5	1.7	50.8
II	50.3	2.4	47.9	II	52.9	1.9	51.0
III	50.8	1.9	48.9	III	53.0	2.0	51.0
IV	52.1	1.3	50.8	IV	53.0	1.7	51.3
1943	53.6	0.9	52.7	1948	53.8	1.8	52.0
I	53.0	1.2	51.8	I	53.5	1.7	51.8
II	53.5	0.9	52.6	II	53.5	1.7	51.8
III	53.7	0.9	52.8	III	54.2	1.8	52.4
IV	54.0	0.6	53.4	IV	54.2	1.8	52.4
1944	54.3	0.6	53.7	1949	54.8	3.0	51.8
I	54.0	0.6	53.4	I	54.7	2.2	52.5
II	54.4	0.6	53.8	II	54.6	2.9	51.7
III	54.2	0.6	53.6	III	54.8	3.3	51.5
IV	54.7	0.4	54.3	IV	55.3	3.6	51.7

TABLE C-2, *continued*

ANNUAL AND QUARTERLY AVERAGES,[a] ADJUSTED FOR SEASONAL VARIATIONS [b]

	Labor Force	Unemployed [b]	Employed		Labor Force	Unemployed	Employed
1950	55.8	2.7	53.1	1954	58.5	2.8	55.7
I	55.6	3.3	52.3	I	58.7	2.6	56.1
II	55.4	2.8	52.6	II	58.4	2.9	55.5
III	55.7	2.4	53.3	III	58.4	2.9	55.5
IV	56.3	2.2	54.1	IV	58.5	2.8	55.7
1951	57.2	1.7	55.5	1955	59.3	2.2	57.1
I	57.0	1.8	55.2	I	58.8	2.4	56.4
II	56.8	1.6	55.2	II	59.1	2.3	56.8
III	57.2	1.5	55.7	III	59.8	2.1	57.7
IV	57.8	1.8	56.0	IV	59.7	2.1	57.6
1952	57.5	1.5	56.0	1956	60.5	1.9	58.6
I	57.6	1.5	56.1	I	60.9	2.0	58.9
II	57.2	1.5	55.7	II	60.3	1.9	58.4
III	57.5	1.6	55.9	III	59.8	1.9	57.9
IV	57.6	1.5	56.1	IV	61.1	2.0	59.1
1953	57.8	1.3	56.5				
I	58.5	1.3	57.2				
II	57.5	1.3	56.2				
III	57.5	1.2	56.3				
IV	57.7	1.5	56.2				

Source and concepts: Appendix Table B-1, Chapter 3, and Appendixes E and F.

[a] The female labor force was converted to adult-male equivalents on the basis of the ratio of the earnings of females to those of males: 0.58 in 1940 and 0.67 in 1950. The ratio was assumed to rise by roughly 0.01 each year during the intervening decade and to be 0.68 during 1951–1954. Adjustment was made for changes in the proportion of children 14–19 without dealing with the 14–19 groups on a quarterly basis, utilizing the ratios established by complete age-sex analysis in April of each year. The changes were instituted annually, in the first quarter. They were not large enough to cause a significant hiatus between the last quarter of each year and the first quarter of the next.

[b] See note *a* to Table B-1. Unemployment was not adjusted for the period 1942–1945, when the seasonal variation in idleness was suspended by high wartime employment.

TABLE C-3

Great Britain:
Labor Force, the Unemployed, and the Employed in Persons 14 and Older and in Adult-Male Equivalents, 1911–1951

(millions)

	1911	1921	1931	1939	1951 [a]
	PERSONS				
Census month [a]					
Labor force	18.2	19.3	21.1	22.9	22.6
Unemployed	0.3 [b]	2.4 [c]	2.6 [d]	1.4 [d]	0.4
Employed	17.9	16.9	18.5	21.5	22.2
Monthly average [e]					
Labor force	18.2	19.3	21.1	22.9	22.7 [f]
Unemployed	0.3	1.8	2.6	1.5	0.4 [f]
Employed	17.9	17.5	18.5	21.4	22.3
	ADULT-MALE EQUIVALENTS [g]				
Monthly average					
Labor force	14.0	15.3	16.9	18.3	19.2
Unemployed	0.2	1.6	2.3	1.3	0.4
Employed	13.8	13.7	14.6	17.0	18.8

Source and concepts: Appendix Table A-9, Chapter 3, and Appendix F.

[a] April in the years 1911, 1931, and 1951; June in 1921 and 1939. The 1951 statistics are from a 1 per cent sample tabulation. *Census 1951, Great Britain, One Percent Sample Tables*, London, General Register Office, 1952, Part I, p. 63.

[b] Not in census returns. Approximated from idleness reported by trade unions. As justification for using the latter in connection with the subsequent employment exchange material, see W. H. Beveridge, *Full Employment in a Free Society*, Norton, 1945, p. 72.

[c] Not published by the census. The number of insured jobless in 1921, as given by the *Nineteenth Abstract of Labour Statistics of the United Kingdom* (London, Ministry of Labour, 1928, Cmd. 3140, pp. 44, 79) differs from the 2.2 million reported by employment exchanges in the *Ministry of Labour Gazette* (London, July 1921, p. 361). According to T. S. Chegwiddin and G. Myrddin-Evans, "It is, however, probable that, at any rate among wage earners, the number of unemployed persons not included in the Ministry of Labour Statistics is inconsiderable." (*The Employment Exchange Service of Great Britain*, London, Macmillan, 1934, p. 59.)

[d] In 1931 the census, utilizing a "not at work" concept, enumerated 0.2 million fewer unemployed than were registered by the insurance plans. The figures in both 1931 and 1939 include the insured and uninsured idle on the register of employment exchanges, and those who were "wholly idle," "temporarily stopped," and "normally in casual employment."

[e] Average population and labor force in each decade year during 1911–1939 were assumed to be the same as those reported by the census, or estimated in this study for the census month.

[f] Reported by the 1951 census from a 1 per cent sample of the enumeration. The average labor force for the year was obtained by multiplying the April figure by the ratio of the average working population at four quarterly dates to that for the end of March (*Monthly Digest of Statistics*, London, Central Statistical Office, No. 74, February 1952, p. 19). Unemployment for the year was assumed to be the same as that for April, on the basis of unemployment exchange data.

[g] For explanation of the weights used in converting the labor force of women and teen-agers to adult-male equivalents, see text of this appendix following Table C-7. The same weights were used for the employed and the unemployed.

349

TABLE C-4

Canada:

Labor Force, the Unemployed, and the Employed in Persons 14 and
Older and in Adult-Male Equivalents, 1911–1951

(millions)

	1911	*1921*	*1931*	*1941*	*1951*
			PERSONS		
June					
Labor force	2.7	3.2	3.9	4.7	5.3
Unemployed a	. . .	0.3	0.6	0.3	0.1
Employed b	. . .	2.9	3.3	4.4	5.2
Monthly average					
Labor force c	2.7	3.2	3.9	4.7	5.3
Unemployed d	. . .	0.3	0.6	0.3	0.1
Employed b	. . .	2.9	3.3	4.4	5.2
		ADULT-MALE	EQUIVALENTS e		
Monthly average					
Labor force	2.3	2.7	3.4	4.0	4.6
Unemployed	. . .	0.3	0.6	0.3	0.1
Employed	. . .	2.4	2.8	3.7	4.5

Source and concepts: Appendix Table A-11, Chapter 3, and Appendix F.

[a] For discussion of unemployment before 1921, see *Administration of Public Employment Offices and Unemployment Insurance*, New York, Industrial Relations Counselors, Inc., 1935, p. 16. The number in 1921 was extrapolated from that in 1931 by an index of trade union joblessness (*Canada Year Book*, Ottawa, Dominion Bureau of Statistics, 1933, p. 769). The source for 1931–1951: *Census of Canada* (Ottawa, Dominion Bureau of Statistics): *1931*, Vol. VI, pp. 3, 1303; *1941*, Vol. VI, pp. 920–921, 1010; *1951*, Vol. IV, Table 1, p. 2.

The idle in 1931–1951 include persons absent from jobs because of illness, accident, holidays, and strikes. New seekers of work in 1931 were assumed to have amounted to the same percentage of gainfully employed wage earners as in 1941. A small allowance for the self-employed was added for the latter year on the basis of their relationship to idle wage and salary workers in the United States in 1930. The ratio was taken from the 1930, instead of the 1940 census because employment conditions in the two countries were more comparable in 1930.

[b] Employment in 1921 and 1931 was derived by subtracting the number of unemployed from the labor force, but in 1941 and 1951 it was enumerated separately.

[c] During 1947–1949, the labor force in June proved to be extremely close to the average for the four quarterly dates. In 1951 it was exactly the same (*The Labor Force*, Ottawa, Dominion Bureau of Statistics, Aug. 18, 1951, p. 12 and March 1952, p. 5). Since there is no reason to suppose that the situation differed in 1911, 1921, 1931, or 1941, the June labor force is taken to represent the annual figure in each of these years.

[d] For 1921, 1931, and 1941, the relationships of annual to June unemployment were calculated from trade union percentages (*Ministry of Labour Gazette*, London, February 1922, p. 220; February 1942, pp. 211, 221; and *Canada Year Book*, *1932*, p. 651). Although the seasonal variation was considerable, the June ratios were found to be so close to the annual ratios that when the final data were rounded no difference in numbers could be detected.

[e] For explanation of the weights used in converting the labor force of women and teen-agers to adult-male equivalents, see text of this appendix following Table C-7. The same weights were used for the employed and the unemployed.

TABLE C-5

Canada:

Labor Force, the Unemployed, and the Employed in Adult-Male Equivalents, Annual and Quarterly Averages, 1945–1956

(in millions,[a] adjusted for seasonal variations [b])

| | | ANNUAL AVERAGES AND QUARTERLY ESTIMATES | | |
		Labor Force	Unemployed	Employed
1945	Nov. 17	4.48	0.17	4.31
1946		4.43	0.13	4.30
	Feb. 23	4.46	0.13	4.33
	June 1	4.44	0.14	4.30
	Aug. 31	4.41	0.15	4.26
	Nov. 9	4.42	0.12	4.30
1947		4.45	0.09	4.36
	Mar. 1	4.39	0.08	4.31
	May 31	4.45	0.10	4.35
	Aug. 16	4.48	0.10	4.38
	Nov. 8	4.49	0.09	4.40
1948		4.52	0.10	4.42
	Feb. 21	4.51	0.09	4.42
	June 5	4.53	0.09	4.44
	Sept. 4	4.50	0.09	4.41
	Nov. 20	4.53	0.11	4.42
1949		4.62	0.13	4.49
	Mar. 5	4.57	0.12	4.45
	June 4	4.60	0.12	4.48
	Aug. 20	4.60	0.13	4.47
	Oct. 29	4.71	0.15	4.56
1950		4.65	0.15	4.50
	Mar. 4	4.73	0.19	4.54
	June 3 [c]	4.44	0.16	4.28
	Aug. 19	4.69	0.13	4.56
	Nov. 4	4.72	0.12	4.60
1951		4.79	0.10	4.69
	Mar. 3	4.80	0.10	4.70
	June 2	4.78	0.10	4.68
	Aug. 18	4.78	0.09	4.69
	Nov. 3	4.81	0.10	4.71
1952		4.88	0.12	4.76
	Mar. 1	4.88	0.12	4.76
	May 31	4.89	0.13	4.76
	Aug. 16	4.87	0.11	4.76
	Nov. 22	4.88	0.12	4.76
1953		4.91	0.13	4.78
	Mar. 21	4.91	0.11	4.80
	May 16	4.88	0.13	4.75
	Aug. 22	4.94	0.12	4.82
	Nov. 21	4.90	0.16	4.74

APPENDIX C

TABLE C-5, *continued*

| | ANNUAL AND QUARTERLY AVERAGES OF MONTHLY ESTIMATES | | |
	Labor Force	Unemployed	Employed
1953	4.91	0.13	4.77
I	4.86	0.11	4.75
II	4.91	0.11	4.80
III	4.94	0.14	4.80
IV	4.91	0.17	4.74
1954	4.96	0.23	4.73
I	4.87	0.19	4.68
II	4.95	0.22	4.73
III	4.98	0.27	4.71
IV	5.02	0.24	4.78
1955	5.13	0.22	4.91
I	5.00	0.24	4.76
II	5.09	0.27	4.82
III	5.28	0.20	5.08
IV	5.15	0.19	4.96
1956	5.20	0.17	5.04
I	5.18	0.25	4.94
II	5.14	0.16	4.99
III	5.23	0.09	5.14
IV	5.27	0.15	5.11

Source and concepts: Appendix Table B-6, Chapter 3, and Appendix F.

[a] The female labor force (both employed and unemployed) was converted to adult-male equivalents on the basis of the ratio of female, to male earnings—0.55 throughout the period; no adjustment was made for children because there were so few of them in the labor force.

[b] For description of the method used in adjusting for seasonal variation, see note *a* to Appendix Table B-1.

[c] Excluding Manitoba which was not enumerated because of flood conditions.

APPENDIX C

TABLE C-6

New Zealand:

Labor Force, the Unemployed, and the Employed in Persons 15 and Older and in Adult-Male Equivalents, 1896–1951

(thousands)

	1896	1901[a]	1906	1911	1921	1926	1936[a]	1945[a]	1951
	PERSONS								
Census enumeration [a]									
Labor force	282	328	383	437	506	548	645	675	701
Unemployed	17	10	9	8	13	13	38	7	9
Employed	265	318	374	429	493	535	607	668	692
Monthly average [b]									
Labor force	282	328	383	437	506	534	650	692	701
Unemployed	17	10	9	8	13	15	44	7	9
Employed	265	318	374	429	493	519	606	685	692
	ADULT-MALE EQUIVALENTS [c]								
Monthly average									
Labor force	257	297	348	394	452	480	582	611	622
Unemployed	16	10	9	8	12	14	43	7	8
Employed	241	287	339	386	440	466	539	604	614

Source and concepts: Appendix Table A-14, Chapter 3, and Appendix F. *Population Census* (Wellington, Census and Statistics Dept.): *1936*, Vol. XI, *Unemployment*, pp. i, 1; *1945*, Vol. IX, p. vi; *1951*, Vol. IV, pp. 9–10.

[a] The census was enumerated in March of 1901 and 1936, in September of 1945, and in April of the other years.

[b] Because data on fluctuations within the year were lacking for 1896–1921, the monthly averages are assumed to be the same as the census enumerations. However, variations in factory employment during 1926 and 1936, in idleness rates of trade union members during 1926 and in the registration of the unemployed during 1936, indicated that the annual data did not differ significantly from those of the censuses. The monthly average for each category in 1951 and that for the unemployed in 1945 are also assumed to be the same as the census enumerations—on the ground that employment in industry, as registered by national employment service statistics in 1951, and unemployment benefits in force in 1945 and 1951 yielded annual averages very close to the census data. *New Zealand Official Year Book: 1929*, p. 860; *1938*, p. 802; *1947–1949*, p. 717; *1951–1952*, p. 868. *Statistical Report for the Year 1926*, p. 64; *Statistical Report on the Factory and Building Production of the Dominion of New Zealand for the Year 1936-7*, p. 35; *Report on Prices, Wages, and Labour Statistics of New Zealand for the Years 1951–52 and 1952–53*, pp. 53, 58–65. All Wellington, Census and Statistics Dept.

[c] For explanation of the weights used in converting the labor force of women and teen-agers to adult-male equivalents, see text of this appendix following Table C-7. The same weights were used for the employed and the unemployed.

TABLE C-7

Germany:

Labor Force, the Unemployed, and the Employed in Persons 14 and Older and in Adult-Male Equivalents, 1895–1950

(millions)

	Post-World War I Boundaries (without Saar)					Federal Republic of Germany (without Berlin)		
	1895	1907	1925	1933	1939	1939	1946	1950
	PERSONS							
Census month [a]								
Labor force	19.4	24.8	31.8	32.2	34.9	20.3 [e]	19.4 [f]	22.1 [g]
Unemployed	0.3 [b]	0.5 [c]	0.6 [d]	5.9 [d]	0.1 [e]	0.0 [e]	1.2 [f]	1.4 [g]
Employed	19.1	24.3	31.2	26.3	34.8	20.3 [e]	18.2 [f]	20.7 [g]
Monthly average								
Labor force	19.4	24.8	31.3	31.6	33.5	19.6 [e]	19.4 [f]	21.9 [g]
Unemployed	0.3 [b]	0.5 [c]	1.3 [d]	5.7 [d]	0.1 [e]	0.1 [e]	1.2 [f]	1.8 [g]
Employed	19.1 [b]	24.3 [c]	30.0 [d]	25.9 [d]	33.4 [e]	19.5 [e]	18.2 [f]	20.1 [g]
	ADULT-MALE EQUIVALENTS [h]							
Monthly average								
Labor force	14.6	18.5	23.7	24.9	25.4	14.9	14.7	17.2
Unemployed	0.2	0.5	1.3	5.2	0.1	0.1	1.0	1.5
Employed	14.4	18.0	22.4	19.7	25.3	14.8	13.7	15.7

Source and concepts: Appendix Table A-17, Chapter 3, and Appendix F; *Vierteljahrshefte zur Statistik des Deutschen Reichs*, Berlin, Kaiserliches Statistisches Amt, 1896, Vol. v, Supplement to Vol. 4, pp. 16, 18.

[a] Census months: 1895–1933, April; 1939, May; 1946, October; 1950, September.

[b] Unemployment was adjusted to that within the post-World War I boundaries on the basis of census data. Averages for employment and unemployment are taken to be the same as the census figures for April 1, the assumption regarding unemployment resting on quarterly material for 1910 and 1911. *Statistisches Jahrbuch*, Berlin, Kaiserliches Statistisches Amt, 1912, p. 404.

[c] The rate of joblessness, 1.6 per cent, reported by trade unions was extended to a percentage of the labor force by multiplying it by the ratio of the census to the trade union percentage in 1925, yielding 1.9 per cent or 0.5 million. For conversion of April, to annual idleness, see previous note.

[d] April figures, reported by the census, were multiplied by ratios of average monthly, to April data reported by health insurance schemes for employment and by trade unions for unemployment. *Statistisches Jahrbuch* (Statistisches Reichsamt), *1926*, p. 294; *1935*, pp. 18, 306. *Weekly Report of the Institut für Konjunkturforschung*, Berlin, February 1934, Third Supplement, Appendix D.

[e] For the Federal Republic of Germany, estimates by the Wirtschaftswissenschaftliches Institut der Gewerkschaften include wage and salary workers and exclude the self-employed. May and yearly employment and unemployment were reported by employment offices for the older and for the enlarged territory. *Statistisches Jahrbuch*, 1941–1942, pp. 410, 426. In determining yearly averages the same percentage rate was attached to the Federal Republic of Germany. *Deutschland in Zahlen*, Köln, Wirtschaftswissenschaftliches Institut der Gewerkschaften, 1951, p. 33.

[f] Census data. *Wirtschaft und Statistik*, Wiesbaden, Statistisches Amt des Vereinigten Wirtschaftsgebietes, February 1950, p. 1168.*

[g] Census data. *Statistik der Bundesrepublik Deutschland, Die Berufliche und Soziale Gliederung der Bevölkerung Nach der Zählung vom 13.9.1950*, Wiesbaden, Statistisches Amt des Vereinigten Wirtschaftsgebietes, Vol. 36, Part 1, No. 2, pp. 14–15; yearly averages from *Wirtschaft und Statistik*, December 1950, p. 1293,* and January 1952 (Statistisches Bundesamt), p. 7.*

[h] For explanation of the weights used in converting the labor force of women and teen-agers to adult-male equivalents, see text following this table. The same weights were used for the employed and the unemployed.

Adjustment to Adult-Male Equivalents

Aside from differences in productivity based on sex and age, women and children earn less than adult males (1) because they ordinarily command lower hourly rates, even for equal work; (2) because they hold the less desirable jobs; and (3) because they work fewer hours and less regularly. This study does not differentiate the variations in pay due to differences in skill, for though the tendency to be in the labor force may be affected by earnings, there is no expectation that these variations would require separate treatment. The purpose here is to ensure that increases in the proportion of women and children who work for low wages do not produce a deflationary effect on average earnings and thus produce in turn a spurious correlation between the labor force and income. Women and children therefore, are weighted merely according to earnings, whatever may be the reason for their lower rates of pay.

UNITED STATES.

The hourly wages of women appear to have ranged between a tenth and a fourth, and to have averaged a sixth, below those of men in the same work.[1] Women generally have never tended to be in the same work: the fact that they normally aspire to less skilled or responsible jobs, and lose more time than men for sickness, shopping, housework, or courting, and vary somewhat in age, explains why their weekly or annual earnings are still lower. For the three decades between 1890 and 1919, there are no separate records for male and female compensation in all industries, but there are enough data on manufacturing to indicate that the relative average weekly pay of female factory workers remained fairly stable—at about 52–54 per cent of that of males. Since 1919, however, the rise in the ratio of female, to male earnings has been appreciable. The pronounced increase since 1939 is

---

[1] For example, see: wage rates cited for men and women labelers and packers in the paint and varnish industries in eleven large cities in August 1947, or those for general and payroll clerks and hand bookkeepers in fifteen manufacturing industries in 1946, in "Equal Pay for Equal Work for Women," in *Subcommittee of House Committee on Education and Labor, on H. R. 4273, H. R. 4408*, Feb. 10, 1948, p. 12; John H. McNeely, "Salaries in Land Grant Universities and Colleges," processed, Office of Education, Pamphlet No. 23, November 1931, p. 3; A. J. Klein, "Survey of Land Grant Colleges and Universities," processed, Office of Education, Bulletin 9, 1930, pp. 386–389; average hourly earnings of employees in radio, electrical, soap, and meat-packing enterprises, in Temporary National Economic Committee, "Hourly Earnings of Employees in Large and Small Enterprises," Monograph No. 14, 1940, 76th Cong., 3rd Sess., p. 14; median full-time earnings of women in relation to those of men in cotton mills, South Carolina and Maine, 1932, in M. E. Pidgeon, "Variations in Wage Rates under Corresponding Conditions," Bulletin of the Women's Bureau, No. 122, 1935, p. 56.

seen not only in factory payrolls but also in the income statistics for households of workers employed in manufacturing. Table C-8 of this appendix presents the approximations used in weighting women in the labor force to adult-male equivalents. The ratios in other industries may differ somewhat from those in manufacturing, but there is no indication that the latter are not representative.

TABLE C-8

United States:

Average Weekly Earnings of Females as Percentage of Those of Males, Manufacturing Industries, 1889–1949

1889	1899	1909	1919	1929	1939	1949
0.52	0.54	0.54	0.54	0.57	0.58	0.67

Source and explanation: Census of the United States: *1900*, Davis R. Dewey (Special Reports), *Employees and Wages, Manufactures*, Part 4, Vol. x, pp. 29–99; *1920*, Paul F. Brissenden, *Earnings of Factory Workers, 1899 to 1927* (Census Monographs X), p. 85; *1940, Wage or Salary Income in 1939, Population, The Labor Force* (Sample Statistics), pp. 133–136. Maurice Leven, *Income in the Various States: Its Sources and Distribution, 1919, 1920, and 1921*, National Bureau of Economic Research, 1925, p. 79; M. A. Beney, *Wages, Hours, and Employment in the United States, 1914–36*, National Industrial Conference Board, 1936, pp. 48–50; *Handbook of Facts on Women Workers*, Dept. of Labor, Bull. 237, 1950, p. 29. Derivation of percentages: *1889*, median weekly earnings of males and females 16 and older, employed in a selected group of 15 manufacturing industries during the year ended June 1, 1890; *1899–1919*, actual annual earnings of males and females 16 and older in all manufacturing industries combined; *1929* and *1939*, weekly earnings of males and females of all ages in 25 manufacturing industries reporting to the N.I.C.B. (the ratio of female, to male earnings in this group is somewhat above the 53 per cent derived from the census household data on 1939 median wages and salaries of workers employed in manufacturing in March 1940); *1949*, average weekly earnings of male and female production workers in manufacturing industries, reported by the N.I.C.B. for 1948 and by the state departments of labor in Illinois and in New York for 1949. Pertinent data for 1949 were not included in the preliminary reports of the 1950 census, but a current population report for 1947 reveals that median income of females in factories was 62 per cent of that of males. Although in both years the percentages based on the census figures were below those of the N.I.C.B. and of the two states, the relative rise for women was the same.

The relative weekly earnings of children showed still lower ratios to those of men—roughly 30 per cent in manufacturing during 1889–1919 for those under 16, and in all industries in 1939 for those 14–19 who worked 12 months of that year.[2] Throughout 1889–1949, a worker under 20 years of age is therefore given a weight in the labor force which is equal to one-third that of an adult male.

GREAT BRITAIN, CANADA, NEW ZEALAND, AND GERMANY.

In other lands women receive wages three-quarters to nine-tenths of those of men in identical or similar jobs, and earn still less in practi-

[2] Census reports of 1900, 1920, and 1940. See source note to Appendix Table C-9.

cal effect.[3] The ratio of female to male earnings in Britain may have made about the same gain as in this country since before World War I, but throughout the period women's wages have remained at appreciably lower relative levels than those which prevailed in the United States. The percentages of adult-male earnings used in weighting the labor force of females 20 and older in Britain are taken to be 40 in 1911; 50 in 1921, 1931, and 1939; and 60 in 1951, approximating in round numbers and dates the percentages in Table C-9. The proportion used for British workers of both sexes under 20 in all of the decades is one-third.

Canada and Germany furnished no information on the earnings of girls and boys. It is assumed here that the pay of young people was the same, in relation to the earnings of men, as in the United States and Britain. The relative pay of females in Canada and Germany has manifested no definite trend over the years; the earnings of those 20 and older have maintained a constant proportion to the earnings of males: 55 per cent.

Data of New Zealand indicate that women earned slightly over five-tenths as much as men at various times during 1914–1945 and about six-tenths as much in 1949 and 1950. These ratios are not greatly different from those in the other countries, but in New Zealand the percentages for boys and girls are definitely above those in the United States or in Britain, and during the period through 1945 boys and girls here are given weights equal to 45 and 35 per cent, respectively, of those of adult males.

Labor Force Adjustments Considered but Not Made

In connection with our interest in measuring labor supply or input, it would have been theoretically desirable to adjust the decennially enumerated labor force as the current estimates were adjusted: deducting the number of persons who were nominally in the labor force but who were not available for work in the week or month of the enumeration, and adding the number of those who were not nominally in the labor force but who were available at that time. But it so happened in 1930 and 1940—the only years for which the data were available to permit such corrections—that the deductions and additions would have offset each other within a few hundred thousand, too few, in view of the imprecision of the data, to warrant an adjustment. For 1950, it would have

[3] Comparison of wages paid women and men in nonindustrial civil service and post-office jobs, teaching, manual work in distribution and non-manual work in private industry as reported in "Highlights of the British Equal Pay Report, Royal Commission on Equal Pay, 1944–1946," processed, Women's Bureau (United States), January 1947, pp. 1–9; *Statistisches Jahrbuch für das Deutsche Reich, 1927*, Herausgegeben vom Statistischen Reichsamt, Berlin, Reimar Hobbing, p. 321.

TABLE C-9

Average Weekly Earnings of Women and Young People in Manufacturing as Percentages of Those of Males, 4 Foreign Countries, Various Periods, 1906–1951

Great Britain	1906 [a]	1924 [b]	1928 [b]	1940 [c]	1951 [d]
Women 18 and older	38	48	48	47	57
Boys under 21	36	...	...	38	39
Girls under 18	22	...	...	27	34

Canada	1911 [e]	1921 [e]	1931 [f]	1939 [g]	1941 [g]	1942 [g]	1943 [g]	1944 [g]	1945 [g]	1946 [g]
Females 10 and older	53	54	53	58	55	55	57	60	57	55

New Zealand [h]	1914	1939	1945	1949	1950
Adult women	50	52	51	60	61
Boys	47	48	47	57	58
Girls	35	41	39	48	50

Germany	1913 [i]	1925 [i]	1936 [j]	1939 [j]	1947 [k]	1950 [k]
Females	54	58	56	54	55	59

[a] Median ratios to adult males, including persons who worked less or more than full time, based on weekly earnings in 37 manufacturing industries in the United Kingdom in the last pay week of September 1906. *Sixteenth Abstract of Labour Statistics of the United Kingdom*, London, Ministry of Labour, 1925, pp. 99–116.

[b] *Twentieth Abstract of Labour Statistics of the United Kingdom*, 1929, pp. 99–100.

[c] All manufacturing, week ended July 20, 1940. *Ministry of Labour Gazette*, London, November 1940, p. 280, and December 1940, p. 306. The ratios were computed by the U.S. Bureau of Labor Statistics. *Monthly Labor Review*, BLS, September 1947, p. 289.

[d] Based on the last pay week in October 1951. The ratios for government and for all industries, including mining, building, and public utilities—very close to those for manufacturing—are: women, 54 per cent; youths, 42 per cent; and girls, 35 per cent. *Ministry of Labour Gazette*, March 1952, p. 82.

[e] Based on the average wages of employees 10 and over, by sex, in all industries during the twelve months prior to June 1, 1911 and 1921. *Canada Year Book, 1936*, Ottawa, Dominion Bureau of Statistics, p. 801.

[f] Based on the average wages of manufacturing employees 10 and over, by sex, in the twelve months preceding June 1, 1931. In all industries the percentage was 60. *Canada Year Book, 1936*, pp. 802–803.

[g] Based on the average annual wages of manufacturing employees. *Canada Year Book, 1950*, p. 625.

[h] *New Zealand Official Year Book, 1950*, Wellington, Census and Statistics Dept., pp. 720–722.

[i] Average ratios of weekly earnings of unskilled female, to skilled male employees in the textile and the Kartonnagen industries. *Statistisches Jahrbuch, Berlin*, Statistisches Reichsamt, 1927, p. 321.

[j] Ratio of female, to male weekly earnings in manufacturing and mining throughout the period 1936–1943 and in March 1944. No data are available for the Federal Republic of Germany in 1939; therefore, the same ratio was used as for total Germany. *Statistisches Handbuch von Deutschland, 1928–1944*, München Länderrat des Amerikanischen Besatzungsgebiets, 1949, p. 469.

[k] Data refer to the Federal Republic of Germany only. *Statistiches Jahrbuch*, Wiesbaden, Statistisches Bundesamt, 1952, p. 412.

been unsafe to make the net reduction called for by the figures (about a million) considering the unknown volume of additions that would surely have been required to make up for omitted entries—respondents who were not explicit as to their labor force status. Since for 1930 and 1940 these omissions have been estimated by the census to have numbered about a half million, and since the 1950 enumeration yielded 3-½ million fewer in the labor force than did the monthly survey for the same month, the omitted entries may, in fact, have necessitated a net addition.[4] Under the circumstances, it seemed preferable to make no adjustment rather than one that might be in the wrong direction. Nevertheless, it seems worth while to present the following brief discussion of the nature and amount of the counter adjustments that could have been made for 1930, 1940, and 1950.

ADDITIONS.

No correction would have been needed in 1940 and 1950 for new job seekers, mainly ex-schoolboys; in both censuses such inexperienced persons were enumerated separately. They were, however, nominally excluded from all previous censuses, supposedly because they would have been unable to claim a customary occupation. That many youths were thus completely without experience, or would not have been classified in the type of work to which they aspired, may be doubted. Had an adjustment been made, the Durand-Goldfield calculation, that about 0.2 million were wrongly omitted in 1930, would have been accepted. Their estimates for the other omitted entries would have been accepted also—entries presumably omitted because of carelessness or lack of information, totaling 0.4 million in 1930 and 0.5 million in 1940.[5]

SUBTRACTIONS.

No deduction was required for persons unavailable because of strikes, since data of the Bureau of Labor Statistics indicate that work stoppages were negligible in 1930, 1940, and 1950.[6] Nor was it necessary to subtract inmates of institutions from the 1940 and 1950 censuses, as they were not reported in these years as gainfully occupied, but 0.2 mil-

---

[4] Clarence D. Long, *The Labor Force in War and Transition: Four Countries,* National Bureau of Economic Research, Occasional Paper 36, 1952, p. 48 n., and "Statistical Standards and the Census," *American Statistician,* February 1952. See also Morris Hansen's reply and Long's rejoinder in the latter publication, same issue.

[5] *Census of Population, 1940,* Alba M. Edwards, *Comparative Occupation Statistics for the United States, 1870 to 1940,* pp. 12, 16. All data were rounded to nearest 100,000.

[6] *Statistical Abstract of the United States, 1951,* Bureau of the Census. Idleness in man-days was computed as a percentage of working time applied to the entire labor force, and the result was rounded to the nearest 100,000.

lion were believed by Durand and Goldfield to have been erroneously included in the labor force in 1930.[7] Persons with jobs or unemployed, but temporarily unavailable for work, could have been deducted here as reported at each census: In 1930, the ill and the disabled were in Unemployment Classes C and D, and the vacationers, in Unemployment Classes E, F, and G.[8] The 1940 and 1950 enumerations fail to

TABLE C-10

United States:

Labor Force Adjustments Considered but Not Made, 1930–1950

(millions)

	1930	1940	1950
Add:			
1. New workers seeking jobs, not enumerated	0.2	0	0
2. Omitted entries	0.4	0.5	...
3. Gross additions	0.6	0.5	...
Subtract persons counted in labor force, but not available for work:			
4. Strikers	a	a	a
5. Inmates doing institutional work	0.2	0	0
6. Temporarily ill persons		0.5	0.7
7. Disabled or retired persons	} 0.4	0	0
8. Persons on vacation	0.3	0.2	0.3
9. Gross subtractions	0.9	0.7	1.0
10. Net subtractions	0.3	0.2	1.0

Source and explanations: See text of this appendix.

a Negligible.

analyze, by reason for idleness, those who had jobs but were not at work. The numbers ill or on vacation have been approximated here on the basis of the proportions 40 and 20 per cent respectively, derived from *Current Population Reports*.[9] All of the disabled or retired work-

[7] *Census of Population, 1940*, Edwards, *op. cit.*

[8] It is possible that there were additional persons in Classes A and B unemployed who were ill, disabled, or vacationing. Though Class A covered persons who were out of a job, *able* to work, and *looking* for work, and Class B, persons having jobs but laid off without pay (excluding those sick or voluntarily idle), a breakdown disclosed that many named vacation, sickness, and disability in explanation of their idleness. While the enumerators may not always have distinguished between the original, and the current reason for unemployment, it was assumed (1) that Classes A and B covered persons genuinely unemployed in April 1930; and (2) that, where reasons for idleness conflicted with this assumption, the explanations given really explained the *original* cause of idleness. *Census of Unemployment, 1930*, Vol. I, pp. 12–13.

[9] *Current Population Reports, Monthly Report on the Labor Force*, Series P-57, No. 94, Bureau of the Census, April 1950, p. 10.

ers in 1940 or 1950 are presumed to have been reported as not being in the labor force and therefore require no adjustment.[10]

Altogether, the gross numbers (in millions) that could have been subtracted were 0.9, 0.7, and 1.0 in 1930, 1940, and 1950, respectively (Table C-10, line 9). Because the censuses before 1930 offer no criteria for correcting the labor force, and any net adjustments in 1930 or 1940 would, therefore, have been slight it may be that the omitted entries would have nearly balanced the unwarranted inclusions in the earlier years as well, and that the number available for work was substantially reflected by the labor force without adjustment.

[10] *Census of Population, 1950, Employment and Income in the United States, by Regions: 1950*, Series PC-7.

APPENDIX D

Earnings and Income

TABLE D-1

United States:

Annual Wage or Salary per Adult-Male Equivalent Employed in 38 Large Cities, 1899–1949

(dollars of buying power in Chicago in 1929)

	Manufacturing [a]			All Industries [a]	
	1899 [b]	1919 [c]	1929 [c]	1939 [c, d]	1949 [c, d]
	BASED ON LOCAL WORKWEEK				
Atlanta	945	898	996	1,275	1,512
Baltimore	1,092	1,215	1,343	1,497	1,893
Birmingham	. . .	1,080	1,130	1,527	1,754
Boston	1,474	1,125	1,444	1,509	1,829
Bridgeport	1,299	1,282	1,344	1,581	1,903
Buffalo	1,204	1,370	1,585	1,751	2,172
Chicago	1,310	1,459	1,615	1,571	2,249
Cincinnati	1,175	1,196	1,521	1,610	1,950
Cleveland	1,232	1,458	1,757	1,610	2,211
Columbus	1,156	1,303	1,603	1,751	2,079
Dallas	. . .	1,055	1,216	1,471	2,000
Denver	1,569	1,265	1,548	1,652	2,039
Detroit	1,130	1,560	1,865	1,885	2,374
Houston	. . .	1,088	1,328	1,586	2,003
Indianapolis	1,109	1,200	1,417	1,697	2,267
Kansas City	1,384	1,285	1,498	1,650	2,210
Los Angeles	1,327	1,326	1,575	1,608	2,062
Louisville	979	1,134	1,231	1,462	2,037
Memphis	1,062	895	1,101	1,240	1,645
Milwaukee	1,137	1,269	1,684	1,726	2,235
Minneapolis	1,232	1,291	1,461	1,687	2,193
Newark	1,310	1,276	1,477	1,588	2,001
New Haven	1,315	1,099	1,305	1,525	1,828
New Orleans	1,137	1,093	1,110	1,206	1,706
New York	1,467	1,408	1,737	1,533	2,178
Norfolk	. . .	1,178	1,240	1,418	1,534
Omaha	1,322	1,398	1,497	1,614	2,042
Philadelphia	1,261	1,338	1,533	1,572	2,026
Pittsburgh	1,322	1,357	1,495	1,647	1,996
Portland	1,320	1,556	1,461	1,872	2,231
Providence	1,216	1,005	1,208	1,502	1,732
Richmond	879	963	1,136	1,471	1,721
Rochester	1,159	1,266	1,642	1,792	2,186
St. Louis	1,239	1,238	1,420	1,544	2,020
St. Paul	1,166	1,309	1,533	1,665	2,247
San Francisco	1,427	1,430	1,598	1,693	2,162
Scranton	1,218	1,059	1,204	1,562	1,853
Seattle	1,618	1,593	1,552	1,895	2,224
Mean—38 Cities	1,241	1,245	1,432	1,591	2,008

TABLE D-1, *continued*

	Manufacturing [a]			All Industries [a]	
	1899 [b]	1919 [c]	1929 [c]	1939 [c, d]	1949 [c, d]

BASED ON 48-HOUR WORKWEEK [e]

Atlanta	723	816	853	1,391	
Baltimore	846	1,215	1,343	1,796	
Birmingham	. . .	864	951	1,788	
Boston	1,199	1,125	1,444	1,685	
Bridgeport	1,038	1,282	1,268	1,897	
Buffalo	995	1,370	1,585	2,101	
Chicago	1,083	1,459	1,615	1,885	
Cincinnati	941	1,196	1,463	1,885	
Cleveland	986	1,402	1,689	1,933	
Columbus	924	1,229	1,541	1,910	
Dallas	. . .	995	1,081	1,502	
Denver	1,197	1,265	1,548	1,802	
Detroit	863	1,530	1,759	2,263	
Houston	. . .	1,066	1,180	1,730	
Indianapolis	860	1,132	1,337	1,986	
Kansas City	1,126	1,285	1,469	1,799	
Los Angeles	1,116	1,326	1,575	1,838	
Louisville	746	1,031	1,161	1,672	
Memphis	810	795	979	1,295	
Milwaukee	867	1,244	1,559	2,072	
Minneapolis	941	1,291	1,461	1,928	
Newark	1,047	1,276	1,477	1,906	
New Haven	1,052	1,037	1,231	1,786	
New Orleans	867	1,071	951	1,315	
New York	1,213	1,408	1,737	1,752	
Norfolk	. . .	1,133	1,148	1,620	
Omaha	1,026	1,398	1,497	1,761	
Philadelphia	993	1,338	1,446	1,887	
Pittsburgh	1,040	1,207	1,410	1,977	
Portland	1,007	1,556	1,461	2,191	
Providence	972	985	1,162	1,802	
Richmond	671	908	1,052	1,642	
Rochester	957	1,266	1,642	2,150	
St. Louis	1,007	1,238	1,392	1,853	
St. Paul	891	1,309	1,533	1,949	
San Francisco	1,199	1,460	1,598	2,032	
Scranton	960	1,038	1,136	1,829	
Seattle	1,235	1,731	1,552	2,274	
Mean—38 Cities	982	1,218	1,376	1,839	

The 38-city study omitted 1890 and 1910 because of the difficulty presented by the probability of varying degrees of overcount or undercount in the different cities in these years. Birmingham, Dallas, Houston, and Norfolk were not covered by the census in 1900.

Source: Text of this appendix following Table D-7 and notes to Appendix Table C-8; Erika H. Schoenberg and Paul H. Douglas, "Studies in the Supply Curve of Labor: The Relation in 1929 between Average Earnings in American Cities and the Proportions Seeking Employment," *Journal of Political Economy*, February 1937, p. 79; Paul H. Douglas, *The Theory of Wages*, Macmillan, 1934, pp. 276–281; Margaret L. Stecker, "Intercity Difference in Cost of Living in March 1935, 59 Cities," *Research Monograph* XII, *Handbook of Labor Statistics, 1941*, Vol. I,

Notes to Table D-1, *continued*

pp. 98–99, and *Monthly Labor Review*, February 1951, p. 153, Bureau of Labor Statistics.

[a] For adjustment to adult-male equivalents, see text in Appendix C following Table C-7.

[b] Adjusted for cost of living in 1899 compared with 1929, but not adjusted for intercity differences in 1899. The lack of an intercity adjustment in 1899 may not have mattered in view of the fact that the associations between income and labor force in 1919, 1929, and 1939 were almost as high for unadjusted, as for adjusted data.

[c] Adjusted for variations in the cost of living over time and among cities at the same time. Within accuracy limits of living-cost indexes, a dollar of earnings in any of the 38 cities in any year has the same purchasing power as in Chicago during 1929. The adjustments for intercity differences in 1919 and 1929 were made by Paul Douglas (Douglas, *op. cit.*, p. 281; Schoenberg and Douglas, *op. cit.*, pp. 66–67). The adjustments for 1939 and 1949 rest on 1935 and 1941 Work Progress Administration indexes among different cities for a 4-person manual worker's family extended by means of indexes of the Bureau of Labor Statistics for individual cities over time. See: Stecker, *loc. cit.; Statistical Abstract of the United States, 1956*, Bureau of the Census, pp. 325–326.

[d] Annual wage or salary per employed male. Data were given separately for males; no adjustment was made for the lower earnings of boys, since the number employed was not large enough to distort the averages.

[e] Hours data were not available for 1949.

TABLE D-2

United States:
Average Hourly Earnings, Weighted by the Industrial Composition of Employment, 1940–1956

	ANNUAL AND QUARTERLY AVERAGES									
	Current Dollars		1929 Dollars [a]				Current Dollars		1929 Dollars [a]	
	Weighted by Employment in:		Weighted by Employment in:				Weighted by Employment in:		Weighted by Employment in:	
	Given Year	1940	Given Year	1940			Given Year	1940	Given Year	1940
1940	0.63	0.64	0.77	0.78	1947		1.17	1.14	0.90	0.88
I	0.63	0.63	0.77	0.77	I		1.13	1.10	0.90	0.87
II	0.62	0.64	0.76	0.78	II		1.15	1.12	0.90	0.88
III	0.62	0.64	0.76	0.78	III		1.17	1.15	0.89	0.88
IV	0.64	0.64	0.78	0.78	IV		1.21	1.18	0.90	0.87
1941	0.69	0.68	0.80	0.80	1948		1.26	1.24	0.90	0.89
I	0.67	0.66	0.81	0.80	I		1.23	1.20	0.90	0.89
II	0.68	0.67	0.81	0.80	II		1.24	1.22	0.89	0.88
III	0.69	0.69	0.79	0.79	III		1.28	1.25	0.90	0.88
IV	0.71	0.71	0.79	0.79	IV		1.30	1.27	0.92	0.90
1942	0.77	0.76	0.81	0.80	1949		1.31	1.30	0.95	0.94
I	0.74	0.73	0.80	0.79	I		1.31	1.29	0.95	0.93
II	0.75	0.74	0.79	0.78	II		1.30	1.29	0.94	0.93
III	0.78	0.77	0.81	0.80	III		1.31	1.30	0.95	0.94
IV	0.80	0.79	0.82	0.81	IV		1.32	1.31	0.96	0.95
1943	0.85	0.83	0.84	0.82	1950		1.37	1.35	0.98	0.96
I	0.83	0.80	0.84	0.81	I		1.35	1.32	0.98	0.96
II	0.84	0.82	0.83	0.81	II		1.35	1.33	0.98	0.96
III	0.85	0.84	0.84	0.83	III		1.38	1.36	0.98	0.96
IV	0.87	0.85	0.86	0.84	IV		1.41	1.39	0.98	0.96
1944	0.90	0.88	0.88	0.86	1951		1.50	1.47	0.99	0.97
I	0.90	0.87	0.89	0.86	I		1.47	1.43	0.98	0.96
II	0.90	0.88	0.88	0.86	II		1.48	1.45	0.98	0.96
III	0.90	0.89	0.87	0.86	III		1.50	1.47	0.99	0.97
IV	0.91	0.89	0.88	0.86	IV		1.53	1.51	0.99	0.98
1945	0.93	0.92	0.88	0.88	1952		1.58	1.55	1.02	1.00
I	0.92	0.90	0.89	0.87	I		1.56	1.53	1.01	1.00
II	0.92	0.91	0.88	0.87	II		1.57	1.53	1.02	0.99
III	0.94	0.93	0.89	0.88	III		1.58	1.55	1.01	0.99
IV	0.94	0.93	0.89	0.88	IV		1.61	1.58	1.03	1.01
1946	1.03	1.02	0.91	0.90	1953		1.66	1.63	1.06	1.04
I	0.97	0.95	0.92	0.90	I		1.64	1.60	1.06	1.03
II	1.01	1.00	0.94	0.93	II		1.65	1.61	1.06	1.03
III	1.05	1.04	0.90	0.89	III		1.67	1.64	1.06	1.05
IV	1.09	1.07	0.88	0.87	IV		1.68	1.65	1.07	1.05

ANNUAL AND QUARTERLY AVERAGES

	Current Dollars		1929 Dollars [a]			Current Dollars		1929 Dollars [a]	
	Weighted by Employment in:		*Weighted by Employment in:*			*Weighted by Employment in:*		*Weighted by Employment in:*	
	Given Year	*1940*	*Given Year*	*1940*		*Given Year*	*1940*	*Given Year*	*1940*
1954	1.72	1.68	1.09	1.07	1956	1.87	1.83	1.18	1.16
I	1.71	1.67	1.09	1.06	I	1.85	1.81	1.18	1.16
II	1.71	1.67	1.09	1.07	II	1.86	1.82	1.18	1.16
III	1.71	1.68	1.09	1.07	III	1.86	1.83	1.17	1.15
IV	1.73	1.70	1.10	1.09	IV	1.91	1.87	1.19	1.16
1955	1.79	1.75	1.15	1.12					
I	1.77	1.72	1.14	1.10					
II	1.78	1.74	1.14	1.12					
III	1.78	1.75	1.14	1.12					
IV	1.82	1.79	1.16	1.14					

Source, coverage, and discussion of method: text at end of this appendix and the following. Data on hourly earnings cover production and related workers in manufacturing and mining; nonsupervisory employees in railroads, public utilities, trade, laundries and cleaning establishments; all employees, including teachers, in government; and wage and salary employees in agriculture, excluding family workers, owner-farmers, and tenant farmers. The types of earnings include full- and part-time, premium, and vacation pay (but they exclude special bonuses in manufacturing, mining, construction, railways, and public utlities), payroll divided by estimated man-hours of employment in government, and average wage rate without board in agriculture.

General sources were the Bureau of Labor Statistics for manufacturing, mining (except for hours in anthracite coal), public utilities, trade, services; Interstate Commerce Commission for railroads; Anthracite Institute for hours in anthracite coal mining; Bureau of the Census, Bureau of Labor Statistics, and laws and directives for hours in government; Agricultural Marketing Service (Bureau of Agricultural Economics) and the census, for agriculture. Specific references were:

Monthly Labor Review, Bureau of Labor Statistics: *January 1941*, p. 258; *May 1941*, p. 1321; *December 1945*, p. 22; *December 1949*, pp. 699–700; *September 1950*, p. 389; *September 1951*, p. 336; *April 1952*, p. 453; *September 1952*, p. 325.

Survey of Current Business, Department of Commerce: *1942 Supplement*, p. 55; *June 1943*, p. 31; *1947 Supplement*, pp. 54–71; *1949 Supplement*, p. 78; *December 1949*, p. S-15; *September 1950*, pp. S-10, 15 ff.; *February 1951*, p. S-11; *May 1951*, p. S-11; *June 1951*, p. S-15; *February 1952*, pp. S-11, 15; *April 1952*, p. 453; *July 1952*, p. S-11; *October 1952*, pp. S-11, 15; *February and November 1953*, pp. S-11, 15; *June 1955*, p. S-11.

Economic Almanac for 1950, National Industrial Conference Board, pp. 302, 345–347. "Hours and Earnings in the United States, 1932–40," Dept. of Labor, *Bull. 697*, p. 133. *Current Population Reports, Labor Force, Employment, and Unemployment in the United States, 1940 to 1946*, Series P-50, No. 2, pp. 18–23, and *Labor Force*, Series P-50, No. 13, p. 25, and Nos. 63–175. *Labor Force Bulletin, April 1947*, p. 11; *Statistical Abstract of the United States, 1949*, p. 908; *Government Employment, State Distribution of Public Employment in 1949*, Series G-GE49-No. 7, and *in 1950*, Series G-GE50-No. 7; *and Public Employment in July 1950, in October 1951, in April 1952, in May 1953, in October 1953, in October 1954, and in January 1955;* all from the Bureau of the Census.

Data on hours of Employment of Government Workers: Act of June 28, 1940 (Public Law 671), of Oct. 21, 1940 (P. L. 873), May 2, 1941 (P. L. 46), June 3, 1941 (P. L. 100), Feb. 10, 1942 (P. L. 450); S. J. Res. 170, Dec. 22, 1942; War Overtime Pay Act, May 7, 1943 (P. L. 49); War and Navy Depts. Exec. Orders of June 18 and August 20, 1941; Presidential memorandum to heads of all departments and agencies, Dec. 23, 1942, establishing general minimum work schedule of 48-hour week; Ismar Baruch, "The Federal Employees Pay Act of 1945," *Public Personnel Review*, October 1945, pp. 201–212.

[a] For description of adjustment for changes in the value of the dollar, see Table D-4, note *c*.

TABLE D-3

Canada:

Average Hourly Earnings, Excluding Agriculture and Government, Weighted by the Industrial Composition of Employment, 1945–1956

	ANNUAL AND QUARTERLY AVERAGES			
	Current Dollars		1929 Dollars [a]	
	Weighted by Employment in:		Weighted by Employment in:	
	Given Year	1945	Given Year	1945
1945	0.68	0.68	0.69	0.69
I	0.68	0.68	0.70	0.70
II	0.68	0.68	0.70	0.70
III	0.68	0.68	0.69	0.69
IV	0.67	0.67	0.68	0.67
1946	0.70	0.70	0.69	0.69
I	0.68	0.68	0.69	0.69
II	0.69	0.69	0.68	0.68
III	0.70	0.70	0.68	0.68
IV	0.73	0.73	0.70	0.70
1947	0.79	0.79	0.71	0.71
I	0.76	0.76	0.72	0.72
II	0.78	0.78	0.71	0.71
III	0.80	0.80	0.71	0.71
IV	0.83	0.83	0.70	0.70
1948	0.90	0.90	0.70	0.70
I	0.86	0.86	0.70	0.70
II	0.88	0.88	0.70	0.70
III	0.91	0.91	0.70	0.70
IV	0.93	0.93	0.71	0.71
1949	0.96	0.96	0.73	0.73
I	0.95	0.95	0.72	0.72
II	0.96	0.96	0.73	0.73
III	0.97	0.96	0.72	0.72
IV	0.97	0.97	0.73	0.73
1950	1.01	1.01	0.74	0.74
I	0.99	0.99	0.74	0.74
II	1.00	1.00	0.74	0.74
III	1.01	1.01	0.73	0.73
IV	1.03	1.03	0.73	0.73
1951	1.12	1.13	0.74	0.74
I	1.06	1.07	0.73	0.74
II	1.10	1.10	0.73	0.74
III	1.14	1.15	0.73	0.74
IV	1.17	1.18	0.75	0.75
1952	1.23	1.24	0.80	0.80
I	1.20	1.21	0.77	0.78
II	1.23	1.24	0.80	0.80
III	1.23	1.24	0.80	0.80
IV	1.23	1.26	0.82	0.83

TABLE D-3, *continued*

	ANNUAL AND QUARTERLY AVERAGES			
	Current Dollars		1929 Dollars [a]	
	Weighted by Employment in:		Weighted by Employment in:	
	Given Year	1945	Given Year	1945
1953	1.30	1.31	0.86	0.86
I	1.28	1.29	0.84	0.85
II	1.30	1.30	0.86	0.86
III	1.31	1.31	0.86	0.86
IV	1.32	1.32	0.86	0.86
1954	1.34	1.35	0.88	0.88
I	1.34	1.35	0.88	0.88
II	1.35	1.36	0.88	0.89
III	1.34	1.35	0.87	0.88
IV	1.34	1.35	0.87	0.88
1955	1.38	1.39	0.90	0.91
I	1.36	1.37	0.89	0.89
II	1.38	1.39	0.90	0.91
III	1.38	1.39	0.90	0.91
IV	1.39	1.40	0.90	0.91
1956	1.45	1.46	0.93	0.94
I	1.42	1.42	0.92	0.93
II	1.45	1.45	0.94	0.94
III	1.46	1.47	0.93	0.94
IV	1.48	1.49	0.93	0.94

Source, coverage, and discussion of method (see also text of this appendix following Table D-7) : Data on hourly earnings cover wage earners in manufacturing, mining, construction, services, transportation, and trade; they do not cover those in government and agriculture. The types of earnings are: gross hourly earnings for manufacturing, mining, construction, and services; hourly rates in local transportation (chiefly street and electric railway) ; and hourly earnings, computed from weekly salaries, for trade. The general sources were the Dominion Bureau of Statistics and the Department of Labour, Ottawa. See *Annual Review of Employment and Payrolls in Canada; Eighth Census of Canada, 1941*, Vol. VI, pp. 578–593; *Canada Year Book, 1948–1949*, pp. 677–678; and *Canadian Statistical Review*, monthly issues beginning with October 1953; all from the Dominion Bureau of Statistics. See also *The Labour Gazette*, monthly issues beginning with January 1946; and *Annual Report on Wage Rates and Hours of Labour in Canada*, beginning with 1948; both from the Department of Labour.

[a] Adjusted for changes in the purchasing value of the dollar on the basis of the index of the Dominion Bureau of Statistics for urban wage earners in cities. *Canada Year Book, 1925*, p. 752; *1945*, p. 898; *1946*, pp. 861–863; *1954*, p. 1049. *Monthly Bulletin of Statistics* (New York, United Nations) : *March 1949*, p. 156; *January 1956*, p. 140; *January 1957*, p. 140.

TABLE D-4

Personal Disposable National Income, 5 Countries, Various Periods, 1890–1951

	Per Adult-Male Equivalent Employed [a] *Three-Year Averages* [b]						
	1890	*1900*	*1910*	*1920*	*1930*	*1940*	*1950*
United States							
Current dollars	533	579	827	1,401	2,048	1,825	3,776
1929 dollars [c]	1,011	1,203	1,418	1,486	2,079	2,293	2,701
			1911	*1921*	*1931*	*1939*	*1951*
Great Britain							
Current pound sterling			144	321	240	261	487
1929 pound sterling [c]			245	229	252	274	338
1929 United States dollars [c]			1,190	1,135	1,224	1,332	1,644
				1921	*1931*	*1941*	*1951*
Canada							
Current Canadian dollars				1,489	1,373	1,441	3,120
1929 Canadian dollars [c]				1,354	1,426	1,651	2,225
1929 United States dollars [c]				1,340	1,411	1,634	2,203
			1901	*1926*	*1936*	*1945*	*1951*
New Zealand							
Current New Zealand pound sterling			117	323	206	425	751
1929 New Zealand pound sterling [c]			214	321	248	369	524
1929 United States dollars [c]			1,040	1,564	1,206	1,798	2,552

	Post-World War I Boundaries without the Saar					*Federal Republic of Germany without Berlin*	
	1895	*1907*	*1925*	*1933*	*1939*	*1939*	*1950*
Germany							
Current Reichsmark	1,574	1,836	2,469	2,559	2,939	3,061	3,910
1929 Reichsmark [c]	3,248	3,243	2,679	3,154	3,603	3,736	3,084
1929 United States dollars [c]	780	779	643	759	866	899	742

TABLE D-4, *continued*

			Per Capita Three-Year Averages [b]				
	1890	1900	1910	1920	1930	1940	1950
United States							
Current dollars	157	170	262	474	644	539	1,297
1929 dollars [c]	298	354	449	502	654	677	928
			1911	1921	1931	1939	1951
Great Britain							
Current pound sterling			48	110	80	94	188
1929 pound sterling [c]			82	79	84	99	131
1929 United States dollars [c]			401	382	409	481	636
				1921	1931	1941	1951
Canada							
Current Canadian dollars				432	404	431	953
1929 Canadian dollars [c]				393	419	493	679
1929 United States dollars [c]				389	415	488	673
			1901	1926	1936	1945	1951
New Zealand							
Current New Zealand pound sterling			42	114	70	153	254
1929 New Zealand pound sterling [c]			77	113	84	133	177
1929 United States dollars [c]			375	550	407	648	862

	Post-World War I Boundaries without the Saar					Federal Republic of Germany without Berlin	
	1895	1907	1925	1933	1939	1939	1950
Germany							
Current Reichsmark	492	600	886	769	1,071	1,153	1,284
1929 Reichsmark [c]	1,016	1,059	962	948	1,313	1,407	1,013
1929 United States dollars [c]	244	255	231	228	316	338	243

TABLE D-4, *continued*

	Per Adult-Male Equivalent Employed Census Years						
	1890	*1900*	*1910*	*1920*	*1930*	*1940*	*1950*
United States							
National Unstandardized for Farm-Nonfarm Composition of Employment							
Current dollars	530	634	886	1,915	1,960	1,894	3,951
1929 dollars c	1,035	1,275	1,417	1,545	2,054	2,370	2,808
National Standardized for Farm-Nonfarm Composition of Employment							
Current dollars	723	749	965	2,038	2,046	1,894	3,830
1929 dollars c	1,412	1,507	1,544	1,644	2,144	2,370	2,722
Farm							
Current dollars	156	302	499	965	614	783	2,557
1929 dollars c, d	306	577	776	652	654	991	1,598
Nonfarm							
Current dollars	869	864	1,085	2,315	2,415	2,180	4,158
1929 dollars c	1,697	1,756	1,738	1,921	2,528	2,726	2,988

	1911	*1921*	*1931*	*1939*	*1951*
Great Britain					
Current pounds sterling	139	311	223	267	507
1929 pounds sterling c	236	226	248	277	329
1929 United States dollars c	1,146	1,096	1,206	1,349	1,597

	1921	*1931*	*1941*	*1951*
Canada				
Current Canadian dollars	1,449	1,288	1,523	3,289
1929 Canadian dollars c	1,358	1,437	1,659	2,170
1929 United States dollars c	1,345	1,423	1,642	2,148

	1901	*1926*	*1936*	*1945*	*1951*
New Zealand					
Current New Zealand pounds sterling	117	323	244	455	874
1929 New Zealand pounds sterling c	214	321	283	391	557
1929 United States dollars c	1,040	1,565	1,379	1,904	2,715

	Post-World War I Boundaries without the Saar					Federal Republic of Germany without Berlin	
	1895	*1907*	*1925*	*1933*	*1939*	*1939*	*1950*
Germany							
Current Reichsmark	1,556	1,906	2,469	2,365	3,123	3,061	4,153
1929 Reichsmark c	3,208	3,367	2,679	3,086	3,814	3,736	3,369
1929 United States dollars c	771	806	643	741	917	899	809

For source and concept, see text of this appendix following Table D-7 and:
United States: Survey of Current Business, Dept. of Commerce: *National Income Supplement, 1951,* pp. 146, 151, 209; *February 1952,* p. S-5; and *July 1952,* pp. 14–

APPENDIX D

Notes to Table D-4, *continued*

15, 30. *Historical Statistics of the United States, 1789–1945,* Bureau of the Census, pp. 14, 99, 233–234. Simon Kuznets, *National Income and Its Composition, 1919–1938,* 1941, pp. 137, 147, and *National Product since 1869,* 1946, p. 119, National Bureau of Economic Research. *Economic Report of the President,* January 1957, p. 136.

United Kingdom: Arthur L. Bowley, *Wages and Income in the United Kingdom since 1860,* London, Cambridge University Press, 1937, p. 83. A. R. Prest, "National Income of the United Kingdom, 1870–1946," London, *Economic Journal,* March 1948, pp. 58–59, Table II. J. N. R. Stone, "The Measurement of National Income and Expenditure," *Economic Journal,* September 1947, p. 286. *National Income Statistics, 1938–1947,* New York, United Nations, 1948, p. 103, Table 3. *Monthly Digest of Statistics, July 1947,* p. 123, Table 133, and *January 1949,* p. 123, Table 146; *Annual Abstract of Statistics, 1937–1947,* p. 221, Table 254, *1952,* pp. 241, 269, 273, *1953,* p. 269, *1954,* pp. 247, 250, Table 325, and *1955,* p. 242. All from the Central Statistical Office, London. *Statistical Abstract for the United Kingdom, 1913 and 1918–1931,* London, Board of Trade, pp. xiii, 115, 130, and *1913 and 1924–1937,* p. 153.

Canada: Colin Clark, *The Conditions of Economic Progress,* London, Macmillan, 1951, p. 54. *Canada Year Book, 1921,* p. 647, Table 28, *1946,* p. 863, Table 3, *1947,* p. 1001, Table 2, *1948–1949,* pp. 1093–1094, Tables 3 and 4, and *1952–1953,* pp. 1084–1085; *Canadian Statistical Review,* April 1952, pp. V, 6, 22; *Estimates of Labour Income in Canada, May 1949,* p. 2, *December 1950,* p. 2, and *May 1953,* p. 2; all from the Dominion Bureau of Statistics, Ottawa. *Monthly Bulletin of Statistics,* New York, United Nations, *March 1949,* p. 156, Table 63, and *August 1952,* p. 136, Table 54.

New Zealand: Clark, *op. cit.,* p. 148. *New Zealand Official Year Book, 1902,* p. 476, *1928,* p. 581, *1939,* pp. 483, 674, 805, *1945,* p. 512, *1947–1949,* pp. 414, 1108–1110, *1954,* p. 874; *Official Estimates of National Income and Sector Accounts, 1938–39 to 1953–54,* p. 24; and *National Income Statistics, 1938–1947,* p. 76, all Wellington, Census and Statistics Dept.

Germany: *Wirtschaft und Statistik,* Wiesbaden, Statistiches Bundesamt, 1952, Vol. IV, pp. 192, 243 *. *Statistisches Jahrbuch,* Berlin, Statistisches Reichsamt, *1927,* pp. 458, 482–483, Table 24; *1933,* p. 494; *1938,* p. 331; *1939–1940,* pp. 339, 576, 579; *1941–1942,* p. 605; *1952* (Wiesbaden, Statistisches Bundesamt), p. 375. *Statistisches Handbuch von Deutschland, 1928–44,* München, Länderrat des Amerikanischen Besatzungsgebiets, 1949, pp. 556, 601. *Deutschland in Zahlen,* Köln, Wirtschaftswissenschaftliches Institut der Gewerkschaften, 1951, pp. 134–135; *Einzelschriften zur Statistik des Deutschen Reichs, Das Deutsche Volkseinkommen vor und nach dem Kriege,* Berlin, No. 24, pp. 31–32, 64–68, 83–85. Maxine Y. Sweezy, *The Structure of the Nazi Economy,* Harvard University Press, 1941, p. 204; Kossuth Kent Kennan, *Income Taxation,* Burdick & Allen, 1910, pp. 104, 129.

[a] For adjustment to adult-male equivalents, see Appendix C, following Table C-7.
[b] Where data were available: averages of the census year and the two preceding years. Where data were not available for these years, income data were based on different years for the following nations:
United States: 1884–1893, 1894–1903, 1904–1913, 1914–1923
New Zealand: 1901–1903, 1925–1926
Germany: 1925; for Federal Republic of Germany without Berlin, 1939, 1949–1950
[c] Conversion of foreign currencies to United States dollars was made at exchange rates of 1929. Adjustment for changes in the purchasing value of the currencies of each nation over time was made on the following bases:
United States: Index of cost-of-living items, variously for working class, wage and clerical, or moderate income families in large cities: *1870–1910,* Paul H. Douglas, *Real Wages in the United States, 1890–1926,* Pollak Foundation for Economic Research, Publication No. 9, 1930, p. 60 (rent was not included during these years). *1920–1950, Historical Statistics of the United States, 1789–1945,* pp. 228–230, 236; *Statistical Abstract of the United States, 1951,* p. 282, and *1956,* p. 324; and *Bulletin* Nos. 375 (1924), and 699 (1941), all from the Bureau of the Census. *Monthly Labor Review,* Bureau of Labor Statistics, September 1935, pp. 819–837. Adjustment for 1929–1950 was based on an implicit price deflator for personal consumption expenditure (*Survey of Current Business, National Income Supplement, 1951,* p. 146).

Notes to Table D-4, *continued*

Great Britain: Index of cost-of-living items of working class families in urban areas. *Guide to Official Sources, No. 1, Labour Statistics,* London, Inter-departmental Committee on Social and Economic Research (rev. August 1950), pp. 14–15. *Nineteenth Abstract of Labour Statistics of the United Kingdom,* London, Ministry of Labour, 1928, pp. 130–134. *Cost of Living of the Working Classes,* London, Ministry of Labour, Report of 1912, Cd. 6955 of 1913. *Monthly Digest of Statistics: Supplement, Definitions and Explanatory Notes, 1950,* pp. 54–55, and *1947,* p. 35; *July 1947,* p. 123, and *January 1949,* p. 123. *Ministry of Labour Gazette,* London, *February 1921,* pp. 69–71, and *August 1947,* p. 255. *Statistical Abstract for the United Kingdom,* Vol. 76, p. 115; Vol. 82, p. 153; Vol. 85, p. 244.

Canada: Index of cost-of-living items for urban wage earners for 1921–1951. *Canada Year Book, 1921,* pp. 646–647, and *1946,* pp. 861–863. *Monthly Bulletin of Statistics, loc. cit. Canadian Statistical Review, April 1952,* p. 22, and *December 1956,* p. 8.

New Zealand: Index of cost-of-living items based on average consumption of the population for 4 or more centers. *New Zealand Official Year-Book: 1945,* pp. 505–506, 512; *1947–49,* pp. 1007–1010; *1954,* p. 874.

Germany: Since 1920, the index of the cost of living has been that of a typical wage earner in urban areas; before 1920 it was based on the price of food. *Wirtschaft und Statistik,* Berlin, Statistisches Reichsamt, *1925,* pp. 159–162; *1935,* pp. 759–762; *1938,* p. 282; *1952* (Wiesbaden, Statistisches Bundesamt), p. 243.* *Statistisches Jahrbuch, 1938,* pp. 331; *1939–1940,* p. 339; *1952,* p. 404.

[a] Adjustment of farm income for changes in the value of the dollar was made on the basis of the Department of Agriculture index covering family maintenance items. The adjustment makes use of wholesale prices for 1890 and 1900. *Historical Statistics of the United States, 1789–1945,* pp. 82, 99, 233–234, and *Economic Report of the President,* January 1957, p. 190.

TABLE D-5

United States:

Personal Disposable National Income, 1940–1956

	Annual and Quarterly Averages, Adjusted for Seasonal Variations [a]			
	Per Adult-Male Equivalent Labor Force [b]		Per Adult-Male Equivalent Employed [b]	
	Current Dollars	1929 Dollars [c]	Current Dollars	1929 Dollars [c]
1940	398	486	467	571
I	388	477	455	559
II	389	475	456	557
III	396	483	466	569
IV	417	509	491	600
1941	472	550	523	609
I	437	531	489	595
II	456	542	509	605
III	485	558	541	622
IV	510	567	552	614
1942	575	605	602	633
I	522	567	561	609
II	555	586	582	616
III	598	624	622	648
IV	626	641	642	657
1943	618	613	629	624
I	611	617	625	631
II	628	617	639	627
III	609	603	619	614
IV	624	615	631	622
1944	677	661	683	668
I	665	657	672	665
II	671	658	678	665
III	681	661	688	668
IV	689	667	694	672
1945	699	667	711	678
I	690	667	698	674
II	698	667	705	674
III	697	660	709	671
IV	712	674	732	692
1946	766	674	795	701
I	736	693	764	719
II	756	702	787	730
III	779	663	808	689
IV	791	639	822	665

TABLE D-5, *continued*

| | Annual and Quarterly Averages, Adjusted for Seasonal Variations [a] | | | |
| | Per Adult-Male Equivalent Labor Force [b] | | Per Adult-Male Equivalent Employed [b] | |
	Current Dollars	1929 Dollars [c]	Current Dollars	1929 Dollars [c]
1947	802	618	831	639
I	789	627	815	648
II	777	609	806	631
III	809	617	841	641
IV	832	617	860	637
1948	875	627	905	648
I	841	615	869	635
II	878	632	907	653
III	891	627	922	649
IV	889	633	920	655
1949	853	618	903	654
I	863	623	899	650
II	857	619	905	654
III	849	615	903	654
IV	844	615	903	658
1950	921	656	968	689
I	892	649	948	690
II	899	650	947	684
III	935	661	977	690
IV	959	664	998	691
1951	983	649	1,013	667
I	956	639	987	659
II	982	650	1,011	668
III	993	654	1,020	671
IV	1,002	651	1,034	671
1952	1,025	661	1,052	679
I	1,000	651	1,027	668
II	1,012	656	1,039	673
III	1,030	661	1,059	680
IV	1,056	677	1,084	695
1953	1,083	694	1,108	710
I	1,060	684	1,084	699
II	1,092	701	1,118	717
III	1,094	697	1,117	712
IV	1,088	693	1,107	712
1954	1,087	694	1,142	729
I	1,075	685	1,125	717
II	1,082	690	1,139	726
III	1,087	693	1,144	730
IV	1,103	706	1,158	741

TABLE D-5, *continued*

	Annual and Quarterly Averages, Adjusted for Seasonal Variations [a]			
	Per Adult-Male Equivalent Labor Force [b]		Per Adult-Male Equivalent Employed [b]	
	Current Dollars	*1929 Dollars* [c]	*Current Dollars*	*1929 Dollars* [c]
1955	1,139	728	1,184	757
I	1,109	711	1,156	741
II	1,135	728	1,181	757
III	1,145	732	1,187	759
IV	1,166	744	1,208	771
1956	1,185	747	1,224	771
I	1,151	737	1,190	762
II	1,181	750	1,219	774
III	1,206	756	1,245	781
IV	1,200	746	1,240	772

Source and concept: See text of this appendix following Table D-7 and notes to Table D-4. Data for the years 1953–1956 are revised (see *Economic Report of the President*, 1957, p. 137).

[a] Seasonally adjusted with indexes which were computed by averaging the ratios of the original figures to four-term moving averages. See Arthur F. Burns and Wesley C. Mitchell, *Measuring Business Cycles*, National Bureau of Economic Research, 1946, pp. 46–50, and text of Appendix B following Table B-7.

[b] For adjustment to adult-male equivalents, see Appendix C, following Table C-7.

[c] For description of adjustment for changes in the value of the dollar, see Table D-4, note c.

TABLE D-6

Canada:

Labor Income, 1946–1956

		Annual and Quarterly Averages, Adjusted for Seasonal Variations [a]			
		Per Adult-Male Equivalent Labor Force [b]		Per Adult-Male Equivalent Employed [b]	
		Current Canadian Dollars	1929 Canadian Dollars [c]	Current Canadian Dollars	1929 Canadian Dollars [c]
1946		300	294	309	303
	I	287	291	295	299
	II	291	287	301	296
	III	302	293	312	303
	IV	320	306	329	315
1947		350	314	357	321
	I	338	322	345	328
	II	341	311	348	319
	III	352	312	359	318
	IV	368	311	375	317
1948		394	309	402	316
	I	373	303	380	309
	II	383	304	391	310
	III	409	316	417	322
	IV	410	313	421	321
1949		422	320	435	329
	I	422	322	433	330
	II	423	322	434	330
	III	426	320	439	329
	IV	418	314	432	325
1950		447	327	461	337
	I	419	314	436	327
	II [d]	460	341	477	353
	III	444	321	457	330
	IV	463	330	475	339
1951		503	331	513	338
	I	472	326	482	333
	II	502	334	512	341
	III	512	330	523	337
	IV	524	334	535	341
1952		551	357	565	367
	I	532	340	546	348
	II	543	352	557	362
	III	552	358	565	367
	IV	575	379	590	389

TABLE D-6, *continued*

	Annual and Quarterly Averages, Adjusted for Seasonal Variations [a]			
	Per Adult-Male Equivalent Labor Force [b]		Per Adult-Male Equivalent Employed [b]	
	Current Canadian Dollars	1929 Canadian Dollars [c]	Current Canadian Dollars	1929 Canadian Dollars [c]
1953	594	390	610	400
I	580	382	593	391
II	600	396	617	407
III	590	386	605	395
IV	603	393	623	406
	Averages of Monthly Estimates			
1953	594	390	611	401
I	585	386	599	395
II	596	394	611	404
III	592	387	609	398
IV	602	393	624	407
1954	601	392	630	410
I	598	392	622	407
II	597	391	625	409
III	598	388	632	410
IV	609	395	639	415
1955	625	406	652	425
I	612	399	642	419
II	625	407	660	430
III	619	403	643	419
IV	641	416	666	431
1956	686	440	708	454
I	649	422	680	442
II	690	447	711	461
III	702	447	716	456
IV	701	442	722	456

Source and concepts: Table D-4 and text of this appendix, following Table D-7.

[a] For method used in adjusting for seasonal variations, see note *a* to Table D-5 of this appendix.

[b] For adjustment to adult-male equivalents, see text of Appendix C following Table C-7.

[c] For description of adjustment for changes in the value of the dollar, see note *c* to Table D-4 of this appendix.

[d] Excluding Manitoba, where no census was taken due to flood conditions.

TABLE D-7

Great Britain:

Annual Personal Disposable Income, 1939–1955

	Per Adult-Male Equivalent Labor Force [a]		Per Adult-Male Equivalent Employed [a]	
	Current Pounds	1929 Pounds [b]	Current Pounds	1929 Pounds [b]
1939	240	249	255	265
1940	260	232	267	238
1941	281	232	282	232
1942	301	247	303	248
1943	310	256	312	257
1944	320	261	320	261
1945	336	271	338	273
1946	359	289	364	293
1947	388	311	392	315
1948	414	311	420	315
1949	436	318	441	322
1950	456	324	460	327
1951	483	313	488	316
1952	532	317	537	320
1953	575	330	581	333
1954	607	341	616	345
1955	653	352	660	355

Source and concept: See following text and notes to Table D-4. "Old Series" 1938–1947; "New Series" 1946–1954. Adjustment was made to reduce the income of the United Kingdom to that of Great Britain, by assuming that Northern Ireland's income was in proportion to its population.

[a] For adjustment to adult-male equivalents, see text of Appendix C. No separate adjustment was made for the earnings of young people. Earnings of the total female working population were adjusted by the ratio of earnings of women 18 and older to the total.

[b] For description of adjustment for changes in the value of the pound, see Table D-4, note c.

Composition and Treatment

The wage or salary coin has two sides: price or cost (to the employer) and income (of the employee). Its price to the employer depends, of course, on the output of labor which, in different places at different times, involves a varying complex of occupations, skills, and paces of work and which, in order to allow for the computation of real labor cost, would have to be translated into man-hours of standard quality and intensity. But this translation is impracticable and unnecessary, for the wage as price, though it helps determine how many workers are hired, can scarcely determine the size of the labor force (unless it can be shown that the number who seek work is significantly affected by the number who are hired). More likely it is the wage as income, in its relation to hours of work and to the standard of living, which can sway the decision of those who ponder the question of seeking employment. The materials on earnings and income to be compared with labor force among areas and over time are appraised in this appendix.

WAGE OR SALARY EARNINGS IN DIFFERENT CITIES AT A GIVEN TIME.

The data on wages and salaries (Table D-1, this appendix) used to test the association of labor force with earnings in 38 large cities in the United States in 1900, 1920, and 1930 derive from payrolls reported by censuses of manufactures for the immediately preceding years: 1899, 1919, and 1929 (Chapter 4, Table 1). They differ in certain respects from wages and salaries reported by households for 1939 and 1949 (the source of data used for these years) in the 1940 and 1950 censuses of population, respectively.

The payroll data are comparatively accurate, in that they rest on records of sums actually disbursed, but they have disadvantages. Covering only factory workers, they neglect four-fifths of the labor force; they do not show an employee's income from other sources, and thereby understate average earnings; and they lump workers together regardless of age, sex, or skill, and consequently vary with the composition of employees at different pay levels.

For 1899, 1919, and 1929, no adjustment could be made for the lack of statistics on income for nonfactory and dual employment. But by weighting women and young people according to relative earnings (Appendix C), it was possible to adjust the payroll figures to earnings per adult-male equivalent, and prevent some of the distortion due to changes in the age and sex composition of the labor force.

For 1939 and 1949, the data on wages and salaries were obtained by census enumerators in household interviews during April 1940 and 1950. This source of figures on earnings also has its disadvantages. It does not reveal profits of employers, fees of the self-employed, or interest, dividends, royalties, and rents—all of which may affect the need or tendency to work (of both actual and prospective members of the labor force). The enumerators must often rely on teen-agers, servants, or landladies, who may relate nothing better than scraps of overheard conversation. They cannot get satisfactory information on earnings from a worker if he does not wish to disclose it or if he has trouble adding figures in his head while the enumerator is tapping his pencil, eager to get on to the next question. They can hardly obtain a full report without having to go into impractical detail.[1] And they are apt to be cluttered with earnings of persons who may have worked only a part of the year as employees and put in the rest as employers or professional practitioners. As a case in point, the figures on annual earnings of farm hands are unusable for this study because of dilution due to the inclusion of many self-employed farmers who worked for other farmers part of the time.

Note that canvasses of households in the censuses of April 1940 and 1950 inquired of each person enumerated (whether employed or idle at the time) what his or her wages, salaries, or commissions had been during the 12 months of the preceding year. Thus the census would report an income for a young woman employed the year before (even though she had ceased work in January 1940 or 1950 to settle down as a housewife or to open a gift shop), but would not report the income of a person not in the labor force before January (though gainfully occupied at the time of the enumeration). Note further that the census reported the labor force activity for early spring, three months after the end, and nine months after the mid-date of the year of the earnings. Such lags offer an advantage, should persons require time to adjust labor force participation to income; but they may lead to tenuous statistical comparisons, should persons really respond immediately to income changes, or if during the interval the income changes are greater in some states or cities than in others. However, the income differentials are substantial and could scarcely change enough in a short period to alter any labor force-income relationship materially.

But the censuses of population for 1940 and 1950 are preferable to the censuses of manufactures. The former provided median earnings, not affected by a comparatively few high incomes. They specify wages

---

[1] However, "the unascertained income is fairly sure to be chiefly in the higher brackets . . . among professional and proprietary groups . . . the total for salaries and earnings of nonfarm workers can be obtained with sufficient precision to make the distribution by size fairly reliable." C. E. Noyes and E. R. Hilgard, "Estimated Income Distribution in Three Surveys of Consumer Requirements," in *Studies in Income and Wealth, Volume Eight,* National Bureau of Economic Research, 1946, pp. 270–271, 277.

and salaries separately for males and females employed 12 months in 1939 or 1949, making it unnecessary to convert the earnings of women and young people to adult-male equivalents. And they are more complete, for the information they obtain in interviews from respondents, who (in theory at least) know all the jobs held during the previous year and can put together a rough total of income including tips and gifts, could never be furnished by an employer for his workers who receive other income or who are on his payroll only part of a day, week, or year.

QUARTERLY AVERAGES OF HOURLY EARNINGS.

Chapter 11 discusses the response of the labor force to quarterly variations in hourly earnings. Hourly earnings do not include dividends, interest, tips, profits of employers, and professional fees. But aside from the influence of premium payments for overtime, they have the merit of not reflecting statistically any variations in full- or part-time unemployment, but of covering, in the United States, the bulk of employees: those in state and local government, service industries, amusement, manufacturing, mining, contract construction, railroads, public utilities, wholesale and retail trade, and farming (except family help and tenants). In Canada they are also fairly comprehensive, but unfortunately do not include earnings of farm and government employees. In both countries, they refer almost entirely to production workers and ordinarily admit overtime premiums and vacation allowances; but they neglect most clerical, supervisory, management, and staff workers, and reject special bonuses or back pay. One series of averages in this study weighted earnings in the various industries according to employees currently on payrolls, and a second, according to employment composition at the start of the period (in order to abstract from shifts between low- and high-wage industries). In the United States the two series were rarely apart by more than 1 to 3 cents per hour, even in the midst of wartime, and in Canada they kept to their common path still more closely (Tables D-2 and D-3 of this appendix). Adjustments were made in both countries for variations in the consumer's price level.

PERSONAL DISPOSABLE INCOME IN THE UNITED STATES.

For decade comparisons in the nation as a whole, incomes were computed for 1920, 1930, 1940, and 1950, and annual average incomes were computed for 1884–1893, 1894–1903, 1904–1913, and 1914–1923. The latter four were each shifted one and a half years so as to center on 1890, 1900, 1910, and 1920 (Table D-4 of this appendix) and, so derived, were very close to unpublished annual estimates made by

Simon Kuznets in 1951. At each of the 7 decade dates, income was divided by the average number of adult-male equivalents employed during the year, and by the average number of adult-male equivalents in the labor force during the year.

Income for 1930–1950—estimated by the Department of Commerce —consisted of wages and salaries, interest and dividends, rents (including those implicit on owner-occupied dwellings) and pay and allowances to the military: they excluded business savings and personal income tax and other payments to the government. Incomes for 1920 were based on Kuznets' calculations of consumer goods expenditures, and were expanded here to include an estimate of personal savings assumed to be, at least during years of peace and fairly high employment, a roughly constant ratio to consumer expenditure: 4.75 (based on an average of 4.7 in 1929 and 4.8 in 1949).[2] In theory, personal disposable income covers such items as honey eaten by the bee-keeper's family, meals consumed by restaurant employees, and the imputed rent a home owner pays himself for living in his own house. They bar capital gains and losses as well as pure transfers (relief, Christmas presents, and gambling earnings), and (insofar as they can be identified) direct proceeds from illegal activities. From these incomes, business savings were taken out by Kuznets, and personal taxes by the author, the latter deductions being based on material of the National Industrial Conference Board.[3] The concept used by Kuznets differed in treatment of rents on owner-occupied houses and subsistence allowances for the armed forces, but it was adapted to comparability with the Department of Commerce series on the basis of relationship during the years when the two series overlapped: 1929–1938.[4] The price adjustments made by the Department of Commerce and by Kuznets relied primarily on indexes of the Bureau of Labor Statistics for broad commodity groups.

Farm income differs here from personal income in that it includes entrepreneurial savings, personal income taxes, and nontax payments to the federal government. Payments to the government, however, have been a real factor only in the last two decades and even then did not greatly affect agriculture. Entrepreneurial savings doubtless merge, in

---

[2] *Survey of Current Business, National Income Supplement*, Dept. of Commerce, 1951. These savings estimates were much lower than those made by Goldsmith, who reclassified personal savings by including part of personal expenditures, such as saving through consumer durable goods. Raymond W. Goldsmith, *A Study of Saving in the United States*, Princeton University Press, 1955, Vol. 1, pp. 353, 357. However, by applying this constant ratio, the estimates for years prior to 1920 were made comparable to those used by the Department of Commerce in later years.

[3] *Economic Almanac for 1948*, National Industrial Conference Board, p. 313.

[4] *Survey of Current Business*, as cited.

the minds of most farmers, with personal savings, so that failure to deduct them might well have turned out for the best. Farm income for 1910–1950—figures of the Department of Commerce—was extended through 1890 on the basis of the N.I.C.B. estimates of realized private production income for agriculture.[5] Conversions to real income rested on a price index of farm living-cost items during 1910–1950 which was computed by the Bureau of Agricultural Economics and on an index of wholesale prices during the earlier period, computed by the Bureau of Labor Statistics. Nonfarm income was the difference between farm and national income. Each set was divided by the average number of adult-male equivalents employed or in the labor force during each decennial year (Appendix C).

Quarterly averages of disposable income for 1940–1955 are comparable, in concept and coverage, to the annual data (Table D-5 of this appendix). They were corrected for seasonal variation by the method of four-term moving averages used for the quarterly averages of the labor force.

PERSONAL DISPOSABLE INCOME IN THE UNITED KINGDOM.

Personal income for 1939 and 1951 as estimated by the Central Statistical Office, omitted corporate profits which were not distributed to stockholders and is further stripped here of income taxes, death duties, and national insurance contributions (Table D-4). The resulting personal disposable income thus comprises profits, interest, rent, income in kind, pay and allowances to the armed forces, social security, and other transfer payments to individuals from government and corporations. The annual income data (Table D-7 of this appendix) for the same period, however, do not exclude death duties and other direct-tax payments. Disposable income for 1911, computed by Arthur Bowley as "the total of incomes that comes into the possession of individuals or corporations in the United Kingdom (less Southern Ireland)," [6] differed from later concepts of income in the United Kingdom and in the United States by omitting taxes paid directly to the government and corporation profits withheld from stockholders. These two items were not approximated by Bowley, but could not have been large in 1911. Since personal income estimates were for the United Kingdom and thus included Northern Ireland, adjustment was made to Great Britain's income by assuming that Northern Ireland's income was proportional to its population. In taking account of changes in the cost of living, it must be kept in mind that the official 1947 index, which

[5] *Economic Almanac for 1948*, p. 249.
[6] A. L. Bowley, *Wages and Income in the United Kingdom since 1860*, Cambridge University Press, 1937, p. 83.

showed a rise of only 29 per cent over 1939, was held down by price controls. This study, guided by Richard Stone's criticism of the official index for 1938–1945,[7] makes an additional computation of real income, using a rise of 60 per cent.

PERSONAL DISPOSABLE INCOME IN CANADA.

Data for 1931, 1941, and 1951 were estimated by the Dominion Bureau of Statistics after deduction of contributions by employers and employees to social insurance or government pension funds, and after further deduction here for individual income taxes. They contain military pay and allowances, net income of unincorporated businesses (including farms), property income, pensions, and charitable contributions to individuals from government and corporations (Table D-4). The figure for 1921 was obtained by using the 1931 estimate by the Dominion Bureau of Statistics as a bench mark and multiplying it by the ratio of Colin Clark's 1921 estimate of national income at market prices (less exports and gold production, plus imports) to his 1931 estimate. The 1911 income was not used, since the figure that Colin Clark secured from R. H. Coats was based on nothing more substantial than impression.[8] Incomes were reduced to constant price by means of the cost-of-living index of the Dominion Bureau of Statistics.

The quarterly averages during 1946–1956 (this appendix, Table D-6) were labor earnings in five fields, plus supplementary labor income, computed by the Dominion Bureau of Statistics. It was not possible to deduct income taxes, or to include property incomes, implicit rents on owner-occupied dwellings, dividends paid to individuals by corporations, or profits and fees enjoyed by small business men and the self-employed.

PERSONAL DISPOSABLE INCOME IN NEW ZEALAND.

Included in personal income here for 1945 were wages and salaries; pay and allowances of the armed forces; social security benefits and pensions; rental value of nonfarm, owner-occupied houses (net of depreciation, mortgage interest, insurance, and maintenance); service and property income of professional men, farmers, and individual traders; and dividends of corporations, assumed to be half of profits (Table D-4). Personal income taxes could be subtracted by averaging the taxes of 1944–1945 and 1945–1946, but contributions to income and

[7] J. N. R. Stone, 'The Measurement of National Income and Expenditure," *Economic Journal*, September 1947, p. 286. "It can be estimated that the [consumer's] price level rose . . . by 57% at market value."
[8] Colin Clark, *The Conditions of Economic Progress*, London, Macmillan, 1951, pp. 55, 58, 59.

pension funds could not. Incomes for 1936 and 1951 were very similar in composition.

Income produced during the period of March 31, 1925–March 31, 1926, as estimated by Clark, was reduced by £3.2 million for income taxes.[9] The estimates for 1901–1903 by Sir Timothy Coghlan, which Clark quoted, refer to average net income produced, less interest on private loans.[10] Neither for 1901–1903 nor for later years could any base be discovered which would allow deduction of profits withheld from shareholders by joint stock companies.

PERSONAL DISPOSABLE INCOME IN GERMANY.

"Privateinkommen" for 1925–1939 comprise wages and salaries (without deduction of employees' contributions to social insurance), returns from agriculture and forestry (counting incomes of self-employed farmers and rents on owner-occupied farm dwellings), incomes from commerce and trade (including earnings in self-employment and in free occupations), and interest on funded debt and rents going to persons (including the implicit rent on owner-occupied dwellings; pensions; insurance benefits; and other transfers). Excluded are employers' contributions to social insurance; undistributed company income; returns from publicly-owned, gainful enterprises, railroads, funded debt, land, and investments of social insurance funds. Personal income taxes were deducted in this study.

Data for 1895 and 1907 derive from national income figures of the German Statistical Office, which extended those of 1913 back to 1891 on the basis of Prussian income-tax assessments, supplemented with the approximations of tax-free income and deductions. The use of this base to extrapolate national income back to earlier years may not have been too risky, for in 1913 income in Prussia was 62 per cent of the German total, and in 1895 and 1907 it bore almost the same relation to 1913 income (51.6 and 79.2 per cent respectively) as analogous data for Saxony. Income taxes, RM 0.3 billion in 1907 and RM 0.1 billion in 1895, were calculated roughly from data of Prussia and other states, there having been no income tax in these two years for the nation. Since the German Statistical Office did not present the national income components, the coverage must be regarded as implicit.

The income data for 1895 and 1907 were reduced for comparison with that after World War I when the following areas, equal to 13.3 per cent of the pre-war territory, were ceded: Alsace-Lorraine, Eupen-Malmedy, northern Schleswig, part of Upper Silesia, almost the entire

[9] *New Zealand Official Year Book,* Wellington, Census and Statistics Dept., 1928, pp. 173 and 759.
[10] Clark, *op. cit.,* pp. 147–148.

province of Posen, West Prussia, the city and hinterland of Memel, the Saar, and Danzig. The adjustment was made on the basis of the ratio, in 1913, between the two sets of national income estimates for the postwar territory (without the Saar) and for the prewar territory (*Statistiches Jahrbuch*, Berlin, Statistisches Reichsamt, 1933, p. 494). The Saar, with a population of about 800,000 persons, was recovered by 1939, but it is not included in these data in order to retain comparability. The territory covered by the data of 1950 (and by the data of 1939 comparable to 1950) consisted of the zones occupied by the United States, Great Britain, and France (54.6 per cent of the area covered by Germany in 1914). Jostock says that there is no material which would allow reduction of the earlier data to comparability with the area of the Bundesrepublik of post-World War II. "A continuous comparison for the entire period . . . has to rely on per capita income figures." [11] No disposable personal income data have been published for the Federal Republic of Germany. These data were estimated on the basis of the increase of the national income of the Federal Republic between 1936 and 1950 and on the basis of published direct tax figures.

[11] Paul Jostock, "The Long-Term Growth of National Income in Germany," in *Income and Wealth*, Series IV, London, Bowes and Bowes for International Association for Research in Income and Wealth, 1955, p. 10.

APPENDIX E

The Concept of Unemployment and Labor Force

"We believe, after all, that nothing is so much disliked as
steady, regular labour; and that the opportunities of idleness afforded by an occupation of irregular employment
are so much more than an equivalent for its anxiety as to
reduce the annual wages of such occupations to below
the common average."

NASSAU W. SENIOR, *An Outline of
the Science of Political Economy*

The Labor Force and Its Components

The concept of *labor force* was developed by the Bureau of the Census
more for demographic, than for economic purposes, but it is surprising how few alterations are required to make it fit the economic notion
of *labor supply*. Of the seven characteristic features of the census' concept, four conform reasonably well with the meaning of marketable
labor:

1. All persons who have jobs or businesses for pay or profit. They
comprise wage and salary earners, salesmen and commission workers,
employers and the self-employed, and even unpaid children or wives
milking cows on the family farm or waiting on customers in the family
store, provided the products of their labor are sold.

2. Employees of government, and private nonprofit institutions.[1]

3. Both the employed and the unemployed. The former are persons
who are occupied as described in point 1; the latter, those who are not
so occupied but are seeking work.

4. All persons who are working or seeking work at any time during
the week with reference to which the labor force is surveyed. (Since
1940 the censuses of the United States have classified individuals on
the basis of their employment status in a given week. However, through
1930, and in Canadian censuses as late as 1941, persons were grouped
according to *whether,* but not precisely *when* they had a customary
occupation. This is still true in other countries.)

The other three particulars of the census' concept differ from the
idea of economic labor supply:

5. The census includes in the labor force persons who are inactive—

---

[1] The censuses of 1850 and 1860 included students aged 16 and older even
though they were not gainfully employed. Solomon Fabricant, "The Changing Industrial Distribution of Gainful Workers: Comments on the Decennial Statistics,
1820–1940," in *Studies in Income and Wealth, Volume Eleven,* National Bureau of Economic Research, 1949, p. 11.

the employed who are ill, on vacation, or weather-bound, and the unemployed who are ill if it is reported that they would otherwise be seeking work. From an economic point of view none of these inactive people should be counted in the current labor supply, since they are not immediately available for productive effort.

6. Before 1940, the census excluded from the labor force (in theory, but not necessarily in practice) people who were seeking employment for the first time and who could not, therefore, claim a customary occupation. The practice since 1940 of including such persons is sound from an economic point of view since they represent a supply of labor even if they are inexperienced.

7. The census has never questioned job seekers on the amount of pay or the type of work they desire or on the kind of jobs they can fill. Yet these preferences and abilities are related to their "willingness" and "ability" to work—in other words, their employability.

But the meaning of unemployment and its relation to employability must be clarified before a reasonably accurate boundary can be drawn to mark off the labor force from the great range of leisure and nongainful activities that lies outside it.

Status of the Concept of Unemployment

Actually, the concept of unemployment furnishes less a boundary than a battleground on which economic and social philosophies are still fighting. This can be seen clearly in the literature on the subject, which falls into three main groups.[2]

The first can hardly be said to have defined unemployment at all; for the writings ranged from implying that the unemployed tend to be unemployable (because they demand higher wages than they are worth) to letting the idle person determine his own status,[3] merely stipulating that a person must first have been a gainful worker, i.e. a member of the labor force, in order to be classified as unemployed. In the local surveys this untidiness of concept persisted well into the Great Depression.

The second group, largely theoretical, has tended to characterize the unemployed as persons willing and able to work but not working. The writers have differed from one another not only in their treatment of such knotty problems as are presented by strikers, the self-employed, family workers, persons temporarily sick or laid off, part-time workers,

[2] Some of the rest of this appendix is a revision of part of the author's article on "The Concept of Unemployment," which appeared in the *Quarterly Journal of Economics* in November 1942 (pp. 1–20). The article refers to the rather extensive literature underlying the present section.

[3] *Occupations at the Twelfth Census* (Special Reports), Bureau of the Census, 1904, pp. ccxxv–ccxxvii, ccl–cclii.

and inexperienced job seekers, but also in their interpretation of willingness and ability to work. Some have conceded that a person's *ability* to work may depend on whether conditions in the labor market are those of a normal, depressed, or booming economy. Others ignore the question of ability, but have insisted that a person's *willingness* to work depends on the wages specified. Even these authors vary widely in the meanings they attach to the term "wages." They speak of wages demanded by the workers, wages that prevail at any given moment, wages that are "reasonable," wages that are not so high as to price the worker out of the market, or wages of a kind not specified. Their theoretical definitions of unemployment have therefore been incomplete, vague, and conflicting.

The third, or statistical group also defines the unemployed as those who term themselves willing and able to work, but the writings vary according to the test applied by the writer himself. And some apply no test at all. Then there are those who use as the criterion the fact that the person is *usually working* or would be if jobs were available. Still others ask if the person is *seeking work*, a question that was included in the United States censuses of 1940 and 1950 and in the monthly sample surveys of the labor force in this country and in Canada. But the censuses, as we have noted, and the surveys usually accept the respondent's statement that the idle person is willing and able to work and is seeking employment, regardless of the economic conditions which may affect his willingness and ability. Are these concepts of unemployment and labor force useful for studying how the labor force responds to economic influence? The answer lies in the meaning of employability and in certain problems of disguised unemployment, such as part-time idleness, the fringe desire to work, and substandard productivity.

Employability

A really rigorous definition of employability must examine carefully the meaning of its components—the willingness and ability to work. Many theoretical, and all statistical definitions give the impression that willingness to work is what mother love ought to be—independent of the character and mood of the subject and of the attractiveness of the object. Ability to work is also usually regarded as an absolute. Yet both of these attributes may be subject to numerous factors—wage rates, non-wage income, working conditions, the cost of living, the difficulty and expense of getting a job,[4] and the outlook for future employment.

[4] Many persons who would be glad to work for current wages under current conditions lose their willingness to work when confronted by fatiguing, embarrass-

The usual statistical practice—of sample surveys as well as the regular censuses—is to let the respondent and the enumerator decide on the worker's employability. The enumeration treats the subject as employable (by classifying him as unemployed) not only if he is seeking work but also if he is not, when it is reported that he would be if work were available. The alternative to this method is to study job histories of the unemployed, an expensive and futile process, since millions of marginal employables are young people who have no histories worth analyzing. Also the judgments of employers necessarily relate to particular jobs; and even a congress of personnel managers could rarely be certain that there was no job in the economy which a particular worker could fill, however sub-standard he might appear to be from many points of view. And employers are apt to be influenced by circumstances—those who would not hire a poor worker during a depression might be glad to do so in wartime.

But the current practice is also far from satisfactory. Some people who may regard themselves as employable may not be in the eyes of the law or of public opinion. Children, for example, might be banned from employment by organized labor when there were not enough jobs for adult men, or by age restrictions in some occupations. Very few children aged 10 to 13 were reported in the labor force in 1930; and they were not enumerated in 1940 or 1950.[5] The 400,000 youths aged 14 to 17 who were unemployed in 1940 and the approximately 225,000 who were unemployed in 1950 might well be kept in a separate classification.

There has been little agreement on the issue of classifying strikers as involuntarily unemployed. Some economists argue that a strike is a refusal of labor to accept going wages and that the resulting idleness is voluntary. But collective bargaining between large unions and big business firms tends to be a power struggle between quasi-monopolies; it provides no precise standard of the "rightful" wage and therefore no

---

ing, expensive, and discouraging job-hunts. The possible relation of labor supply to the attainment of employment applies especially to young women of the middle class, college students, and reasonably well-off married women.

[5] There may not have been many children aged 10–13 in gainful employment in 1940 because jobs were so scarce in cities and because the number of unemployed adults on farms was probably so great that there was no extensive need for child labor in rural areas. By 1950, however, a special sample survey by the Bureau of the Census for the Department of Labor yielded an estimate of over a million children 10–13 working in August, and over 700,000, or about 8 per cent of the population of that age, in October when school was in session. Approximately 40 per cent were working as unpaid family labor for 15 hours or more a week and 60 per cent were working for pay. Most of the latter worked a substantial number of hours per week. More than a tenth of the children 10–13 who were working during the school term were not enrolled in school. *Caution: Children under 14 at Work*, Dept. of Labor, January 24, 1951, pp. 1–4.

indication that strikers are either genuinely, or voluntarily unemployed.[6]

Generally, strikers were reported as unemployed by the census of 1930. The 1940 and 1950 censuses classified most of them in the "with job but not at work" category (employed), and some of them in the "other and unknown" categories. The problem of whether or not strikers are unemployed is further complicated because they do not normally seek work at their regular occupations; they may not look for other work if there is only one industry in their locality or if they expect the strike to be short. Local and special surveys have occasionally included strikers but usually have not classified them. Fortunately, strikes are rarely a major cause of idleness.

The individual's opinion is apt to vary with economic conditions. He may not have the knowledge or emotional stability to distinguish between normal and abnormal conditions, or he may lose self-confidence after a prolonged and fruitless search for work. Or if he were near the margin of employability he might have described himself as unable to work or as too old in 1940, when jobs were tight, because he could not find employment. Two years later, when jobs were plentiful, he might have decided that he was employable after all. It is even conceivable that an employable worker could become unemployable simply as a result of a long period of poverty or unemployment itself.

Actually, there is little evidence that poverty and unemployment are the cause of any extensive disability in this country.[7] Some even hold that the decline in mortality among the whole population during the Great Depression indicates a general improvement in health. However, Collins and Perrott definitely challenge this assumption, pointing out that the most important causes of illness are not the most important causes of death, and that the ratio of illness to death averages more than 100 to 1.[8] Moreover, the great lag between sickness and death could make the drop in mortality a result of the previous prosperity. The 1950 census revealed that the proportion of people who said they were unable to work had decreased since 1940 (as had unemployment) from 5.2 to 4.1 per cent of the population aged fourteen and

[6] Strikers have usually been excluded from unemployment benefits under joint agreement, trade union compensation plans, and unemployment compensation systems in the United States.

[7] For some light on this question, see the eight-city survey made in 1932 by the Public Health Service and the Milbank Memorial Fund, summarized by S. D. Collins and G. S. Perrott, in "The Economic Depression and Sickness," *Proceedings of the American Statistical Association,* March 1934.

[8] *Ibid.,* p. 47.

older [9]—a reduction of 1.25 million disabled persons. And considering the growing number of older persons, who are naturally more subject to disability, the relative decline is accentuated. Thus standardizing the proportion in 1950 according to the age and sex composition of the population unable to work in 1940 reduces the 1950 percentage to 3.6 and brings the decrease in the number of disabled up to 1.8 million. However, such comparisons must be made with caution, for the way in which the census enumerators' questions are posed, or replies tabulated, has much to do with the results. To illustrate: a woman who says she is unable to work may mean that she is too busy caring for young children.[10] These data suggest that a depression may well cause significant increases in disability. But they do not throw a clear light on whether the increases are actual or the spurious result of relying on respondents' opinions which are conditioned by the ease or difficulty of getting and holding jobs. It is suspected that most of the increase is due to the latter.

Thus unemployment as measured in persons willing and able to work may theoretically vary according to economic conditions. The variation would reflect the net effect of two speculative countermovements. One would be the addition of job seekers who are pressed into the labor market by a reduction in family income; the other, the exodus of comfortably situated persons who are normally employable but who may be currently discouraged by the obstacles in the course of a job-hunt, or by depression wages and job conditions. Some economists believe that during depressions the labor force gains more workers than it loses.[11] Woytinsky, for one, has tried to show statistically that the addition of secondary workers accounts for an important part of the general volume of unemployment.[12] However, his method has been

[9] *Census of Population: 1940,* Vol. IV, *Characteristics of Persons Not in the Labor Force,* p. 17; *1950,* Vol. II, *Characteristics of the Population,* p. 99. Some data were reported in the 1930 census also, but since no real attempt was made to count persons unable to work among those not in the labor force, the figures were absurdly low—about a tenth of those in 1940 or 1950.

[10] The dubious reliability of these statistics is disclosed by the discrepancy between the 1950 decennial census, which reported 4.6 million persons unable to work, and the *Current Population Reports,* which found only half this number for the same month, using an almost identical questionnaire. The latter count was, of course, still further below the census of 1940. There were no data on age available from the current reports' enumeration at this writing, but even the distribution by sex varied as between the two census reports for the same month.

[11] *Testimony of Leon Henderson before the Temporary National Economic Committee,* Part 1, *Economic Prologue,* 75th Cong., 3d sess., 1938, p. 162.

[12] W. S. Woytinsky, *Additional Workers and the Volume of Unemployment in the Depression,* Social Science Research Council, Pamphlet Series No. 1, 1940, pp. 1, 17, 26.

criticized by Humphrey on the ground that the results are due to assumption—specifically, that Woytinsky concerned himself only with persons entering the labor market and overlooked persons who were withdrawing.[13]

It has not been proved that depressions cause a net increase in the labor supply. The evidence so far has been to the contrary.[14] Indeed, Chapter 10 of this volume shows that the Great Depression tended to bring about a moderate net decrease.

Hidden Unemployment

PART-TIME EMPLOYMENT.

Census figures are designed to show the number of persons employed regardless of hours actually worked. For example, in the week ending May 14, 1949, the census reported 60.2 million persons in civilian employment, distributed by hours worked in class intervals. Time "lost," both willingly and unwillingly, by the persons who spent less than a full-time workweek (assumed here to be 42 hours) at their jobs, was the equivalent of 7.4 million persons absent 42 hours a week; the aggregate overtime (some persons worked an 80- to 90-hour week) was the equivalent of 8 million extra workers.[15]

In some months, measurement by hours has had a significant effect on the employment figure, e.g. the number of employed persons was 1.1 million greater in February 1951 than in May 1949, but measured in 42-hour equivalents it was 2.3 million less. True, the difference resulted mainly from seasonal variations due to illness and vacations.

PART-TIME UNEMPLOYMENT.

Except for the Voluntary Registration of 1937, a few special surveys, and some census surveys which, until recently, were scheduled only

---

[13] D. D. Humphrey, "Alleged 'Additional Workers' in the Measurement of Unemployment," *Journal of Political Economy*, June 1940, pp. 412–419. See also W. S. Woytinsky, "Additional Workers on the Labor Market in Depressions: A Reply to Mr. Humphrey," *Journal of Political Economy*, October 1940, pp. 735–739.

[14] C. D. Long, *The Labor Force in Wartime America*, National Bureau of Economic Research, Occasional Paper 14, 1944.

[15] The actual full-time week of a large number of people may have fallen below 42 hours. In this week the equivalent part time and the equivalent overtime should have been the same, since the average happened to be the same as the arbitrary figure of 42 hours. The reason for the relatively small discrepancy was that the actual average within each broad hours class was not given and had to be approximated from the mid-points; the census' report of average hours worked was computed from a distribution by single hours of work.

Of course, one person who works 21, and another 63 hours need not be the equivalent in productive efficiency of two persons who each work 42 hours, and one who works 84 hours may not make up for one who does nothing.

occasionally, part-time unemployment has been ignored or it has been merely reflected in data on part-time employment. As we have seen, the 1940 and 1950 censuses and the regular monthly estimates have classified persons as employed if they worked any part of the week of enumeration and reported the hours they worked, and did not report the hours desired or regarded as normal or standard. Yet part-time employment may at times conceal a significant source of involuntary idleness.

The failure to collect and report information on this vital question has been largely due to the difficulties of defining full time, the meaning of which must in general be left up to the worker, whose choice is subject to many outside restrictions. There can, therefore, be no single standard of full time. Depending upon the purpose of the investigation, part-time unemployment may be computed by subtracting the actual hours the worker puts in from the hours he wants currently, or would have wanted to put in if times were normal, the hours that are limited by law, unions, or employers; or the hours that could be sustained in a war emergency.

Part-time unemployment is not, of course, confined to employees working for wages or salary. Non-wage workers, including farmers, unpaid family workers, employers, and the self-employed also suffer involuntary partial idleness not ordinarily reported in the statistics of unemployment.[16] A farmer and his family, say, with little to do in off seasons, may be unable because of isolation or lack of information, to locate nonfarm jobs for which they are suited. Such disguised idleness is never reported in the unemployment statistics, yet these data would be valuable in estimating the amount of labor that might, with skillful management, be made available to the armed forces or to industry.

Occasionally reports have been made since 1947 on partial employment and unemployment; regular reports have been made since 1940 on hours worked by employed persons. An estimate of the number of partially unemployed persons was made for the fifteen scattered months in which the census asked workers employed part time and the unemployed if they wanted full- or part-time work. Although they were not asked the number of hours of work they wanted, the full time desired could be approximated by assuming, arbitrarily, that generally it amounted to 42 hours a week, or the average put in by all persons at work. Converted into full-time equivalents, part-time unemployment ranged from a low of about 2/3 million in November 1950 to a high of 1.2 million in August 1949.[17]

[16] An unpaid family worker could theoretically be counted in the 1940 and 1950 censuses as unemployed, if idle and seeking work.
[17] Regular reports were instituted in February 1955.

FRINGE WORKERS

Fringe workers or the "inactive unemployed" are terms applied to persons who may desire work but do not seek it, believing there is none available. Such persons are classed by the census as being outside the labor force, as are persons who do not want work.

Have there been many inactive unemployed? This question was raised during the 1949 contraction in employment, and again during the contraction of late 1953 and early 1954. (In both instances the census was accused of understating the amount of unemployment.) The census sought the answer by resorting to eight special surveys, conducted between 1946 and 1950.[18]

These surveys, which yielded substantially similar results, have demonstrated how difficult it is to measure accurately the number of borderline unemployed. Regular censuses, asking only a few questions, may not count in the labor force some who are genuinely unemployed. And special surveys, trying to extract the last bit of information, are likely to include a large number of persons who have no more than a nebulous attachment to the labor market. The Bureau of the Census has indicated, "It is probably better to accept the exclusion of small marginal groups from the unemployment estimates rather than probe more deeply and run the risk of including large numbers of persons not actually attached to the labor force." [19] An additional factor has not been mentioned by the census. If adding certain fringe groups now left *out* of the unemployed and labor force classifications is considered, eliminating certain fringe groups now counted *in*, both as employed and unemployed, should also be considered. We have already noted that the census' definition of unemployment is by some criteria very generous, for it admits into the labor force:

1. Some persons who may be physically or temperamentally unemployable.

2. Some persons merely pretending to seek work, possibly in order to collect unemployment insurance.

3. Some persons who wish to work, but for wages and under working conditions that are unrealistic in terms of their abilities.

4. Sick persons who would be seeking work if they were well.

5. Job-seekers who desire only part-time employment.

6. Persons who are about to give up the search for work and leave the labor force.

There is no certainty that the number of such fringe workers is great,

---

[18] For example: *Population, Labor Force Memorandum,* Bureau of the Census, No. 3, June 25, 1948, pp. 3–5.

[19] *Ibid.,* p. 3.

but it may well be as great as the number of fringe workers who are not included in the labor force.

Employment That Is Substandard in Productivity

Persons in jobs that do not utilize their capabilities or that yield no output may in some degree be regarded as representing disguised unemployment.[20] The concept of disguised unemployment must not be so comprehensive as to cover the enormous number of persons who are at all times and in all societies under-utilized by the highest existing standard of efficiency. A sensible concept would cover depression decreases (if any) in output per person or per man-hour employed.[21] There is a fairly common assumption that a depression creates a shift to less productive employment. There are equal grounds for believing that declining profits spur many business firms to get rid of deadwood and make organizational improvements, thus raising the average efficiency of the remaining employees. These conflicting beliefs suggest that a net shift to less productive employment during a depression cannot be assumed; [22] they must be determined by statistical investigation—properly, a study of cyclical fluctuations in productivity. No thoroughgoing study of this kind has yet become available.

Economic Labor Force

Whatever definition of labor force may be needed for sociological, legal, political, or other studies, an ideal one for an economic study should take employment to be the number of persons actually at work (perhaps in terms of time worked or, less satisfactorily, time paid for) and unemployment, the number of persons who are actually seeking

[20] Russell A. Nixon lists the categories of inferior employment as (1) skilled workers in semiskilled and unskilled jobs; (2) workers doing unnecessary work, which makes no addition of goods or services; (3) workers making a bare living on marginal land; (4) workers self-employed on a subsistence basis. *The Problem of Employability: A Consideration of Certain Fundamental Aspects of the Labor Market* (unpublished doctoral dissertation, 1940; manuscript in the Harvard University library), pp. 81–87. J. Douglas Brown has added, in conversation, a fifth class—young persons who are prevented by depression conditions from advancing to jobs in which they would develop skill and a sense of responsibility. See also J. H. G. Pierson, *Full Employment*, Yale University Press, 1941, p. 43.

[21] R. A. Nixon and P. A. Samuelson make the same suggestion: "We would argue the concept of disguised unemployment should not include all deviations from optimal allocation, *but only those which are due to cyclical variations in the level of effective demand.*" "Estimates of Unemployment in the United States," *Review of Economic Statistics*, February 1940, p. 103.

[22] Compare this with Joan Robinson's statement: "In all those occupations which the dismissed workers take up, their productivity is less than in the occupations that they have left. For if it were not so they would have engaged in them already." "Disguised Unemployment," *Essays in the Theory of Employment*, London, Macmillan, 1937, p. 84. This is economic theory at its tautological worst.

work and able to work. Whether willingness and ability to work shall be judged by current or normal labor market standards is a legitimate theoretical question, but it does not seem important in practice. Even in severe depressions the size of the labor force is not much less than in periods of normal or moderately high employment conditions (Chapter 10).

From a strictly economic point of view the present census' concept of the labor force as pointed out in the preceding section and in Chapter 3, has two main operational defects: it includes some persons who are not actually and currently working or available for work and it fails to deal adequately with the problem of part time.

The first defect is remedied in the estimate of the number of persons in the economic labor force in Table E-1 (this appendix). It was computed by adding to the number of persons actually at work in the survey week, the number who were unemployed because of economic factors beyond their control. This is the number of persons who would presumably have been at work if there had been a demand for their service (under conditions that did not alter the supply). During the 8-year period studied, the economic labor force numbered fewer persons than the labor force reported by the census, the difference ranging from 2 to 7 per cent. The main reasons for this difference, and for the variations in the difference, were bad weather and sickness during the winter and vacations—paid or unpaid—in the summer. It should be noted that in the summer months, although the census reports the labor force as rising sharply because of the inflow of students, the *economic labor force* may actually decline because of the vacation exodus of many persons who are normally employed but currently unavailable for productive effort. *But there were no significant variations in the ratio of economic to census-reported labor force between years of recession and years of high employment.*

The second defect of census estimates of the labor force, their failure (admittedly forgivable) to come to grips with the problem of part-time workers, is remedied for rough purposes by converting the number employed into a full-time equivalent (assumed here to be 42 hours per week, about the average hours worked by all the labor force) and adding to it the equivalent full-time unemployment. This economic labor force in full-time equivalents seems to fluctuate more widely from month to month than the census-reported labor force, and again the greater fluctuation appears to be the result of seasonal factors. In February the economic labor force may be below 97 per cent of the census figure. In August there is a sharp rise in the number of persons not at work. In other months there may be a loss of working time because of legal holidays. Aside from these seasonal variations, however, the economic labor force, more strictly speaking, did not seem to have differed greatly from the census-reported labor force during the period, and the ratio of economic, to census-reported labor force did not seem to have responded in any systematic way to either the recession of 1949–1950 or the Korean conflict. The economic labor force was about 1 per cent higher than the census-reported labor force in May 1951 during the Korean operations and in May 1949 during the recession, and about 4 per cent lower in both February 1950 and February 1951.

TABLE E-1

United States:
Adjustment of Census-Reported Unemployment and Labor Force to Arrive at the Number of Persons Unemployed and in the Labor Force for Economic Reasons, 1947–1956

ANNUAL AND QUARTERLY AVERAGES
(*millions*)

	1947					1948			
		I	*II*	*III*	*IV*		*I*	*II*	*III*	*IV*
1) Census-reported unemployment	2.14	2.41	2.31	2.20	1.65	2.06	2.38	2.05	2.02	1.81
2) Add: persons with jobs but not at work because on layoff or not yet called to a new job	0.22	0.15	0.27	0.28	0.16	0.26	0.25	0.30	0.28	0.21
3) Deduct: persons without jobs but unavailable for work because of illness a	0.31	0.30	0.31	0.32	0.30	0.31	0.30	0.31	0.32	0.32
4) Total persons unemployed for economic reasons	2.05	2.26	2.27	2.16	1.51	2.01	2.33	2.04	1.98	1.70
5) Total persons at work	56.99	55.13	57.56	57.15	58.13	57.93	55.99	58.49	57.73	59.52
6) Total persons in the economic labor force (sum of lines 4 and 5)	59.04	57.39	59.83	59.31	59.64	59.94	58.32	60.53	59.71	61.22
Seasonally adjusted										
7) Total persons unemployed for economic reasons	2.05	1.97	2.23	2.18	1.80	2.01	2.03	2.00	2.00	2.02
8) Total persons at work	56.99	55.67	56.99	57.73	57.55	57.93	56.56	57.91	58.31	58.93
9) Total persons in the economic labor force (sum of lines 7 and 8)	59.04	57.64	59.22	59.91	59.35	59.94	58.59	59.91	60.31	60.95

ANNUAL AND QUARTERLY AVERAGES
(millions)

		1949					1950			
		I	II	III	IV		I	II	III	IV
1) Census-reported unemployment	3.39	3.02	3.36	3.71	3.49	3.14	4.43	3.32	2.69	2.14
2) Add: persons with jobs but not at work because on layoff or not yet called to a new job	0.29	0.29	0.29	0.34	0.23	0.21	0.19	0.27	0.21	0.16
3) Deduct: persons without jobs but unavailable for work because of illness a	0.32	0.31	0.32	0.32	0.32	0.32	0.31	0.32	0.33	0.33
4) Total persons unemployed for economic reasons	3.36	3.00	3.33	3.73	3.40	3.03	4.31	3.27	2.57	1.97
5) Total persons at work	57.56	56.88	58.35	56.35	58.68	58.80	56.39	59.29	58.23	61.32
6) Total persons in the economic labor force (sum of lines 4 and 5)	60.92	59.88	61.68	60.08	62.08	61.83	60.70	62.56	60.80	63.29
Seasonally adjusted										
7) Total persons unemployed for economic reasons	3.36	2.50	3.26	3.77	3.95	3.03	3.75	3.27	2.62	2.46
8) Total persons at work	57.56	57.45	57.77	56.92	58.10	58.80	56.96	58.71	58.82	60.72
9) Total persons in the economic labor force (sum of lines 7 and 8)	60.92	59.95	61.03	60.69	62.05	61.83	60.71	61.98	61.44	63.18

TABLE E-1, *continued*

		1951					1952			
		I	II	III	IV		I	II	III	IV
1) Census-reported unemployment	1.88	2.35	1.78	1.68	1.71	1.67	1.98	1.68	1.66	1.37
2) Add: persons with jobs but not at work because on layoff or not yet called to a new job	0.22	0.18	0.24	0.28	0.17	0.26	0.24	0.28	0.32	0.19
3) Deduct: persons without jobs but unavailable for work because of illness [a]	0.33	0.32	0.33	0.34	0.33	0.33	0.33	0.33	0.34	0.33
4) Total persons unemployed for economic reasons	1.77	2.21	1.69	1.62	1.55	1.60	1.89	1.63	1.64	1.23
5) Total persons at work	61.33	59.67	62.03	60.76	62.85	61.92	60.96	62.19	61.06	63.48
6) Total persons in the economic labor force (sum of lines 4 and 5)	63.10	61.88	63.72	62.38	64.40	63.52	62.85	63.82	62.70	64.71
Seasonally adjusted										
7) Total persons unemployed for economic reasons	1.77	1.92	1.66	1.64	1.85	1.60	1.65	1.60	1.66	1.47
8) Total persons at work	61.33	60.27	61.42	61.38	62.23	61.92	61.58	61.57	61.68	62.85
9) Total persons in the economic labor force (sum of lines 7 and 8)	63.10	62.19	63.08	63.02	64.08	63.52	63.23	63.17	63.34	64.32

ANNUAL AND QUARTERLY AVERAGES
(*millions*)

ANNUAL AND QUARTERLY AVERAGES
(millions)

		1953					1954 [b]			
		I	II	III	IV		I	II	III	IV
1) Census-reported unemployment	1.60	1.79	1.48	1.37	1.77	3.23	3.49	3.37	3.23	2.82
2) Add: persons with jobs but not at work because on layoff or not yet called to a new job	0.27	0.22	0.25	0.28	0.33	0.34	0.33	0.42	0.36	0.23
3) Deduct: persons without jobs but unavailable for work because of illness [a]	0.33	0.33	0.33	0.34	0.33	0.34	0.33	0.34	0.34	0.34
4) Total persons unemployed for economic reasons	1.54	1.68	1.40	1.31	1.77	3.23	3.49	3.45	3.25	2.71
5) Total persons at work	62.96	62.54	63.66	62.24	63.40	61.55	61.10	62.17	59.93	63.00
6) Total persons in the economic labor force (sum of lines 4 and 5)	64.50	64.22	65.06	63.55	65.17	64.78	64.59	65.62	63.18	65.71
Seasonally adjusted										
7) Total persons unemployed for economic reasons	1.54	1.46	1.37	1.32	2.10	3.23	3.03	3.38	3.28	3.23
8) Total persons at work	62.96	63.23	63.02	62.86	62.77	61.55	61.78	61.55	60.53	62.38
9) Total persons in the economic labor force (sum of lines 7 and 8)	64.50	64.69	64.39	64.18	64.75	64.78	64.81	64.93	63.81	65.61

TABLE E-1, *continued*

ANNUAL AND QUARTERLY AVERAGES
(*millions*)

	1955[b]					1956[b]			
	I	II	III	IV		I	II	III	IV
1) Census-reported unemployment	2.65	3.30	2.71	2.29	2.32	2.55	2.88	2.70	2.34	2.28
2) Add: persons with jobs but not at work because on layoff or not yet called to a new job	0.22	0.23	0.26	0.15	0.22	0.27	0.24	0.32	0.31	0.22
3) Deduct: persons without jobs but unavailable for work because of illness [a]	0.34	0.33	0.34	0.35	0.35	0.35	0.34	0.35	0.36	0.35
4) Total persons unemployed for economic reasons	2.53	3.20	2.63	2.09	2.19	2.47	2.78	2.67	2.29	2.15
5) Total persons at work	63.30	61.28	63.54	62.84	65.57	64.67	63.38	65.43	63.86	66.01
6) Total persons in the economic labor force (sum of lines 4 and 5)	65.83	64.48	66.17	64.93	67.76	67.14	66.16	68.10	66.15	68.16
Seasonally adjusted										
7) Total persons unemployed for economic reasons	2.53	2.78	2.58	2.11	2.61	2.47	2.42	2.62	2.31	2.56
8) Total persons at work	63.30	61.96	62.91	63.47	64.92	64.67	64.08	64.78	64.51	65.35
9) Total persons in the economic labor force (sum of lines 7 and 8)	65.83	64.74	65.49	65.58	67.53	67.16	66.50	67.40	66.82	67.91

Source: Appendix Table B-1.

[a] An estimate of ½ of 1 per cent of total labor force is based on data reported for 1940–1954. Gertrude Bancroft, "Current Unemployment Statistics of the Census Bureau and Some Alternatives," *The Measurement and Behavior of Unemployment*, Princeton University Press for the National Bureau of Economic Research, 1957, pp. 63–119.

[b] From January 1954 through April 1956 the data were based on the 230-area sample; from May 1956, they were based on the 330-area sample. Through 1953 there were 68 sample areas.

APPENDIX F

Statistical Measures of the Labor Force: Their Content and Comparability

"It is this union of passionate interest in detailed fact with equal devotion to abstract generalization that forms the novelty in our present society. . . . It is the salt that keeps life sweet."

A. N. WHITEHEAD, *Science and the Modern World*

The United States since 1820

The statistics on the labor force in this study derive from two types of survey which are described and appraised in Chapter 3 and referred to throughout the volume: the decennial enumeration of the nation's entire population, and the monthly sample enumeration of 20,000–35,000 interviewed households for population estimates. Both are conducted by the Bureau of the Census by means of interviews in individual dwellings. An alternative source of information—the employment schedules filled out by employers from payroll data—was used only occasonally for comparison.

The household interview has substantial advantages over employers' payroll data in measuring the labor force, just as it has in measuring earnings and income (Appendix D). It eliminates duplication in counting workers. It covers domestic servants, the self-employed, the unemployed, and persons who, though employed, are inactive and not receiving pay—none of whom would be on a business payroll. Moreover, by counting workers in connection with the population, it provides data which allow computation of the rate of participation of various groups classified by age, sex, color, residence, and other factors which affect the statistics on labor force behavior.

The same drawbacks which were discussed in previous chapters apply here. Frequently, when the census agent rings the doorbell, the adults of the family are working or shopping, and answers have to be secured from a fifteen-year-old daughter, or a landlady, not necessarily well posted on whether the subject of the interview is employed, involuntarily idle, laid off, or retired. Even the worker concerned is not always a good source of information about himself. Perhaps he does not know the name of his industry, cannot define it unambiguously, or confuses it with that of his firm. Perhaps he mentions a similar occupation with superior prestige; a high school teacher, anxious for social acceptance but deluded as to how it may best be obtained, may

405

pass himself off as a professor. Perhaps his memory misleads him as to what he did in the previous week, month, or year. Perhaps his response is to some extent suggested by the wording of the questions or the order in which they are put to him. Perhaps his answers are cut short by an interviewer who finds it less confusing, or less time-consuming, to record his own impressions. But household interviews are indispensable in measuring the labor force, and their faults, like those of a new daughter-in-law, must be accepted.

Despite their defects, the United States censuses of the labor force since 1870 have covered with fair uniformity all important groups of people who have been working or seeking work (Table F-1, Part A). They have excluded the retired and the disabled,[1] persons in criminal pursuits (who in any case are not readily identified by house-to-house visits),[2] and students and housewives who do not work for pay. And they have included unpaid family workers and the unemployed. Before 1940 they may have omitted a few new job-seekers (young people from school and college who were inexperienced and did not know what occupation they belonged to),[3] and some who looked upon their work as too incidental—or lowly—to mention.

In 1870 and 1880 the censuses were conducted so haphazardly that their findings were useful only for rough comparison, but before 1870 the data belong to an order of accuracy so inferior as to interest primarily the antiquarian. Discussion commences here with 1820, for the attempts in 1810 to inventory workers by industry "were of little avail . . . and the results, although printed, have but little value."[4]

1820. Only 38.3 per cent of all persons aged 10 and older were recorded as occupied, partly because the enumeration was confined to agriculture, commerce, and manufacturing (including mechanical and hand trades) and partly because, even in these industries, it was guilty of manifest omissions (specially of slaves).[5] The extent of the

---

[1] Specific instructions concerning retired and disabled persons do not appear in the censuses until 1910. *Census of Population, 1910,* Vol. IV, p. 89.

[2] Occasionally disclaiming moral concerns, the census has stressed the practical difficulties of gathering data from those engaged in the seamy modes of livelihood, who will frequently claim some respectable means of support. The fact that bootleggers may have posed as restaurateurs perhaps disposes unofficially of a source of discontinuity during prohibition.

[3] Fabricant doubts that all the new or inexperienced work-seekers were omitted from the census in 1930 or earlier, as Durand and Goldfield assumed. He points out that many would have learned some occupation in school, at odd jobs, or from parents. Solomon Fabricant, "The Changing Industrial Distribution of Gainful Workers: Comments on the Decennial Statistics, 1820–1940," *Studies in Income and Wealth, Volume Eleven,* National Bureau of Economic Research, 1949, pp. 16–17.

[4] Carroll D. Wright and William C. Hunt, *The History and Growth of the United States Census,* S. Doc. 194, 56th Cong., 1st sess., February 24, 1900, p. 38.

[5] Fabricant, *op. cit.,* p. 31, note.

undercount may be deduced from the relatively small number reported as occupied in the larger cities: in Detroit, 1 in 16 out of a total of 1,422 inhabitants; in Albany and Baltimore, 1 in 9 of the populations. An attempt at correction of the United States data has been made by P. K. Whelpton, whose estimate of workers in various services (domestic, personal, and professional), mining, lumbering, and fishing brought the over-all labor force up to 44.4 per cent of the population aged 10 and over. But Whelpton made no allowance for underreporting in the industries covered, and in view of the absurdly low median for fourteen cities—only 13.5 per cent of those aged 10 and over were counted in the labor force—his addition of 6 per cent must also be regarded as inadequate.

1830. This enumeration did not include questions on the labor force.

1840. The coverage of industries was extended in 1840 to include agriculture, mining, trade, navigation, learned professions, and engineering. However, the ratios of the labor force to population in cities remained incredibly low, e.g. 6 per cent of 34,000 residents in Albany, 12 per cent of 102,000 in Baltimore, and 14 per cent of 24,000 in Louisville. Of Detroit's 9,000 residents just 25 workers were reported: 22 in manufacturing, 1 in commerce, and 2 in the learned professions (not counting 6 persons occupied "for revolutionary or military purposes"). Among twenty cities the median percentage was 18.3.[6] Again, Whelpton added a figure for domestic, personal, and professional services; lumbering, and fishing. The addition raised the proportion of those aged 10 and over in gainful occupations from 41.3 to 46.6 per cent but it did nothing to remedy the obvious deficiencies in the groups nominally reported.

1850 and 1860. These enumerations were less adequate than the earlier ones. Both excluded slaves and the former, white females as well, in effect confining the labor force to free males. Whelpton substituted his own interpolations based on the censuses of 1840 and 1870.

1870. The first post-Civil War census, which found 44.4 per cent of those aged 10 and older to be gainfully occupied, did not neglect any sizable groups but obviously it was still not complete. The Census Office (now the Bureau of the Census) itself felt that reconstruction and un-

[6] In 1843 the youthful American Statistical Association complained to Congress that "in returning the people according to their several employments, some of the marshals 'seem to have included the whole population, men, women, and children, in these classes, arranging them, probably, according to the employment of the head of the family, and some seem to have noticed only the males over 21 years of age; others seem to have noticed all who were sufficiently able to perform any service; and, lastly, some seem to have entirely neglected this duty, and have recorded none in some of the employments; and in many counties none are reported to have any employment whatever.'" Wright and Hunt, *op. cit.*, p. 37.

TABLE F-1, Part A

Labor Force Concepts of the Censuses over Time, United States, 1820–1953

	REGULAR DECENNIAL AND MONTHLY SAMPLE ENUMERATIONS					
	Decennial				Monthly Sample	
Coverage as to:	1820–1860 [a]	1870–1930 [b]	1940 [c]	1950 [d]	1940–1945 [e]	1945–1953 [d]
Age [f]	10 and older	10 and older	14 and older	14 and older	14 and older	14 and older
Date of labor force status [g]	vague	vague	March 24–30	week in April	week incl. 15th	week incl. 8th or 15th
Unemployed	yes	yes	yes	yes	yes	yes
Inexperienced work-seekers	no [h]	no [h]	yes	yes	yes	yes
Methods of payment:						
Wages, fees, profits	yes	yes	yes	yes	yes	yes
Room, board, & other goods	yes	yes	yes	yes	yes	yes
Unpaid family labor [i]	yes	yes	yes	yes	yes	yes
Economic status:						
Employees, incl. supervisors	yes	yes	yes	yes	yes	yes
Employers, farmers, self-employed	yes	yes	yes	yes	yes	yes
Corporation officials, paid	yes	yes	yes	yes	yes	yes
Government (incl. armed forces)	yes	yes	yes	yes	yes	yes
Relief workers (WPA, CCC, etc.)	–	–	yes	–	yes, in 1940–1942	–
Inmates of institutions	obscure	yes [j]	no	no	no	no
Persons not working nor seeking work but having job:						
Temporarily ill	obscure	yes	yes	yes	yes	yes
On vacation, paid or unpaid	obscure	yes	yes	yes	yes	yes
On strike	obscure	yes	yes [k]	yes	yes	yes
Laid off temporarily	obscure	yes	yes [k]	yes [k]	yes [k]	yes [k]
Waiting to start new job	obscure	yes	yes	yes	yes	yes

TABLE F-1, Part A, *continued*

| | REGULAR DECENNIAL AND MONTHLY SAMPLE ENUMERATIONS | | | | | |
| | Decennial | | | | Monthly Sample | |
Coverage as to:	1820–1860 [a]	1870–1930 [b]	1940 [c]	1950 [d]	1940–1945 [e]	1945–1958 [d]
Persons not working nor seeking work and having no job:						
Temporarily ill	obscure	yes [1]	yes [1]	yes [1]	yes [1]	yes [1]
Disabled	obscure	no	no	no	no	no
Believe no jobs exist	obscure	yes [1]	yes [1]	yes [1]	yes [1]	yes [1]
Weather-bound	obscure	yes [1]	yes [1]	yes [1]	yes [1]	yes [1]
Part-time work for pay:						
Student or housewife working	m	m	yes	yes	yes	yes
Student or housewife seeking work	obscure	obscure	yes	yes	yes	yes
Industries and occupations:						
Legal [o]	n	all	all	all	all	all
Illegal [o]	no	no	no	no	no	no
Slaves	not in 1850 or 1860	–	–	–	–	–
Armed forces abroad [p]	pr. no	no	no [p]	no [p]	no [p]	no [p]
Sex	free males only in 1850	both	both	both	both	both
Counting of dual job-holders	once	once	once	once	once	once

Source: *1820–1880*, Appendix Table A-1. *Census of 1890, Compendium*, Part 3, p. 382. *Census of Population: 1900*, Vol. II, p. xxxvi; *1910*, Vol. I, p. 310; *1920*, Vol. II, p. 154; *1930*, Vol. II, p. 595; *1940*, Vol. IV, Part 1, pp. 178–182; *1950, Preliminary Reports*, Series PC-7, No. 2, p. 21.

pr. = presumably.
[a] The censuses of 1820 through 1860 were so incomplete as to be of little value. No questions of any kind on the labor force were asked in 1830.

(notes on next page)

Notes to Table F-1, Part A, *continued*

b The 1870 census was the first even to attempt a complete count of occupations, but, owing presumably to the unrest associated with the post-Civil War reconstruction, both population and labor force were almost certainly under-enumerated in the southern states, and possibly in some northern areas as well (see text of this appendix). Women and young people in the labor force may have been undercounted in 1890 and overcounted in 1910, probably because of peculiarities in instructions (see Supplementary Appendix G).

c See text of this appendix and Supplementary Appendix H for discussion on the change in measurement technique, and of its supposed effect for 1940.

d The labor force as reported by the decennial census in April 1950 was below that of the sample survey estimate for the same month by 3.5 million, even though both used the same concept (see text of this appendix).

e The questionnaire used for April 1940 to June 1945 was very similar to that of the 1940 decennial census. The monthly data were subsequently revised upward to make them comparable to the new series begun in July 1945 (see text of this appendix). "Detailed Instructions to Interviewers for Filing Schedule DRS-370C," *Monthly Report of Unemployment*, Federal Works Agency, August 1941. *Sampling Procedures and Method of Operation of the Monthly Report on the Labor Force*, November 1942, and "Enumerator's Instructions for Filing Schedule SS-370 f.," *Current Population Reports, Monthly Report on the Labor Force*, July 1945, and September 20, 1945, No. 39, p. 4, Bureau of the Census.

f These age limits doubtless resulted in the exclusion, except in 1940, of substantial numbers of newspaper delivery boys, or boys and girls working without pay on farms or in stores operated by their parents.

g Although the canvasses usually required a month or more and often referred to some vague period of the recent past, they had the following official dates:

1820, August 7
1840–1900, June 1
1910, April 15
1920, January 1
1930, April 1
1940, March 24–30
1950, April 1

In practice the occupation reported was probably determined by the time of year in which the census was taken. The 1950 census required that the answers to questions must refer to the week preceding the date when the enumerator called—in most households during the first half of April.

h Probably very few persons who were seeking primary work for the first time were left out of the censuses through 1930, for it is likely that most new job-seekers had had some occasional work history and could therefore claim a gainful occupation (see text of this appendix).

i The censuses have always aimed at excluding persons who do home housework or incidental chores. Up to July 1945 this was left to the discretion of the interviewer; thereafter, the number of hours of unpaid work on a family farm or in a family business were reported, and persons working less than fifteen hours in the census week were omitted as part of the editing and tabulating process (see text of this appendix).

j No instruction was given concerning inmates during 1870–1890. In 1900 they were counted as gainfully occupied only if they received a stated wage in addition to board. In 1910–1930 they were included if they had been assigned regular duties.

k Persons laid off were classified as having jobs if they were definitely to return after a specific period: four weeks in the 1940 census,

30 days in the 1950 census and in sample surveys. If no definite period or date had been specified by the employer, the individual was regarded as without a job.

[l] Included if the respondent stated a "usual" occupation (through 1930), or (since 1940) stated he would have sought work, had he been well and believed that work was available.

[m] The specifications were obscure on this matter before 1910. During 1870–1930, working students and housewives could be counted as gainful workers but, except in 1910, the practice was not encouraged "unless the . . . boy or girl . . . is earning money regularly," or unless the student or housewife was spending most of the time in a gainful occupation. Solomon Fabricant notes that censuses in 1850 and 1860 included students aged 16 and older as gainfully occupied, even though they were not paid for studying or not employed part time ("The Changing Industrial Distribution of Gainful Workers," *Studies in Income and Wealth, Volume Eleven*, National Bureau of Economic Research, 1949, p. 11).

In 1900 a working student was regarded as student or worker depending upon which activity took up more of his time (*Census of Population, 1900*, Vol. IV, p. 85). The instructions did not mention working students in 1910, but in 1920 specified that they be classified according to their occupation.

[n] The census of 1820 covered only persons in agriculture, commerce, and manufacturing, and even in these industries skipped large blocks of workers, including slaves. It failed to include workers engaged in services (professional, domestic, and personal), forestry, fishing, and mining. The 1840 census included only persons in mining, agriculture, commerce, manufactures and trade, navigation of the ocean and inland waterways, and learned and engineering professions; it left out domestic and personal services, forestry, and fishing.

[o] Persons in illegal pursuits are barred in theory, but in practice the censuses have probably reported most prostitutes, gamblers, bootleggers, and dope peddlers as being in legal and more reputable callings (see text of this appendix, footnote 2).

[p] Members of the armed forces stationed abroad after 1940, in excess of the normal contingent of 150,000, have been added to the labor force in this study.

TABLE F-1, Part B

SPECIAL SURVEYS MADE DURING THE GREAT DEPRESSION

Coverage as to:	Jan. 2, 1934 Mass.	Feb.–Apr. 1934 Penn.	Jan. 14, 1935 Mich.	Jan. 1936 R.I.	1937 United States Check Census
Age	14 and older	14 and older	15 and older	15 and older	15–74
Date of labor force status	vague	vague	month before enumeration	vague	Nov. 14–20
Unemployed	yes	yes	yes	yes	yes
Inexperienced work-seekers	yes	yes	yes	yes	yes
Methods of payment:					
Wages, fees, profits	yes	yes	yes	yes	yes
Room, board, & other goods	yes	yes	yes	yes	yes
Unpaid family labor	obscure [a]	obscure [a]	yes	yes	no [b]
Economic status:					
Employees, incl. supervisors	yes	yes	yes	yes	yes
Employers, farmers, self-employed	yes	yes	yes	yes	yes
Corporation officials, paid	yes	yes	yes	yes	yes
Government (incl. armed forces)	yes	yes	yes	yes	yes
Relief workers (WPA, CCC, etc.)	yes	yes	yes	yes	yes
Inmates of institutions	no	no	no	no	no
Persons not working nor seeking work but having job:					
Temporarily ill	yes	yes	yes	yes	yes [c]
On vacation, paid or unpaid	yes	yes	yes	yes	yes
On strike	no	yes	yes	yes	no
Laid off temporarily	yes	yes	yes	yes	yes
Waiting to start new job	yes	yes	yes	yes	yes
Persons not working nor seeking work and having no job:					
Temporarily ill	pr. yes	no	yes	yes	yes
Disabled	pr. yes	no	no	yes	no
Believe no jobs exist	pr. yes	pr. yes	pr. yes	pr. yes	yes
Weather-bound	pr. yes	pr. yes	pr. yes	pr. yes	yes
Seasonally idle	pr. yes	no	no	pr. yes	no

TABLE F-1, Part B, *continued*

Coverage as to:	Jan. 2, 1934 Mass.	Feb.–Apr. 1934 Penn.	Jan. 14, 1935 Mich.	Jan. 1936 R.I.	1937 Check Census United States
Part-time work for pay:					
Student or housewife working	pr. yes	yes	yes	yes	yes
Student or housewife seeking work	pr. yes	yes d	yes	yes	yes
Industries and occupations:					
Legal	all	except farm	all	all	all
Illegal	no	no	no	no	no
Armed forces abroad	...	...	...	...	...
Sex	both	both	both	both	both
Counting of dual job-holders	once	once	once	once	once

Source:

Massachusetts: *Report on the Census of Unemployment, Annual Report on the Statistics of Labor*, Massachusetts, Pub. Doc. N 15, November 30, 1934, Part II. The respondent was asked his customary occupation as well as duration of employment.

Pennsylvania: "In general, the emphasis in the present enumeration was on the employment status of workers as demonstrated by their actual employment or availability in the labor market, since it was desired to reflect as accurately as possible the extent and nature of unemployment in a period of severe economic dislocation." Pennsylvania Division of Research and Statistics, State Emergency Relief Administration (*Census of Employable Workers in Urban and Rural Non-Farm Areas of Pennsylvania, 1934*), p. 2.

Michigan: "Age, Sex and Employment Status of Gainful Workers in Five Types of Communities," *Michigan Census of Population and Unemployment*, State Emergency Welfare Relief Commission, December 1936.

Rhode Island: *The Story of the 680,712*, Rhode Island Department of Labor, January 1936.

United States check census: *Census of Partial Employment, Unemployment and Occupation, Final Report*, Vol. IV, *The Enumerative Check Census*, Bureau of the Census, 1937.

pr. = presumably.

ᵃ Not important in Massachusetts because of the small farming population, nor in Pennsylvania because farm areas were not represented in the survey.

ᵇ Unless actively seeking paid employment.

ᶜ The guidance issued to enumerators on the point was obscure and ambiguous. Persons temporarily absent from jobs owing to illness, bad weather, strikes, or vacations were regarded as neither working, nor wanting work, unless actually seeking a job.

ᵈ Unless they indicated that they sought a job solely because other potential workers in the family were unemployed. *Census of Employable Workers in Urban and Rural Non-Farm Areas of Pennsylvania, 1934*, as cited, p. v.

rest in the South may have caused an undercount of about 1.3 million population.[7] In fact, the labor force may have been greater in northern areas than the report showed. In Philadelphia, for example, no more than 80 per cent of the males aged 16–59 were reported as occupied, against 91 per cent for the nation as a whole; and in Detroit (population 80,000), the count was only 10 women workers aged 60 and older and 40 boys aged 10–15 (compared to 146 girls!).

1880. The lack of necessary data on age in the returns for 1880 made it impossible to begin the detailed investigation of the labor force before 1890.

1890–1920. Though reasonable care was used in administering the census from 1890 on, the figures for some decades up to 1920 require adjustments (1) to make uniform the age groupings in 1890–1910; (2) to compensate for a minor undercount in 1890 and an appreciable overcount in 1910 of child and women workers; and (3) to convert the labor force, originally recorded as of June (1890 and 1900) or January (1920) to an April basis (Supplementary Appendix G). The corrections were small and mainly cancelled each other, raising the labor force by a mere 1 per cent of the population of working age in 1890 and 0.2 per cent in 1920, and reducing it by 0.5 per cent in 1900 and 2.5 per cent (mostly teenagers) in 1910.

1930–1950. There were so few working minors aged 10–13 reported by 1930, that the censuses of 1940 and 1950 did not include them in the labor force, though by 1950 it is likely that they were working in significant numbers once again as a result of the high level of employment opportunities. (See Appendix E, footnote 5.) Also dropped from the classification of labor force in 1940 were inmates of jails and asylums —including those who were drawing wages in the manufacture of rope or license plates, for instance. These new practices, however, affected only a few hundred thousand workers at the time. Other changes had more important effects upon the data gathered.

One of these was an improvement in the time-reference, hitherto extremely vague. Beginning in 1940 persons were asked whether they had had a job or had sought one in a certain week, March 24–30. An incidental effect of this innovation was supposed to be the inclusion in the labor force of many persons just out of school and hunting for their first jobs. This group had presumably been overlooked in the enumerations through 1930 because, never having held regular employment, they had too little experience (or imagination) to name an occupation. The main purpose was to eliminate many persons who neither had nor sought work during the reference week but who might have been counted in earlier censuses merely because they had har-

[7] *Historical Statistics of the United States, 1789–1945,* Bureau of the Census, 1949, p. 25.

vested wheat, waited on tables at a resort hotel, or held other seasonal jobs.

To adjust for persons who were supposed to have been overreported by 1940 standards—seasonal workers as they were called—1,156,000 was subtracted from the 1930 labor force figure by John Durand and E. D. Goldfield.[8] This adjustment would not, in any case, have been enough to upset intercensal comparisons. Nevertheless it would seem from the argument in Supplementary Appendix H to have been without very solid foundation.

Another improvement in practice was initiated five years later at the close of World War II. Census technicians suspected that a considerable number of people who had actually been working for pay or profit during some part of the reference week were still being classed as housewives or students, either because their paid labor was very minor or because interviewers, seeing the respondents wearing an apron or reading a book, jumped to the false conclusion that they were not in the labor force. The new schedule led off with a "warm-up" question designed to give a woman a chance to say what she considered her primary occupation. If her reply were, say, that she had been occupied primarily as a housewife, the next question would be: "*In addition*, did you do any work for pay or profit?" If she answered in the negative, the following question was: "Were you looking for work?" Once having gotten off her chest the fact that she regarded herself as a housewife rather than a worker, she presumably would not hesitate to disclose the fact that she had also been active in the past week selling magazine subscriptions, or answering help-wanted ads for beauty parlor work. The census thus undertook to ensure that working housewives, students, and the unemployed were not omitted from the labor force count.

Such was the aim. The actual effect was naturally expected to be obscured by seasonal fluctuations and by impending cut-backs in war production and employment. Therefore, to reveal the effect of the change in technique, the Census Bureau conducted a pretest in April 1945 and thereafter, in the initial month of July, made two calls on identical households, using both old and new schedules.

The change resulted, generally speaking, in increases in the numbers reported as employed and as actively seeking work, and decreases in those classified as inactively unemployed and as not being in the labor force. Subsequently the census used the overlap ratios in various age and sex groups, supplemented by the pretest and by "evidence of other studies," to re-estimate employment and unemployment for each month back to 1940, raising the estimate of labor force for March 30, 1940 by

---

[8] *Census of Population, 1940, Estimates of Labor Force, Employment, and Unemployment in the United States 1940 and 1930*, Vol. IV, p. 2.

1.5 million. This, added to the previous estimated excess of 0.5 million, brought the revised sample results to 2 million above the complete census figure. Some of the intervening monthly figures were increased by larger amounts.[9]

These amendments for 1940–1945 should not escape criticism. First, a less fortunate month for a test than July 1945 would have been hard to choose; the armed forces contained some twelve million men, unemployment was less than a million, and the composition of the civilian labor force by age, sex, and industry was also far from normal. Ratios derived from such an unusual period could not be supposed to apply to the earlier depression years, when as few as 1.3 million were in military camps, when as many as 8 million were idle, and when the occupational and demographic structure of the civilian labor force was more normal (or abnormal in an opposite direction). Second, the overlap between the old and the new data rested upon interviews with members of about 20,000 interviewed households divided into 364 subgroups, some of which, e.g. the unemployed, doubtless comprised no more than a few persons,[10] and must have been subject to enormous errors. Not unmindful of the budgetary limitations under which any statistical agency labors, it is still difficult to understand why the census should have relied upon a small sample overlap, based on one month, to correct data covering sixty months and a full range of seasonal, cyclical, and war and peace variations. The difficulty is not fully resolved by the Bureau of the Census' statement that the overlap was reinforced in some undescribed way by a pretest of unstated size and by "other evidence." [11] Instead of attempting to reconcile the series in this manner would it not have been more sensible (1) to postpone the new schedule to a less hectic time (we were still at war with Japan), and (2) to spread several double-interview canvasses over a few years, taking pains to represent all seasons of the year and various stages of economic fluctuation? The second course would not have been too costly in relation to the $1 million spent each year on sample surveys, and the first would have cost nothing at all.

[9] *Current Population Reports, Labor Force, Employment and Unemployment in the United States, 1940 to 1946*, Bureau of the Census, September 11, 1947, Series P-50, No. 2, pp. 5–6, 9, Tables III, IV. The previous figure was itself a revision of the original estimate of the Work Projects Administration (*Current Population Reports, Monthly Report on the Labor Force*, November 1944, pp. 5–8, 10). The original WPA estimate for which the Census Bureau assumes no responsibility, was 1.4 million above the 1940 census count, though it may have been for mid-April rather than for the last week of March, the date to which the census referred. Oddly enough, the results were much closer in 1940, though the wording of the WPA schedule differed somewhat from that of the census.

[10] This is pure conjecture, since the census does not publish the number of households reporting in these various subgroups.

[11] *Labor Force, Employment and Unemployment in the United States, 1940 to 1946*, as cited, p. 6.

APPENDIX F

THE COMPLETE AND THE SAMPLE ENUMERATION IN APRIL 1950.

The two figures provided by the two types of survey for April 1950 rested on virtually identical questionnaires, and should have differed by no more than a sampling error of a half million; yet the monthly results exceeded the decennial by 3.5 million. Nearly three in six of this number were employed females, two in six were employed youths or men above middle age, and one in six was unemployed. Borderline cases apparently accounted for most of the difference. The estimates of both tallies for persons on full time, especially men aged 25–44, were almost identical. Of the 3.5 million discrepancy, part-time workers accounted for 2.7 million; individuals with jobs but not at work, 0.2 million; and the jobless, 0.6 million.

Census officials do not believe the discrepancy was the result of sampling difficulties, and in support of this position cite similar disparities for a matched sample of 51,000 persons interviewed in both the regular and sample enumerations of April 1940.[12] Rather, it has been attributed to the unqualified 130,000 temporary interviewers employed for the decennial census. The permanent staff, who conduct the sample survey, was a "small, well trained group with, on the average, more than 12 months of specialized experience in the enumeration of the labor force. . . . As was the case a decade earlier, when the monthly survey results were compared with the 1940 Decennial Census data, it appeared that the more skilled interviewers had had greater success in handling the labor force questions for population groups whose activity is difficult to measure and, in consequence, had obtained a more nearly complete count of persons who were employed or looking for work. . . . Both groups of enumerators obtained practically the same result for employed males 25 years of age and over."[13]

It is possible to agree that a skillful sample can come closer to the mark than a less skillful complete count. Still the disparity is disturbing. First, it exceeds any fluctuation in the ratio of labor force to population that has occurred in peacetime since 1890.[14] Second (and this was not explained by the census in pointing to the excess ten years earlier), it went up from 1 per cent of labor force in April 1940 to almost 6 per cent in April 1950, a differential at the latter date of nearly 5 per cent, or roughly 3 million (see footnote 8). Why were the differences on such a lower scale in 1940?

The census has emphasized the fact that the temporary canvasser is hardly an ideal interviewer. Often chosen politically and trained briefly, he is under strong pressure to make "quickie" canvasses be-

[12] Census of Population, 1950 (Special Reports), Employment and Personal Characteristics, Series P-E No. 1A, pp. 16–17.
[13] Census of Population, 1950, Preliminary Reports, Series PC-7, No. 2, p. 1.
[14] See Chapter 12.

417

cause his compensation is at a few pennies per name. So brief are some of the house calls that even at this modest fee, a former official has told the author, enumerators have earned $35 per day. Such agents would scarcely trouble long over stutterers or respondents who recall the events during the census week according to whether it was before or after the visit to Aunt Viola. It is plausible that decennial enumerators have never paid much attention to the elaborate instructions (it has taken the writer a good many years to understand them) and that they have been guided instead by common sense, or by quick impression, i.e. a woman ironing is a housewife—next item! Moreover, the personnel available for temporary work in 1940, when 8 million persons were idle, were doubtless superior to those who could be recruited and retained in 1950, when only 3.5 million persons were out of jobs and when interviewers resigned after finding their earnings were too low to continue.[15] Thus there may have been some deterioration in the practical conduct of the decennial census from 1940 to 1950. At the same time, the sample surveys could, by 1950, have reflected an increase in efficiency gained by experience in the 120 monthly interviews over the decade. They could easily have reported the sampling equivalent of several million extra workers (mostly on part time or unemployed) who in April 1940 would have been left out of the estimate, particularly since the monthly interviews were just beginning and the regular canvassers were only partially rehearsed. Either the new technique had no tendency to switch important numbers of borderline workers into the labor force or, if it had, its theoretical effect in this direction may have been washed out by a possibly greater carelessness of enumeration which resulted in the failure to include many workers in 1950 who would have been covered under the standards of enumeration used in 1940.

The difference between the results of the two labor force counts must also be viewed in the light of their time reference. The sample survey referred to the week ending April 8. The decennial survey began on April 1 and, though two-thirds of the population had been covered by April 15, it was not until the end of April that nine-tenths had been interviewed and the end of June that the count was virtually completed. Since the decennial count in 1950 referred to the week preceding the interviews, it may be said to have had a varying time reference. However, the effect of this variation would not explain the lower figure; on the contrary, the labor force rises seasonally in the spring and the later enumeration of a third of the population should have resulted in a higher figure.

[15] The enumerator first assigned to my own neighborhood quit, so we were informed by the local office, because the homes were too far apart.

YEARS OF SCHOOLING.

The estimates of equivalent full-time years of school completed, underlying Chart 19, were based on three sets of data.

The first set consists of the years of school completed by persons 20 and older as reported for the first time in the 1940 census. These data were projected backward to the earlier censuses by 5-year cohorts. For example, males 70–74 who were enumerated in 1950 as having completed 8 years of education, were assumed to have had the same amount of education in 1930, when they were 60–64; in 1920, when they were 50–54; in 1910, when they were 40–44; in 1900, when they were 30–34; and in 1890, when they were 20–24. And women 40–44 who were enumerated in 1940 as having completed 8.7 years of education, were assumed to have had the same amount of education in 1930, when they were 30–34; and in 1920, when they were 20–24.

This method cannot, of course, provide information on years of school completed by persons too young to have completed their education at the various censuses, nor by persons who were counted by the censuses of 1890–1930, but who died before 1940. For their years of schooling completed, a second set of data were used—e.g., the number of young persons of various ages who were enrolled in school at the various census dates. These statistics, which were summarized in the 1920 census report, cover persons 5–20 by sex and age group for each census back to 1850.

These two types of data made it possible to estimate the nominal years of schooling completed by each five-year age group of males and females from 1890. However, the chief change in educational attainment since 1890 has not been in nominal years of school completed by the average person, but rather in the length of school terms and in actual attendance. This change can be taken roughly into account by means of a third set of data which permit converting each year of schooling into an equivalent full-time school year of 150 days. Data supplied by the Office of Education in the *Statistical Abstract of the United States, 1954* (Bureau of the Census, p. 125), indicate that the average student 5–17, enrolled in elementary and secondary schools, actually attended school about 158 days in 1950; 152 days in 1940; 143 in 1930; 121 in 1920; 113 in 1910; 99 in 1900; 86 in 1890; 81 in 1880; and 78 in 1870. Thus men 70–74 in 1940, in addition to having completed only 8 nominal years of education when they were enrolled in school during the decade or so centering around 1880, had in their youth attended only about 80 days a year and acquired a formal education equal to little more than 4 years of full-time schooling. But women 40–44 in 1940, who had completed 8.7 years of nominal education, had in their youth, around 1910, attended 113 days a year, acquiring a formal education equal to about 6½ years of full-time schooling.

Thus it would seem that the advancing standard of education has benefited the younger persons more than it has the older ones, and, as pointed out in Chapter 9, the ratio of education of the old to that of the young has fallen from about four-fifths at the turn of the century to under two-fifths in 1950.

But granted that the ratio of equivalent full-time years of school completed by the elderly to that of young persons was low in 1940 and 1950, why was it not just as low during 1890 to 1910? The explanation is that the standard of education changed relatively little between 1850 and 1890, so that persons who received their education during these years (and who became the older workers of recent decades) show relatively little increase in educational attainment over those who were elderly around 1900—they received their education before the wave of improvement took place. The younger and middle-aged people of recent decades, on the other hand, were in full position to benefit by the wave—thus the swiftly rising ratio of education of the young and middle-aged to the education of the old.

It is, of course, possible that there are errors in the assumption underlying the method whereby the cohort of males is assumed to have had the same education in 1890, when it was 20–24, as in 1940 when it was 70–74. First, many immigrants of little education entered the country during these fifty years, so that the education of those already here in 1890 must have been somewhat higher than these rough proportions would suggest. Second, many persons of this cohort died, and the survivors in 1940 may not have been entirely representative of those living in 1930, 1920, and 1910, and so on, especially since there seems to have been some tendency for the less well-educated to die at earlier ages. And third, many people doubtless overstate their education to the census taker. These estimates may therefore on balance exaggerate, rather than underestimate, the schooling of people who received their education in the early days.

If there was a variation in the amount of education reported by the same cohort in successive decades, it is rather likely to have been small, for the following comparison shows that those age groups old enough to have completed their education by 1940 reported very similar periods of education in 1950. (Not shown in the comparison are the age groups 20–24 and 25–29 in 1940 which included veterans and others who went on for further schooling, often at government expense. There were small increases in years of education reported by these cohorts in 1950.) The largest variation was a gain of 0.3 years of education for women 65 and older in 1940 who became 75 and older in 1950. But it is at once obvious that the composition of this group must have changed considerably, as an appreciable number of women 65 and older died out of the cohort.

It is also true that the earlier data on days of actual school attendance do not distinguish between males and females; but there is every likelihood that this wave of increase in actual attendance occurred for the females first, so that if adequate adjustment could have been made in this study for differences in actual school attendance by sex, the males would have had still less education to their credit at the turn of the century, compared to females then or now. The reason is that boys, much more than girls, would have been kept at home to help on the farm, in the family store, or in odd jobs for pay. Girls, with less earning power and less physical strength, would have been more easily spared. Indeed abundant instances of this have been related in some of the reports of the state bureaus of labor statistics. And as late as the 1920 census it was reported, "In the whole United States, at each age, a larger proportion among females attends than among males. The differences are slight in the earlier years, increasing to a maximum at 16 and 17 years." (*School Attendance in the United States, 1920, Census Monographs V*, pp. 49–51, 113–114, Tables 30, 31.) Here the census was referring to the number attending at some time during the school year. The census found this to be true for both Negroes and native whites, but apparently not for the foreign born; however, the foreign born of school age were never very numerous. (See also the references to school attendance legislation in Chapter 8 in the section on *Boys and Young Men.*)

Following is a test of the agreement in years of education reported by males and females in ten-year cohorts at the 1940 and 1950 censuses. The center column compares the figure for males aged 34–44 in 1940 with that for males aged 45–54 in 1950, and so on:

| | Years of Education Completed | | Difference between 1940 & 1950 |
	1940	1950	for the Same Cohort
Males			
35–44	8.7		
45–54	8.4	8.7	0
55–64	8.2	8.4	0
65–74		8.1	−0.1
65+	8.0		
75+		7.9	−0.1
Females			
35–44	8.8		
45–54	8.4	8.9	+0.1
55–64	8.1	8.5	+0.1
65–74		8.3	+0.2
65+	7.9		
75+		8.2	+0.3

Young men and women 20–34 were excluded from this particular comparison, because many of them were still attending college and graduate school during the 1940's, and so the excess of the years of school reported in 1950, over that reported in 1940 by the same cohort, would not be a test of accuracy of reporting, but rather a measure of additional years of school acquired by the average member of the cohort during the decade.

Great Britain since 1841

In Britain, as in America, most of the early tallies were incomplete, inaccurate, and vague as to coverage and time reference. The following explains why the censuses of 1801–1831 and 1851–1871 were worthless, and brings together what could be learned from those of 1841, 1881, 1891, and 1911–1951.

1801–1831. The census of 1801 listed only agriculture, trade, manufacturing, handicrafts, and "not employed"; and for these groups there was evidence of gross underreporting. From 1811 through 1831 the same classifications were retained, but whole families were grouped in the same category with no distinction between breadwinners and dependents. And so it was impossible to ascertain how many members of a family were in the labor force and how many were not.

1841. These were the earliest data which were adaptable to this study. Unfortunately some retired persons were included in the labor force under classifications of their former occupations. How great an overcount this amounted to is not known, but with life expectancy shorter in 1841 there must have been fewer older workers at that time than in 1891, when the census classified only 1 per cent of the population as retired. That category could have been offset in 1841 by the excessive numbers classified outside the labor force under "independent means of support." (At least one is entitled to assume so, since 1.4 per cent more individuals were recorded as being in these happy circumstances in 1841 than in 1891.) The two errors are presumed here to cancel each other and therefore to require no correction.

No such offset can be found for the unemployed, a more sizable group, who were not counted in the labor force. To compensate statistically, there is added here a hypothetical 10 per cent based on Thorp's description of 1841 as a depression year with widespread joblessness.[16] This estimate is accompanied by alternative estimates of what the labor force would have been in that year had the involuntary idle been 7 or 13 per cent of the population (Chapter 12, Table 56, lines 11–13).

[16] Willard L. Thorp, *Business Annals,* National Bureau of Economic Research, 1926, p. 161.

1851–1871. These reports lumped the "occupied" and the "unoccupied" together, so the labor force could not be computed.

1881 and 1891. Census coverage was similar to the current practice except that it included in the labor force varying groups of students, paupers under 60, and prison or hospital inmates and classified them under any former trades they may have had. These groups had to be subtracted in the interest of conceptual accuracy and for comparison with other censuses.

1911–1931. Over the period the concept of labor force did not differ materially from that of the United States (Table F-2, Part A, this appendix). The British excluded children under 14 earlier, probably because the need for their labor declined earlier in the less agricultural Britain, and did not stipulate census policy regarding housewives and students employed part time for pay. The United States did not encourage including the two latter classifications unless their gainful occupation was regular and extensive.[17] Also the British census counted, in both the labor force and in the population, the armed forces at sea or stationed abroad. They were left out of the original United States totals, and added here on the basis of department reports.

In Britain, as in this country, the labor force embraced all persons aged 14 and older who were usually gainfully occupied, whether employed in government or private work, self-employed, unemployed, or receiving a wage, salary, fee, profit, or no pay whatsoever (provided the product of their labor was sold). Further similarity was noted in the exclusion from the labor force of the retired and of persons engaged in illegal callings, full-time study, or own housework, and in the vagueness concerning the time element (Supplementary Appendix H).

1939–1952. No official enumeration was made in Britain in the twenty years between June 1931 and April 1951. Estimates for interim years had therefore to be erected upon statistics not originally designed for that purpose: in 1939, those of H. Frankel; and in 1943, 1945, and 1947 those of "working population," compiled in British sources from unemployment insurance registrations, government and civilian agencies, the armed forces, and employers (Appendix B). The working population before 1948 left out women in part-time gainful jobs; men aged 65 and women aged 60 and older; private indoor domestic servants; employers and others in business on their own account; nonmanual employees receiving more than £420 a year; established civil servants; permanent employees of local authorities, railways, and public utility

---

[17] It should be kept in mind that it has never been common for a boy to work his way through high school or college in Great Britain (or in any European country). And few women had worked part time outside the home until after 1939; not a great many have since, in fact, either in Britain or in the United States.

TABLE F-2, Part A

Labor Force Concepts of the Censuses over Time, 4 Foreign Countries, Various Periods, 1841–1952

Coverage as to:	GREAT BRITAIN (ENGLAND, WALES, SCOTLAND), 1841–1952					
	1841	1881, 1891	1911, 1921	1931	1951	1939–1952
Age	10 and older	10 and older	10 or 12 and older [a]	14 and older	15 and older	14 and older
Date of labor force status [b]	vague	vague	vague	vague	vague	vague
Unemployed	no [c]	yes [c]	yes [c]	yes	yes	yes
Inexperienced work-seekers	...	...	...	...	...	no
Methods of payment:						
Wages, fees, profits	yes	yes	yes	yes	yes	yes
Room, board, & other goods	yes	yes	yes	yes	yes	yes
Unpaid family labor	no [d]	yes	yes	yes	yes	yes
Economic status:						
Employees, incl. supervisors	yes	yes	yes	yes	yes	yes
Employers, farmers, self-employed	yes	yes	yes	yes	yes	yes
Corporation officials, paid	yes	yes	yes	yes	yes	yes
Government (incl. armed forces)	yes	yes	yes	yes	yes	yes
Inmates of institutions	yes [e]	yes [e]	yes [e]	yes [e]	pr. no	pr. no
Persons not working nor seeking work but having job:						
Temporarily ill	pr. yes	yes	yes	yes	yes	yes
On vacation, paid or unpaid	pr. yes	yes	yes	yes	yes	yes
On strike	pr. yes	yes	yes	yes	yes	yes
Laid off temporarily	pr. yes	yes	yes	yes	yes	yes
Waiting to start new job	pr. yes	yes	yes	yes	yes	yes
Persons not working nor seeking work and having no job:						
Temporarily ill	pr. yes [f]	pr. yes [f]	pr. yes [f]	yes [f]	...	yes [f]
Disabled	pr. yes [f]	pr. yes [f]	pr. yes [f]	...	...	...
Believe no jobs exist	pr. yes [f]	pr. yes [f]	pr. yes [f]	...	...	...
Weather-bound	pr. yes [f]	pr. yes [f]	pr. yes [f]	...	...	...
Seasonally idle	pr. yes [f]	pr. yes [f]	pr. yes [f]	...	...	...

TABLE F-2, Part A, *continued*

Coverage *as to:*	GREAT BRITAIN (ENGLAND, WALES, SCOTLAND), 1841–1952					
	1841	*1881, 1891*	*1911, 1921*	*1931*	*1951*	*1939–1952*
Part-time work for pay:						
Student or housewife working	...	...	...	no	yes	counted as ½ person
Student or housewife seeking work	...	...	...	...	...	
Industries and occupations:						
Legal	...	all	all	all	all	all
Illegal	...	yes	no	no	no	no
Armed forces abroad	yes	no	yes	yes	pr. yes	yes
Sex	both	both	both	both	both	both
Counting of dual job holders	once	once	once	once	once	once

Source: Census of Great Britain: *1841*, Vol. III, *Occupations; 1851* (condensed form), pp. 56–65. Census of England and Wales: *1881*, Vol. IV, *General Report*, pp. 25–50; *1891*, *General Report*, pp. 35–59; *1911*, *General Report*, p. 97, and *Occupations and Industries*, Part 1, pp. v–cli; *1921*, *General Report*, pp. 85–89; *1931*, *General Report*, pp. 1–2, 104–115; *1951*, *Preliminary Report*, pp. 51–52. Census of Scotland: *1881*, *1911*, *1921*, *1931*. *Statistical Abstract of the United Kingdom*, 1913, 1919–1932, 1924–1937, *Annual Abstract of Statistics*, 1935–1946, No. 84, *Monthly Digest of Statistics*, Nos. 37–42, 1949, and *Definitions of Items and Units in the Monthly Digest of Statistics* (revised January 1947), Central Statistical Office. *National Register*, General Register Office, 1939. *Registrar General's Statistical Review of England and Wales*, 1943, 1945. *Statistics Relating to the War Effort of the United Kingdom*, Ministry of Labour, Cmd. 6564, November 1944, pp. 41–42. *Report for the Years 1939–1946, 1947*, Ministry of Labour and National Service. H. Frankel, "The Industrial Distribution of the Population of Great Britain in July, 1939," *Journal of the Royal Statistical Society*, Parts III–IV, 1945, pp. 392–430. All London.

pr. = presumably.

[a] 10 and older in 1911; 12 and older in 1921.
[b] Official dates of enumeration were:

1841, June 7	1911, April 3	1931, April 26/27
1881, April 4	1921, June 19/20	1951, April 8
1891, April 6		

Annual estimates were made for June 1939–1948.
[c] No specific inquiry as to the unemployed was made before 1931. For 1841, when they were lumped with the residue outside the "occupied," an estimate was used in this study. In 1881–1921 they were counted under their former occupations. Estimates were made for 1911 and 1921, using trade union unemployment data as indexes and unemployment figures reported by the 1931 census as a benchmark.
[d] The data included some family members who had independent means.
[e] Prisoners and inmates of institutions under 60 were listed under their former occupations; those 60 or older were excluded from the labor force. After 1911, the insane and all persons 60 or above were classified as retired.
[f] If the respondent stated a "usual" occupation. Disabled persons in 1841 included retired persons under their former occupations.

TABLE F-2, Part B

Canada, 1911–1952

Coverage as to:	Decennial Enumerations			Sample Surveys
	1911–1931	1941	1951	1945–1952
Age	10 and older	14 and older	14 and older	14 and older
Date of labor force status [a]	vague	vague	1st week in June	varying week [a]
Unemployed	yes [b]	yes [b]	yes	yes
Inexperienced work-seekers	. . .	no	yes	yes
Methods of payment:				
Wages, fees, profits	yes	yes	yes	yes
Room, board, & other goods	yes	yes	yes	yes
Unpaid family labor	yes [c]	yes [c]	yes	yes
Economic status:				
Employees, incl. supervisors	yes	yes	yes	yes
Employers, farmers, self-employed	yes	yes	yes	yes
Corporation officials, paid	yes	yes	yes	yes
Government (incl. armed forces)	yes	yes	yes	yes
Inmates of institutions	no [d]	no	no	no
Persons not working nor seeking work but having job:	pr. yes	pr. yes	yes	yes
Temporarily ill	pr. yes	pr. yes	yes	yes
On vacation, paid or unpaid	pr. yes	pr. yes	yes	yes
On strike	pr. yes	pr. yes	yes	yes
Laid off temporarily	pr. yes	pr. yes	yes	yes
Waiting to start new job	pr. yes	pr. yes	yes	. . .
Persons not working nor seeking work and having no job:	pr. yes [e]	pr. yes [e]	yes [f]	yes [f]
Temporarily ill	pr. yes [e]	pr. yes [e]	yes [f]	yes [f]
Disabled	pr. yes [e]	pr. yes [e]	no	no
Believe no jobs exist	pr. yes [e]	pr. yes [e]	. . .	. . .
Weather-bound	pr. yes [e]	pr. yes [e]	yes [f]	yes [f]
Part-time work for pay:	. . .	. . .	yes	yes
Student or housewife working	. . . [c]	. . . [c]	yes	yes
Student or housewife seeking work	no	no	yes	yes
Industries and occupations:				
Legal	all	all	all	all
Illegal	no	no	no	no
Armed forces abroad	no	no [g]	no [g]	no [g]
Sex	both	both	both	both
Counting of dual job holders	once	once	once	once

Source: *Canada Year Book*, Dominion Bureau of Statistics: *1921*, p. 599; *1929*, p. 140; *1934–1935*, p. 118; *1945* and *1947*, p. 140. Census of Canada: *1911*, Vol. VI, *Occupations*, p. xxvi; *1941*, Vol. VII, *Occupations*, p. 12. *Canadian Statistical Review*, April 1948, p. 15, and *Labour Force Bulletin*, April 1948 and February 1949, Dominion Bureau of Statistics. "Change in Population and in the Labour Force,"

APPENDIX F

Notes to Table F-2, Part B, *continued*

Labour Force Gazette, Supplement, December 1945, p. 18, and *Estimates of the Canadian Labour Force and Its Composition*, Mimeographed, Dept. of Labour, 1941–1947. All Ottawa.

pr.= presumably.

ᵃ Official dates of censuses were: 1911–1931, June 1; 1941, June 2; 1951, June. Annual estimates were made for 1939–1945; annual and quarterly estimates, based on sample surveys, for 1945–1952. From 1945 to the end of 1952, the survey week was typically in early March, early June, mid-August and early November, but sometimes a preceding or subsequent week (see Appendix Table B-6). Since January 1953, the labor force has been surveyed one week each month.

ᵇ Persons with "usual" occupations but unemployed at the time of the census were listed under their occupations when employed. Unemployment in 1911 and 1921 was estimated in this study (Appendix Table C-4).

ᶜ The labor force included family dependents who were engaged in gainful occupations in any capacity, as well as nonschool children who materially assisted their parents outside the home, but it left out school children even though they worked for their parents in the household or on a farm.

ᵈ The 1911 census was not clear concerning inmates of institutions but according to the Director of the Census Division of the Dominion Bureau of Statistics, it may be assumed that they were not regarded as gainfully employed.

ᵉ If the respondent stated a usual occupation.

ᶠ Provided the person would have been seeking employment if he had been well, if he had thought that jobs could be had, and if the weather had been favorable.

ᵍ However, official estimates of armed forces, including those abroad, were added to the civilian population and the labor force for the purpose of this study.

concerns excepted by certificate; teachers; members of H. M. Forces and Women's Services, professional female nurses; police; and farmers' children employed in agriculture.[18] These totals were supplied by calculations based in large part on the ratio, in July 1948, of data from the old working population series, to those from the more comprehensive new social insurance plans. Since the latter registered all wage-earners irrespective of age, and no longer ignored those in better paid, nonmanual callings, private indoor domestic service, or uninsured occupations, they are presumed to measure the total labor force with reasonable accuracy. The June 1948 ratios of the new to the old manpower figures are used here to approximate the number of most of the males and females not in the former series for 1943, 1945, and 1947. However, private domestic servants, men aged 65 and older, and women aged 60 and older required separate computation (Appendix Table B-4).

Extending the school-leaving age from 14 to 15 in April 1947 had no noticeable consequence by June 1947, but had become fully effective a year later.[19]

Canada and New Zealand

CANADA SINCE 1911.

Canada's concept of labor force has also closely resembled that of the United States (Table F-2, Part B). In a formal sense, it has been somewhat more restrictive in that up to 1941 it barred school children, even though they may have worked part time on family farms. It may have been more systematic in ruling out housewives in agriculture, though it shows little difference, actually, so far as unpaid farm women are concerned. On the other hand, it doubtless records many students in summer jobs, since the official census date has been the first part of June (see Appendix Table C-4 for a comparison between the June figure and the annual average). And until recent years, the Canadian instructions may also have been less clear in dealing with the disabled. But in other respects the Dominion Census and Bureau of Statistics have followed American usage, even to the point of adopting, in 1945, a technique similar to the one the United States had initiated in 1940.

NEW ZEALAND, 1896-1951.

This Commonwealth has been inhabited almost entirely by English stock (the Maoris constitute too small a segment of the population to be included in the data of this volume, except in the case of women

[18] The old and new manpower statistics are discussed in *Ministry of Labour Gazette* (London), February 1949, p. 40.
[19] *Ibid.*, p. 41.

428

classified by marital status). The concept of the labor force has apparently varied only slightly over the last half century (Table F-2, Part C). New Zealand has clung to the notion of "usual" or "customary" employment. A modification, which affects comparability over the years, was made in 1945, when the time of the census was switched from late March or mid-April to the last week in September. The effect of this seasonal shift is measured in Appendix Table C-6. In 1951, the census was again enumerated in April.

The New Zealand labor force remained much the same in content for fifty years. Also, it was virtually the same in concept as that of the United States until 1940, except that it included some young children through 1921 and was vague concerning the inexperienced and disabled.

Germany, 1895–1950

Here, too, the concept of labor force does not seem to have altered critically over the five decades (Table F-2, Part D, this appendix). Children under 15 were excluded during the World War II years, and children under 14 and working inmates of prisons, insane asylums, and poorhouses were excluded over the whole period. Censuses were taken in late May or early June, except in 1946 and 1950, when they were shifted to late October and September respectively. Finally, much German territory was lost, restored, and lost again as the result of two World Wars. However, the data appear to be moderately comparable during the interwar years.

For the period of World War II the figures do not justify quite the same confidence (Table F-2, Part D). Those for 1939–1944, derived by the United States Strategic Bombing Survey from the Kriegswirtschaftliche Kraftebilanz of the Statistisches Reichsamt, "were not always reliable, and had frequently changing conceptual and territorial coverage with little or no provision for adjustments to render them comparable." [20] They included all those gainfully occupied except party officials, and, in 1944 for the first time, a small number of home workers, i.e. persons engaged in industrial production at home. The statistics were founded on questionnaires returned by employers and the self-employed, and on the membership lists of industrial, trade, and cultural societies. They are, of course, subject to some gaps and duplications among organizations, and required a number of corrections. [21]

A striking feature, in comparison with the labor force of the United

[20] *The Effects of Strategic Bombing on the German War Economy,* Strategic Bombing Survey, Overall Economic Effects Division, 1945, p. 199.
[21] *Ibid.,* p. 199.

APPENDIX F

TABLE F-2, Part C
New Zealand, 1896–1951

Coverage as to:	1896–1911	1921–1936	1945	1951
Age	15 and older [a]	15 and older [a]	15 and older	15 and older
Date of labor force status [b]	vague	vague	vague	...
Unemployed	yes [c]	yes	yes	yes
Inexperienced work-seekers	...	...	yes	yes
Methods of payment:				
Wages, fees, profits	yes	yes	yes	yes
Room, board, & other goods	yes	yes	yes	yes
Unpaid family labor	yes	yes	yes	yes
Economic status:				
Employees, incl. supervisors	yes	yes	yes	yes
Employers, farmers, self-employed	yes	yes	yes	yes
Corporation officials, paid	yes	yes	yes	yes
Government (incl. armed forces)	yes	yes	yes	yes
Inmates of institutions	no	no	no	no
Persons not working nor seeking work but having job:				
Temporarily ill	pr. yes [d]	yes	yes	yes
On vacation, paid or unpaid	pr. yes [d]	yes	yes	yes
On strike	pr. yes [d]	yes	yes	yes
Laid off temporarily	pr. yes [d]	yes	yes	yes
Waiting to start new job	pr. yes [d]	yes	yes	yes
Persons not working nor seeking work and having no job:				
Temporarily ill	pr. yes [d]	yes [d]	yes [d]	yes [d]
Disabled	pr. yes [d]	yes [d]	yes [d]	yes [d]
Believe no jobs exist	pr. yes [d]	yes [d]	yes [d]	yes [d]
Weather-bound	pr. yes [d]	yes [d]	yes [d]	yes [d]
Seasonally idle	pr. yes [d]	yes [d]	yes [d]	yes [d]
Part-time work for pay:				
Student or housewife working	...	...	...	...
Student or housewife seeking work	...	...	...	...
Industries and occupations:				
Legal	all	all	all	all
Illegal	...	...	...	...
Armed forces abroad	–	–	yes	yes
Sex	both	both	both	both
Counting of dual job holders [e]	once	once	once	once

Source: *Report on the Results of a Census of the Dominion of New Zealand*, Registrar-General's Office, 1911, pp. 58, 62. *Population Census* (Census and Statistics Dept.): *1926*, Vol. IX, p. 6; *1936*, Vol. X, pp. i–vi, 59, and Vol. XI, p. 1; *1945*, Vol. IV, pp. 3, 9, and Vol. IX, pp. i–vii, 50, 61. *New Zealand Official Year Book* (Census and Statistics Office): *1897*, p. 109; *1927*, p. 872; *1951*, II, p. 5, IV, pp. 5–11. All Wellington.

430

Notes to Table F-2, Part C, *continued*

pr. = presumably.

ᵃ It is possible that some very young persons were included.

ᵇ Official census dates were:

1896–1926, April	1945, Sept. 25
1936, Late March	1951, April 17

ᶜ "Employment" and "unemployment" covered only wage and salary workers. The idle self-employed were part of the "occupied" population; they were probably insignificant in number and may be neglected.

ᵈ If the respondent stated a "usual" occupation.

ᵉ Presumably no worker was counted twice, but the census did not provide a specific answer on this question.

TABLE F-2, Part D

Germany, 1895–1950

Coverage as to:	1895–1907 [a]	1925–1939 [a]	1939–1944 [a]	1946	1950
Age	14 and older	14 and older	15 and older	15 and older	15 and older
Date of labor force status	vague [b]	vague [b]	May 31	vague [b]	vague [b]
Unemployed	yes	yes	yes	yes	yes
Inexperienced work-seekers	...	...	...	...	...
Methods of payment:					
Wages, fees, profits	yes	yes	yes	yes	yes
Room, board, & other goods	yes	yes	yes	yes	yes
Unpaid family labor	yes	yes	yes [c]	yes	yes
Economic status:					
Employees, incl. supervisors	yes	yes	yes	yes	yes
Employers, farmers, self employed	yes	yes	yes	yes	yes
Corporation officials, paid	yes	yes	yes	yes	yes
Government (incl. armed forces)	yes	yes	yes	yes	yes
Relief workers	–	... [d]	–	–	–
Inmates of institutions	no	no	no	no	no
Persons not working nor seeking work but having job:					
Temporarily ill	pr. yes	pr. yes	yes	yes	yes
On vacation, paid or unpaid	pr. yes	pr. yes	yes	yes	yes
On strike	pr. yes	pr. yes	yes	yes	yes
Laid off temporarily	pr. yes	pr. yes	yes	yes	yes
Waiting to start new job	pr. yes	pr. yes	yes	yes	yes
Persons not working nor seeking work and having no job:					
Temporarily ill	...	...	...	...	...
Believe no jobs exist	...	...	...	...	...
Weather-bound	...	...	...	...	...
Seasonally idle	...	...	...	...	...
Disabled	...	...	...	...	...

TABLE F-2, Part D, *continued*

Coverage as to:	1895–1907 [a]	1925–1939 [a]	1939–1944 [a]	1946	1950
Part-time work for pay:					
Student or housewife working	yes [e]	yes	yes [f]	...	...
Student or housewife seeking work	yes [e]	yes	...	...	...
Industries and occupations:					
Legal	all	all	all	all	all
Illegal	no	no	no	no	no
Armed forces abroad	no	no	yes	–	–
Sex	both	both	both	both	both
Counting of dual job holders	once	once	once	once	once

Source: *Statistik des Deutschen Reiches*, Berlin, Statistisches Reichsamt, Neue Folge: *Band 103*, pp. 2, 245; *Band 203*, Abteilung II, pp. 2–5; *Band 211*, p. 35; *Band 402*, Abteilung I and II, p. 7; *Band 458*, p. 7. *Statistisches Jahrbuch*, Berlin, Statistiches Reichsamt, *1934*, p. 12; *1935*, p. 11. *Wirtschaft und Statistik*, Berlin, Statistisches Reichsamt: 1940, p. 519; 1941, p. 50; 1952 (Wiesbaden, Statistisches Bundesamt), pp. 256, 352. *The Effects of Strategic Bombing on the German War Economy*, U.S. Strategic Bombing Survey, Overall Economic Effects Division, 1945, pp. 29–41, 199–216. Frank Notestein and others, *The Future Population of Europe and the Soviet Union*, Geneva, League of Nations, 1944, pp. 256–257, 264–265. *Deutschland in Zahlen*, Köln, Wirtschaftswissenschaftliches Institut der Gewerkschaften, 1951, pp. 25–45.

pr. = presumably.

[a] The 1895 and 1907 censuses referred originally to a territory larger than that after World War I, when Germany had been partitioned by the Versailles treaty. To make the over-all series cover the same area, the 1895 and 1907 population and labor force in the amputated areas were deducted on the basis of official German data. The age-sex distribution in this restricted territory may have differed somewhat, but for lack of information it had to be made proportional to that originally reported. By 1946 territory was still more restricted. The 1939 population and labor force include adjustments for males in the military and labor services, originally omitted, which apply only to males aged 14–19, 20–24, and 25–39. Females and the older male groups were probably not much affected.

[b] Official census dates were: mid-June 1895, 1907, 1925, 1933; May 17, 1939; October 29, 1946; September 1950. The Strategic Bombing Survey data refer to May 31, 1939–1944 (see text of this appendix).

[c] Omitted "home workers," i.e. persons doing industrial tasks at home, up to 1943.

[d] Included relief workers in 1933 but not compulsory labor service in 1939.

[e] If the part-time job is a major source of the respondent's income.

[f] Included "helping family members," a group with no counterpart in Anglo-American statistics (*The Effects of Strategic Bombing on the German War Economy*, U.S. Strategic Bombing Survey, 1945, p. 30).

States, was the huge proportion of female farm workers in Germany. It is not known whether this difference was due to a higher rate of participation or to a more liberal classification. Since women undoubtedly tend to work more in the fields in Germany than here, perhaps there should be a larger proportion of such women in the German labor force. But many of them may have performed tasks too trivial to have qualified them as workers in the United States, for this country has very likely ignored female farm workers unless their labor outside the home demanded a substantial part of the week—in recent years, fifteen hours or more. One wonders whether comparing Germany's female labor force with America's is not akin to translating German poetry!

SUPPLEMENTARY APPENDIXES

(Mimeographed; on file at the National Bureau of Economic Research, Inc., and in other economics libraries. Copies will be furnished at cost on special request made to the National Bureau while the supply lasts.)

G Adjustments of United States Labor Force and Population Used in Appendix A

H Rejection of the Durand-Goldfield Adjustments of the United States Labor Force of 1930

I Sampling and Interview Errors in Census Monthly Estimates of Labor Force

INDEX

437

RECENT PUBLICATIONS OF THE
NATIONAL BUREAU OF ECONOMIC RESEARCH

BOOKS

Financial Intermediaries in the American Economy since 1900 (1958)	452 pp.	$ 8.50
Raymond W. Goldsmith		
Corporate Bond Quality and Investor Experience (1958)	566 pp.	10.00
W. Braddock Hickman		
The Income-Tax Burden on Stockholders (1958)	268 pp.	5.00
Daniel M. Holland		
Federal Lending and Loan Insurance (1958)	596 pp.	12.00
R. J. Saulnier, Harold G. Halcrow, and Neil H. Jacoby		
A Critique of the United States Income and Product Accounts (1958)	600 pp.	11.50
Studies in Income and Wealth, Volume 22		
An Appraisal of the 1950 Census Income Data (1958)	460 pp.	10.00
Studies in Income and Wealth, Volume 23		

OCCASIONAL PAPERS

61 *Measuring Recessions* (1958)	$ 1.00
Geoffrey H. Moore	

TECHNICAL PAPERS

13 *The Volume of Mortgage Debt in the Postwar Decade* (1958)	$ 2.00
Saul B. Klaman	

ANNUAL REPORTS (GRATIS)

By Solomon Fabricant

38th. *Investing in Economic Knowledge*	May 1958
37th. *Financial Research and the Problems of the Day*	May 1957
36th. *Basic Research and the Analysis of Current Business Conditions*	May 1956

HOW TO OBTAIN NATIONAL BUREAU PUBLICATIONS

NATIONAL BUREAU BOOKS *are available from bookstores or Princeton University Press, Princeton, New Jersey, except that contributors and subscribers to the National Bureau should order directly from the Bureau.* OCCASIONAL *and* TECHNICAL PAPERS, *and* ANNUAL REPORTS *are available from the National Bureau of Economic Research, 261 Madison Avenue, New York 16, New York.*